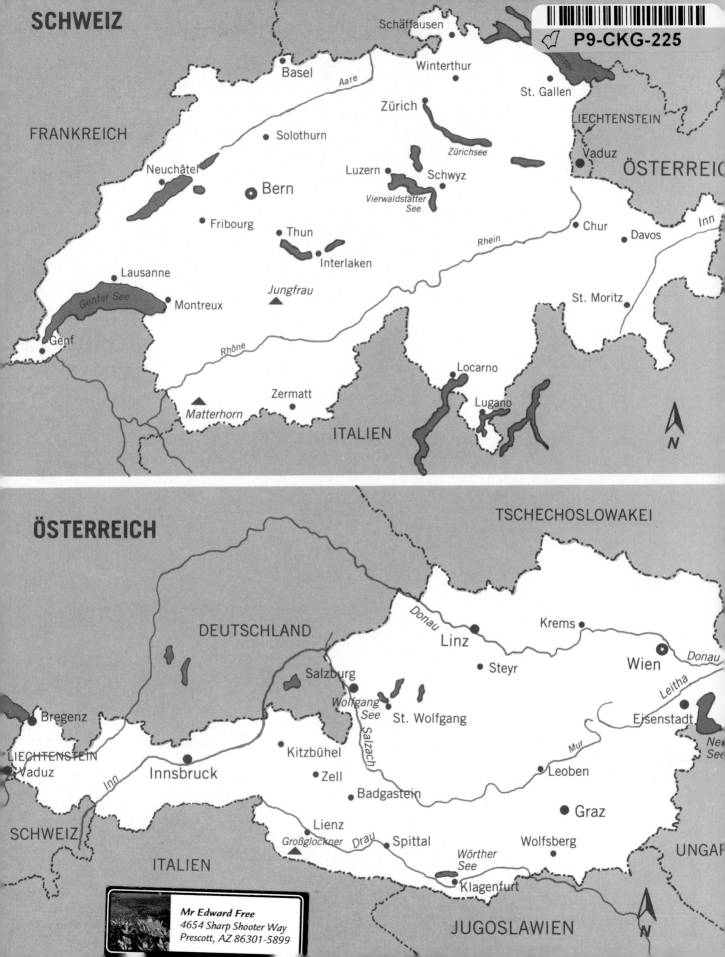

Treffpunkt DEUTSCH

A STUDENT-CENTERED APPROACH

E. Rosemarie Widmaier
McMaster University

Fritz T. Widmaier
McMaster University

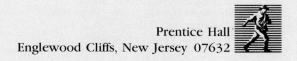

Prentice Hall
Englewood Cliffs, New Jersey 07632

Library of Congress Cataloging-in-Publication Data

WIDMAIER, E. ROSEMARIE (date)
  Treffpunkt Deutsch: a student-centered approach/E. Rosemarie
Widmaier, Fritz T. Widmaier.
    p. cm.
  Includes index.
  ISBN 0–13–051350–4 (with cassette).—ISBN 0–13–051111–0 (w/o
cassette)
  1. German language—Grammar—1950– 2. German language—Textbooks
for foreign speakers—English. I. Widmaier, Fritz (date)
II. Title.
PF3112.W5 1991
438.2'421—dc20   90–49903
                CIP

Acquisitions editor: *Steve Debow*
Development editor: *Cynthia H. Westhof*
Editorial/production supervision: *F. Hubert*
Cover and interior design: *Kenny Beck*
Manufacturing buyer: *Dave Dickey*
Pre-press buyer: *Herb Klein*
Photo editor: *Rona Tuccillo*
Illustrations: *Michael Widmaier*

 © 1991 by Prentice-Hall, Inc.
A Division of Simon & Schuster
Englewood Cliffs, New Jersey 07632

Printed in the United States of America
10 9 8 7 6 5 4 3 2 1

ISBN 0-13-051111-0 (without cassette)
ISBN 0-13-051350-4 (with cassette)

Prentice-Hall International (UK) Limited, *London*
Prentice-Hall of Australia Pty. Limited, *Sydney*
Prentice-Hall Canada Inc., *Toronto*
Prentice-Hall Hispanoamericana, S.A., *Mexico*
Prentice-Hall of India Private Limited, *New Delhi*
Prentcie-Hall of Japan, Inc., *Tokyo*
Simon & Schuster Asia Pte. Ltd., *Singapore*
Editora Prentice-Hall do Brasil, Ltda., *Rio de Janerio*

CONTENTS

FUNKTIONEN UND FORMEN

FUNKTIONEN UND FORMEN

FUNKTIONEN UND FORMEN

FUNKTIONEN UND FORMEN

FUNKTIONEN UND FORMEN

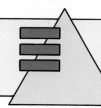

ABOUT THE AUTHORS

Born in Canada, **Rosemarie Widmaier** received her B.A. from the University of Western Ontario in London, and her M.A. from the Johns Hopkins University. She did further graduate work at the University of Southern California. She has taught German at the secondary school and college level. Presently at McMaster University in Hamilton, Ontario, she has taught and coordinated beginning German courses as well as courses in the Methodology of Foreign Language Acquisition.

Born in Stuttgart, Germany, **Fritz Widmaier** received his B.A. from the University of Waterloo and his M.A. and Ph.D. from the University of Southern California. Before coming to Canada, he studied music (violin) at the *Staatliche Hochschule für Musik* in Stuttgart, and was a member of the *Stuttgarter Kammerorchester* under Karl Münchinger. He is presently Associate Professor of German at McMaster University where he teaches Methodology of Foreign Language Acquisition, and is Coordinator of Beginning and Intermediate German courses. He received two major grants from the Ontario Committee on Teaching and Learning for the development of new methods of teaching German, and for many years he served as chairperson of McMaster University's Committee on Teaching and Learning.

The Widmaiers have two sons. Their older son, Michael, who created the line drawings for this text, is studying architecture at the *Technische Universität* in Berlin. Their younger son, Peter, is an honors music student at McMaster University. The Widmaiers live on a farm on the outskirts of Hamilton, where they raise a few sheep in their spare (!) time.

PREFACE

The *Treffpunkt Deutsch* program is designed to transform your classroom into a meeting place where your students will encounter not only the German language, but also the history and culture of the German-speaking countries.

Student-centered, communicative learning is the foundation upon which *Treffpunkt Deutsch* is built. All language models, grammatical examples, and communicative activities use colloquial language in natural settings. The material has been carefully designed to encourage your students to interact spontaneously and meaningfully in German. Language skills are developed through cyclical practice in listening, speaking, reading, and writing. At the end of the course, students will be in command of the basic elements of German language and culture and will be able to function with relative ease in the German-speaking countries of Europe.

ORGANIZATION OF THE TEXT

Treffpunkt Deutsch consists of an *Einleitung* and fourteen chapters. The *Einleitung* is the "warm-up" for the course. Its short conversations give students the opportunity to practice greetings, introductions, and farewells. Each subsequent chapter is structured consistently and moves from topic to topic, activity to activity, as follows:

KOMMUNIKATIONSZIELE. *Kommunikationsziele* are clearly displayed at the beginning of each chapter opener, drawing students' attention to the functional goals of the chapter.

VORSCHAU. The *Vorschau* (chapter-opening material) introduces the structures taught in the chapter in natural, idiomatic German through mini-dramas, short stories, and other listening material. These materials are all recorded, and they are intended to be listened to as well as to be read. The mini-dramas are not conventional dialogues that are to be memorized. Set in situations that students can easily relate to, the mini-dramas are designed to give context to the language and to provide cultural information. Warm-up activities suggested in the *Instructor's Resource Manual* help you set the grammatical context of the mini-dramas without a formal teaching of structures. Glosses help students understand the mini-dramas before vocabulary is actually learned. In later chapters, new vocabulary is indicated with a gloss mark, but students will find translations for these words in the *Anhang*. This innovation will provide you with the option of teaching reading strategies as suggested in the *Instructor's Resource Manual*.

VOM LESEN ZUM SPRECHEN. The activities that follow the mini-dramas are designed to have students work with the vocabulary and structures of the chapter before they are formally introduced. The activities range from recognizing certain features and understanding the situation to talking about ideas in the *Vorschau* that touch students' own lives.

NÜTZLICHE WÖRTER UND AUSDRÜCKE.   This list of active vocabulary presents useful words and expressions that have appeared in the *Vorschau*. Arranged under the headings *Nomen, Verben, Andere Wörter,* and *Ausdrücke,* the individual items are grouped into semantic categories wherever possible. To facilitate mastery of the vocabulary, the section *Wörter im Kontext* gives students the opportunity to use the words in a variety of contexts.

FUNKTIONEN UND FORMEN.   The grammar sections of *Treffpunkt Deutsch* are functionally oriented and focus on basic structures essential to communication. Grammar explanations are clear and concise, contrasting English and German usage wherever possible. The exercises that directly follow each grammar explanation range from contextualized practice to open-ended, creative expression. A large proportion of the exercises are in the form of mini-conversations that are best done by pairs of students. They are designed in such a way that mindless pattern practice is avoided, i.e., that students must *understand* what they are saying. This is frequently achieved by having students choose an answer from a variety of possibilities or by picture-cuing with line drawings. The use of the drawings is also an aid to vocabulary retention. The open-ended, interactive activities that follow the controlled practice give students the opportunity to use the structures in real-life, personal situations.

ZUSAMMENSCHAU.   Each chapter has two *Zusammenschau* sections that synthesize structures and skills learned previously in the chapter. Central to these sections is audio material for which there is no in-text script. This material is included on the cassettes that accompany the text. Through a variety of processing strategies, students are guided from a global to a more detailed understanding of the material and are then given the opportunity to interact with one another in role plays or discussions on a similar topic.

WORT, SINN UND KLANG.   The *Wort, Sinn und Klang* section is divided into three sub-sections:

Wörter unter der Lupe takes a closer look at words by discussing cognates, word families, compound words, suffixes that signal gender, and so on.
Weitere Nützliche Wörter und Ausdrücke groups words that have appeared previously as passive vocabulary into *Sinngruppen*. This second list of vocabulary is again followed by a variety of reinforcing activities.
In the *Zur Aussprache* section, sounds that are potentially difficult for speakers of English are discussed and practiced. Pronunciation practice material is included on the accompanying audio cassettes.

WISSENSWERTES.   Cultural information appears in the *Wissenswertes* sections in each chapter. These vary in length and scope and present a wide range of historical, social, and cultural topics for reading or informal discussion. As the title implies, these sections are simply *things worth knowing*.

SPRACHNOTIZEN.   Scattered throughout the text, the *Sprachnotizen* briefly discuss idiomatic features of colloquial German. They also present discourse strategies that will help students to express themselves in German.

IN-TEXT AUDIO PROGRAM.   The audio program for *Treffpunkt Deutsch* is incorporated into the body of the text, an innovation that facilitates cohesive four skills development. The cassettes that accompany the text contain audio material for the *Vorschau* and the two *Zusammenschau* sections of each chapter. Pronunciation exercises from the *Zur Aussprache* sections have also been recorded. A complete transcript of the recorded material not contained in the student text is printed in the *Instructor's Resource Manual*.

SUPPLEMENTS

ANNOTATED INSTRUCTOR'S EDITION.   Marginal annotations in the *Annotated Instructor's Edition* include warm-up activities, resource notes, cultural information, and suggestions for using and expanding the materials and activities in the student text. The annotations are based on the experiences of the authors and their teaching assistants over many years of class testing.

ARBEITSBUCH.   Each chapter of the *Arbeitsbuch* features a variety of exercises including reading comprehension activities, sentence-building and completion exercises, fill-ins, matching exercises, and realia-based and picture-cued activities. They have been designed to enhance and reinforce the vocabulary, structures and themes in the corresponding chapters of the student text.

DEUTSCH-ON-A-DISK.   Completely integrated with *Treffpunkt Deutsch, Deutsch-on-a-disk* is designed for students with little or no computer experience. This full-color software program consists of 160 tutorial screens and over 500 screens of practice material, including annotated screens with reading comprehension activities. The practice material is supported by detailed hints, two sets of "flash-card" reference files, and a German-English, English-German dictionary containing all the vocabulary used in the program.

TESTING PROGRAM.   The Testing Program consists of two chapter tests for each of the fourteen chapters of the text. Each test utilizes a variety of techniques to address the skill areas of listening, reading, writing, and culture.

SITUATION CARDS.   The Situation Cards, which are coordinated with the themes and structures of the chapters, are designed for oral practice and testing. The cards present situations in which students can use the vocabulary and structures that they have learned as well as practice discourse strategies such as circumlocution.

INSTRUCTOR'S RESOURCE MANUAL

Management system: The management system includes syllabi for three- and five-hour programs. It also gives a description of and a guide to all the components of the *Treffpunkt Deutsch* program.

Transparencies: 20 full-color transparencies with maps, illustrations to inspire speaking activities, grammatical charts, and so on are included to provide visual support for materials in the student text.

Transparency guide: Approximately sixty pages in length, the *Transparency Guide* contains suggested activities for each transparency.

Gradebook: An electronic grade management system, the *Gradebook* organizes course records and calculates grade averages.

THE NEW YORK TIMES CONTEMPORARY VIEW PROGRAM.   Prentice Hall and The New York Times have joined forces to offer you and your students current information concerning events in the German-speaking countries and in Europe. Upon adoption of *Treffpunkt Deutsch,* you will receive a complimentary one-semester subscription for classroom use, and your students will receive a special student supplement containing articles pertinent to the historic events of November, 1989.

ABC NEWS/PRENTICE HALL VIDEO LIBRARY. Prentice Hall and ABC News have collaborated to provide timely and comprehensive video documentaries to enhance your presentation of significant political issues. Taken from "Nightline" and "This Week with David Brinkley," the *ABC/PH Video Library for Treffpunkt Deutsch* is comprised of three hour-long segments featuring coverage of the historic opening of the Berlin Wall and the events surrounding reunification.

ACKNOWLEDGMENTS

Treffpunkt Deutsch is the result of years of class testing, revision, and more class testing in the German section of the Department of Modern Languages at McMaster University. Over the years, countless people have contributed ideas and suggestions for the text. We are deeply indebted to all our teaching assistants, whose enthusiasm and encouragement assisted us in shaping this student-centered program, and also to the host of beginning German students at McMaster, whose candid evaluations clearly showed us what was successful and what needed improvement. We would especially like to thank our colleagues Gerhart Teuscher, Jim Lawson, and Karl Denner for their unwavering support of the project, and Teresa Venitelli and Erica Giese for their cheerful assistance in readying the materials for class testing. We are also grateful to Barbara Bayne, who gave us a great deal of encouragement and constructive criticism in the early stages of the project.

We are greatly indebted to the many people at Prentice Hall who participated in the lengthy development of *Treffpunkt Deutsch.* Foremost, our thanks go to our Editor, Steve Debow, whose boundless energy, enthusiasm, and imagination were a constant source of inspiration. His organizational talents, his ability to focus on what is important, his willingness to listen, and his engaging personality have made him indispensable to this project. He was always there when we needed him most and without him, the project would never have achieved its full potential. Our Developmental Editor, Cynthia Westhof, joined the project in 1989. Cindy expertly guided us through the final revision of the manuscript, and many of her ideas and suggestions have been implemented throughout the book. The overall shape of the text is in large measure her work, and we are very grateful for her consistent attention to detail. Ray Mullaney directed the developmental program with steady, expert comments. His gentle guidance throughout the project is gratefully acknowledged. The addition of Steve Deitmer to our publishing team in its final stages proved of paramount importance. Steve coordinated the project with his usual calming persistence and has contributed a host of fine suggestions and details. Frank Hubert has been brilliant at coordinating a monumental production job. Despite his move to the remote and tranquil hills of Pennsylvania, Frank has kept the project moving from state to state. He never once lost his composure, and exercised skilled judgment and meticulous care in maintaining the integrity of our work.

We owe special thanks to many other people at Prentice Hall who contributed time, assistance, and energy to *Treffpunkt Deutsch:* the imperturbable Maria Felicidad Garcia; Ann Knitel, who oversaw all aspects of the Supplements Program; Chris Freitag, who continues to motivate and inspire the Prentice Hall sales force and Marketing Department; Margaret Lepera, Joe Sengotta, Wendy Alling-Judy, and Suzanne Daghlian in Advertising; Herta Erville for her marvelous copyediting and proofreading; and Florence Silverman, Elaine Rusoff, Lisa Domínguez, Kenny

Beck, and Lorraine Mullaney in the Art Department. We also thank the staff at the German Information Center and Frau Hella Roth at Inter Nationes in Bonn for the use of photographs.

We gratefully acknowledge the input received from the following instructors. The appearance of their names does not necessarily constitute their endorsement of *Treffpunkt Deutsch.*

Lida Daves Baldwin, Washington College; **George Koenig,** SUNY College at Oswego; **Richard L. Morris,** Louisiana State University; **William W. Anthony,** Northwestern University; **Morris Vos,** Western Illinois University.

Helga Bister, University of North Carolina at Chapel Hill; **Arndt A. Krüger,** Trent University, Peterborough, Ontario; **Thomas G. Evans,** Towson State University; **Gerhard F. Strasser,** Pennsylvania State University; **Trudy Gilgengast,** University of Delaware.

Jennifer Ham, Lafayette College; **Kamakshi P. Murti,** University of Arizona; **Barbara Bopp,** University of California at Los Angeles; **John Lalande,** University of Illinois; **Jurgen Froehlich,** Pomona College.

Karl F. Otto, Jr., University of Pennsylvania; **Veronica Richel,** The University of Vermont; **Ronald C. Reinholdt,** Orange Coast College; **Stephen J. Kaplowitt,** The University of Connecticut; **John Austin,** Georgia State University.

Robert Mollenauer, The University of Texas; **Wilfried Voge,** University of California at Los Angeles; **Esther Enns-Connolly,** The University of Calgary; **Michael M. Metzger,** SUNY University at Buffalo; **Richard Whitcomb,** Illinois State University.

Five instructors accepted the task of reading every word of the close-to-final manuscript. Their enthusiasm, constructive comments, and gentle guidance proved indispensable. With heartfelt thanks, and the deepest appreciation, we acknowledge the contributions of the following colleagues:

Christian Hallstein, Carnegie-Mellon University; **Henry F. Fullenwider,** The University of Kansas; **Frauke A. Harvey,** Baylor University; **Helga Van Iten,** Iowa State University; **Suzanne Shipley Toliver,** University of Cincinnati.

Finally our love and deepest appreciation go to our sons Michael and Peter. Michael's superb line drawings are an integral part of this text, and he worked meticulously and tirelessly to execute in art form what was often just an idea in our heads. Our thanks to Peter for putting up with us through it all. His interest and support buoyed our spirits on many an occasion, and we would often have gone hungry had he not taken upon himself the responsibility of doing the grocery shopping and seeing to it that we got a square meal.

Rosemarie Widmaier
Fritz Widmaier

Ludwig-Maximilians-Universität, München

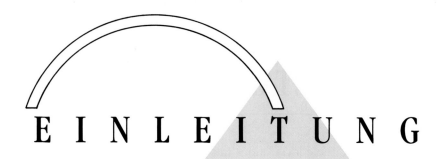

EINLEITUNG

Kommunikationsziele
(Communicative goals)

*In the **Einleitung** you will learn how to:*
address people in the German-speaking countries
greet someone and respond to greetings
inquire about someone's health and respond to such
  an inquiry
ask where someone comes from and say where you
  come from
say good-bye

Sprechsituationen
(Communicative Activities)

Wir lernen einander kennen: Im Klassenzimmer
Wir lernen einander kennen: Im Büro

Wissenswertes *(Things worth knowing)*

Du, ihr, Sie, and their social implications

The following three conversations introduce the main characters in this book, all students at the **Ludwig-Maximilians-Universität** in **München.**

Claudia Berger from Frankfurt

Martin Keller from Mannheim

Stephanie Braun from Chicago

Peter Ackermann from Berlin

📼 BEIM STUDENTENWERK

Martin and Peter meet at the student center, where they are checking the bulletin board for rooms.

MARTIN: Hallo, ich heiße Martin, Martin Keller.

PETER: Und ich bin Peter Ackermann. Woher kommst du, Martin?

MARTIN: Ich komme aus Mannheim. Und du, woher bist du?

PETER: Ich bin aus Berlin.

At the student center – MARTIN: Hello, my name is Martin, Martin Keller. PETER: And I'm Peter Ackermann. Where do you come from, Martin? MARTIN: I come from Mannheim. And where are you from? PETER: I'm from Berlin.

WIR LERNEN EINANDER KENNEN

Walk around the classroom and get to know as many of your classmates as possible. In the German-speaking countries, it is customary to shake hands when greeting someone.

STUDENT 1: Hallo, ich heiße _____. Wie heißt du?

STUDENT 2: Ich heiße _____.

STUDENT 1: Ich komme aus _____. Woher kommst du?

STUDENT 2: Ich komme aus _____. (Ich komme auch° aus _____.) *also*

🎞 IM STUDENTENHEIM

Claudia has already settled into her room in the dorm. Stephanie, her new room-mate, has just arrived.

STEPHANIE: Entschuldigung, bist du Claudia Berger?

CLAUDIA: Ja. Und du, wie heißt du?

STEPHANIE: Ich bin Stephanie Braun aus Chicago.

CLAUDIA: Oh, grüß dich, Stephanie! Wie geht's?

STEPHANIE: Danke, gut.

WIR LERNEN EINANDER KENNEN

Now walk around the classroom again, and see how many of your classmates' names you remember.

S1: Entschuldigung, bist du _____?

S2: Ja, ich bin _____. (Nein, ich bin _____.) Und du, heißt du _____?

S1: Ja, ich heiße _____. (Nein, ich heiße _____.)

In the dormitory — STEPHANIE: Excuse me, are you Claudia Berger? CLAUDIA: Yes. And what's *your* name? STEPHANIE: I'm Stephanie Braun from Chicago. CLAUDIA: Oh hi, Stephanie. How are you? STEPHANIE: Fine, thanks.

▣ IM HÖRSAAL

Peter knows Martin and Martin knows Claudia. Peter would like to get to know Stephanie.

MARTIN: Hallo, Peter! Wie geht's?

PETER: Danke, es geht. — Du Martin, wer ist das?

MARTIN: Das ist Stephanie, Claudias Zimmerkollegin.

CLAUDIA: Komm, Martin. Ich habe Hunger.

MARTIN: Na, dann tschüs, Peter!

PETER: Tschüs, ihr zwei!

WIR LERNEN EINANDER KENNEN

A. Walk up to two classmates and greet one by name. She/he will then introduce you to the other classmate.

S1: Grüß dich, _____! Wie geht's?　　*S2:* Danke, es geht. *(Introducing S3):* Das ist _____.

S1 (to S3): Hallo, _____! Wie geht's?　　*S3:* Danke, gut!

B. The classmate you are about to have lunch with is talking to a friend. Indicate that you want her/him to come now.

S1: Komm, _____! Ich habe Hunger.　　*S2 (to S3):* Na, dann tschüs, _____!

S3: Tschüs, ihr zwei!

Im Hörsaal

Sprachnotizen

In German some things are different

a. In German, all nouns are capitalized: **Zimmerkollegin,** **H**unger.

b. There is no apostrophe in German to show the possessive unless a name ends in an **s**-sound: **Claudias Zimmerkollegin, Thomas' Zimmerkollege.**

c. In addition to the letter **s,** German has another letter to represent the **s**-sound: **ß,** which is called **Eszett.**

d. The letter **ä** in **Universität** is called **a-Umlaut.** The letters **o** and **u** can also be umlauted: **H**ö**rsaal, tsch**ü**s.**

In the lecture hall — MARTIN: Hi, Peter. How are you? PETER: Not bad, thanks. — Hey, Martin, who's that? MARTIN: That's Stephanie, Claudia's roommate. CLAUDIA: Come on, Martin. I'm hungry. MARTIN: Well then, so long, Peter. PETER: So long, you two.

How to say *you* in German

German has more than one way of saying *you*. The familiar **du** is used to address members of the family, close friends, children, and teenagers up to about age sixteen. It is also used among students even if they are not close friends. The plural form of **du** is **ihr.**

When addressing adults who are not close friends, the equivalent of *you* is **Sie.** **Sie** is *always capitalized* and does not change in the plural.

	Singular	**Plural**
Familiar	du	ihr
Formal	Sie	Sie

IM BÜRO

Ms. Meyer has been expecting Mr. Ziegler, a sales representative from Bonn.

HERR ZIEGLER: Guten Tag. Mein Name ist Ziegler.

FRAU MEYER: Wie bitte? Wie heißen Sie?

HERR ZIEGLER: Ich heiße Ziegler.

FRAU MEYER: Oh, Sie sind Herr Ziegler aus Bonn. Ich bin Ruth Meyer. Wie geht es Ihnen, Herr Ziegler?

HERR ZIEGLER: Danke, gut. Und Ihnen, Frau Meyer?

FRAU MEYER: Oh danke, es geht.

WIR LERNEN EINANDER KENNEN

Imagine that you are meeting a business colleague. Introduce yourself, using your last name. Address your partner with **Frau** or **Herr** and don't forget to shake hands!

S1: Guten Tag. Mein Name ist _____.   *S2:* Und ich heiße _____.

S1: Wie geht es Ihnen, Frau/Herr _____?   *S2:* Danke, gut. Und Ihnen, Frau/Herr _____?

S1: Oh danke, es geht.

In the office – MR. ZIEGLER: Hello. My name is Ziegler. MS. MEYER: Pardon? What is your name? MR. ZIEGLER: My name is Ziegler. MS. MEYER: Oh, you are Mr. Ziegler from Bonn. I'm Ruth Meyer. How are you, Mr. Ziegler? MR. ZIEGLER: Fine, thanks. And you, Ms. Meyer? MS. MEYER: Not bad, thanks.

Knowing how to use **Sie,** or **du** and **ihr** appropriately often poses problems for students learning German. Here are some general guidelines:

The pronoun **Sie** basically implies formality and distance. You use it when addressing adults you do not know very well. You also use **Sie** to address your professors, your landlord, and even your next-door neighbors, unless they are your friends.

The pronouns **du** and **ihr** imply informality or a close relationship. You use **du** and **ihr** when addressing relatives, close friends, children, and pets. You also use **du** and **ihr** when addressing your fellow students even if they are not your close friends.

The pronouns **du** and **Sie** can also imply social distinctions in the working world. For example, workers on a construction site address each other with **du** and in this way express working class solidarity. The engineer on the construction site usually addresses the workers with **Sie.** It is, however, possible that an engineer and his workers become such a tightly knit group that they switch to **du.**

If you are in a German-speaking country and are unsure as to which form of address you should use, remember that it is better to err on the side of caution and use **Sie.**

Unlike North Americans, Germans use first names only with close friends. Even neighbors who have lived side by side for many years are likely to address each other as **Herr** or **Frau. Frau** (*Mrs.* or *Ms.)* is used to address married or single women over the age of sixteen. The term **Fräulein** *(Miss)* is on its way out, although many older people still use this term to address young, unmarried women.

In North America it is customary for people to shake hands when they *first* meet each other. In German-speaking countries, people usually shake hands whenever they meet or say good-bye.

Sprachnotizen

Greetings and farewells

In the German-speaking countries, there are various ways of saying hello and good-bye.

	Formal	Less Formal	
Greetings	Guten Tag!	Tag!	*Hello!*
	Guten Morgen!	Morgen!	*Good morning!*
	Guten Abend!	'n Abend!	*Good evening!*
		Hallo!	*Hello!*
		Grüß dich!	*Hello!*
		Grüß Gott! *(So. German)*	*Hello!*
		Grüezi! *(Swiss)*	*Hello!*
Farewells	Auf Wiedersehen!	Wiedersehen!	*Good-bye!*
		Tschüs!	*Good-bye!*
		Gute Nacht!	*Good night!*

Find greetings that are used in the German-speaking countries.

NÜTZLICHE WÖRTER UND AUSDRÜCKE

Informelle Situationen

Grüß dich!	Hi!
Hallo!	Hi!
Tschüs!	So long!
Entschuldigung!	Excuse me!

Woher kommst (bist) du?	Where are you from?
Ich komme (bin) aus . . .	I'm from . . .
Woher kommt (ist) Claudia?	Where is Claudia from?
Sie kommt (ist) aus Frankfurt.	She's from Frankfurt.
Woher kommt (ist) Martin?	Where is Martin from?
Er kommt (ist) aus Mannheim.	He's from Mannheim.

Wie geht's?	How are you?
Danke, gut.	Fine, thanks.
Danke, es geht.	Not bad, thanks.

Wie heißt du?	What is your name?
Ich heiße . . .	My name is . . .
Ich bin . . .	I'm . . .

Wer ist das?	Who's that?
Das ist . . .	That's . . .

ja	yes
nein	no

Formelle Situationen

Guten Tag!	Hello!
Guten Morgen!	Good morning!
Guten Abend!	Good evening!
Auf Wiedersehen!	Good-bye!

Wie heißen Sie?	What is your name?
Ich heiße . . .	My name is . . .
Mein Name ist . . .	My name is . . .

Woher kommen (sind) Sie?	Where are you from?
Wie geht es Ihnen?	How are you?
Wie bitte?	Pardon?

Frau	Mrs., Ms.
Herr	Mr.

Hundewetter!

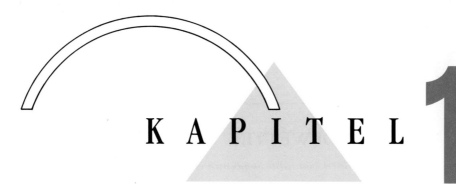

KAPITEL 1

Kommunikationsziele

*In **Kapitel 1** you will learn how to:*
talk about the weather
name things
express negation
count and do simple arithmetic
spell
ask for and give personal information

Hör- und Sprechsituationen

Wie ist das Wetter jetzt?
Ist es warm oder kalt?
Beim Auslandsamt
Wir lernen einander kennen
Ich habe endlich ein Zimmer
Ein Telefongespräch

Strukturen

Singular nouns: gender and definite articles
Position of the verb in German sentences
Position of **nicht**
Numbers from 1 to 100,000
The alphabet

Wissenswertes

Landscapes of the German-speaking countries
German postal and telephone service
Why German and English are similar

🔊 HUNDEWETTER

Claudia is still in bed, and Stephanie is looking out the window.

CLAUDIA: Wie ist das Wetter heute?
STEPHANIE: Gar nicht schön. Es regnet in Strömen.
CLAUDIA: Ist es warm oder kalt?
STEPHANIE: Das Thermometer zeigt zehn Grad.
CLAUDIA: Nur zehn Grad! Was für ein Hundewetter!

🔊 BADEWETTER

Claudia has been working on an essay in the library since early morning and is oblivious to the weather outside.

MARTIN: Hallo, Claudia. Bist du fertig?
CLAUDIA: Ja, gleich. — Sag mal, regnet es noch?
MARTIN: Nein, jetzt ist es wieder schön. Die Sonne scheint, und der Himmel ist blau.
CLAUDIA: Toll! Ist es warm?
MARTIN: Ja, sehr. Fast dreißig Grad.
CLAUDIA: Dreißig Grad! Mensch, das ist ja Badewetter!

Rotten weather – CLAUDIA: What's the weather like today? STEPHANIE: Not nice at all. It's pouring rain. CLAUDIA: Is it warm or cold? STEPHANIE: The thermometer reads ten degrees (Celsius). CLAUDIA: Only ten degrees! What rotten weather!

Swimming weather – MARTIN: Hi, Claudia. Are you finished? CLAUDIA: Yes, just about.—Say, is it still raining? MARTIN: No, now it's nice again. The sun is shining and the sky is blue. CLAUDIA: Fantastic! Is it warm? MARTIN: Yes, very warm. Almost thirty degrees (Celsius). CLAUDIA: Thirty degrees! Wow, that's *swimming* weather!

VOM LESEN ZUM SPRECHEN

WAS PASST ZUSAMMEN? *(What goes together?)* Working with a partner, find the five sentences that describe each of these illustrations.

Heute ist es gar nicht schön.
Heute ist es schön.
Die Sonne scheint.

Es regnet.
Der Himmel ist grau.
Der Himmel ist blau.
Es ist windig.
Es ist windstill.
Das ist Badewetter!
Was für ein Hundewetter!

WIE IST DAS WETTER JETZT?

Working with a partner, read through the following situations. Complete the conversations with appropriate questions and answers from the list below.

Situation A

When your friend went to the library this morning, it was pouring rain. When you come to pick her/him up for lunch, your friend wants to know whether it is still raining. You tell her/him that it's nice out now. Your friend responds appropriately.

S1: Grüß dich, _____. Bist du fertig?

S1: . . .

S2: Ja, gleich. Sag mal, wie ist das Wetter jetzt? . . . ?

S2: . . .

Situation B

When your friend went to the library this morning, the sun was shining. When you come to pick her/him up for lunch, your friend wants to know whether it's still so nice outside. You tell her/him that it's raining now. Your friend responds appropriately.

S1: Grüß dich, _____. Bist du fertig?

S1: . . .

S2: Ja, gleich. Sag mal, wie ist das Wetter jetzt? . . . ?

S2: . . .

Ist es immer noch° so schön?
Regnet es noch?

Nein, gar nicht. Es regnet in Strömen.
Nein, jetzt ist es wieder schön. Die Sonne scheint und der Himmel ist blau.

Toll, das ist ja Badewetter!
Was für ein Hundewetter!

---

immer noch = noch

IST ES WARM ODER KALT?

With a partner, read the following situation and the mini-conversation below it.

You are an American hiking in Austria. The Canadian that you meet in a youth hostel tells you the temperature, but you don't understand the Celsius scale.

approximately

AMERIKANER(IN):[1] Was zeigt das Thermometer?

AMERIKANER(IN): Dreißig Grad? Was ist das in Fahrenheit?

AMERIKANER(IN): Neunzig Grad? Oh, das ist heiß.

KANADIER(IN): Dreißig Grad.

KANADIER(IN): In Fahrenheit? Etwa° neunzig Grad.

- Now adapt the mini-conversation above to the following Celsius temperature readings:

  10°C   0°C   20°C

Das Thermometer zeigt dreißig Grad.

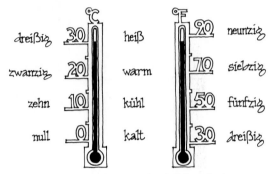

Grad Celsius   Grad Fahrenheit

NÜTZLICHE WÖRTER UND AUSDRÜCKE

Nomen *(Nouns)*

der Himmel	sky	**das Thermometer**	thermometer
die Sonne	sun	**das Wetter**	weather

Andere Wörter *(Other words)*

kalt	cold	**was?**	what?
kühl	cool	**wie?**	how?
warm	warm	**gleich**	just about, right away
heiß	hot	**jetzt**	now
schön	nice, beautiful	**heute**	today
windig	windy	**nur**	only
windstill	calm	**fast**	almost
		sehr	very
		nicht	not
		gar nicht	not at all

Ausdrücke *(Expressions)*

Wie ist das Wetter?	What's the weather like?
Regnet es noch?	Is it still raining?
Es regnet in Strömen.	It's pouring rain.
Das Thermometer zeigt dreißig Grad.	The thermometer reads thirty degrees.
Das ist Badewetter!	That's swimming weather!
Was für ein Hundewetter!	What rotten weather!

Bist du fertig?	Are you finished? Are you ready?	**Mensch!**	Wow! Boy!
Toll!	Fantastic!	**Sag mal, . . . ?**	Say, . . . ?

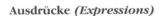

Was zeigt das Thermometer? Und das Barometer?

1. In German, a male American is an **Amerikaner** and a female American is an **Amerikanerin**. Likewise, a male Canadian is a **Kanadier** and a female Canadian is a **Kanadierin**.

Sprachnotizen

The flavoring particle *ja*

Speakers of German often use *flavoring particles* to add spice to what they are saying. When **ja** is used as a flavoring particle, it can add emphasis to an exclamation. In this function, **ja** has no equivalent in English.

Das ist ja Badewetter!   Das ist ja wunderbar!

Discourse strategies

If a speaker uses certain words or phrases to influence the direction a conversation is taking, she/he is employing a *discourse strategy*.

When you talk to your classmates in German, you can often use **du** to attract attention.

PETER: Du Martin, wer ist das?

When you want to ask a question to change the subject, you can use **sag mal**.

MARTIN: Hallo, Claudia. Bist du fertig?
CLAUDIA: Ja, gleich. — Sag mal, regnet es noch?

WÖRTER IM KONTEXT

WAS PASST ZUSAMMEN? In each set, read one of the items in the left column. Your partner gives an appropriate response from the right column. In some instances more than one response is possible.

1. Wie geht's?	Aus Berlin.
2. Die Sonne scheint, und der Himmel ist blau.	Was für ein Hundewetter!
3. Mein Name ist Ziegler.	Das ist heiß.
4. Bist du fertig?	Danke, gut.
5. Das Thermometer zeigt dreißig Grad.	Wie bitte? Wie heißen Sie?
6. Es regnet in Strömen.	Toll!
7. Woher kommst du?	Gleich!
8. Das Thermometer zeigt dreißig Grad.	Das ist Stephanie Braun.
9. Scheint die Sonne?	Nein, jetzt ist es wieder schön.
10. Sag mal, regnet es noch?	Tschüs!
11. Wie ist das Wetter?	Nein, es regnet in Strömen.
12. Wie kalt ist es?	Das ist ja Badewetter!
13. Auf Wiedersehen, Claudia!	Minus zehn.
14. Wer ist das?	Es ist kalt und sehr windig.

Wie heißt das Hotel?

FUNKTIONEN UND FORMEN

1. IDENTIFYING PEOPLE AND THINGS

SINGULAR NOUNS:
GENDER AND DEFINITE ARTICLES

Nouns are used to name people and things. In English all nouns have the definite article *the*. In German every noun has *grammatical gender*, i.e., it is either masculine, feminine, or neuter. Nouns that are masculine have the definite article **der,** nouns that are feminine have the definite article **die,** and nouns that are neuter have the definite article **das.**

Masculine	Feminine	Neuter
der	die	das

Although nouns referring to males are usually masculine (***der* Mann,** ***der* Vater)** and nouns referring to females are usually feminine (***die* Frau,** ***die* Mutter),** the gender of German nouns is not always logical:

der Winter	**die** Sonne	**das** Wetter
der Himmel	**die** Kamera	**das** Thermometer

You should learn each noun with its definite article *as one unit.*

A. WER IST DAS? Identify the members of the Ziegler family.

1. Das ist . . .

2. Das ist . . .

3. Das ist . . .

4. Das ist . . .

die Mutter	der Vater	die Tochter	der Sohn

B. WAS PASST ZUSAMMEN? Name the objects in the illustrations with nouns from the list below.

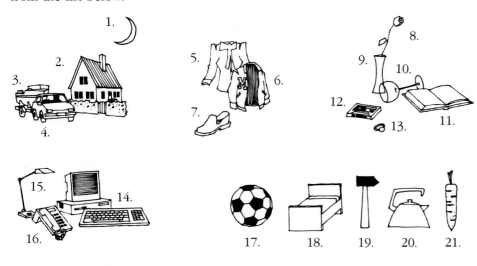

MASCULINE	FEMININE	NEUTER
der Computer	die Bluse	das Auto
der Fußball	die Jacke	das Boot
der Hammer	die Karotte	das Bett
der Mond	die Kassette	das Buch
der Ring	die Lampe	das Weinglas
der Schuh	die Rose	das Haus
der Teekessel	die Vase	das Telefon

2. ASKING QUESTIONS AND RESPONDING TO THEM

POSITION OF THE VERB IN QUESTIONS

a. Information questions

In information questions the verb immediately follows the question word.

Wie **ist** das Wetter heute?	*How **is** the weather today?*
Was **zeigt** das Thermometer?	*What **does** the thermometer **read?***

b. Yes/no questions

In yes/no questions the verb is always the *first element*.

Regnet es noch?	*Is it still **raining?***
Scheint die Sonne?	*Is the sun **shining?***

POSITION OF THE VERB IN STATEMENTS

Statements can be responses to questions. In English statements the verb follows the subject. In German statements the verb is *always the second element.* This basic difference is one of the most common sources of error for English-speaking students of German.

Der Himmel **ist** blau.	*The sky **is** blue.*
Heute **ist** der Himmel blau.	*Today the sky **is** blue.*
Die Sonne **scheint.**	*The sun **is shining.***
Heute **scheint** die Sonne.	*Today the sun **is shining.***

Ja, nein, and conjunctions such as **und** *(and),* **aber** *(but),* and **oder** *(or)* do not count as elements in a sentence.

Regnet es noch?	*Is it still raining?*
Nein, jetzt **scheint** die Sonne, **und** der Himmel **ist** blau, **aber** es **ist** immer noch sehr windig.	*No, now the sun is shining and the sky is blue, but it's still very windy.*

Note that the three forms of the English present tense have only one equivalent in German, i.e., forms like *it is raining* and *it does rain* do not exist.

How often **does** it **rain** in Hamburg?	Wie oft **regnet** es in Hamburg?
It **rains** very often.	Es **regnet** sehr oft.
It **is raining** today.	Es **regnet** heute.

it rains	
it is raining	**es regnet**
it does rain	

please

C. AUF ENGLISCH, BITTE!°

1. Scheint die Sonne hier viel?
   Ja, die Sonne scheint hier sehr viel.
   Die Sonne scheint heute.
2. Woher kommt Peter?
   Peter kommt aus Berlin.
3. Kommt Stephanie heute?
   Nein, Stephanie kommt nicht.

D. WIE IST DAS WETTER? Work with a partner.
Answer your partner's questions according to the illustration.

or

S1: Ist der Himmel blau oder° grau?   *S2:* Der Himmel ist blau.

1. Regnet es oder scheint die Sonne?
2. Ist es heiß oder kalt?
3. Ist es windig oder windstill?
4. Zeigt das Thermometer zwanzig Grad oder dreißig Grad?

E. WIE IST DAS WETTER HEUTE? Again, answer your partner's questions according to the illustration. Begin each answer with **heute.**

S1: Ist der Himmel heute grau oder blau?

S2: Heute ist der Himmel blau.

1. Ist heute Regenwetter oder Badewetter?
2. Ist es heute kalt oder heiß?
3. Zeigt das Thermometer heute zwanzig Grad oder dreißig Grad?
4. Ist es heute windig oder windstill?
5. Scheint heute die Sonne oder regnet es?

✏️ **DAS WETTER.** Look out the window and write a few lines describing what the weather is like today. Read your description to your classmates.

F. AUF DEUTSCH, BITTE! Sometimes Claudia and Stephanie speak English. What would they have said in German?

CLAUDIA:	What's the weather like today?
STEPHANIE:	Today it's cool and very windy.
CLAUDIA:	Is it still raining?
STEPHANIE:	Yes, it's pouring rain.
CLAUDIA:	How cold is it?
STEPHANIE:	The thermometer reads ten degrees.
CLAUDIA:	What rotten weather!

3. EXPRESSING NEGATION (1)

POSITION OF *NICHT*

You can say things negatively by using **nicht** *(not)* with various sentence elements.

a. If **nicht** negates a *specific element* in the sentence other than the verb, it precedes that particular element:

Ist es windig?
Nein, es ist **nicht** windig.

Is it windy?
No, it's not windy.

Regnet es in Las Vegas viel?
Nein, in Las Vegas regnet es **nicht** viel.

Does it rain a lot in Las Vegas?
No, in Las Vegas it doesn't rain a lot.

Regnet es heute sehr?
Nein, heute regnet es **nicht** sehr.

Is it raining hard today?
No, today it isn't raining hard.

Heißt du Stephanie?
Nein, ich heiße **nicht** Stephanie.

Is your name Stephanie?
No, my name is not Stephanie.

b. If the verb *itself* is negated, **nicht** stands at the end of the sentence:

Scheint die Sonne?
Nein, die Sonne scheint **nicht.**

Is the sun shining?
No, the sun isn't shining.

Kommt Stephanie?
Nein, Stephanie kommt **nicht.**

Is Stephanie coming?
No, Stephanie isn't coming.

c. **Nicht** follows adverbs of time like **heute** and **morgen**:

Kommt Stephanie morgen?	*Is Stephanie coming tomorrow?*
Nein, Stephanie kommt morgen **nicht.**	*No, Stephanie isn't coming tomorrow.*

G. TOTAL NEGATIV! Give a negative response to each of your partner's questions.

S1: Ist das Wetter schön? *S2:* Nein, das Wetter ist nicht schön.

1. Ist der Himmel blau?
2. Ist es windstill?
3. Scheint die Sonne?
4. Ist es sehr kalt?
5. Ist es warm?
6. Regnet es?
7. Ist es sehr windig?

8. Ist der Himmel grau?
9. Regnet es sehr?
10. Kommt Peter heute?
11. Kommt Peter aus Hamburg?
12. Ist Claudia fertig?
13. Kommt Stephanie morgen?

said

▨▷ **DAS WETTER: NEGATIV GESAGT°.** Write four sentences describing weather conditions. Each sentence must contain **nicht.**

H. AUF DEUTSCH, BITTE! Stephanie sometimes speaks English with Peter. What would they have said in German?

STEPHANIE:	Tell me, Peter, is it still raining?
PETER:	No, it isn't raining. The sun is shining and it's very nice.
STEPHANIE:	Fantastic! Is it warm?
PETER:	Yes, the thermometer reads thirty degrees.
STEPHANIE:	Boy, that's not warm, that's hot! That's swimming weather!

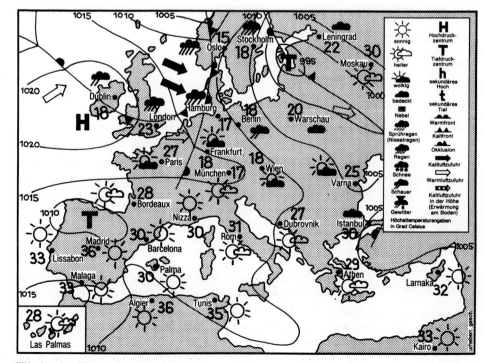

Wie ist das Wetter heute?

 ZUSAMMENSCHAU

BEIM AUSLANDSAMT

at the foreign student's office

⊟ Listen to the conversation of a group of students at a reception organized by the **Auslandsamt** of the **Ludwig-Maximilians-Universität.** Answer the following questions.

1. How many people are speaking?

   1   2   3   4   5

2. Which names do you hear?

   Mark   Martin   Stephanie   Claudia   Peter

3. Which of the following cities are mentioned in the conversation?

   Hamburg   Frankfurt   Toronto   München   Calgary   Chicago

4. How many Americans are among the speakers?

   0   1   2   3   4

5. How many Canadians are among the speakers?

   0   1   2   3   4

✏⟶ Listen to the conversation again. Then write the answers to the following questions in German. Note the German spellings of physics and biology: **Physik, Biologie.**

1. Woher kommt Claudia?
2. Was ist Marks Nationalität? Ist er° Amerikaner? *Nein, er ist . . .*   *he*
3. Kommt Mark aus Toronto? *Nein, er . . .*
4. Wie heißt Claudias Zimmerkollegin, und woher kommt sie?°   *she*
5. Ist Claudias Zimmerkollegin Kanadierin? *Nein, sie . . .*
6. Was studiert Stephanie?
7. Was studiert Mark?
8. Wie ist das Wetter jetzt? Regnet es noch?
9. Ist der Wind immer noch so kühl?
10. Wie warm ist es?

 ## WIR LERNEN EINANDER KENNEN

You are a student at a reception organized by the **Auslandsamt.** Walk around and:

1. introduce yourself to other students and ask what their names are.
2. ask where they come from and say what nationality you are.
3. say what you are majoring in **(Ich studiere . . .)**. Ask what their major is **(Was studierst du?).**
4. use **Sag mal,** . . . to change the subject, and ask a few questions about the weather (e.g., **Sag mal, regnet es noch?**)

Der Rhein bei Bingen

Winter im Schwarzwald

Encompassing 182,082 square miles, the German-speaking countries are approximately one-fortieth the size of the United States and Canada. And yet the topography of these countries is enormously varied.

The journey from the **Friesische Inseln,** a string of islands off the North Sea coast, to the peaks of the German, Swiss, and Austrian Alps in the south offers an abundance of fascinating views. Just south of Hamburg is the quiet beauty of the **Lüneburger Heide** *(Lüneburg Heath),* where you can watch the **Heidschnucken,** a breed of sheep special to the area, grazing in the heather. The North German lowlands soon give way to the Harz mountains with the beautiful towns of Goslar and Stolberg. To the southwest lies the vine-covered **Rheintal** *(Rhine valley),* and following the Rhine south you reach the densely-forested mountains of the **Schwarzwald** *(Black Forest).* From its highest point, the **Feldberg** (4900 ft.), you can see the snow-covered peaks of the Swiss Alps in the distance.

It takes about a day to drive from Freiburg, at the western edge of Germany, to the eastern border of Austria. Follow the Danube as it flows through a succession of culturally significant towns: Regensburg, Passau, Linz, and of course Vienna, the capital of Austria.

It is the quick succession of varying landscapes combined with historically rich architecture that makes the German-speaking countries so interesting. The Alps would lose much of their uniqueness without the picturesque old towns and villages tucked deep down in the steep valleys. The **Odenwald** would be just another mountainous region without an architectural jewel like the medieval market square of Michelstadt, and the Rhine would be just another large river without the vineyards that rise up steeply from its banks, and the castles on the cliffs above.

Beyond the castles, the market squares and cathedrals, the windmills and the thatched roof houses, it is the people who make these landscapes unique. Every region has its own customs and festivals and its own distinctive dialect.

Tourists from the German-speaking countries who visit North America are often impressed by the vastness of the undeveloped landscapes, but are puzzled by the uniformity of the architecture and food. On the other hand, North Americans traveling in the German-speaking countries may feel somewhat claustrophobic in these densely populated, extensively cultivated areas. But the lack of wide open space is amply compensated for by the rapid succession of impressions that the ever-changing landscape, architecture, cuisine, and people offer.

Am Nordseestrand ist es immer (*always*) windig and kühl.

Die Donau (*Danube*) bei Kehlheim.

4. LEARNING HOW TO COUNT

THE NUMBERS FROM 1–100,000

0 null			
1 ein**s**	11 elf	21 ei**nu**ndzwanzig	10 zehn
2 zwei	12 zwölf	22 zweiundzwanzig	20 zwanzig
3 drei	13 dreizehn	23 dreiundzwanzig	30 drei**ß**ig
4 vier	14 vierzehn	24 vierundzwanzig	40 vierzig
5 fünf	15 fünfzehn	25 fünfundzwanzig	50 fünfzig
6 sech**s**	16 se**chz**ehn	26 sech**s**undzwanzig	60 se**chz**ig
7 sieb**en**	17 sie**bz**ehn	27 sieb**en**undzwanzig	70 sie**bz**ig
8 acht	18 achtzehn	28 achtundzwanzig	80 achtzig
9 neun	19 neunzehn	29 neunundzwanzig	90 neunzig
10 zehn	20 zwanzig	30 dreißig	100 hundert

101 (ein)hundertein**s**	200 zweihundert	1000 (ein)tausend
102 (ein)hundertzwei	300 dreihundert	10 000 zehntausend
usw.°	usw.	100 000 hunderttausend

etc.

Note the following:

1. The **-s** in **eins** is dropped in combination with **zwanzig, dreißig,** etc: **einundzwanzig, einunddreißig,** etc.
2. The numbers from the twenties through the nineties are "turned around": **vierundzwanzig** *(four and twenty),* **achtundsechzig** *(eight and sixty),* etc.
3. **Dreißig** is the only one of the tens that ends in **-ßig** instead of **-zig.**
4. The final **s** in **sechs** is dropped in **sechzehn** and **sechzig.**
5. The **-en** of **sieben** is dropped in **siebzehn** and **siebzig.**
6. There is no **und** in **hunderteins, hundertzwei,** etc. (compare English *a hundred **and** one, a hundred **and** two,* etc.).
7. Where English uses a comma to mark off thousands, German uses a space: 10 000.
8. German uses a comma to indicate a decimal: 2,7 **(zwei Komma sieben).**
9. All numbers up to 999,999 are written as one word; e.g., 999 999 = **neunhundertneunundneunzigtausendneunhundertneunundneunzig.**

I. OHNE TASCHENRECHNER, BITTE! *(Without a calculator, please!)*

▶ 2 + 2

how much

S1: Wieviel° (Was) ist zwei plus zwei? **S2:** Zwei plus zwei ist vier.

▶ 2 − 2

S1: Wieviel (Was) ist zwei minus zwei? **S2:** Zwei minus zwei ist null.

1. 10 − 4   5. 44 + 11
2. 11 + 5   6. 71 − 10
3. 99 − 22   7. 9 + 3
4. 50 − 5   8. 14 + 3

J. CELSIUS UND FAHRENHEIT. For an American traveling in Europe, it is important to be familiar with the Celsius scale. With a partner, work on converting Celsius to Fahrenheit.

S1: Was (Wieviel) ist zwanzig Grad Celsius in Fahrenheit?	*S2:* Zwanzig Grad Celsius ist etwa achtundsechzig Grad Fahrenheit.

K. SCHON WIEDER DIE FALSCHE NUMMER! *(The wrong number again!)* It's just not your day. You keep dialing wrong numbers. Do this role play with a partner.

The name and number of the party you reach:	The number you think you dialed:	
▶ Hartmann: 91 08 12	91 08 13	
S1: Hier Hartmann.	*S2:* Hartmann? Ist da° nicht einundneunzig null acht dreizehn?	*there*
S1: Nein, hier ist einundneunzig null acht zwölf.	*S2:* Oh, Entschuldigung. Auf Wiederhören.	

1. Kurz: 58 44 23   58 44 32
2. Huber: 63 37 11   63 36 11
3. Strauß: 42 34 16   41 34 16
4. Schmidt: 78 48 24   48 78 24
5. Fischer: 33 06 18   33 06 17

5. LEARNING HOW TO SPELL

THE ALPHABET

The name of almost every letter in the German alphabet contains the sound represented by that letter. Learning the alphabet is therefore useful not only for purposes of spelling, but also for your pronunciation. Listen carefully to the cassette and to your instructor. Repeat what you hear.

Germans saying the alphabet do not include the three umlauted vowels **ä, ö, ü,** and the **Eszett (ß).**

L. HÖREN SIE GUT ZU UND WIEDERHOLEN SIE! *(Listen carefully and repeat!)*

a	b	c		j	k	l		s	t	u
d	e	f		m	n	o		v	w	x
g	h	i		p	q	r		y	z	

What is the logo of the German Post Office?

In Germany both the telephone system and the postal system are run by the **Deutsche Bundespost** *(Federal German Post Office.)* Phone booths and mailboxes are easy to spot: they are bright yellow, the official color of the **Bundespost.**

Most German telephone numbers are in pairs of digits (e.g., 86 68 22). The area code is called **die Vorwahl.** Although collect calls cannot be made within the country, you can call collect to the USA (but not to Canada). If you are traveling in Germany and want to call home, you can easily do so by going to the window marked **Fernsprechdienst** *(long distance service)* at the **Postamt** *(post office).* You can also dial overseas directly from phone booths marked **International,** but be sure to have enough change to feed the machine.

Telephone etiquette requires that the person answering the phone, as well as the caller, give her/his name. To say good-bye on the phone, many Germans use the phrase **auf Wiederhören** *(until we hear from each other again),* a variant of **auf Wiedersehen** *(until we see each other again).*

Letters are addressed a bit differently in the German-speaking countries. The house number follows the name of the street (e.g., Lindenstraße 29). The postal code **(die Postleitzahl)** in Germany consists of 4 digits and precedes the name of the city. The largest cities have numbers in the even thousands as postal codes, e.g., **1000 Berlin, 8000 München,** whereas smaller towns use the numbers in between, e.g., **7060 Schorndorf, 7055 Ochsenhausen.** In larger cities, sections within the city are indicated by an additional number following the name of the city, e.g., **1000 Berlin 62.**

What do the numbers 16, 8000, and 70 stand for?

M. LESEN SIE! *(Read!)*

VW	Volkswagen
BMW	Bayerische Motorenwerke
DZT	Deutsche Zentrale für Tourismus
BRD	Bundesrepublik Deutschland
USA	Vereinigte Staaten von Amerika[1]

N. BEIM AUSLANDSAMT.
You are the secretary at the **Auslandsamt** who is responsible for making up a list of foreign students. Your partner is one of the students.

▶ Lisa Fawcett
   Helmstraße 13, Berlin 62
   Tel. 6 33 25 17

S1: Ihr° Name, bitte?
S2: Lisa Fawcett. *your*

S1: Fawcett. Wie buchstabieren° Sie das?
S2: F–a–w–c–e–t–t. *spell*

S1: Und die Adresse bitte, Frau Fawcett?
S2: Helmstraße 13, Berlin 62.

S1: Haben Sie Telefon?
S2: Ja, meine Nummer ist 6 33 25 17.

1. Jim Uxbridge
   Lessingstraße 25, Berlin 41
   Tel. 3 65 28 04
2. Sandra Hitchcock
   Lindenstraße 122, Berlin 19
   Tel. 3 92 49 13
3. Peter Quigley
   Winterstraße 11, Berlin 51
   Tel. 3 66 14 27
4. Robert Percival
   Sandstraße 53, Berlin 20
   Tel. 7 91 79 38
5. Lori Jamieson
   Schillerstraße 30, Berlin 45
   Tel. 4 18 17 37
6. John Blizzard
   Bismarckstraße 64, Berlin 33
   Tel. 8 16 44 22

München (0 89)	
Schuh-Center	**80 29 19**
Dr. F. Werner	
(K-M) SchwieberdingerStr.120	
Schuh-Dorn	**62 43 84**
1 Rotebühlpl.37	
Priv. 1 Rosen–	**42 51 17**
gartenstr.87	
Schuh-Fischer	**62 49 39**
1 Silberburgstr.93	
Schuh-Graf	**56 89 97**
Julius Graf 50 Seelbergstr.21	
Fil.	**33 47 00**
60 Widdersteinstr.10	
Schuh-Grau	**29 42 17**
Gustav Grau 1 Hirschstr.14	

Why are there two different phone numbers for Schuh-Dorn?

WIR LERNEN EINANDER KENNEN

Use the model above to find out the last names, addresses, and telephone numbers of two of your classmates. Then report your findings to the class.

▶ *Lindas Familienname ist Hall. H–a–l–l.*
Lindas Adresse ist 89 Oakstraße, Somerville.
Lindas Telefonnummer ist 589-4106.

---

1. Germans use the English abbreviation.

ICH HABE ENDLICH EIN ZIMMER

Listen to the telephone conversation and answer the questions below.

Neue Vokabeln

endlich	*finally*	Minuten	*minutes*
ein Zimmer	*a room*	wann	*when*
nett	*nice*	nach Berlin	*to Berlin*
weit	*far*	Mach's gut!	*Good luck!*
zur Uni	*to the university*		

1. Who is speaking in this conversation?

   Martin Fischer Peter Ackermann Peter Ackermanns Mutter Martin Keller

2. Between which two cities does this call take place?

   Mannheim München Berlin

3. Which of these three students are rooming together?

   Peter Ackermann Martin Fischer Martin Keller

4. In which season of the year does this conversation take place?

   spring summer fall winter

5. When will Peter be seeing his parents again?

   in mid-October in mid-November at the end of November

Listen to the conversation again. Then write the answers to these questions in German.

1. Wer ist Frau Ackermann?
where
2. Wo° in Deutschland ist Frau Ackermann?
3. Wo in Deutschland ist Peter?
4. Heißt Peters Zimmerkollege Fischer oder Keller?
5. Woher kommt Martin Fischer?
6. Woher ist Martin Keller?
7. Was ist Peters Adresse?
from
8. Wie weit ist es von° Peters Zimmer zur Uni?
9. Was ist Peters Telefonnummer?
10. Wie kalt ist es heute in Berlin?

 **EIN TELEFONGESPRÄCH**

You and a partner are friends studying at different universities in Germany. Using the role cards below, make up a short telephone conversation. The numbers on the role cards indicate the order in which you speak.

Student(in) in Hamburg

It is the end of October and the beginning of your first semester at the **Universität Hamburg.**

1. Call your friend in **Stuttgart,** saying her/his phone number to yourself as you dial: 0711/45 32 61.
3. Say hello and identify yourself.
5. Say that you're fine and that you finally have a room now.
7. Your address is **Hagedornstraße 17, 2000 Hamburg 13.** Spell the name of the street.
9. Give your phone number: 040/98 68 53.
11. Describe weather conditions in **Hamburg,** and ask when your friend is coming to **Hamburg. (. . . nach Hamburg).**
13. Express pleasure about her/his impending visit and say good-bye.

Student(in) in Stuttgart

You are studying in your apartment in **Stuttgart** when your phone rings.

2. Answer the phone (as a German would).
4. Say hello and ask how your friend is.
6. Ask for your friend's address. **(. . . deine Adresse?)**
8. Ask for your friend's phone number. **(. . . deine . . . ?)**
10. Mention present weather conditions in **Stuttgart,** and inquire about what the weather is like in **Hamburg.**
12. Give approximate date of your visit to **Hamburg.**
14. Wish your friend good luck and say good-bye.

WORT, SINN UND KLANG

WÖRTER UNTER DER LUPE

GERMAN AND ENGLISH (1)

In reading the dialogues in the *Einleitung* and this chapter you have seen that German and English are closely related languages. Some German words and their English equivalents are completely identical in spelling and meaning: **warm, mild, blind, der Wind, der Hunger, der Ball, der Hammer,** etc. Many other German words are so close in sound and spelling to their English equivalents that you can

---

easily guess their meanings, especially if you look at the context in which they appear. Words in different languages that are identical or similar in form and meaning are called *cognates*.

- Give the English cognates of the following German words.

The family	Descriptive words		Animals
die Mutter	rot	hart	der Fisch
der Vater	grün	lang	die Ratte
der Sohn	blau	laut	die Maus
die Tochter	grau	voll	die Katze
der Bruder	braun	frisch	die Laus
die Schwester	weiß	sauer	der Wurm
	jung	dumm	der Fuchs
Parts of the body	alt	gut	der Bulle
	neu	reich	die Kuh
das Haar			das Lamm

Parts of the body

das Haar
die Nase
die Lippe
die Schulter
der Arm
der Ellbogen
die Hand
der Finger
der Fingernagel
das Knie
der Fuß

Food and drink

das Wasser	der Apfel
das Brot	das Bier
die Butter	der Wein
das Salz	die Milch
der Pfeffer	der Käse

WEITERE NÜTZLICHE WÖRTER UND AUSDRÜCKE

Ländernamen

The names of most countries are neuter and are not normally preceded by an article (e.g., **England, Dänemark, Schweden).** However, when the name of a country is masculine, feminine, or plural, the article must be used.

die Bundesrepublik Deutschland (die BRD)	the Federal Republic of Germany (the FRG)
die Schweiz	Switzerland
Österreich	Austria
die Vereinigten Staaten (die USA)	the United States (the USA)
Kanada	Canada

Nationalitäten

Er ist Deutscher.	He's a German.
Sie ist Deutsche.	She's a German.
Er ist Schweizer.	He's Swiss.
Sie ist Schweizerin.	She's Swiss.
Er ist Österreicher.	He's an Austrian.
Sie ist Österreicherin.	She's an Austrian.
Er ist Amerikaner.	He's an American.

Das Telefon

das Telefon	telephone
die Vorwahl	area code
die Nummer	number
Auf Wiederhören!	Good-bye! *(on the telephone)*

Sie ist Amerikanerin.	She's an American.
Er ist Kanadier.	He's a Canadian.
Sie ist Kanadierin.	She's a Canadian.

Farben (*Colors*)

blau	blue	**lila**	purple
braun	brown	**rosa**	pink
gelb	yellow	**rot**	red
grau	gray	**schwarz**	black
grün	green	**weiß**	white

Das Gegenteil (*The opposite*)

| **der Mann — die Frau** | man, husband—woman, wife |
| **bitte — danke** | please—thank you |

What does the circle of stars stand for?

Konjunktionen

und	and
aber	but
oder	or
usw. (und so weiter)	etc., and so on

WÖRTER IM KONTEXT

1. DIE NATIONALITÄT, BITTE!

a. Herr Karlhuber kommt aus Innsbruck. Er ist _____.
b. Frau Kröger ist aus Hamburg. Sie ist _____.
c. Frau Lawson kommt aus Vancouver. Sie ist _____.
d. Herr Bürgli ist aus Zürich. Er ist _____.
e. Frau Hall ist aus San Franzisko. Sie ist _____.
f. Herr Altmann ist aus Leipzig. Er ist _____.

2. WER WEISS° DIE FARBEN?

knows

a. Schokolade ist _____.
b. Gras ist _____.
c. Butter ist _____.
d. Milch ist _____.
e. Kohle ist _____.

f. Blut ist _____.

g. Die Sonne scheint, und der Himmel ist _____.

h. Der Himmel ist _____, und es regnet.

3. KONJUNKTIONEN, BITTE!

a. Claudia _____ Stephanie studieren in München.

b. Kommt Martin aus Berlin _____ aus Mannheim?

c. Ist es kalt?

Ja, _____ nicht sehr.

d. Ist der Wein weiß _____ rot?

Many of the similarities between English and German can be traced back 1600 years to the time when the Angles and Saxons, Germanic tribes from what is today northern Germany, invaded Britain and settled there.

Around the year 200 A.D. the Roman Empire encompassed not only the countries around the Mediterranean, but also included present-day Austria, Switzerland, Southern Germany, France, and most of the British Isles. But then this vast empire started to crumble and lose its military power. The Germanic tribes, plagued by problems of overpopulation, and lured by the warmer and more civilized areas dominated by the Romans, the Germanic tribes began to invade Roman territory. Sometimes entire tribes migrated from their homelands. This was the case with the Vandals (whose name is preserved in the word *vandalism*) who left their territory along the Oder River and crisscrossed Western Europe, leaving a path of terror and destruction. They finally settled in North Africa, where they were defeated by the Romans in 534 A.D.

The migration of the Angles and the Saxons was far less spectacular, but it had a much more enduring effect. Beginning about the fourth century A.D., shiploads of warriors from these tribes crossed the North Sea to England and attacked the increasingly vulnerable Roman defenses. When the Romans finally retreated from Britain in the fifth century, the Angles and Saxons remained and settled the country. It was the Germanic languages of these tribes that became the foundation for present-day English.

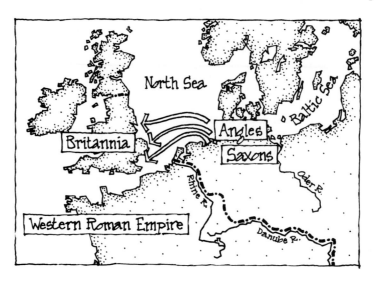

In this chapter you have become acquainted with some sounds and letters that are not found in the English language. They are discussed briefly here and will be discussed again in greater depth in later chapters. As you repeat the German examples bear in mind that the key to good pronunciation is to listen carefully and to imitate the sounds that you hear.

• Hören Sie gut zu und wiederholen Sie!

1. THE UMLAUTED VOWELS *Ä, Ö,* AND *Ü*

The sounds represented by the letter **ä** are close to the sound represented by the letter *e* in English *let.*

   der Bäcker   der Gärtner   der Käse   die Universität

The sounds represented by the letter **ö** have no equivalents in English. Listen carefully to your instructor or the cassette.

   der Mörder   die Wörter   schön   in Strömen

The sounds represented by the letter **ü** also have no equivalents in English. Listen carefully and imitate.

   fünf   Tschüs!   Grüß dich!   grün

2. THE ESZETT

The letter **ß,** which is called **Eszett,** is pronounced like an *s.*

   heiß   heißen   dreißig

3. GERMAN *CH*

After **a, o,** and **u** the sound represented by **ch** resembles a gentle gargling.

   noch   acht

After **i** and **e** the sound represented by **ch** is pronounced like a loudly whispered *h* in *huge.*

   ich   dich   nicht   gleich

The suffix **-ig** is pronounced as if it were spelled **-ich.**

   fertig   windig   zwanzig   dreißig

Das Rathaus *(city hall)* in Hamburg

KAPITEL 2

◼ Kommunikationsziele

*In **Kapitel 2** you will learn how to:*
describe people, places, and things
make comparisons
talk about more than one person or thing
talk about people and things without naming them
ask for information

◼ Hör- und Sprechsituationen

Wie gut bist du in Klimatologie?
Vergleiche
Wie ist der Sommer (der Winter) bei euch?
In der Studentenkneipe
Woher komme ich?
Wie alt bist du? Wie groß bist du?
Farben und Farbtöne
Was ist es?

◼ Strukturen

Adjectives and adverbs
The comparative of adjectives and adverbs
Plural forms of nouns
Ein and **kein**
Personal pronouns
Present tense of **sein**
Question words

◼ Wissenswertes

Hansestadt Hamburg
The climate of the German-speaking countries

📼 KONTRASTE

Sandra Hutton and Günter Schlumberger meet during their Christmas vacation in Florida.

SANDRA:	Ist das nicht toll hier in Florida? Fünfundzwanzig Grad mitten im Winter!
GÜNTER:	Wie kalt ist es jetzt in Montreal?
SANDRA:	Zwanzig unter Null. Und in Hamburg?
GÜNTER:	Dort regnet es.
SANDRA:	Was, Regen an Weihnachten?!°
GÜNTER:	Ja, bei uns° in Hamburg ist der Winter nicht so kalt wie bei euch° in Montreal. Bei uns ist das Klima viel milder. Aber manchmal schneit° es auch in Hamburg.
SANDRA:	Ist der Sommer bei euch sehr heiß?
GÜNTER:	Nein, in Hamburg regnet es auch im Sommer viel. Aber wärmer als in Kanada ist es bestimmt.
SANDRA:	Aber Günter! Bei uns ist es im Sommer sehr heiß, oft über dreißig Grad!
GÜNTER:	Was, über dreißig Grad?! Und im Winter zwanzig unter Null! Was für Extreme!
SANDRA:	Und bei euch nichts als° Regen! Wie deprimierend!
GÜNTER:	Lieber° Regen als Eis und Schnee! Und außerdem scheint auch in Hamburg oft die Sonne.

Christmas
where I come from / where you come from / snows

nothing but
I'd rather have

VOM LESEN ZUM SPRECHEN

RICHTIG ODER FALSCH? *(True or False)* Your instructor will read ten statements based on the conversation above. Decide whether they are **richtig** or **falsch.**

WER WEISS DAS? Your instructor will ask you nine questions that are related to the conversation above. Do you know the correct answers?

WIE GUT BIST DU IN KLIMATOLOGIE?

Work with a partner. Take turns testing your general knowledge about climates in various countries and cities of the world. The numbers on the role cards indicate the order in which you proceed. You can judge your partner's responses with **richtig** or **falsch.**

Student 1:

1. Wo ist der Winter so mild wie in Florida?
3. in Sibirien   in Mexiko   in England
   Wo regnet es so viel wie in Hamburg?
5. in Tel Aviv   in Berlin   in München
   Wo schneit es so viel wie in Montreal?
7. in Kairo   in Los Angeles   in London

Student 2:

2. in Schweden   in Österreich   in Israel
   Wo ist das Klima so extrem wie in Kanada?
4. in Las Vegas   in Seattle   in Athen
   Wo ist es an Weihnachten so warm wie in Miami?
6. in Rom   in Innsbruck   in Madrid
   Wo ist der Winter so deprimierend wie in Hamburg?

VERGLEICHE *(Comparisons)*

The graphs below show the average temperatures in Hamburg, Chicago, Ottawa, and Sydney for the months of January **(der Januar),** April **(der April),** July **(der Juli),** and October **(der Oktober).** Working with a partner, compare the average seasonal temperatures of the four cities.

S1: Wo ist der Januar kälter als in Hamburg? *S2:* In Chicago und in Ottawa.

S1: Wo ist der Januar wärmer als in Chicago? *S2:* In . . .

S1: . . .

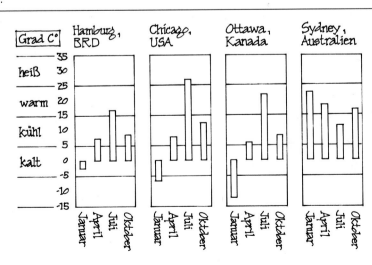

Nina Grunenberg über Helmut Kohl: Balance-Akt am Kaukasus (Seite 3)

DIE ZEIT

Nr. 30   30. Juli 1990, 45. Jahrgang   Preis 3,80 DM   WOCHENZEITUNG FÜR POLITIK · WIRTSCHAFT · HANDEL UND KULTUR   C 7451 C

Hamburg: der Hafen *(harbor)*

Hamburg, located in Northern Germany at the mouth of the Elbe river, is a city of superlatives. It is not only Germany's largest seaport, but also one of the largest in the world. Even though it is located 120 kilometers (75 miles) from the North Sea, the port can service large ocean liners and freighters. About 60 ships enter the harbor every day, adding up to almost 20,000 a year. Hamburg has more canals than Venice: 2125 bridges span these canals and the three rivers that flow through the city, the Elbe, the Alster, and the Bille. Hamburg is Germany's second largest city and it has the reputation of being the country's rainiest city. Finally, many of the most famous German newspapers, magazines,

and tabloids are published in Hamburg. They include the widely-read newspaper **Die Zeit,** the magazines **Der Spiegel,** and **Stern,** and the sensationalist tabloid **Bild-Zeitung** (circulation: 5.4 million).

License plates of cars registered in Hamburg show the letters HH, which stand for **Hansestadt Hamburg.** In medieval times most of the important Northern German cities belonged to the **Hansa,** a powerful league of merchant cities that maintained a large fleet of trading vessels and dominated trade in the North and Baltic Seas for centuries.

NÜTZLICHE WÖRTER UND AUSDRÜCKE

Nomen

das Klima	climate	der Schnee	snow
der Winter	winter	der Regen	rain
der Sommer	summer	das Eis	ice

Andere Wörter

mild	mild, moderate	auch	too, also
extrem	extreme	unter	under, below
		über	over, above
manchmal	sometimes	dort	there
oft	often		
viel	much, a lot	nichts	nothing
bestimmt	certainly; for sure	außerdem	besides

Ausdrücke

mitten im Winter	in the middle of winter
zehn unter Null	ten below zero
Es schneit.	It's snowing.
Was für Extreme!	What extremes!
nichts als Regen	nothing but rain
Wie deprimierend!	How depressing!
Lieber Regen als Eis und Schnee!	I'd rather have rain than ice and snow!
bei uns	where I (we) come from, where I (we) live
bei euch	where you come from, where you live
Wie ist das Klima bei euch?	What's the climate like where you come from?
so kalt wie	as cold as
wärmer als	warmer than

WÖRTER IM KONTEXT

1. WAS PASST ZUSAMMEN?

a. Wie kalt ist es im Winter in Montreal?   Wie deprimierend!

b. In Hamburg regnet es auch im Sommer viel.   Lieber Regen als Eis und Schnee!

c. In Montreal ist es im Sommer sehr heiß, und im Winter zeigt das Thermometer oft 20 unter Null.   Ja, aber manchmal schneit es auch.

d. Was, Regen mitten im Winter?   Was für Extreme!

e. Regnet es im Winter oft in Hamburg?   Nein, bei uns regnet es im Sommer viel.

f. Ist der Sommer bei euch sehr heiß?   Oft zwanzig unter Null.

2. WAS PASST WO?

schneit   dort   mitten   auch   so   viel   wie   viel extremer

a. EVA: Ist das Klima in Rumänien _____ so mild wie in Italien?

   PAUL: Nein, _____ ist das Klima _____.

b. INGRID: _____ es in Hamburg auch _____ in Montreal?

   DAVID: Nein, in Hamburg regnet es oft _____ im Winter.

Schnee   deprimierend   bei euch   als   bei uns   so heiß wie
nichts   kühler

C. STEVE: Ist der Sommer _____ in San Franzisko auch _____ bei uns in Miami?

   CINDY: Nein, _____ ist der Sommer viel _____.

d. SANDRA: _____ als Regen im Winter?! Wie _____!

   GÜNTER: Lieber Regen _____ Eis und _____!

unter   über   das Klima   bestimmt   Sommer   manchmal

e. GÜNTER: Bei euch in Montreal ist _____ bestimmt viel extremer als bei uns in Hamburg.

   SANDRA: Ja, im _____ ist es bei uns oft sehr heiß und im Winter zeigt das Thermometer _____ dreißig _____ Null.

f. FRAU KOCH: Ist es heute sehr heiß?

   FRAU BENN: Ja, _____ _____ dreißig Grad.

FUNKTIONEN UND FORMEN

1. DESCRIBING PEOPLE, PLACES, THINGS, AND ACTIONS

ADJECTIVES AND ADVERBS

Adjectives are words that describe people, places, and things.

In Alaska ist Fisch **billig** und Salat **teuer.**	*In Alaska fish is **cheap** and lettuce is **expensive.***
Berlin ist **groß** und Bonn ist **klein.**	*Berlin is **big** and Bonn is **small.***

Adverbs can be used to describe actions.

In Hamburg regnet es **oft.**	*In Hamburg it rains **often.***

A. DAS GEGENTEIL. Look at the pairs of opposites below and then use them to complete the sentences given. Since you know the meaning of at least one of the pairs, you can easily guess the rest.

kalt—heiß   alt—jung   lang—kurz   dumm—intelligent

1. Spaghetti sind _____, und Makkaroni sind _____.
2. Eis ist _____, und Feuer ist _____.

human being

3. Der Mensch° ist _____, und der Computer ist _____.
4. Das Baby ist _____, und die Großmutter ist _____.

oft—selten   alt—neu   sauer—süß   extrem—mild

5. In Kalifornien ist das Klima _____, und in Kanada ist es _____.
6. Grapefruit ist _____, und Schokolade ist _____.
7. Die Carnegie Hall in New York ist _____, und das Kennedy Center in Washington ist _____.
8. In Hamburg regnet es _____, und in Las Vegas regnet es _____.

teuer—billig   gut—schlecht   viel—wenig   groß—klein

9. Der Elefant ist _____, und die Maus ist _____.
10. Wein ist _____, und Wasser ist _____.
11. Das Buch° ist _____, aber der Film ist _____.   *book*
12. David trinkt _____, und Thomas trinkt _____.

2. MAKING COMPARISONS

THE COMPARATIVE OF ADJECTIVES AND ADVERBS

The comparative forms of adjectives and adverbs are used to compare characteristics and qualities. In contrast to English, German has only one way of forming the comparative: by adding **-er** to the adjective or adverb.

Peter ist ein Jahr **jünger** als Martin.   *Peter is one year **younger** than Martin.*

In Nordamerika ist das Klima **extremer** als in Europa.   *In North America the climate is **more extreme** than in Europe.*

In Hamburg regnet es **öfter** als in Frankfurt.   *In Hamburg it rains **more often** than in Frankfurt.*

Most German one-syllable adjectives or adverbs with the vowels **a, o,** or **u** are *umlauted* in the comparative:

warm—w**ä**rmer   *warm—warmer*
groß—gr**ö**ßer   *big—bigger*
jung—j**ü**nger   *young—younger*

As in English, a few adjectives and adverbs have irregular comparative forms:

gut—besser   *good—better*
viel—mehr   *much—more*
hoch—höher   *high—higher*

Adjectives that end in **-er** or **-el** drop the **e** in the comparative:

Der Orangensaft ist teuer, **teurer** als der Apfelsaft.   *The orange juice is expensive, **more expensive** than the apple juice.*
Tanja ist sehr sensibel, aber Eva ist noch viel **sensibler.**   *Tanja is very sensitive, but Eva is much **more sensitive.***

The German equivalent of *than* is **als:**

intelligenter **als**   *more intelligent **than***

Another way of comparing characteristics and qualities is to use **so . . . wie** *(as . . . as).*

Ist der Fudschijama **so** hoch **wie** die Jungfrau°?   *Is Mt. Fuji **as** high **as** the Jungfrau?*

Was kostet ein Paar Schuhe?

mountain in the Swiss Alps

1282 feet

Nein, die Jungfrau ist 391 Meter höher.   *No, the Jungfrau is 391 meters° higher.*

Nicht so . . . wie can serve as a substitute for the comparative:

Eva ist **freundlicher als** Tina.   =   Tina ist **nicht so freundlich wie** Eva.

B. DER KLIMATOLOGE.   You want to know how the weather in various parts of the world compares to that of Germany. Ask your partner, who is an expert in climatology.

▶ der Sommer/Florida   heiß

S1: Wie ist der Sommer in Florida?   **S2:** Heißer als in Deutschland.

---

1. der Winter / Alaska   kalt
2. das Klima / Kanada   extrem
3. der Sommer / Schweden   kühl
4. der Winter / Kalifornien   mild
5. der Sommer / Spanien   warm
6. das Klima / Italien   mild
7. der Winter / Norwegen   kalt
8. das Klima / Sibirien   extrem

WIE IST DER SOMMER (DER WINTER) BEI EUCH?   Ask your partner how the summer and the winter where she/he comes from compares to that of Germany.

C. VERGLEICHE.   Answer your partner's questions, using the comparative form of the characteristic given.

▶ süß   sauer
  Sind Grapefruits . . . Orangen?   Nein, Grapefruits sind . . . Orangen.

S1: Sind Grapefruits so süß wie Oran-   **S2:** Nein, Grapefruits sind saurer als
gen?   Orangen.

---

1. lang   kurz
   Ist der Februar . . . der Januar?   Nein, der Februar ist . . . der Januar.
2. alt   jung
   Ist Stephanie . . . Peter?   Nein, Stephanie ist . . . Peter.
3. viel   wenig
   Regnet es in München . . . in Ham-   Nein, dort regnet es . . . in Hamburg.
   burg?
4. teuer   billig
   Ist Silber . . . Gold?   Nein, Silber ist . . . Gold.
5. dumm   intelligent
   Ist der Mensch . . . der Computer?   Nein, der Mensch ist . . . der Computer.
6. schlecht   gut
   Ist das Buch . . . der Film?   Nein, das Buch ist . . . der Film.
7. wenig   viel
   Trinkt David . . . Thomas?   Nein, David trinkt . . . Thomas.

8. oft   selten
   Regnet es in München . . . in Ham-   Nein, dort regnet es . . . in Hamburg.
   burg?
9. groß   klein
   Ist Zürich . . . Berlin?   Nein, Zürich ist . . . Berlin.
10. billig   teuer
   Ist Orangensaft . . . Apfelsaft?   Nein, Orangensaft ist . . . Apfelsaft.

◪ ZUSAMMENSCHAU

IN DER STUDENTENKNEIPE

in the student pub

  Günter Schlumberger meets Lori Wilson in a student pub and he's using his favorite conversation opener: talking about the weather. Listen to their conversation.

Neue Vokabeln

Nordkalifornien	*Northern California*
Südkalifornien	*Southern California*
südlich von	*south of*
also	*that's*
direkt am Pazifik	*right on the Pacific*
nie	*never*
zu viel	*too much*
bis Ende August	*until the end of August*

In der Kneipe

- Indicate the order in which you hear the following statements or questions.

    —— San Diego ist direkt am Pazifik.
    —— Bist du Amerikanerin oder Engländerin?
    —— Bis Ende August.
    —— Das ist sehr mild, viel milder als hier in Hamburg.
    —— In Südkalifornien, südlich von Los Angeles.

- Listen to the conversation again and choose the correct answer.

    1. Günter shows his ignorance about the USA by assuming that San Diego is in:

       Northern California   Texas   New Mexico

    2. Günter concludes that it is very hot in San Diego because San Diego is:

       in California   very close to Mexico

    3. The temperatures that are mentioned in connection with the Fahrenheit scale are:

       80°   18°   14°   40°

    4. The temperatures that are mentioned in connection with the Celsius scale are:

       5°   52°   25°

5. The conversation between Lori and Günter takes place in:

San Diego   Los Angeles   Hamburg

✏️ Write full sentences to answer the following questions about Günter's conversation with Lori.

1. Ist Lori Wilson Amerikanerin oder Engländerin?
2. Woher in Amerika ist sie?
3. Ist San Diego in Nordkalifornien oder in Südkalifornien?
4. Ist Los Angeles südlich oder nördlich von San Diego?
5. San Diego ist fast in Mexiko. Warum ist es dann nicht sehr heiß dort?
6. Wie warm ist es im Sommer in San Diego? (in Grad Fahrenheit)
7. Was ist das in Celsius? *In Celsius . . .*
8. Wie kalt ist es im Winter in San Diego? (in Grad Fahrenheit)
9. Was ist das in Celsius? *In Celsius . . .*
10. Ist das Klima in Hamburg auch so mild wie in San Diego? *Nein, in Hamburg . . .*
11. Regnet es in San Diego auch so viel wie in Hamburg? *Nein, in San Diego . . .*
12. Wie lang ist Lori noch in Hamburg?

 **WOHER KOMME ICH?**

Imagine that you are from a well-known city in the USA or Canada that is quite different, both climatically and in size, from the city in which you are presently living. Your partner asks you the following in order to guess the name of the city. Sometimes you may have to answer with **manchmal** or **Ich weiß es nicht.**

Your partner asks you:

1. whether the city **(die Stadt)** is in America or in Canada.
2. whether the state or province **(der Staat, die Provinz)** is bigger or smaller than _____ *[name of state or province where you are at the moment]*.
3. whether the state or province is north, south, east, west northeast, southwest, etc. of here? **(nördlich von hier, südlich von hier, östlich von hier, westlich von hier, nordöstlich von hier, südwestlich von hier, usw.)**
4. whether the summer there is hotter or cooler than here.
5. whether the winter there is colder or warmer than here.
6. whether it rains there. More or less than here? As much as here? When, in summer or in winter?
7. whether it snows there. More or less than here?
8. whether the state or province is called _____.
9. whether the city **(die Stadt)** is bigger or smaller than _____ *[name of your college or university town]*.
10. whether the city is called _____.

The Matterhorn above Zermatt, Switzerland

Even though the German-speaking countries generally have a temperate climate, there can be considerable variation within this relatively small area.

In the north, the weather is influenced by the cool air currents off the North Sea and the Baltic Sea. The summers are only moderately warm and the winters are mild, but often stormy and very wet.

In the central region, between the Northern Lowlands and the Alps in the south, the summers are usually much warmer and the winters much colder than in the north. The highest summer temperatures occur in the protected valleys of the Rhine and Moselle rivers. Here the warm summer sun shines on the steep slopes rising from the river banks, providing perfect growing conditions for the thousands of acres of vineyards that produce the famous white wines of Germany.

To the south, the alpine climate of the mountainous regions of Switzerland and Austria is characterized by high precipitation, shorter summers, and longer winters. But even in these small countries the variation in climate from one area to the next is quite striking. In Switzerland, which is about half the size of the state of Maine, the climate is so varied that a sports enthusiast can go windsurfing and skiing in the space of one summer's day!

Sprachnotizen

German *also*

German **also** does not mean *also* in English. The German word **also** is often used in conversation to draw a conclusion. In this function it means something like *that is* or *so:*

A: Ist San Diego in Nordkalifornien oder in Südkalifornien?

Is San Diego in Northern California or in Southern California?

B: In Südkalifornien, südlich von Los Angeles.

In Southern California, south of Los Angeles.

B: **Also** fast in Mexiko.

So, *almost in Mexico.*

A: Ja, fast in Mexiko.

Yes, almost in Mexico.

You can also use **also** to indicate that you are getting somewhat impatient with the person you're talking to and want her/him to make a decision.

Also kommst du jetzt oder nicht?　　*Are you coming or not?*

Also combined with **dann** is frequently used to introduce a farewell such as **auf Wiedersehen, tschüs, bis morgen.**

Also dann, bis morgen!　　***Well then,*** *see you tomorrow!*

3. IDENTIFYING PERSONS AND THINGS

PLURAL FORMS OF NOUNS

Although a few English nouns have irregular plural forms (e.g., woman, wom*en*; child, child*ren*) the majority of English nouns forms the plural by adding -*s* or -*es* (e.g., student, student*s*; class, class*es*).

German has seven types of plural forms. You must therefore learn each noun not only with its definite article, but also with its plural form.

The definite articles **(der, die, das)** have only *one* plural form: **die.**

Type	Plural Markers	Singular	Plural
1	- (none)	der Amerikaner	die Amerikaner
	¨ (umlaut only)	die Mutter	die Mütter
2	-e	der Freund	die Freund**e**
	-ë	die Maus	die Mäus**e**[1]
3	-n	die Lampe	die Lampe**n**
4	-en	die Frau	die Frau**en**
5	-er	das Kind	die Kind**er**
	¨er	das Land	die Länd**er**
6	-s	das Auto	die Auto**s**
7	-nen	die Freundin	die Freundin**nen**

All nouns of Type 7 are derived from masculine nouns, e.g., **der Student, die Student*in*; der Amerikaner, die Amerikaner*in*.**

Beginning at the end of this chapter, the sections *Nützliche Wörter und Ausdrücke* and *Weitere Nützliche Wörter und Ausdrücke* will contain the plural forms of nouns. To facilitate learning, these forms will be written out in full, as they are above. However, in dictionaries and in the end vocabulary of this book, the plural forms are abbreviated as follows:

der Amerikaner,   die Frau, -en
die Mutter, ¨   das Kind, -er
der Freund, -e   das Land, ¨er
die Maus, ¨e   das Auto, -s
die Lampe, -n   die Freundin, -nen

D. WER WEISS DIE FARBEN? The plural forms below are listed as you would find them in a dictionary. Using the plural forms, say what colors the objects or animals are.

Masculine	Feminine	Neuter
der Ball, ¨e	die Banane, -n	das Auto, -s
der Schuh, -e	die Blume, -n	das Haus, ¨er
der Apfel, ¨	die Katze, -n	das Bett, -en
der Pullover, -	die Maus, ¨e	das Buch, ¨er

Die Vasen sind blau.

---

1. The combination of two vowels in **Maus** is called a diphthong. If the diphthong **au** is umlauted, it is always the **a** that is umlauted.

1.   2.   3.   4.

5.   6.   7.   8.

9.   10.   11.   12.

THE INDEFINITE ARTICLE

The forms of the indefinite article that correspond to **der, die,** and **das** are **ein, eine,** and **ein** (English: *a, an*):

	Definite	**Indefinite**
Masculine	**der** Meter	**ein** Meter
Feminine	**die** Minute	**eine** Minute
Neuter	**das** Auto	**ein** Auto

If the numeral *one* (**eins**) precedes a noun, German uses the indefinite article instead:

Wie viele Kinder hat Frau Koch?	*How many children does Mrs. Koch have?*
Sie hat nur **ein** Kind.	*She has only **one** child.*
Wie viele Katzen hat Bernd?	*How many cats does Bernd have?*
Er hat nur **eine** Katze.	*He has only **one** cat.*

E. WER WEISS DAS?   Test your partner's general knowledge!

▶ Räder°/ Auto *(n)*   *wheels*

S1: Wie viele Räder hat ein Auto?   **S2:** Ein Auto hat vier Räder.

1. Meter / Kilometer *(m)*
2. Zentimeter / Meter *(m)*
3. Millimeter / Zentimeter *(m)*
4. Sekunden / Minute *(f)*
5. Stunden° / Tag *(m)*
6. Tage / Woche° *(f)*
7. Wochen / Jahr *(n)*
8. Tage / Jahr *(n)*
9. Minuten / Stunde *(f)*
10. Sekunden / Stunde *(f)*
11. Monate / Jahr *(n)*
12. Jahre / Jahrhundert *(n)*
13. Räder / Dreirad *(n)*
14. Finger / Mensch *(m)*
15. Räder / Fahrrad° *(n)*

hours
week
bicycle

The Metric System: Length

1 cm = 10 mm   1 m = 100 cm   1 km = 1000 m

F. ALTER UND GRÖSSE *(Age and Height).* Ask your partner about the ages and heights of Claudia, Martin, Peter, and Stephanie.

S1: Wie alt ist Claudia?
S1: Und wie groß ist sie?

S2: Sie ist dreiundzwanzig.
S2: Eins achtundsechzig.

Claudia 23 J. 1,68 m   Martin 22 J. 1,77 m   Peter 21 J. 1,80 m   Stephanie 19 J. 1,60 m

---

Now compare the ages and heights of the four friends. To talk about height in German, use the adjectives **groß** and **klein.**

S1: Wer ist vier Jahre jünger als Claudia?   **S2:** Stephanie.
S1: Wer ist drei Zentimeter kleiner als Martin?   **S2:** . . .
S1: Wer ist ein Jahr älter als Peter?
S1: Wer ist acht Zentimeter größer als Stephanie?
S1: Wer ist . . . ?

WIE ALT BIST DU? WIE GROSS BIST DU?

Move around the classroom and find out similar statistics about your classmates. Use the scale to convert feet and inches to metric measure.

---

then

S1: Wie alt bist du?

S1: Dann° bist du | so alt wie ich. / älter als ich. / jünger als ich.

S1: Und wie groß bist du?

S1: Dann bist du | so groß wie ich. / größer als ich. / kleiner als ich.

S2: Ich bin _____ *[Give your age].*

S2: _____ *[Give your height].*

THE NEGATIVE FORMS OF THE INDEFINITE ARTICLE

In English the negative forms of the indefinite article are *not a, not (any), no.*

In German the negative forms of the indefinite article are **kein** and **keine.**

Das ist **keine** Oboe, das ist eine Klarinette.

*That's **not an** oboe, it's a clarinette.*

Das sind **keine** Orangen, das sind Mandarinen.

*Those are**n't** oranges, they're mandarins.*

Kein Monat ist so kurz wie der Februar.

***No** month is as short as February.*

Masculine	Feminine	Neuter	Plural
ein	eine	ein	————
kein	**keine**	**kein**	**keine**

Note that **kein** has a plural form.

G. WAS FÜR DUMME FRAGEN!° The words to match the illustrations are in the *questions* box below.

▶   ein Glas

S1: Ist das ein Glas?

S2: Nein, das ist kein Glas. Das ist eine Vase.

▶   Lilien

S1: Sind das Lilien?

S2: Nein, das sind keine Lilien. Das sind Tulpen.

1. Weingläser

2. eine Kaffeekanne

3. eine Jacke

4. ein Pullover

5. ein Barometer

6. Mäuse

7. ein Mikroskop

8. Disketten

| ein Sweatshirt | Ratten | eine Teekanne | ein Teleskop |
| eine Bluse | ein Thermometer | Kassetten | Kognakgläser |

4. TALKING ABOUT PERSONS WITHOUT NAMING THEM

What facility does this sign point to?

PERSONAL PRONOUNS

If you want to talk about persons without repeating their names, you use personal pronouns.

You have already seen most of the personal pronouns in the *Einleitung* and *Kapitel 1*. The personal pronouns are categorized under three "persons":

1st person: I / we   *(to talk about oneself)*
2nd person: you / you   *(to talk to a second party)*
3rd person: he / she / it / they   *(to talk about a third party)*

		Singular		Plural
1st person	**ich**	*I*	**wir**	*we*
2nd person	**du**	*you (familiar)*	**ihr**	*you (familiar)*
	Sie	*you (formal)*	**Sie**	*you (formal)*
3rd person	**er**	*he*	**sie**	*they*
	sie	*she*		
	es	*it*		

H. ERGÄNZEN SIE! *(Complete!)* Fill in the blanks using the appropriate personal pronouns.

1. BERND: Wie heißt ihr?
   STEPHANIE: _____ heiße Stephanie und das ist Peter.
   BERND: Und woher kommt _____?
   STEPHANIE: _____ komme aus Chicago und Peter ist aus Berlin.
2. HERR SCHWARZ: Sind _____ Frau Meyer?
   FRAU MÜLLER: Nein, _____ bin Erika Müller.
3. HOLGER: Heißt _____ Claudia?
   STEPHANIE: Nein, _____ heiße Stephanie.
4. KURT: Sind Linda und Jennifer aus England?
   RALF: Nein, _____ sind aus Amerika.
5. BERND: Wie alt ist Stephanie? Ist _____ älter als Claudia?
   PETER: Nein, _____ ist vier Jahre jünger als Claudia.
6. STEPHANIE: Wie groß ist Martin? Ist _____ größer als Peter?
   CLAUDIA: Nein, _____ ist ein bißchen° kleiner als Peter.
7. CLAUDIA: Regnet _____ noch?
   MARTIN: Nein, jetzt ist _____ wieder sehr schön.
8. CLAUDIA: Ich bin Claudia und das ist Stephanie.
   HOLGER: Wohnt ihr° im Studentenheim?
   CLAUDIA: Ja, _____ sind Zimmerkolleginnen.

a bit

do you live

9. EVA: Wie alt bist du?

   INGRID: _____ bin 20.

   EVA: Dann bist _____ ein Jahr älter als ich.

5. EXPRESSING *TO BE*

THE PRESENT TENSE OF *SEIN*

The present tense forms of **sein** *(to be)* are as frequently used and as irregular as their English counterparts. They should be carefully learned.

Singular		Plural	
ich bin	*I am*	wir sind	*we are*
du bist	*you are*	ihr seid	*you are*
er / sie / es ist	*he / she / it is*	sie sind	*they are*
	Sie sind	*you are*	

I. ERGÄNZEN SIE! Read the following conversations, using the proper forms of **sein.**

1. Hallo!

   MARTIN: Hallo! Ich _____ Martin, und das _____ Peter.

   HELGA: _____ ihr Brüder?

   MARTIN: Nein, wir _____ Freunde.

   HELGA: Woher _____ ihr?

   MARTIN: Ich _____ aus Mannheim, und Peter _____ aus Berlin.

2. Wie alt ist Holger?

   JULIA: Wie alt _____ du, Holger? _____ du älter oder jünger als Kathrin?

   HOLGER: Wie alt _____ Kathrin?

   JULIA: Sie _____ so alt wie ich.

   HOLGER: Und wie alt _____ du?

   JULIA: Ich _____ einundzwanzig.

   HOLGER: Dann _____ ihr drei Jahre älter als ich.

   Holger ist _____ Jahre alt.

3. Wo sind Herr und Frau Ziegler?

   FRAU HOLZ: Entschuldigung, _____ Sie Herr und Frau Ziegler aus Bonn?

   FRAU NAGLER: Nein, wir _____ nicht Herr und Frau Ziegler.

   FRAU HOLZ: Sie _____ nicht Herr und Frau Ziegler?

   FRAU NAGLER: Nein, und wir _____ auch nicht aus Bonn.

   FRAU HOLZ: Aber wer _____ Sie dann?

   FRAU NAGLER: Ich _____ Beate Nagler aus Kassel, und das _____ Herr Müger aus Frankfurt.

   FRAU HOLZ: Und wo _____ Herr und Frau Ziegler?

   FRAU NAGLER: Ich glaube,° Zieglers _____ noch im Hotel.   *I think*

J. KLEINE GESPRÄCHE. Supply the correct forms of **sein** and/or the correct personal pronouns.

Stefan   Oliver   Barbara

Holger   Brigitte

Frau Jones   Herr Smith

1. _____ Stefan größer als Barbara?
   Nein, _____ _____ kleiner als _____.
2. _____ Barbara und Stefan größer als Oliver?
   Nein, _____ _____ kleiner als _____.
3. Wie alt _____ _____, Brigitte?
   _____ _____ fünf.
   Und du, Holger, wie alt _____ _____?
   _____ _____ drei.
   Und woher _____ _____ zwei?
   _____ _____ aus Stuttgart.
4. _____ _____ Amerikaner, Herr Smith?
   Nein, _____ _____ Kanadier.
   Und Sie, Frau Jones, _____ _____ auch Kanadierin?
   Nein, _____ _____ Amerikanerin.

K. NAME? ALTER? You are a police officer who needs some information. Begin by asking your partner's name and age. Your partner will respond with first names that correspond to her/his gender.

	▶ Bettina (Oliver) Müller, 45
S1: Wie heißen Sie?	**S2:** Ich heiße Bettina (Oliver) Müller.
S1: Und wie alt sind Sie?	**S2:** Ich bin fünfundvierzig Jahre alt.
	▶ Kathrin (Thomas) Berger, 13
S1: Wie heißt du?	**S2:** Ich heiße Kathrin (Thomas) Berger.
S1: Und wie alt bist du?	**S2:** Ich bin dreizehn Jahre alt.

1. Angelika (Karl-Heinz) Bandmann, 51
2. Christine (Daniel) Kunz, 14
3. Anita (Günter) Stengel, 11
4. Helga (Stefan) Krüger, 66
5. Brigitte (Kurt) Vogel, 12

6. TALKING ABOUT THINGS WITHOUT NAMING THEM

PERSONAL PRONOUNS IN THE THIRD PERSON

In English the pronouns in the 3rd person singular (he, she, it) are usually chosen according to the principle of *natural gender: he* for males, *she* for females, and *it* for things.

In German the *nouns themselves* are either masculine, feminine, or neuter, and the pronouns in the 3rd person singular **(er, sie, es)** are chosen according to the principle of *grammatical gender,* i.e., **er** for all nouns with the article **der, sie** for all nouns with the article **die,** and **es** for all nouns with the article **das:**

Ist **der** Student nett?°	Ist **der** Film lang?	*nice*
Ja, **er** ist sehr nett.	Ja, **er** ist sehr lang.	
Ist **die** Professorin gut?	Ist **die** Suppe heiß?	
Ja, **sie** ist sehr gut.	Ja, **sie** ist sehr heiß.	
Ist **das** Baby süß?	Ist **das** Wetter schlecht?	
Ja, **es** ist sehr süß.	Ja, **es** ist sehr schlecht.	

In the 3rd person plural, the personal pronoun for all three genders is **sie:**

Sind **die** Studenten intelligent?	Sind **die** Tomaten süß?
Ja, **sie** sind sehr intelligent.	Ja, **sie** sind sehr süß.

L. JA ODER NEIN?

▶ Peter / groß

S1: Ist Peter groß?   *S2:* Ja, er ist sehr groß.
                                                   Nein, er ist nicht sehr groß.

---

1. der Kaffee / heiß	Nein, . . .	8. die Äpfel *(pl)* / sauer	Nein, . . .
2. Helga / intelligent	Ja, . . .	9. der Professor / jung	Ja, . . .
3. die Bananen *(pl)* / gut	Ja, . . .	10. die Klassen *(pl)* / groß	Nein, . . .
4. Günter / nett	Nein, . . .	11. der Pullover / warm	Ja, . . .
5. der Wind / kalt	Ja, . . .	12. die Butter / frisch	Ja, . . .
6. das Wetter / schlecht	Ja, . . .	13. das Buch / interessant	Ja, . . .
7. der Wein / süß	Nein, . . .		

FARBEN UND FARBTÖNE°

shades of color

What color or shade of color are your classmates' clothes? Your instructor wants to know your opinion. Use colors or shades of colors from the list below.

LEHRER(IN): Ist Lisas Pullover blau oder
            grün?

S1: Ich denke°, er ist blau.   *think*
S2: Ich denke, er ist grün.
S3: Ich denke, er ist blaugrün.

die Jacke	der Pullover	die Bluse	das Hemd	die Hose

der Rock	das Kleid	die Jeans *(pl)*	die Schuhe *(pl)*	die Socken *(pl)*

schwarz	gelb	grün	blau	braun	rot	grau	
weiß	hellgelb°	hellgrün	hellblau	hellbraun	hellrot	hellgrau	*light yellow*
lila	dunkelgelb°	gelbgrün	dunkelblau	dunkelbraun	dunkelrot	dunkelgrau	*dark yellow*
rosa	goldgelb	blaugrün	schwarzblau	gelbbraun	rosarot	schwarzgrau	
				rotbraun			

---

7. GETTING INFORMATION

Semestermitteilungen hier erhältlich

DM 3,00

For which faculty is this calendar?

QUESTION WORDS

You use question words to find out specific information. In German all question words begin with the letter **w** (pronounced like English *v*):

wann?	*when?*
wie?	*how?*
woher?	*where? (from what place?)*
wo?	*where? (in what place?)*
wohin?	*where? (to what place?)*
wer?	*who?*
was?	*what?*
wieviel?	*how much?*
wie viele?	*how many?*
warum?	*why?*

Note that German uses three words for the word *where,* according to whether it means *from what place, in what place,* or *to what place.*

Woher ist Martin?	*Where is Martin from?*
Aus Mannheim.	*From Mannheim.*
Wo ist Graz?	*Where is Graz?*
In Österreich.	*In Austria.*
Wohin gehst du heute abend?	*Where are you going tonight?*
Heute abend gehe ich ins Kino.	*Tonight I'm going to the movies.*

Be careful to distinguish between **wo** *(where)* and **wer** *(who).* Don't let the English equivalents confuse you.

M. WEISST DU DAS? *(Do you know it?)* Complete the questions with appropriate question words and find out whether your partner knows the answers.

1. _____ ist der Winter kälter, in Deutschland oder in Schweden?
2. _____ ist einunddreißig plus sechs?
3. _____ Stunden hat ein Tag?
4. _____ ist älter, Michael Jackson oder Mick Jagger?
5. _____ kommt Wayne Gretzky, aus Polen oder aus Kanada?
6. _____ ist das Klima in England, mild oder extrem?
7. _____ ist teurer, ein VW oder ein BMW?
8. _____ schneit es in Acapulco nicht?
9. _____ ist null Grad Celsius in Fahrenheit?
10. _____ ist das Wetter heute?
11. _____ in Europa ist Innsbruck?
12. _____ Monate hat ein Jahr?
13. _____ schneit es in Neuseeland, im August oder im Januar?
14. _____ singt besser, Michael Jackson oder Mick Jagger?
15. _____ ist es in Frankfurt wärmer, im April oder im Juli?
16. _____ kommen Monty Python, aus England oder aus Amerika?
17. _____ sind viele Deutsche im Winter in Florida, und _____ nicht im Sommer?
18. _____ gehst du heute abend, ins Konzert, ins Kino, ins Theater, in die Bibliothek,° in die Cafeteria, ins Bett?

library

N. IN DER STUDENTENKNEIPE. Robert and Tina meet Lori in a student pub in Hamburg. Express their conversation in German.

ROBERT: Hello! I'm Robert and this is Tina.
LORI: Are you from Hamburg?
ROBERT: No, we're from Graz.
LORI: From Graz? Where's that?
TINA: Graz is in Austria.
LORI: What's the climate like there? Better than here in Hamburg?
TINA: Much better. In winter it's colder and it snows a lot, and in summer it rains much less.
ROBERT: Where are you from, Lori?
LORI: I'm an American.
ROBERT: What's the climate like where you come from?
LORI: Where I come from it never° snows and in summer it isn't very hot. **nie**
ROBERT: Does it rain a lot?
LORI: No, where I come from the sun almost always° shines. **immer**
TINA: Are you from Florida?
LORI: No, I'm from Southern California.° **Südkalifornien**

◥ ZUSAMMENSCHAU

WAS IST ES?

 Listen to the speakers play a guessing game. As you listen, decide which of the statements in each of the sets below is *most* helpful in identifying the object. The solution is not given. Can you guess what the object is?

Neue Vokabeln

das Ding	*object, thing*	aus Glas	*made of glass*
		aus Holz	*made of wood*
also	*so*	aus Leder	*made of leather*
meistens	*most of the time*	aus Metall	*made of metal*
manchmal	*sometimes*	aus Papier	*made of paper*
immer	*always*	aus Plastik	*made of plastic*
nie	*never*	aus Porzellan	*made of porcelain*
oft	*often*	aus Wolle	*made of wool*
		aus Baumwolle	*made of cotton*

1. Das Ding ist . . .
   a. so groß wie ein Haus.
      so klein wie eine Kassette.
      größer als eine Kassette, aber nicht sehr viel größer.
   b. meistens viel billiger als ein Auto, aber teurer als eine Kassette.
      so teuer wie ein Auto.
      so billig wie eine Kassette.
   c. immer weiß.
      nie schwarz oder weiß, aber oft blau, grün oder gelb.
      manchmal weiß, aber nicht immer.
   d. meistens aus Holz.
      oft aus Porzellan.
      manchmal aus Wolle.

2. Lösung:° Das Ding ist . . .
   a. ein Thermometer.
   b. ein Bierglas.
   c. eine Vase.

For homework write a description of one of the objects below so that a classmate or your instructor can guess what it is. You can work with the vocabulary above, adjectives like **groß, klein, teuer, billig** and their comparative forms, and colors.

ein Auto	ein Buch	eine Kassette	ein Ring
ein Ball	ein Computer	ein Kassettenrecorder	ein Schuh
ein Bett	ein Hammer	eine Lampe	ein Sweatshirt
eine Blume	ein Haus	ein Mikroskop	ein Teekessel
eine Bluse	eine Jacke	eine Pistole	ein Telefon
ein Boot	eine Kamera	ein Pullover	ein Thermometer
	eine Vase	ein Weinglas	

Think of an object in the list above. Use materials, colors, and comparisons of size and price to describe the object that you have in mind. Your partner will guess what the object is.

WORT, SINN UND KLANG

WÖRTER UNTER DER LUPE

GERMAN AND ENGLISH (2)

In *Kapitel 1* you read about the common ancestry of German and English and saw that for many of the related words—the so-called cognates—the use of a dictionary is quite unnecessary. But it has been almost 1500 years since the Angle and Saxon invaders left their continental homelands and settled in England; German and English have diverged considerably since then. Fortunately, some of the changes are quite systematic and if you know the "code", you will be able to add a great many German words to your vocabulary. Some of the "codes" are given below: you should have no trouble "decoding" the German words in each category. Words followed by *(v)* are the infinitive forms of verbs. It helps to *say* German words aloud when you are trying to guess their meanings.

1. German **f** or **ff** is English *p*

   der A**ff**e   das Schi**ff**
   schar**f**   hel**f**en *(v)*
   die Har**f**e   o**ff**en
   rei**f**   ho**ff**en *(v)*

2. German **b** is English *v* or *f*

ha**b**en *(v)*   das Kal**b**
das Gra**b**   une**b**en
hal**b**   das Fie**b**er

3. German **d, t,** or **tt** is English *th*

das Ba**d**   **d**ies
danken *(v)*   die Fe**d**er
das **D**ing   das Le**d**er
dick   die **D**istel
dünn   der **D**orn
der Bru**d**er   **t**ausend
der Va**t**er   das We**tt**er
die Mu**tt**er   die Er**d**e

weint: *is . . . crying*

What message do these graffiti convey?

WEITERE NÜTZLICHE WÖRTER UND AUSDRÜCKE

Die Jahreszeiten und die Monate

das Jahr, die Jahre	year
die Jahreszeit, die Jahreszeiten	season
der Monat, die Monate	month

In German the names of the seasons, the months of the year, and the days of the week are all masculine (exception: ***das* Frühjahr**).

der Winter
der Januar
der Februar
der März

der Frühling
der April
der Mai
der Juni

der Herbst
der Oktober
der November
der Dezember

der Sommer
der Juli
der August
der September

Die Wochentage

die Woche, die Wochen	week
der Tag, die Tage	day
der Montag	Monday
der Dienstag	Tuesday
der Mittwoch	Wednesday
der Donnerstag	Thursday
der Freitag	Friday
der Samstag, der Sonnabend	Saturday
der Sonntag	Sunday

Die Zeit

die Zeit, die Zeiten	time
die Uhr, die Uhren	clock
die Stunde, die Stunden	hour
die Minute, die Minuten	minute
die Sekunde, die Sekunden	second
gestern	yesterday
morgen	tomorrow
heute abend	tonight
morgen abend	tomorrow night
dann	then
meistens	mostly, most of the time

On what day of the week was this ticket purchased?

Fragewörter

wann?	when?	**wieviel?**	how much?
warum?	why?	**wie viele?**	how many?
was?	what?	**woher?**	where? (from what place?)
wer?	who?	**wo?**	where? (in what place?)
wie?	how?	**wohin?**	where? (to what place?)

Wohin gehst du?

in die Vorlesung	to the lecture	**ins Kino**	to the movies
in die Bibliothek	to the library	**ins Konzert**	to a concert
in die Cafeteria	to the cafeteria	**ins Theater**	to the theater
in die Disco	to the disco	**ins Bett**	to bed
in die Kneipe	to the pub		

Das Gegenteil

kalt—heiß	cold—hot	**gut—schlecht**	good—bad
kühl—warm	cool—warm	**teuer—billig**	expensive—cheap
extrem—mild	extreme—mild	**viel—wenig**	much—little
jung—alt	young—old	**dumm—intelligent**	stupid—intelligent
neu—alt	new—old	**süß—sauer**	sweet—sour
lang—kurz	long—short	**hier—dort**	here—there
groß—klein	large—small; tall—short	**oft—selten**	often—seldom
dick—dünn	fat—thin	**immer—nie**	always—never

WÖRTER IM KONTEXT

WAS PASST WO?

Januar   wohin   heute abend   wo   in die Bibliothek   nie   warum
woher   kalt

1. _____ kommt Peter _____ nicht?
2. Auch Martin kommt fast _____.
3. Im _____ ist es hier oft sehr _____.
4. _____ gehst du? In die Cafeteria oder _____?
5. _____ kommst du? Aus Frankfurt oder aus Heidelberg?
6. _____ ist Herr Ziegler heute? In Bonn oder in Frankfurt?

   süß—sauer   oft—selten   alt—neu   jung—alt   lang—kurz

7. Ist die Orange _____ oder _____?
8. Ist Professor Seidlmeyer _____ oder _____?
9. Ist der Winter bei euch _____ oder _____?
10. Kommt Mark _____ oder _____?
11. Ist das Haus _____ oder _____?

    heiß—kalt   dick—dünn   immer—nie   viel—wenig   gut—schlecht

12. Ist der Film _____ oder _____?
13. Lisa kommt fast _____ und David fast _____.
14. Trinkt Thomas _____ oder _____?
15. Ist der Kaffee _____ oder _____?
16. Ist das Buch _____ oder _____?

GERMAN *EI* AND *IE*

Because of the inconsistencies of English spelling and pronunciation (e.g., N*ei*ther of my fr*ie*nds rec*ei*ved a p*ie*ce of p*ie*), English-speaking students of German often confuse the pronunciation and spelling of the German **ie** and **ei** (e.g., **D*ie* Sonne sch*ei*nt.**) When the two vowels appear together, use the second vowel as an indication of how the word is pronounced. To help you keep these two vowel combinations straight, you can also think of "Frankenst*ei*n is a f*ie*nd".

- Hören Sie gut zu und wiederholen Sie!

W**ei**n	W**ie**n°	*Vienna*
n**ei**n	n**ie**	
s**ei**n	s**ie**	
b**ei**	B**ie**r	

- Distinguish between **ei** and **ie** by reading the following sentences aloud.

  1. W**ie**v**ie**l ist dr**ei** und v**ie**r?
     Dr**ei** und v**ie**r ist s**ie**ben.
  2. W**ie** h**ei**ßen S**ie**?
     Ich h**ei**ße Z**ie**gler.
  3. Das ist nicht m**ei**n B**ie**r.
  4. D**ie** Schw**ei**z ist **ei**ne Demokrat**ie**.
  5. Ist D**ie**ter auch so kl**ei**n w**ie** Stephan**ie**?

Ein Straßenkonzert: Musikstudenten verdienen Geld

KAPITEL 3

◼ **Kommunikationsziele**

In Kapitel 3 you will learn how to:

talk about your studies
talk about your hobbies and leisure time activities
talk about nationalities and groups that you belong to
express your likes, dislikes, and preferences
talk about possessions and relationships
talk about your family and friends

◼ **Hör- und Sprechsituationen**

Spielst du ein Instrument?
Was machst du gern?
John Bayne fliegt nach Deutschland
Wie gut kennen wir einander jetzt?
Das ist Jennifer Winkler
Ich und meine Familie
Du und deine Familie

◼ **Strukturen**

Verb: infinitive and present tense
Verb + **gern** or **lieber**
Omission of the indefinite article
Subject and direct object: nominative and accusative
   case
Possessive adjectives
Present tense of **haben**
More about the position of **nicht**
Doch versus **ja**
Word order: time and place

◼ **Wissenswertes**

Bach, Beethoven, and Schoenberg
**Bekannte deutsche, österreichische und
schweizerische Städte**
German license plates

VORSCHAU

WARUM LERNST DU DEUTSCH?

In an evening German course, students have been working on a role-play in groups of three. The topic was "Warum lernst du Deutsch?" Here is the role-play one of the groups has come up with.

MICHAEL:	Guten Abend! Ich heiße Michael.
ANDREA:	Ich bin Andrea.
MICHAEL:	Warum lernst du Deutsch, Andrea?
ANDREA:	Ich studiere nächstes Jahr in Detmold. Und du?
MICHAEL:	Ich fliege° im Sommer nach Deutschland.
ANDREA:	Was machst du° dort?
MICHAEL:	Ich bin Programmierer und arbeite° bei IBM in Stuttgart. Was studierst du in Detmold, Andrea?
ANDREA:	Musik. Ich bin Musikstudentin.
MICHAEL:	Was für ein Instrument spielst du denn?
ANDREA:	Klavier. Hörst du gern° Musik, Michael?
MICHAEL:	Ja, ich habe viele CDs, und ich gehe auch gern ins Konzert.
ANDREA:	Du, ich habe zwei Karten° für morgen abend. Unser° Orchester spielt Bach, Beethoven und Schoenberg. Hast du Lust?°
MICHAEL:	Natürlich. Ich arbeite bis° fünf, und dann . . .
PROFESSOR KUHL:	Sie sprechen° Deutsch miteinander?! Das höre ich gern!
ANDREA:	Wir versuchen° es.
PROFESSOR KUHL:	Sie sprechen schon sehr gut.
ANDREA:	Oh, danke! Ist die Pause schon vorbei,° Frau Kuhl?
PROFESSOR KUHL:	Ja, es ist gleich sieben Uhr.°
MICHAEL:	Na, dann bis nachher,° Andrea.
ANDREA:	Tschüs, Michael.

am flying

will you be doing
I'll be working

do you like to listen to

tickets / our
Do you want to go?
until
are speaking
we are trying

over
o'clock
see you later

VOM LESEN ZUM SPRECHEN

WER WEISS DAS?

Each of the questions below is followed by three responses. Which *two* answers correctly reflect the content of the conversation?

1. Warum lernt Andrea Deutsch?

Sie studiert nächstes Jahr in Detmold.
Sie fliegt nächstes Jahr nach Deutschland.

2. Warum lernt Michael Deutsch?

Er fliegt im Sommer nach Deutschland.
Er arbeitet im Sommer bei IBM in Stuttgart.
Er geht gern ins Konzert.

3. Was macht Andrea in Detmold?

Sie studiert dort Musik.
Sie arbeitet dort bei IBM.
Sie lernt dort besser Deutsch.

4. Was machen Andrea und Michael morgen abend?

Sie gehen ins Konzert.
Sie lernen Deutsch.
Sie hören Bach, Beethoven und Schoenberg.

 RICHTIG ODER FALSCH? Your instructor will read ten statements based on the dialogue above. Decide whether they are **richtig** or **falsch.**

 ## SPIELST DU EIN INSTRUMENT?

Members of your class are planning a musical talent night. They have to know who plays an instrument and how well. Interview three of your classmates.

S1: Spielst du ein Instrument?

S2: Ja, ich spiele _____.
Nein, aber ich singe gern.
Nein, aber ich klatsche sehr gut.

S1: Wie gut spielst du?

S2: Ich spiele gut.
Ich spiele sehr gut.
Ich spiele nicht sehr gut.

• Record your findings and report them to the rest of the class.

---

1. _____ [name of classmate] spielt _____ [name of instrument].
2. Sie / er spielt | gut.
sehr gut.
nicht sehr gut.
3. _____ [name of classmate] spielt kein Instrument, | aber sie / er singt gern.
aber sie / er klatscht sehr gut.

Johann Sebastian Bach (1685–1750)

Descended from a long line of musicians, Bach learned much about composition from copying and arranging the works of other composers. His own compositions represent the epitome of German **Barockmusik.** One of Bach's duties as organist and music director of the **Thomaskirche** *(Church of St. Thomas)* in Leipzig was to compose music for every Sunday of the church year. His **Matthäuspassion, Johannespassion,** and **Weihnachtsoratorium** *(Christmas Oratorio)* are performed every Easter and Christmas all over the world. His **Brandenburgische Konzerte** are among the finest examples of the *concerto grosso.* Bach left a legacy of over one thousand works.

Johann Sebastian Bach.

Ludwig van Beethoven (1770–1827)

Already during his lifetime Beethoven was acknowledged as the greatest composer of his generation. Growing out of the Viennese tradition of Haydn and Mozart, his music is both the culmination of the classical period and the bridge to romanticism. At the age of 30 he started to lose his hearing, and his later works, including the monumental **Neunte Symphonie,** were written when he was totally deaf. His nine symphonies, five piano concertos, his violin concerto, piano sonatas, and chamber music are performed regularly in concert halls all over the world.

Ludwig van Beethoven.

Arnold Schoenberg (1874–1951)

Schoenberg spent his early musical career as a conductor and teacher, moving between Vienna and Berlin. Hitler's rise to power in 1933 forced him to emigrate and he continued his teaching career in Los Angeles at USC and UCLA. Early compositions like **Verklärte Nacht** *(Transfigured Night)* are still written in the traditional major and minor keys. In the 1920s Schoenberg's theoretical studies led him to the development of the twelve-tone technique (based on the twelve pitches of the octave). The best-known of his later works, the *Variations for Orchestra, Opus 31,* is a blending of traditional tonality with the twelve-tone technique.

Arnold Schoenberg

NÜTZLICHE WÖRTER UND AUSDRÜCKE

Nomen

die Musik	music
das Instrument, die Instrumente	instrument
das Klavier	piano
die CD, die CDs	CD, compact disc
das Konzert	concert
die Karte, die Karten	ticket; card; playing card
die Pause, die Pausen	break, intermission

Verben

hören	to hear; to listen to
lernen	to learn; to study (i.e., do homework, prepare for an exam)
studieren	to go to college or university; to major in a subject

machen	to do, to make	fliegen	to fly
arbeiten	to work	spielen	to play
gehen	to go	haben	to have

reisen to travel/take a trip

Andere Wörter

bis	until
schon	already
für	for
natürlich	of course

Ausdrücke

nächstes Jahr	next year
Bis nachher!	See you later!
nach Deutschland	to Germany
Was für ein Instrument spielst du?	What instrument do you play?
Ich spiele Klavier.	I play the piano.
Hörst du gern Musik?	Do you like to listen to music?
Hast du Lust?	Do you want to (go, come, etc.)?
Es ist sieben (Uhr).	It's seven (o'clock).
Ich arbeite bei IBM.	I work for IBM.

Gehst du gern ins Konzert?

Sprachnotizen

The flavoring particle *denn*

The flavoring particle **denn** is frequently added to questions. It expresses curiosity and interest and has no equivalent in English. It usually follows the subject of the sentence.

Warum studierst du **denn** in Detmold?   *Why are you studying in Detmold?*

Do not confuse **denn** with **dann,** which means *then.*

Ich arbeite bis sieben, und **dann** gehe   *I'm working until seven and then I'm*
ich ins Konzert.   *going to a concert.*

WÖRTER IM KONTEXT

1. WAS PASST ZUSAMMEN?   In some instances more than one response is possible.

a. Spielst du ein Instrument?

b. Warum lernst du Deutsch?

c. Wann fliegst du denn nach Deutschland?

d. Sind die Karten für heute abend?

e. Ich gehe gern ins Konzert.

f. Was für ein Instrument spielst du denn?

g. Was studierst du?

h. Wo studierst du nächstes Jahr?

Ich auch.

Ich spiele Gitarre.

In Detmold.

Nein, aber ich habe viele CDs.

Aber natürlich.

Schon im Sommer.

Nein, für morgen abend.

Ich bin Musikstudentin.

Ich arbeite nächstes Jahr in Deutschland.

2. WAS PASST WO?

geht   spielt   macht   arbeitet

a. Michael _____ kein Instrument, aber er _____ sehr gern ins Konzert.

b. Was _____ Michael in Stuttgart?
Er _____ dort bei IBM.

ist   spielt   fliegt   studiert

c. Andrea _____ Musikstudentin und _____ sehr gut Klavier.

d. Nächstes Jahr _____ sie nach Deutschland und _____ in Detmold Musik.

lernen   sprechen   gehen   hören

e. Michael und Andrea _____ Deutsch, und sie _____ schon sehr gut.

f. Morgen abend _____ sie ins Konzert und _____ Bach, Beethoven und Schoenberg.

lernst   gehe   spielst   habe   arbeite

g. _____ du ein Instrument, Michael?
Nein, aber ich _____ viele CDs, und ich _____ auch oft ins Konzert.

h. Warum _____ du Deutsch?
Ich _____ im Sommer in Deutschland.

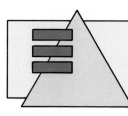

FUNKTIONEN UND FORMEN

 1. EXPRESSING ACTIONS IN THE PRESENT AND FUTURE

THE VERB: INFINITIVE AND PRESENT TENSE

a. The infinitive

In English the infinitive form of the verb is usually signaled by *to: to sing, to learn, to do*. German infinitives consist of a *verb stem* plus the ending **-en** or **-n:**

Infinitive	Stem	Ending
singen	sing	-en
lernen	lern	-en
tun	tu	-n

b. The present tense

In English only the 3rd person singular has an ending in the present tense: he learn*s*, she do*es*, it work*s*. In German *all* the forms of the present tense have endings. These endings are attached to the verb stem:

Singular	Plural
ich lern**e**	wir lern**en**
du lern**st**	ihr lern**t**
er / sie / es lern**t**	sie lern**en**
Sie lern**en**	

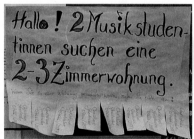

Note: Verbs with the infinitive ending **-n** also have the ending **-n** in the 1st and 3rd person plural and in the **Sie**-form: wir tu**n**, sie tu**n**, Sie tu**n.**

A. KLEINE GESPRÄCHE. Complete the following conversations.

1. NINA: Was mach___ du heute abend, Andrea?
   ANDREA: Von sechs bis sieben lern___ ich Deutsch.
   NINA: Und dann? Was tu___ du dann? Spiel___ du dann Klavier?
   ANDREA: Nein, dann komm___ Michael.
   NINA: Was mach___ ihr heute abend? Geh___ ihr wieder° ins Konzert?   *again*
   ANDREA: Nein, heute abend geh___ wir ins Theater.

2. PROF. KUHL: Warum lern___ Sie Deutsch, Andrea?

   ANDREA: Ich flieg___ nächstes Jahr nach Deutschland.

   PROF. KUHL: Was tu___ Sie dort?

   ANDREA: Ich studier___ in Detmold Musik.

   PROF. KUHL: Was für ein Instrument spiel___ Sie denn?

   ANDREA: Ich spiel___ Klavier.

3. FRANK: Was für ein Instrument spiel___ Andrea?

   MICHAEL: Sie spiel___ Klavier.

   FRANK: Spiel___ sie gut?

   MICHAEL: Ja, sehr gut. Sie studier___ Musik.

   FRANK: Wann flieg___ ihr nach Deutschland?

   MICHAEL: Wir flieg___ Ende Juni.

4. EVA: Warum lern___ Michael und Andrea Deutsch?

   FRANK: Sie flieg___ im Sommer nach Deutschland.

   EVA: Und warum geh___ sie so oft ins Konzert?

   FRANK: Andrea studier___ Musik, und Michael hör___ sehr gern Musik.

   EVA: Ich hör___ auch gern Musik, und heute abend sing___ die Wiener Sängerknaben.°

   FRANK: Gut, dann geh___ wir heute abend ins Konzert.

Vienna Boys Choir

**Kammermusik
für Bläser
mit
Alfred Brendel**

Alfred Brendel, Klavier
Heinz Holliger, Oboe
Louise Pellerin, Oboe
Eduard Brunner, Klarinette
Elmar Schmid, Klarinette
Klaus Thunemann, Fagott
Matthew Wilkie, Fagott
Hermann Baumann, Horn
Radovan Vlatkovic, Horn

Wolfgang Amadeus Mozart
1756 – 1791

Serenade KV 375 Es-Dur
für 2 Oboen, 2 Klarinetten,
2 Hörner und 2 Fagotte

Allegro maestoso
Menuetto
Adagio
Menuetto
Finale. Allegro

Wolfgang Amadeus Mozart
1756 – 1791

Quintett KV 452 Es-Dur
für Klavier, Oboe, Klarinette,
Horn und Fagott

Largo – Allegro moderato
Larghetto
Rondo. Allegretto

Ludwig van Beethoven
1770 – 1827

Quintett op. 16 Es-Dur für
Klavier, Oboe, Klarinette, Horn
und Fagott

Grave – Allegro ma non troppo
Andante cantabile
Rondo. Allegro ma non troppo

Was ist Kammermusik?

c. Expanded and contracted endings

For reasons of pronunciation, the personal endings are sometimes expanded. If a verb stem ends in **d** or **t** (**fin*d*-en, arbei*t*-en**), the personal endings **-st** and **-t** are expanded to **-est** and **-et**.

	Singular	Plural
	ich finde	wir finden
	du find**est**	ihr find**et**
er / sie / es find**et**		sie finden
	Sie finden	

These endings are also expanded if the verb stem ends in certain consonant combinations like the **gn** in **regnen:** es regn**et.**

When a verb stem ends in **s, ß,** or **z,** the personal ending in the 2nd person singular is contracted, i.e., the **-s-** of the ending is dropped because of the **s** or the **s**-like sound in the stem.

	Singular	Plural
	ich heiße	wir heißen
	du hei**ßt**	ihr heißt
er / sie / es heißt		sie heißen
	Sie heißen	

B. ERGÄNZEN SIE! Complete the following conversations.

1. GÜNTER: Wie heiß___ du?
   EVA: Ich heiß___ Eva.
   GÜNTER: Und warum sitz___° du hier und tanz___° nicht?
   EVA: Ich tanz___ nicht gern.

2. SABINE: Was mach___ Vater?
   MUTTER: Er arbeit___ im Garten.
   SABINE: Pflanz___° er Brokkoli?
   MUTTER: Nein, ich glaub___, er ernt___° Tomaten.

3. NINA: Land___ ihr in Frankfurt oder in Düsseldorf?
   NICOLE: Wir land___ in Düsseldorf.
   NINA: Und wie komm___ ihr nach Hannover? Miet___° ihr ein Auto?
   NICOLE: Nein, das kost___ zu viel.

d. The present tense to express future time

German uses the present tense to express future time more frequently than English. However, the context must show clearly that one is referring to the future.

Nächstes Jahr **fliege** ich nach München.   *Next year I'**m flying** to Munich.*
    *Next year I'**ll be flying** to Munich.*

Was **machst** du dort?

Ich **arbeite** im Hotel Astoria.

*What **will you be doing** there?*
*What **are** you **going to do** there?*

*I'**ll be working** at the Hotel Astoria.*
*I'**m going to be working** at the Hotel Astoria.*

C. ZUKUNFTSPLÄNE. Tina quizzes Dieter about his plans for the future. Express their conversation in German. Use **im** with the names of seasons and months and **in** with the names of cities.

in the: **im**

TINA: What will you be doing in the summer?
DIETER: I'm going to fly to Germany.
TINA: What will you be doing there?
DIETER: In July and August I'll be working in the° Hotel Astoria in Munich.
TINA: And then?
DIETER: Then I'll be traveling to Spain.
TINA: And what will you be doing in the fall?
DIETER: In the fall I'll be studying.
TINA: Where? In Munich?
DIETER: No, in Detmold.
TINA: What will you be studying there?
DIETER: Music.
TINA: What instrument do you play?
DIETER: I play the piano and I sing.

D. REISEPLÄNE (1). Jennifer and her friends are traveling in the German-speaking countries. This is what they do in the cities that they visit.

go skiing
celebrate
to the trade fair

buy

In Innsbruck laufen sie Schi.°
In Köln feiern° sie Karneval.
In Leipzig gehen sie auf die Messe.°
In Zürich gehen sie auf die Bank.
In Stuttgart kaufen° sie ein Auto.

▶ Januar | Innsbruck / Schi laufen

S1: Wo seid ihr im Januar? | *S2:* Da sind wir in Innsbruck.
S1: Was macht ihr dort? | *S2:* Dort laufen wir Schi.

1. Februar | Köln / Karneval feiern
2. März | Leipzig / auf die Messe gehen
3. April | Zürich / auf die Bank gehen
4. Mai | Stuttgart / ein Auto kaufen

E. REISEPLÄNE (2). From June to October Jennifer travels by herself.

sailing
lies / on the beach

In Berlin geht sie in die Philharmonie.
In Kiel geht sie segeln.°
In Norderney liegt° sie am Strand.°
In München geht sie aufs Oktoberfest.
In Wien tanzt sie Walzer.

▶ Juni	Berlin / in die Philharmonie gehen
S1: Wo bist du im Juni?	*S2:* Da bin ich in Berlin.
S1: Was machst du dort?	*S2:* Dort gehe ich in die Philharmonie.

1. Juli	Kiel / segeln gehen
2. August	Norderney / am Strand liegen
3. September	München / aufs Oktoberfest gehen
4. Oktober	Wien / Walzer tanzen

2. EXPRESSING LIKES, DISLIKES, AND PREFERENCES

VERB + *GERN* OR *LIEBER*

In German the most common way of saying that you like to do something is to use a verb with **gern.** To say that you don't like to do something, use a verb with **nicht gern.**

Thomas kocht **gern.**	*Thomas **likes to** cook.*
Helga spielt **gern** Golf.	*Helga **likes to** play golf.*
Markus geht **gern** tanzen.	*Markus **likes to** go dancing.*
Günter lernt **nicht gern.**	*Günter does**n't like** studying.*

To express a preference, Germans use a verb plus **lieber,** the comparative form of **gern.**

Was spielst du **lieber,** Schach oder Dame?	*What do you **prefer to** play, chess, or checkers?*
	*What **would** you **rather play,** chess, or checkers?*

F. ICH MACHE DAS GERN. State what you like. Your partner agrees or disagrees with you.

Was ist der deutsche Nationalsport?

▶ spielen: Golf / Tennis / Fußball		
S1: Ich spiele gern Golf.	*S2:*	Ich auch. Ich nicht.

1. trinken: Kaffee / Tee / Milch
2. gehen: ins Konzert / ins Theater / in die Disco
3. hören: Rock / Jazz / Beethoven
4. trinken: Wein / Bier / Cola
5. spielen: Schach / Karten / Dame
6. gehen: schwimmen / Windsurfing / wandern

Ich gehe gern ins Konzert.

Köln

Situated on the banks of the **Rhein** and one of the oldest cities in Germany, **Köln** *(Cologne)* began as a Roman army camp over two thousand years ago. Its skyline is dominated by the twin spires of the **Dom,** one of the most impressive examples of Gothic architecture in Germany. Construction of this huge cathedral spanned centuries: it was begun in 1248 and not completed until 1880. One of Germany's most important industrial cities, **Köln** is also well-known for its **Altstadt** *(old town),* **Kölnisch Wasser** *(eau de Cologne),* and its **Karneval** *(Mardi Gras),* the largest and most boisterous of all the **Karnevals** in the fun-loving Rhineland.

Leipzig

Leipzig was the site in 1989 of the first mass demonstrations against the hard-line communist regime of the former **Deutsche Demokratische Republik.** Leipzig plays host to the **Leipziger Messe,** an internationally renowned trade fair that is held twice a year. It is also the home of the world-famous **Gewandhausorchester** and of the **Thomanerchor,** a boy's choir founded in 1212. It was in Leipzig that the composer Johann Sebastian Bach was organist and music director of the **Thomaskirche** *(Church of St. Thomas)* from 1723 until his death in 1750.

Die Limmat fließt (*flows*) mitten durch Zürich

Zürich

Located in the foothills of the Alps at the western end of the **Zürichsee** *(Lake Zurich),* **Zürich** is the largest city in Switzerland and an important banking center. The **Bahnhofstraße,** with its glittering window displays, is worth a visit for a glimpse of its expensive jewelry and fashions. From downtown **Zürich** it's just a short streetcar ride and a half-hour hike to the top of the **Üetliberg,** where one is rewarded with a panoramic view of the city, the **Zürichsee,** and the Alps.

---

1. When adjectives precede nouns, they take endings. You will learn these endings later.

Berlin

Since 1990, Berlin is once again the capital of Germany. After World War II, the city was divided into **Berlin (West)** and **Berlin (Ost).** This division was intensified in 1961 when the communist regime of East Germany constructed the Berlin Wall **(die Mauer).** The opening of the Wall on November 9, 1989, symbolized the end of the Cold War and marked the beginning of the reunification process of East and West Germany. One of the main tourist attractions in Berlin is the **Kurfürstendamm (Ku'damm),** a broad boulevard of shops, cafés, theaters, nightclubs, and discos that never goes to sleep. The resident orchestra, the **Berliner Philharmoniker,** is one of the best in the world.

Johann Strauß Denkmal (*monument*) in Wien

Die Königsstraße in Stuttgart

Norderney

Norderney is a popular resort town on the East Frisian island of the same name. In spite of cool water temperatures and stiff breezes that constantly blow off the **Nordsee,** thousands of vacationers flock to the island's long, sandy beaches. Popular activities include birdwatching, walking across the **Watt** *(mud-flats)* at low tide, kite-flying, and biking.

Wien

Wien *(Vienna),* the capital of Österreich, was once the capital of the multinational Austro-Hungarian Empire. This cosmopolitan city is one of the most beautiful and historically rich in Europe. Its university, founded in 1365, is the oldest of the German-speaking countries, and over the centuries **Wien** has acquired a special reputation as a city of music, theater, and art. Great composers like Mozart, Beethoven, and Johann Strauß all lived and worked here, and the many museums and galleries in the city house priceless works of art. Situated at the crossroads between Eastern and Western Europe, **Wien** is an important center for international conferences.

Stuttgart

Stuttgart, a major industrial city in south-west Germany, is home to two important car manufacturers: Daimler-Benz and Porsche. Even though it is the hub of a large industrial area, Stuttgart is a pleasant city of parks and cafés and is an important cultural center as well. It is well-known for the **Stuttgarter Ballett** and for the **Staatsgalerie,** which has a particularly interesting collection of German Expressionist and Bauhaus art.

G. ICH MACHE DAS LIEBER. Ask your partner what she/he prefers.

▶ spielen: Golf / Tennis

S1: Spielst du lieber Golf oder Tennis? *S2:* Ich spiele lieber | Golf
Tennis.

1. trinken: Kaffee / Tee
2. gehen: ins Konzert / ins Theater
3. hören: Rock / Jazz
4. trinken: Wein / Bier
5. spielen: Schach / Karten
6. gehen: schwimmen / wandern

WAS MACHST DU GERN?

Find out which sports and games your partner likes to play, what type of music she/he likes to listen to, and what she/he likes to do on weekends.

▶ gehen: schwimmen Windsurfing wandern Schi laufen

S1: Ich gehe gern schwimmen. Und du? *S2:* | Ich gehe auch gern schwimmen.
Ich gehe lieber wandern.

table tennis
badminton

spielen: Golf Tennis Fußball Tischtennis° Baseball
          Basketball Volleyball Federball°
hören: Rock Jazz Beethoven Mozart Schoenberg
spielen: Karten Schach Monopoly Scrabble
gehen: ins Konzert ins Theater ins Kino in die Disco

• Report to the class what you have found out about your partner.

> Sport: _____ *[name of partner]* geht gern _____, und sie / er spielt gern
> _____.
>
> Musik: Sie / er hört gern _____.
> Spiele: Sie / er spielt gern _____.
> Am Wochenende: Am Wochenende geht sie / er gern _____.

 ZUSAMMENSCHAU

JOHN BAYNE FLIEGT NACH DEUTSCHLAND

John Bayne has just received a scholarship to study political science in Germany. Listen as he is being interviewed by a journalist from the California Staats-Zeitung, a German language weekly.

Neue Vokabeln

die Politikwissenschaft	*political science*
politisch	*political*
die Szene	*scene*
faszinierend	*fascinating*
erst Mitte Oktober	*not until the middle of October*
Ich reise per Anhalter.	*I hitchhike*
die Reise	*the trip*
gar nichts	*nothing at all*

• Indicate the order in which you hear the following statements or questions.

___ Im Juli und im August arbeite ich dort im Hotel Astoria.
___ Ich reise sehr gern per Anhalter.
___ Fliegen Sie direkt nach Berlin?
___ Ich studiere Politikwissenschaft.
___ Mieten Sie ein Auto für die Reise nach Italien?

• Listen to the interview again and choose the correct response.

1. Wohin fliegt Herr Bayne im Sommer?

   nach Italien   nach Deutschland

2. Wo studiert er dort?

   in München   in Frankfurt   in Berlin

3. Wo in Deutschland findet Herr Bayne die politische Szene besonders° *especially* interessant?

   in München   in Frankfurt   in Berlin

4. Wann fliegt er nach Deutschland?

   Ende Juli   Ende Juni

5. Wo in Deutschland arbeitet er im Juli und im August?

   in München   in Frankfurt   in Berlin

6. Wann reist er nach Italien?

   im Juli   im August   im September

7. Wann beginnt das Wintersemester in Deutschland?

   im Januar   im April   im September   im Oktober

8. Wann beginnt das Sommersemester in Deutschland?

   im Januar   im April   im September   im Oktober

Ich gehe am Wochenende gern wandern

✏️ Answer the following questions in German in complete sentences.

1. Was studiert Herr Bayne in Berlin?
2. Warum studiert er in Berlin?
3. Wo in Deutschland landet er?
4. Was macht er dann?
5. Warum reist er nach München?
6. Was macht Herr Bayne im September?

7. Warum mietet Herr Bayne kein Auto für die Reise nach Italien?
8. Warum reist Herr Bayne so gern per Anhalter?

WIE GUT KENNEN WIR EINANDER JETZT?

Class activity: Choose one of your fellow students and say everything you know about her/him in German.

> Say: where she/he comes from.
> what she/he is studying.
> whether she/he plays an instrument. If so, which one.
> whether she/he likes to sing.
> what sports she/he likes to play.
> what games she/he likes to play.
> what she/he likes to do on weekends.
> . . .

3. IDENTIFYING NATIONALITY, PROFESSION, OR GROUP MEMBERSHIP

OMISSION OF THE INDEFINITE ARTICLE

When stating someone's membership in a specific group (e.g., her/his nationality, occupation, or religious denomination), German does *not* use the indefinite article.

Michael ist Programmierer.   *Michael is **a** programmer.*
Andrea ist Musikstudentin.   *Andrea is **a** music student.*
Herr Vogel ist Verkäufer.   *Mr. Vogel is **a** sales clerk.*
Frau Wagner ist Methodistin.   *Mrs. Wagner is **a** Methodist.*

sparen: *to save*

If membership is not the issue, the indefinite article has to be used.

Verdient **eine** Polizistin so viel wie **ein** Polizist?

*Does **a** policewoman earn as much as **a** policeman?*

(D)	Deutschland	**Er** ist Deutsch**er.**	**Sie** ist Deutsch**e.**
(A)	Österreich	**Er** ist Österreich**er.**	**Sie** ist Österreicher**in.**
(CH) ¹	die Schweiz	**Er** ist Schweiz**er.**	**Sie** ist Schweizer**in.**
(USA)	Amerika	**Er** ist Amerikan**er.**	**Sie** ist Amerikaner**in.**
(CDN)	Kanada	**Er** ist Kanadi**er.**	**Sie** ist Kanadier**in.**
(GB)	England	**Er** ist Engländ**er.**	**Sie** ist Engländer**in.**
	Hamburg	**Er** ist Hamburg**er.**	**Sie** ist Hamburger**in.**

H. WOHER BIST DU? You want to find out where your partner and her/his friend are from.

▶ Hamburger(in) / aus Berlin   aus Berlin / Frankfurter(in)

S1: Bist du Hamburger?   *S2:* Nein, ich bin aus Berlin.
(Bist du Hamburgerin?)

S1: Und deine° Freundin, ist sie auch   *S2:* Nein, meine Freundin ist Frankfur-   *your*
aus Berlin?   terin.
(Und dein Freund, ist er auch aus   (Nein, mein Freund ist Frankfurter.)
Berlin?)

---

1. Deutscher (Deutsche) / aus Amerika   aus Amerika / Kanadier(in)
2. Engländer(in) / aus Australien   aus Australien / Neuseeländer(in)
3. Amerikaner(in) / aus Kanada   aus Kanada / Deutscher (Deutsche)
4. Wiener(in) / aus Innsbruck   aus Innsbruck / Heidelberger(in)
5. Österreicher(in) / aus Deutschland   aus Deutschland / Schweizer(in)
6. Kalifornier(in) / aus Texas   aus Texas / New Yorker(in)
7. Stuttgarter(in) / aus Tübingen   aus Tübingen / Kölner(in)

---

1. CH stands for **Confoederatio Helvetica.** During the time of the Roman Empire, most of the area that now comprises Switzerland was called **Helvetia.** Present-day Switzerland is therefore a "union of Helvetian states".

In Germany it is fairly easy to recognize where a car comes from by the license plate. Many German travelers on the **Autobahn** like to guess where the other cars on the road are from. The plates depicted are from cities mentioned in the exercise you have just completed. Which plate belongs to which city?

need / money

I. SIE BRAUCHEN° GELD.° You are applying for a loan. Your partner is the bank manager.

teacher

▶ Lehrer° (Lehrerin)
3 500 Mark im Monat

What is your occupation?
earn
Wer sucht die Wohnung ein Mann, oder eine Frau?

S1: Was sind Sie von Beruf?°
S1: Und wieviel verdienen° Sie?

S2: Ich bin Lehrer(in).
S2: Ich verdiene dreitausendfünfhundert Mark im Monat.

ICH SUCHE 2- BIS 3-ZIMMER-WOHNUNG

• Ich bin von Beruf Lektorin
• 32 Jahre alt
• Telefon: 0711/38 58 21

Beruf	Einkommen
1. Automechaniker (Automechanikerin)	2 400 Mark im Monat
2. Busfahrer (Busfahrerin)	1 800 Mark im Monat
3. Polizist (Polizistin)	2 100 Mark im Monat
4. Programmierer (Programmiererin)	2 750 Mark im Monat
5. Professor (Professorin)	6 500 Mark im Monat

Sprachnotizen

Referring to a family by its family name

When referring to a family by its family name, German does not use the definite article:

Wagners fliegen morgen nach Israel.	*The Wagners are flying to Israel tomorrow.*
Morgen abend sind wir bei Schmidts.	*Tomorrow evening we'll be at the Schmidts.*

Naming a musical instrument after *spielen*

When naming a musical instrument after **spielen,** German does not use the definite article before the name of the instrument:

Lutz spielt Gitarre.	*Lutz plays the guitar.*
Spielen Sie Klavier?	*Do you play the piano?*

4. ANSWERING *WHO, WHOM,* OR *WHAT*

SUBJECT AND DIRECT OBJECT

A simple sentence consists of a noun or pronoun *subject* and a *predicate*. The predicate is whatever is said about the subject and consists of a verb or a verb plus other parts of speech.

One of the "other parts of speech" is often a noun or pronoun that answers the question *whom?* or *what?*. This noun or pronoun is called the *direct object* of the verb.

The italicized words in the following examples are the direct objects of the verbs.

Subject	Predicate		
	Verb	**Other Parts of Speech**	
Michael	knows	*Andrea.*	(*Whom* does Michael know?)
He	met	*her* in the German class.	(*Whom* did he meet?)
Michael and Andrea	want to go	to a concert tonight.	
They	need	*tickets.*	(*What* do they need?)
They	have	only *six dollars.*	(*What* do they have?)
They	feel	sad.	
Robert	has	*two tickets.*	(*What* does Robert have?)
He	gives	*them* to Michael and Andrea.	(*What* does he give to Michael and Andrea?)

J. SUBJECT AND DIRECT OBJECT. Name the subjects and direct objects in the following sentences. Note that some sentences have no direct object.

1. Die Sonne scheint, und der Himmel ist blau.
2. Andrea braucht ein Fahrrad.
3. Das Fahrrad kostet viel Geld.

4. Andrea hat nicht viel Geld.
5. Sie kauft es auf Kredit.
6. Michael kennt° Andrea.
7. Kennst du sie auch?

8. Andrea studiert Musik.
9. Sie spielt Klavier.
10. Spielt Michael auch ein Instrument?
11. Nein, aber er singt sehr gut.

NOMINATIVE AND ACCUSATIVE CASE: *EIN* AND *KEIN*

a. The indefinite article: *ein, eine, ein*

In German the form of the indefinite article changes according to whether the noun it accompanies is the subject or object of the verb. The forms of the indefinite article **(ein, eine, ein)** that you learned on page 45 are *subject forms,* i.e., they are used with nouns that are *subjects.*

der Pullover
die Jacke
das Hemd

Ein Pullover° kostet 80 Mark.
Eine Jacke° kostet 120 Mark.
Ein Hemd° kostet 25 Mark.

A pullover costs 80 marks.
A jacket costs 120 marks.
A shirt costs 25 marks.

In the following sentences the indefinite article precedes nouns that are *direct objects* and therefore appears in its *object forms.*

Kurt braucht **einen** Pullover.
Kurt braucht **eine** Jacke.
Kurt braucht **ein** Hemd.

*Kurt needs **a** pullover.*
*Kurt needs **a** jacket.*
*Kurt needs **a** shirt.*

In German grammar the subject forms are said to be in the *nominative case* and the direct object forms in the *accusative case.* Case is often signaled by a change in the form of the article.

In the table below note that the indefinite article differs from the nominative only in the *accusative* masculine. There are no plural forms for **ein, eine,** and **ein** just as there are no plural forms for English *a, an.*

	Masculine	Feminine	Neuter	Plural
Nominative	ein	eine	ein	—
Accusative	ein**en**	eine	ein	—

b. The negative form of the indefinite article: *kein, keine, kein*

Kein has the same endings as **ein.** Note that **kein** has plural forms.

	Masculine	Feminine	Neuter	Plural
Nominative	kein	keine	kein	keine
Accusative	kein**en**	keine	kein	keine

Das ist **kein** Ford, das ist ein Volkswagen.

*That's **not a** Ford, it's a Volkswagen.*

Kurt kauft **keinen** Ford, er kauft einen Volkswagen.

*Kurt is **not** buying **a** Ford, he is buying a Volkswagen.*

Das sind **keine** Orangen, das sind Mandarinen.

*These are **not** oranges, they are mandarins.*

K. BRAUCHST DU DAS? You want to know whether or not your partner needs the
items listed below.

S1: Brauchst du einen Mantel?	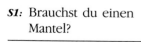	**S2:** Ja, ich brauche einen Mantel. / Nein, ich brauche keinen Mantel.

1.

4.

2.

5.

3.

6.

Pullover *(m)*	Hemd *(n)*	Kamera *(f)*	Bluse *(f)*	Schirm° *(m)*	Ohrringe *(pl)*

umbrella

7.

10.

8.

11.

9.

12.

Hut *(m)*	Jacke *(f)*	Lippenstift *(m)*	Socken *(pl)*	Schuhe *(pl)*	Jeans *(pl)*

5. INDICATING POSSESSION OR RELATIONSHIPS

Which sign says hello and which says good-bye?

POSSESSIVE ADJECTIVES

Adjectives are words that describe people, places, and things, e.g., *a good book, a good friend.* Possessive adjectives indicate possession or relationships, e.g., **my** book, **my** friend.

In *Kapitel 2* you learned the personal pronouns. The corresponding possessive adjectives are:

	Singular			Plural	
ich	**mein**	*my*	wir	**unser**	*our*
du	**dein**	*your*	ihr	**euer**	*your*
er	**sein**	*his*			
sie	**ihr**	*her*	sie	**ihr**	*their*
es	**sein**	*its*			
			Sie	**Ihr**	*your*

Note that just like the formal **Sie,** the formal **Ihr** is always capitalized.

The possessive adjectives take the same case endings as the indefinite articles **ein** and **kein.** Together with **ein** and **kein** they are called **ein**-words.

Warum verkaufen Sie **Ihren** Wagen, Frau Schulz?	*Why are you selling **your** car, Mrs. Schulz?*
Ich brauche **keinen** Wagen mehr.	*I don't need **a** car anymore.*

In the following chart the possessive adjective **mein** is used to show the nominative and accusative forms of *all* possessive adjectives.

	Masculine	Feminine	Neuter	Plural
Nominative	mein	mein**e**	mein	mein**e**
Accusative	mein**en**	mein**e**	mein	mein**e**

The **e** before the **r** is dropped when an ending is added to **euer.**

Ist **eure** Professorin Schweizerin?	*Is **your** professor Swiss?*

L. SYLVIA. Supply the correct forms of **mein.**

both

Ich bin Sylvia, und ich studiere Physik. _____ Eltern arbeiten beide.° _____ Vater ist Polizist und _____ Mutter ist Sozialarbeiterin. _____ Brüder heißen Mark und Oliver. Sie sind jünger als ich, und sie gehen beide noch in die Schule. _____ Schwester heißt Martina. Sie ist zwei Jahre älter als ich und studiert Biochemie. _____ Freund heißt Stefan. Er ist so alt wie _____ Schwester. Stefan studiert auch *for that reason / see / every* Physik, und deshalb° sehe° ich _____ Freund fast jeden° Tag.

M. FAMILIE HAAG. Supply the correct forms of **unser.**

Wir sind Herr und Frau Haag. _____ Kinder sind siebenundzwanzig und dreiundzwanzig Jahre alt. _____ Tochter Nicole ist Architektin und arbeitet in Bremen, und _____ Sohn Florian studiert in Bochum Philosophie. Wir sehen _____ Tochter und _____ Sohn nur sehr selten, und _____ Haus ist jetzt viel zu groß.

N. WARUM DENN? Supply the correct forms of **dein, euer,** or **Ihr.**

1. Warum verkaufst du denn _____ Gitarre (f), Bernd?
2. Warum verkaufen Sie denn _____ Computer (m), Frau Haag?
3. Warum verkauft ihr denn _____ Fahrräder (pl)?
4. Warum verkaufen Sie denn _____ Kamera (f), Herr Weber?
5. Warum verkaufst du denn _____ Volkswagen (m), Ingrid?
6. Warum verkauft ihr denn _____ Segelboot (n)?

O. WARUM DENN? (2) Supply the correct forms of **sein** or **ihr.**

1. Warum verkaufen Zieglers denn _____ Segelboot (n)?
2. Warum verkauft Frau Müller denn _____ Mercedes (m)?
3. Warum verkauft Tina denn _____ Trompete (f)?
4. Warum verkauft Michael denn _____ CDs (pl)?
5. Warum verkaufen Meyers denn _____ Haus (n)?
6. Warum verkauft Ralf denn _____ Klarinette (f)?

P. BESUCHE. Everyone is going to visit relatives and friends.

▶ Anita / am Wochenende   sie / Schwester

S1: Was macht Anita am Wochenende?   **S2:** Da besucht° sie ihre Schwester.   *is visiting*

---

1. du / am Samstag   ich / Großeltern°   *grandparents*
2. Müllers / im Januar   sie / Sohn in Frankfurt
3. ihr / im Sommer   wir / Freunde in Berlin
4. Kurt / am Sonntag   er / Freundin
5. Sie / morgen abend   ich / Bruder
6. Bettina / am Wochenende   sie / Freund
7. Stefan / am Sonntag   er / Großvater
8. Maiers / im Juli   sie / Tochter in Hamburg
9. ihr / morgen   wir / Onkel
10. du / im August   ich / Eltern
11. Claudia / am Samstag   sie / Vater
12. Sie / heute abend   wir / Kinder

Q. IST DAS IHR HUND? Your partner takes the roles of the people indicated. Ask whether she/he owns the items shown.

▶ Ist das . . . ?   Frau Meyer: Ja, das . . .

S1: Ist das Ihr Hund?   **FRAU MEYER:** Ja, das ist mein Hund.

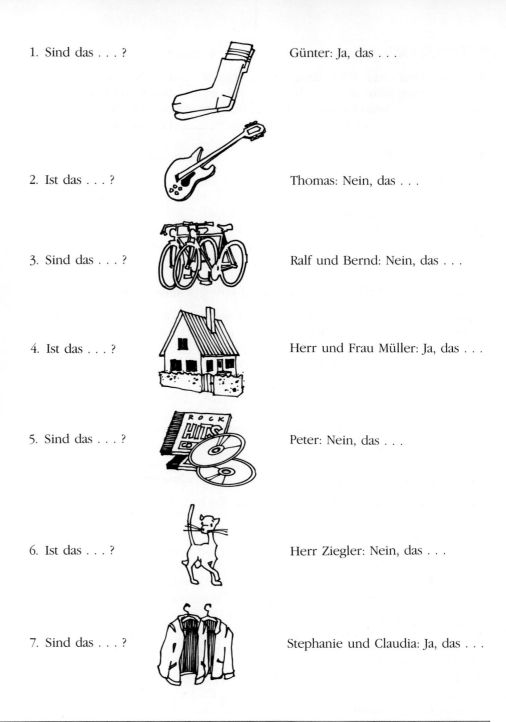

1. Sind das . . . ?   Günter: Ja, das . . .

2. Ist das . . . ?   Thomas: Nein, das . . .

3. Sind das . . . ?   Ralf und Bernd: Nein, das . . .

4. Ist das . . . ?   Herr und Frau Müller: Ja, das . . .

5. Sind das . . . ?   Peter: Nein, das . . .

6. Ist das . . . ?   Herr Ziegler: Nein, das . . .

7. Sind das . . . ?   Stephanie und Claudia: Ja, das . . .

| Fahrräder | Gitarre *(f)* | CDs | Katze *(f)* | Jacken | Haus *(n)* | Socken |

THE PRESENT TENSE OF *HABEN*

The verb **haben** is often used to indicate possession or relationships between people and corresponds to the English verb *to have*. In the present tense of **haben,** the **b** of the verb stem is dropped in the 2nd and 3rd person singular.

Singular	Plural
ich habe	wir haben
du **hast**	ihr habt
er / sie / es **hat**	sie haben
Sie haben	

Haben and *sein*

Müllers haben **einen** Esel.   *The Müllers have a donkey.*

In the example above, the noun **Esel** answers the question *What do the Müllers have?* **Esel** is the direct object and is therefore in the accusative case. The verb **haben** always takes an accusative object.

Günter ist **ein** Esel.[1]   *Günter is an idiot.*

In this example, **Esel** also answers the question *what?* But here **Esel** is used with the linking verb **sein** to *describe* what the subject is. It therefore appears in the same case as the subject, i.e., the nominative.

R. FRAGEN! FRAGEN! Your partner gives a negative response to each of your questions.

▶ haben / Martin / Motorrad *(n)*

S1: Hat Martin ein Motorrad?   ***S2:*** Nein, er hat kein Motorrad.

---

1. haben / du / Wagen° *(m)*
2. sein / das / Volkswagen *(m)*
3. haben / Zieglers / Mercedes *(m)*
4. sein / Günter / Genie° *(n)*
5. haben / Thomas / Freundin *(f)*
6. sein / das / BMW *(m)*
7. haben / Monika / Freund *(m)*
8. sein / Thomas / Esel *(m)*
9. haben / Sie / Geschwister° *(pl)*
10. haben / du / Gitarre *(f)*
11. haben / Schneiders / Kinder *(pl)*
12. sein / Martin / Dummkopf° *(m)*

car

brothers and sisters
genius

dimwit

6. EXPRESSING NEGATION (2)

MORE ABOUT THE POSITION OF *NICHT*

On page 17 you learned that **nicht** usually follows adverbs of time.

Warum arbeitest du **heute nicht?**   *Why aren't you working **today?***

However, if the expression of time itself is negated, **nicht** precedes that expression.

Ich arbeite **nicht immer** so viel.   *I don't **always** work so much.*
Ich arbeite **nicht jeden Samstag.**   *I don't work **every Saturday.***

---

1. Names of animals are often used to characterize people. Here **Esel** *(donkey)* is a slightly friendlier way of saying *idiot.*

Nicht precedes expressions of place.

Warum geht ihr denn **nicht ins Kino?**	*Why aren't you going to the movies?*
Eva ist **nicht zu Hause.**	*Eva is not at home.*

Nicht usually follows the direct object.

Kennst du Martins Freundin?	*Do you know Martin's girlfriend?*
Nein, ich kenne **Martins Freundin nicht.**	*No, I don't know Martin's girlfriend.*

S. IMMER NEGATIV! Your partner responds negatively to each of your questions.

S1: Besuchst du deine Großeltern jeden Sommer?

S2: Nein, ich besuche meine Großeltern nicht jeden Sommer.

1. Kaufen Zieglers das Segelboot?	Nein, sie kaufen . . .
2. Ist Monika im Garten?	Nein, sie ist . . .
3. Geht ihr heute abend ins Kino?	Nein, wir gehen . . .
4. Geht ihr jeden Samstag ins Kino?	Nein, wir gehen . . .
5. Kaufen deine Eltern das Haus?	Nein, sie kaufen . . .
6. Fliegen Meyers nach Spanien?	Nein, sie fliegen . . .
7. Trinkt Peter immer so viel?	Nein, er trinkt . . .
8. Kennst du Brigitte Koch?	Nein, ich kenne . . .
9. Sind Sie morgen in Stuttgart?	Nein, ich bin . . .
10. Sind Sie jeden Montag in Stuttgart?	Nein, ich bin . . .
11. Brauchst du mein Buch?	Nein, ich brauche . . .
12. Arbeitest du morgen abend?	Nein, ich arbeite . . .
13. Studiert Stephanie in Berlin?	Nein, sie studiert . . .
14. Fliegt Herr Ziegler oft nach Berlin?	Nein, er fliegt . . .

DOCH VERSUS *JA*

To respond affirmatively to a negative question or statement, German uses **doch** instead of **ja.** By using **doch** in the response, the speaker contradicts the assumption implied in the preceding question or statement. In this context **doch** sometimes corresponds to English *of course.*

Haben Zieglers **keine** Haustiere?	*Don't the Zieglers have any pets?*
Doch, sie haben eine Katze.	*Yes, they have a cat.*
Stefan kommt heute abend **nicht.**	*Stefan isn't coming tonight.*
Doch, er kommt.	*Of course he is.*

T. DOCH, JA ODER NEIN? Respond either affirmatively with **doch** or **ja** or negatively with **nein.**

▶ _____, sie ist aus Chicago.

S1: Ist Stephanie aus Amerika?

S2: Ja____, sie ist aus Chicago.

1. Spielst du kein Instrument?   _____, ich spiele Trompete.
2. Ist es heute nicht so heiß wie gestern?   _____, das Thermometer zeigt jetzt schon dreißig Grad.

3. Trinken Sie ein Glas Bier? _____, ich habe keinen Durst.° *thirst*
4. Trinken Sie keinen Kaffee? _____, aber bitte koffeinfrei.
5. Hast du eine Kamera? _____, eine Minolta.
6. Hat Frau Meyer keinen Wagen? _____, sie hat einen Audi 4000.
7. Habt ihr keinen Hund? _____, aber eine Katze.

7. EXPRESSING TIME AND PLACE

WORD ORDER: EXPRESSIONS OF TIME AND PLACE

In German expressions of time precede expressions of place. In English it is the
reverse.

PETER: Gehst du **jetzt in die Cafete-** *Are you going **to the cafeteria now?***
ria?

MARTIN: Nein, ich gehe **jetzt in die** *No, I'm going **to class now.***
Vorlesung.

U. WOHIN GEHST DU JETZT? Your partner isn't going where you expect her/him
to go.

▶ du / jetzt  ich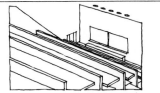

S1: Gehst du jetzt in die Cafeteria? **S2:** Nein, ich gehe jetzt in die Vorlesung.

1. du / heute abend  ich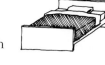

2. Peter / heute abend  er

3. Stephanie /
heute nachmittag°  sie 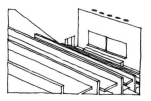 *this afternoon*

4. Claudia /
   heute abend

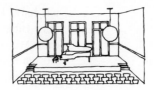

sie

5. du / jetzt

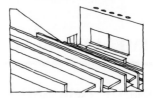

ich

6. Michael /
   morgen abend

er

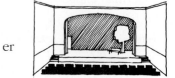

7. du / heute abend

ich

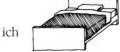

8. Günter /
   heute abend

er

9. Günter /
   morgen abend

er

 ZUSAMMENSCHAU

DIE FAMILIE

The following children's rhyme describes one family. Read the poem. Then study the family tree and answer the questions.

Ein Stammbaum

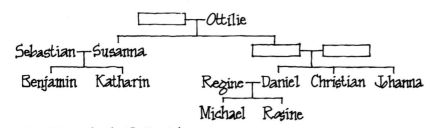

Der Vater, der heißt Daniel,
der kleine Sohn heißt Michael,
die Mutter heißt Regine,
die Tochter° heißt Rosine,
der Bruder, der heißt Christian,
der Onkel heißt Sebastian,
die Schwester heißt Johanna,
die Tante° heißt Susanna,
der Vetter,° der heißt Benjamin,
die Kusine, die heißt Katharin,
die Oma° heißt Ottilie —
jetzt kennst du die Familie.

daughter

aunt
(male) cousin

grandma

1. Wie heißen Johannas Brüder?
2. Wie heißen Susannas Kinder?
3. Wie heißt Michaels Schwester?
4. Wie heißen Daniels Geschwister?
5. Wie heißen Katharins Vettern?
6. Wie heißt Ottilies Tochter?
7. Wie heißt Benjamins Kusine?

8. Wie heißen Rosines Tanten?
9. Wie heißt Michaels Onkel?
10. Wie heißt Benjamins Vater?
11. Wie heißt Rosines Mutter?
12. Wie heißt Johannas Großmutter?
13. Wie heißen Katharins Eltern?
14. Wie heißt Sebastians Sohn?

DAS IST JENNIFER WINKLER

Jennifer Winkler is to be profiled in the next edition of the German Club newsletter. Listen as she is being interviewed by another German student.

Neue Vokabeln

Was ist dein Hauptfach?	*What is your major?*
Er ist in Österreich geboren.	*He was born in Austria.*
leben	*to live*
Ich wohne noch zu Hause.	*I still live at home.*
leider	*unfortunately*

1. Check the names that you hear.

   Mark   Daniel   Tina   Michael   Tanja   Jennifer

2. What subjects do you hear?

   Deutsch   Physik   Soziologie   Mathematik   Medizin   Chemie

3. What cities do you hear?

   Innsbruck   Wien   Chicago   Seattle   Graz   Boston

- Listen to the interview again and choose the correct response.

   1. Wo studiert Jennifer nächstes Jahr?

      in Deutschland   in Österreich

   2. Wo ist Jennifers Vater geboren?

      in Wien   in Graz   in Seattle

   3. Wo wohnt Jennifer?

      zu Hause   im Studentenheim

   4. Wie viele Geschwister hat Jennifer?

      zwei   drei   vier

   5. Wie viele Jahre jünger ist Jennifer als ihre Schwester?

      zwei   drei   vier

   6. Wer ist älter, Mark oder Jennifer?

      Mark   Jennifer

   7. Wer ist Daniel?

      Tanjas Freund   Jennifers Freund   Jennifers Bruder

Write the answers to the following questions about Jennifer's interview.

was . . . noch: *what else?*

   1. Was ist Jennifers Hauptfach?
   2. Was studiert sie noch?°
   3. Warum lernt sie Deutsch?
   4. Woher ist Jennifers Vater, und wo lebt er jetzt?
   5. Wohnt Jennifer im Studentenheim?
   6. Was ist Jennifers Vater von Beruf?
   7. Was ist Jennifers Mutter von Beruf?
   8. Ist Jennifer älter oder jünger als ihre Schwester?
   9. Wie heißt Jennifers Schwester, und was macht sie?
   10. Wohnt sie auch zu Hause?
   11. Wie heißt Jennifers Bruder, und was macht er?
   12. Wie alt ist Jennifer, und wie alt ist Tanja?
   13. Was sind Jennifers Hobbys? Was macht sie gern?
   14. Wie heißt Jennifers Freund, und was macht er?

ICH UND MEINE FAMILIE. For homework write a paragraph about yourself, your studies, your family, your friends, and your hobbies. You will find pertinent vocabulary about fields of study, occupations and hobbies in the reference section.

DU UND DEINE FAMILIE

Ask your partner about her/his family and report your findings to the class. You may want to refer to the list of professions and hobbies in the reference section.

Was ist deine Mutter / dein Vater von Beruf?

Wie viele Geschwister hast du? Wie heißen sie? Wie alt sind sie? Sind sie jünger oder älter als du?

Was machen deine Geschwister? Arbeiten sie, studieren sie, oder gehen sie noch in die Schule? Wo arbeiten sie? Wo und was studieren sie? Wohnen sie noch zu Hause?

Sind deine Geschwister verheiratet?° Haben sie Kinder?   *married*

Was für Hobbys haben deine Geschwister? Was für Instrumente spielen sie? Was für Musik hören sie gern? Gehen sie oft ins Konzert, ins Theater, ins Kino, in die Disco? Spielen sie gern Schach, Monopoly, Scrabble usw.? Sind sie sportlich, oder sitzen sie viel vor dem Fernseher°?   *in front of the TV*

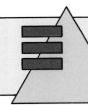

Wort, Sinn und Klang

Wörter unter der Lupe

GERMAN AND ENGLISH (3)

In *Kapitel 2* you saw that it is often quite simple to "decode" the English meanings of certain cognates. Below is another list with the "codes" that will help you figure out the English meanings. Don't forget that in some cases, it helps to say the German words. Words followed by *(v)* are verbs in their infinitive form.

1. German **s, ss,** or **ß** is English *t* or *tt*

das Wa**ss**er	verge**ss**en *(v)*
ha**ss**en *(v)*	wei**ß**
ra**ss**eln *(v)*	der Fu**ß**
be**ss**er	die Nu**ß**
der Ke**ss**el	wa**s**

2. German **z** or **tz** is English *t* or *tt*

se**tz**en *(v)*	die Hi**tz**e
si**tz**en *(v)*	die Ka**tz**e
der Si**tz**	das Sal**z**
gli**tz**ern *(v)*	das Ne**tz**
zehn	grun**z**en *(v)*
zwölf	die War**z**e
die **Z**unge	**z**u

3. German **pf** is English *p* or *pp*

der A**pf**el	der **Pf**ennig
der Kram**pf**	die **Pf**lanze (**z** = *t*!)
die **Pf**anne	der **Pf**osten
der **Pf**ad (**d** = *th*!)	das **Pf**und
die **Pf**eife (**f** = *p*!)	der **Pf**effer (**f** = *p*!)

WEITERE NÜTZLICHE WÖRTER UND AUSDRÜCKE

Was machen die Leute hier?

Die Familie

die Großeltern *(pl)*	grandparents
die Großmutter, die Großmütter	grandmother
die Oma, die Omas	grandma
der Großvater, die Großväter	grandfather
der Opa, die Opas	grandpa
die Eltern *(pl)*	parents
der Vater, die Väter	father
die Mutter, die Mütter	mother
das Kind, die Kinder	child
der Sohn, die Söhne	son
die Tochter, die Töchter	daughter
der Bruder, die Brüder	brother
die Schwester, die Schwestern	sister
die Geschwister *(pl)*	brothers and sisters
der Onkel, die Onkel	uncle
die Tante, die Tanten	aunt
der Vetter, die Vettern	*(male)* cousin
die Kusine, die Kusinen	*(female)* cousin
der Hund, die Hunde	dog
die Katze, die Katzen	cat

Fahrzeuge *(Vehicles)*

der Wagen, die Wagen	car
das Auto, die Autos	car
das Motorrad, die Motorräder	motorcycle
das Fahrrad, die Fahrräder	bicycle
der Zug, die Züge	train
der Bus, die Busse	bus
das Flugzeug, die Flugzeuge	airplane
das Segelboot, die Segelboote	sailboat

Hobbys

das Hobby, die Hobbys	hobby	**Windsurfing gehen**	to go windsurfing
Schi laufen	to go skiing	**Schach spielen**	to play chess
Tennis spielen	to play tennis	**kochen**	to cook
wandern gehen	to go hiking	**backen**	to bake
schwimmen gehen	to go swimming	**tanzen**	to dance
segeln gehen	to go sailing		

Getränke *(Beverages)*

der Kaffee	coffee	**das Bier**	beer
der Tee	tea	**der Wein**	wine
die Milch	milk	**der Apfelsaft**	apple juice
das Wasser	water	**der Orangensaft**	orange juice
die Cola	cola		

Was sind Sie von Beruf?

Was sind Sie von Beruf?	What do you do for a living?
der Beruf, die Berufe	occupation, profession
das Einkommen	income
das Geld	money

Wichtige Verben

verdienen	to earn	**reisen**	to travel
kosten	to cost	**besuchen**	to visit
brauchen	to need	**leben**	to live *(in a country or city)*
kaufen	to buy	**wohnen**	to live *(in a building or a street)*
verkaufen	to sell		

kennen	to know, to be acquainted with
antworten	to answer
wiederholen	to repeat
finden	to find
tun	to do, to make
singen	to sing
trinken	to drink

WÖRTER IM KONTEXT

1. DIE FAMILIE. What are the male or female counterparts?

die Kusine   der Vater   der Opa   der Onkel

die Schwester   der Sohn   die Großmutter

2. WAS PASST NICHT? One in each group does not quite match.

a. das Motorrad
   das Auto
   das Segelboot
   das Fahrrad

b. das Flugzeug
   der Wagen
   der Zug
   der Bus

3. WAS PASST WO?

besuchen   Sohn   kosten   von Beruf   reisen   verdienen   Geld   kaufen

a. Was ist Michael _____?
   Er ist Programmierer, und er _____ viel _____.

b. Warum _____ Sie den Wagen nicht, Frau Ziegler?
   Er _____ viel zu viel.

c. Wohin _____ Frau Ackermann denn?
   Nach München. Sie _____ dort ihren _____ Peter.

In English the spelling of a word is often a poor indicator of how that word is pronounced and vice versa (e.g., pl**ou**gh, thr**ou**gh, thor**ou**gh, en**ou**gh; b**e**, s**ee**, bel**ie**ve, rec**ei**ve; etc.). This is not the case in German. For the most part the German spelling system is an excellent indicator of pronunciation. Once you have mastered a few basic principles, you will have no trouble pronouncing any new words that you encounter. You will also be able to correctly spell any new German words that you hear.

THE VOWELS *A, E, I, O,* AND *U*

In a *stressed syllable* each of these five vowels is either *long* or *short*. Listen carefully to the pronunciation of the following words and sentences and at the same time note the spelling. You will see that there are certain orthographic markers that indicate quite reliably whether a vowel in a stressed syllable is long or short.

1. A doubled vowel is always long: H**aa**r, T**ee**, B**oo**t.
2. A vowel followed by an **h** is long: J**a**hr, es g**e**ht, S**o**hn, **U**hr. Note that in this case the **h** is used as a length marker and is therefore silent.
3. **i** followed by an **e** or by an **eh** is long: B**ie**r, s**ie**ben, er st**ieh**lt.°
4. A vowel followed by a consonant plus another vowel is long: N**a**se, w**e**nig, M**o**nat, Min**u**te.
5. A vowel followed by a doubled consonant is always short: W**a**sser, W**e**tter, L**i**ppe, S**o**mmer, S**u**ppe.
6. Usually, a vowel followed by two or more consonants is short: l**a**nden, M**e**nsch, tr**i**nken, T**o**chter, St**u**nde.

- Hören Sie gut zu und wiederholen Sie!

a (lang)	a (kurz)
Haar	hart
lahm°	Lamm
Kater°	Katze°
Mein Name ist Beate Mahler.	Tanja tanzt gern Tango.
Mein Vater ist aus Saalfeld.	Walter tanzt lieber Walzer.

e (lang)	e (kurz)
Schnee	schnell°
gehen	gestern
Esel	essen°
Peter geht im Regen segeln.	Ein Student hat selten Geld.
Peter ist ein Esel.	

i (lang)	i (kurz)
Liebe°	Lippe
Miete	Mitte
schief°	Schiff°
Verdienen Sie viel, Herr Schmied?	Fischers Fritz fischt frische Fische.

steals

lame
tomcat / cat

quick

to eat

love

crooked / ship

o (lang)

Sohn
Ofen
doof°

Warum ist Thomas so doof?

o (kurz)

Sonne
offen°   *stove*
Dorf°   *stupid / village*

Am Sonntag kommt Onkel Otto.

u (lang)

Schule
Stuhl°
super

Utes Pudel frißt° nur Nudeln.

u (kurz)

Schulter
Stunde   *chair*
Suppe

In Ulm und um Ulm und um Ulm   *eats*
herum.

Das Münster in Ulm. Der
Turm ist 161 Meter (*528
ft.*) hoch.

Wieviel Uhr ist es?

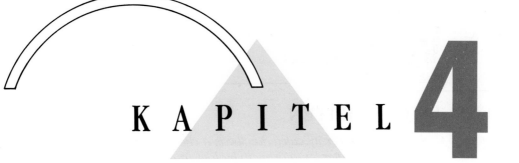

K A P I T E L 4

■ **Kommunikationsziele**

*In **Kapitel 4** you will learn how to:*
talk about your daily routine
talk about what you eat for breakfast, lunch, and
  dinner
talk about your abilities
talk about what you would like to do
give second-hand information
tell time

■ **Hör- und Sprechsituationen**

Wie lange schläfst du morgens?
Was ißt du zum Frühstück?
Was darfst du / kannst du / mußt du / sollst
  du / möchtest du tun?
Was darfst du / willst du nicht tun?
Kaspar Müller hat ein Problem
Mein Freund / Meine Freundin
Brigittes Tageslauf
Mein Tageslauf

■ **Strukturen**

Modal verbs
Present tense of irregular verbs
Telling official and colloquial time
Expressions of time

■ **Wissenswertes**

Entrance requirements for university study in
  Germany
German universities
The German railway system
Local transportation and air travel in Germany

VORSCHAU

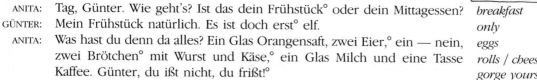

LEBENSGEWOHNHEITEN

life styles

Anita has just joined Günter in the university cafeteria. She is a chemistry major who takes her studies quite seriously. Günter is majoring in biology and tries not to let his studies get in the way of his extra-curricular activities.

ANITA:	Tag, Günter. Wie geht's? Ist das dein Frühstück° oder dein Mittagessen?	*breakfast*
GÜNTER:	Mein Frühstück natürlich. Es ist doch erst° elf.	*only*
ANITA:	Was hast du denn da alles? Ein Glas Orangensaft, zwei Eier,° ein — nein, zwei Brötchen° mit Wurst und Käse,° ein Glas Milch und eine Tasse Kaffee. Günter, du ißt nicht, du frißt!°	*eggs* *rolls / cheese* *gorge yourself*
GÜNTER:	Soll° ich hungern und einen Becher Joghurt frühstücken wie° du?	*should / like*
ANITA:	Das ist nicht mein Frühstück, das ist mein Mittagessen.	
GÜNTER:	Du ißt morgens um elf zu Mittag? Ja, sag mal, wann frühstückst du dann?	
ANITA:	Um Viertel nach° sieben.	*after*
GÜNTER:	Und was ißt du zum Frühstück?	
ANITA:	Ich esse eine Scheibe Toast, und ich trinke eine Tasse Kaffee dazu.	
GÜNTER:	Ohne° Milch und Zucker, nicht?	*without*
ANITA:	Ja, natürlich.	
GÜNTER:	Du bist verrückt,° Anita. Du ißt zu wenig und arbeitest zu viel. Ich frühstücke erst° um halb elf.	*crazy* *not until*
ANITA:	Dann ißt du wohl gar nicht zu Mittag?	
GÜNTER:	Aber natürlich esse ich zu Mittag. Ich spiele nachmittags immer Tennis, und da muß ich doch vorher etwas° essen.	*something*
ANITA:	Ißt du mittags auch so viel?	
GÜNTER:	Was heißt° so viel? Ich esse meistens einen Teller Suppe mit ein paar Scheiben Brot,° einen Hamburger mit zwei Portionen Pommes frites° und trinke ein oder zwei Glas¹ Milch dazu. Zum Nachtisch° esse ich dann noch ein Stück Kuchen°. — Übrigens,° was machst du heute nachmittag? Möchtest du° nicht ein bißchen Tennis spielen?	*what do you mean* *bread / French fries* *dessert* *cake / by the way* *would you . . . like*
ANITA:	Ich kann nicht, Günter. Ich muß ein Referat° schreiben.	*report*
GÜNTER:	Menschenskind, Anita! Du ißt nichts, du treibst° keinen Sport, du . . .	*participate in*
ANITA:	Was soll das heißen, ich esse nichts? Ich esse abends sehr viel.	
GÜNTER:	Wirklich? Darf° ich fragen, was?	*may*
ANITA:	Fleisch oder Hüttenkäse° und viel Salat.	*cottage cheese*
GÜNTER:	Kein Brot? Keine Kartoffeln?°	*potatoes*
ANITA:	Brot und Kartoffeln machen doch dick. Ich will° doch nicht dick werden.°	*want to* *get*
GÜNTER:	Lieber krank°, nicht? — Was machst du denn abends? Gehst du wenigstens früh° ins Bett?	*sick* *early*
ANITA:	Ich gehe meistens noch in die Bibliothek. Ich lese° dort oft bis nachts um elf.	*read*

---

1. When **Glas** is used as a unit of measurement, it remains singular: **zwei Glas Milch** (*two glasses of milk*).

GÜNTER: Du lebst sehr ungesund,° Anita. Du ißt und schläfst° zu wenig, und du *unhealthy / sleep*
arbeitest zu viel.

ANITA: Und du, Günter, du ißt und schläfst zu viel, und arbeitest zu wenig.

VOM LESEN ZUM SPRECHEN

WAS PASST WO?

1. kann   lebt   frühstückt   will   ißt   muß
   a. Anita ———— morgens schon um Viertel nach sieben.
   b. Anita ———— schon um elf zu Mittag.
   c. Anita ———— heute nicht Tennis spielen. Sie ———— ein Referat schreiben.
   d. Anita ———— nicht dick werden.
   e. ———— Anita ungesund?
2. möchte   treibt   ißt   frühstückt   schläft   frißt
   a. Günter ———— erst um elf.
   b. Günter ———— nicht, er ————.
   c. Günter ———— viel mehr Sport als Anita.
   d. Günter ———— mit Anita Tennis spielen.
   e. Günter ———— viel mehr als Anita.

WER MACHT DAS, GÜNTER ODER ANITA?

Your teacher will read fourteen questions beginning with **wer.** Answer with **Anita** or **Günter.**

WIE LANGE SCHLÄFST DU MORGENS, UND WAS ISST DU ZUM FRÜHSTÜCK?

Find out how long your partner sleeps in the morning and what she/he has for breakfast.

S1:

1. Wie lange schläfst du an Wochentagen?

2. Wie lange schläfst du am Wochenende?

3. Was frühstückst du an Wochentagen?
   Was trinkst du?
   Was ißt du?

4. Trinkst du deinen Kaffee (Tee) mit oder ohne Milch und Zucker?

5. Warum ißt du so wenig (so viel)?

S2:

Meistens bis ———— Uhr. Nur am ———— (und am ————) kann ich nicht so lange schlafen, denn° meine Vorlesungen *because* beginnen da schon um ————.

Am Wochenende schlafe ich bis ———— Uhr.

Ich trinke ———— Glas . . . und/oder ———— Tasse(n) . . .
Ich esse . . .

Ich trinke meinen ———— mit (ohne) . . .
Ich trinke meinen ———— nur mit . . .

Ich will nicht dick werden.
Ich bin zu dünn und möchte ein bißchen dicker werden.

Record what you find out and report your findings to the rest of the class.

1. An Wochentagen schläft [Name] meistens bis _____ Uhr. Aber am _____ (und am _____) kann sie/er nicht so lange schlafen, denn ihre/seine Vorlesungen beginnen da schon um _____ Uhr.
2. Am Wochenende schläft [Name] bis _____ Uhr.
3. Zum Frühstück trinkt [Name] Glas . . . und/oder _____ Tasse(n) . . . Sie/er ißt . . .
4. Sie/er trinkt ihren/seinen Kaffee/Tee mit/ohne Milch und Zucker (nur mit Milch/Zucker).
5. [Name] ißt so wenig/viel, denn sie/er | will nicht dick werden.
   | ist zu dünn und möchte ein bißchen dicker werden.

In Germany, the percentage of young people attending university is much smaller than in the United States. In order to be considered for university admission, students must have successfully completed the **Abitur,** a series of exams given in the last year of a **Gymnasium,** a college preparatory high school. However, having the **Abitur** does not guarantee a place **(Studienplatz)** either at the university or in the discipline of one's choice. In the most popular fields like medicine or architecture, enrollment is restricted by **numerus clausus** (literally, *closed number*). For these disciplines the **Zentralstelle für die Vergabe von Studienplätzen** (a central clearing house for university applicants) assigns students to universities on the basis of grades and/or the length of time they have waited to be admitted.

Students pay no **Studiengebühren** *(tuition)*. If neither the student nor the parents are able to pay for living expenses, the state helps with a loan administered under the **Bundesausbildungsförderungsgesetz** or **BAFöG** *(the Federal Education Promotion Act)*. Parents are obligated to pay for their children's education if they can afford it and can be sued by their children for not doing to. The government subsidizes meals in the **Mensa** *(university cafeteria),* making them very inexpensive, and also subsidizes dormitories.

Freie Universität Berlin: Mensa

NÜTZLICHE WÖRTER UND AUSDRÜCKE

Nomen

das Frühstück	breakfast
das Ei, die Eier	egg
die Scheibe, die Scheiben	slice
das Brot	bread; sandwich
das Brötchen, die Brötchen	roll
die Tasse, die Tassen	cup
das Glas, die Gläser	glass
der Zucker	sugar
das Mittagessen	lunch, noon meal
der Teller, die Teller	plate
die Suppe, die Suppen	soup
die Portion, die Portionen	helping, serving, order
das Fleisch	meat
die Wurst	sausage; cold cuts
die Kartoffel, die Kartoffeln	potato
der Salat, die Salate	salad
der Käse	cheese
der Hüttenkäse	cottage cheese
der Nachtisch	dessert
das Stück, die Stücke	piece
der Kuchen, die Kuchen	cake
die Vorlesung, die Vorlesungen	lecture
das Referat, die Referate	report, paper
die Bibliothek, die Bibliotheken	library
die Cafeteria	university cafeteria *(for light meals and snacks)*
die Mensa	university cafeteria *(for full meals)*

Recycling in Deutschland

Verben

frühstücken	to eat breakfast, to have breakfast	**schreiben**	to write
sagen	to say, to tell	**essen**	to eat
fragen	to ask *(a question)*		

Andere Wörter

etwas	something	**wirklich**	really
verrückt	crazy	**früh**	early
krank	sick, ill	**vorher**	before *(adverb)*
gesund	healthy	**mit**	with
ungesund	unhealthy	**ohne**	without
übrigens	by the way	**wie**	like
wohl	probably		

Ausdrücke

Menschenskind!	Good grief!
ein bißchen	a bit
ein paar	a couple of, a few
zu wenig	too little
zum Frühstück	for breakfast
ein Glas Orangensaft	a glass of orange juice
ein Becher Joghurt	a carton of yogurt
Was frühstückst du am Sonntag?	What do you have for breakfast on Sunday?

. . . und zum Nachtisch
ein Stück Kuchen

Wann eßt ihr zu Mittag (zu Abend)?	When do you eat lunch (supper)?
ein Teller Suppe	a bowl of soup
eine Scheibe Brot	a slice of bread
eine Portion Pommes frites	an order of French fries
zum Nachtisch	for dessert
eine Tasse Kaffee und ein	a cup of coffee and a piece of cake with it
Stück Kuchen dazu	
Kuchen macht dick.	Cake is fattening.
Günter treibt viel Sport.	Günter is very active in sports.

Sprachnotizen

The flavoring particle *doch*

The flavoring particle **doch** is often used for emphasis. In English it is approximately equivalent to *you know*.

Ich kann heute abend nicht ins Kino. Ich muß **doch** ein Referat schreiben.	*I can't go to the movies tonight. I have to write a report, **you know**.*
Brot und Kartoffeln machen **doch** dick.	*Bread and potatoes are fattening, **you know**.*

Nicht? nicht wahr?

When statements are followed by **nicht?** or **nicht wahr?**, they are changed into questions that ask for confirmation.

Du trinkst deinen Kaffee ohne Milch und Zucker, **nicht?**	*You drink your coffee without milk and sugar, **right**? You drink your coffee without milk and sugar, **don't you**?*

WÖRTER IM KONTEXT

1. WAS PASST NICHT?   Find the word in each group that does not fit.

a. das Fleisch	b. die Bibliothek	c. die Kartoffel	d. die Scheibe
der Salat	die Cafeteria	der Hüttenkäse	das Brot
der Käse	die Mensa	der Salat	das Stück
die Wurst	das Referat	der Zucker	die Portion

2. WAS PASST?   Select the correct words to fit the context.

a. Anita trinkt morgens nur eine _____ Kaffee.

  Glas   Scheibe   Tasse   Becher

b. Kurt trinkt morgens ein _____ Orangensaft und zwei _____ Milch.

  Stück   Tasse   Teller   Glas

c. Mittags ißt Anita nur einen _____ Joghurt.

  Portion   Teller   Becher   Stück

d. Kurt ißt mittags einen _____ Suppe mit drei _____ Brot und einen Hamburger mit zwei _____ pommes frites.

Becher   Scheiben   Portionen   Teller

e. Zum Nachtisch ißt Kurt ein _____ Kuchen.

Portion   Scheibe   Teller   Stück

FUNKTIONEN UND FORMEN

1. EXPRESSING PERMISSION, ABILITY, NECESSITY, OBLIGATION, DESIRE, AND LIKES

MODAL VERBS

a. Meaning and position of modal verbs

Modal verbs are a small group of verbs (six in German) that modify the meaning of other verbs. They express such ideas as permission, ability, necessity, obligation, desire, and likes. The modals take the regular position of the verb. The verbs modified by the modals appear in the infinitive form at the very end of the sentence.

permission:	**dürfen** *to be allowed to, be permitted to, may*	Gehen wir jetzt? **Dürfen** wir jetzt gehen?	*Are we going now?* ***May*** *we go now?*
ability:	**können** *to be able to, can*	Kommt ihr heute abend? **Könnt** ihr heute abend kommen?	*Are you coming tonight?* ***Can*** *you come tonight?*
necessity:	**müssen** *to have to, must*	Wir gehen jetzt. Wir **müssen** jetzt gehen.	*We're going now.* *We* ***have to*** *go now.*
obligation:	**sollen** *to be supposed to, should*	Wir fliegen morgen nach New York. Wir **sollen** morgen nach New York fliegen.	*We're flying to New York tomorrow.* *We* ***are supposed to*** *fly to New York tomorrow.*
desire:	**wollen** *to want to*	Warum lernt ihr Deutsch? Warum **wollt** ihr Deutsch lernen?	*Why are you learning German?* *Why do you* ***want to*** *learn German?*
likes:	**mögen** *to like*	**Mögen** Sie Spinat? Warum **mögt** ihr Dieter nicht?	*Do you* ***like*** *spinach?* *Why don't you* ***like*** *Dieter?*

Note that **mögen** is mostly used without an infinitive.

The **möchte**-form of **mögen** is more frequently used than **mögen** itself. It expresses desire more politely than **wollen.**

Ich **möchte** in München studieren.   *I **would like to** study in Munich.*

The modal verb **sollen** expresses not only obligation, but can also convey the idea that the speaker is relying on a third party for her/his information.

Müllers sollen sehr reich sein.   *The Müllers are said to be very rich.*
Morgen soll es sehr heiß werden.   *Tomorrow it's supposed to get very hot.*

A. ERGÄNZEN SIE! Supply the appropriate modal verb.

1. Warum _____ ihr denn schon gehen? (mögen / müssen)
2. _____ Sie Ihren Kaffee mit oder ohne Milch und Zucker, Frau Meyer? (möcht- / müssen)
3. Warum _____ ihr Tanja nicht? (sollen / mögen)
4. Wann _____ ihr morgen frühstücken? (dürfen / wollen)
5. _____ wir jetzt gehen? (möcht- / dürfen)
6. Du _____ doch nicht so viel trinken, Günter! (sollen / möcht-)
7. _____ ihr uns° nächstes Wochenende besuchen? (können / sollen)
8. Was _____ Sie lieber, Herr Ziegler? Fisch oder Fleisch? (mögen / können)
9. Studenten _____ viel zu viel lernen. (dürfen / müssen)
10. _____ wir das Haus kaufen? (sollen / mögen)

us

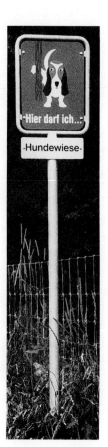

b. Omission of the infinitive after modal verbs

If the meaning of a sentence containing a modal is clear without an infinitive, the infinitive is often omitted:

Ich möchte nächstes Jahr nach Europa.   *I would like to **go** to Europe next summer.*

B. WAS PASST ZUSAMMEN? Match the sentences with the correct "understood" infinitives.

1. Wir müssen jetzt in die Vorlesung.
2. Möchten Sie ein Stück Kuchen?   trinken
3. Können deine Eltern Deutsch?   gehen
4. Warum wollt ihr nicht ins Kino?   essen
5. Wollt ihr Bier oder Wein?   sprechen
6. Mögen Sie Sauerkraut?   fliegen
7. Möchtest du auch nach Deutschland?

c. Position of *nicht* in sentences with modal verbs

In *Kapitel 1* you learned that if **nicht** negates the *verb,* it is at the end of the sentence. In a sentence with a modal and an infinitive, **nicht** becomes the *second to last* element, since the infinitive must be at the end of the sentence. The other rules that you learned about the position of **nicht** still apply (see pages 17 and 83).

Warum kommt ihr **nicht?**   *Why aren't you coming?*
Warum könnt ihr **nicht** kommen?   *Why can't you come?*

C. TOTAL NEGATIV! Your partner gives negative responses to each of your questions.

S1: Möchte dein Bruder studieren?   *S2:* Nein, er möchte nicht studieren.

1. Möchte dein Bruder in München, studieren?   Nein, er möchte . . .
2. Wollt ihr fliegen?   Nein, wir wollen . . .
3. Wollt ihr mit Swissair fliegen?   Nein, wir wollen . . .
4. Müßt ihr morgen arbeiten?   Nein, wir müssen . . .
5. Müßt ihr jeden Samstag arbeiten?   Nein, wir müssen . . .
6. Könnt ihr heute abend kommen?   Nein, wir können . . .
7. Können deine Eltern gut Deutsch?   Nein, sie können . . .
8. Dürfen wir den Kuchen essen?   Nein, ihr dürft . . .
9. Dürfen wir morgen abend ins Kino?   Nein, ihr dürft . . .
10. Mögt ihr das Bier?   Nein, wir mögen . . .
11. Mögt ihr Sabine sehr?   Nein, wir mögen . . .

THE PRESENT TENSE OF THE MODAL VERBS

The modals have no personal endings in the *1st* and *3rd* person singular of the present tense. All but one of the modals **(sollen)** have an irregular stem vowel in the singular.

dürfen *to be allowed to, may*

ich **darf**	wir **dürfen**
du **darfst**	ihr **dürft**
er / sie / es **darf**	sie **dürfen**
	Sie **dürfen**

Hunde dürfen nicht in den Essraum

D. Meet the Zieglers: here's what they aren't allowed to do.

1. Herr und Frau Ziegler _____ keinen Kaffee trinken.
2. Ihre Tochter Helga ist erst° fünfzehn und _____ noch nicht Auto fahren.°   *only / drive*
3. Ihr Sohn Uwe ist zwölf und _____ nicht nach° zehn nach Hause° kommen.   *after / **nach Hause:** home*

S1: Und du? Was __ du nicht trinken?   *S2:* Ich __ alles . . . / Ich __ kein__ . . .

S1: Und du? __ du Auto fahren?   *S2:* Aber natürlich __ . . . / Nein, ich __ . . .

S1: Und du? __ du nach zehn nach Hause kommen?   *S2:* Aber natürlich __ . . . / Nein, ich __ nicht . . .

können *to be able to, can*

ich **kann**	wir **können**
du **kannst**	ihr **könnt**
er / sie / es **kann**	sie **können**
	Sie **können**

E. The Zieglers are a very talented family.

1. Herr und Frau Ziegler _____ sehr gut Französisch und Spanisch.
2. Helga _____ sehr gut tanzen.
3. Uwe _____ sehr gut kochen.

S1: Und du? Was _____ du?   **S2:** Ich _____ sehr gut . . .

müssen *to have to, must*

ich **muß**[1]	wir **müssen**
du **mußt**	ihr **müßt**
er / sie / es **muß**	sie **müssen**

Sie **müssen**

F. There are a lot of things that the Zieglers have to do.

every
homework

1. Herr und Frau Ziegler _____ beide arbeiten und Geld verdienen.
2. Helga und Uwe _____ jeden° Morgen in die Schule, und jeden Abend _____ sie ihre Hausaufgaben° machen.

clean

3. Herr Ziegler _____ jeden Morgen das Frühstück machen und jeden Samstag das Haus putzen.°
4. Frau Ziegler _____ jeden Abend kochen und jeden Samstag waschen.

S1: Und du? Was _____ du tun?   **S2:** Ich _____ . . .

sollen *to be supposed to, should; to be said to be*

ich **soll**	wir **sollen**
du **sollst**	ihr **sollt**
er / sie / es **soll**	sie **sollen**

Sie **sollen**

G. Here's what the Zieglers are supposed to do next Saturday.

1. Frau Ziegler und Helga _____ nächsten Samstag Oma Ziegler besuchen.
2. Uwe _____ nächsten Samstag Vaters Wagen waschen.
3. Herr Ziegler _____ nächsten Samstag die Waschmaschine reparieren.

S1: Und du? Was _____ du nächsten Samstag tun?   **S2:** Ich _____ nächsten Samstag . . .

H. This is what the Zieglers are said to be like.

intelligent

1. Herr Ziegler _____ sehr praktisch sein.
2. Frau Ziegler _____ sehr klug° sein.
3. Helga und Uwe _____ sehr musikalisch sein.

wollen *to want to*

ich **will**	wir **wollen**
du **willst**	ihr **wollt**
er / sie / es **will**	sie **wollen**

Sie **wollen**

I. Here are things that the Zieglers don't want to happen!

1. Herr Ziegler _____ nicht dick werden.
2. Frau Ziegler _____ nicht jeden Sommer campen gehen.

relatives

3. Helga und Uwe _____ nicht jeden Sonntag Verwandte° besuchen.

---

1. At the end of a word or before a consonant **ss** is replaced by **ß.**

S1: Und du? Was _____ du nicht?   *S2:* Ich _____ nicht . . .

mögen *to like*

ich **mag**	wir **mögen**
du **magst**	ihr **mögt**
er / sie / es **mag**	sie **mögen**
	Sie **mögen**

J. The Zieglers have very definite ideas about what they don't like to eat!

1. Herr Ziegler _____ keine Kartoffeln und keine Nudeln.
2. Die beiden Kinder _____ kein Gemüse und keinen Salat.
3. Frau Ziegler _____ kein Fleisch.

S1: Und du? Was __ du nicht?   *S2:* Ich __ kein__ . . .

Note the different conjugation of the alternate form of **mögen** with the stem
möcht- (ich möchte *I would like to*):

ich **möchte**	wir **möchten**
du **möchtest**	ihr **möchtet**
er / sie / es **möchte**	sie **möchten**
	Sie **möchten**

K. If the Zieglers were rich, this is what they would like to have and to do.

1. Frau Ziegler _____ einen Porsche.
2. Herr Ziegler _____ eine Weltreise machen.
3. Uwe _____ ein Segelboot.
4. Helga _____ in Princeton studieren.

S1: Und du? Was _____ du?   *S2:* Ich _____ . . .

L. KLEINE GESPRÄCHE. Complete the mini-conversations with the appropriate
modal verbs.

1. müssen / können
   FLORIAN: Warum _____ du denn nicht   LINDA: Ich _____ Deutsch lernen.
   mit uns tanzen gehen?
2. müssen / möcht-
   HERR SPOHN: _____ Sie noch ein Glas   FRAU MEYER: Nein danke, ich _____ doch
   Wein, Frau Meyer?   fahren.
3. wollen / können
   BARBARA: Warum _____ Sylvia nicht   SABINE: Sie _____ kein Spanisch.
   mit uns nach Mexiko?
4. mögen / dürfen / mögen
   FRAU METZGER: Warum essen Sie denn   HERR BERGER: Natürlich _____ ich es.
   so wenig, Herr Ber-   Aber ich _____ nicht noch
   ger? _____ Sie mein   dicker werden.
   Essen nicht?
5. können / müssen / können / möcht-
   CLAUDIA: Gehst du heute abend mit   STEPHANIE: Ich _____ gern, aber ich
   uns ins Kino?   _____ nicht.

CLAUDIA: Warum _____ du denn nicht?   STEPHANIE: Ich _____ heute abend arbeiten.

M. KLEINE GESPRÄCHE. Express the following mini-conversations in German.

1. MARTIN: Should we go dancing tonight?
   CLAUDIA: I can't, Martin. I have to write a report.

der Hamburger

2. GÜNTER: I would like a hamburger° and two orders of French fries.
   ANITA: But Günter, you're not supposed to eat so much! (*Flavor with* **doch** *before* **nicht**.)

nur / von

3. GÜNTER: You have to eat meat and potatoes, Anita. You can't just° live on° orange juice and yogurt.
   ANITA: But I don't want to get fat! (*Flavor with* **doch** *before* **nicht**.)

4. FRAU MEYER: Why are you eating so little meat, Mr. Ziegler? Don't you like it?
   HERR ZIEGLER: Of course I like it, but I'm not allowed to eat much meat.

noch ein

5. HERR MEYER: Would you like another° glass of wine, Mr. Ziegler?
   HERR ZIEGLER: May I, Brigitte?
   FRAU ZIEGLER: Yes, but then you may not drive.

6. THOMAS: Why do you want to sell your car, Ralf?
   RALF: I don't want to, Thomas, I have to. I need money.

2. EXPRESSING ACTIONS IN THE PRESENT AND FUTURE (2)

THE PRESENT TENSE OF IRREGULAR VERBS

Modals are not the only verbs with irregular forms in the present tense.

Sprechen and **schlafen** are examples of the other two groups of verbs with irregular forms in the present tense. Note that the irregularities that differentiate them from the regular verb **lernen** occur only in the *2nd* and *3rd* person singular.

		lernen	**sprechen**	**schlafen**
	1. ich	lerne	ich spreche	ich schlafe
Singular	2. du	lernst	du sprichst	du schläfst
	3. er	lernt	er spricht	er schläft
	1. wir	lernen	wir sprechen	wir schlafen
Plural	2. ihr	lernt	ihr sprecht	ihr schlaft
	3. sie	lernen	sie sprechen	sie schlafen
	Sie	lernen	Sie sprechen	Sie schlafen

Most verbs with irregularities in the 2nd and 3rd person singular belong to one of the two groups below.

Stem vowel change from *e* to *i* or *ie*

essen	*to eat*	ich esse	du ißt	er ißt
fressen	*to eat*[1]	ich fresse	du frißt	er frißt

---

1. **Essen** is used for people; **fressen** is used for animals (or for people who eat too much).

geben	to give	ich gebe	du gibst	er gibt
lesen	to read	ich lese	du liest	er liest
nehmen	to take	ich nehme	du ni**mm**st[1]	er ni**mm**t
sehen	to see	ich sehe	du siehst	er sieht
sprechen	to speak	ich spreche	du sprichst	er spricht
vergessen	to forget	ich vergesse	du vergißt	er vergißt
werden	to become, get	ich werde	du wi**rst**	er wi**rd**

Stem vowel change from *a* to *ä*

backen	to bake	ich backe	du bäckst	er bäckt
fahren	to drive	ich fahre	du fährst	er fährt
fallen	to fall	ich falle	du fällst	er fällt
fangen	to catch	ich fange	du fängst	er fängt
halten	to hold; to stop	ich halte	du häl**tst**	er häl**t**
laden	to load	ich lade	du lä**dst**	er lä**dt**
lassen	to let; leave	ich lasse	du läßt	er läßt
schlafen	to sleep	ich schlafe	du schläfst	er schläft
waschen	to wash	ich wasche	du wäschst	er wäscht
laufen[2]	to run	ich laufe	du läufst	er läuft
saufen	to drink heavily	ich saufe	du säufst	er säuft

Verbs with these stem vowel changes are usually listed as follows:

sprechen (spricht)	to speak
fahren (fährt)	to drive
usw.	

Sprachnotizen

How to say *there is* and *there are*

From the verb **geben** comes the expression **es gibt.** Its English equivalent is *there is* or *there are.* **Es gibt** always has an accusative object.

When used with a food term, **es gibt** expresses what will be served.

| Ich glaube, **es gibt** Apfelstrudel zum Nachtisch. | *I think **there is** apple strudel for dessert.* |
| Morgen **gibt es** keinen Nachtisch. | *Tomorrow **there is** no dessert.* |

In other contexts **es gibt** is used to speak about the existence of things in a very general way.

| In Kanada **gibt es** Tausende von Seen. | *In Canada **there are** thousands of lakes.* |
| Wie viele McDonald's **gibt es** in München? | *How many McDonald's **are there** in Munich?* |

If one speaks about the physical presence of a person or thing in a very specific way, one does not use **es gibt.**

---

1. The letters in boldface show further irregularities.

2. **Laufen** and **saufen** are the only verbs with the diphthong **au** that are irregular in the present tense.

Da ist keine Milch im Kühlschrank. ***There is*** no milk in the fridge.
Da sind zwei riesige Hunde im Garten! ***There are*** two huge dogs in the garden!

N. EIN SAMSTAGNACHMITTAG BEI ZIEGLERS

fährt   wäscht   fängt   schläft   liest   bäckt

tired

1. Helga _____ ein Buch.
2. Oma Ziegler _____ einen Kuchen.
3. Zieglers Katze ist im Garten und _____ Mäuse.

to town
that's why

4. Herr Ziegler ist müde.° Er liegt im Bett und _____.
5. Frau Ziegler _____ heute in die Stadt.°
6. Deshalb° _____ Uwe ihren Wagen.

O. HERR ZIEGLER KRITISIERT HEUTE ALLES!

sprichst   gibt   wäschst   frißt   fährst   nimmst

1. Warum _____ du denn so viel Fleisch, Uwe?

finally

2. Warum _____ du denn nicht ein bißchen lauter, Helga?
3. Warum _____ es heute keinen Nachtisch?

4. Warum _____ die Katze die Maus hier im Haus?
5. Wann _____ du denn endlich° meinen Wagen, Uwe?
6. Wohin _____ du denn schon wieder, Brigitte?

P. ZUM THEMA° „ESSEN"

topic

essen   esse   ißt   eßt

late

1. Sie _____ zu viel Fleisch, Herr Ziegler!
2. _____ du immer so wenig, Helga?
3. Uwe ist fünfzehn. Er _____ nicht, er frißt.

4. _____ ihr immer so spät° zu Mittag?
5. Heute _____ wir bei McDonald's.
6. Ich _____ gern Kaviar.

S1: Was _____ du gern?

S2: Ich _____ gern . . .

Q. ZUM THEMA „FAHREN"

fahren   fahre   fährst   fährt   fahrt

1. Herr Ziegler _____ einen Audi.
2. _____ du heute mit Vater zur Schule?
3. Nein, heute _____ ich mit Mutter.

4. Was für einen Wagen _____ Sie, Frau Ziegler?
5. Morgen _____ wir nach Berlin.
6. _____ ihr nächsten Sommer wieder nach Italien?

S1: Was für einen Wagen _____ dein Vater/deine Mutter?

S2: Mein Vater/meine Mutter _____ . . .

S1: Und was _____ du?

S2: Ich _____ . . ./Ich habe keinen . . .

R. ERGÄNZEN SIE DIE MINIDIALOGE!

1. hält / läufst

Sabine: Warum _____ du denn so schnell?
Holger: Der Zug _____ hier nur eine Minute.

2. fällt / läßt

   Kurt: Das Barometer _____. Ich glaube, es regnet bald.°   *soon*
   Eva: Warum _____ du dann alle Fenster° offen?   *windows*

3. fahren / laden / lädt

   Frau Borchert: Was _____ Ihr Schiff denn, Herr Kapitän?
   Kapitän Krüger: Wir _____ Autos. Und morgen _____ wir nach Amerika.

4. säuft / vergißt

   Frau Eisenbraun: Warum _____ der alte Herr Huber denn immer alles?
   Frau Schaufler: Ich glaube, er trinkt zu viel.
   Herr Schaufler: Er trinkt nicht, er _____!

5. sehen / wird

   Frau Schaufler: _____ Sie Ihren Sohn oft, Frau Eisenbraun?
   Frau Eisenbraun: Nein, er studiert jetzt in Berlin. Er _____ Architekt.

S. WAS PASSIERT HIER? Use the verbs on pages 106–107 to describe what's happening in each picture.

▶ schlecht

S1: Warum braucht Dieter eine Brille?°   *S2:* Er sieht schlecht.   *glasses*

1. Was macht Herr Fischer?

4. Wie kommt Barbara zur Uni?°

mit Ralf

zur Uni:[1] *to the university*

2. Was macht Helga?

ein Bad

5. Was macht Frau Schneider?

ein Buch

3. Was gibt's zum Nachtisch?

6. Was macht die Katze?

---

1. **Uni** is the abbreviation for **Universität.** Students always use the abbreviated form.

---

7. Was macht die Katze?

8. Was macht Sylvia?

9. Was macht Stefan?

10. Was macht Tina?

11. Was macht Monika?

12. Was macht das Taxi?

nicht!

13. Was macht Bettina?

14. Was macht Markus?

ins Wasser

15. Was macht Tanja?

ZUSAMMENSCHAU

KASPAR MÜLLER HAT EIN PROBLEM

Read the following story carefully. Then test your problem solving skills.

farmer
goat / German
shepherd / barley

Es ist Samstag, und in Hinterkingen ist Wochenmarkt. Kaspar Müller, ein Bauer° aus Dillingen, kauft eine Ziege,° einen Schäferhund° und einen Sack Gerste,° trinkt ein paar Glas Bier und geht dann nach Hause. Aber zwischen° Hinterkingen und Dillingen ist die Donau,° und es gibt hier keine Brücke,° sondern° nur ein kleines Boot. In das Boot passen° nur Kaspar und die Ziege oder Kaspar und der Schäferhund oder Kaspar und die Gerste, und Kaspar muß deshalb mehrmals° über die Donau fahren. Aber da gibt es zwei Probleme:

between
Danube River / bridge / but
fit
several times

1. ohne Kaspar frißt der Schäferhund die Ziege.
2. ohne Kaspar frißt die Ziege die Gerste.

Kaspar bringt deshalb zuerst° die Ziege über die Donau, denn° Schäferhunde fressen keine Gerste. Aber was soll er jetzt holen,° den Schäferhund oder die Gerste? Was soll der arme° Kaspar tun?

first / because
get
poor

Answer the thirteen questions that you hear about the story. Question 9 contains a word with which you may not be familiar:

Question 9:   **man**   *one, you* (as in **man braucht** *one needs, you need*)

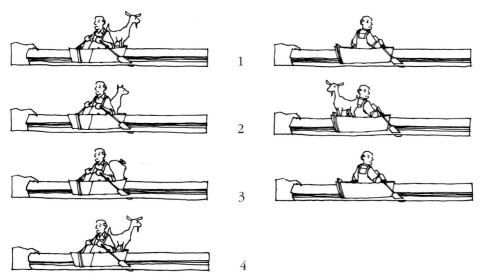

1

2

3

4

WIE LÖST° KASPAR SEIN PROBLEM?   Listen carefully to four additional questions. These questions and the accompanying sketches will show you how Kaspar gets his animals and the bag of barley across the river. You will find the answer to the first question in the story. To answer the other three, look at the sketches. Questions 2 and 4 contain words with which you may not be familiar:

does . . . solve

Question 2:   **zurück**   *back*
Question 4:   **zuletzt**   *last*

3. TELLING TIME

WIEVIEL UHR IST ES? WIE SPÄT IST ES?

what time is it?

In German there are two ways of telling time. The one used in everyday conversation is not unlike the English system. The other system counts the day from 0 to 24 hours and is used for scheduling anything official such as transit timetables, etc.

Es ist 14.07 Uhr

Because Germans see and hear this way of telling time every day of their lives, it is common to use these official forms in colloquial German as well.

		Official	**Colloquial**
	13.00 Uhr	dreizehn Uhr	eins (ein Uhr)
	13.05 Uhr	dreizehn Uhr fünf	fünf nach eins
	13.15 Uhr	dreizehn Uhr fünfzehn	Viertel nach eins
	13.20 Uhr	dreizehn Uhr zwanzig	zwanzig nach eins
	13.25 Uhr	dreizehn Uhr fünfundzwanzig	fünf vor halb zwei
	13.30 Uhr	dreizehn Uhr dreißig	halb zwei
	13.35 Uhr	dreizehn Uhr fünfunddreißig	fünf nach halb zwei
	13.40 Uhr	dreizehn Uhr vierzig	zwanzig vor zwei
	13.45 Uhr	dreizehn Uhr fünfundvierzig	Viertel vor zwei
	13.55 Uhr	dreizehn Uhr fünfundfünfzig	fünf vor zwei
	14.00 Uhr	vierzehn Uhr	zwei (zwei Uhr)

EXPRESSIONS OF TIME REFERRING TO PARTS OF THE DAY (1)

German has no equivalents for the terms A.M. and P.M. In colloquial German the following adverbs of time are used to refer to specific periods during a day without specifying the particular day. Note that all these adverbs of time end in **-s!**

morgens	in the morning
vormittags	in the morning
mittags	(at) noon
nachmittags	in the afternoon
abends	in the evening
nachts	at night

T. WIEVIEL UHR IST ES? Your partner wants to know what time it is. First answer in colloquial time, then in official time.

▶ abends

Colloquial **S1:** Wieviel Uhr ist es? (Wie spät ist es?) **S2:** Es ist fünf nach sechs.

Official **S1:** Wie spät ist es? (Wieviel Uhr ist es?) **S2:** Es ist achtzehn Uhr fünf.

1. nachmittags

2. vormittags

3. nachts

4. morgens

5. abends

6. vormittags

7. nachmittags

8. nachts

9. abends

10. nachmittags

Picture caption (right): *Was ist „werktags"?*

EXPRESSIONS OF TIME REFERRING TO PARTS OF THE DAY (2)

When referring to a part of a specific day, you must first specify the day (e.g., **gestern, heute, Sonntag**) and then mention the part of the day (this time without an **-s**).

gestern mittag	yesterday noon
gestern nacht	last night

Für schnelle Züge braucht man eine Zuschlagskarte (*additional ticket*)

Wobin fährt der Eilzug?

Wie weit ist es von Heidelberg nach Hamburg?

The state-owned **Deutsche Bundesbahn** *(Federal Railway)* provides excellent passenger service with many different types of trains to choose from:

the **EC (Eurocity-Zug),** an international express train that runs daily between major European cities,

the **IC (Intercity-Zug),** an express train within Germany that runs between major cities,

the **FD-Zug,** the **D-Zug,** and the **Eilzug,** which are slightly less expensive and make more frequent stops,

the **Nahverkehrszug,** which stops at all small towns and villages, and

the **S-Bahn (Schnellbahn),** a rapid transit train for commuters traveling short distances.

The punctuality of German trains is legendary: when the minute hand of the station clock snaps to the departure time, the train starts to pull out of the station. Foreign tourists who are not used to such punctuality often miss their trains. Connections are excellent and departures are frequent, e.g., express trains leave the Stuttgart **Hauptbahnhof** *(main railway station)* for **München** every hour.

Some major cities also have subways (called **U-Bahn** or **Untergrundbahn**) and all large towns and cities have **Straßenbahn** *(streetcar)* and/or city bus systems.

Lufthansa (**Luft** = *air*), Germany's national airline, takes its name from the medieval Northern German trading league, the **Hansa.**

heute morgen	this morning
morgen früh[1]	tomorrow morning
(am) Montag nachmittag	(on) Monday afternoon
(am) Dienstag abend	(on) Tuesday evening

There is a difference between time expressions such as **nachmittags** and **nachmittag.**

The adverb **nachmittags** is used to describe a repeated or habitual event:

Ich gehe **nachmittags** immer schwimmen.　　*I always go swimming in the afternoon.*

---

1. To avoid the awkwardness of **morgen morgen** German substitutes **früh.**

The adverb **nachmittag** is used to describe a single event on a particular day:

Heute **nachmittag** gehe ich schwimmen. *This afternoon I'm going swimming.*

U. UM WIEVIEL UHR? Your partner talks about time as if she/he works for the Deutsche Bundesbahn.

▶ Um wieviel Uhr° fährt unser Bus heute morgen, um . . . ?   *what time*

S1: Um wieviel Uhr fährt unser Bus heute morgen, um halb zehn?   **S2:** Ja, Punkt° neun Uhr dreißig.   *on the dot*

1. Um wieviel Uhr beginnt unsere erste° Vorlesung heute vormittag, um . . . ?   *first*

2. Um wieviel Uhr essen wir heute zu Mittag, um . . . ?

3. Um wieviel Uhr fährt unser Bus heute nachmittag, um . . . ?

4. Um wieviel Uhr beginnt das Konzert am Sonntag abend, um . . . ?

5. Um wieviel Uhr frühstücken wir morgen früh, um . . . ?

6. Um wieviel Uhr fährt unser Zug morgen nacht, um . . . ?

7. Um wieviel Uhr fliegt unsere Maschine° am Mittwoch morgen, um . . . ?   *plane*

V. GÜNTER SCHLUMBERGERS STUNDENPLAN. Look at Günter's timetable and then answer the questions below.

1. Was hat Günter am Montag von acht bis zehn?
2. Wann hat Günter Genetik?
3. Wann beginnt Günters Genetische Übung am Montag?
4. Wann ist sie zu Ende?
5. Was macht Günter am Mittwoch von elf bis eins?
6. Was macht Günter am Freitag von zwölf bis zwei?
7. Wo ist Günter am Samstag und am Sonntag?
8. Wie viele Freundinnen hat Günter?

	Mo	Di	Mi	Do	Fr	Sa	So
8.00	Zoologie II			Bio-chemie	Genetik I	Bei Helga	Bei Tina
9.00			Mikro-biologie I				
10.00		Botanik II					
11.00			Tennis mit Helga		Mathe Übung		
12.00					Tennis mit Tina		
13.00			Mathe-matik II				
14.00							
15.00	Genetik I			Botanik II			
16.00	Übung			Übung			
17.00							

Übung: *seminar*

Wo sind diese Studenten?

Students at universities in the German-speaking countries receive much less guidance than students at North American universities and colleges. Attendance at **Vorlesungen** *(lectures)* is not mandatory and there are no semester finals. The first exams **(Zwischenprüfungen)** are taken after the fourth semester. The **Zwischenprüfungen** are important exams: passing them allows a student to continue her/his studies. More advanced courses include **Übungen,** classes in which students receive practical experience in a given subject, and **Seminare,** discussion groups in which students are usually required to write a **Referat** or **Seminararbeit** *(seminar paper).*

The **Wintersemester** begins in mid-October and ends in mid-February. The semester break is long by North American standards and the next semester, the **Sommersemester,** lasts from the middle of April to the middle of July. German students talk about where they are at in their studies according to semesters, not by year, as North American students do. (**Ich bin im vierten Semester.** *I am in my sophomore year.*)

W. MEIN FREUND KURT.
Express in German Monika's description of her boyfriend.

nett
be = become

ganz

**musikalisch /
Klavierstunden
perfekt
der Geburtstag
trotzdem**

My boyfriend's name is Kurt. He is from Regensburg and he is very nice.° He is studying chemistry and biology and he wants to be° teacher. Kurt is very active in sports: in summer he swims and plays tennis and in winter he goes skiing. He likes to eat, he cooks and bakes, and his apple cake is absolutely° fantastic.

Kurt is very intelligent. He reads a lot and he speaks English like an American. Kurt is also very musical.° He takes piano lessons° and he plays Mozart and Beethoven.

But Kurt is not perfect.° He has a motorcycle and he drives much too fast. He often sleeps too long. And sometimes he forgets my birthday.° But I like my Kurt anyway.°

MEIN FREUND/MEINE FREUNDIN. Beschreiben° Sie jetzt Ihren Freund/Ihre *describe*
Freundin.

◣ ZUSAMMENSCHAU

BRIGITTES TAGESLAUF

Brigitte's daily routine

Read the description of Brigitte's daily routine.

Ich esse sehr gern, aber dick werden will ich natürlich nicht. Deshalb gehe ich
jeden Morgen um halb sieben joggen. Dann dusche° ich und frühstücke (nur ein   *take a shower*
Glas Milch!), und um Viertel vor acht fährt mein Bus. Meine erste Vorlesung
beginnt um Viertel nach acht, und sie ist um Viertel vor zehn zu Ende.° Dann gehe   *over*
ich in die Cafeteria, denn jetzt bin ich wirklich hungrig. Ich esse ein Ei und ein
Brötchen mit Butter und Käse und trinke zwei Glas Milch dazu (Milch soll sehr
gesund sein!). Um halb elf gehe ich schwimmen (das ist auch sehr gesund!) und
um halb zwölf in die Bibliothek. Dort lese ich bis halb zwei. Dann bin ich sehr
hungrig, gehe in die Cafeteria und darf jetzt ein bißchen mehr essen, meistens zwei
Knackwürste mit Brötchen und dazu zwei oder drei Glas Milch.

Nachmittags von halb drei bis halb fünf habe ich wieder Vorlesungen, und um
fünf komme ich dann nach Hause und mache meine Hausaufgaben. Aber vorher
muß ich natürlich etwas essen. Ich koche sehr gern, und ich esse oft einen Teller
Suppe, ein Schnitzel,° ein bißchen Reis (Reis soll nicht so dick machen wie Kartof-   *cutlet*
feln oder Nudeln), viel Salat und viel Gemüse° mit ein bißchen Butter (Gemüse ist   *vegetables*
sehr gesund, aber ohne Butter schmeckt° es nicht so gut). Dazu trinke ich wieder   *taste*
viel Milch. Zum Nachtisch esse ich meistens ein Stück Kuchen (ich backe sehr
gern) und trinke eine Tasse Kaffee dazu. Aber ich will natürlich nicht dick werden,
und ich trinke deshalb meinen Kaffee ohne Milch und ohne Zucker.

▭ Answer the questions you hear about Brigitte's daily routine.

You and a partner assume the roles of the interviewer and Brigitte.

1. Wie beginnst du deinen Tag,
   Brigitte?

3. Wann beginnt deine erste
   Vorlesung?

2. Joggen, das macht hungrig. Was ißt
   du denn alles zum Frühstück?

4. Und wann ist sie zu Ende?

5. Was machst du dann?

6. Trinkst du jetzt wieder nur ein Glas Milch?

7. Hast du dann wieder eine Vorlesung?

8. Von wann bis wann?

9. Joggen um halb sieben, Schwimmen um halb elf. Warum das alles?

10. Was machst du um half zwölf?

11. Wie lange lernst du dort?

12. Und was kommt dann?

13. Was ißt du denn jetzt?

14. Von wann bis wann hast du nachmittags Vorlesungen?

15. Um wieviel Uhr kommst du nach Hause?

16. Machst du dann gleich deine Hausaufgaben?

MEIN TAGESLAUF For homework write a paragraph about your **Tageslauf** (especially your eating habits). Make use of the vocabulary you have already learned and the vocabulary in the reference section. Try to use as many modal verbs as possible.

Tell your classmates about your daily routine.

WORT, SINN UND KLANG

WÖRTER UNTER DER LUPE

1. WORDS AS CHAMELEONS: *ERST*

Just as a chameleon changes its color according to its environment, certain words change their meaning according to their context. One of these is **erst.**

a. In its adverb form **erst** means *first, only*[1] or *not until*:

Kurt trinkt **erst** eine Cola, und dann macht er seine Hausaufgaben.	***First*** *Kurt drinks a cola and then he does his homework.*
Es ist **erst** zehn Uhr.	*It's **only** ten o'clock.*
Heute kommt Dieter **erst** um elf nach Hause.	*Today Dieter is**n't** coming home **until** eleven.*

b. In its adjective form **erst** always means *first*:

Wann fährt der **erste** Bus?	*When does the **first** bus leave?*

- Give the correct meaning of **erst.**

1. Sonntags frühstücken wir **erst** um elf oder halb zwölf.   not until / first
2. Thomas ist **erst** siebzehn.   only / not until
3. Anita geht morgens **erst** joggen und dann nimmt sie ein Bad.   not until / first
4. Ich kann **erst** um zehn kommen.   first / not until
5. Freitags beginnt meine **erste** Vorlesung schon um acht.   not until / first
6. Ist es wirklich **erst** Viertel vor sieben?   only / first
7. Sollen wir **erst** eine Tasse Kaffe trinken?   not until / first
8. Ist Brigitte wirklich Günters **erste** Freundin?   not until / first

2. PREDICTING GENDER

The gender of many German nouns is indicated by their suffixes. Here are some examples:

a. Nouns with the suffixes **-or** and **-ent** are *masculine*.

der Profess**or**
der Stud**ent**

---

1. For the difference between **nur** and **erst** see *Kapitel 5,* page 153.

b. Nouns with the suffix **-in** which are derived from masculine nouns are *feminine:*

die Professor**in** *female professor*
die Student**in** *female student*

c. Nouns with the suffix **-ment** are *neuter:*

das Instru**ment**

d. Nouns with the diminutive suffixes **-chen** and **-lein** are *neuter.* These two suffixes (compare English *-let* in star*let,* book*let,* and pig*let*) can be affixed to virtually every German noun to express smallness. This also explains why both **Mädchen** (*girl*) and **Fräulein** *(Miss, young lady)* are neuter.

der Tisch *table*   **das** Tisch**lein** *little table*
die Schwester *sister*   **das** Schwester**chen** *little sister*

The vowels **a, o, u,** and the diphthong **au** are umlauted when a diminutive suffix is added to the noun. Remember that with the diphthong **au** it is the **a** that is umlauted:

der Bruder *brother*   **das** Brüder**chen** *little brother*
das Haus *house*   **das** Häus**chen** *little house*

- Say the following nouns with their definite articles. If a noun has a corresponding feminine form, give that form and the corresponding article.

1. Präsident
2. Dokument
3. Motor
4. Direktor
5. Assistent
6. Agent
7. Kätzchen
8. Fischlein
9. Parlament
10. Projektor
11. Autor
12. Inspektor

3. *BESSER* VERSUS *LIEBER*

Besser, the comparative form of **gut,** is used to make qualitative comparisons:

Er spielt **besser** als ich.   *He plays **better** than I do.*

Lieber, the comparative form of **gern,** is used to express a preference:

Was magst du **lieber,** Äpfel oder Birnen?   *What do you **prefer,** apples or pears?*
          *What do you like **better,** apples or pears?*

English sometimes uses **better** to express a preference. The German **besser** is restricted to qualitative comparisons.

- Decide whether the context of the sentences given suggests a preference or a comparison of quality. Use **besser** or **lieber** as appropriate.

1. Möchtest du heute abend ins Kino?
   Nein, ich lese _____ ein Buch.
2. Warum ißt du Apfelkuchen, Julia? Der Käsekuchen ist doch viel _____.
   Das kann sein, aber ich mag Apfelkuchen viel _____.
3. Was können Sie _____, Herr Ziegler, Italienisch oder Spanisch?
   Italienisch kann ich _____, aber Spanisch spreche ich viel _____.
4. Möchtest du ein Glas Wein, Helga?
   Nein, ich möchte _____ ein Tasse Kaffee.
5. Ich mag Ralf viel _____ als Kurt.

6. Der Weißwein ist _____ als der Rotwein, Herr Müller.

   Ich trinke aber _____ Rotwein.

7. Möchtet ihr _____ ins Kino oder in die Disco?

8. Spricht Ralf so gut Englisch wie Kurt?

   Nein, Kurt spricht viel _____.

9. Gehst du auch noch ein Glas Bier trinken?

   Nein, ich gehe _____ nach Hause.

10. Was magst du _____, Nudeln oder Reis?

    Nudeln mag ich _____, aber Reis ist besser für meine Gesundheit.°   *health*

WEITERE NÜTZLICHE WÖRTER UND AUSDRÜCKE

Wichtige Verben

dürfen, er darf	to be allowed to, may
können, er kann	to be able to, can
mögen, er mag	to like
müssen, er muß	to have to, must
sollen, er soll	to be supposed to, should; to be said to be
wollen, er will	to want to
ich möchte	I would like to
essen, er ißt	to eat
fressen, er frißt	to eat *(of animals)*
geben, er gibt	to give
lesen, er liest	to read
nehmen, er nimmt	to take
sehen, er sieht	to see
sprechen, er spricht	to speak
vergessen, er vergißt	to forget
werden, er wird	to get, to become

backen, er bäckt	to bake	**lassen, er läßt**	to let, to leave
fahren, er fährt	to drive	**schlafen, er schläft**	to sleep
fallen, er fällt	to fall	**waschen, er wäscht**	to wash
fangen, er fängt	to catch	**laufen, er läuft**	to run
halten, er hält	to hold, to stop	**saufen, er säuft**	to drink heavily
laden, er lädt	to load		

Die Uhrzeit

Wieviel Uhr ist es?	What time is it?	**Punkt elf**	eleven on the dot
Wie spät ist es?	What time is it?	**um wieviel Uhr?**	(at) what time?
Viertel vor	a quarter to	**um zwei Uhr**	at two o'clock
Viertel nach	a quarter after	**um vierzehn Uhr**	at two p.m.
halb zwölf	eleven thirty	**von zehn bis elf**	from ten to eleven

Die Tageszeiten

morgens	in the morning	**abends**	in the evening
vormittags	in the morning	**nachts**	at night
mittags	at noon	**heute morgen**	this morning
nachmittags	in the afternoon	**morgen früh**	tomorrow morning

Andere Zeitausdrücke

am Montag, usw.	on Monday, etc.
vorgestern	the day before yesterday

übermorgen	the day after tomorrow
Es ist erst elf.	It's only eleven.
Ich komme erst um elf.	I'm not coming until eleven.
zu Ende sein	to be over
bald	soon
immer noch	still
noch nicht	not yet
erst, zuerst	first
erst	only; not until

your house - at home

Andere Wörter und Ausdrücke

schnell	fast, quick(ly)	**nach Hause gehen**	to go home
müde	tired	**es gibt**	there is, there are
nett	nice	**deshalb**	therefore; that's why

WÖRTER IM KONTEXT

1. WAS PASST WO?

immer noch   bald   deshalb   erst   Viertel

Eva: Kurt ist _____ nicht hier. Glaubst du, er kommt _____?
Paul: Nein, er hat heute bis _____ nach sechs Vorlesungen und kommt _____ _____ um sieben.

nachts   nachmittags   abends   morgens   vormittags   mittags

    a. 23.00 Uhr: _____   c. 16.45 Uhr: _____   e. 20.00 Uhr: _____
    b. 7.00 Uhr: _____   d. 11.15 Uhr: _____   f. 12.00 Uhr: _____

2. WAS PASST NICHT?

a. schnell	b. deshalb	c. nachmittags	d. am Sonntag
bald	noch nicht	übermorgen	morgen früh
immer noch	zuerst	abends	übermorgen
müde	vorgestern	nachts	vorgestern

ZUR AUSSPRACHE

THE VOWELS Ä, Ö, AND Ü

The vowels **a, o,** and **u,** can be umlauted: **ä, ö,** and **ü.** These umlauted vowels can also be long or short. Listen carefully and you will hear the difference between **a, o, u,** and their umlauted equivalents.

• Hören Sie gut zu und wiederholen Sie!

a (lang)	ä (lang)
Glas	Gläser
Rad	Räder
Vater	Väter

a (kurz)	ä (kurz)
alt	**ä**lter
k**a**lt	k**ä**lter
l**a**ng	l**ä**nger

o (lang)	ö (lang)	o (kurz)	ö (kurz)
T**o**n	T**ö**ne	**o**ft	**ö**fter
S**o**hn	S**ö**hne	T**o**chter	T**ö**chter
gr**o**ß	gr**ö**ßer	W**o**rt	W**ö**rter

If you have trouble producing the sound **ö,** round your lips to say a German **o** (as in **O**ma), hold your lips in that position and try to say a German **e** (as in **E**sel).

u (lang)	ü (lang)	u (kurz)	ü (kurz)
B**u**ch	B**ü**cher	M**u**tter	M**ü**tter
Br**u**der	Br**ü**der	j**u**ng	j**ü**nger
F**u**ß	F**ü**ße	d**u**mm	d**ü**mmer

If you have trouble producing the sound **ü,** round your lips to say a German **u** (as in **Br**u**der**), hold your lips in that position and try to say a German **i** (as in **di**e).

▦ DAS RÜBENZIEHEN° In the following story, long and short vowels, including umlauts, stand in sharp contrast to one another. Listen carefully and try to imitate the speaker.   *pulling out a turnip*

Väterchen hat Rüben gesät.° Er will eine dicke Rübe herausziehen;° er packt° sie beim Schopf,° er zieht und zieht und kann sie nicht herausziehen. Väterchen ruft° Mütterchen: Mütterchen zieht Väterchen, Väterchen zieht die Rübe, sie ziehen und ziehen und können sie nicht herausziehen.   *sown / pull out / grabs* *by the top / calls*

    Kommt das Söhnchen: Söhnchen zieht Mütterchen, Mütterchen zieht Väterchen, Väterchen zieht die Rübe, sie ziehen und ziehen und können sie nicht herausziehen.

    Kommt das Hündchen: Hündchen zieht Söhnchen, Söhnchen zieht Mütterchen, Mütterchen zieht Väterchen, Väterchen zieht die Rübe, sie ziehen und ziehen und können sie nicht herausziehen.

    Kommt das Hühnchen:° Hühnchen zieht Hündchen, Hündchen zieht Söhnchen, Söhnchen zieht Mütterchen, Mütterchen zieht Väterchen, Väterchen zieht die Rübe, sie ziehen und ziehen und können sie nicht herausziehen.   *little hen*

    Kommt das Hähnchen:° Hähnchen zieht Hühnchen, Hühnchen zieht Hündchen, Hündchen zieht Söhnchen, Söhnchen zieht Mütterchen, Mütterchen zieht Väterchen, Väterchen zieht die Rübe: sie ziehen und ziehen — schwupps,° ist die Rübe heraus, und das Märchen° ist aus.°   *little rooster* *whoops* *fairy tale / over*

München ist eine schöne Stadt

KAPITEL 5

HEUTE HABEN WIR FREI

Stephanie and Claudia discuss what they have planned for a day away from their books.

CLAUDIA:	Warum stehst° du denn schon auf, Stephanie? Es ist doch erst halb acht.
STEPHANIE:	Peter kommt um acht und holt° mich ab.
CLAUDIA:	Um acht?! Ja, was habt° ihr denn vor?
STEPHANIE:	Wir fahren zum Starnberger See. Peter hat jetzt ein Surfbrett. Das wollen wir ausprobieren.°
CLAUDIA:	Wie kriegt° ihr das Ding denn nach Starnberg? Ihr habt doch keinen Wagen.
STEPHANIE:	Wir haben den Wagen von Bernd.
CLAUDIA:	Den Wagen von Bernd? Braucht der ihn° heute nicht selbst?
STEPHANIE:	Bernd muß sein Referat für Professor Seidlmeyer fertigschreiben.
CLAUDIA:	Armer Bernd. Aber gut für euch.°
STEPHANIE:	Was machst du heute, Claudia?
CLAUDIA:	Erst schlafe° ich mal richtig aus, so bis elf oder halb zwölf, und dann rufe° ich Martin an.
STEPHANIE:	Und weckst ihn auf.
CLAUDIA:	Ja, sonst° schläft er den ganzen° Tag.
STEPHANIE:	Schleppt er dich dann wieder ins Deutsche Museum?
CLAUDIA:	Ja denkste! Das mache ich nicht nochmal mit.° Heute machen wir mal, was ich will.
STEPHANIE:	Und das ist?
CLAUDIA:	Erst gehen wir Weißwürste essen beim Donisl am Marienplatz . . .
STEPHANIE:	Mmm, die sind gut dort.
CLAUDIA:	Dann will ich bei Karstadt° ein paar Kleider° anprobieren° . . .
STEPHANIE:	Armer Martin!
CLAUDIA:	Dann gehen wir in die Alte Pinakothek und schauen° Bilder° von Dürer an. Und zum Schluß° gehen° wir dann im Englischen Garten ein bißchen spazieren.
STEPHANIE:	Geht ihr dort schwimmen?
CLAUDIA:	Ich nicht, denn der Eisbach ist immer noch viel zu kalt. Aber vielleicht geht° Martin rein.
STEPHANIE:	Bis dahin° braucht er die Erfrischung, der arme Kerl!°
CLAUDIA:	Wie lustig.° — Sag mal, wann kommt° ihr heute abend zurück?
STEPHANIE:	So gegen° sieben.
CLAUDIA:	Schon gegen sieben. Dann können wir ja noch tanzen gehen!
STEPHANIE:	Ja, sicher. In Schwabing, nicht?
CLAUDIA:	Klar. — Du, dort hupt° jemand.° Ist das Peter?
STEPHANIE:	Ja, das ist er. Also dann, bis heute abend!

stehst. . .auf: *are . . . getting up* / **holt. . .ab:** *is picking . . . up* / **habt. . .vor:** *do . . . have planned* / *try out* / *are . . . getting*

it

you

schlafe. . .aus: *am sleeping in* / **rufe. . .an:** *am calling*

or else / *all*

I'm not putting up with that again.

a department store chain / *dresses* / *try on*

schauen. . .an: *look at* / *paintings* / *finally* / **gehen . . . spazieren:** *go for a walk*

geht. . .rein: *is going in* / *by that time* / *guy*

funny / **kommt. . .zurück:** *are . . . coming back around*

is honking / *somebody*

VOM LESEN ZUM SPRECHEN

WAS PASST ZUSAMMEN?

1. Warum steht Stephanie heute so früh auf?
2. Wohin fahren Stephanie und Peter heute?
3. Woher haben sie einen Wagen?
4. Warum fahren sie zum Starnberger See?
5. Warum braucht Bernd seinen Wagen heute nicht selbst?
6. Was macht Claudia heute vormittag?
7. Wo will Claudia heute Weißwürste essen?
8. Warum will sie am Nachmittag zu Karstadt?
9. Warum will Claudia im Englischen Garten nicht schwimmen gehen?
10. Wann kommen Stephanie und Peter heute abend zurück?
11. Was haben Claudia, Stephanie, Martin und Peter heute abend vor?

Sie will dort ein paar Kleider anprobieren.
Sie wollen tanzen gehen.

So gegen sieben.
Der Eisbach ist immer noch viel zu kalt.

Zum Starnberger See.

Sie wollen dort Peters Surfbrett ausprobieren.
Von Bernd.

Peter kommt um acht und holt sie ab.

Beim Donisl im Marienplatz.

Er muß sein Referat fertigschreiben.

Erst schläft sie mal richtig aus, und dann ruft sie Martin an.

Der Englische Garten: Ein Treffpunkt für Studenten

WER MACHT DAS? Your teacher will read fourteen questions about *Heute haben wir frei* beginning with **wer.** Answer with the appropriate name(s).

WANN STEHST DU AUF? WANN KOMMST DU HEIM?

Find out more about your partner's life style.

S1:

1. Wann stehst du morgens auf?
2. Warum stehst du so früh/spät auf?
3. Wann kommst du nachmittags / abends heim?
4. Gehst du oft aus?

5. Warum gehst du so oft/selten aus?
6. Was hast du heute abend vor?

S2:

Ich stehe meistens° schon/erst um . . .   *usually*
Ich . . .
Ich komme nachmittags/abends meistens schon/erst um . . .
Ja, ich _____ sehr oft _____.
Nein, ich _____ nur sehr selten _____.
Ich . . .
Heute abend lerne ich Deutsch!
Heute abend . . .

BMW in München

München, the beautiful capital of **Bayern** (Bavaria), is one of Germany's major cultural centers. During the Second World War Munich was almost totally destroyed, and returning the city to its former glory seemed an impossible task. But today it is more beautiful than ever: all the buildings that made it a center of art and culture have been carefully restored. With over 40 theaters and 6 resident orchestras, Munich has cultural offerings unequaled by any other German city. It has become world-renowned in the area of the visual arts. Its art collections are housed in over 25 art galleries and museums, the best known being the **Alte Pinakothek** and the **Neue Pinakothek.** Munich is also the home of the largest technical museum in the world, the **Deutsches Museum.**

With over 50,000 students, the **Ludwig-Maximilians-Universität** in Munich is the largest in the Federal Republic. Adjoining the university is the **Englischer Garten,** a 925-acre park right in the heart of the city. The park is a favorite playground for students, who spend sunny days strolling, cycling, sunbathing, or swimming in the chilly waters of the **Eisbach.**

Munich is also an important industrial center. Best known of its industries is **BMW (Bayerische Motorenwerke),** the maker of an automobile admired the world over for its engineering and design. The city has also become the hub for the microelectronics industry. The area around Munich is Germany's equivalent of California's Silicon Valley.

München is also well-known for its **Oktoberfest,** a 16-day **Volksfest** that attracts visitors from all over the world with its beer tents, music, and carnival rides.

• Report in German what you have found out about your partner to the rest of the class.

Say:

when your partner usually gets up.
why she/he gets up so early/late.
when your partner comes home in the afternoon/evening.
whether your partner goes out often/rarely.
why your partner goes out so often/so rarely.
what your partner has planned for this evening.

NÜTZLICHE WÖRTER UND AUSDRÜCKE

Nomen

das Surfbrett, die Surfbretter	surfboard, windsurfing board
das Ding, die Dinge	thing
das Kleid, die Kleider	dress
die Kleider	clothes
das Bild, die Bilder	picture
der Kerl, die Kerle	guy

Verben

aus•schlafen[1], er schläft aus	to sleep in
auf•stehen	to get up
vor•haben	to plan, to have planned
an•rufen	to call *(on the telephone)*
ab•holen	to pick up
spazieren•gehen	to go for a walk
an•schauen	to look at
an•probieren	to try on
aus•probieren	to try out
zurück•kommen	to come back
hupen	to honk
kriegen	to get
schleppen	to drag
denken	to think

Ruf doch mal an!

Andere Wörter

jemand	somebody
selber, selbst	himself, herself, myself, etc.
richtig	right; really; properly
lustig	funny; happy
arm	poor
wieder	again
vielleicht	perhaps
sonst	or else, otherwise
sicher	sure, certainly; probably
denn	because, for

Ausdrücke

Heute habe ich frei.	Today I have a day off.
den ganzen Tag	all day
Klar!	Of course!
Das mache ich nicht nochmal mit.	I'm not putting up with that again.
zum Schluß	finally; to top it off
Bis heute abend!	See you tonight!
gegen sieben (Uhr)	around seven (o'clock)

---

1. In vocabulary lists in this text, a raised dot indicates a separable-prefix verb. The use of the dot is *not* a German practice.

Sprachnotizen

The flavoring particle *mal*

Mal is the shortened form of **einmal** *(once)*, and it is often used in colloquial German to make a statement or question sound more casual. This usage has no equivalent in English.

Wann besuchst du uns **mal** wieder?   *When are you going to visit us again?*

Mal can also mean *for a change* or *for once.*

Heute machen wir **mal,** was ich will.   *Today we're doing what I want **for a change.***

WÖRTER IM KONTEXT

1. WAS PASST ZUSAMMEN?

a. Was habt ihr morgen vor?
b. Warum nehmt ihr nicht den Wagen von Bernd?

c. Kann ich Müllers jetzt anrufen?

d. Da hupt jemand. Ist das für dich?
e. Was machst du denn bei Karstadt?
f. Schleppt Martin dich morgen wieder ins Deutsche Museum?
g. Ist Monika schon hier?
h. Was machst du morgen?

Nein, die schlafen doch noch.
Erst schlafen wir mal richtig aus, und dann gehen wir vielleicht ein bißchen spazieren.
Ja denkste! Das mache ich nicht nochmal mit!
Da schlafe ich den ganzen Tag.
Das ist sicher Peter. Der holt mich ab.
Ich will ein paar Kleider anprobieren.

Der braucht ihn heute selbst.
Nein, die kommt erst gegen halb acht.

2. WAS PASST WO?

gehen . . . spazieren   schlafe . . . aus   schauen . . . an
rufe . . . an   stehe . . . auf

a. Ich _____ jeden Morgen um sieben _____, aber nächsten Sonntag _____ ich mal richtig _____.
b. Am Nachmittag _____ ich Ralf _____.
c. Wir _____ dann zuerst im Englischen Garten ein bißchen _____.
d. Später gehen wir in die Alte Pinakothek und _____ schöne Bilder _____.

probieren . . . an   kommen . . . zurück   hast . . . vor
probieren . . . aus   holt . . . ab

e. Was _____ du heute nachmittag _____?
f. Heute nachmittag um halb zwei kommt Sabine und _____ mich _____.
g. Wir _____ zuerst ihren neuen Computer _____.
h. Später gehen wir in die Stadt und _____ bei Karstadt Kleider _____.
i. Wir _____ erst gegen sechs wieder _____.

The area south of **München** is popular with tourists. It is an area of many lakes (**Starnberger See, Ammersee, Chiemsee,** etc.), mountains, beautiful towns and villages, and fairy-tale castles. Three of the most extravagant castles were built during the 23-year reign of Ludwig II of Bavaria (1845–86), who became king at the young age of 18. He had little interest in matters of state, but was an ardent admirer and patron of Richard Wagner and his music. He depleted the royal coffers by having castles built that mirrored his lavish, romantic taste in art and architecture. The castles **Neuschwanstein, Linderhof,** and **Herrenchiemsee** (a small Versailles) are the legacy of his fanciful mind.

Alarmed by Ludwig's extravagance with state funds, his ministers demanded that he abdicate. He refused, and shortly afterwards, at the age of 41, Ludwig II was declared insane and was deposed. A few days later he died a mysterious death in the **Starnberger See.**

Neuschwanstein

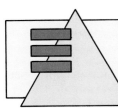

FUNKTIONEN UND FORMEN

1. EXPRESSING ACTIONS IN THE PRESENT AND FUTURE

SEPARABLE-PREFIX VERBS

In English the meaning of certain verbs can be modified or changed by adding a preposition or an adverb:

to go *out*
to go *away*
to come *back*
to come *home*

to try *on*
to try *out*
to get *up*

The same effect is achieved in German by adding a *prefix* to the verb:

ausgehen	*to go **out***	**an**probieren	*to try **on***
weggehen	*to go **away***	**aus**probieren	*to try **out***
zurückkommen	*to come **back***	**auf**stehen	*to stand **up;***
heimkommen	*to come **home***		*to get **up***

In the infinitive form, the prefix is attached to the front of the verb. In the present tense, the prefix is separated from the verb and is placed at the end of the sentence:

Gehst du heute abend **aus?**	*Are you **going out** tonight?*
Warum **kommst** du immer so spät **heim?**	*Why **do** you always **come home** so late?*

In a sentence in which the verb is negated, **nicht** precedes the separable prefix:

Heute abend gehe ich **nicht** aus.	*Tonight I'm **not** going out.*

When used with a modal, the separable-prefix verb appears in its infinitive form at the end of the sentence:

Wann **mußt** du morgen früh **aufstehen?**	*When **do** you **have to get up** tomorrow morning?*
Heute abend **will** ich **nicht ausgehen.**	*Tonight I **don't want to go out.***

Separable-prefix verbs are not usually as similar to their English equivalents as the examples given above:

anfangen	*to begin, to start*	**fertig**schreiben	*to finish writing*
aufhören	*to end, to stop*	**kennen**lernen	*to get to know*
anhören	*to listen to*	**mit**nehmen	*to take along*
ankommen	*to arrive*	**aus**trinken	*to finish drinking*
abfahren	*to depart, to leave*	**aus**essen	*to finish eating*

A. WAS PASST ZUSAMMEN? Complete the sentences by choosing an appropriate prefix. In some instances, more than one prefix is possible.

1. Wer ruft denn so früh morgens _____?
2. Heute abend kommen wir erst sehr spät _____.
3. Ich kann Sie erst gegen sieben _____holen.
4. Stehst du immer so spät _____?
5. Warum gehen Sie denn schon _____?
6. Willst du meinen Computer _____probieren?
7. Warum probierst du das Kleid denn nicht _____?
8. Was habt ihr morgen abend _____?
9. Wann kommt Stephanie _____, im Juli oder im August?
10. Morgen früh schlafe ich mal richtig _____.
11. Monika will nicht mit Günter _____gehen.

weg
aus
vor
an
zurück
auf
ab
heim

B. FREIZEITPLÄNE. You want to know what your partner will be doing at certain times and in certain places. Your partner responds by matching the activities listed below to the illustrations.

▶ du heute nachmittag

mein neues Album anhören

S1: Was machst du heute nachmittag? **S2:** Da höre ich mein neues Album an.

1. du am Samstag
   abend

2. ihr im Deutschen
   Museum

3. du am Sonntag
   vormittag

4. du morgen abend

5. ihr bei Karstadt

---

alte Maschinen anschauen	wollen / mal richtig ausschlafen
mit Claudia ausgehen	wollen / ein paar Kleider anprobieren
müssen / mein Referat für Professor Seidlmeyer fertigschreiben	

6. du heute abend

7. ihr am Sonntag
   nachmittag

8. du in Starnberg

9. du am Samstag
   morgen

10. ihr am Freitag
    abend

---

noch nichts vorhaben	mein Surfbrett ausprobieren
erst um elf aufstehen	sollen / meine Eltern anrufen
im Englischen Garten spazierengehen	

WAS MACHST DU DEN GANZEN TAG?

Answer your partner's questions about your daily routine. Say when you get up, when you leave for classes, when your lectures start, what you have planned for this evening, and when you are coming home. Use the verbs in the list below.

S1:

1. Wann _____ du morgens _____?
   _____ du jeden Morgen so früh/so spät _____?
2. Um wieviel Uhr _____ du _____?
3. Wann _____ deine erste Vorlesung _____?
   _____ deine Vorlesungen jeden Tag so früh/so spät _____?
4. Was _____ du heute abend _____?
5. Wann _____ du heute abend _____?
   _____ du jeden Abend so spät/so früh _____?

S2:

Ich _____ um . . . _____.
. . .

Ich _____ um . . . _____.
Meine erste Vorlesung _____ um . . . _____.
. . .

Heute abend . . .
Heute abend _____ ich um . . . _____.
. . .

| 1. aufstehen | 2. weggehen | 3. anfangen | 4. vorhaben | 5. heimkommen |

VERBS WITH INSEPARABLE PREFIXES

The meaning of German verbs can also be changed by adding inseparable prefixes. As their name implies, inseparable prefixes are never separated from the verb stem. Three of the most common inseparable prefixes are **be-**, **er-**, and **ver-**:

kommen:	Kommst du heute abend?	*Are you coming tonight?*
bekommen:	Warum bekomme ich kein Bier?	*Why don't I get any beer?*
schreiben:	Stefan schreibt nicht sehr leserlich.	*Stefan doesn't write very legibly.*
beschreiben:	Können Sie die Frau beschreiben?	*Can you describe the woman?*
trinken:	Was trinkst du da?	*What are you drinking?*
ertrinken:	Hilfe! Ich ertrinke!	*Help! I'm drowning!*
stehen:	Warum stehst du im Regen?	*Why are you standing in the rain?*
verstehen:	Ich verstehe kein Wort.	*I don't understand a word.*
suchen:	Was suchen Sie denn?	*What are you looking for?*
besuchen:	Wann besucht ihr uns mal?	*When are you going to visit us?*
versuchen:	Warum versuchst du es nicht?	*Why don't you try it?*

Separable prefixes are always *stressed* in pronunciation. Inseparable prefixes are always *unstressed* in pronunciation.

C. WANN? Your partner wants to know when certain things are going to happen.

▶ aufstehen / du morgens	ich / müssen / schon um halb sieben . . .
S1: Wann stehst du morgens auf?	*S2:* Ich muß schon um halb sieben aufstehen.

1. verkaufen / Thomas sein Motorrad — er / wollen / es erst im Herbst . . .
2. heimfahren / Sandra heute abend — sie / wollen / schon um Viertel vor fünf . . .
3. bekommen / du die fünfhundert Mark — ich / sollen / sie schon morgen . . .
4. ausgehen / ihr heute abend — wir / können / nicht vor° halb zehn . . .   *before*
5. wegfliegen / Peter — er / mögen (*möchte*-Form!) / schon im April . . .
6. bestellen° / du deine Bücher — ich / müssen / sie noch heute nachmittag . . .   *to order*
7. besuchen / Kathrin ihre Großeltern — sie / wollen / sie Ende Juni . . .
8. weggehen / du morgen früh — ich / müssen / schon um Viertel vor acht . . .
9. heimkommen / Kurt heute nacht — er / dürfen / nicht nach halb eins . . .
10. ankommen / ihr in Frankfurt — wir / sollen / schon morgens um Viertel nach fünf dort . . .

NOUNS THAT FUNCTION LIKE SEPARABLE PREFIXES

Some verbs are so closely associated with a noun that they function like separable-prefix verbs. This happens most frequently with the verbs **spielen, laufen,** and **fahren.**

Im Sommer **spielt** Claudia fast jeden Nachmittag **Tennis.**	*In summer Claudia plays tennis almost every day.*
Im Winter **läuft** sie fast jedes Wochenende **Schi.**	*In winter she skis almost every weekend.*

If a modal is present, these verb-noun combinations again function like separable-prefix verbs. The noun precedes the infinitive at the end of the sentence.

Kann deine Schwester jetzt **Auto fahren?**	*Can your sister drive now?*

On page 84 you learned that **nicht** usually follows the direct object. With verb-noun combinations **nicht** *precedes* the noun.

Veronika kann **nicht Tennis** spielen.	*Veronica can't play tennis.*

Nouns that are part of verb-noun combinations cannot be replaced with a pronoun.

Spielen Sie **Klavier?**	*Do you play the piano?*
Nein, ich spiele nicht **Klavier.**	*No, I don't play the piano.*

But:

Kaufen Sie **das Klavier?'**	*Are you going to buy the piano?*
Nein, ich kaufe **es** nicht.	*No, I'm not going to buy it.*

D. IMMER NEGATIV! Your partner responds negatively to each of your questions.

S1: Spielst du Cello?   *S2:* Nein, ich spiele nicht Cello.
S1: Kaufst du das Cello?   *S2:* Nein, ich kaufe es nicht.

1. Läufst du Schi?   Nein, ich . . .
2. Kaufst du Stefans Fahrrad?   Nein, ich . . .
3. Magst du mein Motorrad?   Nein, ich . . .
4. Kannst du Motorrad fahren?   Nein, ich . . .
5. Spielt Sabine Saxophon?   Nein, sie . . .
6. Möchtest du das Saxophon?   Nein, ich . . .
7. Fährt Helga Auto?   Nein, sie . . .
8. Magst du Florians Auto?   Nein, ich . . .
9. Spielt Frau Ziegler Klavier?   Nein, sie . . .
10. Kaufen Zieglers euer Klavier?   Nein, sie . . .

E. AUF DEUTSCH, BITTE! Express these exchanges in German.

1. PAUL: When does our train arrive in Frankfurt?
   DAVID: At 6:40 p.m. *(Use official time.)*
2. KATHRIN: When do you leave in the morning?
   MARTINA: At quarter to eight.
   KATHRIN: And when do you come home in the evening?
   MARTINA: At half past six.

mit•kommen
in
aus•essen

3. PETER: We're playing tennis this afternoon. Are you coming along?°
   HOLGER: No, I have (to go) to° the library.
4. MUTTER: Why doesn't Tilmann want to finish° his soup?
   VATER: He doesn't like it.
   MUTTER: Then he's not getting any dessert.

beschreiben
der Schnurrbart

5. POLIZIST: Can't you describe° the man a bit better?
   FRAU HAUCK: He's tall, blond and has a moustache.°

fertig•schreiben

6. ANDREAS: Why can't Tobias go out tonight?
   RALF: He has to finish writing° his report.
7. VERKÄUFERIN: Would you like to try the dress on?
   FRAU VOGEL: No thanks. It's much too expensive.

uns

8. DIETER: Why don't you want to play cards?
   ULI UND KURT: We're going out tonight. Frank is picking us° up.

 ZUSAMMENSCHAU

AUSREDEN   *excuses*

Look at Monika's diary for the week of
July 15 and answer the following questions.

1. Was hat Monika am Montag um neunzehn Uhr dreißig?
2. Was macht Monika am Dienstag morgen um neun Uhr dreißig?
3. Was macht sie am Mittwoch um neunzehn Uhr?
4. Was macht sie am Donnerstag um zwanzig Uhr?
5. Was für ein Film läuft da?
6. Was macht Monika am Freitag abend?
7. Was macht sie am Samstag?

Juli 1991   23 Arbeitstage   29. Woche

15 Montag   196-202. Tag

19³⁰h *Chorprobe°*   *choir practice*

16 Dienstag 9³⁰h H 303
Test° in Physik   **der Test**

17 Mittwoch
19⁰⁰h *Tennis mit Sylvia*

18 Donnerstag 20⁰⁰h *Kino mit David*
„*Zurück in die Zukunft°"*   *future*

19 Freitag
21³⁰h *Disco mit David*

20 Samstag
nach Hause fahren

🔊 Listen to the telephone conversation between Monika and Günter Schlumberger and compare what Monika says with the entries in her calendar. Indicate for which days she is telling or not telling the truth by checking **wahr** (*true*) or **unwahr** (*untrue*) in the box below. *Note that the conversation takes place late Sunday afternoon.*

Wochentag	wahr	unwahr
Montag	———	———
Dienstag	———	———
Mittwoch	———	———
Donnerstag	———	———
Freitag	———	———
Samstag	———	———

🔊 **WIR GEHEN MORGEN SEGELN.** Just after Monika's conversation with Günter, the phone rings again. This time it is Alexander Wolff. Listen to the conversation between Monika and Alexander.

Neue Vokabeln

Ratzeburger See	*lake 35 miles northeast of Hamburg*
der Platz	*room*
außerdem	*besides*
genug	*enough*
Da hast du eigentlich recht.	*Actually you're right.*

✏️ Now answer the questions.

1. Wohin fahren Alexander und seine Freunde?
2. Warum ruft Alexander Monika an?
3. Wie heißen Alexanders Freunde?
4. Warum fahren Alexander und seine Freunde zum Ratzeburger See?

Wir gehen morgen segeln

5. Wie warm soll es morgen sein?
6. Warum hat Monika keine Zeit?
7. Wann will Alexander morgen abend wieder zurück sein?
8. Warum kann Monika morgen abend nicht lernen?
9. Wann soll Monika am Dienstag früh aufstehen?
10. Was hat Monika heute abend vor?
11. Wann soll Monika für ihren Test lernen?
12. Wann fahren die vier Freunde morgen weg?

about

• Was sagt Monika über° ihre Pläne für heute (Sonntag) abend?

a. Zu Günter sagt sie: _____

b. Zu Alexander sagt sie: _____

GEHST DU MIT?

Try to persuade a friend to join you and some other friends in an activity.

Sie

1. Say that Lisa, David, and you are planning an activity tonight (going to the movies, to the disco, etc.). Ask your friend to come along.

ab•geben

3. Ask when your friend's test is (when she/he has to hand in° the report).

5. Suggest to your friend that she/he can study (write her/his report) tomorrow.

eine Abwechslung

7. Tell your friend that she/he works too much. She/he needs a change.°

Ihre Freundin/Ihr Freund

2. Say that you can't go. You have to study for a test (write a report).

4. Your test is the day after tomorrow (you have to hand in the report the day after tomorrow).

6. Say that you don't have time tomorrow. You have lectures, you have to go to the library, and you have to fix° your bicycle.

reparieren

8. Say that you would like to go along, but you can't (*or* that you do need a change, and that you will go along).

Sprachnotizen

Two meanings of *da*

When **da** is used as an adverb of time, it means *then*. When used to express location, **da** is a synonym of **dort**. As the examples show, the English equivalents are not always expressed. Omitting **da** in the German responses would make them sound very abrupt.

Was machst du nächste Woche?	*What are you doing next week?*
Da bin ich in Regensburg.	*I'll be in Regensburg.*
Was machst du **da?**	*What will you be doing there?*
Da besuche ich meine Großeltern.	*I'll be visiting my grandparents.*

2. ANSWERING *WHO, WHOM* OR *WHAT*

NOMINATIVE AND ACCUSATIVE CASE: THE DEFINITE ARTICLE AND *DER*-WORDS

a. The definite article

The definite article has nominative and accusative forms just like the indefinite article.

Nominative

Der Roman „Der Steppenwolf" ist von Hermann Hesse.	*The novel "Der Steppenwolf" is by Hermann Hesse.*

Accusative

Ich lese gerade **den** Roman „Der Steppenwolf" von Hermann Hesse.	*I'm just reading the novel "Der Steppenwolf" by Hermann Hesse.*

As with the indefinite article, only the accusative masculine differs from the nominative.

	Masculine	**Feminine**	**Neuter**	**Plural**
Nominative	der (ein)	die (eine)	das (ein)	die (keine)
Accusative	d**en** (ein**en**)	die (eine)	das (ein)	die (keine)

F. DU BIST MAL NEUGIERIG!° You are inquisitive to the point of nosiness. Your partner gives very patient answers.   *inquisitive*

▶ trinken / der Apfelsaft / zu sauer

> Ich habe nur keinen Durst.

S1: Warum trinkst du den Apfelsaft nicht? Ist er zu sauer?

S2: Nein, zu sauer ist er nicht. Ich habe nur keinen Durst.

1. kaufen / das Fahrrad / zu teuer
2. fertiglesen / der Roman / zu langweilig°   *boring*
3. essen / die Suppe / zu heiß
4. nehmen / der Ring / zu teuer
5. essen / das Steak / zu zäh°   *tough*

to finish drinking / strong   6. austrinken° / der Tee / zu stark°
                                  7. essen / die Wurst / zu fett
                                  8. kaufen / der Pullover / zu teuer
                                  9. trinken / das Bier / zu warm

Ich habe nur nicht so viel Geld.	Ich habe nur keinen Hunger.
Ich habe nur nicht genug° Zeit.	Ich habe nur keinen Durst.

enough

b. *Der*-words

The endings of words like **dieser** *(this)*, **jeder** *(each, every)*, and **welcher** *(which)* correspond closely to the forms of the definite article. For this reason these words, along with the definite article, are called **der**-words.

Kennst du **diesen** Mann?   *Do you know **this** man?*

Nicht **jeder** Bäcker macht so gute Brötchen.   *Not **every** baker makes such good rolls.*

Welches Kleid soll ich anprobieren?   ***Which** dress should I try on?*

	Masculine	Feminine	Neuter	Plural
Nominative	dies**er** (d**er**)	dies**e** (di**e**)	dies**es** (da**s**)	dies**e** (di**e**)
Accusative	dies**en** (d**en**)	dies**e** (di**e**)	dies**es** (da**s**)	dies**e** (di**e**)

G. ERGÄNZEN SIE!   Complete with the correct forms of **dieser, jeder,** or **welcher.**

1. In Deutschland hat fast _____ Familie einen Wagen.
2. _____ Wagen fährst du lieber, den Opel oder den Audi?
3. Wie finden Sie _____ Brot?
4. _____ Schuhe soll ich kaufen?
5. Fast _____ Kind mag Schokolade.
6. Woher hast du _____ Rose *(f)*?
7. Entschuldigung, _____ Bus fährt nach Hohenheim?
8. Sind _____ Brötchen frisch?
9. Nicht _____ Professor ist so nett wie Professor Seidlmeyer.

3. ASKING *WHO*, *WHOM*, OR *WHAT*

THE INTERROGATIVE PRONOUNS *WER*, *WEN*, AND *WAS*

The interrogative pronouns **wer, wen,** and **was** are the equivalents of English *who, whom,* and *what.* **Wer** is a nominative form:

Wer korrigiert unsere Prüfungen, die Professorin oder der Assistent?	**Who** *corrects our exams, the professor or the assistant?*

Wen is an accusative form:

Wen magst du lieber, den Professor oder die Assistentin?	**Whom** *do you like better, the professor or the assistant?*

Was is either nominative or accusative:

Was riecht denn so gut?	**What** *smells so good?*
Was liest du denn?	**What** *are you reading?*

Note the close correspondence between the definite article forms **der, den,** and **das** and the interrogative pronouns **wer, wen,** and **was:**

	Definite Article	Interrogative Pronoun	Definite Article	Interrogative Pronoun
Nominative	d**er**	**wer**	d**as**	w**as**
Accusative	d**en**	**wen**	d**as**	w**as**

H. WER ODER WAS? Begin each question with **wer** or **was.**

> ▶ laut sprechen Professor Seidlmeyer
>
> *S1:* Wer spricht denn da so laut? *S2:* Das ist sicher Professor Seidlmeyer.

1. schnell fahren	dein verrückter Bruder	
2. schlecht riechen°	Professor Seidlmeyers Zigarre	*to smell*
3. toll Klavier spielen	Andrea	
4. laut schreien°	unser neuer Nachbar°	*to scream / neighbor*
5. schrecklich° stinken	Irmas neues Parfüm	*awful*

I. WEN ODER WAS? Ask your partner what her/his personal preferences are.

> ▶ lieber mögen: Martin oder Günter
>
> *S1:* Wen magst du lieber, Martin oder Günter? *S2:* Ich mag Martin lieber.
> Ich mag Günter lieber.

1. lustiger finden: Bill Cosby oder Steve Martin?
2. lieber lesen: Romane° oder Kurzgeschichten?° *novels / short stories*
3. lieber essen: Kartoffeln oder Nudeln?
4. öfter anrufen: deine Eltern oder deinen Freund (deine Freundin)?

5. lieber hören: Rock oder Jazz?
6. attraktiver finden: Meryl Streep oder Glenn Close?
7. lieber trinken: Bier oder Cola?

4. TALKING ABOUT PERSONS OR THINGS WITHOUT NAMING THEM

PERSONAL PRONOUNS IN THE ACCUSATIVE CASE

In English the object forms of the personal pronouns are often different from the subject forms, e.g., *I don't like **him**. He doesn't like **me** either.*

Similarly, in German the accusative forms of the personal pronouns are often different from the nominative forms:

Ich kenne **ihn,** aber er kennt **mich** nicht.

*I know **him** but he doesn't know **me**.*

Warum liest du **den Roman** nicht? Ich finde **ihn** langweilig.

*Why don't you read **the novel**? I find **it** boring.*

Personal Pronouns			
Nominative		**Accusative**	
ich	*I*	**mich**	*me*
du	*you*	**dich**	*you*
er	*he*	**ihn**	*him*
sie	*she*	**sie**	*her*
es	*it*	**es**	*it*
wir	*we*	**uns**	*us*
ihr	*you*	**euch**	*you*
sie	*they*	**sie**	*them*
Sie	*you*	**Sie**	*you*

J. UNGLÜCKLICHE LIEBE *(UNREQUITED LOVE).*
Ergänzen Sie die Personalpronomen!

1. KURT: Ich liebe _____, Eva, liebst du _____ auch?
   EVA: Ich mag _____, Kurt, aber ich liebe _____ nicht.
2. TINA: Liebst du Eva?
   KURT: Ja, ich liebe _____, ich liebe _____ sehr.
   TINA: Und Eva? Liebt sie _____ auch?
   KURT: Sie sagt, sie mag _____, aber sie liebt _____ nicht.
3. TINA: Liebst du Kurt?
   EVA: Nein, ich mag _____, aber ich liebe _____ nicht.
   TINA: Und Kurt? Liebt er _____?
   EVA: Er sagt, er liebt _____ sehr.

K. GLÜCKLICHE LIEBE.

Ergänzen Sie die Personalpronomen!

STEFFI UND MORITZ: Wir mögen _____ Mutti. Magst du _____ auch?
MUTTI: Ja, Kinder, ich mag _____ sehr.
STEFFI UND MORITZ: Und Vati? Mag er _____ auch?
MUTTI: Er mag _____ genau so sehr° wie ich.   **genau so sehr:** *just as much*
STEFFI UND MORITZ: Mögt ihr auch den Hund und die Katze und unsere Fische?
MUTTI: Ja natürlich mögen wir _____ auch, aber _____ zwei mögen wir noch lieber.

L. MEINUNGEN (OPINIONS).

Ergänzen Sie die Personalpronomen!

1. SABINE: Wie findest du Sylvias Freund?
    MONIKA: Ich finde _____ sehr arrogant.
2. SABINE: Wie findest du diesen Artikel?
    MONIKA: Ich finde _____ sehr interessant.
3. MARTIN: Wie findest du unsere Biologieprofessorin?
    CLAUDIA: Ich finde _____ sehr gut.
4. MARTIN: Wie findest du meine Suppe?
    CLAUDIA: Ich finde _____ sehr gut.
5. PETER: Wie findest du Martin und Claudia?
    STEPHANIE: Ich finde _____ sehr nett.
6. PETER: Wie findest du Martins Witze?°   *jokes*
    STEPHANIE: Ich finde _____ ziemlich° doof.   *rather*
7. FRAU KUHN: Kennen Sie den Film *Die Blechtrommel,*° Frau Benn?   *the Tin Drum*
    FRAU BENN: Nein, ich kenne _____ nicht, aber ich kenne den Roman.
    FRAU KUHN: Und wie ist der Roman?
    FRAU BENN: Ich finde _____ sehr interessant.

DIE GESCHMÄCKER SIND VERSCHIEDEN   *tastes differ*

What do you think about the appearance of your classmates: their clothes, their hair cuts, etc.?

S1: Wie findest du Lisas Pulli?   *S2:* Ich finde ihn sehr schick.
                                             Ich finde ihn nicht sehr schön.

Below are some words to help you express your opinions. You can qualify your opinions with the words in parentheses.

geschmackvoll (sehr, nicht sehr)   todschick°   *very stylish*
schön (sehr, nicht sehr)   ganz toll
elegant (sehr, nicht sehr)   ziemlich verrückt
schick (sehr, nicht sehr)

die Jacke

die Jeans

der Schnurrbart

der Pullover

die Hose

der Ring, -e

die Bluse

die Schuhe

der Ohrring, -e

das Hemd

die Frisur

das Armband, "er

das Kleid

der Haarschnitt

die Halskette

der Rock

der Bart

die Brille

DER, *DIE*, AND *DAS* USED AS PRONOUNS

In *Kapitel 2* you learned that **er, sie, es** (and **sie** in the plural) are used to replace nouns. In colloquial German the definite articles **der, die, das** (and **die**) are often used instead. In this function **der, die,** and **das** are not articles, but pronouns. They usually appear at the beginning of the sentence even if they are in the accusative case. These pronouns are often used for emphasis and depending on the context, they can also mean *this one* or *that one*.

Was macht Peter?	*What is Peter doing?*
Der schläft noch.	***He's** still sleeping.*
Wo ist Claudia?	*Where is Claudia?*
Die nimmt gerade ein Bad.	***She's** just taking a bath.*
Kann ich deinen Kassettenrecorder borgen?	*Can I borrow your cassette recorder?*
Nein, **den** brauche ich heute selbst.	*No, I need **it** myself today.*
Welchen Pulli möchtest du? **Den** da?[1]	*Which sweater would you like? **This one?***
Nein, **den** da.	*No, **that one.***

M. WELCHEN RING MÖCHTEST DU? Your partner points to one of two items and asks you if you would like it. Respond according to your preference.

S1: Welchen Ring möchtest du? Den da?		*S2:* Ja, den möchte ich. Der ist sehr schön. Nein, ich möchte lieber den da. Der ist viel schöner.

1.

2.

3.

4.

5.

6.

7.

8.

der Rock	der Pulli	die Bluse	Schuhe
das Armband	Ohrringe	die Halskette	das Kleid

---

1. **Da** is usually added if the speaker is pointing to something or someone.

5. FORMING PHRASES LIKE *THROUGH THE PARK, FOR ME, AROUND SEVEN O'CLOCK*

ACCUSATIVE PREPOSITIONS

A preposition is a word that combines with a noun or pronoun to form a phrase:

Are these roses *for Sarah* or *for me*?

The noun or pronoun in the prepositional phrase is called the *object* of the preposition. After the following German prepositions the noun or pronoun object appears in the *accusative* case:

durch	*through*	Diese Straße geht mitten **durch den** Park	*This street goes through the middle of the park.*
für	*for*	**Für wen** sind diese Rosen? **Für uns?**	*For whom are the roses? For us?*
gegen	*against*	Was hast du **gegen ihn?**	*What do you have against him?*
	around	Ich bin **gegen** sechs wieder zurück.	*I'll be back again around six.*
ohne	*without*	Warum fliegt Frau Müller immer **ohne ihren Mann** nach Europa?	*Why does Mrs. Müller always fly to Europe without her husband?*
um	*at*	Morgen stehe ich **um** zehn auf.	*Tomorrow I'm getting up at ten.*
	around	Ich jogge jeden Morgen zweimal **um den Stadtpark.**	*I jog twice around the city park every morning.*

In the examples above, there are two German equivalents for *around*.

gegen	*around* in a temporal sense	**gegen** sechs Uhr
um	*around* in a local sense	**um** den Stadtpark

In colloquial German the prepositions **durch, für,** and **um** are often contracted with the article **das: durchs, fürs, ums.**

Da läuft eine Maus **durchs** Zimmer!	*There's a mouse running through the room!*
Fürs Auto hast du immer Geld.	*You always have money for the car.*
Warum pflanzt ihr keine Bäume **ums** Haus?	*Why don't you plant any trees around the house?*

N. Ergänzen Sie **durch, für, gegen, ohne** oder **um!**

1. _____ dich gehen wir nicht tanzen.
2. Sind Sie _____ oder _____ den Kapitalismus?
3. Warum trinkst du deinen Kaffee _____ Milch und Zucker?
4. _____ wen machst du den Toast? _____ mich?

5. Wie willst du denn in Deutschland Arbeit finden?
   _____ meinen Onkel natürlich.
6. Hier ist ein Brief° _____ dich. *letter*
7. Wo wohnt Bernd?
   Gleich _____ die nächste Ecke.° *corner*
8. Die neue Straße soll mitten _____ den Park gehen.
9. Spielen die Kanadier morgen _____ die Amerikaner oder _____ die Schweden?
10. Heute müßt ihr _____ mich schwimmen gehen.
11. Fährt der Zug nach München _____ 17.35 Uhr oder _____ 18.35 Uhr?
12. _____ sieben ist nicht Punkt sieben. Es ist ein bißchen vor oder nach sieben.

Fußball *(soccer)* is to Europeans what baseball is to Americans or hockey to Canadians. In Germany almost every village has a **Fußballmannschaft** *(soccer team),* and the **Deutscher Fußball-Bund** *(German Soccer Federation)* has a membership of 4.6 million. **Fußball** is unrivaled as a spectator sport, and the top players of the professional **Bundesliga** *(Federal League)* enjoy tremendous popularity. The German team has been in the finals of the **Weltmeisterschaft** *(World Cup)* several times and it has won the World Cup three times (1954, 1974, 1990).

O. FÜR WEN KAUFST DU DEN WEIN? Ask your partner questions beginning with **durch, für,** and **gegen.**

▶ für / kaufst du den Wein / dein Vater	mein Onkel
S1: Für wen kaufst du den Wein? Für deinen Vater?	**S2:** Nein, für meinen Onkel.

1. für / bestellst du das Buch / deine Freundin — mein Bruder
2. durch / bekommt ihr die Theaterkarten / die Sekretärin — unser Professor
3. für / bäckst du den Kuchen / dein Freund — unsere Deutschlehrerin
4. gegen / spielt Deutschland am Samstag / Italien — Brasilien
5. für / stimmst° du am Sonntag / die CDU — die SPD — *are . . . voting*
6. durch / verkauft ihr euer Haus / ein Makler° — die Zeitung° — *newspaper* / *real estate agent*

Achtung Fußballfreunde!
Stuttgarter Kickers 2. Amateurmannschaft sucht für die Saison 89/90 noch interessierte Spieler.
Anfragen bei: Kanther 0711/453686 (abends)

Im Bundestag

Germany can be described as a social democracy, i.e., a state that has legislated a wide range of social programs, such as health insurance, employment protection, and pension provisions.

There are five political parties represented in the **Bundestag.** The **CDU (Christlich-Demokratische Union)** and the **CSU (Christlich-Soziale Union)** in Bavaria are the conservative parties. At the national level these two parties form one block. Helmut Kohl, the present **Bundeskanzler** *(Federal Chancellor),* is the leader of the **CDU.** The party with a more socialist platform is the **SPD (Sozialdemokratische Partei Deutschlands).** The **CDU-CSU** and the **SPD** share the greatest percentage of the popular vote. The **FDP (Freie Demokratische Partei)** is a small, middle-of-the-road party that never receives more than 5–10% of the popular vote. It is nevertheless an important party on the German political scene. Because the **CDU-CSU** and the **SPD** rarely receive a clear majority, the support of the **FDP** as a coalition partner is often necessary to form a government.

Germany's youngest party, **die Grünen** *(the Green Party)* sent its first elected representatives to the **Bundestag** in 1983. **Die Grünen** developed out of a protest movement concerned with the protection of the environment. Finding most of its supporters among the younger generation, the Greens are against nuclear energy, German membership in NATO, and they champion women's rights.

Germans are extremely interested in politics. Elections are always held on Sundays to give everyone the opportunity to vote.

6. EXPRESSING WHEN SOMETHING OCCURS

EXPRESSIONS OF TIME IN THE ACCUSATIVE CASE

To specify definite points in time, German often uses time phrases in the accusative case. Note that in these time phrases adjectives also have **der**-word endings: nächst**en** Sommer, letzt**es** Jahr.

Ich gehe **jeden Morgen** joggen.	*I go jogging every morning.*
Nächste Woche fahren wir in die Schweiz.	*Next week we're going to Switzerland.*
Günter wird **dieses Jahr** sechsundzwanzig.	*Günter will be twenty-six this year.*

WORD ORDER: EXPRESSIONS OF TIME

If more than one expression of time occurs in a sentence, the more general precedes the more specific.

Ich stehe **im Sommer jeden Morgen um sechs** auf.	*I get up at six every morning in the summer.*

P. KLEINE GESPRÄCHE. Express these exchanges in German.

1. SABINE: Do you need the car every Saturday? (Use **Wagen.**)
   HOLGER: No, next Saturday you can have it.
2. HELGA: Ingrid goes to Mannheim every weekend. (Use **fahren.**)
   SILKE: Whom does she visit there?
   HELGA: Her boyfriend.
3. TINA: Robert is working in Austria this summer.
   OLIVER: Who is he working for there? (For whom . . .)
   TINA: For his uncle.
4. MICHAEL: I can't go to the movies tonight.
   DAVID: You have to come along. The film is excellent.°   **ausgezeichnet**
5. FLORIAN: Next summer we're hiking through Switzerland.
   MORITZ: Fantastic! Will you take me along?°   *to take along:* **mit•nehmen**
6. MONIKA: Holger gets up at six thirty every morning.
   INGRID: Why does he get up so early? (Flavor with **denn.**)
   MONIKA: He goes jogging.

ZUSAMMENSCHAU

AUCH MARTIN MACHT PLÄNE

Martin's plans for his day off are quite different from the ones that Claudia made in her conversation with Stephanie at the beginning of the chapter. After you have read the paragraph below, you and a partner assume the roles of Martin and Peter. The questions are given; the illustrations will cue the answers.

Morgen habe ich frei. Was mache ich da? Na, erst schlafe ich mal richtig aus, so bis zwölf oder halb eins. Dann rufe ich Claudia an und sage, ich hole sie gleich ab. Wir essen dann beim Schnellimbiß° eine Knackwurst und gehen von dort ins Deutsche Museum. Ich finde dieses Museum ganz toll, aber Claudia mag es nicht so sehr. Deshalb bleiben° wir nur bis vier oder halb fünf, gehen dann ins Café Stöpsel und trinken ein Glas Bier. Dann fahren wir zum Englischen Garten und gehen schwimmen. Der Eisbach ist jetzt im Juni noch eiskalt, aber das mag ich, und Claudia sitzt gern ein bißchen im Gras.—Schwimmen macht hungrig. Deshalb gehen wir dann wieder zu Claudia zurück und machen zusammen° das Abendessen. Dann will Claudia sicher wieder tanzen gehen. Aber heute machen wir mal, was ich will, und gehen ins Kino.

stand selling hot snacks

stay

together

 Peter fragt Martin:

Martin antwortet:

1. Was machst du morgen den ganzen Tag?

2. Bis wann denn?

3. Und dann?

4. Was habt ihr vor?

einen Stadtbummel machen: *to stroll through town*

5. Und dann? Macht ihr dann einen Stadtbummel°?

I hope

6. Arme Claudia! Hoffentlich° bleibt ihr nicht zu lange.

somewhere

7. Aber dann geht ihr doch sicher irgendwo° etwas trinken?

Peter fragt Martin:

8. Was macht ihr dann?

9. Geht ihr dort schwimmen?

10. Schwimmen macht hungrig. Geht ihr
dann irgendwo essen?

11. Und dann will Claudia sicher
tanzen gehen.

WIE GUT IST IHR GEDÄCHTNIS?°   As you have seen, Claudia's and Martin's plans for   *memory*
their day off are quite different. The statements below, describing their plans, are
completely mixed up. Working with a partner, first decide which statements describe Claudia's plans and which ones describe Martin's plans. Then read them in
their proper sequence.

___ Ich will dort ein paar Kleider anprobieren.
___ Und am Abend gehen wir dann natürlich noch ins Kino.
___ Am Abend gehen wir dann mit Stephanie und Peter nach Schwabing und tan-
   zen dort bis spät in die Nacht.
___ Erst schlafe ich mal bis elf oder halb zwölf.
___ Erst schlafe ich mal bis zwölf oder halb eins.
___ Dort essen wir Weißwürste und trinken ein Glas Bier dazu.
___ Dann rufe ich Claudia an.
___ Vom Deutschen Museum gehen wir ins Café Stöpsel und trinken ein Glas Bier.
___ Dort gehe ich schwimmen, und Claudia sitzt solange im Gras.
___ Um halb zwei hole ich sie ab, und wir essen beim Schnellimbiß eine Knack-
   wurst.
___ Vom Schnellimbiß gehen wir gleich ins Deutsche Museum.
___ Um halb eins holt Martin mich ab, und wir gehen zum Donisl am Marienplatz.
___ Dann fahren wir zum Englischen Garten.
___ Dann gehen wir im Englischen Garten ein bißchen spazieren, und vielleicht
   geht Martin dort sogar schwimmen.
___ Von Karstadt gehen wir in die Alte Pinakothek.

— Dann gehen wir zu Claudia und kochen ein tolles Abendessen.
— Am Nachmittag gehen wir zu Karstadt.
— Dann rufe ich Martin an.
— Dort schauen wir Bilder von Dürer an.
— Dort schauen wir alte Maschinen an.

✏️ HEUTE HABE ICH FREI. Write a paragraph about what you do on a day off. The following list of leisure activities may help you map out your day.

to go window-shopping
bubble bath
to skip
bike

to
to invite
to watch TV
soap operas

mal richtig ausschlafen
bis zwölf Uhr schlafen
ein Schaumbad° nehmen
das Frühstück ausfallen lassen°
  ich lasse das Frühstück ausfallen
ein gutes Buch lesen
meine CDs (Kassetten) anhören
einen Brief an° meine Eltern
  (meinen Freund, meine
  Freundin) schreiben
fern•sehen°
  ich sehe stundenlang fern
Seifenopern° anschauen
meinen Freund (meine Freundin,
  meine Freunde) besuchen

einen Stadtbummel machen
einen Schaufensterbummel machen°
ein paar CDs kaufen
Kleider (Jeans, Schuhe) kaufen
mein Rad° reparieren
meinen Wagen waschen
schwimmen gehen
Tennis (Fußball, Golf, usw.) spielen
meinen Freund (meine Freundin,
  meine Freunde) ein•laden°
ein gutes Essen kochen
einen Kuchen backen
ins Kino (ins Konzert, usw.) gehen
tanzen gehen

Tell your classmates how you spend a free day.

Sprachnotizen

Discourse strategies

If you want to find out more about the plans of the person you are talking to, the question **Und dann?** will keep her/him going. You can use it by itself or as an introduction to a more exact question.

Und dann? Was machst du dann?
Und dann? Wen besuchst du dann?
Und dann? Wohin geht ihr dann?

A variation is to follow **Und dann?** with a question that contains an assumption or a suggestion.

Und dann? Gehst du dann in die Bibliothek und schreibst dein Referat?

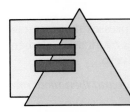

WORT, SINN UND KLANG

WÖRTER UNTER DER LUPE

1. *NUR* VERSUS *ERST*

The English adverb *only* has two equivalents in German: **nur** and **erst.** They are both used to say that a quantity is limited. **Erst** carries the further implication that this limited quantity is expected to increase. **Erst** is therefore used with clock times and age, since they are always increasing.

Wir bleiben **nur** einen Tag in Bonn. *We are staying in Bonn for **only** a day.*
Wir sind **erst** einen Tag in Bonn. *We have been in Bonn for **only** a day.*

* Ergänzen Sie **nur** oder **erst.**

  1. Wir essen _____ selten Kaviar.
  2. Warum stehst du denn schon auf? Es ist doch _____ halb sieben.
  3. Stephanie ist _____ neunzehn.
  4. Anita trinkt morgens _____ ein Glas Milch.
  5. Schmidts wollen _____ ein Kind.
  6. Bauers wollen vier Kinder.
     Und wie viele haben sie schon?
     _____ eins.
  7. Heute habe ich _____ sehr wenig Zeit.
  8. Warum geht ihr denn schon? Es ist doch _____ halb elf.
  9. Wir brauchen zweitausend Mark.
     Und wieviel habt ihr schon?
     _____ fünfhundert.
  10. Wieviel Geld brauchst du?
      _____ fünfzig Mark.

2. *DENN* VERSUS *DANN*

The words **denn** and **dann** occur very frequently in German. Because these words are so similar in sound and appearance and because **denn** has two very different meanings, they deserve a closer look.

a. The flavoring particle **denn** occurs only in questions. It expresses curiosity and it has no equivalent in English. It usually follows the subject.

   Wann stehst du **denn** endlich auf? *When are you finally going to get up?*

b. The conjunction **denn** introduces a clause that states the reason for something. Its English equivalents are *because* and *for.* Like **und, oder,** and **aber,** this **denn** does not count as an element in the clause it introduces; it therefore does not affect word order.

   Bergers sind oft in Stuttgart, **denn** *The Bergers are often in Stuttgart, be-*
   sie haben Freunde dort. *cause they have friends there.*

c. The adverb **dann** is an equivalent of English *then*. It expresses that a certain thing or action follows another thing or action. **Dann** *does* count as an element in the sentence and therefore affects the position of the verb.

Zuerst gibt es Suppe und **dann** Fleisch und Kartoffeln.

First there'll be soup and then meat and potatoes.

Ich habe noch eine Vorlesung, und **dann** esse ich zu Mittag.

I have one more lecture and then I'm going to have lunch.

- Ergänzen Sie **denn** (*flavoring particle*), **denn** (*conjunction*) oder **dann** (*adverb*).

1. HEIKE: Was schreibst du _____ da?
   SYLVIA: Einen Brief an meine Eltern.
   HEIKE: Und _____? Was machst du _____?
   SYLVIA: _____ rufe ich Holger an, _____ er muß mich Punkt fünf hier abholen.
2. SONJA: Wann rufst du _____ endlich deinen Bruder an?
   MARTINA: Erst heute nachmittag, _____ _____ ist er bestimmt nicht mehr im Bett.
3. THOMAS: Mittwochs kommt Günter erst um sechs nach Hause, _____ seine Botanikübung ist erst um halb sechs zu Ende. Er ißt _____ sehr schnell zu Abend, _____ er muß schon um halb sieben bei Tina° sein.
   DIETER: Bei Tina? Ja warum _____ bei Tina? Heißt seine Freundin _____ nicht Helga?
   THOMAS: Nachmittags ist Helga seine Freundin. Aber am Abend geht er _____ mit Tina aus.
4. RUTH: Ich trinke jetzt eine Tasse Kaffee.
   BRIGITTE: Und was machst du _____?
   RUTH: _____ gehe ich in die Bibliothek, _____ mein Referat muß heute fertig werden.
5. MUTTI: Jetzt lernst du zuerst deine deutschen Wörter, und erst _____ gehst du aus.
   FRANK: Aber warum? Ich kann die Wörter doch morgen abend lernen.
   MUTTI: Morgen abend ist es zu spät, _____ das Quiz ist schon morgen früh um acht.

at Tina's

3. THE ADJECTIVE SUFFIXES *-IG, -LICH,* AND *-ISCH*

German and English create many adjectives by adding suffixes to other words. The German adjectives with the suffixes **-ig, -lich,** and **-isch** often have English equivalents with the suffixes *-y, -ly,* and *-ish:*

windig   *windy*
weltlich   *worldly*
schottisch *Scottish*

Wann kann man hier frische Eier kaufen?

- What are the English equivalents?

-ig = -y

sonnig	wurmig
schattig	haarig
eisig	fettig
wässerig	blutig
salzig	stinkig
rostig	sandig
ölig	grasig
schleimig	buschig
schlüpfrig	schläfrig
schäbig	
lausig	

-lich = -ly

freundlich
stündlich
täglich
wöchentlich
monatlich
jährlich
mütterlich
väterlich
brüderlich
ältlich
kränklich

-isch = -ish

kindisch
höllisch
irisch
schwedisch
türkisch
polnisch

WEITERE NÜTZLICHE WÖRTER UND AUSDRÜCKE

Lesestoff *(reading material)*

das Buch, die Bücher	book
der Roman, die Romane	novel
die Zeitung, die Zeitungen	newspaper
der Artikel, die Artikel	article
der Brief, die Briefe	letter
das Wort, die Wörter	word

Präfixe erweitern den Wortschatz *(prefixes expand vocabulary)*

ein•laden (lädt ein)	to invite
aus•gehen	to go out
heim•kommen	to come home
kennen•lernen	to get to know
fern•sehen (sieht fern)	to watch TV
an•hören	to listen to
fertig•schreiben	to finish writing
mit•nehmen (nimmt mit)	to take along
aus•essen (ißt aus)	to finish eating
aus•trinken	to finish drinking
bekommen	to get
beschreiben	to describe
bestellen	to order
verstehen	to understand
versuchen	to try

Die Akkusativpräpositionen

durch	through
für	for
gegen	against; around
ohne	without
um	at; around

Welche Zeitungen kann man hier kaufen?

Die der-Wörter

dieser, diese, dieses	this
jeder, jede, jedes	each, every
welcher, welche, welches	which

Das Gegenteil

jemand—niemand	somebody—nobody
ab•fahren—an•kommen	to depart—to arrive
weg•gehen—zurück•kommen	to go away—to come back
an•fangen—auf•hören	to start—to stop
gehen—kommen	to go—to come
suchen—finden	to look for—to find
früh—spät	early—late
schnell—langsam	fast—slow
langweilig—interessant	boring—interesting
arm—reich	poor—rich
richtig—falsch	right—wrong
wichtig—unwichtig	important—unimportant

Hunger und Durst

der Hunger	hunger
Ich habe Hunger.	I'm hungry.
Ich habe keinen Hunger.	I'm not hungry.
der Durst	thirst
Ich habe Durst.	I'm thirsty.
Ich habe keinen Durst.	I'm not thirsty.

Warum muß man hier langsam fahren?

Sprachnotizen

More on separable prefixes

a. When the adverb **fertig** is prefixed to a verb, the resulting combination usually means to *finish* doing something: **fertiglesen** *to finish reading;* **fertigkochen** *to finish cooking;* etc.

Warum **liest** du den Roman nicht **fertig?**

*Why don't you **finish reading** the novel?*

b. As a prefix, the preposition **mit** often means *along:* **mitgehen** *to go along;* **mitkommen** *to come along;* etc.

Wir gehen schwimmen. **Kommst** du **mit?**

*We're going swimming. Are you **coming along?***

c. When used as a prefix, the adverb **zurück** *(back)* usually keeps its basic meaning: **zurückrufen** *to call back;* **zurückhalten** *to hold back;* etc.

Ich **rufe** dich in zehn Minuten **zurück.**

*I'll **call** you **back** in ten minutes.*

WÖRTER IM KONTEXT

WAS PASST WO?

weg   ab   an   heim   auf   an

a. Wann fängt das Konzert heute abend _____, und wann hört es _____?
b. Wann fährt der Zug in Frankfurt _____, und wann kommt er in Hannover _____?
c. Wann gehst du morgens _____, und wann kommst du abends _____?

    einladen   verstehen   kennenlernen   bestellen

d. Warum willst du das Buch denn _____? Du kannst es ja doch nicht _____.
e. Soll ich Daniel auch _____?
   Ja, natürlich. Ich möchte ihn doch gern _____.

    ohne   interessant   bekommen   welche   ausgehen   durch   finde
anhören

f. Die Karten _____ Sie _____ die Sekretärin.
g. Ich _____ diesen Artikel sehr _____.
h. _____ CD sollen wir jetzt _____?
i. Warum kannst du denn nicht mal _____ mich _____?

██ 📼 ZUR AUSSPRACHE

THE DIPHTHONGS

A diphthong is a combination of two vowel sounds. There are three diphthongs in German. The diphthong **ei** (also spelled **ey, ai, ay**) is pronounced like the *i* in *mine.*

- Hören Sie gut zu und wiederholen Sie!

   eins zw**ei** dr**ei**   Herr M**ey**er Herr S**ai**ler Herr B**ay**er

H**ei**ke B**ay**er und H**ei**nz Fr**ey** h**ei**raten° am zw**ei**ten M**ai.**   *are getting married*

The diphthong **au** is pronounced like the *ou* in *house.*

  laufen **kau**fen s**au**fen   B**au**er M**au**er° s**au**er   *wall*
        bl**au** br**au**n gr**au**

P**au**l, du bist zu l**au**t.
Ich gl**au**be, du bist bl**au.**°   *drunk*

The diphthong **eu** (also spelled **äu**) is pronounced like the *oy* in *boy.*

  h**eu**te t**eu**er n**eu**   Fr**äu**lein H**äu**schen M**äu**schen

Wer ist Fr**äu**lein Z**eu**ners n**eu**er Fr**eu**nd?
Ein Verk**äu**fer° aus Bayr**eu**th.[1]   *salesman*

------

1. A town in Bavaria, famous for the **Bayreuther Festspiele,** the annual Richard Wagner Opera Festival.

Deutsche Auswanderer im Hamburger Hafen

KAPITEL 6

■ **Kommunikationsziele**

*In **Kapitel 6** you will learn how to:*
talk about events in the past
talk about your heritage and ancestry
talk about what and whom you know
talk about job qualifications
write a letter
act as an interpreter

■ **Hör- und Sprechsituationen**

Meine Vorfahren
Was hast du gestern gemacht?
Was hast du letzten Samstag gemacht?
Martin sucht einen Ferienjob
Ich suche einen Ferienjob
Ein deutscher Einwanderer sucht Arbeit
Kannst du dolmetschen?

■ **Strukturen**

Wissen and **kennen**
The perfect tense
    with **haben** as auxiliary
    with **sein** as auxiliary
    of verbs with prefixes
The simple past of **haben** and **sein**

■ **Wissenswertes**

Immigration to North America from the German-speaking countries
The apprenticeship system in the German-speaking countries

VORSCHAU

EIN BISSCHEN FAMILIENGESCHICHTE

The following conversation between Claudia and Stephanie took place back in October as they were settling into their dormitory room. While Stephanie unpacks her suitcases, Claudia writes a postcard to her parents.

CLAUDIA: *(liest laut):* „ ... Brief folgt bald. Herzlichst,° Eure Claudia" — So! Fertig ist die Postkarte! Briefmarke drauf und weg damit!° — Hast du eigentlich schon nach Hause geschrieben, Stephanie?   *lots of love* / *A stamp on it and off with it!*

STEPHANIE: Aber Claudia, ich habe ja noch nicht mal meine Koffer° ausgepackt!   *suitcases*

CLAUDIA: Eine Postkarte mit „Bin gut angekommen, Brief folgt bald" braucht noch keine°...   *doesn't even take*

STEPHANIE: Aber Claudia, meine Eltern wollen einen Brief. Sie wollen wissen: „Wo und wie wohnst du? Wie heißt deine Zimmerkollegin? Wie alt, woher und wie ist sie?" Und das weiß ich ja alles noch gar nicht.

CLAUDIA: Kein Problem, Stephanie. Du weißt, ich heiße Claudia, Claudia Maria Berger. Ich bin aus Frankfurt und bin sehr, sehr nett. — Weißt du, du bist eigentlich viel interessanter, Stephanie: Amerikanerin aus Chicago, jung, schön, reich ...

STEPHANIE: Ach Quatsch!°   *nonsense*

CLAUDIA: Und dann dieser Name, „Stephanie Braun"! So exotisch, so typisch amerikanisch! — Sag mal, ist dein Vater eigentlich Deutscher? Ist er ausgewandert?

STEPHANIE: Nein, nicht mein Vater, mein Großvater. Er war° arbeitslos, weißt du, und in Deutschland hat° es damals° immer mehr Arbeitslose gegeben. 1932 waren es° über sechs Millionen! Da sind Tausende nach Amerika ausgewandert.   *was* / **hat es... gegeben:** *there were / at that time*

CLAUDIA: Und hat dein Großvater dort gleich Arbeit gefunden?

STEPHANIE: Zuerst war er im Norden, in Kanada, als Holzfäller.° Das war sehr schwer° für ihn, denn er war eigentlich Bäcker von Beruf. Einmal° ist er sogar fast erfroren.° Drei Jahre später hat er dann durch einen Freund in New York Arbeit gefunden. Diesmal° als Bäcker. Und deshalb ist er dann 1935 in die USA eingewandert. In New York hat er auch meine Großmutter kennengelernt und geheiratet.   *lumberjack* / *hard / once* / *froze to death* / *this time*

CLAUDIA: Ist deine Großmutter auch aus Deutschland?

STEPHANIE: Nein, sie ist in New York geboren. Aber ihre Eltern waren Deutsche. 1939 ist dann mein Vater zur Welt gekommen.° Er ist auch Bäcker geworden° und hat später in Chicago eine Bäckerei gekauft.   *... was born* / *became*

CLAUDIA: So bist du also in Chicago geboren.

STEPHANIE: Ja, am ersten September 1972.

CLAUDIA: Sag mal, Stephanie, wie hast du eigentlich so gut Deutsch gelernt?

STEPHANIE: Meine Großmutter ist früh gestorben,° und Großvater ist dann auch nach Chicago gekommen und hat im Geschäft° mitgearbeitet. Er hat bei uns° gewohnt und mit Vater immer Deutsch gesprochen. Ich habe also schon als Kind viel Deutsch gehört.   *died* / *business* / *with us*

CLAUDIA: Nur gehört? Nicht gesprochen?

STEPHANIE: Nicht zu Hause,° denn meine Mutter versteht fast kein Deutsch. Aber im College hatten wir eine tolle Professorin, und wir haben da sehr viel Deutsch gesprochen. Und jetzt bin ich hier in München und spreche Deutsch. Ich kann's kaum glauben.° *at home*

believe

CLAUDIA: Und ich habe mein Schulenglisch schon fast vergessen. Können wir manchmal Englisch sprechen, Stephanie? Ich möchte doch auch etwas lernen.

STEPHANIE: Ja, natürlich. — So tell me about yourself, Claudia Maria Berger. Why are you studying in Munich?

VOM LESEN ZUM SPRECHEN

WAS PASST ZUSAMMEN?

1. Warum hat Stephanie noch nicht nach Hause geschrieben?
2. Warum hat sie ihre Koffer noch nicht ausgepackt?
3. Warum ist Stephanies Großvater nach Kanada ausgewandert?
4. Ist er gleich in die USA eingewandert?
5. War Stephanies Großvater in Deutschland auch Holzfäller von Beruf?
6. Warum ist er 1935 nach New York gekommen?
7. Wo hat er Stephanies Großmutter kennengelernt?
8. War Stephanies Großmutter auch aus Deutschland?
9. Wo ist Stephanie geboren?
10. Warum spricht Stephanie so gut Deutsch?

Nein, dort war er Bäcker.

In New York.

Nein, die Großmutter nicht, aber ihre Eltern.

In Chicago.

Sie hat noch keine Zeit gehabt.

Er hat in Deutschland keine Arbeit gefunden.

Sie hat es schon als Kind viel gehört, und im College hat sie dann viel Deutsch gesprochen.

Nein, zuerst hat er im Norden von Kanada als Holzfäller gearbeitet.

Er hat dort durch einen Freund Arbeit gefunden.

ancestors

STEPHANIES DEUTSCHE VORFAHREN°. Wer ist in Deutschland geboren und wer in Amerika?

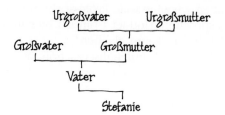

 WAS SIND DIE RICHTIGEN ANTWORTEN? Your instructor will read two questions for each set of responses. On the basis of what Stephanie tells Claudia in *Ein bißchen Familiengeschichte,* decide which *two* responses in each set are correct.

1. a. In Chicago.
   b. In Kanada.
   c. In München.
2. a. Aus Frankfurt.
   b. Aus New York.
   c. Aus Deutschland.
3. a. Zu Hause.
   b. Im College.
   c. Im Gymnasium.°

4. a. Stephanies Großvater.
   b. Stephanies Vater.
   c. Stephanie.
5. a. Stephanies Großmutter.
   b. Stephanies Mutter.
   c. Stephanie.
6. a. 1932
   b. 1935
   c. 1939

high school

 **WOHER SIND DEINE VORFAHREN?**

MEINE VORFAHREN. Draw your family tree and indicate where your ancestors were born.

• Using questions similar to those on the next page, find out more about your partner's ancestors.

Zuerst war er im Norden, in Kanada, als Holzfäller.

Wo ist dein Vater/deine Mutter geboren?
Wo ist dein Großvater/deine Großmutter väterlicherseits/mütterlicherseits geboren?
Wann ist dein Großvater/deine Großmutter nach Amerika ausgewandert?
Wo ist dein Urgroßvater/dein Ururgroßvater geboren?

• Using the following description of Lisa's heritage as a guide, report your findings to the rest of the class.

Lisas Eltern und ihre Großeltern mütterlicherseits sind in Amerika geboren.
Ihre Großeltern väterlicherseits sind in Irland geboren. Sie sind 1935 nach Amerika ausgewandert.
Ihr Urgroßvater mütterlicherseits ist in Schweden geboren.
Er ist etwa 1925 nach Amerika ausgewandert.

NÜTZLICHE WÖRTER UND AUSDRÜCKE

Nomen

der Freund, die Freunde	*(male)* friend; boyfriend
die Freundin, die Freundinnen	*(female)* friend; girlfriend
die Postkarte, die Postkarten	post card
die Briefmarke, die Briefmarken	stamp
der Koffer, die Koffer	suitcase
die Schule, die Schulen	school
das Problem, die Probleme	problem
die Arbeit	work

Verben

glauben, hat geglaubt	to believe, to think
wissen (weiß), hat gewußt	to know
aus•wandern, ist ausgewandert	to emigrate
ein•wandern, ist eingewandert	to immigrate
aus•packen, hat ausgepackt	to unpack
heiraten, hat geheiratet	to marry, to get married
sterben (stirbt), ist gestorben	to die

Andere Wörter

arbeitslos	unemployed
laut	loud, aloud
typisch	typical
schwer	hard, difficult; heavy
einmal, zweimal, dreimal, usw.	once, twice, three times, etc.
diesmal	this time
immer mehr	more and more
kaum	scarcely, hardly

Zieglers fahren nach Hause

Zieglers sind zu Hause

eigentlich	actually, as a matter of fact
etwa	approximately, about

Ausdrücke

Ich bin am 1. (ersten) September 1972 geboren.	I was born on September 1, 1972.
bei uns / bei euch / bei Monika	at our house / at your house / at Monika's (house)
Bist du heute abend zu Hause?	Will you be (at) home tonight?
Wann gehst du heute abend nach Hause?	When are you going home tonight?
als Kind	as a child
gleich jetzt	right now
Quatsch!	Nonsense!

Sprachnotizen

1. The flavoring particle *eigentlich*

Like **denn,** the flavoring particle **eigentlich** expresses curiosity and interest. It has no equivalent in English.

Hast du **eigentlich** schon nach Hause geschrieben?	*Have you written home yet?*

As an adverb **eigentlich** means *actually.*

Da hast du **eigentlich** recht.	***Actually,*** *you're right.*

2. *Immer* + the comparative

Immer is used with the comparative form of adjectives and adverbs to express ideas like *more and more, better and better, faster and faster.*

Meine Zensuren werden **immer besser.**	*My grades are getting **better and better.***
Ich lerne **immer mehr** Deutsch.	*I'm learning **more and more** German.*

WÖRTER IM KONTEXT

1. WAS PASST WO?

nach Hause   zu Hause

a. Wann kommt Stephanie heute abend _____?
b. Ist Claudia immer noch nicht _____?
c. Geht ihr heute abend aus, oder eßt ihr _____?
d. Stephanie hat _____ sehr viel Deutsch gehört.
e. Fliegst du an Weihnachten _____, Stephanie?
f. Wohnt Günter immer noch _____?
g. Ich muß jetzt _____.
h. Ich muß Punkt sieben _____ sein.

Over a thousand cities and towns in North America are named after the German, Swiss, and Austrian birthplaces of their founders. The first German settlers, 13 Pietist families from northern Germany, came to the New World in 1683 seeking freedom from religious persecution. They came at the invitation of William Penn, a Quaker who had founded a colony where all religions were tolerated. Many such immigrants followed, among them the Mennonites, who also settled in Pennsylvania and later branched out into Canada. Not all of these immigrants came to North America for religious reasons, but all who came were optimistic and hard-working. Many of them fought against Great Britain in the American War of Independence. Ironically, they often had to fight against fellow Germans, because the British had purchased 30,000 soldiers from the

George Szell

rulers of Hesse in Germany to help fight on the British side. Understandably, the loyalty of many of these Hessian troops was less than firm: when offered land by the Americans, a good 7000 of them did not hesitate to desert the army. After the British were defeated, thousands more stayed and began new lives in America.

Cataclysmic events in Europe started the second great wave of immigration to America. In the 1840s famine struck Europe and drove many farmers to seek a better life in the New World. Other immigrants were adventurers, lured to California by the Gold Rush. Still others were young liberals who had fought in the unsuccessful German Revolution of 1848. These so-called "Forty-eighters" were often academics, scientists, and highly skilled crafts-

Albert Einstein

men who had a profound influence on almost every facet of American life.

The third big wave of immigration came in the 1930s. Many immigrants came during the period of massive unemployment following the Great Depression of 1929. They were looking for a better life in the vast reaches of this **Land der unbegrenzten Möglichkeiten** *(land of unlimited opportunity)*. Many others were intellectuals, scientists, writers, and artists who fled Hitler's totalitarian and anti-Semitic regime; their emigration was an immeasurable loss to Germany. Among those who came at this time were the physicist Albert Einstein, writers like Thomas Mann *(The Magic Mountain, Death in Venice)* and Bertolt Brecht *(The Three-Penny Opera),* and the composers Kurt Weill (who wrote the musical score for Brecht's *Three-Penny Opera*), Arnold Schoenberg, and Paul Hindemith. Other immigrants who greatly contributed to the cultural life in their new country were the conductor George Szell, who made the Cleveland Orchestra world-famous, and the architects Walter Gropius (Harvard Graduate Center, Pan Am Building in New York) and Ludwig Mies van der Rohe (Chicago Federal Center, Toronto Dominion Center), whose work influenced a whole generation of architects.

hat ... geheiratet   hast ... ausgepackt   ist ... ausgewandert

i. Warum ____ Stephanies Großvater nach Kanada ____?
j. Wann ____ Stephanies Großvater ____?
k. Warum ____ du denn deine Koffer noch nicht ____?

ist ... geboren   ist ... gestorben   ist ... eingewandert

l. Stephanies Großmutter ____ sehr früh ____.
m. Wann ____ Stephanie ____?
n. Stephanies Großvater ____ 1935 in die USA ____.

2. WAS PASST ZUSAMMEN?

a. Warum will Herr Berger auswandern?	Am ersten Mai 1972.
b. Warum packst du denn deine Koffer nicht aus?	Etwa zwei- oder dreimal.
c. Wann bist du geboren?	Nächstes Jahr.
d. Günter sagt, du liebst ihn.	Ich glaube, er kann hier keine Arbeit finden.
e. Ist die Party heute wieder bei Bernd?	Ja, sehr.
f. Haben wir noch Briefmarken?	Das ist doch alles Quatsch, was der sagt.
g. Wann heiratet ihr eigentlich?	Kaum eine halbe Stunde.
h. Wie oft waren Sie schon in Berlin, Frau Ziegler?	Ja, ich glaube, wir haben noch ein paar.
i. Ist der Koffer schwer?	Ich will erst ein paar Postkarten schreiben.
j. Wie lange warst du eigentlich bei Monika?	Nein, ich glaube, diesmal ist sie bei Monika.

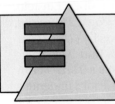

FUNKTIONEN UND FORMEN

1. TALKING ABOUT WHAT AND WHOM YOU KNOW

THE VERBS *WISSEN* AND *KENNEN*

The present tense of **wissen** *(to know)* is irregular in the singular:

Singular	Plural
ich weiß	wir wissen
du weißt	ihr wißt
er/sie/es weiß	sie wissen
Sie wissen	

Wissen can be followed either by a direct object or by a clause:

Weißt du Ralfs Telefonnummer?	*Do you know Ralf's telephone number?*
Nein, aber ich weiß, wo er wohnt.	*No, but I know where he lives.*

A. ERGÄNZEN SIE!

1. KURT: _____ deine Eltern, wie schlecht deine Zensuren° sind?   *grades*
   GÜNTER: Meine Mutter _____ es, aber mein Vater _____ es noch nicht.
2. TOURISTIN: Entschuldigung, _____ Sie vielleicht, wohin dieser Bus fährt?
   TOURIST: Nein, ich _____ es leider° auch nicht.   *unfortunately*
3. THOMAS: _____ du Stefans Adresse?
   BRIGITTE: Nein, seine Adresse _____ ich nicht, aber ich _____ seine Telefonnummer.
4. BERND: _____ ihr, wo Peter ist?
   MARTIN: Nein, das _____ wir auch nicht.
   CLAUDIA: Warum fragst du nicht Stephanie? Die _____ es bestimmt.
5. FRAU KUHN: Warum _____ du denn nicht, wie man Sauerkraut kocht?
   HERR KUHN: Ich kann doch nicht alles _____.

Whereas **wissen** means *to know something as a fact,* **kennen** means *to know* in the sense of *to be acquainted with someone* or *to be familiar with something.* **Kennen** is always followed by a direct object. It cannot be followed by a clause.

Kennst du Bernds neue Freundin?	*Do you **know** Bernd's new girlfriend?*
Ja, ich **kenne** sie sehr gut.	*Yes, I **know** her very well.*
Weißt du, wie alt sie ist?	*Do you **know,** how old she is?*
Nein, das **weiß** ich nicht.	*No, I don't **know** that.*

B. ERGÄNZEN SIE WISSEN ODER KENNEN!

1. FRAU LANG: _____ Sie Frau Ziegler?
   FRAU KURZ: Ja, ich _____ sie sehr gut.
2. FRAU HOFER: _____ Sie vielleicht, wieviel Uhr es ist?
   FRAU LANG: Genau° _____ ich es nicht, aber ich glaube, es ist fast fünf.   *exactly*
3. GÜNTER: _____ du Monika?
   PETRA: Ja, natürlich _____ ich sie.
   GÜNTER: Und _____ du, wo sie wohnt?
   PETRA: Nein, das _____ ich nicht.
4. FRAU BENN: _____ Sie Berlin?
   FRAU HAAG: Ja, ich _____ es sehr gut.
   FRAU BENN: Dann _____ Sie doch sicher, wo die Grimmstraße ist.
   FRAU HAAG: Nein, das _____ ich leider nicht.
5. RALF: _____ du den Mann dort?
   HEINZ: Ja, den _____ ich, aber ich _____ nicht, wie er heißt.
6. HOLGER: _____ du diese Oper?
   THOMAS: Ich glaube, sie ist von Mozart, aber ich _____ nicht, wie sie heißt.
7. SYLVIA: _____ ihr, wo Günter ist?
   MARKUS: Ich glaube, er ist bei Eva.
   SYLVIA: Bei Eva?! Ja, woher _____ er denn die?
   THOMAS: Das _____ wir auch nicht.

8. FRAU JAHN: _____ du, wie schlecht Franks Zensuren sind?
   HERR JAHN: Nein, ich _____ es nicht, und ich will es auch nicht _____.
9. FRAU VOGEL: Sind Ihre neuen Nachbarn nett, Frau Vogel?
   FRAU BRAUN: Wir _____ es nicht. Wir _____ sie noch nicht.

2. TALKING ABOUT EVENTS IN THE PAST

THE PERFECT TENSE: REGULAR VERBS

In German the perfect tense is mainly used to talk about past events in *conversational* situations. English normally uses the simple past for this purpose.

Was **hast** du gestern abend **gemacht?**	*What **did** you **do** last night?*
Ich **habe** meine deutschen Vokabeln **gelernt.**	*I **learned** my German vocabulary.*

The perfect tense consists of an *auxiliary verb* (usually **haben**) that takes personal endings, and a *past participle* that remains unchanged:

Singular	Plural
ich habe gelernt	wir haben gelernt
du hast gelernt	ihr habt gelernt
er / sie / es hat gelernt	sie haben gelernt
Sie haben gelernt	

The German perfect tense can correspond to the following English verb forms:

ich habe gelernt	I learned I have learned I have been learning I was learning I did learn

a. The past participle of regular verbs

Most German verbs form the past participle by adding the prefix **ge-** and the ending **-t** or **-et** to the verb stem. The ending **-et** is used if the verb stem ends in **d, t,** or certain consonant combinations.

	Prefix	Verb Stem	Ending
machen	ge	mach	t
arbeiten	ge	arbeit	et
baden	ge	bad	et
regnen	ge	regn	et

Past participles of verbs ending in **-ieren** do *not* have the prefix **ge-**:

	Prefix	Verb Stem	Ending
studieren		studier	t

b. Position of auxiliary and past participle in the sentence

The auxiliary verb takes the regular position of the verb. The past participle appears at the *end* of the sentence or clause.

auxiliary verb	past participle
Sandra **hat** heute morgen das Frühstück **gemacht.**	

Heute morgen **hat** Sandra das Frühstück **gemacht.**	*This morning Sandra made breakfast.*
Hat Sandra heute morgen das Frühstück **gemacht?**	*Did Sandra make breakfast this morning?*
Wer **hat** heute morgen das Frühstück **gemacht?**	*Who made breakfast this morning?*
Ich **habe** die Fenster **geputzt,** den Rasen **gemäht,** und erst dann **habe** ich **gefrühstückt.**	*I cleaned the windows, mowed the lawn and only then did I have breakfast.*

c. Position of *nicht*

If a verb in the perfect tense is negated, **nicht** precedes the past participle:

Warum hat Sandra **nicht** gefrühstückt?	*Why didn't Sandra have breakfast?*

C. WAS HABEN ZIEGLERS GESTERN GEMACHT? Supply the perfect tense of the verbs given.

1. Gestern _____ Frau Ziegler nur sehr wenig Zeit _____.
   haben
2. Sie _____ deshalb gestern früh nicht _____, sondern nur _____.
   baden
   duschen
3. Um halb acht _____ sie schnell _____ und im Radio die Nachrichten° _____.
   frühstücken
   hören — *news*
4. Dann _____ Frau Ziegler ihre Post° _____ und mit Kunden° _____.
   öffnen° — *mail / customers / to open*
   telefonieren
5. Herr Ziegler _____ gestern nicht _____.
   arbeiten
6. Er _____ deshalb die Betten _____, den Toaster und den Rasenmäher° _____, und das Mittagessen _____.
   machen
   reparieren / kochen — *lawn mower*
7. Nachmittags _____ Herr Ziegler dann Holz° _____ und den Rasen _____.
   spalten° — *wood / to split*
   mähen
8. Uwe _____ gestern nachmittag stundenlang Fußball _____ und dann noch schnell die Fenster _____.
   spielen
   putzen
9. Helga _____ am Nachmittag Klavier _____ und ihre englischen Vokabeln _____.
   üben° — *to practice*
   lernen
10. Uwe _____ seine Hausaufgaben erst spät abends _____.
    machen
11. Und wer _____ gestern abend die Katze _____?
    füttern° — *to feed*

WAS HAST DU GESTERN GEMACHT?

Your partner uses past participles from the list below to tell you what she/he did yesterday. Take notes and then report her/his activities to the rest of the class.

- Your partner's story:

  ▶ Gestern morgen habe ich zuerst ... Dann habe ich ...
  Gestern nachmittag habe ich zuerst ... Dann habe ich ...
  Gestern abend habe ich zuerst ... Dann habe ich ...

- Your report:

  ▶ Gestern morgen hat Lisa ...

geduscht	gebadet	gefrühstückt	gefüttert	gehabt	gekauft
gespielt	geübt	telefoniert	repariert	geputzt	
gearbeitet	gekocht	gemacht	gelernt	gehört	

lazy / people

D. MORGEN, MORGEN, NUR NICHT HEUTE, SAGEN ALLE FAULEN° LEUTE.°

deine deutschen Vokabeln lernen	Tennis spielen

S1: Hast du deine deutschen Vokabeln gelernt?
Ja, was hast du denn gemacht?

S2: Nein, noch nicht.

Ich habe Tennis gespielt.

1.

2.

3.

den Rasen mähen	Fußball spielen
das Holz spalten	baden
das Fahrrad reparieren	Gitarre spielen

4.

5.

6.

7.

deinen Koffer packen	eine Zigarette rauchen
die Fenster putzen	mit Monika telefonieren
den Hund füttern	frühstücken
Klavier üben	Radio hören

THE PERFECT TENSE: IRREGULAR VERBS

Irregular verbs are a small but important group of verbs. Past participles of these verbs end in **-en.** The verb stem often undergoes a vowel change and sometimes a consonant change as well.

	Prefix	Verb Stem	Ending
finden	ge	**fu**nd	en
nehmen	ge	n**omm**	en
schlafen	ge	schlaf	en

The list below shows the past participles of some common irregular verbs.

schneiden	geschn**itt**en	to cut
schreiben	geschr**ie**ben	to write
streichen	gestr**i**chen	to paint
gießen	ge**goss**en	to water
finden	ge**fu**nden	to find
singen	ges**u**ngen	to sing
trinken	getr**u**nken	to drink
nehmen	gen**omm**en	to take
sprechen	gespr**o**chen	to speak
essen	ge**g**essen	to eat
lesen	gelesen	to read
sehen	gesehen	to see
backen	gebacken	to bake
waschen	gewaschen	to wash
schlafen	geschlafen	to sleep
stehen	gest**and**en	to stand
sitzen	ge**ess**en	to sit
liegen	gel**eg**en	to lie

E. WAS HAT EVA GESTERN GEMACHT? Supply the perfect tense of the verbs given.

1. Gestern morgen _____ Eva nur bis halb sieben _____. — schlafen
2. Sie _____ dann gleich ein Bad _____. — nehmen
3. Um sieben _____ sie eine Tasse Kaffee _____ und die Zeitung _____. — trinken / lesen
4. Dann _____ sie ihre Zimmerpflanzen _____. — gießen
5. Später _____ sie einen Brief an ihre Eltern _____ aber die Briefmarken nicht _____. — schreiben / finden
6. Um halb zwölf _____ Eva mit Professor Seidlmeyer _____. — sprechen
7. Um zwölf _____ sie mit Kurt zu Mittag _____. — essen
8. Am Nachmittag _____ Eva zuerst ihre Pullis° _____ und dann einen Kuchen _____. — waschen / backen

sweaters

9. Von fünf bis sieben _____ sie im Studentenchor _____. — singen
10. Am Abend _____ Eva dann vor dem Fernseher _____ und einen tollen Film _____. — sitzen / sehen
11. Kurz nach elf _____ sie dann wieder im Bett _____. — liegen

WAS HAST DU GESTERN GEMACHT?

Your partner uses past participles from the list below to tell you what she/he did yesterday. Take notes and then report her/his activities to the rest of the class.

- Your partner's story:

  ▶ Gestern morgen habe ich ... Dann habe ich ...
  Mittags habe ich ...
  Gestern nachmittag habe ich zuerst ... Dann habe ich ...
  Gestern abend habe ich zuerst ... Dann habe ich ...

- Your report:

  ▶ Gestern morgen hat Lisa ...

geschlafen	gesessen	getrunken	gegossen	(ein Bad) genommen
geschrieben	gelesen	gesprochen	gewaschen	gebacken
gesungen	gesehen	gelegen	(vor dem Fernseher) gesessen	

F. DU SCHIEBST IMMER ALLES AUF DIE LANGE BANK.

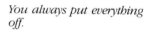
You always put everything off.

die Blumen gießen	ein Buch lesen

S1: Hast du die Blumen gegossen?   *S2:* Nein, noch nicht.
Ja, warum denn nicht?   Ich habe ein Buch gelesen.

1.

2.

3.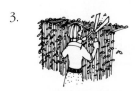

dein Referat schreiben	ein Stück Kuchen essen
den Wagen waschen	eine halbe Stunde schlafen
die Hecke schneiden	die Zeitung lesen

4.

5.

6.

mit Professor Seidlmeyer sprechen	ein Bad nehmen
den Zaun streichen	mit Helga eine Tasse Kaffee trinken
einen Kuchen backen	im Gras liegen

THE VERB *SEIN* AS AUXILIARY IN THE PERFECT TENSE

a. Verbs that express a change of location

English *always* uses the verb *to have* as the auxiliary in the perfect tense. German *usually* uses **haben,** but for verbs that express a *change of location* **sein** is used:

Bist du schon mal mit Lufthansa **geflogen?** ***Have** you ever **flown** with Lufthansa?*

Ist Sabine schon nach Hause **gegangen?** ***Has** Sabine **gone** home already?*

Singular	Plural
ich bin gegangen	wir sind gegangen
du bist gegangen	ihr seid gegangen
er/sie/es ist gegangen	sie sind gegangen
Sie sind gegangen	

b. *Sein* and *bleiben*

There are two very common verbs that use **sein** as an auxiliary although they do *not* express a change of location: **sein** *(to be)* and **bleiben** *(to stay, to remain)*.

Wo **bist** du **gewesen?**	*Where **have** you **been?***
Warum **ist** Sylvia zu Hause **geblieben?**	*Why **did** Sylvia **stay** at home?*

c. Verbs with *sein* or *haben* as auxiliaries

You have just learned that verbs that express a change of location use **sein** as an auxiliary. However, when verbs like **fahren** or **fliegen** are followed by an *accusative object,* they use **haben:**

Ist Sabine mit Ralf zur Uni **gefahren?**	*Did Sabine **drive** to the university with Ralf?*
Warum **hast** du **den Wagen** nicht in die Garage **gefahren?**	*Why **did**n't you **drive the car** into the garage?*

G. AUS FRAU ZIEGLERS TAGEBUCH:° EINE FERIENREISE° NACH SPANIEN. Ergänzen Sie **haben** oder **sein!**

diary / vacation trip

1. Diesen Sommer ＿＿＿ Klaus und ich mal nach Spanien **gereist.**
2. Dort ＿＿＿ ich aber für mein Tagebuch nie Zeit **gehabt,** und deshalb sitze ich jetzt hier und schreibe.
3. Wir ＿＿＿ diesmal leider nur zwei Wochen Ferien **gehabt** und ＿＿＿ deshalb nicht den Zug **genommen,** sondern ＿＿＿ mit Iberia Air nach Madrid **geflogen.**
4. Wir ＿＿＿ zwei Tage in Madrid **geblieben,** und wir ＿＿＿ dort sehr viel **gesehen.**
5. Von Madrid ＿＿＿ uns ein Freund an die Costa Dorada **gefahren.**
6. Dort ＿＿＿ wir jeden Tag zwei- oder dreimal schwimmen **gegangen,** ＿＿＿ viel Tennis und Minigolf **gespielt** und viel und gut **gegessen.**
7. Mittags ＿＿＿ es oft sehr heiß **gewesen.**
8. Wir ＿＿＿ dann meistens im Hotel **geblieben** und ＿＿＿ ein paar Stunden **geschlafen.**
9. Abends ＿＿＿ wir fast immer tanzen **gegangen** und oft sehr spät nach Hause **gekommen.**
10. Wir ＿＿＿ selten vor zwei oder halb drei ins Bett **gegangen** und ＿＿＿ morgens immer sehr lange **geschlafen.**
11. Am letzten Morgen ＿＿＿ man uns schon um sieben **geweckt.**
12. Wir ＿＿＿ schnell ein Bad **genommen,** ＿＿＿ ein letztes Mal° gut **gefrühstückt** und ＿＿＿ dann per Taxi nach Barcelona **gefahren.**

time

13. Von Barcelona _____ uns Iberia Air wieder nach Frankfurt **geflogen.**
14. Von dort _____ wir schnell mit Oma, Helga und Uwe **telefoniert** und _____
dann den Intercity nach Bonn **genommen.**

H. CLAUDIAS MITTWOCH: DAS STUDENTENLEBEN IST SCHWER! Describe how
Claudia spent her Wednesday, using the pictures as a guide.

▶ Am Mittwoch hat Claudia bis neun geschlafen. Dann ...

◼ ZUSAMMENSCHAU

MARTIN SUCHT EINEN FERIENJOB

Martin has just finished his exams and goes to the **Studentenwerk** *(student center)* to look for a job for the holidays. Listen to Martin's conversation with Frau Borg, the woman in charge of student employment.

Neue Vokabeln

Herein!	*Come in.*
Bitte schön?	*May I help you?*
der Tagesjob	*job for a day*

zum Beispiel	*for example*
den Rasen mähen	*mowing the lawn*
die Hecke schneiden	*clipping the hedge*
den Zaun streichen	*painting the fence*
Interessiert Sie das?	*Does that interest you?*
sicher	*certainly*
die Kenntnisse *(pl)*	*work experience*
der Maler	*painter*
Bitte schön!	*You're welcome!*

Beim Studentenwerk

- Indicate the order in which you hear the following statements or questions.

— Ja, Herr Keller, warum sind Sie denn da nicht früher gekommen?
— Interessiert Sie das?
— Sie haben nichts mehr? Gar nichts?
— Ja, natürlich, ja. Und vielen Dank auch.
— Mein Name ist Keller.
— Ich rufe gleich dort an.
— Auch keine Tagesjobs?
— Als Maler. Das ist gut. Das ist sehr gut.
— Drei Monate also.

 Listen to the conversation between Martin and Frau Borg again and answer the following questions.

1. Warum geht Martin zum Studentenwerk?
2. Von wann bis wann will er arbeiten?
3. Ist es jetzt Juni oder Juli?
4. Warum ist Martin nicht früher zum Studentenwerk gegangen?
5. Warum nimmt Martin auch einen Tagesjob?
6. Was für ein Wochentag ist heute?
7. Für wen und wo kann Martin morgen und übermorgen arbeiten?
8. Was für Arbeit ist das? Was muß er dort zum Beispiel tun?
9. Was verdient er dort?
10. Was für Kenntnisse hat Martin?
11. Warum findet Frau Borg das so gut?
12. Was soll Martin von jetzt ab° jeden Tag tun?

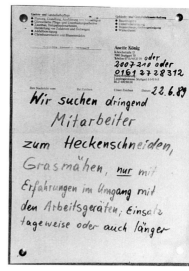

Was für Jobs gibt es hier?

from now on

ICH SUCHE EINEN FERIENJOB

You have just finished exams and are at the **Studentenwerk** looking for a summer job. Your partner, who is a job counselor there, tries to help you. She/he asks your name, age, address, telephone number, and what your job qualifications are (**Was für Kenntnisse haben Sie?**).

```
Ich habe letzten Sommer | im Krankenhaus gearbeitet.
                        | im Büro
                        | im Supermarkt
                        | im Hotel
                        | . . .
```

factory worker
waiter / waitress

```
Ich habe letzten Sommer | als Fabrikarbeiter/in° gearbeitet.
                        | als Kellner/in°
                        | als Koch/Köchin
                        | als Gärtner/in
```

construction worker

```
                        | als Bauarbeiter/in°
                        | als Maler/in
                        | als Discjockey
```

cashier, teller

```
                        | als Kassierer/in°
                        | . . .
```

```
Ich kann | Auto fahren
         | tippen
         | Deutsch, Spanisch usw.
```

drums

```
         | Klavier (Saxophon, Schlagzeug° usw.) spielen
         | . . .
```

Sprachnotizen

Bitte, bitte schön, wie bitte?

The basic meaning of **bitte** or **bitte schön** is *please.*

Können sie mich **bitte** in fünf Minuten zurückrufen?	*Can you **please** call me back in five minutes?*

Bitte! or **Bitte schön!** is also used as a response to **Danke!** or **Vielen Dank!** to mean *You're welcome!* or *Don't mention it!*

Vielen Dank für Ihre Hilfe! **Bitte schön!**	*Thanks a lot for your help!* ***You're welcome!***

Bitte schön? is often used by salespersons or by serving personnel in restaurants to mean *May I help you?* or *What would you like?*

Guten Tag. **Bitte schön?**	*Hello. **May I help you?***

Wie bitte? and **Bitte?** both mean *I beg your pardon?*

Mein Name ist Ziegler. **Wie bitte?** Wie heißen Sie?	*My name is Ziegler.* ***I beg your pardon?*** *What is your name?*

3. TALKING ABOUT EVENTS IN THE PAST

THE PERFECT TENSE: SEPARABLE-PREFIX VERBS

Separable-prefix verbs can be regular or irregular. The prefix is *not* separated in the past participle. It is affixed to the past participle of the base verb.

Infinitive	Past Participle
aufhören	**auf**gehört
anprobieren	**an**probiert
aufstehen	**auf**gestanden
anrufen	**an**gerufen

I. WAS HAT CLAUDIA AM LANGEN SAMSTAG GEMACHT? Supply the perfect tense.

Letzten Samstag morgen hat es geregnet.

1. Claudia _____ deshalb mal richtig _____ und _____ erst um halb zwölf _____.
2. Sie _____ dann gleich ihre neue Kaffeemaschine _____.
3. Beim Frühstück _____ sie ihre Lieblingsplatte° _____.
4. Um zwölf _____ der Regen _____, und Claudia _____ Martin _____.
5. Um halb eins _____ Martin sie _____.
6. Zuerst _____ sie (pl) im Englischen Garten ein bißchen _____.
7. Dann _____ Claudia bei Karstadt Kleider _____, und Martin _____ solange° Jacken und Jeans _____.
8. Bei Spar° _____ sie noch schnell Wurst und Käse _____ und _____ dann _____.
9. Beim Abendessen _____ sie ein bißchen _____.
10. Dann _____ Martin _____, und Claudia _____ ihr Referat _____.

ausschlafen
aufstehen
ausprobieren
anhören   *favorite record*
aufhören
anrufen
abholen

spazierengehen
anprobieren
anschauen   *in the meantime*
einkaufen   German supermarket chain
heimgehen
fernsehen
heimgehen
fertigschreiben

WAS HAST DU LETZTEN SAMSTAG GEMACHT?

Your partner uses past participles from the list below to tell you what she/he did last Saturday. Take notes and then report her/his activities to the rest of the class.

▶ Letzten Samstag ... ich ...

ausschlafen	aufstehen	anrufen	abholen	anhören	aufhören
ausprobieren	anprobieren	anschauen	spazierengehen		einkaufen
heimgehen	fernsehen	fertigschreiben	ausgehen	heimkommen	

J. WAS HAST DU LETZTE WOCHE GEMACHT?
Answer your partner's questions about what you did last week by matching the activities listed below to the illustrations.

▶ du am Sonntag vormittag

mal richtig ausschlafen

S1: Was hast du am Sonntag vormittag gemacht?

S2: Da habe ich mal richtig ausgeschlafen.

1. du in Starnberg

4. ihr im Deutschen Museum

2. du gestern abend

5. ihr bei Karstadt

3. ihr am Sonntag nachmittag

6. ihr am Donnerstag abend

stundenlang Kleider anprobieren
mein neues Surfbrett ausprobieren
im Englischen Garten spazierengehen

mein Referat fertigschreiben
alte Maschinen anschauen
fernsehen

7. du am Samstag abend

8. du gestern nachmittag

9. du am Samstag morgen

10. ihr am Montag abend

Wieviel kosten die Karten für dieses Konzert?

| im Studentenchor mitsingen | mit Claudia ausgehen |
| mein neues Album anhören | erst um elf aufstehen |

THE PERFECT TENSE: VERBS WITH INSEPARABLE PREFIXES

Verbs with inseparable prefixes can be regular or irregular. They do not add **ge-** to the past participle:

Infinitive	Past Participle
besuchen	besucht
verstehen	verstanden

K. KLEINE GESPRÄCHE. Supply the perfect tense.

1. _____ du letzten Sommer gut _____?
   Ja, mein Boß _____ mich sehr gut _____.
2. _____ Sie Rickers Apfel-Orange-Nektar schon _____?
   Ja, und ich _____ auch gleich zwanzig Flaschen° _____.
3. _____ Professor Schneider das Experiment gut _____?
   Ja, ich _____ fast alles _____.
4. Für wieviel _____ Bergers ihr Haus _____?
   Ich glaube, sie _____ fast eine Million _____.
5. Wann _____ Stephanie euch ihre Familiengeschichte _____?
   Gestern abend. Sie _____ uns gestern abend _____.

verdienen
bezahlen°   *to pay*
versuchen
bestellen   *bottles*
erklären°   *to explain*
verstehen
verkaufen
bekommen
erzählen°   *to tell*
besuchen

THE PERFECT TENSE:
VERBS DENOTING A CHANGE OF STATE

You have learned that verbs denoting a *change of location* form the perfect tense with **sein** (see page 174):

Wann **ist** Stephanies Großvater **ausgewandert?**
Ist er gleich nach Amerika **gekommen?**

The verbs in the examples below express a *change of state*. They also use **sein** as the auxiliary in the perfect tense.

Wann **ist** Beethoven **gestorben?**	*When did Beethoven die?*
Wann **bist** du einundzwanzig **geworden?**	*When did you turn twenty-one?*
Warum **sind** Sie Polizist **geworden,** Herr Köhler?	*Why did you become a policeman, Mr. Köhler?*
Gestern nacht **bin** ich um ein Uhr **aufgewacht** und **bin** erst um vier wieder **eingeschlafen.**	*Last night I woke up at one o'clock and didn't fall asleep again until four.*
Letzten Winter **sind** alle unsere Rosen **erfroren.**	*Last winter all our roses froze.*
Letztes Jahr **ist** hier jemand **ertrunken.**	*Last year somebody drowned here.*
Warum sind hier so viele Polizisten? Was **ist** denn **passiert?**	*Why are there so many policemen here? What happened?*

L. WAS PASST WO? Complete the exchanges with the perfect tense of the following verbs.

ertrinken   passieren   aufwachen   einschlafen   erfrieren   sterben
werden

1. INGRID: Ist es draußen° sehr kalt?   *outside*
   EVA: Ja, ich _____ fast _____.
2. BERND: Wie _____ Helga denn so krank _____?
   RALF: Sie ist im Regen segeln gegangen.
3. MARTIN: Warum bist du heute morgen nicht joggen gegangen?
   CLAUDIA: Ich _____ zu spät _____.
4. HOLGER: Warum habt ihr ein Aquarium und keine Fische?
   BERND: Die Fische _____ leider alle _____.
5. KURT: Warum bist du denn so müde?
   RALF: Ich _____ erst um vier Uhr morgens _____.
6. INGRID: Wie ist Ludwig der Zweite gestorben?
   HOLGER: Ich glaube, er _____ im Starnberger See _____.
7. JUTTA: Dein neuer Wagen ist kaputt? Wie _____ denn das _____?
   VOLKER: Ich habe ihn gegen einen Baum° gefahren.   *tree*

THE SIMPLE PAST: *SEIN* AND *HABEN*

For most verbs, the perfect tense is used to talk about past events in conversational situations. **Sein** and **haben** are exceptions. Although it is not incorrect to use the perfect tense of these verbs **(ich bin gewesen, ich habe gehabt),** most Germans use the simple past. The simple past stem of **sein** is **war.** There are no personal endings in the 1st and 3rd person singular.

Singular	Plural
ich war	wir war**en**
du war**st**	ihr war**t**
er/sie/es war	sie war**en**
Sie war**en**	

The simple past stem of **haben** is **hatt-.**

Singular	Plural
ich hatt**e**	wir hatt**en**
du hatt**est**	ihr hatt**et**
er/sie/es hatt**e**	sie hatt**en**
Sie hatt**en**	

M. WO WART IHR GESTERN ABEND? Answer your partner by matching the activities listed below to the illustrations.

▶ ihr am Samstag abend   bei Michael

Karten spielen

S1: Wo wart ihr am Samstag abend?   *S2:* Da waren wir bei Michael.
Was habt ihr da gemacht?   Da haben wir Karten gespielt.

1. du gestern früh   zu Hause

2. Sylvia heute morgen   im Garten

3. Sie gestern nacht um halb zwölf   zu Hause

4. Müllers im Januar   in Innsbruck

5. ihr gestern nachmittag   im Biergarten

German supermarket chain 6. Holger am Freitag nachmittag   bei Tengelmann°

---

gerade° zu Bett gehen	im Gras liegen und ein Buch lesen
Lebensmittel° einkaufen	mein Fahrrad reparieren
viel zu viel Bier trinken	Schi laufen

just
groceries

WO WARST DU LETZTEN SAMSTAG? Find out where your partner was last Saturday and last summer. What did she/he do there?

N. WARUM DENN NICHT? Choose an appropriate response to tell your partner why certain things weren't done.

▶ du / nicht zu Mittag essen   keinen Hunger

S1: Warum hast du nicht zu Mittag   **S2:** Ich hatte keinen Hunger.
gegessen?

---

1. ihr / nicht zu Bernds Party kommen   keinen Durst
2. Sie / den Wagen nicht kaufen   keine Zeit
3. ihr / gestern abend nicht tanzen   heute morgen um acht ein Examen
   gehen   keinen Hunger
4. Holger / sein Bier nicht austrinken   keine Lust
                                                 nicht genug Geld

5. Professor Beck / nicht zu eurer Debatte kommen
6. du / nicht zu Professor Seidlmeyers Seminar kommen
7. ihr / gestern nicht Tennis spielen
8. du / in Berlin deinen Onkel nicht besuchen
9. Helga / ihr Suppe nicht ausessen
10. Günter / sein Referat nicht fertigschreiben
11. ihr / die Bücher nicht gleich bezahlen

O. KLEINE GESPRÄCHE. Express these exchanges in German.

1. SYLVIA: How did you get to know your boyfriend?
   MARTINA: He worked for my father.
2. VATER: Did Martin finish writing his letter?
   MUTTER: Yes, but he hasn't sent° it away.
   VATER: Why not? (*Flavor with* **denn.**)
   MUTTER: He can't find the stamps.

to send away: **weg•schicken**

3. FRAU SMITH: Where are you from?
   FRAU JONES: I'm from Munich.
   FRAU SMITH: Why did you emigrate to America?
   FRAU JONES: My husband is an American.
4. THOMAS: Why did you come so late?
   MATTHIAS: I drove my sister to the university.
5. FRAU HUBER: How much did you pay for this car, Frau Kunz?
   FRAU KUNZ: I got it very cheaply.
6. ERIKA: We were at° Sylvia's party° last night.
   STEFAN: How long did you stay?
   DAVID: Until three o'clock in the morning!

auf / die Party

4. WRITING A LETTER

There are certain conventions in writing letters. In German, dates are written as follows: **München, den 10. Oktober 1990.** Note that the day, followed by a period, precedes the month. There is no comma between the month and the year.

All personal pronouns and possessive adjectives that refer to the person or persons addressed in the letter are capitalized (*Du, Ihr, Dein, Euer*).

Writing a personal letter is considered a conversational situation. The writer frequently uses the perfect tense to relate past events.

P. STEPHANIE SCHREIBT NACH HAUSE. Complete Stephanie's letter by supplying past participles or simple past forms of the verbs given.

München, den 10. Oktober 1990

Liebe Eltern und lieber Opa:

Munich suburb / customs

Heute vormittag kurz vor zehn ist mein Flugzeug in München-Riem° _____. Der Zoll° _____ kein Problem, ein Taxi habe ich auch gleich _____, und so _____ ich noch vor elf im Studentenheim. Meine Zimmerkollegin heißt Claudia. Sie ist vier Jahre älter als ich, kommt aus Frankfurt und ist sehr nett. Sie hat viel _____, und ich habe meine Koffer _____, und _____. Um eins _____ wir dann beide Hunger und sind deshalb in die Stadt _____. Wir haben gut zu Mittag _____, haben dann noch einen Stadtbummel _____ und sind erst spät nachmittags wieder ins Studentenheim _____. München ist eine tolle Stadt, und es gibt schon jetzt so viel zu erzählen. Aber ich habe letzte Nacht im Flugzeug keine Sekunde _____ und bin deshalb

dead tired

todmüde.° Wir gehen jetzt noch schnell zum Abendessen in die Cafeteria, und dann gehe ich ins Bett und schlafe mal richtig aus. Morgen oder übermorgen kriegt Ihr dann einen viel längeren Brief, und Du, Mutti, bekommst einen Extrabrief auf englisch.

landen / sein
finden / sein

fragen
auspacken / erzählen
haben
gehen / essen
machen
zurückkommen

schlafen

Viele liebe Grüße
Eure

Stephanie

 LIEBE ELTERN … You are on a holiday. Write a postcard to your parents or to a friend, describing what you have done or seen in the past few days.

ZUSAMMENSCHAU

EIN DEUTSCHER EINWANDERER SUCHT ARBEIT

The passport below was issued to Hans Keilhau two weeks before he emigrated to America. Look at the passport and answer the questions.

1. Was ist die Kurzform von „Johannes"?
2. Wann hat Herr Keilhau diesen Paß bekommen? *(Er hat ihn am …)*
3. Wo in Deutschland hat Herr Keilhau im Juni 1930 gewohnt?
4. Wann ist er geboren? *(Er ist am …)*
5. Wo ist er geboren?
6. Ist er groß, klein oder mittelgroß?
7. Welche Form hat sein Gesicht?
8. Welche Farbe haben seine Augen?
9. Welche Farbe hat sein Haar?

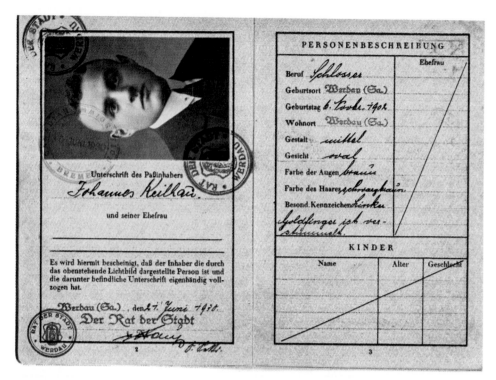

PERSONENBESCHREIBUNG

	Ehefrau
Beruf *Schlosser*	
Geburtsort *Werdau (Sa.)*	
Geburtstag *6. Nove. 1902*	
Wohnort *Werdau (Sa.)*	
Gestalt *mittel*	
Gesicht *oval*	
Farbe der Augen *braun*	
Farbe des Haares *schwarzbraun*	
Besond. Kennzeichen *linken*	
Goldfinger ich ver-	
stümmelt	

KINDER

Name	Alter	Geschlecht

Sa. = Sachsen (province in Germany)

verstümmelt: *injured*

10. Wie heißt der Ringfinger in Hans Keilhaus Paß?
11. Was für besondere Kennzeichen° hat Herr Keilhau? (*Sein ... *)
12. Herr Keilhau ist nicht verheiratet. Woher wissen wir das? (*Er hat ... *)

special characteristics

Hans Keilhau ist Schlosser von Beruf.

Hans Keilhau came to America in the thirties, the time of the Great Depression in Europe and North America. Like most immigrants, he spoke very little English. The interview that you hear takes place in the personnel office of Hutton Machine and Tool Co. in Trenton, New Jersey, where Hans has applied for a job. Since the personnel manager doesn't speak German, the interview has to be conducted through an interpreter, an employee of the firm who happens to speak German.

Neue Vokabeln

eine Lehre machen	*to serve an apprenticeship*
südlich von	*south of*
die Firma	*company*
die Arbeitslosigkeit	*unemployment*
die Arbeitslosen	*unemployed people*
der Gärtner	*gardener*
Ich habe Schlosser gelernt.	*I learned toolmaking.*
schicken	*to send*

✏️ Write the answers to the following questions about the interview.

1. Wo ist Hans Keilhau geboren?
2. Wie alt ist er?
3. Was ist Hans von Beruf?
4. Wo hat er seine Lehre gemacht?
5. Wo in Deutschland ist Lüneburg?
6. Warum ist Hans Schlosser geworden?
7. Wie lange hat Hans in Deutschland als Schlosser gearbeitet?
8. Warum ist er nach Amerika ausgewandert?
9. Wie lange war er arbeitslos?
10. Wo in New Jersey hat er Arbeit gefunden?
11. Was macht er bei Garden State Nurseries?
12. Warum möchte er lieber bei Hutton Machine and Tool Co. arbeiten?
13. Wer hat ihn zu Hutton Machine and Tool Co. geschickt?

interpret

KANNST DU DOLMETSCHEN?°

In groups of three, play the roles of Hans Keilhau, the personnel manager, and the interpreter.

The personnel manager (student 1) conducts the interview in English, using the questions below.

The interpreter (student 2) translates the questions into German. She/he must not forget to use **Sie** to translate *you*.

Hans Keilhau (student 3) answers the questions *in German* on the basis of the biographical information given in the previous interview.

The interpreter (student 2) then translates Hans Keilhau's answers back into English.

1. Are you from Germany or from Austria, Mr. Keilhau?
2. And how old are you?
3. What is your trade?
4. Where did you serve your apprenticeship?
5. Why did you become a toolmaker, Mr. Keilhau?
6. How long did you work in Germany as a toolmaker?
7. How long were you out of work?
8. And have you found work here in New Jersey?
9. Why would you like to work for Hutton Machine and Tool Co.?
10. Who sent you here?
11. Paul Richter?! Then you can start tomorrow.

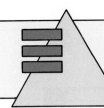

WORT, SINN UND KLANG

WÖRTER UNTER DER LUPE

WORDS AS CHAMELEONS: *GANZ*

The word **ganz** is very frequent, especially in conversational German. Depending on the context, it can have any one of the following meanings: *all, all of, whole, very, quite,* or *completely.*

- What is the correct English equivalent of **ganz** in each of the sentences below?

  1. Meine Eltern haben nur ein ganz kleines Haus. *whole / very / all*
  2. Ich habe ganz vergessen, wann das Konzert beginnt. *all of / very / completely*
  3. Letzten Sommer sind wir durch ganz Europa getrampt.° *all of / quite / very*   °*hitchhiked*
  4. Keinen Zucker, bitte, und nur ganz wenig Milch. *completely / all / very*
  5. Bist du ganz allein durch Europa gereist? *quite / all / whole*
  6. Ich glaube, du verstehst das nicht ganz. *quite / very / whole*
  7. Ralf hat wieder den ganzen Kuchen gegessen. *completely / whole / quite*
  8. Ralf spricht viel zu viel, aber sonst ist er ganz nett. *all / quite / completely*
  9. Die Suppe ist schon ganz kalt. *whole / all of / completely*

Warum fährt man hier lieber nicht so schnell?

Skilled tradesmen from the German-speaking countries played an important role in the development of industry and technology on this continent. This is in large part due to the quality of the vocational training they received in their native countries.

Today vocational training is still a very important part of the educational system in Europe. In Germany, for example, all children start **Grundschule** *(grammar school)* at age six, and receive the same education until the fourth grade. In the fifth grade, students are channeled into various secondary schools according to their goals and abilities. Most children attend a **Hauptschule,** which ends at the ninth or tenth grade, or a **Realschule,** which ends at the tenth grade and is more demanding. Ninety percent of the graduates of these two types of schools serve an apprenticeship **(Lehre)** of some sort, which takes about 3 years. Apprentices (**Auszubildende,** or **Azubis** for short) alternate on-the-job training, often in small firms, with classes in vocational schools. Private enterprise and the Ministry of Education are jointly responsible for vocational training. Apprentices are paid a modest wage **(Ausbildungsgeld)** while they learn. Upon passing an exam at the end of their apprenticeship, they become **Gesellen** *(journeymen/journeywomen)* and are then full-fledged, well-paid members of the work force. For some of them, further training and study leads to a second and final examination, the **Meisterprüfung.** The title **Meister** is very prestigious: only those who receive a **Meisterbrief** *(master craftsman's diploma)* are qualified to train **Auszubildende.** The **Meisterbrief** is displayed with great pride by machinists, bakers, butchers, hair dressers, carpenters, and so on.

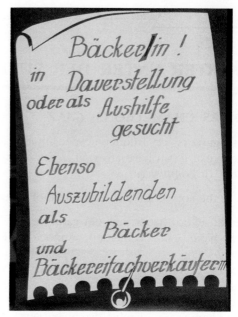

Wie viele Leute sucht diese Bäckerei?

Ein Konditor bäckt kein Brot, sondern Kuchen und Torten.

WEITERE NÜTZLICHE WÖRTER UND AUSDRÜCKE

Haus und Garten

das Haus, die Häuser	house
der Garten, die Gärten	garden, yard
der Zaun, die Zäune	fence
die Hecke, die Hecken	hedge
der Baum, die Bäume	tree
das Gras	grass
der Rasen	lawn
der Rasenmäher, die Rasenmäher	lawnmower

Leute

die Leute *(pl)*	people
der Mensch, die Menschen	person, man, human being; *plural:* people
man	one, you, they, people
In Bayern trinkt man viel Bier.	In Bavaria they (people) drink a lot of beer.

Wichtige Verben

baden	to swim; to take a bath
duschen	to shower
mähen	to mow
öffnen	to open
putzen	to clean
rauchen	to smoke
reparieren	to repair
telefonieren (mit)	to talk on the phone (with)
trampen	to hitchhike
üben	to practice
bezahlen	to pay, to pay for
erzählen	to tell *(a story)*
erklären	to explain
auf•passen	to pay attention
ein•kaufen	to shop, to go shopping
bleiben, ist geblieben	to stay, to remain
schneiden, hat geschnitten	to cut
streichen, hat gestrichen	to paint
gießen, hat gegossen	to water
fern•sehen (sieht fern), hat ferngesehen	to watch TV
sitzen, hat gesessen	to sit
stehen, hat gestanden	to stand
liegen, hat gelegen	to lie, to be situated
werden (wird), ist geworden	to become, to get

Andere Wörter

leider	unfortunately
endlich	finally, at last
gerade	just, just now
genug	enough

Ein typischer deutscher Gartenzaun

Ausdrücke

Bitte schön?	May I help you?
Bitte schön!	You're welcome!
zur Uni	to the university
zum Beispiel (z.B.)	for example (e.g.)

Das Gegenteil

faul — fleißig	lazy—hard-working
erst — letzt	first—last
auf•wachen — ein•schlafen	to wake up—to fall asleep

WÖRTER IM KONTEXT

WAS PASST ZUSAMMEN? Match the verbs in each group with the appropriate noun or expression.

a.
öffnen	die Rosen
streichen	der Brief
gießen	die Familiengeschichte
erzählen	der Zaun

d.
reparieren	das Kind
baden	die Zigarette
mähen	der Rasenmäher
rauchen	der Rasen

b.
erklären	die Hecke
einkaufen	das Fahrrad
putzen	Brot und Milch
schneiden	das Experiment

e.
werden	im Bett
liegen	mit Peter
telefonieren	viel Geld
bezahlen	zwanzig Jahre alt

c.
üben	Klavier
arbeiten	schon um sechs
trampen	im Garten
aufwachen	durch ganz Europa

f.
einschlafen	zur Uni
fernsehen	erst nachts um eins
fahren	bis nachts um eins
sein	faul

 ## ZUR AUSSPRACHE

GERMAN *CH*

German **ch** is one of the few consonant sounds that has no equivalent in English.

1. **ch** after **a, o, u,** and **au**

   When **ch** follows the vowels **a, o, u,** or **au,** it resembles the sound of a gentle gargling.

   Frau Ba**ch** kommt Punkt a**ch**t.
   Am Wo**ch**enende ko**ch**t immer meine To**ch**ter.
   Warum su**ch**st du denn das Ko**ch**buch?
   Ich will versu**ch**en, einen Ku**ch**en zu backen.
   beer belly   Hat Herr Rau**ch** au**ch** so einen Bierbau**ch**° wie Herr Strau**ch**?

2. **ch** after all other vowels and after consonants

The sound of **ch** after all other vowels and after consonants is similar to the sound of a loudly whispered *h* in *huge* or *Hugh*.

Mi**ch**aels Kätz**ch**en mö**ch**te ein Teller**ch**en Mil**ch**.

The ending **-ig** is pronounced as if it were spelled **-ich,** unless it is followed by a vowel.

Es ist sonni**g,** aber sehr windi**g.**

The two types of **ch** sounds are often found in the singular and plural forms of the same noun.

die Na**ch**t	die Nä**ch**te
die To**ch**ter	die Tö**ch**ter
das Bu**ch**	die Bü**ch**er
der Bierbau**ch**	die Bierbäu**ch**e

3. The combination **-chs** is pronounced like English *x*.

das Wa**chs**
se**chs**
der **Ochs**e
der Fu**chs**

Weihnachtsmarkt in Stuttgart

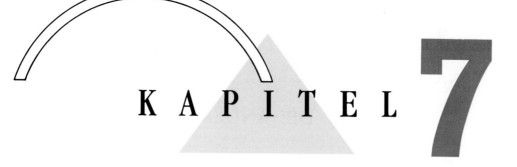

KAPITEL 7

■ **Kommunikationsziele**

*In **Kapitel** 7 you will learn how to:*

talk about chores
express commands and requests
express to whom or for whom something is done
express personal opinions
purchase a gift for someone
return defective merchandise

■ **Hör- und Sprechsituationen**

Weihnachtsgeschenke
Im Blumengeschäft
Rosen zum Geburtstag
Ein paar persönliche Fragen
Seit wann?
Welche Frisur gefällt dir besser?
Die Geschmäcker sind verschieden
Das Loch im Pulli
Gibt es denn gar keine Qualität mehr?

■ **Strukturen**

The imperative
The dative case: indirect object
Dative prepositions
Idiomatic uses of the dative case

■ **Wissenswertes**

Christmas in the German-speaking countries
Other religious and secular holidays in the German-
    speaking countries
Mitbringsel
Gastarbeiter in Germany

EINE HAND WÄSCHT DIE ANDERE°

In Hamburg ist das Wetter heute sehr schön. Anita sitzt° beim Eingang° zur Bibliothek und liest. Jetzt ist es Viertel vor zwölf. Günter kommt aus der Bibliothek und sieht Anita.
Günter (ruft): Anita!
Anita und antwortet nicht liest weiter°.
Günter (ruft noch einmal, und lauter): Anita!

ANITA: Oh, Günter! Was ist denn los?°
GÜNTER: Warum hast du mir denn nicht gleich geantwortet?
ANITA: Ich habe dich nicht gehört.
GÜNTER: Gehst du mit mir zum Mittagessen?
ANITA: Du lädst mich wohl ein?
GÜNTER: Ja, natürlich! Aber nach dem Essen hilfst° du mir doch wieder bei meinem Referat. Mir fällt einfach nichts ein.°—Komm, ich bezahle.
ANITA: Aber Günter, ich esse doch mittags nur einen Teller Suppe. Den kann ich noch selbst bezahlen.
GÜNTER: Und was ist mit meinem Referat?
ANITA: *(sarkastisch)* Schreib's° doch einfach aus Büchern ab!
GÜNTER: Und Professor Weber gibt es mir wie letztes Mal ohne Zensur zurück! Nein, das probiere ich nicht noch einmal! Gott sei Dank° hast du mir dann geholfen.° Und du hilfst mir doch wieder, nicht? Du mußt mir helfen!
ANITA: Sag mal, Günter, bist du mit dem Wagen hier?
GÜNTER: Ja. Warum?
ANITA: Nimmst du mich heute abend mit?
GÜNTER: Natürlich. Wohin willst du denn?
ANITA: Zu meiner Freundin nach Bergedorf.
GÜNTER: Das ist weit. Aber Kurt Kröger fährt gern ein bißchen spazieren.
ANITA: Was?! Kurt Kröger fährt mit dir?! Dann fahrt ihr ohne mich. Ich kann den Kerl nicht ausstehen.°
GÜNTER: Aber ihr wart doch mal ganz dicke Freunde.
ANITA: Von wem weißt du das?
GÜNTER: Von Kurt selbst.
ANITA: Und dem glaubst du? Der lügt wie gedruckt.° Wohin fährst du ihn eigentlich?
GÜNTER: Zur Disco beim Hotel Merkur.
ANITA: Was will er dort?
GÜNTER: Er trifft° seine Freundin dort.
ANITA: Seine Freundin? Wie heißt sie denn?
GÜNTER: Bettina Hofstetter.
ANITA: Die Philosophiestudentin?
GÜNTER: Ja, die.
ANITA: Günter, ich fahre doch mit euch.
GÜNTER: Wirklich?

Margin glosses:
You scratch my scratch yours.
entrance

continues reading

What's the matter?

are going to help
I can't think of a thing.

schreib...ab: *copy*

thank God
helped

stand

He lies through his teeth.

is meeting

ANITA: Und ich helfe dir auch bei deinem Referat.
GÜNTER: Jetzt plötzlich°?   *suddenly*
ANITA: Und dafür° lädst du mich heute abend zum Tanzen ein—in die Disco   *in exchange*
       beim Hotel Merkur!

VOM LESEN ZUM SPRECHEN

WAS PASST ZUSAMMEN?

1. Wann soll Anita Günter bei seinem Referat helfen?   Mit Bettina Hofstetter.

2. Warum soll Anita Günter bei seinem Referat helfen?   Er hat es aus Büchern abgeschrieben.

3. Von wem hat Günter sein letztes Referat ohne Zensur zurückbekommen?   Ihre Freundin.

4. Warum hat Günter sein letztes Referat ohne Zensur zurückbekommen?   Günter fällt einfach nichts ein.

5. Wer hat ihm dann geholfen?   Nach dem Mittagessen.

6. Wen will Anita in Bergedorf besuchen?   Kurt Kröger.

7. Warum will Anita plötzlich nicht mehr mitfahren?   Mit Günter.

8. Wem soll Günter nicht glauben?   Anita.

9. Mit wem geht Kurt heute abend in die Disco beim Hotel Merkur?   Von Professor Weber.

10. Mit wem will Anita heute abend in die Disco beim Hotel Merkur?   Sie sagt, sie kann Kurt Kröger nicht ausstehen.

WER? WEN? WEM? Your instructor will read fourteen questions starting with **wer**, **wen**, or **wem**. Answer with **Anita, Günter, Bettina,** or **Kurt**.

EINE HAND WÄSCHT DIE ANDERE

Trying to get others to help out or do things that you don't like to do often requires exchanging chores. Using the example below, write about three chores that you, your friends, or members of your family exchange. Then report to the class.

▶ Meine Zimmerkollegin putzt nicht gern. Deshalb putze ich einmal die Woche unser Zimmer, und sie muß dafür die Wäsche waschen.

		Referate tippen
		kochen
to do the dishes		ab•waschen°
to tidy up the kitchen	ich	die Küche auf•räumen°
	meine Zimmerkollegin	einkaufen gehen
apartment	mein Zimmerkollege	die Wohnung°auf•räumen
	meine Freundin	die Wohnung putzen
	mein Freund	die Fenster putzen
	meine Mutter	die Betten machen
	mein Vater	den Wagen waschen
	meine Schwester	die Garage auf•räumen
	mein Bruder	die Wäsche waschen
	. . .	den Rasen mähen
to iron		bügeln°
to mend		flicken°
		. . .

zum GEBURTSTAG-
eine ÜBERRASCHUNG

GUTSCHEIN
für meine Mutter:

Ich übernehme am ..3. 4....
und am 3.5... oder am ..8. 6....

⊗ Kochen
O Frühstück
O Tisch decken
⊗ Abwasch
O Schuhe putzen
O Großeinkauf
⊗ Betten machen
O Mülleimer leeren
⊗ Fenster putzen
O ....

Datum ..2. 4....

Unterschrift ..Peter....

Was will Peter an diesen Tagen für seine Mutter tun?

NÜTZLICHE WÖRTER UND AUSDRÜCKE

Nomen

das Hotel, die Hotels	hotel
der Eingang, die Eingänge	entrance
das Essen	lunch, dinner, supper; meal
die Disco, die Discos	disco
die Zensur, die Zensuren	grade, mark

Verben

abschreiben, hat abgeschrieben	to copy
helfen (hilft), hat geholfen	to help
treffen (trifft), hat getroffen	to meet
weiter•lesen (liest weiter), hat weitergelesen	to continue reading

Verben

spazieren•fahren (fährt spazieren),	
ist spazierengefahren	to go for a ride
rufen, hat gerufen	to call; to exclaim
probieren	to try

Andere Wörter

ander-	other; different	**plötzlich**	suddenly, all of a sudden
weit	far	**einfach**	simply, just

Ausdrücke

noch einmal, nochmal	(over) again, once more
Was ist denn los?	What's the matter?
Mir fällt nichts ein.	I can't think of a thing.
Ich kann den Kerl nicht ausstehen.	I can't stand that guy.
Er lügt wie gedruckt.	He lies through his teeth.
Eine Hand wäscht die andere.	You scratch my back, I'll scratch yours.

Sprachnotizen

Weiter

The adverb **weiter** can be prefixed to many verbs. The resulting combination usually means to *continue* doing something.

Warum will Moritz nicht **weiter-studieren?**	*Why doesn't Moritz want to **continue studying?***
Arbeiten wir heute nachmittag **weiter?**	*Are we going to **continue working** this afternoon?*

WÖRTER IM KONTEXT

1. WAS PASST WO? Use the correct forms of the appropriate verbs.

   probieren   anprobieren   ausprobieren

a. Darf ich das Kleid noch einmal _____, bitte?
b. Hast du deine neue Kamera schon _____?
c. Kannst du Motorrad fahren?
   Ich weiß nicht. Ich habe es noch nie _____.

   rufen   anrufen   zurückrufen

d. Warum hat Eva mich nicht gehört?
   Du hast nicht laut genug _____.
e. Kurt hat _____. Du sollst ihn bitte gleich _____.

   stehen   aufstehen   ausstehen   verstehen

f. Warum bist du denn so spät _____?
g. Wir haben stundenlang im Regen _____.
h. Bernd findet Frau Müller sehr nett.
   Das kann ich nicht _____. Ich kann diese Frau nicht _____.

2. WAS PASST ZUSAMMEN?

a. Was ist denn los? Warum schreibst du denn nicht weiter?

Ich glaube, ihr Freund hilft ihr.

b. Hat Günter wirklich gesagt, er hat das Referat nicht aus Büchern abgeschrieben?

Beim Eingang zur Disco.

c. Warum bekommt Eva denn plötzlich so gute Zensuren?

Mir fällt einfach nichts mehr ein.

d. Wo triffst du deinen Freund heute abend?

Ja, aber ich glaube, er lügt wie gedruckt.

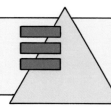

FUNKTIONEN UND FORMEN

1. EXPRESSING COMMANDS AND REQUESTS

IMPERATIVES

The imperative is a form of the verb used to express commands and requests. Since English has only one form of address *(you)*, it has only one imperative form. German has three forms of address **(du, ihr, Sie)** and consequently it has three imperative forms. In written German, imperative sentences usually end with an exclamation mark.

Komm!	
Kommt!	Come!
Kommen Sie!	

a. The *du*-imperative

The **du**-imperative is simply the stem of the verb.

Komm schnell, Thomas! Die Vorlesung hat schon angefangen.

Come quickly, Thomas! The lecture has already started.

Sei still!

Be quiet!

Verbs that have a stem vowel change from **e** to **i** or **ie** in the 2nd and 3rd person singular of the present tense (e.g., **ich spreche, du sprichst, er spricht**) use the *changed* stem in the **du-**imperative.

Nimm doch nicht so viel Fleisch!

Don't take so much meat!

Lies mal bitte diesen Brief!

Please read this letter.

Iß *ja* nicht wieder den ganzen Kuchen!   *Don't you dare eat all the cake again!*

Verbs that have a stem vowel change from **a** to **ä** (e.g., **ich fahre, du fährst, er fährt**) do *not* use the changed stem.

Fahr doch bitte nicht so schnell!   *Please don't drive so fast!*

Imperative sentences frequently contain flavoring particles. The particles **doch** and **mal** soften the command somewhat. The particle **ja,** strongly stressed, has the opposite effect. It gives the command an almost threatening note: *Don't you dare . . . !* The addition of **bitte** to an imperative sentence introduces a friendly note and transforms a command into a request.

Verbs with a stem ending in certain consonant clusters such as **ordnen** *(to put in order)* and **öffnen** *(to open)* add an **-e** in the **du**-imperative. The same is true of verbs with a stem ending in **-d** or **-t.**

Öffne sofort die Tür!   *Open the door immediately!*

Antworte bitte so bald wie möglich!   *Please answer as soon as possible.*

The prefix of separable verbs appears at the end of the imperative sentence:

Hol mich bitte Punkt sieben **ab!**   *Please pick me up at seven on the dot.*

Komm *ja* nicht wieder so spät **heim!**   *Don't come home so late again!*

A. MACH BITTE, WAS ICH SAGE! You are in charge of your younger sister/brother. Use the verbs given to tell her/him what and what not to do.

1. _____ doch endlich _____!   aufstehen
2. _____ mal ein bißchen schneller!   essen
3. _____ doch endlich deine Milch _____!   austrinken
4. _____ deine Bücher nicht!   vergessen
5. _____ mich bitte um zwölf _____!   anrufen
6. _____ mal deine Suppe _____!   ausessen
7. _____ doch nicht so schnell!   sprechen
8. _____ bitte gleich meinen Wagen!   waschen
9. _____ *ja* nicht ohne mich _____!   wegfahren
10. _____ doch bitte ein bißchen schneller!   arbeiten
11. _____ mal nicht so frech!   sein
12. _____ *ja* nur ein Stück Kuchen!   nehmen
13. _____ doch nicht immer nur mit Robert und Jürgen _____!   ausgehen
14. _____ *ja* vor Mitternacht zu Hause!   sein

B. STEH DOCH ENDLICH AUF! You and your roommate are running late and tell each other what to do. Match correctly in each set.

▶ aufstehen   bitte den Kaffee
  machen   doch endlich

S1: Steh doch endlich auf!   *S2:* Mach bitte den Kaffee!

impatient	1. kommen	doch endlich zum Frühstück
	sein	doch nicht so ungeduldig°
	2. essen	bitte meine Hausaufgaben
	durchlesen	doch nicht so langsam
	3. nehmen	doch nicht so laut
	sprechen	doch nicht so viel Zucker
	4. austrinken	doch endlich deinen Kaffee
	vergessen	deine Bücher nicht
	5. wegfahren	doch nicht so nervös
	sein	*ja* nicht ohne mich

✏️➡ **SEI DOCH NICHT IMMER SO PESSIMISTISCH!** As much as we like our family and friends, some of their habits keep annoying us. What commands would you give to try and stop their irritating behavior? Write three commands in the **du**-imperative and share them with your classmates. The phrases below may give you some ideas.

to spend

> so spät nach Hause kommen   so spät aufstehen   so schnell fahren
> so viel Geld ausgeben°   nur mit David ausgehen   so laut sprechen
> nur vor dem Fernseher sitzen   nur Comics lesen   so schnell essen
> so taktlos sein   so ungeduldig sein . . .

Was ist Müll?

b. The *ihr*-imperative

The **ihr**-imperative is identical to the **ihr**-form of the present tense, but without the pronoun:

Kommt, Kinder! Wir müssen jetzt gehen.   *Come on, children! We have to go now.*

Seid doch bitte nicht so laut!   *Please don't be so loud.*

Ladet *ja* Günter nicht **ein!**   *Don't invite Günter!*

C. IHR MACHT EIN PICKNICK?   Your friends are going on a picnic. You like to tell them what to do and give last-minute instructions.

sandwiches

a large, soft pretzel.

1. ＿＿ genug Brote° ＿＿!	einpacken
2. ＿＿ noch irgendwo ein paar Brezeln!°	kaufen
3. ＿＿ genug Bier ＿＿!	mitnehmen
4. ＿＿ bitte nicht zu viel!	trinken
5. ＿＿ das Frisbee nicht!	vergessen
6. ＿＿ bitte nicht so schnell!	fahren
7. ＿＿ bitte gegen sechs wieder zurück!	sein
8. ＿＿ bitte nicht wieder erst um halb neun ＿＿!	heimkommen
9. ＿＿ doch ein bißchen schneller°!	machen
10. ＿＿ doch endlich ＿＿!	abfahren

schnell machen: *to hurry up*

Was darf man hier alles nicht?

✐ **SCHONT UNSERE ANLAGEN!** *(Protect our parks!)* Look at the sign in the illustration. Using the phrases below in the **ihr**-imperative, write four commands that express what one is not allowed to do in this park. Each command must contain the negatives **nicht** or **kein**. Express your commands very forcefully by using the pattern: _____ **hier ja . . . !**

rad•fahren	Blumen pflücken
Fußball spielen	eure Hunde frei laufen lassen

D. IHR MACHT UNS NOCH VERRÜCKT! You and your partner are the exasperated parents of teenagers. Take turns telling them what and what not to do. Match correctly in each set.

▶ aufstehen   bitte gleich eure Betten
  machen   doch nicht immer so spät

S1: Steht doch nicht immer so spät auf!   *S2:* Macht bitte gleich eure Betten!

1. einladen   *ja* nicht wieder den ganzen Kuchen
   aufessen   diesen Kerl *ja* nicht nochmal
2. aufhängen   doch bitte eure Jacken
   machen   bitte gleich eure Hausaufgaben
3. vergessen   bitte keinen Alkohol
   trinken   eure warmen Jacken nicht
4. kommen   *ja* nicht wieder so spät nach Hause
   sein   bitte vor Mitternacht zu Hause

c. The *Sie*-imperative

The **Sie**-imperative is the infinitive of the verb followed directly by the pronoun **Sie**:

Kommen Sie bitte schnell, Herr Doktor!   *Please come quickly, doctor!*

Rufen Sie mich doch bitte heute abend **an!**   *Please call me tonight.*

The verb **sein** is slightly irregular in the **Sie**-imperative:

Sei**en** Sie doch nicht so unfreundlich!   *Don't be so unfriendly.*

Was soll man hier tun oder nicht tun?

E. IN PROFESSOR KUHLS DEUTSCHKLASSE. Professor Kuhl is giving instructions to her German class.

1. _____ bitte gut _____!   zuhören
2. _____ bitte, was ich sage!   wiederholen
3. _____ das bitte noch einmal!   sagen
4. _____ diesen Satz° bitte an die   schreiben
   Tafel°!

sentence
blackboard

5. _____ dieses Wort bitte!   buchstabieren
6. _____ bitte _____, Andrea!   weiterlesen
7. _____ doch bitte ein bißchen lauter!   sprechen
8. _____ bitte _____, Michael!   aufwachen
9. _____ diesen Dialog bis morgen   durchlesen
   genau _____!
10. _____ diese Übung bitte schriftlich°!   machen   *in writing*
11. _____ doch bitte nicht so laut!   sein
12. Michael! _____ doch nicht schon   einschlafen
    wieder _____!

F. ENTSCHEIDUNGEN! *(Decisions!)* The persons indicated don't know what to do. Take on their roles and ask your partner for advice. Begin your questions with **was, wen, wann,** or **wo.**

▶ HERR UND FRAU BERG: ___ sollen wir   einen Opel
kaufen, einen Audi oder einen
Opel?

Here: you'd be better off   **S1:** Was sollen wir kaufen, einen Audi   **S2:** Kaufen Sie lieber° einen Opel.
oder einen Opel?

---

1. HERR BERG: _____ soll ich anrufen, die Polizei   einen Arzt
                       oder einen Arzt?°

doctor

2. FRAU BRAUN: _____ soll ich studieren, in   in Freiburg
                       Freiburg oder in Berlin?

3. EVA UND TANJA: _____ sollen wir fliegen, am   am Freitag
                       Donnerstag oder am Freitag?

4. SYLVIA UND INGE: _____ sollen wir mitnehmen,   Helga
                       Brigitte oder Helga?

5. RALF: _____ soll ich trinken, Rotwein   Weißwein
                       oder Weißwein?

6. BERND: _____ soll ich lesen, ein Buch oder   ein Buch
                       die Zeitung?

7. KLAUS UND SILKE: _____ sollen wir kommen, um zwei   schon um zwei
                       oder um drei?

8. ZWEI TOURISTEN: _____ sollen wir essen, beim   beim Donisl
                       Donisl oder bei McDonald's?

9. JENNIFER: _____ soll ich einladen, Thomas   Thomas
                       oder Stefan?

2. INDICATING THE PERSON *TO WHOM* OR *FOR WHOM* SOMETHING IS DONE

THE DATIVE CASE: THE INDIRECT OBJECT

In *Kapitel 3* you learned that many verbs take a *direct object:*

Professor Seidlmeyer needs *a new tie.*

You also learned that in German the *direct object* is signaled by the *accusative case:*

Professor Seidlmeyer braucht **einen neuen Schlips.**

Some verbs take not only a direct object but also an *indirect object.* As the examples below show, the indirect object indicates *to whom* or *for whom* something is done. The indirect object is almost always *a person.*

The students buy *the professor* a new tie.
(The students buy a new tie *for the professor.*)
They give *the professor* the tie for his birthday.
(They give the tie *to the professor* for his birthday.)

In German the *indirect object* is signaled by the *dative case:*

Die Studenten kaufen **dem Professor** einen neuen Schlips.
Sie schenken° **dem Professor** den Schlips zum Geburtstag.   *give (as a gift)*

It is important to remember that German signals the indirect object with the dative case, not with the preposition **zu** *(to).*

	Masculine		**Feminine**		**Neuter**		**Plural**	
Nominative	der	Vater	die	Mutter	das	Kind	die	Kinder
	mein	Vater	meine	Mutter	mein	Kind	meine	Kinder
Accusative	den	Vater	die	Mutter	das	Kind	die	Kinder
	meinen	Vater	meine	Mutter	mein	Kind	meine	Kinder
Dative	**dem**	Vater	**der**	Mutter	**dem**	Kind	**den**	Kinder**n**
	mein**em**	Vater	mein**er**	Mutter	mein**em**	Kind	mein**en**	Kindern

In the dative plural all nouns take the ending **-n** unless the plural form already ends in **-n (die Freundinne*n*, den Freundinne*n*)** or if it ends in **-s (die Discjok-keys, den Discjockeys).**

G. SUBJEKT, DIREKTES OBJEKT ODER INDIREKTES OBJEKT? Decide whether the words in bold are subjects, direct objects or indirect objects. All the subjects in this exercise are people and you can identify them by asking the question *who.* Identify the direct objects by asking the questions *whom* or *what* and the indirect objects by asking the questions *to whom* or *for whom.*

1. **Martin** hat **ein Referat** geschrieben. Heute nachmittag will **er es Claudia** zeigen,° denn **Claudia** schreibt sehr gut und findet **alle seine Fehler.°** Mor-   *show / mistakes* gen früh um halb zehn muß **Martin das Referat** dann **Professor Seidlmeyers Sekretärin** geben.
2. **Stephanie** schreibt **ihrer Schwester** oft **lange Briefe,** aber **ihrem Bruder** hat **sie** erst einmal geschrieben, und nur **eine Postkarte.**
3. Heute schickt **Stephanie ihrer Familie ein Paket. Ihrer Mutter** schickt **sie ein Paar Ohrringe** und **ihrer Schwester einen Dirndlrock,°** **ihrem Vater**   *full, colorful skirt typical of* und **ihrem Bruder** schickt sie je° **einen Bierstein.**   *Bavaria or Austria / each*

4. **Peter** war drei Wochen in Berlin und fährt morgen wieder nach München. Deshalb kauft **er** noch schnell **ein paar Geschenke.°** **Seiner Freundin Stephanie** kauft **er ein Sweatshirt. Claudia** bekommt **zwei Tafeln Schokolade°** und **seinem Freund Martin** kauft **Peter drei frische Berliner Pfannkuchen.°**

Sprachnotizen

Ein Paar and *ein paar*

Ein Paar means *a pair,* i.e., *two* of something.

Stephanie hat ihrer Mutter **ein Paar** Ohrringe gekauft.	*Stephanie bought her mother **a pair** of earrings.*

Ein *paar* means *a couple of* in the sense of *a few.*

Ich muß noch **ein paar** Geschenke kaufen.	*I still have to buy **a couple of** presents.*

THE DATIVE CASE: THE INTERROGATIVE PRONOUN

The dative form of the interrogative pronoun **wer** has the same ending as the dative form of the masculine definite article:

	Interrogative Pronoun	Definite Article
Nominative	wer	der
Accusative	wen	den
Dative	**wem**	**dem**

Wer ist der Mann dort? Der Briefträger.	*Who is that man there? The mailman.*
Wen hat Müllers Hund gebissen? Den Briefträger.	*Whom did the Müllers' dog bite? The mailman.*
Wem schenken Müllers die Flasche Kognak? **Dem** Briefträger.	***To whom** are the Müllers giving the bottle of cognac? **To the** mailman.*

H. WAS PASST ZUSAMMEN?

1. Wer holt dich ab?
2. Wen rufst du an?
3. Wem schenkst du dieses Buch?

Meiner Mutter.	Mein Onkel.
Mein Freund.	Meiner Tante.
Meinem Bruder.	Meinen Vater.
Meiner Kusine.	Meinen Eltern.
Meine Eltern.	Meine Zimmerkollegin.
Meine Freundin.	Meiner Klavierlehrerin.
Meinen Großeltern.	Meinem Vetter.

I. WEM SCHENKST DU DAS ALLES? Your roommate displays all the Christmas gifts that she/he has just bought. You ask who they are for.° *for whom*

 ►   mein ___ Mutter

S1: Wem schenkst du die Weingläser?   **S2:** Die schenke ich meiner Mutter.

1.   mein___ Vater

2.   mein___ Schwester

3.   mein___ beiden Brüder _____

4.   mein___ Großeltern

5.   mein___ Kusine Silke

die zwei Armbanduhren	die Flasche Parfüm	das Armband
den Teekessel	den Geldbeutel	

6.   mein___ beiden Vettern

7.   mein___ Tante Brigitte

8.   mein___ Onkel Albert

9.   mein___ Freundinnen

den Hammer	die zwei Tennisschläger
die Gießkanne	die drei Kugelschreiber

THE DATIVE CASE: PERSONAL PRONOUNS

English personal pronouns have only one object form. This one form can function as a direct object and as an indirect object.

German personal pronouns have two object forms: an *accusative form* for the *direct object,* and a *dative form* for the *indirect object.*

Warum habt ihr **mich** nicht eingeladen?	*Why didn't you invite **me?***
Kannst du **mir** deinen Kassettenrecorder leihen?	*Can you lend **me** your cassette recorder?*
	*(Can you lend your cassette recorder **to me?**)*
Kannst du **mir** eine Tasse Kaffee machen?	*Can you make **me** a cup of coffee?*
	*(Can you make a cup of coffee **for me?**)*

Nominative	Accusative	Dative
ich	mich	**mir**
du	dich	**dir**
er	ihn	**ihm**
sie	sie	**ihr**
es	es	**ihm**
wir	uns	**uns**
ihr	euch	**euch**
sie	sie	**ihnen**
Sie	Sie	**Ihnen**

J. WAS SOLL ICH MEINER MUTTER SCHENKEN? You ask your roommate what you should give your friends and relatives for Christmas. She/he responds by matching the illustrations with the words listed below.

▶ mein___ Mutter

S1: Was soll ich meiner Mutter schenken?

S2: Schenk ihr doch ein Paar warme Hausschuhe.

1. mein___ Vater

2. mein___ Schwester

3. mein___ kleinen Bruder

4. mein___ beiden Vettern

5. mein___ Freundin

---

ein Paar Ohrringe   ein paar Tafeln Schokolade
einen schönen Pullover   einen Hockeyschläger
eine elegante Bluse

---

6. mein___ Onkel Hermann

7. mein___ Kusine Ute

8. mein___ Tante Elisabeth

9. mein___ Großeltern

10. unser___ Briefträger

---

ein paar Flaschen Wein   zwanzig Mark
eine CD   ein Paar Handschuhe
einen neuen Toaster

THE PRONOUNS *DER, DIE, DAS* IN THE DATIVE

In *Kapitel 5* you learned that in colloquial German the definite articles **der, die,** and **das** often function as pronouns. Note that the dative plural of the pronoun is **denen.**

	Masculine	Feminine	Neuter	Plural
Nominative	der	die	das	die
Accusative	den	die	das	die
Dative	**dem**	**der**	**dem**	**denen**

Was schenkst du deinen Eltern zu Weihnachten?
Meinen Eltern? **Denen** schenke ich eine schöne Lampe.

What are you giving your parents for Christmas?
*My parents? I'm giving **them** a nice lamp.*

K. WAS SCHENKST DU DEINER FAMILIE UND DEINEN FREUNDEN?

▶ dein___ Bruder

S1: Was schenkst du deinem Bruder?   **S2:** Dem schenke ich ein Sweatshirt.

1. dein___ Schwester

2. dein___ Eltern

3. dein___ Kusine

4. dein___ Vetter

5. dein___ Großeltern

ein Armband	einen Toaster	eine Bluse	eine Lampe
	eine CD		

6. dein___ Freundin

7. dein___ Freund

8. dein___ Tante Brigitte
und dein ___ Onkel Albert

9. dein___ Klavierlehrerin

10. dein___ Onkel Gerhard

eine Zimmerpflanze	ein paar Flaschen Wein
eine Flasche Parfüm	ein Flasche Kognak
einen schönen Kugelschreiber	

Haben Sie besondere Wünsche "Sprechen Sie mit uns"

Weihnachten *(Christmas)* is celebrated in a similar way in all the German-speaking countries. Beginning on December 1, many children count down the twenty-four days until Christmas Eve with an **Adventskalender.** Each day they open a little door or window on the calendar, behind which are pictures related to Christmas. Many families have an **Adventskranz** *(Advent wreath)* with four candles that are lit on the four Sundays before Christmas. On the eve of **Nikolaustag** (December 6), children put their shoes outside their bedroom door for **St. Nikolaus,** the protector of children, to fill with candy, chocolate, and nuts.

As in other countries that celebrate Christmas, **Weihnachten** is associated with a Christmas tree and gift-giving. The **Weihnachtsbaum** *(Christmas tree)* is not put up until December 24 and is a **Tannenbaum** *(a fir or spruce tree).* Many families decorate their tree with real candles and light them for the first time when the **Bescherung** *(gift-giving)* takes place on Christmas Eve **(Heiliger Abend).** Children believe that the **Christkind** or the **Weihnachtsmann** (the helper of the **Christkind**) brings the gifts. Christmas Eve is usually a quiet celebration for the immediate family and many families attend church before or after the **Bescherung.**

Am vierten Adventssonntag

Both December 25 **(der erste Weihnachtsfeiertag)** and 26 **(der zweite Weihnachtsfeiertag)** are holidays. On the 25th, families gather over a **Festessen** *(feast)* that often centers around a **Weihnachtsgans** *(Christmas goose).* They wish each other **Frohe Weihnachten!**

New Year's Eve **(Silvester)** is the night for parties and revelry. The new year is ushered in with the greeting **Ein gutes, neues Jahr!**

Frohe
Weihnachten
und ein
gutes
neues Jahr

WEIHNACHTSGESCHENKE

christmas presents

Ask your partner what she/he is going to give her/his family and friends (and you!) for Christmas. Take notes and report to the class.

WORD ORDER: SEQUENCE OF OBJECTS

The following examples show the normal sequence of the direct and indirect object in German.

If both objects are *nouns,* the indirect object (the person) normally precedes the direct object (the thing):

Geben Sie **Ihrem Sohn dieses Hustenmittel** dreimal am Tag.	*Give **your son this cough medicine** three times a day.* *Give **this cough medicine to your son** three times a day.*

If both objects are *pronouns,* English and German word order is identical: the direct object (accusative) precedes the indirect object (dative).

Geben Sie **es ihm** dreimal am Tag.	*Give **it to him** three times a day.*

If one object is a *noun* and the other a *pronoun,* the pronoun *always* precedes the noun:

Geben Sie **ihm** dieses Hustenmittel dreimal am Tag.	*Give **him** this cough medicine three times a day.* *Give this cough medicine **to him** three times a day.*
Geben Sie **es** Ihrem Sohn dreimal am Tag.	*Give **it** to your son three times a day.*

L. WAS PASST WO? Complete the exchanges by supplying the direct and indirect objects in the correct order.

1. KIND: Kaufst du _____ _____, Vati?   das Fahrrad   mir

   VATER: Nein, ich kaufe _____ _____ nicht.   es   dir

2. MUTTER: Sollen wir _____ _____ kaufen?   diese Kamera   unserem Sohn

   VATER: Ja, ich glaube wir kaufen _____ _____.   sie   ihm

3. HERR ZIEGLER:	Kannst du ____ ____ bügeln, Brigitte?	ein Hemd	mir
FRAU ZIEGLER:	Mach's doch selber. Ich muß ____ schnell ____ schreiben.	eine Postkarte	meinen Eltern
4. CLAUDIA:	Ich kaufe ____ ____ zu Weihnachten.	ein Buch	Stephanie
MARTIN:	Und ich schenke ____ ____.	eine Schallplatte	ihr
5. BERND:	Kannst du ____ ____ leihen, Eva?	dein Biologiebuch	mir
EVA:	Ja, aber du mußt ____ ____ morgen früh wieder zurückgeben.	es	mir
6. FRAU ZIEGLER:	Hast du ____ ____ gezeigt?	deine Zensuren	Vati
UWE:	Nein, ich zeige ____ ____ lieber erst morgen.	sie	ihm
7. FRAU BERG:	Letztes Jahr haben Müllers ____ ____ gekauft.	eine Schreibmaschine	ihrer Tochter
FRAU WILD:	Ja, und dieses Jahr wollen sie ____ ____ schenken.	einen Computer	ihr

M. WER BEKOMMT WAS? Onkel Gustav is an eccentric old bachelor who loves to play practical jokes. Last Christmas he gave everyone in the family a gift that was obviously intended for someone else. Help the family redistribute the gifts.

skates
razor
cane
rocking chair

Letzte Weihnachten hat Onkel Gustav der Oma ein Paar Schlittschuhe° geschenkt, dem Opa ein Dreirad, der Mutti einen Rasierapparat,° dem Vati einen Teddy, der Sabine einen Stock,° der Christine eine Flasche Parfüm und dem Kurtchen einen Schaukelstuhl.°

S1: Wem gibt Oma die Schlittschuhe?	*S2:* Sie gibt sie der Sabine.

1. ____ gibt Sabine d__ Stock (*m*)? | Sie gibt ____ d__ Opa.
2. ____ gibt Opa d__ Dreirad (*n*)? | Er gibt ____ d__ Christine.
3. ____ gibt Christine d__ Flasche Parfüm (*f*)? | Sie gibt ____ d__ Mutti.
4. ____ gibt Mutti d__ Rasierapparat (*m*)? | Sie gibt ____ d__ Vati.
5. ____ gibt Vati d__ Teddy (*m*)? | Er gibt ____ d__ Kurtchen.
6. ____ gibt Kurtchen d__ Schaukelstuhl (*m*)? | Er gibt ____ d__ Oma.

ZUSAMMENSCHAU

IM BLUMENGESCHÄFT°

flower shop

Stephanie hat morgen Geburtstag. Peter möchte ihr Blumen schenken und ist deshalb im Blumenhaus Dieterich. Hören Sie bitte gut zu!

Neue Vokabeln

Sie wünschen?	*May I help you?*
Blumen	*flowers*
Sie hat morgen Geburtstag.	*It's her birthday tomorrow.*
besonders	*particularly*
zeigen	*to show*
fünf Mark das Stück	*five marks a piece*
schicken	*to send*
warten	*to wait*
ein•schlagen	*to wrap*

1. Welche Farben hören Sie?

   weiß   gelb   rosa   rot   blau

2. Welche Zahlen hören Sie?

   2   4   5   10   15   20   25

3. Welche Imperativformen hören Sie?

   Kommen Sie!   Schicken Sie!   Geben Sie!   Warten Sie!   Schenken Sie!

Hören Sie Peters Gespräch° mit der Verkäuferin noch einmal an, und beantworten Sie dann die folgenden zehn Fragen!   *conversation*

1. Warum möchte Peter seiner Freundin Blumen schenken?
2. Warum sagt die Verkäuferin, Peter soll seiner Freundin Rosen schenken?
3. Was für Rosen will Peter seiner Freundin schenken?
4. Warum sagt die Verkäuferin: „Bitte, kommen Sie"?
5. Was kosten die Rosen?
6. Findet Peter das billig oder teuer?
7. Wie viele Rosen kauft Peter?
8. Warum schenkt er seiner Freundin nicht zehn oder fünfzehn Rosen?
9. Warum soll die Verkäuferin der Freundin die Rosen nicht schicken?
10. Warum soll Peter noch einen Moment warten?

When invited for **Kaffee und Kuchen** (often on a Sunday afternoon) or for dinner in a German-speaking country, it is customary to take along a **Mitbringsel** *(small gift)* for the hostess or host. The most common choices are a bouquet of flowers, a box of chocolates, or a bottle of wine.

There are certain customs associated with giving flowers in the German-speaking countries. A small bouquet should contain an uneven number. The selection of flowers is also important. Red roses are a token of love; chrysanthemums or white flowers are for solemn occasions.

Meistens kauft man Blumen als Mitbringsel.

ROSEN ZUM GEBURTSTAG

Sie möchten Ihrer Freundin (Mutter, Schwester) Rosen zum Geburtstag schenken und gehen deshalb in ein Blumengeschäft.

Sie

1. Enter the florist's shop and say hello.
3. Say that it's your girlfriend's (mother's, sister's) birthday tomorrow and that you would like to give her some flowers.
5. Say that you would like red roses.
7. Say that you like the roses and ask how much they cost.
9. Say that you find this very expensive.
11. Say that you don't have much money. Then state how many roses you would like.
13. Say that you would rather give them to her yourself. Hand the salesperson the money, saying how much it is.
15. Thank the salesperson in return and say good-bye.

Verkäufer/in

2. Return the greeting and ask your customer what she/he would like to have.
4. Suggest to your customer that she/he give roses. Say that you have particularly nice fresh roses today and mention some colors.
6. Ask whether you may show your customer the red roses. Ask her/him to come with you.
8. Tell your customer the price.
10. Agree that this isn't cheap, but stress the quality and beauty of the roses. Ask how many you may give your customer.
12. Ask whether you may send the roses to your customer's girlfriend (mother, sister).
14. Say thank you. Ask the customer to wait for a moment because you would like to wrap the roses for her/him.

3. FORMING PHRASES LIKE *WITH MY FRIENDS,*
AFTER THE LECTURE

THE DATIVE PREPOSITIONS

In *Kapitel 5* you learned the prepositions that are followed by an object in the accusative case: **durch, für, gegen, ohne, um.** There are other prepositions that are always followed by an object in the *dative case:* **aus, außer, bei, mit, nach, seit, von, zu.** The basic meanings of these prepositions are given below.

aus	*out of*	Nimm bitte die Milch **aus dem Kühlschrank.**	*Please take the milk out of the refrigerator.*
	from	Herr Schweri ist **aus der Schweiz.**	*Mr. Schweri is from Switzerland.*
außer	*except for*	**Außer deinem Bruder** waren gestern alle hier.	*Except for your brother everybody was here yesterday.*
bei	*at*	Arbeitet Herr Herder immer noch **bei der Post?**	*Is Mr. Herder still working at the post office?*
	at the home of	Ist die Fete **bei dir** oder **bei deinem Bruder?**	*Is the party at your place or at your brother's?*
	near	Bergedorf liegt **bei Hamburg.**	*Bergedorf is near Hamburg.*
mit	*with*	**Mit wem** geht Günter heute abend aus?	*With whom is Günter going out tonight?*
	by	Fahren Sie **mit dem Zug** oder **mit dem Bus?**	*Are you going by train or by bus?*
nach	*after*	Was machst du **nach dieser Vorlesung?**	*What are you doing after this lecture?*
	to	Fährt dieser Zug **nach Stuttgart?**	*Does this train go to Stuttgart?*
seit	*since*	Mein Onkel wohnt **seit dem Krieg** in Wien.	*My uncle has been living in Vienna since the war.*
	for	Er lebt schon **seit vielen Jahren** dort.	*He has been living there for many years.*
von	*from*	**Von wem** sind diese Rosen?	*From whom are these roses?*
	of	Er ist ein guter Freund **von mir.**	*He is a good friend of mine.*
zu	*to*	Heute abend kommen wir alle **zu dir.**	*Tonight we're all coming to your place.*
	for	Was hast du **zu Weihnachten** gekriegt?	*What did you get for Christmas?*

Was darf man hier alles nicht?

During the 1950s and 1960s, the period of reconstruction after World War II, West Germany experienced a period of remarkable economic growth which came to be known as the **Wirtschaftswunder** *(economic miracle)*. To ease the severe labor shortages that ensued, foreign workers **(Gastarbeiter)** were recruited from Italy, Yugoslavia, Greece, Spain, and Turkey. Currently the **Gastarbeiter** and their families number approximately 4.5 million, most of whom are from Turkey.

The slow-down of the economy in the mid-seventies and the resulting increase in unemployment led to a rise in **Ausländerfeindlichkeit** *(resentment against foreigners)*. Some Germans think the unemployment problem would best be solved by sending the **Gastarbeiter** back home. Fortunately most Germans recognize the responsibility the country has to integrate those who, in

Türkische Gastarbeiter

contributing to its economic growth, have put down roots and started families far from their native country.

N. REISEPLÄNE. Ergänzen Sie **mit, seit, von** oder **zu** und die Dativendungen!

1. _____ w__ hast du den Pullover, Peter? _____ dein__ Eltern?
2. Ja, den haben sie mir _____ Weihnachten geschenkt.
3. Übrigens, hier ist ein Brief _____ ihnen!
4. Sie sind _____ d__ ersten April wieder in Berlin.
5. Meine Mutter schreibt, ich soll bald mal _____ dir _____ ihnen nach Berlin kommen.
6. Sollen wir _____ d__ Zug fahren oder _____ mein__ alten Golf?
7. Meine Eltern leben schon _____ zwanzig Jahr__ in Berlin.
8. Hier ist ein Foto _____ mein__ Eltern mit mir und Stefan.
9. Stefan ist ein guter Freund _____ mir.
10. Ich bin _____ ihm in die Schule gegangen. Er lebt _____ ein paar Jahr__ in Braunschweig.
11. _____ Braunschweig nach Berlin ist es gar nicht weit.
12. Warum fahren wir nicht _____ d__ Wagen _____ Stefan, bleiben ein paar Tage bei ihm und fahren dann _____ dort _____ d__ Zug nach Berlin?

O. MEINE TÜRKISCHE FREUNDIN. Ergänzen Sie **aus, außer, bei** oder **nach** und die Dativendungen!

1. Heute abend bin ich _____ mein__ Freundin Azat Gürlük zum Essen eingeladen.
2. Azats Eltern sind _____ d__ Türkei (*f*) und sind gerade für zwei Wochen _____ Istanbul geflogen.
3. Azat kocht sehr gut, und _____ d__ Cola ist das Essen _____ ihr immer echt° *typically* türkisch.

4. _____ d__ Essen wollen wir dann im Odeon einen türkischen Film anschauen.
5. Azats Vater arbeitet _____ d__ Deutschen Bundesbahn, und ihre Mutter ist Verkäuferin _____ Hertie°.

German department store chain

6. Gürlüks haben drei Kinder. _____ mein__ Freundin Azat leben sie aber nicht mehr _____ d__ Eltern.
7. Ich bin _____ d__ Vorlesungen oft _____ Gürlüks, und Frau Gürlük holt mir dann immer gleich eine Cola _____ d__ Kühlschrank.
8. Gürlüks wohnen in Gundelfingen _____ Freiburg. Sie haben einen kleinen Garten, aber _____ Tomaten wächst° dort nur türkisches Gemüse.

grow

9. Die Tomaten _____ Gürlüks Garten sind viel besser als die _____ unser__ Supermarkt.

4. INDICATING DESTINATION, ORIGIN, AND A POINT/PERIOD IN TIME

MORE ON DATIVE PREPOSITIONS

a. *Nach* versus *zu*

Nach and **zu** can both mean *to*. **Nach** is used to indicate that the point of destination is a city or a country. **Zu** is used to indicate that the point of destination is a building, an institution, someone's business, or place of residence.[1]

Wie lange arbeitet Dr. Huber am Freitag?

P. KLEINE GESPRÄCHE. Ergänzen Sie **nach** oder **zu** und die Dativendungen!

1. OLIVER: Wie weit ist es _____ eur__ Wochenendhaus?
   THOMAS: Fast doppelt so weit wie _____ Salzburg.
2. FRAU ROTH: Was soll ich denn tun, Frau Ziegler? Ich habe Zahnschmerzen,° und unser Zahnarzt° ist _____ Spanien geflogen.
   FRAU ZIEGLER: Gehen Sie doch _____ unser__ Zahnarzt.

a toothache
dentist

3. ANITA: _____ welch__ Disco fährst du deinen Freund Uwe?
   GÜNTER: _____ der beim Hotel Merkur.
4. FRAU KRÖGER: Warum fährt Herr Meyer denn so oft _____ Wien?
   FRAU SCHELL: Er geht dort _____ ein__ berühmten° Psychiater.

famous

5. CLAUDIA: Fährst du im April wieder _____ dein__ Onkel, Stephanie?
   STEPHANIE: Nein, diesmal fahre ich mit Peter _____ Berlin.

b. *Aus* versus *von*

Aus and **von** can both mean *from*. **Aus** is used to indicate that the point of origin is a city or a country. **Von** is used to indicate that the point of origin is a person, building, or an institution. **Von** is also used to indicate a point of departure as in *from point A to point B.*

---

1. The idiomatic expressions **nach Hause** and **zu Hause** which you learned in *Kapitel 6* do not conform to these rules: **ich gehe nach Hause** *I'm going home;* **ich bin zu Hause** *I'm at home.*

Q. KLEINE GESPRÄCHE. Ergänzen Sie **aus** oder **von** und die Dativendungen!

1. LISA: Ist diese schwedische Vase nicht schön?

   SYLVIA: Ja, sehr schön. _____ wem hast du sie?

   LISA: _____ ein_ Freund. Er ist _____ Stockholm.

2. CLAUDIA: Hier ist ein Brief für dich, Stephanie.

   STEPHANIE: Ist er _____ d_ Uni?

   CLAUDIA: Nein, er kommt _____ Amerika.

3. FRAU MEYER: Sind Sie Herr Ziegler _____ Bonn?

   HERR ZIEGLER: Ja, der bin ich.

   FRAU MEYER: Und Sie fahren morgen nach München?

   HERR ZIEGLER: Ja. Sagen Sie mal, wie lange braucht denn der Intercity _____ Stuttgart nach München?

Wie weit ist es von Stuttgart nach München?

		Erster Geltungstag	Zur Hinfahrt	Zur Rückfahrt	Ausgabe-Nr
DB				gültig bis einschließlich	
		30.06.86	29.08.86	29.08.86	183701
Klasse	2	HIN- UND RUECKFAHRT***		halber Preis	
	von	STUTTGART			
	nach	MUENCHEN HBF			
	über	DON/MM			143
Verkaufsstelle			Z A	km	DM
STUTTGART HBF			XX	0240	***70,00
				29037965	Bitte Rückseite beachten

R. WOHER? WO? WOHIN? Begin your questions with **woher, wo,** or **wohin;** your partner begins her/his answers with **aus, bei, nach, von,** or **zu.**

S1. Wohin fährt dieser Zug?   *S2.* Nach München.

---

1. _____ ist Stephanie?   _____ d_ USA.
2. _____ fliegen Bergers nächsten Sommer?   _____ Kanada.
3. _____ bist du nächsten Sonntag?   _____ mein_ Eltern.
4. _____ geht ihr?   _____ Helga.
5. _____ ist Thomas?   _____ sein_ Freundin.
6. _____ fliegen Sie diesen Winter, Frau Koch?   _____ Israel.
7. _____ kommt diese Schokolade?   _____ d_ Schweiz.
8. _____ ist die Party morgen abend?   _____ Brigitte.
9. _____ sollen wir heute essen?   _____ McDonald's.
10. _____ kommt ihr denn?   _____ Professor Seidlmeyer.
11. _____ geht ihr jetzt?   _____ mein_ Freundin.
12. _____ hast du diesen Ring?   _____ mein_ Freund.
13. _____ ist Martin?   _____ Professor Seidlmeyer.
14. _____ ist dieses Bier?   _____ München.
15. _____ fahrt ihr mit eurem Surfbrett?   _____ unser_ Wochenend-
                                                 haus (*n*) am Starnberger
                                                 See.
16. _____ gehst du?   _____ Professor Seidlmeyer.

EIN PAAR PERSÖNLICHE FRAGEN

a. Ask your partner from whom she/he got a certain piece of jewelry or article of clothing.

S1: Von wem hast du	den Ring?	*S2:* Den habe ich von . . .	
	die Halskette?	Die . . .	
	das Armband?	Das . . .	
	die Armbanduhr?	Die . . .	
	den Ohrring?	Den . . .	
	die Ohrringe?	Die . . .	
	den Pulli?	Den . . .	
	. . .		

b. Ask your partner about some of her/his plans.

S1: Was machst du nach	dieser Deutschstunde?	*S1:* Nach dieser Deutsch-stunde? Da . . .	
	dem Mittagessen?	Nach dem Mittagessen? Da . . .	
	dem Abendessen?	Nach dem Abendessen? Da . . .	
	den Schlußprüfun-gen?°	Nach den Schlußprüfun-gen? Da . . .	*final exams*

S1: Bei wem ist deine nächste Party?　　　　*S2:* Bei . . .
Bei wem war deine letzte Party?　　　　　Bei . . .

c. **The preposition *seit***

When **seit** refers to a *point in time* its English equivalent is *since;* when it refers to a *period of time* its English equivalent is *for.*

Seit wann haben Sie diesen Ford, Herr Schwarz?　　　　***How long have*** *you* ***had*** *this Ford, Mr. Schwarz?*
Seit einem Jahr.　　　　***For*** *a year.*

Seit wann haben Sie diesen BMW, Frau Stermann?　　　　***How long have*** *you* ***had*** *this BMW, Mrs. Stermann?*
Seit Montag.　　　　***Since*** *Monday.*

As the examples show, the preposition **seit** is used when talking about actions or situations that have begun in the past and continue in the present. Whereas English uses a perfect tense in such contexts, German uses the present tense.

S. SEIT WANN? You want to know how long certain people have been doing things. Your partner knows the answer.

▶ sein/Frau Burgmüller im Krankenhaus   ein Monat

S1: Seit wann ist Frau Burgmüller im Krankenhaus?   *S2:* Seit einem Monat.

---

car accident
engaged
party

1. fahren/du mit dem Bus zur Uni   mein Autounfall°
2. sein/Karin verlobt°   eine Woche
3. ausgehen/Sandra mit Holger   die Fete° bei Sylvia
4. haben/du diesen Computer   ein Vierteljahr
5. kennen/Sie Frau Huber   ein Jahr
6. haben/du dieses tolle Fahrrad   mein Geburtstag

heart attack

7. joggen gehen/Sie jeden Morgen   mein Herzanfall°
8. arbeiten/Sie hier bei Bosch   zwanzig Jahre
9. trinken/Stephanie Bier   ihr Jahr in München
10. haben/du diesen Kassettenrecor-   Weihnachten
    der

SEIT WANN?

Find out how long your classmates have been doing or how long they have had certain things.

S1: Spielst du ein Instrument?   *S2:* Ja, ich spiele . . .
      Seit wann?   Seit . . . Jahren
                                                (Monaten, usw.).
                                                Seit 1987 (September,
                                                usw.).

      Arbeitest du? Wo? Seit wann?   . . .
      Treibst du Sport? Seit wann?   . . .
      Hast du einen Freund/eine Freundin? Seit wann?   . . .
               einen Computer?
driver's license   einen Führerschein°?
               einen Wagen?
               . . .

CONTRACTIONS

The following preposition-article contractions are common. Consider these contractions mandatory for the time being.

hairdresser

Wo ist Brigitte?—**Beim** Friseur.°   **beim** = bei + dem
Sind diese Eier direkt **vom** Bauer?   **vom** = von + dem

airport

Fährt dieser Bus **zum** Flughafen?°   **zum** = zu + dem
Fährst du heute mit dem Auto **zur** Uni?   **zur** = zu + der

---

T. WO GEHST DU HIN? The German question words **woher** and **wohin** are often split. The question then begins with **wo** and ends with **hin** or **her.** In the following exercise you use **wo, wo . . . her,** or **wo . . . hin** in the questions. Your partner uses the contractions **beim, vom, zum,** or **zur** in the responses.

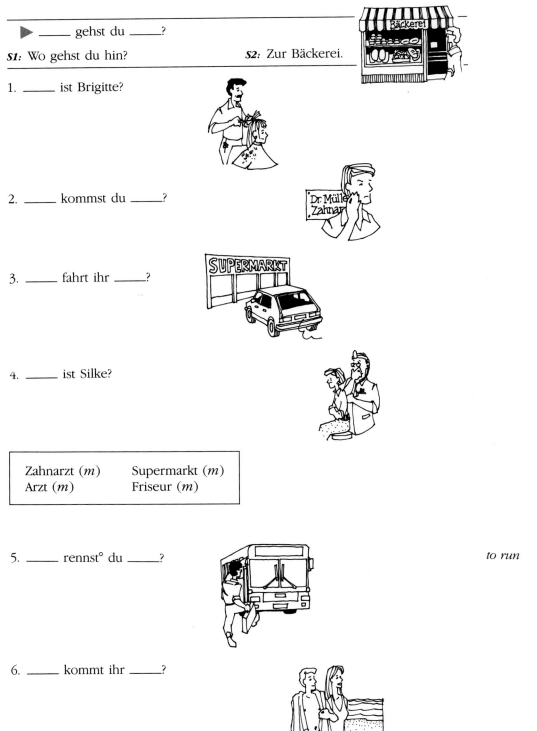

▶ _____ gehst du _____?

S1: Wo gehst du hin?   *S2:* Zur Bäckerei.

1. _____ ist Brigitte?

2. _____ kommst du _____?

3. _____ fahrt ihr _____?

4. _____ ist Silke?

Zahnarzt (*m*)	Supermarkt (*m*)
Arzt (*m*)	Friseur (*m*)

5. _____ rennst° du _____?   *to run*

6. _____ kommt ihr _____?

---

7. _____ gehst du _____?

8. _____ sind Bernd
und Sabine?

9. _____ fahrt ihr _____?

Fleischerei (*f*)	Bus (*m*)
Baden (*n*)	Flughafen (*m*)
	Mittagessen (*n*)

SPRACHNOTIZEN

Word order: time, manner, place

You have already learned that expressions of time precede expressions of place.

Wir sind **letztes Wochenende nach Starnberg** gefahren.

When expressions of manner are added, the order is *time, manner, place*.

Wir sind letztes Wochenende **mit Bernds Wagen** nach Starnberg gefahren.

5. USING VERBS LIKE *ANTWORTEN, DANKEN,* AND *HELFEN*

DATIVE VERBS

There are a few German verbs that always take a *dative* object.

antworten	*to answer*	Warum hast du **mir** nicht geantwortet?	*Why didn't you answer me?*
danken	*to thank*	Ich kann **Ihnen** nicht genug danken.	*I can't thank you enough.*

glauben	to believe	Warum glaubst du **ihm** nicht?	*Why don't you believe him?*
helfen[1]	to help	Hilf **mir** doch bitte bei meinem Referat.	*Please help me with my report.*
gehören	to belong to	Gehört dieser Wagen **dir?**	*Does this car belong to you?*
gefallen[1]	to like	Wie gefällt **euch** mein neuer Pullover?	*How do you like my new sweater?* (Literally: *How does my new sweater appeal to you?*)

U. WAS PASST WO?   Note that some of the verb forms are used more than once.

antwortet   glaubt   danken   gehört   helfen   gefällt

1. Warum sagst du uns nicht, wo du warst?
   Ihr _____ mir ja doch nicht.
2. Wem _____ dieser tolle Wagen?
   Meiner Freundin.
3. Warum schreibst du denn deiner Kusine Christa nie?
   Sie _____ mir ja doch nicht.
4. Wie findest du mein neues Kleid?
   Es _____ mir gar nicht.
5. Warum kommst du denn nicht zu unserer Party?
   Ich muß meinem Vater _____.
6. Warum schenkst du deiner Klavierlehrerin Blumen?
   Ich möchte ihr für den guten Unterricht° _____.   *lessons*
7. Sind Krögers sehr reich?
   Ja, denen _____ fast die halbe Stadt°.   *town*
8. Wie _____ dir meine neue Jacke?
   Ich finde sie sehr schön.
9. Ist das dein Mantel?
   Ja, der _____ mir.
10. Warum _____ ihr Kurt nicht?
    Der Kerl lügt doch wie gedruckt.

V. DIR ODER DICH?

1. Ich muß _____ etwas fragen.
2. Ich kann _____ jetzt nicht helfen.
3. Komm, ich lade _____ zum Mittagessen ein.
4. Ich glaube _____ nicht.
5. Wie gefällt _____ mein neuer Wagen?
6. Wann soll ich _____ abholen?
7. Der Wagen gehört _____ doch gar nicht.
8. Hat Tina _____ angerufen?

---

1. **Helfen** and **gefallen** are irregular verbs: **helfen (hilft), hat geholfen; gefallen (gefällt), hat gefallen.**

9. Sie will _____ für die schönen Rosen danken.
10. Hat Irene _____ immer noch nicht geantwortet?
11. Vielleicht mag sie _____ nicht.

WELCHE FRISUR GEFÄLLT DIR BESSER?

🔲🔲 Ask your partner to compare the hairdos (haircuts, glasses, earrings) of two classmates and say which she/he likes better.

S1: Welche Frisur gefällt dir besser, die von Cindy oder die von Lisa?   *S2:* Die von Lisa gefällt mir besser.

| die Frisur | *hairdo* | die Brille (*singular!*) | *glasses* |
| der Haarschnitt | *haircut* | die Ohrringe | *earrings* |

6. EXPRESSING PERSONAL OPINIONS

THE DATIVE CASE WITH ADJECTIVES AND IN IDIOMATIC EXPRESSIONS

The dative case is often used with adjectives in expressions like the following.

Das ist **ihm** sehr wichtig.   *That's very important **to him.***
Das ist **mir** zu früh (zu spät, zu teuer usw.).   *That's too early (too late, too expensive etc.) **for me.***

reason **W. WAS IST DER GRUND°?** Complete your questions with the verbs provided. Your partner chooses appropriate adjectives from the list below in her/his responses.

▶ Warum _____ Claudia diesen Joghurt nicht **(mögen)**   Er ist _____ zu _____.

S1: Warum mag Claudia diesen Joghurt nicht?   *S2:* Er ist ihr zu sauer.

---

1. Warum _____ David den Wagen nicht? **(kaufen)**   Er ist _____ zu _____.
2. Was _____ Eva denn gegen ihre neue Zimmerkollegin? **(haben)**   Sie ist _____ zu _____.
3. Warum _____ dir Stephanies neues Kleid nicht? **(gefallen)**   Es ist _____ zu _____.
4. Warum _____ deine Eltern denn keine Rockmusik? **(mögen)**   Sie ist _____ zu _____.
5. Warum _____ Ingrid ihren Wein nicht _____? **(austrinken)**   Er ist _____ zu _____.
6. Was _____ Monika denn gegen Günter? **(haben)**   Er ist _____ zu _____.
7. Warum _____ du den Roman nicht _____? **(fertiglesen)**   Er ist _____ zu _____.
8. Warum _____ ihr Bernd nicht _____? **(einladen)**   Er ist _____ zu _____.

9. Warum _____ deine Eltern das Haus nicht? Es ist _____ zu _____.
   (kaufen)
10. Was _____ dein Vater gegen deine Freunde? Sie sind _____ zu _____.
    (haben)
11. Warum _____ ihr denn nicht _____? **(spazieren-** Es ist _____ zu _____.
    gehen)
12. Warum _____ du denn deinen Kaffee nicht? Er ist _____ zu _____.
    (trinken)

kurz	sauer	teuer	klein	heiß	langweilig
frech	kalt	doof	laut	groß	lang

The dative case also appears in the following common idiomatic expressions:

Es tut **mir** leid.   *I'm sorry.*

Das ist **mir** egal.   *I don't care. It's all the same to me.*

Wie geht es **Ihnen?**   *How are you?*

Mir fällt nichts ein.   *I can't think of anything.*

Steht **mir** diese Jacke?   *Does this jacket look good on me?*

X. WAS PASST ZUSAMMEN?

1. Wie gefällt dir meine neue Jacke, Claudia?

   Nein, es steht mir nicht.

2. Warum schreibst du den Brief denn nicht fertig, Peter?

   Ja, aber ich glaube, das ist ihm ganz egal.

3. Ist deine Mutter immer noch so krank, Sybille?

   Mir fällt nichts mehr ein.

4. Stephanie geht es heute gar nicht gut.

   Ja, aber ihr Name fällt mir im Moment nicht ein.

5. Warum kaufst du das Kleid nicht? Ist es dir zu teuer?

   Nein, es geht ihr schon wieder viel besser.

6. Kennst du die Frau dort, Antje?

   Sie steht dir sehr gut.

7. Weiß Günter, wie traurig° Helga ist?

   Das tut mir sehr leid.   *sad*

DIE GESCHMÄCKER SIND VERSCHIEDEN

If you were buying Christmas gifts for your classmates, what would you buy them? Give a reason for your choice. The words and expressions below may give you some ideas.

S1: Was schenkst du Lisa?   *S2:* Lisa? Der schenke ich einen Pulli. Ihr Pulli ist mir nicht flott genug.

too loud (of colors)	viel zu konservativ	ein bißchen zu knallig°
stylish	nicht flott° genug	ein bißchen zu verrückt
old-fashioned	ein bißchen zu altmodisch°	usw.

die Jacke	das Hemd	die Schuhe
der Pullover	das Kleid	ein Paar Schuhe
das Sweatshirt	der Rock	die Ohrringe
die Bluse	die Hose	ein Paar Ohrringe
		usw.

 ## ZUSAMMENSCHAU

hole

DAS LOCH° IM PULLI

Lesen Sie Claudias Brief an ihre Eltern!

München, den 28. Oktober 1991

Liebe Eltern,

in order

Ich bin doch nicht so dumm, wie Ihr denkt, und ich glaube, ich komme auch ganz gut allein durchs Leben. Aber vielleicht erzähle ich Euch alles der Reihe nach.°

you see/one/skirt
put on

Gestern nachmittag habe ich bei Karstadt für sechzig Mark einen grauen Pulli gekauft. Ich brauche nämlich° einen° zu meinem grauen Rock.° Heute morgen habe ich den Pulli dann zum erstenmal angezogen,° und da habe ich ein Loch gefunden. Ich bin deshalb gleich nach meiner letzten Vorlesung zu Karstadt zurückgegangen und habe der Verkäuferin das Loch gezeigt. Sie hat den gleichen°

same

grauen Pulli nochmal gesucht, hatte aber nur noch braune, rote und grüne Acht-

size thirty-eight
mend
mending yarn
okay/tough

unddreißiger.° Da habe ich gesagt, ich brauche den grauen Pulli, und sie sollen ihn flicken.° Sie flicken aber nicht bei Karstadt, und so hat die Verkäuferin mir einfach ein bißchen graue Flickwolle° gegeben und geglaubt, dann ist alles in Ordnung.° Da bin ich aber energisch° geworden. „Na hören Sie mal!" habe ich gesagt, „da muß ich zweimal hierherkommen, soll das Loch selber flicken und noch den vollen Preis bezahlen!? Da geben Sie mir den Pulli lieber mal ein ganz schönes bißchen billiger!"

department manager

Natürlich ist die Verkäuferin dann erst zum Abteilungsleiter° gegangen. Aber ich habe Schwein gehabt.[1] Sie ist von dort ganz lustig zurückgekommen und hat mir volle zwanzig Mark zurückgegeben!—Habe ich das nicht gut gemacht?

that's all

Heute nachmittag habe ich das Loch schön geflickt, und jetzt gehe ich dann gleich im grauen Rock und grauen Pulli auf eine Party. Deshalb Schluß° für heute.

Viele liebe Grüße

Eure

Claudia

---

1. **Schwein haben** is a colloquial equivalent for **Glück haben** (*to be lucky*). Owning a fat pig was once considered to be a sign of prosperity and good fortune.

WAS SIND DIE RICHTIGEN ANTWORTEN?   Your instructor will read two questions for each set of responses. On the basis of Claudia's letter to her parents, decide which *two* responses in each set are correct.

1. a. Heute morgen.
   b. Gestern nachmittag.
   c. Heute nach ihrer letzten Vorlesung.
2. a. Sie hatte keine grauen Achtunddreißiger mehr.
   b. Sie braucht ihn zu ihrem grauen Rock.
   c. Ihr Pulli hat ein Loch.
3. a. Zwanzig Mark.
   b. Vierzig Mark.
   c. Sechzig Mark.
4. a. Auf eine Party.
   b. Zu Karstadt.
   c. Zum Abteilungsleiter.
5. a. Claudia.
   b. Der Verkäuferin.
   c. Ihren Eltern.
6. a. Die Verkäuferin.
   b. Ihre Eltern.
   c. Claudia.

Listen to Claudia's conversation with the salesperson at Karstadt's. Identify the speaker and indicate the order in which you hear the following statements or questions.

___ Na, ich kann ja fragen. Ich kann den Abteilungsleiter fragen.

___ Sagen Sie, können Sie flicken?

___ Achtunddreißig, Größe achtunddreißig, und wieder in Grau, bitte.

___ Sie haben aber mal Glück!

___ Nein, nein, der Pulli gefällt mir. Es ist nur dieses Loch.

___ Zwanzig Mark, das ist nicht schlecht!

___ Sie flicken Ihren Pulli selber, und alles ist in Ordnung, nicht?

___ Das tut mir aber leid. Wir haben diesen Pulli aber sicher nochmal.

___ Aber ich brauche den Pulli doch. Kann man das Loch denn nicht flicken?

___ Da geben Sie mir den Pulli lieber mal ein ganz schönes bißchen billiger.

Write Claudia's reactions to the following statements or questions of the salesperson.

1. Wir haben diesen Pulli aber sicher nochmal. Oder wollen Sie lieber Ihr Geld zurück?
2. Da habe ich noch braun, rot und grün . . . , aber grau . . . ?
3. Sagen Sie, können Sie flicken?
4. Ja, dann gebe ich Ihnen doch ein bißchen Flickwolle. Sie flicken Ihren Pulli selber, und alles ist in Ordnung, nicht?
5. Sie haben aber mal Glück!

Write the salesperson's reactions to Claudia's statements or questions.

1. Sehen Sie, hier! . . . Da habe ich dieses Loch gefunden.
2. Aber ich brauche den Pulli doch. Kann man das Loch denn nicht flicken?
3. Ja, natürlich kann ich flicken.
4. Da geben Sie mir den Pulli lieber mal ein ganz schönes bißchen billiger.
5. Zwanzig Mark, das ist nicht schlecht!

GIBT ES DENN GAR KEINE QUALITÄT MEHR?

You are dissatisfied with a piece of merchandise that you bought yesterday, and you are returning it to the store. Your partner plays the role of the salesperson.

Some expressions that may be helpful to the customer:

> Gestern habe ich hier bei Ihnen dies___ _____ gekauft.
> Sehen Sie mal, hier!
> Er/sie/es hat ein Loch.
> ist ganz zerrissen°.   *ripped*
>
> ist kaputt.
> schon ganz rostig.
> ganz verkratzt°.   *scratched*
>
> läuft nicht.
> funktioniert nicht.
> Ich möchte einen neuen (eine neue, ein neues) _____.
> Ich möchte lieber mein Geld zurück.

ripped

scratched

Some expressions that may be helpful to the salesperson:

easily

> Das kann doch gar nicht sein.
> Wirklich, das ist . . .
> Das tut mir aber leid.
> Das können wir leicht° reparieren.
> Wir haben dies___ _____ sicher nochmal (leider nicht nochmal).
> Da muß ich erst den Abteilungsleiter fragen.

Apart from **Weihnachten,** other religious holidays **(Kirchliche Feiertage)** are observed throughout the German-speaking countries. Good Friday **(Karfreitag),** Easter **(Ostern),** a two-day holiday celebrated on **Ostersonntag** and **Ostermontag,** Ascension Thursday **(Christi Himmelfahrt),** and Pentecost **(Pfingsten),** which is celebrated on the seventh Sunday and Monday after Easter.

There are important secular holidays as well. May 1, International Workers' Day **(Tag der Arbeit),** is a holiday in all the German-speaking countries. Since 1965, Austrians have set aside October 26 as **Tag der Fahne** (*Flag Day*) to commemorate the day in 1955 when Austria became a neutral, non-aligned state. On August 1, the Swiss commemorate the founding of the **Confoederatio Helvetica** in 1291.

Viele Feiertage sind kirchliche Feiertage.

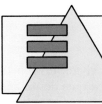

WORT, SINN UND KLANG

WÖRTER UNTER DER LUPE

1. PREDICTING GENDER

Infinitive forms of verbs are often used as nouns. Such nouns are always *neuter* and they are, of course, capitalized. Their English equivalents usually end in *-ing.*

Wann gibst du endlich **das Rauchen** auf?

When are you finally going to give up ***smoking?***

Wie heißt diese Organisation in Nordamerika?

When the contraction **beim** is followed by such a noun, it often means *while.*

Gestern abend bin ich **beim Fernsehen** eingeschlafen.   *Last night I fell asleep **while watching TV.***

- Complete the following sentences with the correct nouns from the list below.

  (das) Schwimmen   (das) Wissen   (das) Leben
  (das) Einkaufen   (das) Trinken   (das) Schreiben

1. Dieses faule ＿＿＿ gefällt mir.
2. Gestern haben wir beim ＿＿＿ fast fünfhundert Mark ausgegeben.
3. Fang doch endlich mit deinem Referat an! Vielleicht fällt dir beim ＿＿＿ etwas ein.
4. Das viele ＿＿＿ hat diesen Mann krank gemacht.
5. Helga ist gestern abend ohne Günters ＿＿＿ mit Holger ausgegangen.
6. ＿＿＿ ist sehr gesund.

2. GIVING LANGUAGE COLOR

Like other languages, German has many colorful expressions to characterize people. Many of these expressions make use of the real or imagined qualities of animals. The expressions below use the following animals.

sheep
snake

der Bär   das Schaf°
der Fuchs   die Schlange°
der Wolf   die Ratte
der Wurm

- Ergänzen Sie!

sly
*sheepskin/**der Kopf:** head*

eine falsche Schlange   ein Bücherwurm   eine Leseratte
ein schlauer° Fuchs   Wasserratte   Schlafratte
ein Wolf im Schafspelz°   Bärenhunger   Schafskopf°
das schwarze Schaf

1. Steh doch endlich auf, du . . . ! Es ist schon fast ein Uhr nachmittags.
2. Heike hat gesagt, sie liebt mich, und jetzt ist sie mit Kurt ausgegangen.
   Ich habe dir doch gleich gesagt, sie ist . . .
3. Dieter ist . . . Er verdient 5 000 Mark im Monat und bezahlt keinen Pfennig
   Steuer°.   *tax*
4. Mein Bruder ist so . . . Er liest von morgens bis abends.
   Genau wie meine Schwester! Die ist auch so . . .
5. Mit seinen miserablen Zensuren ist Christian . . . in dieser intellektuellen
   Familie.
6. Was?! Du willst mit Günter ausgehen?
   Ja, warum denn nicht? Er ist doch ein netter Kerl.
   Ja denkste! . . . ist er, dieser nette Kerl.
7. Antje ist eine richtige . . . Sie ist den ganzen Tag im Swimmingpool.
8. Was gibt's zu essen? Ich habe einen . . . !
9. Aber Bernd! Du machst ja alles falsch, du . . . !

WEITERE NÜTZLICHE WÖRTER UND AUSDRÜCKE

Kleidungsstücke *(Articles of clothing)*

das Hemd, die Hemden	shirt
der Schlips, die Schlipse	tie
die Hose, die Hosen	pants
ein Paar Hosen	a pair of pants
die Jeans (*pl*)	jeans
die Socke, die Socken	sock
der Schuh, die Schuhe	shoe
der Mantel, die Mäntel	coat
der Schal, die Schals	scarf
der Pullover, die Pullover	sweater
der Pulli, die Pullis	
das Sweatshirt, die Sweatshirts	sweatshirt
die Bluse, die Blusen	blouse
der Rock, die Röcke	skirt
das Kleid, die Kleider	dress
der Hut, die Hüte	hat
der Handschuh, die Handschuhe	glove
die Jacke, die Jacken	jacket
der Hausschuh, die Hausschuhe	slipper

Das Gegenteil

an•ziehen, hat angezogen—aus•ziehen,	to put on—to take off
hat ausgezogen	

Festtage und Geschenke (*Special days and gifts*)

das Weihnachten	Christmas
zu Weihnachten	for Christmas
das Weihnachtsgeschenk, die	Christmas present
Weihnachtsgeschenke	
der Geburtstag, die Geburtstage	birthday
zum Geburtstag	for one's birthday

der Ohrring, die Ohrringe	earring
das Armband, die Armbänder	bracelet
die Armbanduhr, die Armbanduhren	wrist watch
das Parfüm	perfume
der Geldbeutel, die Geldbeutel	wallet
der Rasierapparat, die Rasierapparate	razor
der Kugelschreiber, die Kugelschreiber	ball-point pen
eine Flasche Wein	a bottle of wine

Verben mit zwei Objekten

geben (gibt), hat gegeben	to give
schenken	to give (*as a gift*)
schicken	to send
zeigen	to show

Dativverben

antworten	to answer
danken	to thank
glauben	to believe
helfen (hilft), hat geholfen	to help
gehören	to belong to
gefallen (gefällt), hat gefallen,	to please
Deine Jeans gefallen mir.	I like your jeans.

Die Dativpräpositionen

aus	out of; from
außer	except for
bei	at, at the home of
mit	with; by
nach	after; to
seit	since, for (*a period of time*)
von	from; of
zu	to, to the home of

Ausdrücke

Es tut mir leid.	I'm sorry.
Das ist mir egal.	I don't care.
Steht mir diese Jacke?	Does this jacket suit me (look good on me)?
Du hast Glück.	You're lucky.
in Ordnung	O.K.

WÖRTER IM KONTEXT

1. WAS PASST NICHT?

a. der Schuh	b. das Hemd	c. die Jacke	d. die Jeans	e. der Geburtstag
der Hausschuh	die Hose	das Armband	der Rock	der Rasierapparat
der Handschuh	die Bluse	der Mantel	die Hose	der Geldbeutel
die Socken	der Pulli	das Kleid	die Bluse	der Kugelschreiber

2. WAS PASST WO?

gefallen   gehören   zeigen   schicken   schenken

a. Meine Eltern _____ mir jeden Monat ein Paket.°   *parcel*
b. Was soll ich dir zu Weihnachten _____?
c. Eva will uns heute abend ihre neue Wohnung° _____.   *apartment*
d. Wie _____ dir meine neuen Ohrringe?
e. Wem _____ diese Handschuhe hier, dir oder Peter?

3. WAS PASST ZUSAMMEN?

a. Mir geht es heute gar nicht gut.   Da hast du aber Glück gehabt.
b. Ich habe den Pulli ganze zwanzig   Sie steht dir sehr gut.
   Mark billiger bekommen.
c. Soll ich meiner Schwester ein Arm-   Das tut mir aber leid.
   band oder ein Paar Ohrringe
   schenken?
d. Wie gefällt dir meine neue Jacke?   Das ist mir egal.

ZUR AUSSPRACHE

GERMAN *L*

In English the sound represented by the letter *l* varies according to the vowels and consonants surrounding it. (Compare the *l* sound in *leaf* and *feel.*) In German the sound represented by the letter *l* *never* varies and it is very close to the *l* in English *leaf.* Try to maintain the sound quality of the *l* in *leaf* throughout the exercise below.

• Hören Sie gut zu und wiederholen Sie!

Lilo **l**ernt **L**atein.
Latein ist manchma**l l**angwei**l**ig.
Lilo **l**ernt Phi**l**ipp kennen.
Phi**l**ipp hi**l**ft **Li**lo **L**atein **l**ernen.
Phi**l**ipp b**l**eibt **l**ange bei **Li**lo.
Lilo **l**ernt vie**l**.
Lilo **l**ernt Phi**l**ipp **l**ieben.°   *to love*

LATEINPROBLEME? – Höchste Erfolgsquote durch bewährtes Intensivprogramm. Der Pauker. 0 55 74/25 27 65. 5552/U

Ein süddeutsches Gasthaus

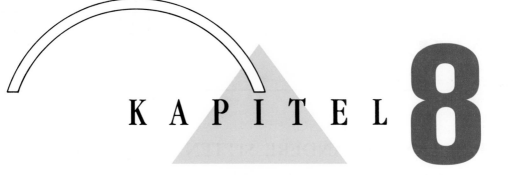

KAPITEL 8

■ **Kommunikationsziele**

*In **Kapitel 8*** you will learn how to:
discuss cultural differences
order a meal in a restaurant
talk about plans and intentions
talk about lifestyles
hold your own in an argument

■ **Hör- und Sprechsituationen**

Andere Länder, andere Sitten
Was machen deine Eltern selbst? Was lassen sie
  machen?
Was hast du heute abend vor?
Im Gasthaus
Da ist ein Haar in der Suppe!
Lebst du gesund oder ungesund?
Was gefällt Ihnen an Ihren Mitstudenten/Mitstuden-
  tinnen?
Günter Schlumberger soll einkaufen gehen
Eine kleine Auseinandersetzung

■ **Strukturen**

The verb **lassen:** *to have something done*
Infinitive phrases
**um . . . zu, ohne . . . zu, nicht
  brauchen . . . zu**
Coordinating and subordinating conjunctions
Indirect questions

■ **Wissenswertes**

Eating in restaurants
Apotheke, Drogerie, Reformhaus
Table etiquette
Würstchenbuden, Schnellimbiß
Supermarkets and specialty stores

VORSCHAU

📼 ANDERE LÄNDER, ANDERE SITTEN°   *customs*

Claudias Lieblingstante° lebt in Leonberg bei Stuttgart und hat Claudia und Ste-   *favorite aunt*
phanie auf ein paar Tage zu sich° eingeladen. Heute früh sind die beiden mit der   *to her house*
S-Bahn von Leonberg nach Stuttgart gefahren. Sie haben den ganzen Vormittag
Schaufenster angeschaut und sind jetzt recht müde und hungrig.

STEPHANIE:	Du, jetzt habe ich aber Hunger. Weißt du, wo man hier gut ißt?	
CLAUDIA:	Ja, gleich um die Ecke ist ein gutes Gasthaus°. Schau, dort hängt die Speisekarte°.	*restaurant* *menu*
STEPHANIE:	Ich habe Lust auf° Fisch. Mal sehen, ob° die das haben. Ja, hier: Schellfisch° gebacken mit Kartoffelsalat. Das esse ich.	*I feel like having / whether* *haddock*
CLAUDIA:	Gut, gehen wir hinein!	
STEPHANIE:	Du, das ist aber voll. Da ist ja gar kein Tisch° frei.	*table*
CLAUDIA:	Das macht doch nichts°. Dort sind zwei freie Plätze. Komm. — Entschuldigung, sind diese beiden Plätze noch frei?	*that doesn't matter*
FRAU:	Ja, bitte.	
STEPHANIE:	Endlich mal wieder sitzen, das tut gut.	
KELLNER:	Guten Tag. Was darf's sein, meine Damen?	
STEPHANIE:	Ich möchte Schellfisch mit Kartoffelsalat und eine Cola.	
KELLNER:	Und Sie, meine Dame?	
STEPHANIE:	Iß doch Wiener Schnitzel°, das magst du doch so.	*breaded veal cutlet*
FRAU:	Das Wiener Schnitzel ist heute sehr gut.	
CLAUDIA:	Ja, dann bringen Sie mir doch ein Wiener Schnitzel und ein kleines Bier.	
STEPHANIE:	Sag mal, Claudia, ich verstehe da was° nicht so ganz. Im Studentenheim und auch bei deiner Tante sind immer alle Türen° zu°, und um die Gärten habt ihr überall Zäune und Hecken. Das wirkt° so unfreundlich, weißt du. Aber hier im Gasthaus sitzt ihr eng° zusammen und eßt ganz freundlich miteinander. Da stimmt doch was nicht ganz°, oder?	colloquial for **etwas** *doors / closed* *makes an impression* *close* *that doesn't quite make sense*
CLAUDIA:	Was soll denn da nicht stimmen, Stephanie? Das ist doch ganz normal.	
FRAU:	Ich verstehe, was Ihre Freundin meint°. Sie sind aus Amerika, nicht? Ich war letztes Jahr in Amerika und habe Freunde besucht. Da waren immer alle Türen offen im Haus, und die Gärten hatten keine Zäune und keine Hecken. Aber im Gasthaus waren fast alle Tische halb leer°, weil drüben° niemand° mit Fremden° zusammen essen möchte.	*means* *empty* *over there / nobody / strangers*
STEPHANIE:	Ja, so ist es bei uns. Zu Hause sind wir Amerikaner frei und offen, aber im Gasthaus brauchen wir unsere Privatsphäre.	
CLAUDIA:	Gibt es da Gründe° für diese Unterschiede°? Da muß es doch Gründe geben.	*reasons / differences*
FRAU:	Ja, sicher gibt es Gründe. Ich habe da auch so meine Theorien, aber ich weiß natürlich nicht, ob sie richtig sind.	

CLAUDIA:	Sagen Sie uns doch, was Sie denken.	
FRAU:	Na, Sie wissen ja, daß° wir hier immer sehr viele Menschen hatten und sehr wenig Land. Und so hat jeder um sein bißchen Land einen Zaun gebaut°, und wenn° er überhaupt ein eigenes° Zimmer hatte, dann hat er die Tür zugemacht°, um endlich mal allein zu sein.	*that* *built / if / own* *closed*
STEPHANIE:	Ja, und dann sind diese Leute aus dem engen Europa in das riesige° Amerika gekommen und hatten plötzlich so viel Land und so viel Platz. Da haben sie natürlich keine Zäune mehr gebraucht.	*huge*
CLAUDIA:	Das klingt° recht überzeugend°. Aber warum sind die Amerikaner dann im Gasthaus so reserviert? Das paßt doch nicht.	*sounds / convincing*
FRAU:	Nein, reserviert sind die Amerikaner natürlich nicht. Aber sie haben auch im Gasthaus mehr Platz als wir. Bei uns müssen die Gäste oft zusammenrücken°, wenn sie etwas zu essen bekommen wollen.	*move closer together*
STEPHANIE:	Eine interessante Theorie.	
FRAU:	Ja, aber sehr wissenschaftlich° ist sie natürlich nicht.	*scientific*
KELLNER:	Entschuldigung. Einmal Schellfisch, bitte schön.	
STEPHANIE:	Mmm, das sieht aber gut aus.°	**sieht . . . aus:** *looks*
KELLNER:	Und ein Wiener Schnitzel.	
CLAUDIA:	Danke schön.	
FRAU:	Na, dann wünsche° ich Ihnen mal einen recht guten Appetit!	*wish*

VOM LESEN ZUM SPRECHEN

WO IST DAS, IN DEUTSCHLAND ODER IN AMERIKA?   On the basis of *Andere Länder, andere Sitten* indicate which country is being referred to.

1. Hier machen die Studenten im Studentenheim ihre Türen meistens zu.
2. Hier bauen die meisten Leute um ihr bißchen Land einen Zaun.
3. Hier denken die Leute, das Gasthaus ist voll, wenn kein ganzer Tisch mehr frei ist.
4. Hier ist ein Gasthaus erst dann ganz voll, wenn gar keine Plätze mehr frei sind.
5. Hier haben die meisten Gärten keine Zäune und keine Hecken.
6. Hier sitzen die Leute im Gasthaus oft mit Fremden zusammen.
7. Hier gibt es sehr viele Menschen und sehr wenig Land.
8. Hier lassen die Studenten im Studentenheim ihre Türen meistens offen.
9. Hier pflanzen die Leute oft Hecken um ihre Gärten.
10. Hier gibt es in Privathäusern oft nicht viel Privatsphäre.

The German-speaking countries have restaurant customs that differ from those in North America. The menu is usually posted outside a **Restaurant** or **Gasthaus** for people to study before deciding whether or not to go inside. If all the tables in a restaurant are occupied, it is common to approach a person at a table with empty places and ask if you may sit there. One would say **Entschuldigung, ist dieser Platz noch frei?** However, for more formal dining, it is customary to reserve a private table.

Der Kaffee ist ja teurer als der Kuchen!

Essen Sie gern türkische Spezialitäten?

A glass of ice water is not commonly served in the German-speaking countries and ice is also not served in soft drinks. There is a small charge for bread and butter. When one asks for the check at the end of a meal, the server figures out the bill directly at the table, repeating aloud what has been ordered. The price of the meal includes a service charge **(Bedienungsgeld)** of 15%. One pays immediately upon receiving the bill and the server gives change from a purse that she/he carries. As an extra tip **(Trinkgeld)** it is customary to round the bill off (e.g., paying 13 marks if the bill comes to 12.35). Tips are not left on the table.

 WAS SIND DIE RICHTIGEN ANTWORTEN? Your instructor will read eight questions. On the basis of *Andere Länder, andere Sitten,* decide whether *a.* or *b.* is the correct response.

1. a. Weil sie heute früh mit der S-Bahn nach Stuttgart gefahren sind.
   b. Weil sie den ganzen Vormittag Schaufenster angeschaut haben.

2. a. Weil sie Wiener Schnitzel so mag.
   b. Weil sie Lust auf Fisch hat.

3. a. Weil im ganzen Gasthaus kein freier Tisch mehr ist.
   b. Weil die Frau so interessante Theorien hat.
4. a. Weil sie müde und hungrig ist.
   b. Weil sie noch nie in Amerika war.
5. a. Weil sie aus Amerika kommt.
   b. Weil sie müde und hungrig ist.
6. a. Weil sie letztes Jahr drüben war.
   b. Weil sie aus Amerika ist.
7. a. Weil die Amerikaner viel mehr Land haben als die Deutschen.
   b. Weil die Deutschen so wenig Land haben.
8. a. Weil sie unfreundlich sind.
   b. Weil sie auch mal allein sein wollen.

 ## ANDERE LÄNDER, ANDERE SITTEN

Interview a classmate who is from a different country/region or who has visited a different country/region. In your interview concentrate on cultural differences. Take notes and report your findings to the rest of the class. Below are some questions that you could ask.

Woher bist du?	**Wo warst du?**
Seit wann bist du hier?	Wann war das?
Was ist hier anders als bei euch?	Wie lange warst du dort?
Welche Sitten gefallen dir hier besonders gut? Warum?	Was hast du dort gemacht?
Welche Sitten gefallen dir hier nicht so gut? Warum?	Was war dort anders als hier?
Was hat dir bei euch zu Hause besser gefallen?	Welche Sitten haben dir dort besonders gut gefallen? Warum?
	Welche Sitten haben dir dort nicht so gut gefallen? Warum?

NÜTZLICHE WÖRTER UND AUSDRÜCKE

Nomen

das Gasthaus, die Gasthäuser	restaurant
der Gast, die Gäste	guest; customer *(in a restaurant)*
der Kellner, die Kellner	waiter
die Kellnerin, die Kellnerinnen	waitress
der/die Fremde, die Fremden	stranger
die Dame, die Damen	lady
der Tisch, die Tische	table
der Platz, die Plätze	place, seat; space
die Speisekarte, die Speisekarten	menu
die Ecke, die Ecken	corner

Nomen

die Tür, die Türen	door
das Schaufenster, die Schaufenster	display window
die Theorie, die Theorien	theory
der Grund, die Gründe	reason
der Unterschied, die Unterschiede	difference

Verben

hinein•gehen, ist hineingegangen	to go in
zu•machen	to close
meinen	to mean; to think
wünschen	to wish
bauen	to build

Andere Wörter

beide	both; two
zusammen	together
miteinander	with each other
drüben, dort drüben	over there
überall	everywhere
recht	quite; very

Ausdrücke

Das tut gut.	That feels good.
Das macht nichts.	That doesn't matter.
Das sieht gut aus.	That looks good.
Was darf's sein?	What would you like?
Ich habe Lust auf Fisch.	I feel like having fish.
Guten Appetit!	Enjoy your meal!
gleich um die Ecke	right around the corner
auf ein paar Tage	for a few days

Das Gegenteil

voll — leer	full — empty
offen — zu	open — closed

*Was essen Sie lieber,
Butter oder Margarine?*

Sprachnotizen

1. Expressing *favorite*

The noun **Liebling** means *darling* or *favorite*. With the addition of an **s (Lieblings-)**, it can be prefixed to many nouns to express that someone or something is one's favorite:

Was ist deine **Lieblings**farbe?	*What's your **favorite** color?*
Rosen sind meine **Lieblings**blumen.	*Roses are my **favorite** flowers.*

2. The flavoring particle *aber*

In colloquial German, **aber** is often used to add emphasis to a statement:

Das tut mir **aber** leid.	*I'm **so** sorry.*
Jetzt habe ich **aber** Hunger.	*I'm **really** hungry now.*

1. WAS PASST NICHT?

a. der Kellner   b. der Tisch   c. der Unterschied
   die Theorie   der Platz   die Ecke
   das Gasthaus   der Grund   das Schaufenster
   die Speisekarte   der Gast   die Tür

2. WAS PASST WO?

dort drüben   machen . . . zu   gehen . . . hinein   leer   beide   Lust

a. Das Gasthaus ist halb _____. _____ wir _____?
b. _____ Sie doch bitte die Tür _____!
c. Hast du _____ auf ein Stück Kuchen?
d. Wem gehört denn das Haus _____?
e. Habt ihr denn wirklich _____ keine Zeit?

recht   auf ein paar Tage   wünsche   offen   gleich um die Ecke   voll

f. Zieglers fahren morgen _____ nach Wien.
g. Dieses Gasthaus ist leider _____.
   Das macht nichts. _____ ist noch ein gutes Gasthaus.
   Ich weiß, aber das hat heute leider nicht _____.
h. Ich _____ Ihnen einen _____ guten Appetit!

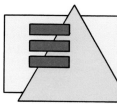

FUNKTIONEN UND FORMEN

1. EXPRESSING *TO LEAVE; TO LET; TO HAVE SOMETHING DONE*

THE VERB *LASSEN*

The verb **lassen (läßt), hat gelassen,** is a frequently used verb in German. It has three basic meanings.

a. *to leave*

Laß die Schlüssel nicht im Wagen!   *Don't **leave** the keys in the car!*

b. *to let, to allow*

In this meaning **lassen** functions like a modal verb, i.e., the infinitive appears without **zu** at the end of the sentence.

Warum **läßt** du mich nie **fahren**?   *Why don't you ever **let** me **drive**?*

c. *to have something done*

Here **lassen** functions like a modal verb as well:

Wo **lassen** Sie Ihren Wagen **reparieren?**   *Where do you **have** your car repaired?*

Lassen has two past participle forms: **gelassen** and **lassen**. The form **gelassen** is used when **lassen** is the main verb in the sentence:

Wo **habe** ich denn meine Brille **gelassen?**   *Where **did** I **leave** my glasses?*

The form **lassen** is used when the infinitive of another verb is present in the sentence. This is called a *double infinitive construction.*

Warum **hast** du Sabine nicht **fahren
lassen?**   *Why **didn't** you **let** Sabine **drive?***

Wo **hast** du deinen Computer **repa-
rieren lassen?**   *Where **did** you **have** your computer repaired?*

A. AUF ENGLISCH, BITTE!

1. Warum läßt du mich nie kochen?
2. Wo haben Sie das Kleid machen lassen?
3. Warum läßt du immer die Tür offen?
4. Leben und leben lassen.
5. Verflixt!° Jetzt habe ich mein Referat zu Hause gelassen.
6. Ich muß noch schnell den Wagenwaschen lassen.
7. Laßt doch den Hund zu Hause!
8. Laß mich doch auch etwas sagen!
9. Hast du den Toaster rereparieren lassen?
10. Laß mich bitte schlafen!

Darn it!

B. KÖNNEN DIESE LEUTE DENN GAR NICHTS SELBST MACHEN?

▶ Haben Sie   Nein, wir haben sie . . .

| Ihre Hecke schneiden |

S1: Haben Sie Ihre Hecke selber
geschnitten?   *S2:* Nein, wir haben sie schneiden lassen.

1. Habt ihr   Nein, wir haben es . . .

2. Haben Sie    Nein, ich habe es . . .

3. Hast du    Nein, ich habe es . . .

4. Haben Sie    Nein, wir haben ihn . . .

das Zimmer tapezieren	den Zaun streichen
euer Haus bauen	das Kleid machen

5. Hast du    Nein, ich habe es . . .

6. Haben Sie    Nein, ich habe ihn . . .

7. Habt ihr   Nein, wir haben ihn . . .

8. Hast du    Nein, ich habe es . . .

dein Fahrrad reparieren	den Geburtstagskuchen backen
dein Referat tippen	Ihren Wagen waschen

WAS MACHEN DEINE ELTERN SELBST? WAS LASSEN SIE MACHEN?

Ask your partner these two questions and make a list of things her/his parents do themselves and things they prefer to have done. You may want to inquire about some of the activities listed below. Use the following pattern when you report your findings to the class.

▶ Den Wagen waschen Lisas Eltern selbst.
Die Fenster lassen sie putzen.
. . .

den Wagen waschen	die Fenster putzen	die Zimmer tapezieren
das Haus streichen	den Rasen mähen	den Wagen reparieren
das Haus / die Wohnung putzen		. . .

2. CONNECTING IDEAS (1)

INFINITIVE PHRASES

Ideas can often be expressed more elegantly by connecting sentences.

Hast du Zeit? Gehst du mit uns schwimmen?	*Do you have time? Are you going swimming with us?*
Hast du Zeit, mit uns schwimmen **zu gehen?**	*Do you have time **to go** swimming with us?*

As the example shows, sentences can be connected by using a **zu**-infinitive, which closely parallels the use of the English infinitive with *to*. Note that the **zu**-infinitive appears at the end of its phrase and is marked off by a comma.
With separable-prefix verbs, **zu** is inserted between the prefix and the verb:

Fällt es dir nicht schwer, jeden Morgen um halb sieben **aufzustehen?**	*Don't you find it difficult **to get up** at half past six every morning?*

If there are two or more infinitives at the end of the phrase, **zu** precedes the last infinitive:

Es macht mir gar keinen Spaß, jedes Wochenende so viel **lernen zu müssen.**	*I don't at all enjoy **having to study** so much every weekend.*

C. ERGÄNZEN SIE DIESE KLEINEN GESPRÄCHE!

1. GÜNTER: Hast du vor, mit dem Wagen zur Uni _____? fahren

   MONIKA: Ja, möchtest du _____? mitfahren
2. EVA: Hast du Lust, heute abend mit uns _____? ausgehen

   PAUL: Lust schon, aber ich habe leider viel zu viel tun

   _____.

3. STEFAN: Macht es dir Spaß, jeden Morgen zwei Kilometer _____? joggen

   BRIGITTE: Spaß nicht, aber ich will doch fit _____. bleiben

4. STEPHANIE: Ist es nicht schön, morgen mal richtig _____? ausschlafen können

   CLAUDIA: Ja, aber vergiß nicht, am Nachmittag dein Referat _____. fertigschreiben

5. RALF: Habt ihr Zeit, heute nachmittag mit uns _____? schwimmen gehen

   KURT: Nein, wir müssen leider Hausaufgaben _____. machen

6. OLIVER: Ist es nicht toll, Ferien _____, und keine Referate mehr _____? haben / schreiben müssen

   HEIKE: Ja, und jeden Nachmittag _____, ist auch nicht schlecht. segeln gehen können

7. HELGA: Warum fängst du denn nicht endlich an, deine Koffer _____? auspacken

   ANTJE: Ich muß erst meinen Eltern _____. schreiben

8. MARKUS: Warum soll ich denn Günter nicht _____ einladen

   TINA: Es fällt mir schwer, zu ihm noch freundlich _____. sein

9. PETER: Hast du vor, den ganzen Tag im Bett _____? bleiben

   MARTIN: Sei still, und laß mich _____! schlafen

Wie soll man die Parkanlagen schonen?

D. SIND IHRE ELTERN AUCH SO? With two classmates, play the roles of Sabine and her parents. Sabine begins each of her responses with **zum, zur,** or **nach.**

▶ gehen   die Bibliothek

VATER: Wo gehst du hin?   *SABINE:* Zur Bibliothek.

deine Bücher zurückgeben

MUTTER: Dann vergiß auch nicht, deine Bücher zurückzugeben.

1. gehen   der Bäcker
2. fliegen   Hamburg
3. fahren   die Post
4. fliegen   München
5. fahren   der Fleischer

deinen Regenschirm° mitnehmen	aufs Oktoberfest gehen
frische Brötchen mitbringen	Briefmarken kaufen
mir hundert Gramm Leberwurst mitbringen	

umbrella

6. gehen	die Apotheke
7. fahren	die Bank
8. fliegen	Bonn
9. gehen	die Drogerie
10. fahren	Innsbruck

das Herz: *heart*

Zahnpasta und Shampoo kaufen	das Beethovenhaus anschauen
deine Schier mitnehmen	meine Herztabletten° abholen
mir ein neues Scheckheft mitbringen	

The typical North American drugstore, where everything from prescription drugs to school supplies is sold, does not exist in the German-speaking countries. Prescription drugs are sold only at an **Apotheke;** non-prescription drugs, toilet articles, and sundries are sold at a **Drogerie.**

Reformhäuser *(health food stores)* have been a part of German culture for many years. People in the German-speaking countries are very conscious of what they eat and many prefer their food without chemical additives and preservatives.

Apotheke am Kirchplatz

465

Werner Horn
Inhaber Michael Knüttel
7063 Welzheim
Telefon 0 71 82 / 88 19

Kaufe Arzneimittel nur in der Apotheke!

Was sind Arzneimittel?

WAS HAST DU HEUTE ABEND VOR?

Ask about your partner's plans, what she/he enjoys doing, and what she/he finds difficult to do.

S1: Was hast du heute abend vor?
Was hast du am Wochenende vor?
Was macht dir Spaß?
Was fällt dir schwer?

S2: Heute abend habe ich vor, . . .
Am Wochenende habe ich vor, . . .
Es macht mir viel Spaß, . . .
Es fällt mir schwer, . . .

INFINITIVE PHRASES INTRODUCED BY *UM*

A **zu**-infinitive introduced by **um** expresses purpose or intention. The English equivalent of **um . . . zu** is *in order to*. English often uses *to* instead of *in order to*. In German the word **um** is rarely omitted.

Warum war Silke hier?
Um dir für die Blumen **zu danken.**

Why was Silke here?
(In order) to thank you for the flowers.

Warum hat Tanja angerufen?
Um uns ins Konzert **einzuladen.**

Why did Tanja call?
(In order) to invite us to a concert.

E. WOZU° BRAUCHST DU DENN DAS ALLES?

what . . . for

▶ der Hammer diesen Nagel ein•schlagen°

to drive in

S1: Wozu brauchst du einen Hammer?   *S2:* Um diesen Nagel einzuschlagen.

1. der Dosenöffner

2. der Korkenzieher

3. der Bohrer

4. der Flaschenöffner

diese Bierflasche öffnen	diese Dose Thunfisch öffnen
Löcher in diese Bretter° bohren	den Korken aus dieser Weinflasche heraus•ziehen

boards

5. das Bügeleisen

6. die Waschmaschine

7. die Nähmaschine

8. die Kaffeemaschine

nicht mehr zum Waschsalon gehen müssen
endlich mal eine gute Tasse Kaffee machen können
meine Hemden selbst bügeln können
meine Kleider selbst nähen können

F. ALLES HAT SEINE GRÜNDE *(There's a reason for everything)*

▶ Claudia / schreiben   Um uns für die hundert Mark . . .

> danken

S1: Warum hat Claudia geschrieben?   *S2:* Um uns für die hundert Mark zu danken.

1. Monika / anrufen   Um uns zum Abendessen . . .
2. du / heute morgen so früh aufstehen   Um noch eine halbe Stunde Klavier . . .
3. Peter und Stephanie / nach Starn-   Um Peters neues Surfbrett . . .
   berg fahren
4. Anita / zu Günter gehen   Um ihm bei seinem Referat . . .
5. Bettina / in die Stadt fahren   Um Weihnachtsgeschenke . . .

> üben können   helfen   einkaufen   einladen   ausprobieren

INFINITIVE PHRASES INTRODUCED BY *OHNE*

A **zu**-infinitive introduced by **ohne** expresses *without . . . -ing*.

Wie kannst du meinen Wagen nehmen, **ohne** mich **zu fragen?**   *How can you take my car **without asking** me?*

Kommt ja nicht, **ohne** uns vorher **an-zurufen.**   *Don't come **without calling** us beforehand.*

G. GEGEN ALLE ERWARTUNGEN!° *expectations*

die Zähne putzen

▶ Ist Brigitte wieder ins Bett gegan-   Nein, diesmal hat sie sie . . .
gen, ohne . . . ?

S1: Ist Brigitte wieder ins Bett gegan-   **S2:** Nein, diesmal hat sie sie geputzt.
gen, ohne die Zähne zu putzen?

1. Ist Kathrin wieder weggefahren,   Nein, diesmal hat sie . . .
ohne . . . ?

2. Bist du wieder zur Uni gegangen,   Nein, diesmal habe ich sie . . .
ohne . . . ?

3. Seid ihr wieder spazierengegangen,   Nein, diesmal haben wir ihn . . .
ohne . . . ?

4. Sind Müllers wieder zu Besuch   Nein, diesmal haben sie uns vorher . . .
gekommen, ohne . . . ?

5. Ist Tilmann wieder in die   Nein, diesmal hat er . . .
   Klavierstunde gegangen, ohne . . . ?

---

den Hund mitnehmen   üben   frühstücken   die Katze füttern
euch vorher anrufen

NICHT BRAUCHEN + *ZU*-INFINITIVE

The basic meaning of **brauchen** is *to need:*

Ich **brauche** einen neuen Wintermantel.	*I **need** a new winter coat.*

However, when **brauchen** is used *negatively* with a **zu**-infinitive, it is the negative of **müssen** and means *not to have to:*

Müssen wir alle diese Wörter lernen? Nein, Sie **brauchen** sie **nicht** alle **zu lernen.**	*Do we have to learn all these words? No, you **don't have to learn** them all.*

H. SAGEN SIE DAS AUF DEUTSCH!

die Hilfe

1. You have to help me, Anita!
2. This time you don't have to help me, Anita.
3. I don't need any help.°
4. When do we have to be home?
5. You don't have to come tomorrow, Mr. Krüger.
6. How much money do you need, Mr. Krüger?

I. SO VIEL GELD HABEN WIR NICHT!

das Zimmer tapezieren

▶ Aber Sabine, du brauchst . . . !   Ja, glaubst du denn, wir haben Geld,
                                             es . . . ?

S1: Aber Sabine, du brauchst das Zim-   *S2:* Ja, glaubst du denn, wir haben Geld,
mer doch nicht selbst zu tapezieren!   es tapezieren zu lassen?

1. Aber Sabine, du brauchst . . . !   Ja, glaubst du denn, wir haben Geld, ihn . . . ?

2. Aber Thomas, du brauchst . . . !   Ja, glaubst du denn, wir haben Geld, ihn . . . ?

3. Aber Sabine, du brauchst . . . !   Ja, glaubst du denn, wir haben Geld, ihn . . . ?

4. Aber Thomas, du brauchst . . . !   Ja, glaubst du denn, wir haben Geld, sie . . . ?

die Hecke schneiden   den Rasen mähen   den Garten um•graben
den Ast° ab•sägen

branch

5. Aber Thomas, du brauchst . . . !   Ja, glaubst du denn, wir haben Geld, es . . . ?

6. Aber Sabine, du brauchst . . . !   Ja, glaubst du denn, wir haben Geld, es . . . ?

7. Aber Thomas, du brauchst . . . !   Ja, glaubst du denn, wir haben Geld, ihn . . . ?

8. Aber Thomas, du brauchst . . . !   Ja, glaubst du denn, wir haben Geld, ihn . . . ?

den Wagen waschen	das Holz spalten	das Fahrrad reparieren
	den Zaun streichen	

Table etiquette and customs are similar in all the German-speaking countries. Most eating activities occur around a table, even **Kaffee und Kuchen**. When dining, people in the German-speaking countries keep both hands (but not arms) on the table. To have one hand under the table is considered rude. Cutlery **(das Besteck)** is used differently than in North America. The fork **(die Gabel)** is held in the left hand and the knife **(das Messer)** in the right hand throughout the meal, not just for cutting food. At the beginning of a meal, people usually wish one another **Guten Appetit!**

So hält man in Deutschland Messer und Gabel.

 # ZUSAMMENSCHAU

 ## IM GASTHAUS

Martin und Peter sind heute in Düsseldorf und haben den ganzen Morgen die Stadt besichtigt°. Jetzt haben sie Hunger und suchen ein Gasthaus.

toured

- Hören Sie gut zu! In welcher Reihenfolge° hören Sie die folgenden Aussagen° und Fragen?

sequence / statements

Neue Vokabeln

Herr Ober!	*Waiter!*
das Tagesgericht	*special of the day*
Kaßler Rippchen, Kaßler	*smoked pork chop*
Die Kartoffeln sind nicht durch.	*The potatoes are not done.*
rohe Kartoffeln	*raw potatoes*
Wir müssen weiter.	*We have to get going.*
welche	*some*
getrennt	*separate*

—— Rohe Kartoffeln. Das mag ich gar nicht.
—— Vielen Dank. Und das mit den Kartoffeln, das tut mir wirklich leid.
—— Was geht denn besonders schnell? Wir haben nicht viel Zeit.

Und wer bekommt den Kaffee, bitte?

— Also, zweimal Kaßler, ein Bier und eine Cola.

— Ja, komm. Ich habe einen Bärenhunger.

— Du, was machen wir denn heute nachmittag? Fahren wir nach Köln?

— Kaßler, acht Mark fünfzig. Gut, das nehme ich.

— Alles in Ordnung, meine Herren?

— Zusammen, bitte. Dann geht's schneller.

— Hier ist auch schon das Kaßler, meine Herren. Und ein Bier und eine Cola.

✐▷ Hören Sie das Gespräch jetzt noch einmal an, und beantworten Sie dann die folgenden Fragen!

does . . . advise

1. Warum rät° der Kellner den beiden Gästen, das Tagesgericht zu nehmen?
2. Was ist heute das Tagesgericht?
3. Wieviel kostet das Tagesgericht?
4. Was trinkt Peter?
5. Was trinkt Martin?
6. Was haben Peter und Martin heute nachmittag vor?
7. Warum haben sie morgen so wenig Zeit?
8. Warum kommt das Tagesgericht so schnell?
9. Was ist mit den Kartoffeln los?
10. Warum soll Martin das dem Kellner nicht sagen?
11. Warum bezahlen Martin und Peter nicht getrennt?

tip

12. Wieviel kostet alles zusammen, und wieviel Trinkgeld° gibt Peter dem Kellner?

DA IST EIN HAAR IN DER SUPPE!

Personen: zwei Studenten
ein Kellner

complain

- Rufen Sie den Kellner **(Herr Ober!),** und bestellen Sie etwas zu essen. Der Kellner bringt das Essen, und Sie beginnen beide zu essen. Aber leider ist das Essen nicht ganz in Ordnung. Rufen Sie den Kellner, und reklamieren° Sie!

use

Sie können die folgenden Ausdrücke verwenden°:

sauce
oversalted

Da ist ein Haar in der Suppe.
Die Suppe (die Soße°, das Fleisch usw.) ist versalzen°.

tough

Das Fleisch ist noch halb roh.
Das Fleisch ist zäh° wie Leder.

pork roast
spicy

Der Schweinebraten° ist viel zu fett.
Das Gulasch ist viel zu scharf° (nicht scharf genug).

Das Bier (der Weißwein) ist viel zu warm.
Der Rotwein ist viel zu kalt.
Der Kaffee (der Tee) ist ganz kalt.
. . .

SPEISEKARTE

TAGESMENÜ I . . . . DM 10,80   TAGESMENÜ II. . . . . DM 12,–

Tagessuppe	Tagessuppe
Wiener Schnitzel mit Kartoffelsalat	Sauerbraten mit Kartoffelpüree und Salat
Vanilleeis	Vanilleeis

SUPPEN

Tagessuppe . . . . DM 3,–

Nudelsuppe . . . . DM 3,30

HAUPTGERICHTE

1. Bratwurst mit Sauerkraut und Bratkartoffeln . . . . DM 8,–
2. Ungarisches Gulasch, Eiernudeln und gemischter Salat . . . . DM 9,30
3. Schweinebraten mit Rotkraut und Salzkartoffeln . . . . DM 10,50
4. Hühnchen mit Weinsoße, Reis und Tomatensalat . . . . DM 12,40
5. Filetsteak gegrillt mit Champignons, Pommes frites
   und Gurkensalat . . . . DM 18,40

ZUM NACHTISCH

Schokoladenpudding . . . . DM 2,80

Fruchtsalat mit frischen Früchten . . . . DM 3,30

Apfelstrudel . . . . DM 3,40

Schwarzwälder Kirschtorte . . . . DM 4,–

GETRÄNKE

Limonade . . . . DM 1,80

Apfelsaft . . . . DM 2,–

Kaffee, Tasse . . . . DM 2,20

Kaffee, Kännchen . . . . DM 3,80

Tee, Kännchen . . . . DM 3,60

Bier, vom Faß (0,33 l) . . . . DM 2,50

Weißwein, Mosel (0,2 l) . . . . DM 3,–

Rotwein, Beaujolais (0,2 l) . . . . DM 3,10

Würstchenbuden, the precursors of the fast-food industry, have always been a part of German eating culture. They are situated in railway stations and other busy areas of larger cities and they serve sausages like **Bockwurst, Knackwurst,** and **Currywurst** on a **Brötchen** with **Senf** (mustard). A **Schnellimbiß** serves not only **Wurst** but also other fast food items such as **Hamburger** and **Gulaschsuppe.** A snack that has become very popular is the Turkish specialty **Döner Kebab** (pita bread filled with meat roasted on a spit, lettuce, tomatoes, and onions). **Pizzerias** can be found everywhere in the German-speaking countries, and now most large cities also have a McDonald's or a Wendy's.

Eine Wurst mit Brötchen und Senf

3. CONNECTING IDEAS (2)

COORDINATING CONJUNCTIONS

Coordinating conjunctions are words that connect clauses, phrases, or words. The five most common coordinating conjunctions are:

und	*and*	**aber**	*but, however*
oder	*or*	**sondern**	*but, but rather*
denn	*because*		

When coordinating conjunctions connect clauses, word order is not affected. The conjunctions **denn, aber,** and **sondern** are *always* preceded by a comma. Before **und** and **oder** there is a comma only if a complete clause with subject and verb follows.

Möchten Sie Bier **oder** Wein?	*Would you like beer **or** wine?*
Ich trinke ein Bier, **und** mein Freund möchte ein Glas Wein.	*I'll have a beer **and** my friend would like a glass of wine.*
Ich möchte lieber eine Cola, **denn** ich muß später alle nach Hause fahren.	*I would prefer a soda, **because** later I have to drive everybody home.*

Be careful to distinguish between **aber** *(but, however)* and **sondern** *(but, but rather)*. Note that **sondern** is always preceded by a negative statement.

Ich möchte gern ins Kino, **aber** ich muß leider lernen.	*I would like to go to the movies, **but** unfortunately I have to study.*
Claudia möchte heute mal nicht in die Disco, **sondern** ins Kino.	*Claudia doesn't want to go to the disco today **but** to the movies.*

J. ABER, SONDERN?

1. Das ist kein Zucker, _____ Salz.
2. Zucker haben wir noch viel, _____ Salz mußt du kaufen.
3. Der Pulli ist sehr schön, _____ viel zu teuer.
4. Ich möchte keinen roten Pulli, _____ einen grauen.
5. Frau Kuhl ist noch nicht hier, _____ sie kommt sicher gleich.
6. Ich habe nicht mit Frau Kuhl gesprochen, _____ mit ihrer Sekretärin.
7. Diesen Sonntag fahren wir nicht weg, _____ schlafen mal richtig aus.
8. Claudia liegt noch im Bett, _____ ich glaube, sie schläft nicht mehr.
9. Morgen spielen wir mal nicht Tennis, _____ gehen schwimmen.
10. Peter möchte auch schwimmen gehen, _____ er hat morgen keine Zeit.

K. UND, ODER, DENN?

1. MARTIN: Sollen wir den Bus nehmen _____ zu Fuß gehen?
   PETER: Ich nehme den Bus, _____ meine Vorlesungen beginnen schon in zehn Minuten.
2. EVA: David hat ein tolles Gasthaus gefunden _____ möchte uns alle zum Mittagessen einladen.
   MICHAEL: Ich kann jetzt noch nicht essen, _____ ich habe erst um elf gefrühstückt.
3. KURT: Fährt Thomas den alten Mercedes noch, _____ hat er ihn verkauft?
   BERND: Er hat ihn verkauft _____ fährt jetzt mit dem Fahrrad zur Uni.
4. DIETER: Wer holt dich in Frankfurt ab, deine Eltern _____ dein Bruder?
   TANJA: Mein Bruder, _____ meine Eltern kommen erst am Abend von der Arbeit.
5. KLAUS: Kommt Silke heute abend, _____ kommt sie nicht?
   GABI: Sie kommt nicht, _____ sie ist krank _____ liegt im Bett.

SUBORDINATE CLAUSES AND SUBORDINATING CONJUNCTIONS

A subordinate clause is a clause that depends on a main clause to complete its meaning. Subordinating conjunctions introduce subordinate clauses and connect these clauses to the main clauses.

In a German subordinate clause, the verb appears at the end of the clause, and the clause is always marked off by a comma.

Four important subordinate conjunctions are:

weil	*because*	**wenn**	*when*
daß	*that*	**wenn**	*if*

Main Clause	Subordinate Clause
Sabine lernt Englisch,	**weil** sie nächstes Jahr in Amerika **studiert.**
Sabine is learning English	***because*** *she* ***is studying*** *in America next year.*

Federal Express. Wenn es absolut notwendig ist, daß es rechtzeitig ankommt.

IHRE NÄCHSTGELEGENE FEDERAL-EXPRESS-FILIALE FINDEN SIE IN DEN GELBEN SEITEN.

Separable-prefix verbs are not separated in subordinate clauses.

Ruf mich bitte gleich an,	**wenn** du aus den Ferien **zurückkommst.**
Please call me immediately	***when** you **get back** from your vacation.*

The modals and the auxiliaries **haben** and **sein** also appear at the end of subordinate clauses.

Ruf mich an,	**wenn** du nicht kommen **kannst.**
Call me	***if** you **can**'t come.*
Es tut mir leid,	**daß** ich nicht früher geschrieben **habe.**
I'm sorry	***that** I **haven**'t written earlier.*
Stephanie schreibt,	**daß** sie gut angekommen **ist.**
Stephanie writes	***that** she **has** arrived safely.*

L. WEIL ODER WENN? Beginnen Sie die Antwort mit der richtigen Konjunktion!

▶ Warum ißt du denn so schnell?	Meine Vorlesung fängt in fünf Minuten an.
S1: Warum ißt du denn so schnell?	*S2:* Weil meine Vorlesung in fünf Minuten anfängt.

1. Warum hast du heute morgen nicht gefrühstückt?   Ich bin zu spät aufgestanden.
2. Wann stehst du denn endlich auf?   Du hast das Frühstück gemacht.
3. Lädst du mich zum Abendessen ein?   Du reparierst mein Fahrrad.
4. Wann sprichst du mit Helga?   Sie kommt von der Vorlesung zurück.
5. Warum gibst du denn das Rauchen nicht auf?   Ich will nicht dick werden.
6. Darf ich das Buch mitnehmen?   Du gibst es mir morgen wieder zurück.

7. Wann heiratet ihr?   Ich bin mit meinem Studium fertig.
8. Warum lernst du Deutsch?   Ich will in Deutschland studieren.
9. Darf ich den Brief lesen?   Ich kann ihn finden.
10. Wann fahren Sie nach Österreich?   Das Semester ist vorbei.°   *over*
11. Gehst du morgen abend auch ins Konzert?   Ich muß nicht zu viel lernen.
12. Warum ist Sandra so unfreundlich?   Wir haben sie nicht eingeladen.
13. Geht ihr heute nachmittag mit uns schwimmen?   Es regnet nicht.

LEBST DU GESUND ODER UNGESUND?

Find out whether your partner has a healthy lifestyle or not. Report your findings to the class.

S1: Rauchst du?

Warum rauchst du nicht? Warum rauchst du?

S2: Nein, ich rauche nicht. / Ja, ich rauche.
Weil . . .

Rauchst du?	Ich will fit bleiben.	
Trinkst du Kaffee?	Der Arzt hat es mir verboten.	
Trinkst du Alkohol?	Ich kann dann besser denken.	
Trinkst du viel Milch?	Ich will nicht ewig° leben.	*forever*
Frühstückst du jeden Morgen?	Ich bin zu faul.	
Ißt du drei Mahlzeiten° am Tag?	Ich habe keine Zeit.	*meals*
Ißt du viel Fleisch?	Ich will schlank° bleiben.	*slim*
Machst du ab und zu° eine	Ich will gesund bleiben.	*now and then*
Schlankheitskur?°	Ich will nicht krank werden.	*diet*
Nimmst du Vitamine?	Ich kann ohne Kaffee (ohne Zigaretten)	
Treibst du Sport?	nicht leben.	
. . .	Ich bin sowieso° viel zu nervös.	*anyway*
	. . .	

M. IMMER DIESE KRITIK!

▶ Ich kritisiere sie immer.   ein bißchen weniger kritisch sein

S1: Meine Freundin mag es gar nicht, daß ich sie immer kritisiere.   **S2:** Dann versuch doch mal, ein bißchen weniger kritisch zu sein.

1. Ich komme immer zu spät.	ein bißchen pünktlicher sein	
2. Ich gebe so viel Geld aus.	ein bißchen sparsamer° sein	*thriftier*
3. Ich bin so dünn.	ein bißchen mehr essen	
4. Ich kann ihre Verwandten° nicht ausstehen.	ein bißchen toleranter sein	*relatives*
5. Ich bin so ernst.°	ein bißchen lustiger sein	*serious*
6. Ich rieche° so nach Tabak.	ein bißchen weniger rauchen	*to smell*

WAS GEFÄLLT IHNEN AN° IHREN MITSTUDENTEN° / MITSTUDENTINNEN?

S1: Was gefällt dir an Lisa?

Und was gefällt dir an _____?

S2: An Lisa gefällt mir, daß sie so sportlich ist.

. . .

lively
quiet

helpful / cheerful / well-prepared

lebhaft°	ernst	lustig
ruhig°	praktisch	elegant
interessiert	sportlich	immer so pünktlich
hilfsbereit°	fröhlich°	immer so gut vorbereitet°
fleißig	freundlich	. . .

SUBORDINATE CLAUSE PRECEDING MAIN CLAUSE

When the subordinate clause precedes the main clause, the entire subordinate clause becomes the *first* element in the sentence. The main clause then begins with the conjugated verb (i.e., the verb with personal endings). The conjugated verbs of both clauses thus appear side by side, separated by a comma.

Subordinate Clause	Main Clause
Wenn du mich nach Hause **fährst,**	**bezahle** ich dir das Mittagessen.
If you drive me home,	*I'll pay for your lunch.*
Weil Eva mich nach Hause gefahren **hat,**	**habe** ich sie zum Essen eingeladen.
Because Eva drove me home,	*I invited her for dinner.*

N. WAS PASST ZUSAMMEN? Match correctly in each set and change the position of the conjugated verb in the main clause.

▶ Wenn der Pulli Ihrer Freundin nicht gefällt,
Weil der Pulli ein Loch hatte,

Ich bin gleich wieder zu Karstadt zurückgegangen.
Sie kann ihn natürlich zurückbringen.

S1: Wenn der Pulli Ihrer Freundin nicht gefällt, kann sie ihn natürlich zurückbringen.

S2: Weil der Pulli ein Loch hatte, bin ich gleich wieder zu Karstadt zurückgegangen.

1. Weil wir nicht viel Zeit hatten,

Wenn du nicht viel Zeit hast,

Wir haben beide das Tagesgericht bestellt.
Du kannst ja nach einer halben Stunde wieder gehen.

Wer täglich

arbeitet wie ein Pferd

fleißig ist wie eine Biene

abends müde ist wie ein Hund

der sollte zum Tierarzt gehen - es könnte sein -

daß er ein Kamel ist!

Kamel bedeutet hier „Dummkopf".

2. Weil mein Steak so zäh war,
   Wenn das Steak zu zäh ist,

   Du mußt den Kellner rufen.
   Ich habe den Kellner gerufen.

3. Wenn das Wetter mitmacht°,
   Weil das Wetter so schlecht war,

   Wir gehen nächste Woche Schi laufen.   *cooperates*
   Wir sind gestern den ganzen Tag zu
   Hause geblieben.

4. Weil Stephanie so Durst hatte,
   Wenn Claudia richtig Durst hat,

   Sie trinkt ganz gern mal ein Glas Bier.
   Sie hat drei Glas Orangensaft
   getrunken.

5. Wenn du Geld brauchst,
   Weil Martin Geld braucht,

   Er sucht einen Ferienjob.
   Du mußt es mich bald wissen lassen.

INDIRECT QUESTIONS

Indirect questions are questions that are preceded by an introductory clause. In indirect questions the question words act as subordinating conjunctions and the verb appears at the end of the clause.

Direct question: **Wie komme** ich zum Bahnhof?

How do I *get* to the railway station?

Indirect question: Können Sie mir bitte sagen, **wie** ich zum Bahnhof **komme?**

*Can you please tell me **how** I **get** to the railway station?*

Indirect yes/no questions are introduced by the subordinating conjunction **ob** (*whether*):

Direct question: **Ist** Professor Seidlmeyer schon da?

Is Professor Seidlmeyer here yet?

Indirect question: Weißt du, **ob** Professor Seidlmeyer schon da **ist?** schon da **ist?**

*Do you know **whether** Professor Seidlmeyer **is** here yet?*

O. KÖNNEN SIE MIR BITTE SAGEN, . . . ? Change the direct questions into indirect questions. Your partner answers by matching the illustrations with phrases from the list below.

▶ Fährt dieser Bus zum Bahnhof?
  Können Sie mir bitte sagen, . . .   Nein, er fährt . . .

zum Zoo

S1: Können Sie mir bitte sagen, ob dieser Bus zum Bahnhof fährt?   *S2:* Nein, er fährt zum Zoo.

1. Wo ist Brigitte?
   Weißt du, . . . ?   Ich glaube, sie ist . . .

2. Ist Professor Seidlmeyer schon da?
   Wißt ihr, . . . ?

   Ja, er arbeitet . . .

3. Wohin fährt dieser Zug?
   Können Sie mir bitte sagen, . . . ?

   Das ist der
   Intercity . . .

4. Ist Claudia heute abend zu Hause?
   Weißt du, . . . ?

   Nein, heute abend
   geht sie mit Mar-
   tin . . .

5. Was soll sie ihrer Kusine morgen
   nachmittag zeigen?
   Stephanie möchte wissen, . . . ?

   Sie soll doch mal
   mit ihr . . .

---

beim Friseur	nach Hannover	ins Deutsche Museum	ins Kino
	in seinem Büro		

6. Hat Günter schon gefrühstückt?
   Weißt du, . . . ?

   Nein, der
   liegt noch . . .

7. Wann fängt das Konzert heute
   abend an?
   Können Sie mir bitte sagen, . . . ?

   Soviel° ich weiß,
   beginnt es . . .

as far as

8. Sind Fischers wieder zurück?
   Wissen Sie, . . . ?

   Nein, sie sind
   immer noch . . .

9. Warum ist Silke nicht hier?
   Weißt du, . . . ?

   Ich glaube, sie ist heute . . .

10. Fährst du morgen nachmittag mit
    ihnen nach Starnberg?
    Kurt und Ralf möchten wis-   Nein, ich muß morgen
    sen, . . . ?   nachmittag leider . . .

| in Italien | zum Zahnarzt | im Bett | beim Arzt | um 20,30 Uhr |

P. KLEINE GESPRÄCHE. Auf deutsch, bitte!

1. SABINE: When are you going to have the car washed?
   THOMAS: I had it washed this morning.

2. CLAUDIA: Do you have time to go to the movies with us tonight?
   STEPHANIE: Unfortunately not. I have too much to do.

3. BRIGITTE: Why did Silke call?
   TINA: To thank you for the tickets.

4. STEPHANIE: Why are you reading the menu out here?°   *out here:* **hier draußen**
   PETER: I never go into° a restaurant without first looking at the menu.   **in**

5. STEPHANIE: What do your grandparents write?
   PETER: They want to know whether I'm going to visit them next summer.

6. KATHRIN: Were you at Bettina's last night?
   MICHAEL: Yes, but I went home early because it was so boring.

 # ZUSAMMENSCHAU

GÜNTER SCHLUMBERGER SOLL EINKAUFEN GEHEN

*Günter Schlumberger lebt immer noch bei seinen Eltern. Er ist kein sehr rück-   considerate
sichtsvoller° Mensch, und er hat die Tendenz, alles besser zu wissen als seine Eltern.
Seine Eltern sehen° nicht ein, warum sie wegen° Günter ihre Gewohnheiten° än-   **sehen . . . ein:** see /
dern° sollen. Deshalb kommt es bei Schlumbergers manchmal zu kleinen   because of / habits /
Auseinandersetzungen.°*   change / arguments

• Sie hören später eine solche° Auseinandersetzung. Lesen Sie aber zuerst die   such a
  folgenden Standpunkte!°   points of view

Günters Standpunkt

Ich studiere seit zwei Jahren hier in Hamburg Biologie und wohne immer noch
zu Hause. Meine Eltern sind beide berufstätig,° aber meine Mutter kommt über   working
die Mittagszeit kurz nach Hause. Mittwochs muß ich erst nachmittags um drei
zur Uni, und Mutti und ich essen dann meistens zusammen zu Mittag.

Mein Vater kauft jeden Samstag für die ganze Woche ein. Aber weil Brot,
Wurst, Obst° und Gemüse nicht so lange frisch bleiben, muß ich jeden Mittwoch   fruit
ein bißchen einkaufen gehen. Das paßt mir gar nicht,° denn am Donnerstag früh   doesn't suit me at all
habe ich immer eine wichtige Übung, und ich habe am Mittwoch sehr viel
vorzubereiten.° Ich gehe deshalb nie, ohne vorher lebhaft zu protestieren.   to prepare

Bäcker Hagner bäckt die besten Brezeln.

things / just as
schlage . . . vor: *suggest /*
save

Bei Tengelmann — so heißt unser Supermarkt — gibt es alles. Meine Eltern wollen aber die Wurst nur vom Fleischer und das Brot nur vom Bäcker. Das braucht viel Zeit, und diese Sachen° sind bei Tengelmann genauso° gut. Deshalb schlage° ich meiner Mutter jedesmal vor, mich doch Zeit sparen° und alles schnell bei Tengelmann kaufen zu lassen.

after all

Heute ist wieder mal Mittwoch, und weil ich gestern ein Referat fertiggeschrieben habe, habe ich für meine Übung morgen früh noch gar nichts vorbereitet. Warum bin ich nur gestern abend mit Helga ins Kino gegangen?! Aber schließlich° kann man ja nicht immer nur lernen! Vielleicht kann Mutti heute mal selbst einkaufen gehen, oder ich gehe morgen gleich nach meiner Übung zu Tengelmann.

Jetzt ruft Mutti mich gerade zum Essen, Hoffentlich ist da noch Leberwurst. Ich habe einen Bärenhunger, und ich esse so gern Leberwurst.

decide

 Sie hören acht Aussagen zu *Günters Standpunkt.* Entscheiden° Sie, ob diese Aussagen richtig oder falsch sind!

Frau Schlumbergers Standpunkt

for

 Heute ist Mittwoch. Ich bin gerade auf° eine Stunde nach Hause gekommen und habe gleich für Günter und mich etwas zu essen gemacht. Da war aber kaum noch

refrigerator
ham sausage / all gone

Schwarzbrot, und im Kühlschrank° war nur noch ein bißchen Käse und ein kleines bißchen Schinkenwurst.° Die Leberwurst war alle,° und mein Mann und Günter essen sie doch so gern! Mein Mann arbeitet sehr schwer, und er braucht jeden Morgen Käse und Wurst für seine Brote. Deshalb habe ich gleich diese Einkaufsliste geschrieben:

Tengelmann :
2 Kilo Bananen
1 Kilo Tomaten
1 Kopfsalat
200 g Schweizerkäse
Fleischer :
250 g Leberwurst
250 g Schinkenwurst
Bäcker :
1 Schwarzbrot

Ich weiß, daß Günter gar nicht gern einkaufen geht und daß er mittwochs sehr viel zu tun hat. Aber ich habe tagsüber° wirklich keine Zeit, und abends nach der Arbeit sind die Läden° zu. Außerdem hat Günter es sehr gut bei uns. Er wohnt und ißt hier umsonst,° und dafür kann er doch wirklich einmal die Woche für uns einkaufen gehen. Warum ist er auch gestern abend mit Helga ins Kino gegangen und warum steht er immer so spät auf?

during the day
stores
for nothing

Günter will sicher wieder Zeit sparen und alles bei Tengelmann kaufen. Aber da bin ich hart,° denn die Wurst und das Brot vom Supermarkt sind nie so frisch und so gut wie die Wurst von unserem Fleischer und das Brot von unserem Bäcker.

firm

Frau Schlumberger kauft ihre Wurst nur im Fleischer-Fachgeschäft.

 Sie hören acht Aussagen zu *Frau Schlumbergers Standpunkt.* Entscheiden Sie, ob diese Aussagen richtig oder falsch sind!

 Hören Sie jetzt Günters Auseinandersetzung mit seiner Mutter!

Wie reagiert Günter auf° die folgenden Aussagen und Fragen von Frau Schlumberger?

to

1. Da, nimm dir Brot! Und hier ist Butter und Käse.
2. Du mußt nach dem Essen auch gleich einkaufen gehen.
3. Und was nimmt Vati morgen mit?
4. Zu viel zu tun? Warum bist du dann gestern abend mit Helga ausgegangen?

• Wie reagiert Frau Schlumberger auf Günters Aussagen?

1. Aber ich habe doch keine Zeit, Mutti.
2. Dann geh doch nach der Arbeit!
3. Heute kaufe ich aber alles bei Tengelmann, das spart viel Zeit.
4. Tengelmanns Wurst und Brot sind doch genauso gut.

The introduction of supermarkets in Europe has had a tremendous impact on shopping habits in the German-speaking countries. Not too long ago a **Hausfrau**'s daily routine included a morning walk to several specialty stores to buy what she needed to prepare the meals for the day. Now most Germans, Austrians, and Swiss shop less frequently, but many still like to go to the **Fleischerei** (called **Metzgerei** in Southern Germany) or **Bäckerei** that makes their favorite **Wurst** or **Brot.** Most towns also have a **Wochenmarkt,** where one can

Obst/Gemüse		
Ital. **Trauben** Regina Vigneti Kl. 1	kg	**2.99**
Ital. **Wassermelonen**	kg	**-.99**
Tschech. **Bohnen** Kl. 1	kg	**1.99**
frz. **Tomaten** ROMA KL. 2	kg	**1.99**
Ficus Benjamini 120 cm hoch	Stk.	**14.99**

Suchard Milka Schokolade 100 g	**-.89**
Toblerone 100 g	**-.89**
Pepsi Cola, Mirinda, Schwip Schwap 0,33 l Ds.	**-.49**
Sunkist Slim Line 3×0,2 l	**1.79**
Frankenbrunnen Mineralwasser + DM 6,60 Pf. 12×0,7 l	**5.49**

Langer Samstag Familieneinkaufstag!

Aus welchen Ländern kommt das Obst und das Gemüse?

In Deutschland sind Spargel *(asparagus)* nicht grün, sondern weiß.

purchase fresh fruit, vegetables, eggs, and other locally-grown produce direct from the grower. Supermarkets in the German-speaking countries are usually not as large as North American supermarkets. Customers are often not permitted to touch or pick out fruits and vegetables and there is a charge for the plastic shopping bags.

Shopping hours in a German-speaking country take some getting used to. By law, stores may be open only from 7 A.M. to 6:30 P.M. from Monday to Friday and many smaller stores are closed over the lunch hour. They must close no later than 2 P.M. on Saturdays. In Germany, they may stay open until 6 P.M. one Saturday each month **(langer Samstag).** Stores are closed on Sundays.

 Hören Sie die Auseinandersetzung zwischen Günter und seiner Mutter noch einmal, und beanworten Sie die folgenden Fragen!

1. Warum soll Günter so schnell zum Mittagessen kommen?
   Weil seine . . .

2. Warum kann Frau Schlumberger heute nachmittag nicht einkaufen gehen?
   Weil sie Punkt . . .

schlägt . . . vor:
does . . . suggest

3. Günter hat heute wirklich sehr wenig Zeit. Was für einen Kompromiß schlägt° er seiner Mutter deshalb vor?
   Er schlägt vor, morgen . . .

4. Warum akzeptiert Frau Schlumberger Günters Kompromißvorschlag nicht?
   Weil Herr Schlumberger . . .

5. Warum denkt Günter, daß Vatis Brote kein Problem sind?
   Weil da . . .

6. Warum denkt Frau Schlumberger, daß ihr Mann keine Schinkenwurstbrote mitnehmen will?
   Weil sie weiß, daß . . .

7. Warum glaubt Frau Schlumberger nicht, daß Günter gestern abend zu viel zu
   tun hatte?
   Weil sie weiß, daß . . .

8. Was meint Frau Schlumberger, wenn sie sagt, eine Hand wäscht die andere?
   Sie meint, daß Günter . . . und daß er dafür . . .

 **EINE KLEINE AUSEINANDERSETZUNG**

Übernehmen Sie die Rolle von Frau Schlumberger. Ihr Gesprächspartner spielt die
Rolle von Günter. Die folgenden Argumente sollen Ihnen bei Ihrer Auseinandersetzung helfen.

Ein paar Argumente für Frau Schlumberger

Jemand muß mittwochs Brot, Wurst, Obst und Gemüse einkaufen, weil diese
Sachen nicht die ganze Woche frisch bleiben.

Heute ist Mittwoch, und der Kühlschrank ist wieder mal fast leer.

Herr Schlumberger braucht Wurst und Käse für seine Brote. Im Kühlschrank
ist noch ein bißchen Schinkenwurst, aber die mag er nicht.

Frau Schlumberger hat nur eine Stunde Mittagspause, und abends nach der
Arbeit sind die Läden zu.

Frau Schlumberger denkt, daß das Brot beim Bäcker und die Wurst beim
Fleischer besser und frischer sind als bei Tengelmann.

Günter wohnt und ißt zu Hause, muß nichts dafür bezahlen und soll deshalb
manchmal ein bißchen helfen.

Warum ist Günter gestern abend mit Helga ausgegangen? Er weiß doch, daß
er donnerstags eine wichtige Übung hat und mittwochs ein bißchen
einkaufen gehen muß.

. . .

WORT, SINN UND KLANG

WÖRTER UNTER DER LUPE

1. COMPOUND NOUNS

A compound noun is a combination of:

two or more nouns (**der Nachttisch** *night table,* **die Nachttischlampe** *bedside lamp*);
an adjective and a noun (**der Rotwein** *red wine*);
a verb and a noun (**der Schreibtisch** *desk*);
a preposition and a noun (**der Vorname** *first name*).

In German these combinations are always written as *one* word. The last element of a compound noun is the base word and determines the gender of the compound noun. All preceding elements are modifiers that define the base word more closely.

der Kaffee + **die** Tasse = **die** Kaffeetasse
der Tisch + das Tennis + **der** Ball = **der** Tischtennisball
der Fuß + der Ball + **das** Spiel = **das** Fußballspiel

- In the following exercise, supply the definite articles for the compound nouns and match the nouns with their English equivalents.

1. d___ Wochenendhaus   *superintendent (of a building)*
2. d___ Hausschuh   *family doctor*
3. d___ Haustür   *cottage*
4. d___ Reformhaus   *house husband*
5. d___ Kaufhaus   *slipper*
6. d___ Hausmeister   *department store*
7. d___ Hausaufgabe   *single family dwelling*
8. d___ Krankenhaus   *health food store*
9. d___ Hausarzt   *homework assignment*
10. d___ Einfamilienhaus   *hospital*
11. d___ Hochhaus   *front door*
12. d___ Hausmann   *high-rise*

13. d___ Tagebuch   *dictionary*
14. d___ Taschenbuch°   *bookend*   **die Tasche:** *pocket*
15. d___ Bücherwurm   *reader*
16. d___ Wörterbuch   *diary*
17. d___ Sparbuch   *bookworm*
18. d___ Buchhandlung°   *screenplay*   **die Handlung:** *shop*
19. d___ Lesebuch   *paperback*
20. d___ Drehbuch°   *bankbook*   **drehen:** *to turn*
21. d___ Bücherregal°   *bookstore*   **das Regal:** *shelves*
22. d___ Bücherstütze°   *bookshelves*   **die Stütze:** *support*

Was kauft man im Reformhaus?

2. GIVING LANGUAGE COLOR

In *Kapitel* 7 you saw how names of animals are used to characterize people. The idiomatic expressions below will show you that the names of common foods can also be used metaphorically. Some of the items are marked with an asterisk. These expressions are quite colloquial and should not be used in more formal situations or with people you don't know very well.

Es ist alles in Butter!*	*Everything is A-okay.*
Das ist mir Wurst.*	*I could care less.*
Er will immer eine Extrawurst.*	*He always wants special treatment..*
Das ist doch alles Käse!*	*That's all baloney!*

pure
to pour

Ich glaube, ich muß ihm reinen° Wein einschenken.° — *I think I have to tell him the truth.*

Er gleicht seinem Bruder wie ein Ei dem anderen. — *He and his brother are as alike as two peas in a pod.*

cherries
tree trunk

Mit dem ist nicht gut Kirschen° essen. — *He's not an easy man to get along with.*

Der Apfel fällt nicht weit vom Stamm.° — *Like father, like son.*

WAS PASST ZUSAMMEN?

1. Alle anderen kommen mit dem Bus, aber Jutta sollen wir mit dem Auto abholen.

   Mit dem ist nicht gut Kirschen essen.

2. Stefan ist wie sein Vater. Er fängt immer tausend Projekte an und macht nie etwas fertig.

   Nein, aber ich will ihm heute noch reinen Wein einschenken.

3. Was? Du gehst schon wieder mit Ralf aus? Weiß er denn eigentlich, daß du verlobt° bist?

   Sie will doch immer eine Extrawurst.

engaged

4. Wie ist denn dein neuer Boß?

   Der Apfel fällt nicht weit vom Stamm.

5. Wie sieht Claudias Schwester aus?

   Das ist mir Wurst.

6. Sollen wir ins Kino gehen oder in die Disco?

   Sie gleicht ihr wie ein Ei dem anderen.

7. Günter sagt, daß du heute abend mit ihm ins Kino gehst.

   Nein, jetzt ist alles wieder in Butter.

8. Hast du immer noch Probleme mit deiner Hauswirtin?°

   Das ist doch alles Käse, was der sagt.

landlady

EIN WORTRÄTSEL

What are the opposites of the following words? The first letters of these opposites will give you the German equivalent of the English proverb "All's well that ends well". The double slashes indicate the beginning of a new word in the German proverb.

aufwachen / ja / intelligent / letzt / / schlecht / über / Nacht / / jung / schnell / kurz / letzt / süß / / nehmen / wichtig / billig

WEITERE NÜTZLICHE WÖRTER UND AUSDRÜCKE

Die Stadt

die Stadt, die Städte	town, city
in die Stadt	to town
das Rathaus	city hall
die Straße, die Straßen	street
der Laden, die Läden	store
der Supermarkt	supermarket
das Obst	fruit
das Gemüse	vegetables
die Fleischerei	butcher shop
der Fleischer	butcher
die Bäckerei	bakery
der Bäcker	baker
das Kaufhaus	department store
die Buchhandlung	bookstore
das Blumengeschäft	flower shop
die Blume, die Blumen	flower
die Drogerie	drugstore
die Apotheke	pharmacy
die Post	post office
die Bank	bank
das Krankenhaus	hospital
der Arzt, die Ärzte	(*male*) doctor
die Ärztin, die Ärztinnen	(*female*) doctor
der Hausarzt	family doctor
der Zahnarzt	dentist
der Bahnhof	train station
der Flughafen	airport

Geschirr und Besteck

das Geschirr	dishes, china
die Tasse, die Tassen	cup
die Untertasse, die Untertassen	saucer
der Teller, die Teller	plate
das Besteck	cutlery
das Messer, die Messer	knife
die Gabel, die Gabeln	fork
der Löffel, die Löffel	spoon

Wichtige Verben

sparen	to save
aus•geben (gibt aus), hat ausgegeben	to spend
leihen, hat geliehen	to lend, to borrow
lassen (läßt), hat gelassen	to leave, to let; to have something done
riechen, hat gerochen	to smell

Andere nützliche Wörter

hoffentlich	hopefully, I hope
umsonst	for nothing; in vain

Koordinierende Konjunktionen

und	and
oder	or
denn	for, because
aber	but, however
sondern	but, but rather

Subordinierende Konjunktionen

weil	because
wenn	if
wenn	when
daß	that
ob	whether

Ausdrücke

zu Besuch kommen	to come for a visit, to visit
zu Fuß gehen	to walk
Es macht mir Spaß, Geld auszugeben.	I enjoy spending money.
Es fällt mir schwer, immer so früh aufzustehen.	I find it hard to get up so early all the time.

WÖRTER IM KONTEXT

1. WAS PASST ZUSAMMEN?

a. der Flug   arzt
    die Zahn   hof
    der Bahn   ärztin
    der Haus   hafen

b. die Unter   markt
    die Buch   haus
    der Super   tasse
    das Kauf   handlung

2. ASSOZIATIONEN. Pair the words in each group.

a. die Straße   die Rose
   die Fleischerei   das Porzellan
   das Blumengeschäft   das Auto
   das Krankenhaus   die Karotten
   das Gemüse   die Wurst
   das Geschirr   der Arzt

b. die Drogerie   das Brot
   das Obst   das Penizillin
   die Bäckerei   die Briefmarke
   die Apotheke   die Suppe
   die Post   der Apfel
   der Löffel   das Shampoo

c. das Messer   trinken
   die Tasse   sparen
   die Stadt   gut riechen
   der Laden   leben
   die Bank   schneiden
   die Blume   einkaufen

3. WAS PASST WO?

Spaß   ausgegeben   außerdem   spare   zu Fuß   hoffentlich   umsonst

a. _____ hast du für die Karten nicht wieder so viel Geld _____.
   Nein, diesmal have ich sie _____ bekommen.

b. Ich gehe jetzt immer _____ zur Uni. Es macht mir _____, ich _____ Geld, und
   _____ ist es sehr gesund.

   lassen   geliehen   zu Besuch   schwer

c. Warum hast du Günter schon wieder 100 Mark _____?
   Weil es mir _____ fällt, nein zu sagen.

d. Warum willst du denn das Wohnzimmer neu tapezieren _____?
   Weil Tante Emma nächste Woche _____ kommt.

▣ ZUR AUSSPRACHE

GERMAN *R*

A good pronunciation of the German **r** will go a long way to making you sound like
a native speaker. Don't let the tip of the tongue curl upward and backward as it
does when pronouncing an English *r,* but keep it down behind the lower teeth.
When followed by a vowel, the sound of a German **r** is not unlike the sound of **ch**
in **auch.** When it is not followed by a vowel, the German **r** takes on a vowel-like
quality.

• Hören Sie gut zu und wiederholen Sie!

1. **R**ita und **R**icha**r**d sitzen imme**r** im Zimme**r**.
   Rita und **R**icha**r**d sehen ge**r**n fe**r**n.

   Robe**r**t und **R**osi spielen Ka**r**ten im Ga**r**ten.
   Robe**r**t und **R**osi t**r**inken Bie**r** fü**r** vie**r**.

2. Geste**r**n wa**r** **R**alf hie**r** und do**r**t,
   Mo**r**gen fäh**r**t e**r** wieder fo**r**t.°   **fort•fahren:** *to leave*

3. Ho**r**st ist hie**r**,
   Ho**r**st will Wu**r**st,
   Ho**r**st will Bie**r**
   fü**r** seinen Du**r**st.

Einfamilienhaus in Kaisersbach bei Stuttgart.

KAPITEL 9

■ **Kommunikationsziele**

*In **Kapitel 9** you will learn how to:*
talk about how and where you live
talk about location and destination
negotiate with a landlord/landlady
talk about possessions and relationships
describe people, places, and things
give opinions and react to opinions

■ **Hör- und Sprechsituationen**

Die möblierte Wohnung
Wo wohnst du?
Mein Zimmer
Wo warst du vor der Deutschstunde?
Zimmersuche
Zimmer zu vermieten
Gelüste
Zimmersorgen
Wohnmöglichkeiten

■ **Strukturen**

Two-case prepositions
stellen/stehen; legen/liegen; hängen
an, in, vor, and **zwischen** in time phrases
The genitive case
The genitive prepositions
N-nouns
Adjective endings after **der**-words and **ein**-words

■ **Wissenswertes**

Housing in the German-speaking countries
Schrebergärten
Student housing in the German-speaking countries

VORSCHAU

📼 DIE MÖBLIERTE° WOHNUNG

Martin und Peter sind schon lange unzufrieden° mit ihrer Einzimmerwohnung in der Zennerstraße. Sie suchen seit Monaten eine größere Wohnung, und vorgestern haben sie endlich etwas gefunden. Die Besitzerin° dieser Wohnung fliegt auf ein Jahr zu ihrem Sohn nach Texas, und gestern hat sie Peter noch die letzten Anweisungen° gegeben. Jetzt ist gerade Claudia zur Tür hereingekommen, um die neue Wohnung der beiden Freunde zu bewundern°.

MARTIN: Nun, Claudia, wie gefällt dir unsere neue Wohnung? Vollständig° möbliert für nur 400 Mark im Monat!

CLAUDIA: Nicht schlecht, Martin. Nur, die Möbel stehen alle am falschen Platz.

MARTIN: Tut mir leid, Claudia, aber wir haben Frau Wild versprochen°, nichts umzustellen.°

CLAUDIA: Ist Frau Wild nicht schon weggeflogen?

PETER: Ja, heute morgen um halb acht.

CLAUDIA: Also vor zwei Stunden°, und nach Texas, nicht?

MARTIN: Ja, zu ihrem Sohn nach Texas.

CLAUDIA: Na, dann können wir ja anfangen. Nimm doch mal die Stehlampe hier, Martin, und stell° sie neben die Couch.

MARTIN: Aber Claudia . . .

CLAUDIA: Da ist ein Ozean zwischen euch und Frau Wild, und sie kommt erst in einem Jahr wieder zurück. Ihr dürft nur nicht vergessen, wie alles gestanden hat.

PETER: Du bist echt schlau°, Claudia. Und wir haben ja auch beide ein ziemlich gutes Gedächtnis°.

CLAUDIA: Na, dann mal los! Nehmt mal den Teppich° hier, und legt ihn vor die Couch! So, das sieht schon gleich viel besser aus. Und die häßliche° alte Uhr dort auf dem Büfett, was machen wir nur mit der?

PETER: Die Uhr ist ihr sehr lieb, sagt Frau Wild. Sie hat sie von ihren Eltern zur Hochzeit° bekommen, und wir dürfen *ja* nicht vergessen, sie jeden Morgen aufzuziehen°. Sonst geht sie kaputt.

CLAUDIA: Dann nimm sie doch in die Küche, und stell sie auf den Kühlschrank. Ihr seht sie dann immer beim Frühstück und könnt sie nicht vergessen.

PETER: Da war doch noch etwas, was wir nicht vergessen dürfen. Ach ja, die Zimmerpflanzen, die brauchen natürlich Wasser.

CLAUDIA: Und *wie* die Wasser brauchen! Schau mal die Kakteen hier, die sind ja ganz ausgetrocknet°.

PETER: Ja, die sollen wir tüchtig° gießen, alle° zwei Tage, sagt Frau Wild. Und die Orchideen dort drüben . . .

CLAUDIA: Warum stehen denn die nicht am Fenster? Das ist doch viel zu dunkel dort, wo die stehen.

PETER: Da hast du recht. Komm, Martin, wir stellen sie ans Fenster neben die Kakteen. Wir dürfen sie übrigens nur alle vierzehn Tage gießen, sonst gehen sie kaputt.

furnished

dissatisfied

owner

instructions
admire

completely

promised
to rearrange

two hours ago

put

smart
memory
carpet
ugly

wedding
to wind

dried out
thoroughly / every

CLAUDIA: Was ist denn mit der Katze dort auf dem Balkon? Gehört die auch zur Wohnung?

MARTIN: Ja, das ist die alte Maunz. Was müssen wir der füttern, Peter?

PETER: Sie bekommt jeden Morgen eine Dose Katzenfutter und jeden Abend ein bißchen warme Milch. Sonst wird sie krank, sagt Frau Wild.

MARTIN: Jetzt geh mal raus auf unseren Balkon, Claudia!

CLAUDIA: *(geht auf den Balkon)* Du, die haben aber tolle Geranien hier nebenan°.   *next door*

PETER: Die gehören Pleikes, die Geranien. Das sind richtig nette Leute, sagt Frau Wild. Und wenn wir Probleme haben, sollen wir *ja* nur zu Pleikes gehen.

MARTIN: Du Peter, wer ist denn die Frau dort unten? Die sieht ja wie Frau Wild aus.

PETER: Du, das gibt's doch nicht°! Das *ist* Frau Wild!   *That's impossible!*

CLAUDIA: Ich denke, Frau Wild ist auf dem Weg° nach Texas.   *way*

MARTIN: Das ist Frau Wild, und sie kommt zu uns. Stell sofort die Uhr wieder aufs Büfett, Peter!

CLAUDIA: Ich stelle die Stehlampe wieder in die Ecke, und du, Martin, legst den Teppich wieder . . .

VOM LESEN ZUM SPRECHEN

Beantworten Sie diese Fragen!

1. Wieviel Uhr ist es jetzt?
2. Warum ist die Uhr Frau Wild so lieb?
3. Warum müssen Martin und Peter sie jeden Morgen aufziehen?
4. Wie oft müssen sie die Orchideen gießen und wie oft die Kakteen?
5. Warum stellen Martin und Peter die Orchideen ans Fenster?
6. Wie heißt Frau Wilds Katze? Was kriegt sie morgens, und was bekommt sie abends?
7. Was sollen Peter und Martin machen, wenn sie Probleme haben?

Die haben aber tolle Geranien hier nebenan!

WIE GUT HAT PETER AUFGEPASST? Hören Sie, was Frau Wild gestern zu Peter gesagt hat. Beantworten Sie dann jede Frage zweimal: a. Was hat Frau Wild gestern zu Peter gesagt? b. Was hat Peter heute zu Claudia und Martin gesagt?

1. Von wem hat Frau Wild die Uhr?
2. Wie oft sollen Martin und Peter die Uhr aufziehen?
3. Wie oft sollen sie die Kakteen gießen, und wie oft brauchen die Orchideen Wasser?
4. Wie heißt Frau Wilds Katze?
5. Was bekommt die Katze morgens, und was kriegt sie abends?
6. Was für Leute sind Pleikes?
7. Zu wem sollen Martin und Peter gehen, wenn sie Probleme haben?
8. Wann fliegt Frau Wild weg?

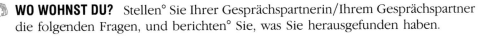

WO WOHNST DU? Stellen° Sie Ihrer Gesprächspartnerin/Ihrem Gesprächspartner die folgenden Fragen, und berichten° Sie, was Sie herausgefunden haben.   *ask*   *report*

S1: Wo wohnst du?	**S2:** Ich wohne	im Studentenheim.
Wie gefällt es dir, wo du wohnst?		(mit einer Freundin/ einem Freund zusam- men) in einer [Zwei-] zimmerwohnung.
Warum gefällt es dir dort so gut (nicht sehr gut)?		mit [zwei] Studenten zusammen in einer Wohngemeinschaft°.
shared housing		noch zu Hause.
	Ich habe	ein Zimmer in einem Privathaus.
		. . .

Owning a home is a dream of many families in the German-speaking countries, but all too often it remains just a dream. Together these countries are about the size of California but have almost five times California's population. The density of the population as well as strict laws for the preservation of green space put real estate at a premium. In addition, building costs are very high. The combination of these factors makes owning a house **(Ein- familienhaus)** or even a condominium apartment **(Eigentumswohnung)** impossible for well over half of the population. There is a saying in Swabian, a Southern German dialect, that aptly expresses the hardship involved in acquiring a home: **Schaffe, spare, Häusle baue, — verrecke!** *(Work, save, build your house—croak!)*

DHH heißt „Doppelhaushälfte". Wie heißen solche Häuser in Amerika?

NÜTZLICHE WÖRTER UND AUSDRÜCKE

Wohnung und Möbel

die Wohnung, die Wohnungen	apartment
die Möbel *(pl)*	furniture
das Wohnzimmer, die Wohnzimmer	living room
der Couchtisch, die Couchtische	coffee table
der Sessel, die Sessel	armchair
die Stehlampe, die Stehlampen	floor lamp
die Couch, die Couches	sofa
die Stereoanlage, die Stereoanlagen	stereo
das Bücherregal, die Bücherregale	bookcase
der Balkon, die Balkone	balcony

Wohnung und Möbel

der Schreibtisch, die Schreibtische	desk
das Büfett, die Büfetts	buffet
der Fernseher, die Fernseher	television set
der Papierkorb, die Papierkörbe	wastepaper basket
das Schlafzimmer, die Schlafzimmer	bedroom
der Teppich, die Teppiche	carpet
die Kommode, die Kommoden	dresser
das Fenster, die Fenster	window
die Lampe, die Lampen	lamp
das Bett, die Betten	bed
das Bild, die Bilder	picture
der Schrank, die Schränke	closet
die Zimmerpflanze, die Zimmerpflanzen	houseplant
die Küche, die Küchen	kitchen
der Fußboden, die Fußböden	floor
die Wand, die Wände	wall
die Decke, die Decken	ceiling
der Tisch, die Tische	table
der Stuhl, die Stühle	chair
der Kühlschrank, die Kühlschränke	refrigerator
der Herd, die Herde	stove
das Spülbecken, die Spülbecken	sink
das Badezimmer (das Bad), die Badezimmer[1]	bathroom
das Waschbecken, die Waschbecken	wash basin
die Dusche, die Duschen	shower
die Badewanne, die Badewannen	bathtub
die Toilette, die Toiletten[1]	toilet, lavatory
das Klo, die Klos	toilet
der Flur, die Flure	hall
die Treppe, die Treppen	staircase
die Tür, die Türen	door
die Garderobe, die Garderoben	front hall closet

Verben

legen	to put *(in a horizontal position)*, to lay (down)
stellen	to put *(in an upright position)*, to stand
um•stellen	to rearrange
füttern	to feed
versprechen (verspricht), hat versprochen	to promise

Andere Wörter

möbliert	furnished
lieb	dear
ziemlich	fairly, quite, rather
sofort	immediately

---

1. In many German homes the bathtub, shower, and washbasin are in one room **(das Bad)** and the toilet in another **(die Toilette).**

Ausdrücke

vor zwei Stunden	two hours ago
Das gibt's doch nicht!	That's impossible! That can't be!
alle vierzehn Tage	every two weeks

Das Gegenteil

hell — dunkel	light—dark
schön — häßlich	beautiful—ugly
zufrieden — unzufrieden	satisfied—dissatisfied

WÖRTER IM KONTEXT

ASSOZIATIONEN. Was paßt zusammen?

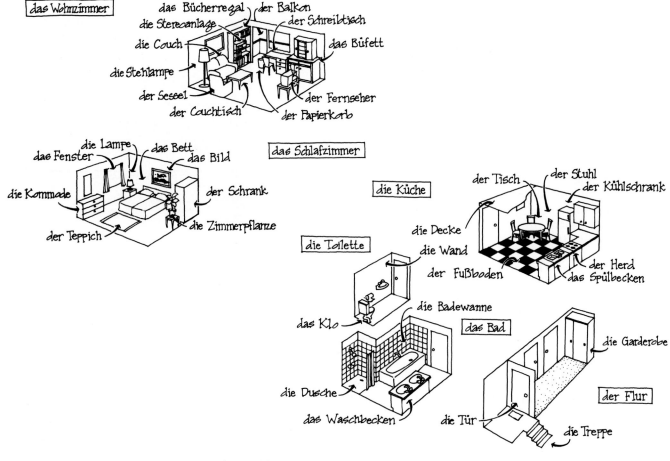

a. der Stuhl	kochen	c. die Wand	der Mantel
das Bett	gießen	das Spülbecken	der Teppich
die Zimmerpflanze	schlafen	der Fußboden	das Wasser
der Herd	sitzen	die Garderobe	das Bild
b. der Kühlschrank	laut	d. lieb	die Nacht
die Stereoanlage	müde	dunkel	die Stehlampe
das Schlafzimmer	frisch	hell	der Hund

Schrebergärten bei
Stuttgart

Many people in the German-speaking countries are avid gardeners. Those who live in apartments often lease or buy a **Schrebergarten,** a small plot of land at the edge of town where they can go on weekends to grow a few flowers and vegetables, or just to relax. The concept of **Schrebergärten** dates back to the nineteenth century. Daniel Schreber, a doctor and professor in Leipzig, created playgrounds with adjoining gardening plots for children and their parents. The love for growing things is also evident in the windows and on the balconies of apartments, which are often fitted with window boxes full of flowers and hanging plants.

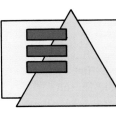

FUNKTIONEN UND FORMEN

1. TALKING ABOUT LOCATION AND DESTINATION

WO AND WOHIN: A REVIEW

In *Kapitel 2* you learned that the English question word *where* has three equivalents in German: **wo** *(in what place)*, **wohin** *(to what place)*, and **woher** *(from what place)*. Since **wo** and **wohin** will play an important role in subsequent sections of this chapter, you will have to fine-tune your feeling for the difference between them.

The use of **wo** or **wohin** is obvious in the following questions:

Wo ist mein Mantel?
Wohin gehst du?
Wohin geht diese Straße?

Where is my coat? (*in* what place?)
Where are you going? (*to* what place?)
Where does this road go? (*to* what place?)

Wohin geht es nach rechts, und wohin nach links?

For speakers of English it is less obvious whether to use **wo** or **wohin** in the following examples:

Where should I hang my coat? (*in* what place? or *to* what place?)
Where did you put my briefcase? (*in* what place? or *to* what place?)

For both of these questions, speakers of German think in terms of moving something (e.g., the coat, the briefcase) from point A to point B. The German equivalent for *where* in these two questions is therefore **wohin:**

Wohin soll ich meinen Mantel hängen?   *Where (to what place) should I hang my coat?*

Wohin hast du meine Aktentasche gestellt?   *Where (to what place) did you put my briefcase?*

A. WO ODER WOHIN?

1. _____ gehst du?
2. _____ hast du in Berlin gewohnt?
3. _____ ist Sylvia?
4. _____ geht diese Straße?
5. _____ habe ich meine Handschuhe gelegt?
6. _____ wohnt deine Freundin?
7. _____ hast du das schöne Kleid gekauft?
8. _____ soll ich den Brief schicken?
9. _____ hast du meine Aktentasche° gestellt?
10. _____ arbeitet Tina?
11. _____ sind denn meine Handschuhe?
12. _____ hast du diesen Artikel gefunden?
13. _____ fliegst du nächsten Sommer?
14. _____ hast du meine Schlüssel° gelegt?
15. _____ spielt ihr morgen Fußball?
16. _____ soll ich meinen Mantel hängen?
17. _____ triffst du deinen Freund?
18. _____ fährt dieser Bus?
19. _____ geht diese Tür?
20. _____ spielen die Kinder?

keys

briefcase

TWO-CASE PREPOSITIONS

You have already learned that there are accusative prepositions and dative prepositions.

Accusative Prepositions		Dative Prepositions	
durch	ohne	aus	nach
für	um	außer	seit
gegen		bei	von
		mit	zu

There is another group of prepositions that is followed by *either* the dative case *or* the accusative case:

an	at; to *(the side of)*, on *(a vertical surface)*	**neben**	beside
auf	on *(a horizontal surface)*	**über**	over, above
hinter	behind	**unter**	under, below
in	in, into, to	**vor**	in front of
		zwischen	between

When these two-case prepositions signal *location*, they answer the question **wo?** and are followed by the *dative* case. When they signal *destination*, they answer the question **wohin?** and are followed by the *accusative* case.

location	wo?	preposition + dative
destination	wohin?	preposition + accusative

B. IN DER NEUEN WOHNUNG. Using **wo** or **wohin,** ask your partner where the items in the illustration are, or are being placed. She/he answers using two-case prepositions.

Was ist ein Bauernhof?

▶ _____ hängt Antje das Poster? _____ d__ Küchentür. *(f)*

S1: Wohin hängt Antje das Poster? **S2:** An die Küchentür.

1. _____ hängt der Picasso? _____ d__ Wand *(f)* über der Couch.
2. _____ steht die Zimmerpflanze? _____ d__ Bücherregal. *(n)*
3. _____ springt° die Katze? _____ d__ Couch. *(f)*   *is . . . jumping*
4. _____ steht der Herd? _____ d__ Küche. *(f)*
5. _____ geht die offene Tür? _____ d__ Küche.
6. _____ steht der Karton mit den Büchern? _____ d__ Bücherregal. *(n)*
7. _____ legt Kurt den Teppich? _____ d__ Couch. *(f)*
8. _____ ist die Stehlampe? _____ d__ Sessel. *(m)*
9. _____ huscht° die Maus? _____ d__ Couch. *(f)*   *is . . . scurrying*
10. _____ hängt Uli das Landschaftsbild?° _____ d__ Schreibtisch. *(m)*   *landscape painting*
11. _____ hängt der Picasso? _____ d__ Couch. *(f)*
12. _____ liegt der Ball? _____ d__ Schreibtisch. *(m)*
13. _____ krabbelt° das Baby? _____ d__ Schreibtisch.   *is . . . crawling*
14. _____ stellt Helga den Papierkorb? _____ d__ Schreibtisch.
15. _____ ist der Lichtschalter?° _____ d__ Küchentür. *(f)*   *light switch*
16. _____ hängt der Kalender? _____ d__ Picasso *(m)* und d__ Landschaftsbild. *(n)*
17. _____ stellt Thomas die Vase? _____ d__ Zimmerpflanze *(f)* und d__ Radio. *(n)*

Contractions

The prepositions **an** and **in** normally contract with the articles **das** and **dem**:

an + das = ans	Hast du unseren Poster **ans** schwarze Brett gehängt?	*Did you hang our poster **on** the bulletin board?*
an + dem = am	Hängt unser Poster schon **am** schwarzen Brett?	*Is our poster hanging **on** the bulletin board yet?*
in + das = ins	Heute abend gehen wir **ins** Konzert.	*Tonight we're going **to** a concert.*
in + dem = im	Gestern abend waren wir **im** Kino.	*Last night we were **at** the movies.*

In colloquial German the article **das** is also contracted with other two-case prepositions: **aufs, hinters, übers, unters, vors.**

C. KONTRAKTIONEN. Beginnen Sie die Fragen mit **wo, wohin** oder **was.** Ihr Gesprächspartner verwendet in den Antworten **am, ans, im** oder **ins.**

S1:

1. _____ geht diese Tür?
2. _____ soll ich diesen Kaktus stellen?
3. _____ ist Claudia?
4. _____ wart ihr gestern abend?
5. _____ machst du heute abend?
6. _____ soll ich mit diesem Poster machen?
7. _____ ist denn Andrea?
8. _____ kochst du heute abend?
9. _____ ist Peter?

S2:

Die geht _____ Schlafzimmer.

Den stellst du _____ Fenster, der braucht viel Sonne.

Sie sitzt _____ Computer und arbeitet an ihrem Referat.

Wir waren _____ Kino und haben einen tollen Film gesehen.

Ich glaube, ich gehe mal früh _____ Bett.

Häng es bitte gleich _____ schwarze Brett.

Ich glaube, sie sitzt wieder _____ Klavier und übt.

Gar nichts. Heute abend essen wir mal _____ Gasthaus.

Ich glaube, er liegt noch _____ Bett.

German *an, auf, in,* and English *to*

In *Kapitel 7* you learned that both **zu** and **nach** can mean *to.* The prepositions **an, auf,** and **in** can also mean *to* if they answer the question **wohin.**

a. **An** is used to indicate that your point of destination is next to something, such as a door, a telephone, or a body of water:

Geh bitte **an** die Tür.	*Go **to** the door, please.*
Geh **ans** Telefon!	*Go **to** the phone.*
Wir fahren jeden Sommer **ans** Meer.	*We go **to** the ocean every summer.*

b. **In** is generally used if your point of destination is within a place, such as a room, a house, a concert hall, or a mountain range:

Geht doch bitte **ins** Wohzimmer.	*Go **to** the living room, please.*
Heute abend gehen wir **in** die Oper.	*Tonight we're going **to** the opera.*
Warum fahren wir nicht mal **in** die Berge?	*Why don't we go **to** the mountains for a change?*

c. **In** is used instead of **nach** to express that you are going to a country if the name of the country is feminine or plural:

Morgen fliegen wir **in** die USA.	*Tomorrow we're flying **to** the USA.*

d. **Auf** is often used instead of **zu** to express that you are going to a building or an institution like the bank, the post office, the city hall, especially to do business:

Ich muß heute nachmittag **aufs** Rathaus.	*I have to go **to** the city hall this afternoon.*

D. WAS PASST ZUSAMMEN? Beginnen Sie Ihre Fragen mit **Wohin geht man, wenn . . .** Ihr Gesprächspartner verwendet in den Antworten die Präpositionen **an, auf** oder **in.**

▶ Man will Schwyzerdütsch° hören.

> die Schweiz

dialect word for Swiss German

S1: Wohin geht man, wenn man Schwyzerdütsch hören will?

S2: Da geht man in die Schweiz.

1. Man braucht Geld.
2. Man will mit dem Bürgermeister° sprechen.
3. Das Telefon klingelt.°
4. Man braucht Briefmarken.
5. Jemand klopft.°
6. Man will ein Symphonieorchester hören.
7. Man will in den Ferien in Salzwasser schwimmen.
8. Man will schlafen.
9. Man will Shakespeares „Hamlet" sehen.

mayor

rings

knocks

> die Tür   die Bank   das Theater   das Rathaus   die Post
> das Telefon   das Konzert   das Bett   das Meer°

ocean

10. Man möchte Mozarts „Don Giovanni" sehen.
11. Man möchte einen Film sehen.
12. Man will etwas kochen.
13. Man will mal nicht kochen.
14. Man braucht frisches Obst und Gemüse.
15. Man muß seine Steuern° bezahlen.
16. Man will eine Flasche Wein holen.
17. Man möchte bergsteigen.°
18. Man möchte amerikanisches Englisch hören.

taxes

go mountain climbing

> das Gasthaus   die USA   der Weinkeller   das Finanzamt°   das Gebirge°
> der Wochenmarkt   die Oper   das Kino   die Küche

tax office / mountains

The verbs *stellen, legen, hängen*

In English the verb *to put* can mean *to put something in a vertical, horizontal, or hanging position:*

Put the wine glasses on the table.
Put your coats on the bed.
Put your jacket in the closet.

German uses three separate verbs to describe the action conveyed by the English *to put:*

stellen	*to put in an upright position, to stand*	**Stell** die Weingläser auf **den** Tisch!
legen	*to put in a horizontal position, to lay (down)*	**Legt** eure Mäntel auf**s** Bett!
hängen	*to hang (up)*	**Häng** deine Jacke in **die** Garderobe!

When these verbs are followed by a two-case preposition, the object of the preposition appears in the *accusative* case.

move
discuss

E. UNSERE NEUE WOHNUNG (I). Sie ziehen° mit Ihrer Gesprächspartnerin/Ihrem Gesprächspartner in eine neue Wohnung. Besprechen° Sie mit ihr/ihm, wohin Sie Ihre Sachen stellen (legen, hängen) wollen.

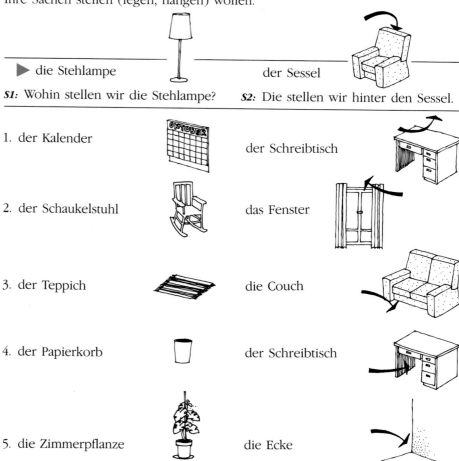

▶ die Stehlampe   der Sessel

S1: Wohin stellen wir die Stehlampe?   *S2:* Die stellen wir hinter den Sessel.

1. der Kalender   der Schreibtisch

2. der Schaukelstuhl   das Fenster

3. der Teppich   die Couch

4. der Papierkorb   der Schreibtisch

5. die Zimmerpflanze   die Ecke

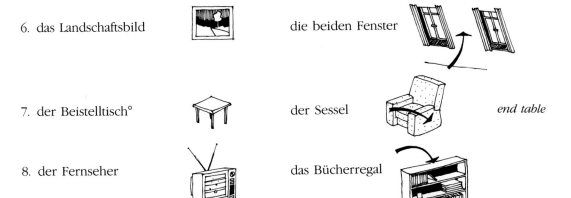

6. das Landschaftsbild   die beiden Fenster

7. der Beistelltisch°   der Sessel   *end table*

8. der Fernseher   das Bücherregal

The verbs *stehen, liegen, hängen*

English normally uses the verb *to be* when describing the position of an object.

The wine glasses *are* on the table.
Your coats *are* on the bed.
Your jacket *is* in the closet.

German tends to be more exact when describing these positions:

stehen	*to be standing*	Die Weingläser **stehen** auf **dem** Tisch.
liegen	*to be lying*	Eure Mäntel **liegen** auf **dem** Bett.
hängen	*to be hanging*	Deine Jacke **hängt** in **der** Garderobe.

When these verbs are followed by one of the two-case prepositions, the object of the preposition appears in the *dative* case.

F. UNSERE NEUE WOHNUNG (II). Eine Freundin/ein Freund ruft sie an und möchte wissen, wo Ihre Sachen stehen (liegen, hängen).

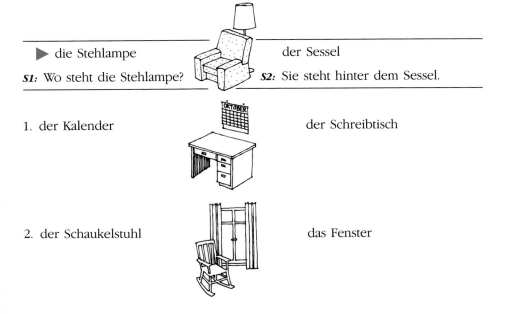

▶ die Stehlampe   der Sessel

S1: Wo steht die Stehlampe?   *S2:* Sie steht hinter dem Sessel.

1. der Kalender   der Schreibtisch

2. der Schaukelstuhl   das Fenster

3. der Teppich  die Couch

4. der Papierkorb der Schreibtisch

5. die Zimmerpflanze die Ecke

6. das Landschaftsbild die beiden Fenster

7. der Beistelltisch der Sessel

8. der Fernseher  das Bücherregal

 **MEIN ZIMMER**

draw / floor plan
to indicate

Zeichnen° Sie einen Grundriß° von Ihrem Zimmer, *ohne* Möbel, aber mit allen Türen und Fenstern. Vergessen Sie nicht anzudeuten,° wo Norden, Süden, Osten und Westen sind.

    Geben Sie diesen Grundriß Ihrer Gesprächspartnerin/Ihrem Gesprächspartner. Beschreiben Sie ihr/ihm, wo Ihre Sachen stehen (liegen, hängen). Sie/er zeichnet° dann alles ein.

zeichnet ... ein: *sketches*
... in

Nützliches Vokabular

An der Nordwand (der Südwand, der Ostwand, der Westwand) steht (hängt) . . .

on the left
on the right

Links° neben . . . steht . . .
Rechts° neben . . . steht . . .
Zwischen . . . und . . . steht . . .

G. HOLGERS ZIMMER. Sagen Sie das auf deutsch!

1. Mother comes into Holger's room.
2. Holger is sitting in front of the TV.
3. Mother says: "Holger, I don't understand you.
4. How can you live in such° a pigpen?°   **so / der Schweinestall**
5. Your clothes are lying on the floor.
6. Why can't you hang them in the closet?
7. Your notebooks° are lying on the bed.   **die Hefte**
8. Please put them on the desk.
9. And on the dresser (there) are five cola cans!°   **die Coladosen**
10. Didn't I tell you that you're not supposed to put your cola cans on the dresser?!"

✏️ **ICH UND MEIN ZIMMER.** Beschreiben Sie Ihr Zimmer. Was gefällt Ihnen an° Ihrem Zimmer besonders?° Warum?   *about / especially*

2. SAYING WHEN SOMETHING OCCURS

THE TWO-CASE PREPOSITIONS *AN, IN, VOR,* AND *ZWISCHEN* IN TIME PHRASES

Phrases with the prepositions **an, in, vor,** and **zwischen** often answer the question **wann.** The objects of these prepositions are then *always* in the dative case. Note that in time expressions **vor** can mean *before* or *ago.*

Wann sind Sie geboren?	**When** *were you born?*
Am ersten April 1969.	**On** *April first 1969.*
Wann fliegst du nach Deutschland?	**When** *are you flying to Germany?*
Im September.	**In** *September.*
Wann sprichst du mit Professor Seidlmeyer?	**When** *are you going to talk to Professor Seidlmeyer?*
Vor der Vorlesung.	**Before** *the lecture.*
Wann hast du mit Professor Seidlmeyer gesprochen?	**When** *did you talk to Professor Seidlmeyer?*
Vor einer Viertelstunde.	*Fifteen minutes* **ago.**
Wann kommt Tante Esther?	**When** *is Aunt Esther coming?*
Zwischen dem ersten und **dem** fünften Mai.	**Between** *the first and fifth of May.*

H. WANN ODER WOHIN?

▶ _____ warst du in Berlin?   Vor ein__ Jahr.

S1: Wann warst du in Berlin?   *S2:* Vor einem Jahr.

---

1. _____ geht ihr nach der Vorlesung?   In__ Kino.
2. _____ beginnt das Wintersemester?   I__ Oktober.
3. _____ soll ich diesen Sessel stellen?   Zwischen d__ Schreibtisch und d__ Couch.

---

4. _____ gehst du in die Stadt? Zwischen mein__ Biologievorlesung und d__ Mittagessen.

5. _____ besuchst du deine Eltern? A__ Wochenende.

6. _____ hängst du das Landschafts-bild? Zwischen d__ Tür und d__ Fenster.

7. _____ gehst du auf die Post? Vor d__ Mittagessen.

8. _____ soll ich das Poster hängen? An d__ Schlafzimmertür.

9. _____ habt ihr diesen Film gesehen? Vor ein__ Woche.

10. _____ legen wir den Perserteppich? Vor d__ Couch.

11. _____ rufst du an? In ein__ halben Stunde.

12. _____ geht ihr zwischen Weih-nachten und Neujahr? In d__ Schweiz.

13. _____ fahrt ihr in die Türkei? Zwischen d__ zehnten und d__ fünfzehnten Juli.

14. _____ seid ihr aus Italien zurück-gekommen? Vor ein__ Monat.

15. _____ geht ihr nach dem Konzert? In__ Café Mozart.

16. _____ hast du Brigitte zuletzt gesehen? An ihr__ neunzehnten Geburtstag.

17. _____ warst du in den USA? Vor zwei Jahr__.

 WO WARST DU VOR DIESER DEUTSCHSTUNDE? Fragen Sie Ihre Gesprächspartnerin/Ihren Gesprächspartner, wo sie/er vor dieser Deutschstunde war, und wohin sie/er nachher° geht. Berichten Sie der Klasse, was Sie heraus-gefunden haben!

afterwards

ZUSAMMENSCHAU

ZIMMERSUCHE

didn't get enough studying done / decided

has . . . rung the doorbell

Stephanie hat sehr gern im Studentenheim gewohnt, aber sie weiß auch, daß sie dort nicht genug zum Lernen gekommen ist°. Sie hat deshalb beschlossen°, ein ruhiges Zimmer in einem Privathaus zu suchen. Beim Studentenwerk hat sie eine Adresse in der Ebersbergerstraße bekommen, und sie steht jetzt dort vor der Haus-tür und hat gerade geklingelt°.

- Lesen Sie bitte zuerst die *Neuen Vokabeln,* und hören Sie dann, was Stephanie und Frau Kuhn miteinander sprechen.

Neue Vokabeln

vermieten	*to rent (out)*
hoch	*up*
rechts	*on the right*
hinaus•gehen	*to go out*
da unten	*down there*
benutzen	*to use*
stören	*to disturb*
die Kochplatte	*hot plate*
frei•halten	*to hold*

Wieviel möchte Gerhard für Zimmer und Heizung ausgeben?

- Was ist die richtige Antwort?

1. Was ist groß und hell?   die Treppe / das Zimmer
2. Was findet Stephanie wunderbar?   den Balkon / die Möbel
3. Was benutzt Frau Kuhn nicht?   die Badewanne / die Dusche
4. Wie viele Personen wohnen in diesem Haus?   eine / zwei
5. Was darf Stephanie nicht benutzen?   die Kochplatte / die Küche
6. Wo ist die Kochplatte?   in der Küche / in dem freien Zimmer
7. Nimmt Stephanie das Zimmer?   ja / vielleicht

Hören Sie das Gespräch jetzt noch einmal, und beantworten Sie die folgenden Fragen!

1. Warum geht Stephanie zu Frau Kuhn? *Weil Frau Kuhn . . .*
2. Warum gefällt Stephanie das Zimmer so gut? *Weil . . .*
3. Von wo schaut Stephanie in den Garten?
4. Für wen ist die Badewanne, und für wen ist die Dusche?
5. Was kostet das Zimmer, und was sagt Stephanie zu diesem Preis?
6. Warum fragt Stephanie, ob es hier auch wirklich ruhig ist? *Weil sie . . .*
7. Was darf Stephanie bei Frau Kuhn nicht?
8. Wie kann Stephanie hier Wasser für Kaffee oder Tee heiß machen?
9. Bis wann möchte Frau Kuhn wissen, ob Stephanie das Zimmer nimmt?

ZIMMER ZU VERMIETEN

Sie suchen ein Zimmer und haben beim Studentenwerk eine Adresse bekommen. Sie sind gleich hingefahren, und Sie sprechen jetzt mit der Hauswirtin°/dem Hauswirt°. Natürlich finden Sie heraus, daß das Zimmer, wie alle Zimmer, seine Vorteile° und seine Nachteile° hat. Verwenden Sie Vorteile und Nachteile aus der folgenden Liste, um das Gespräch interessanter zu machen.

       landlady
       landlord
       advantages / disadvantages

Vorteile und Nachteile

Das Zimmer ist | nicht sehr teuer / sehr teuer.
               groß und hell / klein und dunkel.
               sehr ruhig / ziemlich laut.

Die Wände sind | frisch gestrichen / ziemlich schmutzig°.   *dirty*

Die Möbel sind | ganz neu / alt und ziemlich schäbig°.   *shabby*

Von hier zur Uni ist es | gar nicht weit / sehr weit.

Die Fenster gehen auf | den Garten / die Straße.

Sie haben | Küchenbenutzung° / keine Küchenbenutzung, aber Sie haben eine   *kitchen privileges*
          Kochplatte in Ihrem Zimmer.

Sie dürfen | das Badezimmer benutzen / das Badezimmer nicht benutzen, aber Sie
          haben ein Waschbecken in Ihrem Zimmer.
          Besuch haben, so lange Sie wollen / nur bis 22 Uhr Besuch haben.

3. INDICATING POSSESSION OR RELATIONSHIPS

Was ist eine Baustelle?

THE GENITIVE CASE

The genitive case is used to express the idea of possession or the idea of belonging together in a more general sense. You are already familiar with one form of the genitive:

Claudia**s** Fahrrad   *Claudia's bike*
Frau Meyer**s** Schirm   *Ms. Meyer's umbrella*

In German this form of the genitive is used only with proper names. Note that the ending **-s** is not preceded by an apostrophe.

For nouns other than proper names a different form of the genitive must be used. Note that this form of the genitive *follows* the noun it modifies.

das Buch **des** Lehrer**s**   *the teacher's book*
der Wagen mein**er** Schwester   *my sister's car*
der IQ dies**es** Kind**es**   *this child's IQ*
die Freunde mein**er** Kinder   *my children's friends*

English generally uses the possessive *-'s* only for persons while showing the belonging together of *things* with the preposition *of.* German uses the genitive for persons *and* things.

das Fahrrad mein**es** Bruder**s**   *my brother's bicycle*
das Dach unser**es** Haus**es**   *the roof **of** our house*

	Masculine		Feminine		Neuter		Plural	
Nominative	der	Lehrer	die	Schwester	das	Kind	die	Kinder
	ein	Lehrer	eine	Schwester	ein	Kind	meine	Kinder
Accusative	den	Lehrer	die	Schwester	das	Kind	die	Kinder
	einen	Lehrer	eine	Schwester	ein	Kind	meine	Kinder
Dative	dem	Lehrer	der	Schwester	dem	Kind	den	Kindern
	einem	Lehrer	einer	Schwester	einem	Kind	meinen	Kindern
Genitive	d**es**	Lehrer**s**	d**er**	Schwester	d**es**	Kind**es**	d**er**	Kinder
	ein**es**	Lehrer**s**	ein**er**	Schwester	ein**es**	Kind**es**	mein**er**	Kinder

One syllable masculine and neuter nouns add **-es** in the genitive singular. Masculine and neuter nouns with more than one syllable add **-s** in the genitive singular. Feminine nouns and the plural forms of all nouns have no genitive ending.

The genitive form of the interrogative pronoun **wer** is **wessen:**

Wessen Jacke ist das?   **Whose** *jacket is that?*

I. WESSEN HANDSCHUHE SIND DAS?

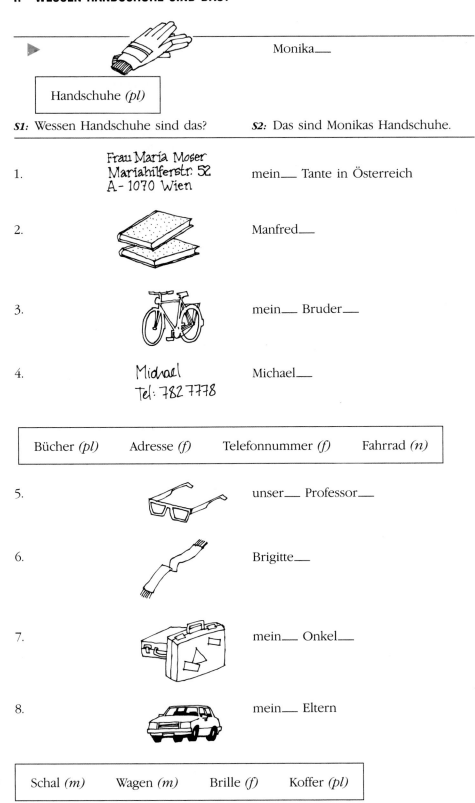

Monika___

Handschuhe *(pl)*

S1: Wessen Handschuhe sind das?   *S2:* Das sind Monikas Handschuhe.

1. Frau María Moser
    Maríahilferstr. 52
    A - 1070 Wien   mein___ Tante in Österreich

2. Manfred___

3. mein___ Bruder___

4. Michael
    Tel: 782 7778   Michael___

| Bücher *(pl)* | Adresse *(f)* | Telefonnummer *(f)* | Fahrrad *(n)* |

5. unser___ Professor___

6. Brigitte___

7. mein___ Onkel___

8. mein___ Eltern

| Schal *(m)* | Wagen *(m)* | Brille *(f)* | Koffer *(pl)* |

J. DAS FAMILIENALBUM. Sie sind Frau Kuhn und Ihre Gesprächspartnerin/Ihr Gesprächspartner ist Frau Stolz. Zeigen Sie Frau Stolz Ihr Familienalbum.

▶ mein Großvater   der Vater Ihr___ Mutter?
    mein___ Vater___

FRAU KUHN: Das ist mein Großvater.   *FRAU STOLZ:* Der Vater Ihrer Mutter?
FRAU KUHN: Nein, der Vater meines
           Vaters.

1. meine Tante   die Schwester Ihr___ Vater___?
    mein___ Mutter

nephew   2. mein Neffe°   der Sohn Ihr___ Schwester?
    mein___ Bruder___

3. mein Onkel   der Bruder Ihr___ Mutter?
    mein___ Vater___

niece   4. meine Nichte°   die Tochter Ihr___ Bruder___?
    mein___ Schwester

grandchildren   5. meine Enkelkinder°   die Kinder Ihr___ Tochter?
    mein___ Sohn___

Von + dative

In colloquial German the idea of possession or of belonging together is often expressed by the preposition **von** + a dative object instead of the genitive case.

Ist das der Wagen **von** dein**em** Bruder?
Herr Berger ist ein guter Freund **von** mein**em** Vater.

N-nouns

N-nouns are a group of *masculine* nouns that take the ending **-n** or **-en** in all cases except the nominative singular. The following chart shows an **n**-noun in all four cases.

		Singular		Plural
Nominative	der	Student	die	Student**en**
Accusative	den	Student**en**	die	Student**en**
Dative	dem	Student**en**	den	Student**en**
Genitive	des	Student**en**	der	Student**en**

K. Ergänzen Sie die richtige Form von **Student!**

1. Kennen Sie diesen _____?
2. Woher kommt dieser _____?
3. Warum protestieren diese _____?
4. Dieser _____ kommt aus Ghana und spricht kaum Deutsch.
5. Wir müssen diesem _____ helfen.
6. Die Zensuren dieser beiden _____ sind sehr gut.

In most dictionaries, the nominative singular of a noun is followed by the changes (if any) that occur in the genitive singular and in the plural:

Nominative singular	Genitive singular	Plural
der Mann	-es	¨er
die Frau	-	-en

This clearly identifies **n**-nouns:

der Student	-en	-en
der Nachbar	-n	-n

Some other **n**-nouns:

der Assistent, -en, -en   der Idiot, -en, -en

der Präsident, -en, -en   der Herr, -n, -en

der Kollege, -n, -n   der Junge,° -n -n   *boy*

der Athlet, -en, -en   der Kunde,° -n, -n   *customer*

der Polizist, -en, -en   der Nachbar, -n, -n

der Tourist, -en, -en   der Mensch, -en, -en

der Patient, -en, -en   der Elefant, -en, -en

der Pilot, -en, -en   der Bär,° -en, -en

Woher wissen Sie, daß in Klosterhof 13 eine Arztpraxis und Geschäfte sind?   *bear*

Note that the singular forms of **Herr** end in **-n** (except for the nominative). The plural forms end in **-en**.

L. Ergänzen Sie die richtigen Nomen!

▶ Studienkollege / Präsident
Sie kennen den _____ persönlich?   Ja, er war ein _____ von mir.

S1: Sie kennen den Präsidenten per-   *S2:* Ja, er war ein Studienkollege von
sönlich?   mir.

---

1. Nachbar / Junge
Wie viele Kinder haben Ihre _____?   Zwei Mädchen und einen _____.

2. Kollege / Pilot
Wie sind Sie denn ins Cockpit   Ja, er ist der Bruder eines _____ von
gekommen, Herr Ziegler? Kennen   mir.
Sie den _____?

3. Assistent / Herr
Wer sind die zwei jungen _____ dort?   Das sind meine beiden _____.

4. Tourist / Polizist
Können Sie mir bitte sagen, wo der   Ich bin leider auch Tourist. Aber fragen
Bahnhof ist, oder sind Sie auch   Sie doch den _____ dort drüben. Der
_____?   weiß es bestimmt.

5. Eisbär / Junge
Wie war's im Zoo, mein _____?   Toll! Ich habe sogar einen richtigen°   *real*
                                           _____ gesehen.

6. Patient / Mensch

brave

Wie geht es dem _____ heute? Leider nicht sehr gut, aber ich habe noch nie einen so tapferen° _____ gesehen.

7. Kunde / Herr

Woher kennen Sie diesen _____? Er ist ein alter _____ von mir.

puzzles / appropriate

M. WAS IST DAS? Beschreiben Sie die folgenden Drudel° mit den passenden° Wortpaaren **(Das ist *das Dach eines Hauses*)**.

1.

3.

2.

4.

roof / handle
trunk / paws

das Dach° / ein Haus	der Henkel° / eine Tasse
der Rüssel° / ein Elefant	die Pfoten° / ein Bär

5.

7.

6.

8.

neck
humps

der Hals° / eine Giraffe	der Bizeps / ein Athlet
der Hals / eine Flasche	die Höcker° / ein Kamel

4. FORMING PHRASES LIKE *DURING THE WEEK, BECAUSE OF THE STORM*

PREPOSITIONS WITH THE GENITIVE CASE

The following prepositions require a *genitive* object in *formal* written and spoken German. However, in *colloquial* German they tend to take a *dative* object.

statt	instead of
trotz	in spite of
während	during
wegen	because of

FORMAL GERMAN:	Wegen **des Schnee-sturms** waren gestern alle Schulen geschlossen.	*Because of the snow-storm all schools were closed yesterday.*
COLLOQUIAL GERMAN:	Bist du **wegen dem Schneesturm** zu Hause geblieben?	*Did you stay home because of the snow-storm?*

Warum soll man hier so langsam fahren?

N. Ergänzen Sie **statt, trotz, während** oder **wegen!**

1. Warum warst du nicht in der Vorlesung?
   _____ meiner Erkältung.°   *cold*
2. Ist Beate _____ ihrer Erkältung schwimmen gegangen?
3. _____ der großen Hitze° fallen° heute nachmittag alle Vorlesungen aus.   *heat / **fallen ... aus:** are canceled*
4. Möchten Sie lieber Salat _____ der Suppe?
5. _____ der Woche habe ich leider keine Zeit, dir zu helfen.
6. Direktor Großmann geht _____ seines Alters° noch jeden Winter Schi laufen.   *age*
7. Bist du _____ deinem Referat so spät ins Bett gegangen?
8. _____ des Vizepräsidenten ist gestern der Präsident selbst nach Moskau geflogen.
9. _____ der Arbeitszeit ist das Rauchen verboten.°   *forbidden*
10. Ich habe _____ dem tollen Essen schon wieder Hunger.
11. Diesmal habe ich meinem Bruder _____ einer CD einen Pulli zum Geburtstag gekauft.
12. _____ des Semesters sind Professor Seidlmeyers Sprechstunden montags und mittwochs von 14 bis 15 Uhr.
13. Warum will Renate diesen Kerl heiraten?
    _____ seinem Geld natürlich.
14. Herr Motz raucht _____ seiner Krankheit° jeden Tag zwei Packungen Zigaret-   *illness*
    ten.

5. DESCRIBING PEOPLE, PLACES, AND THINGS

ADJECTIVE ENDINGS AFTER *DER*-WORDS

In German, adjectives that precede nouns have endings. After **der**-words (such as **der, dieser, jeder, welcher**) an adjective can take one of two endings: **-e** or **-en.** The ending **-e** appears:

a. in the nominative singular (masculine, feminine, and neuter):

der jung**e** Mann	dies**er** jung**e** Mann
die jung**e** Frau	jed**e** jung**e** Frau
das klein**e** Kind	welch**es** klein**e** Kind

b. in the accusative singular (feminine and neuter):

die jung**e** Frau	dies**e** jung**e** Frau
das klein**e** Kind	dies**es** klein**e** Kind

The ending **-en** appears in all other instances.

	Masculine		Feminine		Neuter		Plural	
Nominative	der	jung**e** Mann	die	jung**e** Frau	das	klein**e** Kind	die	klein**en** Kinder
Accusative	den	jung**en** Mann	die	jung**e** Frau	das	klein**e** Kind	die	klein**en** Kinder
Dative	dem	jung**en** Mann	der	jung**en** Frau	dem	klein**en** Kind	den	klein**en** Kindern
Genitive	des	jung**en** Mannes	der	jung**en** Frau	des	klein**en** Kindes	der	klein**en** Kinder

If more than one adjective precedes a noun, they all have the same ending:

Wer ist dieser nett**e,** alt**e** Mann?

In the comparative, adjectives that precede nouns also take endings:

Was studiert der älter**e** Sohn von Frau Müller?

O. DIE REICHEN MÜLLERS. Ergänzen Sie die Adjektivendungen!

1. Dieser reich___, alt___ Mann heißt Müller.

swanky

2. Dieses groß___, protzig___° Haus gehört dem reich___, alt___ Müller.

only

3. Das ist die einzig___° Tochter dieses reich___, alt___ Mannes.

4. Diese beid___ weiß___ Pudel gehören der einzig___ Tochter des reich___, alt___ Müller.

5. Das ist der klein___ Sohn der einzig___ Tochter dieses reich___, alt___ Mannes.

6. Diese beid___ süß___ Hamster gehören dem klein___ Sohn der einzig___ Tochter des reich___, alt___ Müller.

7. Das ist der schön___, neu___ Käfig der beid___ süß___ Hamster des klein___ Sohnes der einzig___ Tochter dieses reich___, alt___ Mannes.

P. WAS?! DU KENNST DIE REICHEN MÜLLERS NICHT? Ergänzen Sie die Adjektivendungen!

S1:

1. Kennst du den alt___ Mann dort? Den mit der groß___ Nase und der dick___ Zigarre.
2. Wem gehört dieses groß___, protzig___ Haus?
3. Wer ist denn die jung___ Frau dort? Die mit der lang___ Nase und den kurz___ Haaren.
4. Wem gehören diese beid___ weiß___ Pudel?
5. Kennt ihr den klein___ Jungen dort? Den mit dem dünn___ Hals und den groß___ Ohren.
6. Wem gehören diese beid___ süß___ Hamster? Die in dem schön___, neu___ Käfig.

S2:

Welchen alt___ Mann? Ja klar, das ist doch der reich___, alt___ Müller. Das gehört dem reich___, alt___ Müller.

Welche jung___ Frau? Das ist die einzig___ Tochter des reich___ alt___ Müller. Die gehören der jung___ Frau dort mit der lang___ Nase und den kurz___ Haaren.

Welchen klein___ Jungen? Ja klar, das ist doch der klein___ Sohn der einzig___ Tochter des reich___, alt___ Müller. Welche süß___ Hamster?

Die gehören dem klein___ Jungen dort mit dem dünn___ Hals und den groß___ Ohren.

ADJECTIVE ENDINGS AFTER *EIN*-WORDS

As you have already seen, **ein**-words have no endings in three instances:

in the nominative singular masculine:	**Mein** Mann ist Amerikaner.
in the nominative singular neuter:	Das ist **mein Haus**.
in the accusative singular neuter:	Wir haben **ein** Haus.

When an adjective follows an **ein**-word without an ending, the adjective takes the case ending of the **der**-word:

d**er** liebe Mann	dies**es** alte Haus
mein lieb**er** Mann	ein alt**es** Haus

All other adjective endings after **ein**-words are identical to those after **der**-words:

	Masculine		Feminine		Neuter		Plural	
Nominative	*mein*	lieb**er** Mann	seine	lieb**e** Frau	*ein*	alt**es** Haus	keine	alt**en** Häuser
Accusative	meinen	lieb**en** Mann	seine	lieb**e** Frau	*ein*	alt**es** Haus	keine	alt**en** Häuser
Dative	meinem	lieb**en** Mann	seiner	lieb**en** Frau	einem	alt**en** Haus	keinen	alt**en** Häuser
Genitive	meines	lieb**en** Mannes	seiner	lieb**en** Frau	eines	alt**en** Haus	keiner	alt**en** Häuser

Q. LIESCHEN MAIERS HUND. Ergänzen Sie die Adjektivendungen!

Lieschen Maier hat einen klein___, weiß___ Hund. Es ist ein sehr schön___, weiß___ Hund, und Lieschen liebt ihn sehr.

leash
own

Wegen ihres klein___, weiß___ Hundes steht Lieschen jeden Morgen schon um sieben auf. Sie gibt ihm eine klein___ Dose Hundefutter und geht dann in die Schule. Wenn Lieschen nach der Schule mit ihrem klein___, weiß___ Hund im Park spazierengeht, hat sie ihn immer an einer lang___ Leine.° Und in Lieschens Schlafzimmer steht neben ihrem eigen___° Bett das Bettchen ihres klein___, weiß___ Hundes.

Lieschen tut alles für ihren klein___, weiß___ Hund, denn sie denkt, kein ander___ klein___, weiß___ Hund soll es so gut haben, wie ihr klein___, weiß___ Hund.

R. FRITZCHEN MÜLLERS KATZE

Fritzchen Müller hat eine groß___, schwarz___ Katze. Es ist eine sehr schön___, schwarz___ Katze, und Fritzchen liebt sie sehr.

Wegen seiner groß___, schwarz___ Katze steht Fritzchen jeden Morgen schon um sieben auf. Er gibt ihr eine groß___ Dose Katzenfutter und geht dann in die Schule. Wenn Fritzchen nach der Schule mit seiner groß___, schwarz___ Katze im Park spazierengeht, hat er sie immer an einer lang___ Leine. Und in Fritzchens Schlafzimmer steht neben seinem eigen___ Bett das Bettchen seiner groß___, schwarz___ Katze.

Fritzchen tut alles für seine groß___, schwarz___ Katze, denn er denkt, keine ander___ groß___, schwarz___ Katze soll es so gut haben, wie seine groß___, schwarz___ Katze.

S. UNSER KROKODIL

Wir haben ein riesig___, grün___ Krokodil. Es ist ein sehr schön___, grün___ Krokodil, und wir lieben es sehr.

Wegen unseres riesig__, grün__ Krokodils stehen wir jeden Morgen schon um sieben auf. Wir geben ihm eine riesig__ Dose Krokodilfutter und gehen dann in die Schule. Wenn wir nach der Schule mit unserem riesig__, grün__ Krokodil im Park spazierengehen, haben wir es immer an einer lang__ Leine. Und in unserem Schlafzimmer steht neben unserem eigen__ Bett das Bettchen unseres riesig__, grün__ Krokodils.

Wir tun alles für unser riesig__, grün__ Krokodil, denn wir denken, kein ander__ riesig__, grün__ Krokodil soll es so gut haben, wie unser riesig__, grün__ Krokodil.

GELÜSTE

cravings

Was möchten Sie gern essen und trinken. Beschreiben Sie mit einem oder zwei passenden Adjektiven, was Sie ausgesucht° haben!

selected

LISA: Worauf hast du Lust,° David?

DAVID: Ich habe Lust auf einen großen, knackigen° Apfel.

DAVID: Und du, Tanja, was möchtest du?

TANJA: Ich möchte ein riesiges Glas Orangensaft.

TANJA: Worauf hast du Lust, . . . ?

What do you feel like having?
crisp

groß	ein __ Glas Apfelsaft
riesig	ein __ Glas Orangensaft
kalt	ein __ Glas Tomatensaft
eiskalt	ein __ Glas Mineralwasser
heiß	ein __ Glas Milch
superlang	einen __ Kaffee
saftig°	eine __ Cola
zart°	ein __ Bier
süß	. . . ?
knackig°	
reif	
. . . ?	

saftig° → *juicy*
zart° → *tender*
knackig° → *crisp*

einen __ Teller Spaghetti
einen __ Teller Sauerkraut
eine __ Portion Pommes frites
einen __ Hamburger
einen __ Hotdog
eine __ Knackwurst
ein __ Steak
ein __ Schnitzel
ein __ Stück Pizza
. . . ?

eine __ Banane
einen __ Apfel
eine __ Birne°
eine __ Tafel Schokolade
ein __ Stück Kuchen
ein __ Stück Käsekuchen
ein __ Stück Apfelkuchen
ein __ Stück Schwarzwälder
  Kirschtorte
einen __ Becher Fruchtjoghurt
einen __ Becher Softeis
einen __ Becher Schokoladeneis
einen __ Becher Vanilleeis
. . . ?

pear

T. KLEINE GESPRÄCHE. Sagen Sie das auf Deutsch!

das Labor

1. PROFESSOR MÜLLER: What does your assistant do all day, Mr. Seidlmeyer?
   PROFESSOR SEIDLMEYER: He works in the lab,° he reads my students' reports, and sometimes he helps the assistant of a colleague.

2. POLIZIST: Do you know this boy, Mrs. Koch?
   FRAU KOCH: Yes, he's the son of our new neighbors.

hell
winzig

3. DAVID: How big is your new apartment, Silke?
   SILKE: I have a big, bright° living room with a balcony, a small bedroom, and a tiny° kitchen.

4. CLAUDIA: What should I wear, Stephanie? My grey sweater or my blue jacket?
   STEPHANIE: I like your grey sweater better. (Use **gefallen.**)

wertvoll / antik
das Möbelstück

5. HEIKE: How much did you pay for this ugly, old chair, Dieter?
   DIETER: This is no ugly, old chair, but a very valuable,° antique° piece of furniture.°

Sprachnotizen

Discourse strategies

A personal opinion is often introduced by phrases such as:

Ich denke, (daß)...	*I think (that)...*
Ich finde, (daß)...	*I think (that)...*
Ich bin der Meinung, daß...	*I'm of the opinion that...*
Meiner Meinung nach...	*In my opinion...*

To agree with someone (or to disagree in a polite way), you can use the following expression:

Da hast du recht, (aber)...	*You are right (but)...*

MONIKA: **Ich denke, daß** jeder Student mal ein Jahr lang im Studentenheim leben soll.

BERND: **Ich finde** WGs besser als Studentenheime, weil in einer WG nicht so viele Studenten zusammenleben.

STEPHANIE: **Da hast du recht, aber** ein Zimmer in einem Privathaus ist noch besser, weil man da wirklich ganz konzentriert lernen kann.

STEFAN: **Ich bin der Meinung, daß** man nicht immer nur lernen soll.

OLIVER: **Da hast du recht.** Außerdem lernt man **meiner Meinung nach** in der Kneipe oft mehr als aus Büchern.

 ZUSAMMENSCHAU

rooming problems

ZIMMERSORGEN°

Am Ende von Zimmersorgen *finden Sie unter* Zur Orientierung und zum Zusammenfassen *ein paar Fragan zu diesem Text. Lesen Sie die Fragen zu jedem der vier*

Paragraphen, bevor Sie den Paragraphen lesen. Beantworten Sie die Fragen, nach-
dem Sie den Paragraphen gelesen haben.

In ihrem ersten Semester waren Stephanie und Claudia Zimmerkolleginnen, und sie sind bald auch gute Freundinnen geworden. Sie sind mehr oder weniger regelmäßig° in die Vorlesungen gegangen, aber sie haben auch viel vor dem Fernseher gesessen oder gequatscht°. Abends waren sie oft mit Freunden
5 in der Kneipe und haben wichtige Probleme diskutiert oder Karten gespielt. Das war alles sehr schön und sehr interessant, aber am Ende des Wintersemesters haben sie beide beschlossen°, ihr Studium nächstes Semester viel ernster° zu nehmen. Sie haben deshalb vor, aus dem Studentenheim auszuziehen° und noch vor Beginn des Sommersemesters eine Wohnung oder
10 ein Zimmer zu suchen.

Jetzt ist es Anfang April. Stephanie sitzt in der Cafeteria und trinkt eine Tasse Kaffee. Sie hat heute morgen ein Zimmer in einem Einfamilienhaus in der Ebersbergerstraße angeschaut. Die Hauswirtin ist eine sehr nette, alte Dame. Sie wohnt ganz allein im Haus, und das Zimmer ist groß, hell, schön möbliert und vor allem° sehr ruhig. „Bei mir stört° Sie niemand", hat die alte Dame
15 gesagt, „und hier können Sie lernen, so viel Sie wollen." Das ist Stephanie sehr wichtig, weil sie natürlich nicht zu Hause in Amerika das ganze Jahr wiederholen will. Weil das Zimmer aber ziemlich teuer ist — es kostet 350 Mark im Monat — und weil Stephanie die Küche nicht benutzen° darf, hat sie nicht sofort ja gesagt, sondern versprochen, die alte Dame noch vor dem Abendessen
20 anzurufen. Stephanie möchte natürlich auch noch gern mit Claudia sprechen, aber sie hat noch nicht herausgefunden, ob Claudia schon aus den Ferien° zurück ist.

Claudia ist seit vorgestern wieder in München. Gestern früh hat sie Bernd getroffen, und Bernd hat ihr erzählt, daß er nach langem Suchen eine ziemlich
25 ordentliche° Fünfzimmerwohnung gefunden hat. Zwei Zimmer hat er schon weitervermietet°, und die beiden anderen hat er für Claudia und Stephanie reserviert. Claudia hat sofort eines der beiden Zimmer genommen, und sie nimmt° an, daß Stephanie in das andere einzieht°, sobald sie aus den Ferien zurück ist. In Bernds WG haben alle ihre separaten Zimmer, und natürlich
30 können sie auch alle die Küche benutzen. Und wenn Claudia lernen will, so denkt sie, macht sie einfach die Tür zu, und alles ist in Ordnung. Die zwei anderen Studenten sind Monika Bachmann und Stefan Wehrle. Sie haben letztes Semester auch im Studentenheim gewohnt und haben nichts als Feten° im Kopf gehabt. Aber Claudia denkt, daß auch diese beiden ihr Studium dieses
35 Semester viel ernster nehmen wollen.

Bernd muß für die Wohnung 1000 Mark im Monat bezahlen, und jedes der fünf Zimmer kostet also nur 200 Mark. Claudia weiß, daß Stephanie sparen muß, und sie denkt, daß sie gern wieder mit den alten Freunden aus dem Studentenheim zusammen sein möchte. Sie sucht sie deshalb überall und
40 findet sie schließlich in der Cafeteria.

	regularly
	talked (gabbed)
	decided
	more seriously
	to move out
	above all / will disturb
	use
	vacation
	decent
	sublet
	nimmt an: *assumes / will move*
	parties

ZUR ORIENTIERUNG UND ZUM ZUSAMMENFASSEN°   *for summing up*

1. Z.° 1–10: Warum haben Stephanie und Claudia vor, aus dem Studentenheim auszuziehen?   **Z. = Zeile:** *line*

2. Z. 11–23: Stephanie sucht ein ruhiges Zimmer. Was hat das mit Amerika zu tun? Warum nimmt Stephanie das Zimmer nicht sofort?

Finding a place to live in a university town in the German-speaking countries is always a challenge for a student. Very few universities are situated on a campus. University buildings are often scattered all over town, and the few dormitories that do exist do not nearly meet the housing needs of students. In the Southern German university town of Tübingen, for example, students account for one-third of the population, and finding a place to live is a difficult and sometimes almost impossible task. It has happened that students have had to withdraw from their studies because they could not find living accommodations.

Wohngemeinschaften or **WGs** are a popular and economical type of living accommodation: students rent an apartment jointly and share responsibility for meals and household chores. Of course, many students also rent rooms in private homes, where they may or may not have **Küchenbenutzung** *(kitchen privileges)*.

Dieses Hochhaus ist ein Studentenheim.

3. Z. 24–36: Wie findet Claudia ein Zimmer? Claudia denkt, daß sie in diesem Zimmer besser lernen kann als im Studentenheim. Warum ist das vielleicht ein bißchen zu optimistisch?
4. Z. 37–Ende: Warum sucht Claudia ihre Freundin Stephanie?

 Sie hören zwölf Aussagen zu *Zimmersorgen*. Entscheiden Sie, ob diese Aussagen richtig oder falsch sind!

 Hören Sie jetzt Claudias Unterhaltung mit Stephanie in der Cafeteria!

 Wer sagt das, und was ist die Reaktion?

1. Ja, gar nicht weit von der Uni, in einer WG.
2. Ich finde, daß man in einer WG auch nicht besser lernen kann als im Studentenheim.
3. Und für all das bezahlt jeder nur zweihundert Mark im Monat. Ist das nicht billig?
4. Hast du Küchenbenutzung?

5. Also meiner Meinung nach ist dreihundert Mark einfach zu viel für ein Zimmer ohne Küchenbenutzung.
6. Ja, also da ist Bernd . . .
7. Du weißt doch, daß die nichts als Feten im Kopf haben!
8. Also kommst du?

WOHNMÖGLICHKEITEN°

types of living accommodation

ÜBERREDUNGSKÜNSTE°. Sie haben in Ihrer WG noch ein Zimmer frei, und Sie möchten, daß Ihre Gesprächspartnerin/Ihr Gesprächspartner dort einzieht. Sie wissen, sie/er ist der Meinung, daß man in einer WG nicht richtig lernen kann. Versuchen Sie trotzdem°, sie/ihn zu überreden°.

persuasive skills

anyway / persuade

EINE KLEINE DISKUSSION. Wo wohnen Sie? Im Studentenheim, in einer WG, in einer Wohnung, bei Ihren Eltern, oder haben Sie ein Zimmer in einem Privathaus? Machen Sie eine Liste von den Vorteilen und Nachteilen Ihrer Unterkunft°. In der nächsten Deutschstunde diskutieren Sie dann mit Ihren Klassenkameraden, welche Wohnmöglichkeit die beste ist.

living accommodation

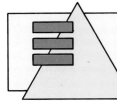

WORT, SINN UND KLANG

WÖRTER UNTER DER LUPE

1. PREDICTING GENDER

In German and in English the suffix **-er** is used to form *agent nouns,* i.e., nouns representing the doer of the action described by the verb. An agent noun with the suffix **-er** is always masculine. Some of these nouns take an umlaut.

arbeiten   *to work*   **der** Arbeit**er**   *worker*
tanzen   *to dance*   **der** T**ä**nz**er**   *dancer*

If an agent noun refers to a woman, the suffix **-in** is added to the masculine suffix **-er.**

der Arbeiter   *(male) worker*   **die** Arbeiter**in**   *(female) worker*
der Tänzer   *(male) dancer*   **die** Tänzer**in**   *(female) dancer*

- Choose appropriate infinitives to create German equivalents of the following English nouns. The article provided indicates whether the noun is to refer to a female or male. Note that the infinitives are not in the correct order.

▶ baker   der _____   backen (umlaut!)
           der Bäcker

reader	die _____	fahren
beginner	der _____	auswandern
narrator	der _____	können
immigrant	der _____	lesen
driver	die _____	kennen
tailor	der _____	erzählen
connoisseur	der _____	sprechen
visitor	die _____	anfangen (umlaut!)
emigrant	der _____	schneiden
speaker	die _____	einwandern
expert	der _____	besuchen

2. GIVING LANGUAGE COLOR

In this chapter you have learned vocabulary that deals with housing and furnishings. The names of parts of a house and pieces of furniture are the source of many idiomatic expressions. The two expressions marked with an asterisk are very colloquial and should not be used in a more formal setting.

Die Kinder haben wieder mal das ganze Haus auf den Kopf gestellt.	*The children have turned the whole house upside down again.*
Schürers sind ganz aus dem Häuschen, weil sie eine Reise nach Hawaii gewonnen haben.	*The Schürers are all excited because they won a trip to Hawaii.*
roof Er hat vom Manager eins aufs Dach° gekriegt.	*He was bawled out by the manager.*
der Schaden: *damage* Du hast wohl einen kleinen Dachschaden°!*	*You must be crazy!*
draw Mal° den Teufel nicht an die Wand!	*Don't speak of the devil (or he will appear)!*
hinge Über solche Probleme kann man nicht zwischen Tür und Angel° sprechen.	*You can't talk about such things in a cursory way.*
wirft ... hinaus: *throws out* Thomas wirft° sein ganzes Geld zum Fenster hinaus.	*Thomas wastes all his money.*
Setz ihm doch den Stuhl vor die Tür!	*Throw him out!*
to stick Du kannst doch nicht ewig die Füße unter unseren Tisch stecken.°	*You can't be dependent on us forever.*
Du hast wohl nicht alle Tassen im Schrank.*	*You must be crazy!*

- Was paßt zusammen?

about 1. Haben Sie schon mit Frau Holz über° dieses Problem gesprochen?	Die hat wohl nicht alle Tassen im Schrank!

2. Was soll ich denn machen, Frau Kluge? Mein Mann kommt jede Nacht betrunken nach Hause.
3. Warum soll ich denn immer Vaters Wagen waschen, Mutti?
4. Julia fährt übers Wochenende mit Günter nach Kiel.
5. Glaubst du, daß Tante Emma uns bald wieder mal besuchen kommt?

Mal doch bitte den Teufel nicht an die Wand!

Setzen Sie ihm doch einfach den Stuhl vor die Tür!
Ja, aber nur so zwischen Tür und Angel.

Solange du bei uns die Füße unter den Tisch steckst, kannst du wahrhaftig° auch ein bißchen was für uns tun.   *surely*

6. Was hat Brigitte zu ihrer Eins° in Chemie gesagt?
7. Warum ist die Fete diesmal nicht wieder bei Kathrin?
8. Eva denkt, du liebst sie.
9. Warum arbeitet Herr Weiß denn plötzlich so fleißig?
10. Warum schickst du Robert kein Geld mehr?

Die hat wohl einen kleinen Dachschaden!   *A (grade)*
Weil er es doch nur zum Fenster hinauswirft.
Weil er von Direktor Horch eins aufs Dach gekriegt hat.
Sie war ganz aus dem Häuschen.

Weil wir letztes Mal das ganze Haus auf den Kopf gestellt haben.

WEITERE NÜTZLICHE WÖRTER UND AUSDRÜCKE

Wohnen

das Haus, die Häuser	house
das Hochhaus, die Hochhäuser	high-rise
das Studentenheim, die Studentenheime **(das Studentenwohnheim)**	student residence, dormitory
die WG, die WGs **(die Wohngemeinschaft, die Wohngemeinschaften)**	shared housing
das Einfamilienhaus, die Einfamilienhäuser	single family dwelling
die Garage, die Garagen	garage
das Wochenendhaus, die Wochenendhäuser	cottage
die Adresse, die Adressen	address
die Telefonnummer, die Telefonnummern	telephone number
der Nachbar, des Nachbarn, die Nachbarn	neighbor

Mieten

der Hauswirt, die Hauswirte	landlord
die Hauswirtin, die Hauswirtinnen	landlady
die Miete, die Mieten	rent
die Küchenbenutzung	kitchen privileges
die Kochplatte, die Kochplatten	hot plate

An der Wand

der Lichtschalter, die Lichtschalter	light switch
das Bild, die Bilder	picture
das Poster, die Poster	poster
der Kalender, die Kalender	calendar
das schwarze Brett	bulletin board

Andere Nomen

die **Brille**	(eye) glasses
die **Aktentasche**, die **Aktentaschen**	briefcase
die **Dose**, die **Dosen**	can

Sprechen

quatschen	to talk; to gab
diskutieren	to discuss

Das Gegenteil

der **Junge** — das **Mädchen**	boy—girl
mieten — **vermieten**	to rent—to rent out
ein•ziehen, ist eingezogen — **aus•ziehen, ist ausgezogen**	to move in—to move out
auf•machen — **zu•machen**	to open—to close
ruhig — **laut**	quiet—loud
regelmäßig — **unregelmäßig**	regular—irregular
zuerst — **zuletzt**	first—last

Die Dativ-Akkusativpräpositionen

an	at; to *(the side of)*; on *(a vertical surface)*
auf	on *(a horizontal surface)*
in	in, into, to
vor	in front of, before; ago
hinter	behind
über	over, above
unter	under, below
neben	beside, next to
zwischen	between

Die Genitivpräpositionen

statt	instead of
trotz	in spite of
während	during
wegen	because of

WÖRTER IM KONTEXT

1. WAS PASST WO?

laut   vermieten   an   zumachen   neben   das Bild   über

a. Die Lampe hängt _____ dem Tisch.
b. _____ hängt _____ der Wand.
c. Es ist so _____ hier. Kannst du bitte das Fenster _____?
d. In dem Haus _____ der Bäckerei Maier ist ein Zimmer zu _____.

aufmachen   vor   den Kalender   vor allem   zwischen   während

e. Hängen Sie _____ bitte _____ das Bild und das Poster.
f. Es ist so heiß hier. Kannst du bitte das Fenster _____?

g. _____ der Woche komme ich selten _____ acht Uhr abends nach Hause.

h. Wenn Sie gesund bleiben wollen, müssen Sie _____ regelmäßig Sport treiben.

2. ASSOZIATIONEN. Was paßt zusammen?

a. die Brille   öffnen   b. die Kochplatte   nett
   die Dose   Fußball spielen   die Miete   schwer
   die Miete   besser sehen   die Hauswirtin   heiß
   der Junge   bezahlen   die Aktentasche   teuer

3. Was paßt so zusammen wie *die Flasche* und *der Wein?*

die Dose   die Studenten
die Garage   die Cola
die Aktentasche   der Wagen
die WG   die Bücher

 ## ZUR AUSSPRACHE

GERMAN *ST* AND *SP*

At the beginning of a word or word stem, **s** in the combinations **st** and **sp** is pronounced like English *sh*. Otherwise it is pronounced like English *s* in *list* and *lisp*.

- Hören Sie gut zu und wiederholen Sie!

a. st

1. **St**efan ist **St**udent.
   Stefan **st**udiert in **St**uttgart.
   Stefan findet das **St**udentenleben **st**ressig.

2. Ha**st** du Lu**st** auf eine Wur**st**,
   Und auf Mo**st**° für deinen Dur**st**?   *cider*

b. sp

1. Herr **Sp**ielberg **sp**richt gut **Sp**anisch.

2. Auf° was **sp**art Frau **Sp**ohn?   *for*
   Auf einen **Sp**ortwagen.
   Die **sp**innt° ja!   *is crazy*

3. Unser Ka**sp**ar li**sp**elt ein bißchen.

Es war einmal . . .

K A P I T E L 10

■ **Kommunikationsziele**

*In **Kapitel 10** you will learn how to:*
narrate past events
write a resumé
talk about events that precede other events in the
  past
ask and respond to questions in a job interview
talk about your childhood
modernize a fairy tale
tell a story from pictures

■ **Lesestücke**

Eine Geschichte aus dem sechzehnten Jahrhundert
Der Hase und der Igel

■ **Hör- und Sprechsituationen**

Sympathie und Moral
Manchmal sollte man gar nicht erst aufstehen
Mein Lebenslauf
Ich suche einen Ferienjob
Was ich gestern alles machte
Als ich klein war, . . .
Es allen recht machen

■ **Strukturen**

The simple past tense
The past perfect tense
Mixed verbs
Distinguishing between **wann, wenn,** and **als**
Hin and **her**

■ **Wissenswertes**

Hans Sachs
Martin Luther
Die Brüder Grimm

EINE GESCHICHTE AUS DEM SECHZEHNTEN JAHRHUNDERT
nach° Hans Sachs

adapted from

In dieser alten Geschichte sprechen drei Personen: ein schlauer Student, ein reicher Bauer und seine gutherzige aber ein bißchen einfältige° Frau. Der erste Mann der Bauersfrau ist vor ein paar Jahren gestorben, und obwohl° er jetzt im Himmel ist, spielt er eine wichtige Rolle in dieser Geschichte.

simple-minded

although

Auf Seite 316 finden Sie unter Vom Lesen zum Sprechen *ein paar Fragen zu den drei Hauptabschnitten° dieser Geschichte. Beantworten Sie die Fragen nach jedem Abschnitt.*

main sections

Im sechzehnten Jahrhundert studierte einmal ein deutscher Student in Paris. Im Juli war das Sommersemester zu Ende, und der Student wollte in den Ferien zu seinen Eltern nach Deutschland zurück. Weil er aber sehr arm war, konnte er kein Pferd° kaufen, sondern mußte zu Fuß nach Deutschland wan-
5 dern. (Busse und Züge gab es° damals natürlich noch nicht.)

horse

there were

Das Wetter war schön und nicht zu warm, und schon nach einer Woche kam unser Student zur deutschen Grenze.° Als° er dann durch das erste deutsche Dorf° wanderte, war es gerade Mittag. Bei einem großen Bauernhaus arbeitete eine Frau im Garten, und weil der Student heute noch keinen Bissen° gegess-
10 sen hatte, blieb° er stehen und sagte: „Guten Tag, liebe Frau. Haben Sie vielleicht etwas zu essen für mich? Ich bin heute schon so weit gewandert und habe noch nicht mal gefrühstückt."

border / when

village

bite

blieb . . . stehen: *stopped*

Weil die Bauersfrau ganz allein zu Hause war und weil sie den jungen Mann noch nie gesehen hatte, hatte sie ein bißchen Angst° vor ihm. Deshalb fragte
15 sie: „Wer sind Sie denn, und woher kommen Sie?"

hatte . . . Angst vor: *was afraid of*

„Ich bin ein armer Student," antwortete er, „und ich komme von Paris."

Nun war die gute Frau zwar sehr fromm,° aber nicht sehr intelligent. Sie ging° jeden Sonntag in die Kirche,° und sie hörte dort viel vom Paradies, aber von Paris hatte sie noch nichts gehört. Und so verstand sie nicht *Paris,* sondern
20 *Paradies.*

pious / went

church

„Oh, Sie kommen vom Paradies!" rief° die Frau. „Dann kennen Sie doch sicher meinen ersten Mann. Er war gut und fromm und ist sonntags immer mit mir in die Kirche gegangen. Er ist jetzt sicher im Paradies."

exclaimed

„Wie heißt er denn?" fragte der schlaue Student.

25 „Hans," antwortete die Bauersfrau, „Hans Krüger."

„Oh, der Hans!" rief der Student. „Aber natürlich kenne ich den. Er ist sogar ein guter Freund von mir."

„Wie geht es ihm denn im Paradies?" fragte die einfältige Frau den Studenten.

„Leider nicht sehr gut," antwortete der. „Hans ist sehr arm. Er hat fast kein
30 Geld, ist in Lumpen° gekleidet° und hat oft nicht mal genug zu essen." *rags / dressed*

„Oh, mein armer Hans," weinte° da die gute Frau, „du hast kein Geld und *cried*
keine Kleider und mußt oft hungern und frieren.° Aber vielleicht kann ich dir *be cold*
helfen. Mein zweiter Mann ist reich und gut." Dann fragte sie den Studenten:
„Wann gehen Sie denn wieder ins Paradies zurück, lieber Mann?"

35 „Meine Ferien sind übermorgen zu Ende," antwortete der, „und ich wandere
schon morgen wieder ins Paradies zurück."

„Können Sie vielleicht für meinen armen Hans ein bißchen Geld und ein paar
gute Kleider mitnehmen?" fragte die Frau.

„Aber natürlich," antwortete der Student, „das mache ich gern. Holen Sie nur
40 das Geld und die Kleider, dann muß Ihr Hans bald nicht mehr hungern und
frieren."

Da war die gute Frau sehr glücklich.° Sie lief° schnell ins Haus, und bald kam *happy / ran*
sie mit einem Mantel, einer Jacke, einem Paar Hosen, einem Hemd, mit
Schuhen und Socken, mit zehn Goldstücken und mit einem großen Stück Brot
45 wieder zurück. Das Brot gab° sie dem Studenten. Die Goldstücke steckte sie in *gave*
die Taschen° der Hose, und dann machte sie aus den Kleidern ein schönes *pockets*
Bündel. Das gab sie dem Studenten und sagte: „Bitte, geben Sie meinem Hans
dieses Bündel und grüßen Sie ihn von mir. Ich habe zwar wieder geheiratet,
aber meinen Hans werde° ich nie vergessen." *will*

50 Der Student dankte der Bauersfrau für das Brot, nahm° das Bündel, sagte auf *took*
Wiedersehen und wanderte so schnell wie möglich° weiter. *possible*

Nach einer halben Stunde kam der Bauer vom Feld. Die glückliche Frau erzählte ihm alles. Er sagte aber kein Wort, sondern lief schnell in den Stall,° *stable*
sattelte sein Pferd und galoppierte dem Studenten nach.

55 Der Student war° mit seinem Bündel schon weit gewandert, als er plötzlich *had*
ein Pferd galoppieren hörte. Da nahm er das Bündel schnell vom Rücken° und *back*
versteckte° es in einem Busch. *hid*

Der Bauer kam, hielt° sein Pferd an, und fragte: „Haben Sie vielleicht einen **hielt . . . an:** *stopped*
Studenten mit einem Bündel auf dem Rücken gesehen?"

60 „Ja," log° unser schlauer Student, „wir sind hier zusammen gewandert. Aber *lied*
als er Ihr Pferd hörte, ist er schnell in den Wald° gelaufen." *woods*

„Halten Sie doch bitte mein Pferd!" rief da der Bauer. „Ich muß diesen Studenten fangen." Und er stieg schnell ab° und lief in den Wald. **stieg . . . ab:** *dismounted*

Der Student holte das Bündel aus dem Busch, stieg° auf das Pferd, und ritt° *climbed /* **ritt . . . weg:**
65 schnell weg. *rode away*

Der Bauer fand niemand im Wald, und als er wieder zurückkam, fand er auch
den Studenten und das Pferd nicht mehr. Da wurde° ihm alles klar, und er *became*
ging langsam zu Fuß nach Hause zurück.

Zu Hause fragte ihn seine Frau: „Warum kommst du zu Fuß zurück? Wo ist
70 denn dein Pferd?"

„Der arme Student mußte das schwere Bündel zu Fuß ins Paradies tragen,"° *carry*
antwortete da der Bauer, „und so habe ich ihm auch noch mein Pferd
gegeben. Mit dem Pferd kommt er schneller ins Paradies."

Hans Sachs (1494–1576) apprenticed as a cobbler and became a master shoemaker in his native Nürnberg in 1520. Like many of the craftsmen of his day, he also became a "master" poet **(Meistersinger).** In the fifteenth century, the craftsmen in the emerging cities tried to imitate the great courtly poets of the Middle Ages and believed that by "serving an apprenticeship" in the art of writing poetry they could learn how to compose verse just as they had learned how to make shoes, tailor clothes, or bake bread. There were hundreds of **Meistersinger,** but only Hans Sachs rose above the rigid rules and restrictive forms of the **Meistergesang** (*poetry of the* **Meistersinger**) to produce lively and humorous pieces of dramatic, epic, and lyric poetry.

Hans Sachs was a staunch supporter of Martin Luther and the Protestant Reformation. He felt that it was his obligation to instruct as well as entertain and almost every one of his poems ends with a moral. He adapted many themes from the Bible and from Greek, Latin, and Renaissance poetry, putting them into the context of people's daily life. He also wrote many **Fastnachtspiele,** plays performed just before the beginning of the Lenten season. The story at the beginning of this chapter, originally entitled **Der farend Schüler im Paradeiß,** is one of the most famous of these **Fastnachtspiele.** With a collection of almost 6000 pieces of poetry, it is sur-

Wann wurde Hans Sachs geboren?

prising that Hans Sachs ever found the time to cobble his shoes!

Hans Sachs has been immortalized by Richard Wagner, a nineteenth-century operatic composer. Sachs is the hero of Wagner's opera **Die Meistersinger von Nürnberg.**

VOM LESEN ZUM SPRECHEN

1. Z. 1–20: Warum will der Student nach Deutschland? Warum wandert er zu Fuß nach Deutschland? Warum ist er jetzt so hungrig? Was will er von der Bauersfrau? Warum hat die Bauersfrau ein bißchen Angst vor ihm? Warum versteht die Bauersfrau *Paradies* statt *Paris?*

2. Z. 21–51: Warum glaubt die Bauersfrau, daß ihr erster Mann jetzt im Paradies ist? Wie reagiert der Student, als die Frau ihn fragt, ob er ihren ersten Mann kennt? Was erzählt der Student von Hans Krüger? Wie will die Frau ihrem ersten Mann helfen? Was macht sie aus den Kleidern, und was macht sie mit den Goldstükken? Was bekommt der Student zu essen?

3. Z. 52–73: Wie reagiert der Bauer, als die Frau ihm von dem Studenten und dem Bündel erzählt? Warum weiß der Bauer nicht, daß er mit dem Studenten spricht? *does . . . ask* Warum bittet° der Bauer den Studenten, das Pferd zu halten? Warum geht der Bauer später zu Fuß nach Hause? Wie erklärt der Bauer seiner Frau, warum er zu Fuß nach Hause kommt?

WAS PASST WO?

arbeitete   sagte   fragte   kam

1. Als der Student zu dem großen Bauernhaus _____, _____ die Bauersfrau gerade im Garten. Der Student _____ guten Tag und _____: „Haben Sie vielleicht etwas zu essen für mich?"

verstand   ging   sagte   hörte

2. Der Student _____ *Paris,* aber weil die Frau jeden Sonntag in die Kirche _____ und dort so viel vom Paradies _____, _____ sie *Paradies* statt *Paris.*

hörte   lief   holte   zurückging

3. Als die Frau _____, daß der Student schon morgen wieder ins Paradies _____, _____ sie schnell ins Haus und _____ Geld, Kleider und ein Stück Brot.

steckte   zurückkam   gab   machte

4. Als sie wieder _____, _____ sie dem Studenten das Brot. Dann _____ sie das Geld in die Taschen der Hose und _____ aus den Kleidern ein Bündel.

ritt   sattelte   erzählte   rannte

5. Als die Frau später ihrem Mann _____, was sie getan hatte, _____ der in den Stall, _____ sein Pferd und _____ dem Studenten nach.

hörte   fragte   versteckte   schickte

6. Als der Student ein Pferd galoppieren _____, _____ er das Bündel schnell in einem Busch. Und als der Bauer dann nach dem Studenten _____, _____ der Student ihn in den Wald.

fand   holte   stieg   ritt

7. Der Bauer _____ dort natürlich niemand. Der Student aber _____ das Bündel aus dem Busch, _____ auf das Pferd und _____ schnell weg.

Sie hören jetzt zwölf Zitate° aus der *Geschichte aus dem sechzehnten Jahrhundert.* Sagen Sie zuerst, wer das sagt (der Student, die Bauersfrau oder der Bauer) und dann, ob der Sprecher / die Sprecherin glaubt, was sie / er sagt, oder ob sie / er bewußt° die Unwahrheit° sagt.

quotations

knowingly / untruth

SYMPATHIE° UND MORAL. Zu welchen der drei Personen passen die folgenden Adjektive: klug, dumm, moralisch, unmoralisch? Welche der drei Personen in dieser Geschichte finden Sie sympathisch, und welche finden Sie unsympathisch? Warum? Arbeiten Sie zu zweit°, und vergleichen° Sie Ihre Resultate mit den Resultaten Ihrer Mitstudenten.

likeability

with a partner / compare

NÜTZLICHE WÖRTER UND AUSDRÜCKE

Nomen

die Geschichte, die Geschichten	story
die Wahrheit	truth
das Jahrhundert, die Jahrhunderte	century

Power to the Bauer

Nomen

die Ferien *(pl)*	holidays, vacation
der Wald, die Wälder	woods, forest
das Feld, die Felder	field
der Busch, die Büsche	shrub, bush
die Grenze, die Grenzen	border
das Dorf, die Dörfer	village
die Kirche, die Kirchen	church
der Bauer, des Bauern, die Bauern	farmer
der Stall, die Ställe	stable
das Pferd, die Pferde	horse
die Tasche, die Taschen	pocket

Verben

stehen·bleiben, ist stehengeblieben	to stop
steigen, ist gestiegen	to climb
reiten, ist geritten	to ride
frieren, hat gefroren	to be cold
lügen, hat gelogen	to tell a lie
fangen (fängt), hat gefangen	to catch
tragen (trägt), hat getragen	to carry
grüßen	to greet, to say hello
holen	to get, to fetch
hungern	to go hungry
stecken	to put, to stick
verstecken	to hide

Andere Wörter

glücklich	happy
möglich	possible
damals	then, at that time
als	when

Ausdrücke

so schnell wie möglich	as quickly as possible
Angst haben (vor + *dative*)	to be afraid (of)

WÖRTER IM KONTEXT

1. WAS PASST WO?

friere   Kirche   fängt   Bauern   Angst   holen

a. Warum _____ unsere Katze denn keine Mäuse?
   Ich glaube, sie hat _____ vor ihnen.
b. Kannst du mir einen Pullover _____? Ich _____.
c. In diesem Dorf gehen die meisten _____ noch jeden Sonntag in die _____.

2. WAS PASST ZUSAMMEN?

a. Viele Tage ohne Vorlesungen sind   ein Jahrhundert.
b. Viele Bäume sind   ein Dorf.
c. Hundert Jahre sind   Ferien.
d. Viele Häuser sind   eine Geschichte.
e. Viele Wörter sind   ein Wald.

The figure who dominated the sixteenth century was Martin Luther, the father of the Protestant Reformation. Luther wanted to make the Word of God accessible to all people, and to do this he translated the Bible into a German that could be understood by educated and uneducated alike. Of his method of translation he said "one must listen to the mother in the home, the children in the street, the common man in the marketplace and observe how they express themselves, and then translate accordingly". Because of this, the Luther translation is full of colorful expressions and images. Since the Luther Bible was the most widely read book in Germany for many centuries, it played a tremendous role in shaping the German language. To this day, no other German translation has been able to match Luther's.

Martin Luther

3. DEFINITIONEN. Was paßt zusammen?

a. hungern	guten Tag sagen
b. lügen	nicht weitergehen
c. reiten	nichts zu essen haben
d. grüßen	nicht die Wahrheit sagen
e. stehenbleiben	auf einem Pferd sitzen

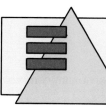

FUNKTIONEN UND FORMEN

1. NARRATING PAST EVENTS

THE SIMPLE PAST TENSE

The simple past is used mainly in written German to describe a series of connected events in the past. It is found mostly in narratives, novels, newspaper reports and newscasts, and is therefore sometimes called *the narrative past*.

In German the simple past is formed in a similar way to the simple past in English.

For regular verbs, a past tense marker is added to the verb stem:

German		English	
lernen:	**ich lernte**	**to learn:**	**I learned**

For irregular verbs, the simple past is signaled by a stem change:

German		English	
kommen:	**ich kam**	**to come:**	**I came**

THE SIMPLE PAST OF REGULAR VERBS

In German the simple past of regular verbs is formed by inserting the past tense marker **-t-** between the infinitive stem and the personal endings:

Singular		Plural	
ich	lernte	wir	lernten
du	lerntest	ihr	lerntet
er / sie / es	lernte	sie	lernten
	Sie lernten		

The German simple past has more than one English equivalent.

ich lernte	I learned I did learn I was learning

Verb stems that end in **d, t, (land-en, arbeit-en),** or certain consonant combinations **(öffn-en)** add an **e** before the past tense marker **-t-**:

Singular		Plural	
ich	arbeitete	wir	arbeiteten
du	arbeitetest	ihr	arbeitetet
er / sie / es	arbeitete	sie	arbeiteten
	Sie arbeiteten		

THE SIMPLE PAST OF IRREGULAR VERBS

The simple past of German irregular verbs is always signaled by a stem change. Note that there is no personal ending in the 1st and 3rd person singular:

Singular		Plural	
ich	kam	wir	kamen
du	kamst	ihr	kamt
er / sie / es	kam	sie	kamen
	Sie kamen		

THE SIMPLE PAST OF SEPARABLE VERBS

In the simple past, the prefix of separable verbs functions just as it does in the present tense.

In a main clause, the prefix is separated and appears at the end of the clause:

Der Bauer sattelte sein Pferd und **galoppierte** dem Studenten **nach.**

*The farmer saddled his horse and **galloped after** the student.*

In a subordinate clause, the unseparated verb appears at the end of the clause:

Als der Bauer wieder **zurückkam,** war der Student weg.

*When the farmer **returned,** the student was gone.*

Sie hörte dort viel vom Paradies.

A. EINE KURZFASSUNG° DER „GESCHICHTE AUS DEM SECHZEHNTEN JAHRHUN-DERT." Lesen Sie diese Kurzfassung, und setzen Sie alle Präsensformen ins Präteritum.° Das Präteritum der unregelmäßigen Verben ist unten° gegeben.

shortened version

simple past / below

1. Das Wetter ist schön und warm, und schon nach einer Woche wandert unser Student durch das erste deutsche Dorf.
2. Bei einem großen Bauernhaus arbeitet eine Frau im Garten.
3. Die Bauersfrau geht jeden Sonntag zur Kirche, und sie hört dort viel vom Paradies.
4. Der Student sagt *Paris,* aber die Bauersfrau versteht *Paradies.*
5. Die Bauersfrau gibt dem Studenten ein Stück Brot. Die Goldstücke steckt sie in die Taschen der Hose, und dann macht sie aus den Kleidern ein schönes Bündel.
6. Der Student dankt der Frau, nimmt das Bündel, sagt auf Wiedersehen und wandert so schnell wie möglich weiter.
7. Der Bauer läuft schnell in den Stall, sattelt sein Pferd und galoppiert dem Studenten nach.
8. Der Student hört das Pferd des Bauern, nimmt das Bündel vom Rücken und versteckt es in einem Busch.
9. Der Student holt das Bündel aus dem Busch, steigt auf das Pferd und reitet schnell weg.

---

10. Der Bauer findet niemand im Wald, und als er wieder zurückkommt, findet er auch den Studenten und das Pferd nicht mehr.

geben—gab	finden—fand	laufen—lief	sein—war
nehmen—nahm	verstehen—verstand	reiten—ritt	
kommen—kam	gehen—ging	steigen—stieg	

B. WARUM STAATSKASSEN° IMMER LEER SIND. Lesen Sie diese Geschichte, und setzen Sie alle kursiv gedruckten° Verben ins Präteritum. Das Präteritum der unregelmäßigen Verben ist unten gegeben.

Obwohl der gute König Otto ein großes, reiches Land mit vielen, fleißigen Menschen *regiert,°* hat er nie Geld in der Staatskasse. Deshalb *ruft* er eines Tages° alle seine Generäle und Minister zusammen und *fragt* sie: „Wo bleibt denn nur das ganze Geld?" Er *bekommt* aber keine Antwort. Die Generäle *schütteln°* nur den Kopf, und die Minister *machen* ein dummes Gesicht.°

Da *sagt* der König: „Wenn ihr alle so dumm seid, dann muß ich meinen Narren° kommen lassen und ihn fragen."

Der Narr *kommt,* und der König *fragt:* „Narr, wo bleibt denn nur das ganze Geld?" „Wenn du das wirklich wissen willst", *sagt* da der Narr, „dann gib mir einen Klumpen Butter."

Da *läßt* der König einen Butterklumpen holen, und es *ist* ein großer Klumpen. Den *gibt* der Narr dem Ministerpräsidenten in die Hand und *sagt:* „Geben Sie den Klumpen doch bitte weiter, Exzellenz!" Und so *geht* nun der Butterklumpen von Minister zu Minister und von General zu General rings° um den großen Tisch herum. Als der Klumpen dann endlich wieder beim Narren *ankommt,* da *ist* das kein großer Klumpen mehr, sondern nur noch ein ganz miserables Klümpchen. Fast die ganze Butter *klebt°* an den großen, warmen Händen der Minister und der Generäle!

Da *sagt* der Narr zum guten König Otto: „Siehst du jetzt, wo dein Geld ist?—Es ist dort, wo auch die Butter ist."

geben—gab	haben—hatte	rufen—rief	sein—war
kommen—kam	lassen—ließ	gehen—ging	

Margin glosses:
- state treasuries
- **kursiv gedruckt:** *italicized*
- *rules / one day*
- *shake*
- *face*
- *court jester*
- **rings um . . . herum:** *all around*
- **klebt . . . an:** *is sticking to*

THE SIMPLE PAST OF MODAL VERBS

Like the regular verbs, the modals add the past tense marker **-t-** to the verb stem. For the modals **dürfen, können, mögen,** and **müssen,** the umlaut of the infinitive form is dropped in the simple past. Note that the **g** of **mögen** becomes **ch.**

dürfen	**können**	**mögen**	**müssen**	**sollen**	**wollen**
ich d**u**r**te**	ich k**onn**te	ich m**ocht**e	ich m**u**ß**te**	ich soll**te**	ich woll**te**

	Singular		Plural
ich	k**onn**te	wir	k**onn**ten
du	k**onn**test	ihr	k**onn**tet
er / sie / es	k**onn**te	sie	k**onn**ten
	Sie k**onn**ten		

As is the case with **sein** and **haben,** the simple past of the modals is used not only as a *narrative* tense, but is also common in conversation.

Narrative situation:

Als das Sommersemester zu Ende war, **wollte** der Student zu seinen Eltern nach Deutschland zurück. Weil er aber sehr arm war, **konnte** er kein Pferd kaufen, sondern **mußte** zu Fuß nach Deutschland wandern.

*When the summer semester was over, the student **wanted** to go back to this parents' home in Germany. Because he was very poor, he **could** not buy a horse, but **had to** go to Germany on foot.*

Conversational situation:

STEFAN: Warum **konntest** du nicht zu unserer Fete kommen?

*Why **couldn't** you come to our party?*

BERND: Weil ich meine Eltern zum Flughafen fahren **mußte.**

*Because I **had to** drive my parents to the airport.*

C. WOHNPROBLEME. Ergänzen Sie das Präteritum der passenden Modalverben!

1. Martin _____ gestern zur Uni und _____ deshalb nicht mit Peter zu Frau Wild.

   können / müssen

2. Peter _____ Martin sagen, was sie in Frau Wilds Wohnung alles nicht tun _____.

   dürfen / sollen

3. Claudia _____ die Wohnung, aber sie meinte, Martin und Peter _____ gleich alle Möbel umstellen.

   sollen / mögen

4. Obwohl Stephanie und Claudia das Leben im Studentenheim sehr _____, _____ sie am Ende des ersten Semesters dort ausziehen.

   wollen / mögen

5. Im Studentenheim war es oft so laut, daß Stephanie nicht lernen _____ und in die Bibliothek gehen _____, wenn sie lernen _____.

   können / wollen / müssen

6. Bei Frau Kuhn _____ Stephanie lernen, so viel sie _____.

   wollen / können

7. Aber sie _____ es gar nicht, daß sie dort die Küche nicht benutzen _____.

   dürfen / mögen

8. Stephanie _____ Frau Kuhn noch vor dem Abendessen anrufen und ihr sagen, ob sie das Zimmer _____ oder nicht.

   sollen / wollen

9. Wenn Claudia in ihrer WG lernen _____, _____ sie nur die Tür zumachen.

   müssen / wollen

10. Stephanie _____ nicht mit schlechten Zensuren nach Amerika zurückkommen, weil sie sonst das ganze Jahr wiederholen _____.

    dürfen / müssen

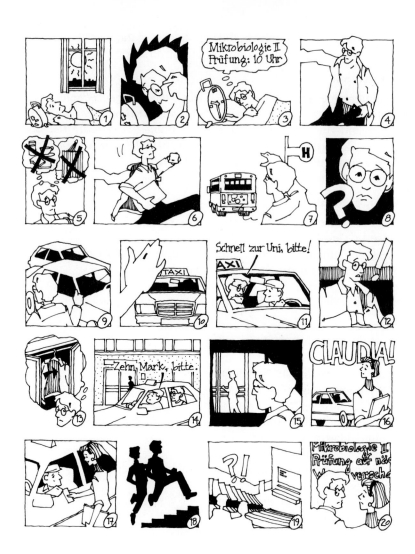

not even

D. MANCHMAL SOLLTE MAN GAR NICHT ERST° AUFSTEHEN. Suchen Sie auf der nächsten Seite den passenden Satz zu jeder der zwanzig Zeichnungen!

stopped —Punkt zehn hielt° das Taxi vor der Uni, und der Fahrer sagte: „Zehn Mark, bitte."

thought —„Was jetzt?" dachte° Martin.

—„Verflixt! Der steckt ja zu Hause in meiner anderen Jacke!"

—Als Martin gestern morgen aufwachte, schien die Sonne hell durchs Fenster.

up —Zusammen rannten sie dann die Treppe zum Hörsaal hinauf.°

—Er versuchte es per Anhalter, aber niemand hielt.

—Schnell sprang er aus dem Bett und zog Hemd und Hose an.

traffic —Und als der Wagen dann durch den Verkehr° raste, holte Martin schon seinen
that is Geldbeutel aus der Tasche—das heißt,° or *wollte* seinen Geldbeutel aus der
Tasche holen.

alarm clock —Und als er auf seinen Wecker° schaute, konnte er kaum glauben, was er sah.

blackboard / it said —Und an der Tafel° stand:° Mikrobiologie II: Prüfung auf nächste Woche
postponed verschoben.°

—Schnell steckte er den Kopf durchs Fenster und schrie:° „Claudia!"   *shouted*

—Wie verrückt rannte er zur Bushaltestelle.°   *bus stop*

—Da blieb zu nichts mehr Zeit—weder° zum Duschen noch zum Frühstück.   **weder . . . noch:** *neither . . . nor*

—Aber obwohl es schon fünf nach zehn war, war der Hörsaal leer!

—Aber natürlich kam er zu spät: der Bus fuhr gerade um die Ecke.

—Es war schon halb zehn, und um zehn hatte er eine wichtige Prüfung!

—Schließlich stoppte er ein Taxi.

—Und Gott sei Dank hörte sie ihn, und sie hatte sogar zehn Mark.

—Aber da sah Martin auch schon die Lösung seines Problems: das war doch Claudia dort vor dem Eingang!

—„Schnell zur Uni, bitte!" rief er, als er einstieg.°   *got in*

 # ZUSAMMENSCHAU

MARTIN SUCHT EINEN FERIENJOB (2)

Als Martin gestern die Stellenangebote° der Süddeutschen Zeitung durchstudierte, fand er die folgende Anzeige:°   *employment section* / *ad*

> Größere Münchener Firma sucht Studenten für interessante und gut bezahlte Ferienarbeit. Vielseitige Arbeitserfahrung,° gute Englischkenntnisse und Führerschein erwünscht.°
>
> Bewerbung° mit Lebenslauf° an
> F. Scheer und Co.
> Postfach 30 10 20, 8000 München 30

work experience / *desirable*

application / resumé

Martin holte deshalb sofort Papier und Kugelschreiber und schrieb diesen Lebenslauf.

LEBENSLAUF

Ich, Martin Keller, wurde am 10. August 1968 in Mainz geboren. Mein Vater ist Wirtschaftsprüfer,° und meine Mutter arbeitet in einem Reisebüro. Von 1974 bis 1978 besuchte ich in Mainz die Grundschule. Im Sommer 1978 zogen° meine Eltern nach Mannheim, und ich ging dort von 1978 bis 1988 aufs Gymnasium. Von 1986 bis 1987 war ich als Austauschschüler° ein Jahr in Seattle, USA, und ich spreche deshalb fast perfekt Englisch. Mein Abitur° machte ich mit einer Gesamtnote° von 2, und seit Herbst 1989 studiere ich auf der Ludwig-Maximilians-Universität hier in München Biologie und Chemie.

accountant / *moved*

exchange student[1] / *high school diploma* / *average*

---

1. In the German-speaking countries students are called **Schüler** up to the end of high school. It is only at the university level that they are called **Studenten.**

In Mannheim arbeitete ich im Sommer 1984 und im Sommer 1985 in einer Schuhfabrik. Meinen Zivildienst° leistete° ich in verschiedenen° Krankenhäusern und Altersheimen in Mannheim und Heidelberg. Im vergangenen° Sommer arbeitete ich als Malergehilfe in Grünwald.

Außer ausgezeichneten Englischkenntnissen und dreimonatiger Erfahrung als Lieferwagenfahrer° habe ich auch Erfahrung mit verschiedenen Textverarbeitungssystemen.°

✎ MEIN LEBENSLAUF

Das Semester ist fast zu Ende, und Sie suchen einen Ferienjob. Schreiben Sie deshalb Ihren Lebenslauf, und vergessen Sie nicht, alle wichtigen Qualifikationen zu erwähnen,° z.B:

Wann und wo wurden Sie geboren?
Was machen Ihre Eltern?
Wo besuchten Sie die Grundschule und das Gymnasium?
Mit was für einer Gesamtnote machten Sie Ihr Abitur?
Was studieren Sie?
Was für Arbeitserfahrung haben Sie?
Was für Sprachkenntnisse haben Sie?
Haben Sie einen Führerschein?
Haben sie Computererfahrung?

ICH SUCHE EINEN FERIENJOB

Sie sind Personalchef bei einer deutschen Firma, und Ihre Gesprächspartnerin / Ihr Gesprächspartner sucht einen Ferienjob. Stellen Sie ähnliche° Fragen wie die obigen,° um herauszufinden, ob diese Bewerberin° / dieser Bewerber die richtigen Qualifikationen hat.

2. TALKING ABOUT EVENTS THAT PRECEDE OTHER EVENTS IN THE PAST

THE PAST PERFECT TENSE

Like the English past perfect, the German past perfect is used to refer to an event that precedes another event in the past. It is formed with the simple past of the auxiliaries **haben** or **sein** and the past participle:

Der Student war sehr hungrig, denn er **war** schon weit **gewandert** und **hatte** noch nicht mal **gefrühstückt.**

*The student was very hungry, because he **had** already **traveled** far and **had** not even **had breakfast** yet.*

Singular			Plural		
ich	war	gewandert	wir	waren	gewandert
du	warst	gewandert	ihr	wart	gewandert
er	war	gewandert	sie	waren	gewandert
	Sie waren gewandert				

Singular			Plural		
ich	hatte	gefrühstückt	wir	hatten	gefrühstückt
du	hattest	gefrühstückt	ihr	hattet	gefrühstückt
er	hatte	gefrühstückt	sie	hatten	gefrühstückt
	Sie hatten gefrühstückt				

The past perfect tense is often used in subordinate clauses that are introduced by the conjunction **nachdem** *(after).*

Nachdem Frau Schneider den ganzen Tag im Büro **gearbeitet hatte,** mußte sie noch das Abendessen kochen und den Kindern bei den Hausaufgaben helfen.

*After Mrs. Schneider **had worked** at the office all day, she had to make supper, and help the children with their homework.*

E. ALTE FREUNDE. Ergänzen Sie das Plusquamperfekt° der gegebenen Verben! *past perfect*

1. Nachdem ich _____ und _____, setzte ich mich an den Schreibtisch und schrieb den ganzen Morgen Briefe.

   aufstehen / frühstücken

2. Nachdem ich den letzten Brief _____, ging ich auf die Post.

   fertigschreiben

3. Nachdem ich die Briefe _____ und _____, machte ich noch einen kleinen Stadtbummel.

   frankieren° / wegschicken   *to put postage on*

4. Da traf ich dann Tanja. Sie sah sehr schick aus, denn sie kam gerade von Karstadt, wo sie einen tollen Mantel _____.

   kaufen

5. Weil wir einander schon lange nicht mehr _____, gingen wir zusammen ins Café Mozart.

   sehen

6. Nachdem wir dort Kaffee und Kuchen _____, erzählte Tanja, daß sie vor einem Jahr _____, und jetzt in Münster lebte.

   bestellen / heiraten

7. Sie _____ gestern auf ein paar Tage nach Köln _____, um hier ihre Eltern zu besuchen.

   kommen

F. PETER ERZÄHLT, WAS ER GESTERN ALLES MACHTE. Verwenden Sie jedesmal zuerst das Plusquamperfekt und dann das Präteritum. Sie brauchen die folgenden unregelmäßigen Formen des Präteritums: **fuhr, ging, aß,** and **trank.**

▶ Nachdem ich _____, _____ ich ein Bad.
Nachdem ich aufgestanden war, nahm ich ein Bad.

                      aufstehen / nehmen

1. Nachdem ich ein Bad _____, _____ ich.   nehmen / frühstücken

2. Nachdem ich _____, _____ ich zur Uni.   frühstücken / fahren

3. Nachdem ich dort _____, _____ ich schnell in die Vorlesung.   ankommen / gehen

4. Nachdem ich zwei Stunden in der Vorlesung _____, _____ ich in der Mensa zu Mittag.   sitzen / essen

5. Nachdem ich zu Mittag _____, _____ ich in der Bibliothek an meinem Referat.   essen / arbeiten

6. Nachdem ich ein paar Stunden an meinem Referat _____, _____ ich mit Martin Kaffee trinken.   arbeiten / gehen

7. Nachdem wir eine Tasse Kaffee _____, _____ wir Tennis spielen.   trinken / gehen

8. Nachdem wir zwei Stunden lang Tennis _____, _____ wir mit dem Bus zu Claudias WG.   spielen / fahren

9. Nachdem wir dort ein paar CDs _____, _____ Martin uns etwas zu essen.   hören / machen

10. Nachdem wir zu Abend _____, _____ wir Stefanie _____ und _____ zusammen ins Kino.   essen / abholen / gehen

11. Nachdem wir dort einen tollen Wildwestfilm _____, _____ wir in einer netten Kneipe ein Glas Bier.   anschauen / trinken

12. Nachdem wir bis Mitternacht in der Kneipe _____ und _____, _____ wir nach Hause.   sitzen / quatschen / gehen

✎ **WAS ICH GESTERN ALLES MACHTE.** Erzählen Sie Ihren Tageslauf! Beginnen Sie jeden Satz mit **nachdem.** (Die unregelmäßigen Verbformen finden Sie im *reference section* *Anhang°*.)

▶ Nachdem ich aufgestanden war und geduscht hatte, frühstückte ich.
Nachdem ich gefrühstückt hatte, . . .
 . . .
Nachdem ich . . . , ging ich ins Bett.

G. EIN UNGLÜCKLICHER VORMITTAG.

Verwenden Sie das Plusquamperfekt, wenn ein Vorgang° früher stattfindet° als ein anderer. Verwenden Sie das Präteritum, wenn die Vorgänge gleichzeitig° stattfinden.

event / takes place at the same time

1. Als ich gestern morgen _____, war es schon Viertel nach zehn. — **aufwachen**

2. Weil ich so spät _____, trank ich nur schnell ein Glas Milch zum Frühstück. — **aufstehen**

3. Als ich zum Bus rannte, _____ es in Strömen. — **regnen**

4. Weil ich meinen Schirm _____, wurde ich ziemlich naß°. — **vergessen** — *wet*

5. Weil der Bus schon längst° _____, als ich zur Bushaltestelle kam, nahm ich ein Taxi. — **abfahren** — *long ago*

6. Als ich den Taxifahrer bezahlen wollte, merkte° ich, daß ich meinen Geldbeutel _____. — **vergessen** — *noticed*

7. Weil ich so schnell wie möglich in die Vorlesung _____, gab ich dem Taxifahrer meine Armbanduhr. — **müssen**

8. Als das Taxi gerade _____, fiel mir ein, daß ich einen Brief mit hundert Mark von meinen Eltern in der Jakkentasche hatte. — **wegfahren**

9. Als ich in den Hörsaal _____, war kein Mensch dort. — **kommen**

Was bedeutet das „H"?

10. Da fiel mir ein, daß es Karfreitag° war und daß Ralf mich am Abend vorher angerufen und mir das _____. — **sagen** — *Good Friday*

---

3. EXPRESSING ACTION IN DIFFERENT TIME FRAMES

THE PRINCIPAL PARTS OF IRREGULAR VERBS

In German and in English, all tenses of *regular* verbs are derived from the stem of the infinitive. They are completely predictable.

Infinitive	Tenses			
	Present	Simple Past	Present Perfect	Past Perfect
lernen	**er *lernt***	**er *lernte***	**er hat *gelernt***	**er hatte *gelernt***
to learn	***he learns***	***he learned***	***he has learned***	***he had learned***

In both German and English all tenses of *irregular* verbs are derived from a set of *principal parts*. These principal parts are not derived from the infinitive and sometimes look quite different from the infinitive. Below are the principal parts of **gehen** *(to go)* and the tenses derived from them.

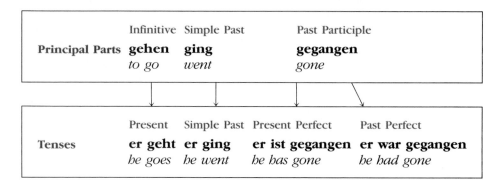

	Infinitive	Simple Past	Past Participle	
Principal Parts	**gehen**	**ging**	**gegangen**	
	to go	*went*	*gone*	

	Present	Simple Past	Present Perfect	Past Perfect
Tenses	**er geht**	**er ging**	**er ist gegangen**	**er war gegangen**
	he goes	*he went*	*he has gone*	*he had gone*

For German verbs with an irregularity in the present tense, there is an additional principal part.

Infinitive	Irregularity In Present Tense	Simple Past	Past Participle
geben	er **gibt**	gab	gegeben
fahren	er **fährt**	fuhr	gefahren

You will find a list of the irregular verbs used in this book in the reference section.

MIXED VERBS

a. There is a small group of *mixed* verbs that have characteristics of both the regular and the irregular verbs. In the simple past and in the past participle they have a stem change like the irregular verbs, but they take the **-t-** marker and the personal endings of the regular verbs. Five very common verbs in this group are:

bringen	**brachte**	**hat gebracht**	*to bring; to take*
denken	**dachte**	**hat gedacht**	*to think*
rennen	**rannte**	**ist gerannt**	*to run*
kennen	**kannte**	**hat gekannt**	*to know* (to be acquainted with)
wissen (weiß)	**wußte**	**hat gewußt**	*to know* (a fact)

b. The verb **werden** has characteristics of mixed verbs and irregular verbs:

werden (wird)	**wurde**	**ist geworden**	*to become*

The simple past is very similar to that of mixed verbs: **ich wurde, du wurdest, er wurde,** etc. The past participle is that of an irregular verb: **geworden.**

H. DER FALSCHE TAG. Ergänzen Sie die passenden gemischten Verben! Verwenden Sie das Präteritum oder das Partizip Perfekt°.   *past participle*

1. Als Ralf seinem Freund Günter sagte, daß Tina heute Geburtstag hatte, _____ Günter gleich zum nächsten Blumengeschäft.
2. Warum hatte er denn nicht _____, wann Tina Geburtstag hatte?
3. Er _____ sie doch schon so viele Jahre.
4. Die beiden hatten einander schon als Kinder _____.
5. Tina _____ ganz genau, wann Günter Geburtstag hatte.
6. Zu seinem letzten Geburtstag hatte sie ihm einen Kuchen mit einundzwanzig Kerzen _____.
7. Günter war nämlich einundzwanzig Jahre alt _____.
8. Auf dem Weg zum Blumengeschäft _____ Günter, daß er Tina einundzwanzig rote Rosen kaufen sollte.
9. Tina _____ heute nämlich auch einundzwanzig.
10. Aber dann waren die Rosen leider viel teurer, als Günter _____ hatte.
11. Kurz vor zwölf _____ Günter seiner Freundin Tina dann fünf wunderschöne rote Rosen.
12. Und weil Günter so außer Atem° war, fragte Tina: „Warum bist du denn so _____, Günter? Mein Geburtstag ist doch erst morgen."   *out of breath*

4. EXPRESSING *WHEN* IN GERMAN

WANN, WENN, AND *ALS*

Although **wann, wenn,** and **als** can all be translated by English *when,* they are not interchangeable.

a. **wann:** *when? at what time?*

Wann is a question word that introduces direct and indirect questions.

Wann kommen Müllers aus Portugal zurück?	**When** *are the Müllers coming back from Portugal?*
Ich weiß nicht, **wann** Müllers aus Portugal zurückkommen.	*I don't know* **when** *the Müllers are coming back from Portugal.*

b. **wenn:** *when, at the time when* (in the present or future)

Wenn is a conjunction that introduces subordinate clauses referring to events in the present or future.

Ich kann nicht lernen, **wenn** ich so müde bin.	*I can't study* **when** *I'm so tired.*
Ruf uns bitte gleich an, **wenn** du in Frankfurt ankommst.	*Please call us right away* **when** *you arrive in Frankfurt.*
Wenn du deine Hausaufgaben gemacht hast, gehen wir ins Kino.	**When** *you have finished your homework, we're going to the movies.*

c. wenn: *when, whenever*

Wenn also introduces subordinate clauses referring to repeated events.

Wenn Tante Emma zu Besuch kommt, bringt sie uns immer Schweizer Schokolade mit.	*When Aunt Emma comes to visit, she always brings us Swiss chocolate.*
Wenn Tante Emma zu Besuch kam, brachte sie uns immer Schweizer Schokolade mit.	*When Aunt Emma came to visit, she always brought us Swiss chocolate.*

d. als: *when, at the time when* (in the past)

Als is a conjunction that introduces subordinate clauses referring to a *single event in the past*. The verb in an **als**-clause is in the simple past or in the past perfect tense.

Als ich den Krimi fertiggelesen hatte, merkte ich, daß es drei Uhr morgens war.	*When I had finished reading the thriller, I noticed that it was three o'clock in the morning.*
Als es anfing, hell zu werden, bin ich endlich eingeschlafen.	*When it started to get light, I finally fell asleep.*

I. WANN, WENN ODER ALS? Ergänzen Sie die Fragen und Antworten!

S1:

1. _____ fliegen Müllers nach Portugal?
2. _____ sind Müllers nach Portugal geflogen?
3. Weißt du, _____ Monika bei IBM anfängt?
4. Weißt du, _____ Monika bei IBM angefangen hat?
5. Warum sagst du mir nicht, _____ du heute abend nach Hause kommst?
6. _____ hat Tina dir das Buch zurückgegeben?
7. _____ gibst du mir das Buch zurück?
8. Warum warst du nicht auf dem Bahnhof, _____ Monika aus Italien zurückkam?
9. Können Sie mir sagen, _____ wir unseren nächsten Test schreiben, Frau Professor?
10. _____ rufst du Bernd an?
11. _____ hat Stefan angerufen?
12. _____ gehst du in die Bibliothek?

S2:

_____ es ihnen hier zu kalt wird.

_____ es ihnen hier zu kalt wurde.

_____ sie aus Italien zurückkommt.

_____ sie aus Italien zurückkam.

Weil ich nicht weiß, _____ das Konzert zu Ende ist.

_____ sie mich gestern nachmittag besuchte.

_____ ich es fertiggelesen habe.

Weil ich nicht wußte, _____ sie ankommt.

_____ wir mit diesem Kapitel fertig sind.

_____ ich nach Haus komme.

_____ ich gerade zu Bett gegangen war.

_____ ich meinen Kaffee ausgetrunken habe.

horseback rider

J. EIN TOLLER REITER.° Erzählen Sie diese kleine Geschichte auf deutsch!
When I was little, we lived in Berlin. In the summer (of) 1970 we visited my

grandfather in Schleswig-Holstein.[1] He was a farmer and had a beautiful horse. Every morning, when we were finished in the stable, I was allowed to ride on this horse. My little brother was afraid of horses. When grandfather got the horse out of the stable, Uli always ran into the house. But when we were in Berlin again, he told his friends: "I am a fantastic horseback rider!"

✏️➤ **ALS ICH KLEIN WAR, . . .** Was machten Sie in den Sommerferien, als Sie klein waren? Was spielten Sie mit den Nachbarskindern? Wohin reisten Sie mit Ihren Eltern? Schreiben Sie eine kleine Geschichte zu diesem Thema.

5. INDICATING DIRECTION *AWAY FROM* AND *TOWARD*

HIN AND *HER* AS DIRECTIONAL PREFIXES

You already know that **hin** and **her** are attached to or used in combination with the question word **wo.**

Wo bist du?	*Where are you?*
Wohin gehst du? (**Wo** gehst du **hin**?)	*Where are you going (to)?*
Woher kommst du? (**Wo** kommst du **her**?)	*Where are you coming from?*

Hier darf ich nicht hinein

> **hin** indicates motion or direction away from the speaker
> **her** indicates motion or direction toward the speaker

Hin and **her** are also used as prefixes or parts of prefixes of separable verbs.

Fährst du mit dem Bus zum Flughafen? Nein, Ralf **fährt** mich **hin.**	*Are you taking the bus to the airport? No, Ralf **is driving** me (**there**).*
Wie bist du so schnell zu uns gekommen?	*How did you get to our house so fast?*
Ralf hat mich **hergefahren.**	*Ralf **drove** me (**here**).*
Sollen wir **hineingehen** oder sollen wir warten, bis Dieter **herauskommt?**	*Should we **go in** or should we wait until Dieter **comes out?***

---

1. The most northerly state in Germany, bordering on Denmark. The world's most productive milking cow, the Holstein, originates from here.

speech bubbles

K. WAS GEHÖRT IN DIE SPRECHBLASEN?° Ergänzen Sie die Sätze! Verwenden Sie die unten gegebenen Verben!

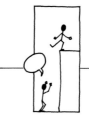

herunterfallen

▶ Passen Sie auf, daß Sie nicht _____!
Passen Sie auf, daß Sie nicht herunterfallen!

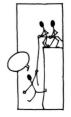

1. _____ Sie doch _____, bitte.

4. Warum _____ Sie mich denn nicht endlich _____?

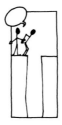

2. Warum _____ Sie denn nicht _____?

5. Sollen wir _____?

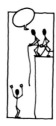

3. Keine Angst! Wir _____ Sie gleich _____.

hereinkommen   hinaufziehen   hinüberspringen   hineingehen   heraufziehen

6. Warum _____ Sie denn nicht _____?   8. _____ Sie sofort _____!

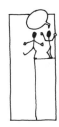

7. _____ Sie sofort _____!   9. Passen Sie auf, daß Sie nicht _____!

hinunterfallen	herauskommen	herüberspringen	hinausgehen

Sprachnotizen

Expressing *away from* and *toward* in colloquial German

In colloquial German, the prefixes **hinaus-, herein-, hinauf-, herunter-,** etc. are (somewhat illogically) abbreviated to **raus-, rein-, rauf-, runter-,** etc.

Sollen wir **hineingehen,** oder sollen wir warten, bis Dieter **herauskommt?**
Sollen wir **reingehen,** oder sollen wir warten, bis Dieter **rauskommt?**

ZUSAMMENSCHAU

DER HASE° UND DER IGEL°
nach einem Märchen der Brüder Grimm

hare / hedgehog[1]

Die drei „Personen" in diesem Märchen sind ein Hase, ein Igel und die Frau des Igels. Der Hase denkt, daß Hasen etwas viel Besseres sind als Igel, und er ist taktlos genug, das dem Igel ins Gesicht zu sagen. Lesen Sie, was in dieser Geschichte mit einer so taktlosen Person passiert.

---

1. A small animal with spines on its back and sides, much like the North American porcupine.

Beantworten Sie nach jedem der vier Hauptabschnitte die Fragen unter Zur Orientierung und zum Zusammenfassen.

harvest time	
larks	
air / bees / were buzzing	

happy	
crossed	
was humming / song	
to himself / softly	

set out
met
cabbage

mockingly
are walking around
laughed / crooked / legs
made angry / tremendously
even if

said
run a race / finish line
if you like
What are you betting?
agreed / shake on it
start / hurry

with these words / in agreement

*with me / **fing . . . an:***
began
concern

furrow
up there / down here

Es war an einem Sonntagmorgen zur Erntezeit.° Die Sonne schien hell vom blauen Himmel, der Morgenwind ging warm über die Felder, die Lerchen° sangen in der Luft,° die Bienen° summten° in den Blumen, und die Leute gingen in ihren Sonntagskleidern in die Kirche, und alle Kreatur war
5 vergnügt,° und der Igel auch.

Der Igel aber stand vor seiner Tür, hatte die Arme untergeschlagen,° schaute in den Morgenwind hinaus und summte° ein kleines Liedchen° vor sich hin.° Als er nun so stand und halb leise° vor sich hin sang, da fiel ihm plötzlich ein, daß er ja noch Zeit zu einem kleinen Spaziergang hatte, während
10 seine Frau die Kinder wusch und das Frühstück machte. „Da kann ich noch schnell aufs Feld und meine Rüben anschauen", dachte er, nahm seinen Spazierstock und ging los.°

Als der Igel zum Rübenfeld kam, traf° er seinen Nachbarn, den Hasen. Der machte einen Spaziergang, um seinen Kohl° anzuschauen. Der Igel sagte
15 freundlich „Guten Morgen". Aber der Hase grüßte nicht zurück, sondern sagte nur ganz spöttisch:° „Wie kommt es denn, daß du hier am frühen Morgen auf dem Feld herumläufst?"° „Ich gehe spazieren", sagte der Igel. „Spazieren?" lachte° der Hase, „du, mit deinen kurzen, krummen° Beinen?"°

Diese Antwort ärgerte° den Igel ganz ungeheuer,° denn für einen Igel hatte
20 er sehr schöne Beine, auch wenn° sie von Natur kurz und krumm waren. „Denkst du vielleicht", sagte er zum Hasen, „daß du mit deinen langen, dünnen Beinen schneller laufen kannst als ich?" „Ja, das denke ich", sagte der Hase. „Das müssen wir erst mal ausprobieren", meinte° der Igel. „Ich glaube, wenn wir um die Wette laufen,° bin ich zuerst am Ziel.° „Das ist ja zum
25 Lachen", sagte der Hase, „aber meinetwegen° können wir laufen, wenn du so große Lust hast. Was gilt die Wette?° „Ein Goldstück und eine Flasche Schnaps", sagte der Igel. „Angenommen",° rief der Hase, „schlag ein,° und dann kann's gleich losgehen."° „Nein, so große Eile° hat es nicht", meinte der Igel, „ich will erst noch nach Hause gehen und ein bißchen frühstücken. In
30 einer halben Stunde bin ich wieder zurück."

Damit° ging der Igel, denn der Hase war einverstanden.° Unterwegs dachte der Igel: „Der Hase kann zwar schneller laufen, aber die Wette gewinne ich, denn er hat die langen Beine, aber ich habe den klugen Kopf." Als nun der Igel zu Hause ankam, sagte er zu seiner Frau: „Frau, zieh schnell eine von meinen
35 Hosen an, du mußt mit mir aufs Feld." „Eine von deinen Hosen? Ja was ist denn los?" fragte seine Frau. „Ich habe mit dem Hasen um ein Goldstück und eine Flasche Schnaps gewettet. Ich will mit ihm um die Wette laufen, und du sollst mit dabei° sein."„O mein Gott, Mann", fing° da die Frau an zu schreien, „bist du nicht ganz recht im Kopf? Wie kannst du mit dem Hasen um die Wette
40 laufen wollen?" „Laß das mal meine Sache° sein", sagte da der Igel. „Zieh jetzt die Hose an, und komm mit."

Als sie dann unterwegs waren, sagte der Igel zu seiner Frau. „Nun paß mal auf, was ich dir sage. Siehst du, auf dem langen Feld dort wollen wir unseren Wettlauf machen. Der Hase läuft in der einen Furche° und ich in der anderen,
45 und von dort oben° fangen wir an zu laufen. Du aber sitzt hier unten° in der Furche, und wenn der Hase hier ankommt, springst du auf und rufst: ,Ich bin schon da.' "

Als der Igel am oberen Ende des Feldes ankam, war der Hase schon da. „Können wir endlich anfangen?" fragte der Hase. „Jawohl", sagte der Igel.

50 Dann ging jeder zu seiner Furche. Der Hase zählte: „Eins, zwei, drei" und
rannte wie ein Sturmwind über das Feld. Der Igel aber blieb ruhig auf seinem
Platz.

Als nun der Hase in vollem Lauf° am unteren Ende des Feldes ankam, *at top speed*
sprang die Frau des Igels auf und rief. „Ich bin schon da!" Der Hase war
55 verblüfft,° denn die Frau des Igels sah natürlich genauso° aus wie ihr Mann. Er *baffled / exactly*
dachte. „Das kann doch gar nicht sein!" Er rief: „Einmal ist nicht genug!" Und
zurück raste er wie ein Sturmwind, daß ihm die Ohren am Kopf flogen. Die
Frau des Igels aber blieb ruhig auf ihrem Platz. Als der Hase am oberen Ende
des Feldes ankam, sprang der Igel auf und rief: „Ich bin schon da!" Der Hase
60 war ganz außer sich° und schrie: „Noch einmal!" „Meinetwegen so oft wie du *beside himself*
Lust hast", antwortete der Igel. So lief der Hase noch dreiundsiebzigmal, und
jedesmal, wenn er oben oder unten ankam, riefen der Igel oder seine Frau:
„Ich bin schon da!"

Das letzte Mal aber kam der Hase nicht mehr zum Ende, sondern stürzte
65 mitten auf dem Feld tot zur Erde. Der Igel aber nahm das Goldstück und die
Schnapsflasche, rief seine Frau, und beide gingen vergnügt nach Hause, und
wenn sie nicht gestorben sind, so leben sie noch heute.

ZUR ORIENTIERUNG UND ZUM ZUSAMMENFASSEN

1. Z. 1–12: Warum waren alle Menschen und Tiere° an diesem Sonntagmorgen so *animals*
   glücklich? Was zeigt, daß der Igel kein moderner Mann war? Wohin wollte der
   Igel und warum?
2. Z. 13–30: Warum machte der Hase einen Spaziergang? Warum fand der Hase es
   so lächerlich,° daß der Igel spazierenging? Was schlug° der Igel vor, als der Hase *ridiculous / schlug . . .*
   ihn verspottete?° Der Igel wollte nicht sofort mit dem Hasen um die Wette *vor: did . . . suggest /*
   laufen. Wie erklärte er das dem Hasen? *ridiculed*
3. Z. 31–47: Warum glaubte der Igel, daß er die Wette gewinnen konnte? Warum
   schrie seine Frau: „O mein Gott, Mann, bist du nicht ganz recht im Kopf?"
   Warum mußte die Frau des Igels eine Hose von ihrem Mann anziehen?
4. Z. 48–67: Was machte der Igel, als der Hase losrannte? Warum merkte der Hase
   nicht, daß er es mit zwei verschiedenen° Igeln zu tun hatte? Warum kam der *different*
   Hase beim letzten Mal nicht mehr zum Ende des Feldes?

WER MACHT DAS? Sie hören vierzehn Fragen zu *Der Hase und der Igel.*
Beantworten Sie die Fragen mit **der Igel, die Frau des Igels, der Igel und
seine Frau, der Hase, der Hase und der Igel!**

 **WIR MODERNISIEREN EIN MÄRCHEN**

Moderne Leser finden den zweiten Paragraphen dieses Märchens chauvinistisch,
und viele moderne Leser finden den letzten Paragraphen zu grausam.° Sprechen *cruel*
Sie mit ein paar Klassenkameraden über diese beiden Paragraphen, und versuchen
Sie, modernere und humanere Versionen auszuarbeiten. Lesen Sie der Klasse Ihre
Versionen vor.

Welches Grimmsche Märchen erzählen diese Briefmarken?

The nineteenth-century linguists and folklorists Jacob and Wilhelm Grimm are known the world over for their **Kinder- und Hausmärchen.** This collection of fairy tales has been translated into 140 languages and is the second most published German book after the Luther Bible. The Grimm Brothers were not the authors of the fairy tales. For six years they traveled from village to village, painstakingly collecting old tales like **Rotkäppchen, Schneewittchen, Der Hase und der Igel,** and **Sterntaler.** These stories had been handed from generation to generation by word of mouth, but they had never been written down. The brothers reworked the stories for publication, always maintaining the simple style of the folk tale. Many of their fairy tales begin with: **Es war einmal . . .** *(Once upon a time . . .).*

The Grimm Brothers are famous not only for their fairy tales, but also for their work in linguistics. They initiated a grand project, the **Deutsches Wörterbuch,** a monumental dictionary that took several generations of scholars more than 100 years to complete.

---

trying to please everybody

ES ALLEN RECHT MACHEN °
nach einer Fabel von Äsop

1. Die folgenden Zeichnungen zeigen eine Geschichte von einem Vater, seinem vierzehnjährigen Sohn und seinem Esel. Sagen Sie, wer in den Silhouetten (Bilder 1, 3, 5, 7 und 9) reitet und wer zu Fuß geht.
2. In Bildern 2, 4, 6 und 8 sehen Sie vier weitere Personen: einen Bäcker, einen

tailor

Fleischer, einen Schneider° und einen Bauern.

   a. Bild 2: Der Bäcker spricht mit dem Vater. Was für einen Effekt hat das, was er zu ihm sagt? (Siehe Silhouetten 1 und 3!) Was hat der Bäcker wohl gesagt?
   b. Bild 4: Der Fleischer spricht mit dem Sohn. Was für einen Effekt hat das, was er zu ihm sagt? (Siehe Silhouetten 3 und 5!) Was hat der Fleischer wohl gesagt?
   c. Bild 6: Der Schneider spricht mit dem Vater und mit dem Sohn. Was für einen Effekt hat das, was er zu ihnen sagt? (Siehe Silhouetten 5 und 7!) Was hat der Bäcker wohl gesagt?

d. Bild 8: Der Bauer spricht mit dem Vater und mit dem Sohn. Was für einen Effekt hat das, was er zu ihnen sagt? (Siehe Silhouetten 7 und 9!) Was hat der Bauer wohl gesagt?

Hören Sie die Fabel!

Neue Vokabeln

vor vielen Jahren	*many years ago*	kurz darauf	*shortly afterwards*
vierzehnjährig	*fourteen-year-old*	rechts	*on the right*
		links	*on the left*
nach einiger Zeit	*after a while*	banden . . . zusammen	*tied together*
begegneten (+ *dative*)	*met*	steckten . . . hindurch	*put through*
erkannte	*recognized*		
stärker	*stronger*	der Stock	*stick*
stieg . . . vom Esel ab	*got off the donkey*	trugen	*carried*
		das Tier	*animal*
ließ	*let*	Schultern	*shoulders*
trafen	*met*		
schüttelte den Kopf	*shook his head*		

Schauen Sie die Zeichnungen an, und erzählen Sie die Fabel! Beginnen Sie die fünf Abschnitte der Fabel wie folgt:

Bild 1: Vor vielen Jahren . . .   Bild 6: Kurz darauf . . .
Bild 2: Nach einiger Zeit . . .   Bild 8: Als sie fast zu Hause waren . . .
Bild 4: Eine Viertelstunde später . . .

WORT, SINN UND KLANG

1. WORDS AS CHAMELEONS: *ALS*

You have learned that **als** has a variety of meanings:

a. When **als** follows the comparative form of an adjective or adverb it means *than*.

Herr Schneider ist acht Jahre älter **als** seine Frau.	*Mr. Schneider is eight years older **than** his wife.*

b. As a conjunction, **als** means *when*.

Bernd war noch im Bett, **als** ich kam.	*Bernd was still in bed **when** I came.*

c. In expressions like **als Kind, als** means *as*.

Als Kind bin ich hier oft schwimmen gegangen.	***As** a child I often went swimming here.*

d. After the negatives **nichts** and **niemand, als** means *but*.

Wir haben nichts **als** Ärger mit diesem Wagen.	*We have nothing **but** trouble with this car.*
Niemand **als** Peter versteht meine Probleme.	*Nobody **but** Peter understands my problems.*

- What is the correct English equivalent of **als** in each of the sentences below: *than, when, as,* or *but?*

1. Als Mensch ist Professor Huber sehr nett.
2. Professor Huber ist viel netter, als ich dachte.
3. Von Professor Seidlmeyer habe ich viel mehr gelernt als von Professor Huber.
4. Niemand als Kathrin hatte das Buch fertiggelesen.
5. Als ich nach Hause kam, hatte Kathrin das Buch schon fertiggelesen.
6. In Hamburg hatten wir leider nichts als Regenwetter.
7. Meine Frau war schon als Mädchen oft in Hamburg.
8. Diesen Juni hat es in Hamburg mehr geregnet als letztes Jahr im ganzen Sommer.
9. Als wir in Hamburg waren, regnete es fast jeden Tag.
10. Im Juli war das Wetter viel besser als im Juni.

2. PREDICTING GENDER

All nouns with the suffix **-ung** are *feminine*. Like most English nouns with the suffix *-ing*, most of these nouns are derived from verbs:

warnen	*to warn*	**die** Warn**ung**	*warning*
landen	*to land*	**die** Land**ung**	*landing*

However, many English equivalents of German nouns with the suffix **-ung** do not have the suffix *-ing*:

prüfen	*to examine*	**die** Prüf**ung**	*examination*
lösen	*to solve*	**die** Lös**ung**	*solution*
üben	*to practice*	**die** Üb**ung**	*exercise*
wohnen	*to live*	**die** Wohn**ung**	*apartment*
erzählen	*to tell*	**die** Erzähl**ung**	*story*

Wohin geht der Junge?

- Form nouns from the following verbs and give their English equivalents.

1.	planen	*to plan*	9.	öffnen	*to open*
2.	mischen	*to mix*	10.	einwandern	*to immigrate*
3.	erklären	*to explain*	11.	übersetzen	*to translate*
4.	schwellen	*to swell*	12.	bedeuten	*to mean*
5.	vorlesen	*to read to*	13.	verbessern	*to correct*
6.	heilen	*to heal*	14.	regieren	*to rule*
7.	beschreiben	*to describe*	15.	automatisieren	*to automate*
8.	ordnen	*to put in order*	16.	heizen	*to heat*

EIN WORTRÄTSEL

What are the opposites of the following words? The first letters of these opposites will give you the German equivalent of the English proverb "The early bird gets the worm." The double slashes indicate the beginning of a new word within the German proverb.

abends / selten / arm / schlecht / letzt / immer / langsam / billig / über / alles / intelligent // schön / fragen / Nacht // klein / mit / voll / dick // langweilig / weniger // Frau / freundlich /geben / bitte

WEITERE NÜTZLICHE WÖRTER UND AUSDRÜCKE

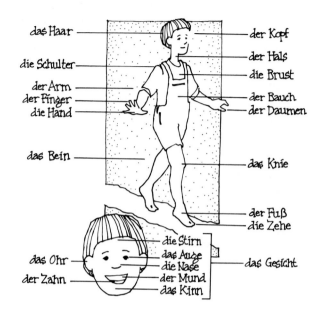

Die Körperteile *(Parts of the body)*

der Körper	body
der Kopf	head
das Haar, die Haare	hair
das Gesicht	face
die Stirn	forehead
das Auge, die Augen	eye
das Ohr, die Ohren	ear
die Nase	nose
der Mund	mouth
die Lippe, die Lippen	lip
der Zahn, die Zähne	tooth
das Kinn	chin
der Hals	neck
die Schulter, die Schultern	shoulder
die Brust	chest
der Bauch	stomach, belly
der Arm, die Arme	arm
die Hand, die Hände	hand
der Finger, die Finger	finger
der Daumen, die Daumen	thumb
das Bein, die Beine	leg
das Knie, die Knie	knee
der Fuß, die Füße	foot
die Zehe, die Zehen	toe

Schule und Universität

die Grundschule, die Grundschulen	elementary school
das Gymnasium, die Gymnasien	academic high school
der Lehrer, die Lehrer	teacher *(male)*
die Lehrerin, die Lehrerinnen	teacher *(female)*
der Schüler, die Schüler	pupil; student in a high school *(male)*
die Schülerin, die Schülerinnen	pupil; student in a high school *(female)*
die Tafel, die Tafeln	blackboard
die Hausaufgabe, die Hausaufgaben	homework
das Abitur	high school diploma
die Universität, die Universitäten	university
der Hörsaal, die Hörsäle	lecture hall
die Übung, die Übungen	exercise, seminar
die Prüfung, die Prüfungen	exam

Ich suche einen Ferienjob

der Lebenslauf	resumé
die Bewerbung, die Bewerbungen	application
die Anzeige, die Anzeigen	ad
das Stellenangebot, die Stellenangebote	job offer
die Arbeitserfahrung	work experience
die Sprachkenntnisse *(pl)*	knowledge of foreign languages
die Fabrik, die Fabriken	factory
das Büro, die Büros	office
der Führerschein	driver's license

Andere nützliche Wörter

einander	each other
schließlich	finally
obwohl	although
weder . . . noch	neither . . . nor

Das Gegenteil

der Anfang—das Ende	beginning—end
das Problem—die Lösung	problem—solution
die Frage—die Antwort	question—answer
lachen—weinen	to laugh—to cry
freundlich—unfreundlich	friendly—unfriendly
naß—trocken	wet—dry
oben—unten	at the top—at the bottom
links—rechts	left—right
taktvoll—taktlos	tactful—tactless
gleich—verschieden	same—different
bevor—nachdem	before *(conjunction)*—after *(conjunction)*

WÖRTER IM KONTEXT

1. WAS PASST ZUSAMMEN?

a. Mit dem Kopf   riecht man.   b. der Regen   links
Mit den Augen   geht man.   die Decke   naß
Mit den Ohren   spricht man.   der Fußboden   weiß
Mit der Nase   denkt man.   die Sahara   oben
Mit dem Mund   hört man.   die Zähne   trocken
Mit der Hand   sieht man.   der Sozialist   unten
Mit den Beinen   schreibt man.

2. WAS PASST WO?

Grundschule   weder . . . noch   bevor   Führerschein
Hausaufgaben   Sprachkenntnisse

a. Deutsche Kinder gehen ein Jahr in den Kindergarten, _____ sie in die _____ kommen.
b. Ich habe _____ Zeit _____ Lust, dir bei deinen _____ zu helfen.
c. Wenn man in Österreich studieren will, braucht man deutsche _____.
d. Ohne _____ darf man nicht Auto fahren.

Problem   Arbeitserfahrung   Anzeigen   Lösung   Bewerbung   Stellenangeboten

e. Wenn man keine _____ hat, ist es nicht leicht, einen guten Ferienjob zu finden.
f. Ich glaube nicht, daß es für dieses _____ eine _____ gibt.
g. Heute sind in der Zeitung viele _____ mit _____.
h. Hast du den Lebenslauf für deine _____ schon geschrieben?

🔲 ZUR AUSSPRACHE

GERMAN S-SOUNDS

Before vowels the sound represented by the letter **s** is *voiced,* i.e., it is pronounced like English *z* in **z**ip.

- Hören Sie gut zu und wiederholen Sie!

die **Insel:** *island*
slang: lousy weather

1. Wohin rei**s**en **S**u**s**e und **S**abine?
   Auf eine **s**onnige **S**üd**s**eein**s**el.°
2. **S**o ein **S**auwetter!°
   Seit **S**onntag keine **S**onne!

Before consonants and at the end of a word, the sound represented by the letter **s** is *voiceless,* i.e., it is pronounced like *s* in **s**ip. Exception: the combinations **st** and **sp** at the beginning of a word or word stem (see page 311).

The sounds represented by **ss** and **ß** (Eszett) are also *voiceless.*

- Hören Sie gut zu und wiederholen Sie!

    1. Der Mensch ist, was er ißt.
    2. Ist das alles, was du weißt?
    3. Wo ist hier das beste Restaurant?

The sound represented by the letter **z** is pronounced like English *ts* in *hits.*

- Hören Sie gut zu und wiederholen Sie!

    1. Der **Z**ug nach **Z**ürich fährt um **z**ehn.
    2. Wann kommt Hein**z** aus Main**z z**urück?
    3. **Z**ahnär**z**te **z**iehen **Z**ähne.

Contrasting German *s*-Sounds

- Hören Sie gut zu und wiederholen Sie!

so	Zoo	Gras	Graz°	*city in Austria*
seit	Zeit	Schweiß°	Schweiz	*sweat*
Saal°	Zahl	Kurs	kurz	*hall*
selten	zelten°	heißen	heizen°	*to camp / to heat*
Sieh!	Zieh!	beißen	beizen°	*to stain wood*
Seen	Zehen			

Sprachnotizen

A note on the use of *ss* and *ß*

Between two vowels, **ss** indicates that the preceding vowel is short, and **ß** indicates that the preceding vowel is long:

Short Vowels	**Long Vowels**
m**üss**en	gr**üß**en
essen	gi**eß**en
russisch	h**eiß**en
Kassel	Stra**ß**e

At the end of a word or before a consonant, **ss** changes to **ß**:

mü**ss**en:	ich mu**ß**	
e**ss**en:	er i**ß**t	
ru**ss**isch°:	Ru**ß**land	*Russian*
Ka**ss**el:	Ka**ß**ler	

Und neues Leben blüht aus den Ruinen (Friedrich Schiller)

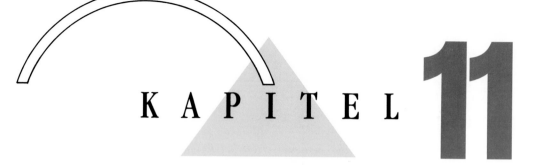

KAPITEL 11

■ **Kommunikationsziele**

In Kapitel 11 you will learn how to:

compare the qualities and characteristics of more
  than two things
rank things
describe what people are wearing
plan a vacation
make inquiries at a travel agency

■ **Hör- und Sprechsituationen**

Zum Thema Kollektivschuld
Was hast du alles?
Persönliche Daten
Günter Schlumberger will verreisen
Im Reisebüro
Modenschau in der Deutschklasse
Urlaubspläne

■ **Strukturen**

Ein-words used as pronouns
Ordinal numbers
More about adjectives:
  The superlative
  Adjectival nouns
  Endings of unpreceded adjectives
  Participles used as adjectives

■ **Wissenswertes**

Hitler und das Dritte Reich
Liechtenstein
der Bodensee
Youth hostels

EINE BÖSE° ZEIT   *bad, evil*

Stephanie verbringt° den größten Teil° der Semesterferien bei ihrem Großonkel — *spends / part*
Udo, dem jüngsten Bruder ihres Großvaters. Er lebt in Köln, und Stephanie hat dort
auch viele Verwandte in ihrem Alter. Während des Tages zeigen die Kusinen und
Vettern ihr die Stadt und die Umgebung,° und am Abend erzählt Onkel Udo ihr oft — *surrounding area*
von alten Zeiten. Und so kommen sie eines Abends auch auf die Zeit zu sprechen,
wo ein anderes Deutschland die Welt in Angst und Schrecken versetzte.° — **in . . . versetzte:** *terrorized*

STEPHANIE: Sag mal, Onkel Udo, du warst doch damals schon ein junger Mann.

ONKEL UDO: Du meinst in der Hitlerzeit?

STEPHANIE: Ja. Wie war das eigentlich? Oder sprichst du lieber nicht davon?° — *about it*

ONKEL UDO: Warum nicht, Stephanie? Es waren böse Zeiten damals, schon vor
Hitler. Wir hatten über sechs Millionen Arbeitslose in Deutschland.
Auch dein Großvater und ich waren ohne Arbeit, und die Regierung° — *government*
hat uns nicht geholfen.

STEPHANIE: Ja, deshalb ist Opa dann nach Amerika ausgewandert. Er hat das oft
erzählt.

ONKEL UDO: Nur die Nazis und die Kommunisten haben uns Arbeit versprochen.
Wir mochten die Nazis nicht, aber vor den Kommunisten hatten wir
Angst. Sie hatten 1932 bereits° 100 Sitze im Reichstag,° und natürlich — *already / Parliament*
hatten wir auch 1917 nicht vergessen.

STEPHANIE: 1917?

ONKEL UDO: Da war die kommunistische Revolution in Rußland.

STEPHANIE: Ach so.

ONKEL UDO: Immer mehr Deutsche glaubten jetzt, daß nur ein „starker° Mann" wie — *strong*
Hitler sie vor° den „Roten" retten° konnte. Deshalb und wegen der — *from / save*
schrecklichen Arbeitslosigkeit stimmten viele von uns für Hitler, und
so ist dieser Mann dann 1933 an die Macht° gekommen. — *to power*

STEPHANIE: Habt ihr dann Arbeit bekommen?

ONKEL UDO: Ja, Stephanie. 1936 waren nur noch eine Million Menschen ohne Arbeit, und bald haben auch die wieder gearbeitet.

STEPHANIE: Aber für den Krieg, so habe ich gelesen. Hitler ließ Autobahnen und
Volkswagen bauen, alles für den Krieg.

ONKEL UDO: So haben wir es damals nicht gesehen, Stephanie. Ich habe auch für
einen Volkswagen bezahlt, einen Volkswagen für mich und meine
Familie, nicht für den Krieg. Ich habe ihn nie bekommen. Hitler hat
mich betrogen.° Er hat das ganze deutsche Volk° betrogen. — *cheated / nation*

STEPHANIE: Und die Juden,° wie war denn das? Sechs Millionen! Das müßt ihr — *Jews*
doch gewußt haben.

ONKEL UDO: Wir haben Gerüchte° gehört, aber — *rumors*
wir wollten sie nicht glauben.

STEPHANIE: Ihr wolltet sie nicht glauben?

ONKEL UDO: Das ist Feindpropaganda,° haben die Nazis uns gesagt. Das haben wir lieber geglaubt. Jetzt wissen wir alles, aber jetzt ist es zu spät. Die meisten° Deutschen haben nichts Böses getan und sind doch mitschuldig° geworden. Es war eine böse Zeit, Stephanie.

enemy propaganda

most
guilty along with others

VOM LESEN ZUM SPRECHEN

ZUR ORIENTIERUNG UND ZUM ZUSAMMENFASSEN

1. Mit welchem Adjektiv beschreibt Onkel Udo die Zeit vor Hitler? Warum?
2. Welche zwei Parteien haben versprochen, den Arbeitslosen zu helfen? Warum hatten viele Deutsche so Angst vor den Kommunisten? Wie hat Hitler den Arbeitslosen geholfen? Geben Sie zwei Beispiele!
3. Was sagten die Nazis über die Gerüchte von den Judenmorden in den Konzentrationslagern? Mit welchem Adjektiv beschreibt Onkel Udo die Hitlerzeit?

 Sie hören neun Aussagen zu *Eine böse Zeit*. Entscheiden Sie, ob diese Aussagen richtig oder falsch sind!

 ## ZUM THEMA KOLLEKTIVSCHULD

Als Stephanie in dem Gespräch mit ihrem Großonkel auf den Holocaust zu sprechen kam, sagte Onkel Udo: „Die meisten Deutschen haben nichts Böses getan und sind doch mitschuldig geworden."

a. Besprechen Sie mit Ihrer Gesprächspartnerin/Ihrem Gesprächspartner den folgenden Fragebogen°, und füllen Sie ihn dann aus. Sie sollten Ihre Meinungen erklären können.

questionnaire

FRAGEBOGEN ZUM THEMA KOLLEKTIVSCHULD Meinungen von:	mitschuldig		nicht mitschuldig	
	S1	S2	S1	S2
Wer vom Holocaust gewußt hat, ist:	____	____	____	____
Wer Gerüchte von einem Holocaust gehört hat, aber nicht glauben konnte, daß so etwas in einem zivilisierten Land wie Deutschland passiert, ist:	____	____	____	____
Wer zur Zeit des Holocausts noch ein Kind war oder erst später geboren wurde, aber doch zum deutschen Volk gehört, ist:	____	____	____	____

b. Diskutieren Sie das Thema Kollektivschuld mit Ihren Klassenkameraden!

Der Reichstag steht in Flammen

Adolf Hitler (1889–1945) was Austrian by birth. As a youth he dreamed of being an artist, but was not accepted into the Academy of Fine Arts in Vienna. He lived in the Austrian capital as a drifter, earning a livelihood by painting postcards. It was here, among the down-and-outers of Vienna, that Hitler was introduced to the racist and anti-Semitic literature in vogue at the time. By 1913 he was making enough money with his art to emigrate to Germany, which he considered the **Vaterland** of the "Aryan race". When the First World War broke out in 1914, Hitler volunteered to serve in the German army.

In the final months of the war Germany was torn by internal chaos. The success of the Communist revolution in Russia inspired Marxist insurrections all over Germany. The Emperor fled to Holland and the monarchy was replaced by a democracy led by Social Democrats. It was this young democratic government that surrendered to the Allies in 1918 and accepted the humiliating and economically debilitating conditions of the Treaty of Versailles.

Hitler fought valiantly during the war and felt that the army's efforts had been betrayed by Marxists and Social Democrats. He decided to become a politician and used his hypnotic oratorial skill and extraordinary organizational talent to build up his own party, the **Nationalsozialistische Deutsche**

Nützliche Wörter und Ausdrücke

Nomen

die Welt	world
der Krieg, die Kriege	war
der Weltkrieg, die Weltkriege	world war
der Feind, die Feinde	enemy
die Macht, die Mächte	power
das Gerücht, die Gerüchte	rumor
das Volk, die Völker	nation, people
die Regierung, die Regierungen	government
der Sitz, die Sitze	seat
die Umgebung	surrounding area
die Autobahn, die Autobahnen	freeway

Arbeiterpartei. The platform of this party was nationalist, anti-Communist, and anti-Semitic. It promised a better life for all Germans by restoring Germany to its former greatness. Hitler blamed the constantly changing leadership (twenty governments in fifteen years) for all of Germany's postwar problems: the reparations that Germany had to pay to the Allies; the rampant inflation that reduced the value of the German mark to an unimaginable 4 trillionth of a US dollar; and unemployment that reached over six million by 1932. On January 30, 1933, Adolf Hitler, as leader of the strongest of a multitude of political parties became Chancellor of Germany. A month later, the **Reichstag,** the parliament building in Berlin, was set on fire, allegedly by a Dutch Communist. The Nazi propaganda machine portrayed this event as the beginning of a Communist uprising and used it to force the fateful **Ermächtigungsgesetz** through parliament. Presented as a "temporary" emergency measure to enable the Chancellor to deal more effectively with the Communist threat, this law gave Hitler dictatorial powers. He could now legally jail his opponents and suspend freedom of the press. In July of 1933, just six months after he had become Chancellor, Hitler declared the Nazi party the only party in Germany and established a dictatorship in which he as the **Führer** was the highest and final authority. From then on the German people were under the sole influence of Nazi ideology and propaganda, and in a few years this disciplined and politically inexperienced nation was transformed into one of the most frightening war machines of all history.

Hitler used cunning and ruthless diplomacy to bring Austria and Czechoslovakia into the Nazi empire, but his military attack on Poland led to World War II. His armies soon occupied most of western and northern Europe, and in 1941 they reached the gates of Leningrad and Moscow in the east. At the same time the **SS** began to set up the death camps where they were to carry out Hitler's insane plan to rid Europe of all Jews.

The end of this brutal dictatorship came in the spring of 1945 when the American, British, and French armies crossed the Rhine, and the Soviets advanced toward Berlin. Tens of millions of soldiers and civilians had lost their lives and much of Europe lay in ruins. And while Russian grenades exploded on top of the **Führerbunker** in Berlin, Adolf Hitler staged a melodramatic exit by first marrying his mistress and then joining her in suicide to avoid "the shame of capitulation".

Nomen

die Presse	press
der Teil, die Teile	part
der Fragebogen, die Fragebogen	questionnaire
der (die) Verwandte, die Verwandten	relative

Verben

meinen	to mean, to think, to say
besprechen, besprach, hat besprochen	to discuss
entscheiden, entschied, hat entschieden	to decide
stimmen (für)	to vote (for)
aus·füllen	to fill out

Verben

betrügen, betrog, hat betrogen	to betray, to deceive, to cheat
retten	to save
verbringen, verbrachte, hat verbracht	to spend (time)

Andere Wörter

böse	bad, evil
schrecklich	terrible
stark	strong
frei	free
bereits	already

WÖRTER IM KONTEXT

WAS PASST WO?

Macht   Krieg   starker   retten   gestimmt   Volk   Autobahnen

a. Warum haben 1932 so viele Deutsche für Hitler _____?
   Weil sie glaubten, daß nur ein _____ Mann wie Hitler Deutschland von den Kommunisten _____ konnte.
b. Nachdem Hitler an die _____ gekommen war, ließ er _____ und Volkswagen bauen. Aber die Volkswagen waren nicht für das _____, sondern für den _____.

Gerüchte   Weltkriegs   Feindpropaganda   Regierung   schreckliche

c. Gegen Ende des zweiten _____ hörte man in Deutschland _____ Gerüchte.
d. Die Nazis sagten: „Das ist _____."
e. Die meisten Deutschen glaubten der _____, weil sie diese _____ nicht glauben wollten.

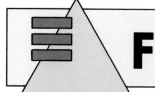

FUNKTIONEN UND FORMEN

1. TALKING ABOUT PERSONS AND THINGS WITHOUT NAMING THEM

EIN-WORDS USED AS PRONOUNS

Hat Kathrin jetzt ein Zimmer?	*Does Kathrin have a room now?*
Ja, ich glaube, sie hat **eins**.	*Yes, I think she has **one**.*
Warum ziehst du keinen Mantel an?	*Why don't you put on a coat?*
Ich habe **keinen**.	*I don't have one. (= I have **none**.)*
Mit wem spielst du heute abend Tennis? Mit deinem Freund?	*With whom are you playing tennis tonight? With your boyfriend?*
Nein, mit **deinem**.	*No, with **yours**.*

As the examples show, **ein-**words **(ein, kein, mein, dein, sein, ihr, unser, euer, ihr, Ihr)** can be used as pronouns. As pronouns, **ein-**words take **der-**word endings. These pronouns do not occur in the genitive.

	masculine	feminine	neuter	plural
nominative	mein**er**	meine	mein**(e)s**	meine
accusative	meinen	meine	mein**(e)s**	meine
dative	meinem	meiner	meinem	meinen

Note that the neuter ending in the nominative and accusative singular is usually **-s** instead of **-es.**

A. HABT IHR IMMER NOCH KEINEN FERNSEHER? Ihre Gesprächspartnerin/Ihr Gesprächspartner beantwortet Ihre Fragen positiv.

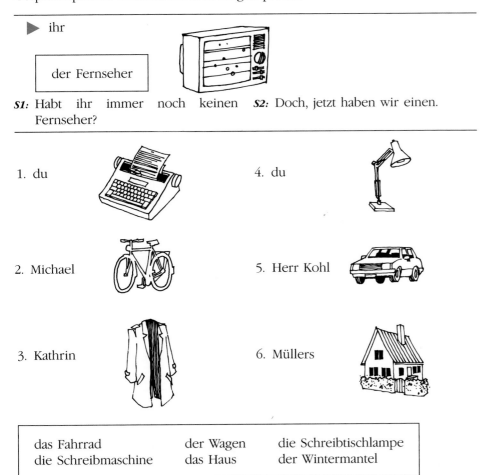

▶ ihr

| der Fernseher |

S1: Habt ihr immer noch keinen Fernseher? *S2:* Doch, jetzt haben wir einen.

1. du

2. Michael

3. Kathrin

4. du

5. Herr Kohl

6. Müllers

| das Fahrrad | der Wagen | die Schreibtischlampe |
| die Schreibmaschine | das Haus | der Wintermantel |

B. HABT IHR JETZT EINEN FERNSEHER? Ihre Gesprächspartnerin/Ihr Gesprächspartner beantwortet Ihre Fragen negativ. Verwenden Sie das Bildmaterial von Übung A noch einmal.

ihr

> der Fernseher

S1: Habt ihr jetzt einen Fernseher?   *S2:* Nein, wir haben noch keinen.

C. GEHÖRT DAS MIR ODER DIR? Ihre Gesprächspartnerin/Ihr Gesprächspartner sagt Ihnen, wo Ihre Sachen **stehen, liegen** oder **hängen.**

> die Aktentasche

S1: Ist das meine Aktentasche oder deine?   *S2:* Das ist meine. Deine steht dort drüben.

1.   4.

2.   5.

3.   6.

| das Bier | der Kugelschreiber | das Buch | der Regenmantel |
| die Cola | das Hemd | | |

OMITTING THE NOUN AFTER AN ADJECTIVE

Welchen Schal möchtest du, den **roten** oder den **blauen?**	*Which scarf would you like, the **red one** or the **blue one?***
Ich möchte lieber **den blauen.**	*I would rather have the **blue one.***

In the example above, it is clear that the adjectives **rot** and **blau** refer to the noun **Schal.** Therefore, adjective endings must be supplied as if the noun were following. Note that English replaces the noun with *one.*

D. WELCHE HANDSCHUHE MÖCHTEST DU?

▶ wollen / ledern

die Handschuhe

S1: Welche Handschuhe möchtest du, die wollenen oder die ledernen?   **S2:** Ich möchte lieber die | wollenen. | ledernen.

1.  grau / braun

4. rot / blau

2.  deutsch / japanisch

5. teuer / billig

3. rot / gelb

| die Rosen | der Pullover | der Schlips | der Tennisschläger | die Kamera |

6. groß / klein

9. deutsch / englisch

7. golden / silbern

10. weiß / blau

8. braun / schwarz

| das Fahrrad | die Aktentasche | das Hemd | die Vase | die Ohrringe |

Finden Sie heraus, was Ihre Gesprächspartnerin/Ihr Gesprächspartner alles hat oder nicht hat! Berichten Sie der Klasse, was Sie herausgefunden haben!

S1: Hast du einen Wagen?

S2: Nein, ich habe keinen.
Ja, ich habe einen, und sogar einen ganz tollen.
Ja, ich habe einen, aber nur einen ganz alten.

einen Fernseher	sehr gut	ganz schlecht
ein Fahrrad	sehr teuer	ganz billig
ein Motorrad	ganz toll	ganz klein
ein Klavier	ganz neu	ganz alt
eine Gitarre	sehr nett	. . .
einen Freund/eine Freundin	. . .	
eine Kamera		
einen Computer		
ein Surfbrett		
. . .		

2. COMPARING THE QUALITIES AND CHARACTERISTICS OF MORE THAN TWO PERSONS OR THINGS

THE SUPERLATIVE

In *Kapitel 2* you learned how to compare the qualities and characteristics of two persons or things. In German there is only one way of forming the comparative: by adding **-er** to the adjective or adverb.

Beim Bäcker ist das Brot **frischer** als im Supermarkt.

*Bread is **fresher** at the baker's than at the supermarket.*

Ist die **teurere** Wurst wirklich die **bessere?**

*Is the **more expensive** sausage really the **better** one?*

The superlative is used to compare the qualities and characteristics of more than two persons or things. In German there is only one way of forming the superlative: by adding **-(e)st** to the adjective or adverb.

Superlative adjectives that precede nouns take endings.

Liechtenstein ist das **kleinste** deutschsprachige Land.

*Liechtenstein is the **smallest** German-speaking country.*

Köln ist eine der **ältesten** deutschen Städte.

*Cologne is one of the **oldest** German cities.*

Das war der **schönste** Tag meines Lebens.

*That was the **most beautiful** day of my life.*

The superlative of adverbs is formed by using the pattern **am -(e)sten.**

Nestled in the Alps between Switzerland and Austria lies the principality of Liechtenstein (capital: Vaduz). With an area of only 61 square miles, it is the smallest of the German-speaking countries. Liechtenstein has its own government and constitution, but since 1920 it has been using Swiss currency, the Swiss postal system, and Swiss diplomatic services.

The 26,000 inhabitants of Liechtenstein enjoy a high standard of living, and taxes are so low that many foreign companies are located there. In fact, there are more companies registered in Liechtenstein than there are inhabitants.

Liechtenstein is well-known to anyone who collects stamps. Its thriving philatelic industry does over 10 million dollars worth of business annually.

Unter Briefmarkensammlern ist Liechtenstein sehr bekannt.

Können Sie mir sagen, wie ich **am schnellsten** nach München komme?

*Can you tell me the **fastest** way to get to Munich?*

Da nehmen Sie **am besten** den Intercity.

*Your **best** bet is to take the Intercity.*

Predicate adjectives[1] in the superlative occur either in the **am -(e)sten** pattern or with the definite article and adjective endings.

Der teuerste Hut ist | **der schönste.** / **am schönsten.**

*The most expensive hat is the **nicest**.*

Note that the **e** before **st** is added if the adjective or adverb ends in **d, t,** an **s**-sound or a *vowel* (e.g., **der kälteste Tag, am heißesten, am neuesten**). Most one-syllable adjectives or adverbs with the stem vowels **a, o,** or **u** are umlauted in the superlative (e.g., der **wärmste Tag, am jüngsten**).

A few adjectives and adverbs have irregular superlative forms.

Was ist eine Fernsehvorschau?

gut	besser	**best-**
viel	mehr	**meist-**
groß	größer	**größt-**
gern	lieber	**liebst-**

Wenn es heiß ist, trinke ich **am liebsten** ein kaltes Bier.

*When it's hot, I like drinking a cold beer **best**.*

Die **meisten** Studenten in unserem Studentenheim fahren am Wochenende nach Hause.

***Most** students in our dorm go home on weekends.*

---

1. A predicate adjective is an adjective that complements verbs like *to be* (e.g., *intelligent* in *Helga is very intelligent.*)

E. SUPERLATIV. Verwenden Sie den Superlativ in allen Fragen und Antworten!

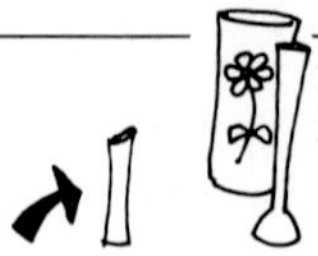

klein

▶ Welche von den drei Vasen gefällt dir am _____? (gut)   Die _____.

S1: Welche von den drei Vasen gefällt dir am besten?   **S2:** Die kleinste.

1. Welches von den drei Hemden
   findest du am _____? (schön)   Das _____.

2. Welcher von den drei Weinen
   kostet am _____? (viel)   Der _____.

3. Welche von den drei Würsten
   magst du am _____? (gern)   Die _____.

comfortable

4. Welcher von den drei Sesseln
   ist am _____? (bequem°)   Der _____.

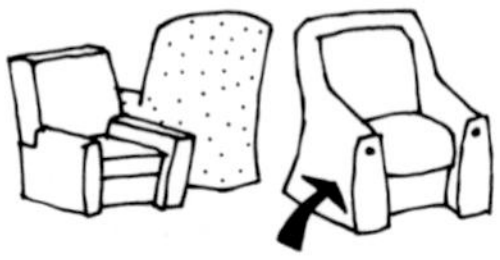

5. Welches von den drei Messern
   ist am _____? (scharf)   Das _____.

| groß | dick | kurz | teuer | alt |

6. Welcher von den drei kleinen
   Jungen ist am _____? (nett)   Der _____.

7. Welche von den drei Sängerinnen
   singt am _____? (laut)   Die _____.

8. Welche von den drei Katzen hast du schon am _____? (lang)

Die _____.

9. Welches von den drei Autos fährt am _____? (schnell)

Das _____.

10. Welche von den drei Jacken ist am _____? (warm)

Die _____.

| billig | dünn | dick | modern | jung |

EIN PAAR PERSÖNLICHE FRAGEN

Stellen Sie Ihrer Gesprächspartnerin/Ihrem Gesprächspartner die folgenden Fragen! Verwenden Sie den Superlativ!

▶ An welchem Tag mußt du am _____ aufstehen? (früh)

Am _____.

S1: An welchem Tag mußt du am frühesten aufstehen?

S2: Am Freitag.

An welchem Tag hast du die _____ Vorlesungen? (viel)   Am _____.
An welchem Tag hast du die _____ Vorlesungen? (wenig)   . . .
Welches von deinen Fächern° findest du am _____? (interessant)   *courses*
An welchem Tag kommst du am _____ nach Hause? (spät)
Für welches Fach mußt du am _____ lernen? (viel)
Was ißt du am _____? (gern)
Was trinkst du am _____? (gern)
Was für Musik hörst du am _____? (gern)
Was für einen Wagen möchtest du am _____? (gern)
Welche Sprache sprichst du am _____? (gut)

Welches Auto möchtest du am liebsten?

3. RANKING PEOPLE AND THINGS

Wie macht das Restaurant seine Gäste „happy"?

ORDINAL NUMBERS AND DATES

a. Ordinal numbers

Ordinal numbers are used to indicate the position of people and things in a sequence (e.g., the first, the second, etc.). For the numbers 1 through 19, the ordinal numbers are formed by adding **-t-** and adjective endings to the cardinal number. Irregular forms are indicated in boldface.

der **erste**	der **siebte**	der dreizehnte
der zweite	der **achte**	der vierzehnte
der **dritte**	der neunte	der fünfzehnte
der vierte	der zehnte	der sechzehnte
der fünfte	der elfte	der siebzehnte
der sechste	der zwölfte	der achtzehnte
		der neunzehnte

From the number 20 on, the ordinal numbers are formed by adding **-st-** to the cardinal numbers.

der zwanzig**ste**
der einundzwanzig**ste**
der zweiundzwanzig**ste**
der dreißig**ste**
usw.

b. Dates

In dates, ordinals are usually written as numbers. When written as a number, an ordinal number is indicated by a period.

der 1. Mai (der erste Mai)

Dates on letterheads are in the accusative case. Note that the day always precedes the month.

Köln, den 17. Juni 1990 (den siebzehnten Juni 1990)

The month is also frequently written as an ordinal number.

Köln, den 17. 6. 1990 (den siebzehnten sechsten 1990)

The following expressions are used to ask for and give the date:

Der wievielte ist heute?
Den wievielten haben wir heute?   *What's the date today?*

Heute ist der fünfzehnte.
Heute haben wir den fünfzehnten.   *Today is the fifteenth.*

Wann bist du geboren?   *When were you born?*
Am 26. Juli 1969.   *On July 26, 1969.*

When saying a year, the word *hundred* is frequently omitted in English. In German the word **hundert** must be expressed.

1999 neunzehn**hundert**neunund-   *nineteen (hundred and) ninety-nine*
neunzig

F. DATEN. Stellen Sie Ihrer Gesprächspartnerin/Ihrem Gesprächspartner die folgenden Fragen!

S1:

1. Den wievielten haben wir heute?
2. Der wievielte ist morgen?
3. Der wievielte ist nächsten Sonntag?
4. Den wievielten hatten wir letzten Sonntag?
5. Am wievielten ist unsere nächste Deutschstunde?
6. Am wievielten war unsere letzte Deutschstunde?
7. Wann ist der Heilige Abend?
8. Wann ist Weihnachten?
9. Wann ist Silvester?
10. Wann ist Neujahr?

S2:

Heute haben wir _____.
Morgen ist _____.
Nächsten Sonntag ist _____.
Letzten Sonntag hatten wir _____.

Unsere nächste Deutschstunde ist _____.

Unsere letzte Deutschstunde war _____.

Der Heilige Abend ist _____.
Weihnachten ist _____.
Silvester ist _____.
Neujahr ist _____.

PERSÖNLICHE DATEN. Sagen Sie der Reihe nach, wann sie Geburtstag haben.

S1: Ich habe am zehnten siebten Geburtstag.
S2: Mein Geburtstag ist am einundzwanzigsten fünften.
S3: Ich habe . . .

G. KLEINE GESPRÄCHE. Sagen Sie das auf deutsch!

1. LEHRER: When did the First World War begin?
   SCHÜLER: On the 28th of July 1914.
2. LEHRER: When is the shortest day of the year?
   SCHÜLER: On the 21st of December.
3. PAUL: Why don't you buy a bicycle?
   STEFAN: I don't need one.
4. FRAU MEYER: What is your oldest son going to be doing this summer, Mrs. Schultz?
   FRAU SCHULTZ: He's going to visit our relatives in the USA.
5. OLIVER: To whom does this fantastic car belong? (use **Wagen.**)
   UWE: That's ours.
6. TOURIST: How do I get° to the railway station the fastest?
   POLIZIST: With the subway° you'll be there in ten minutes.

Mit der U-Bahn sind Sie in zehn Minuten dort.

to get: **kommen**

die U-Bahn

ZUSAMMENSCHAU

ZUSAMMENSCHAU

take a trip

GÜNTER SCHLUMBERGER WILL VERREISEN°

Das Sommersemester ist bald zu Ende, und Günter Schlumberger denkt oft mehr an die Sommerferien als an sein Studium. Von Freunden hat er gehört, daß das Reisebüro Westermann dieses Jahr die besten Sonderangebote° für Studenten hat und daß es höchste Zeit ist, diese preisgünstigen° Reisen zu buchen.

special packages
inexpensive

employee

• Lesen Sie zuerst die *Neuen Vokabeln,* und hören Sie dann das Gespräch zwischen Günter und der Angestellten° im Reisebüro Westermann.

Neue Vokabeln

denken an	*to think of*
Geht das?	*Is that possible?*
ausgebucht	*booked up*
Schade.	*That's too bad.*
die Halbpension	*half-board* (bed, breakfast, and a light supper)
die Übernachtung	*bed*
die Busfahrt	*bus trip*
mit eingeschlossen	*included*
günstig	*inexpensive, reasonable*
zum Strand	*to the beach*
an·zahlen	*to pay down*
vor Reisebeginn	*before the beginning of the trip*
fällig	*due*
vorbei·kommen	*to come by*

Hier gibt es die besten Sonderangebote für Studenten.

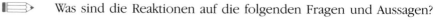

Was sind die Reaktionen auf die folgenden Fragen und Aussagen?

1. Dachten Sie an acht oder an vierzehn Tage?
2. Und in der ersten und zweiten Woche im August, geht es da?
3. Wie sind denn die Hotels?
4. Können Sie uns vielleicht zwei Plätze reservieren?
5. Gut, Herr Schlumberger, dann bis heute nachmittag.

• Hören Sie das Gespräch noch einmal an, und beantworten Sie dann die folgenden Fragen!

1. Wann wollte Günter in die Ferien fahren?
2. Warum geht das nicht?
3. Wo in Spanien sind die beiden billigen Hotels?
4. Was ist Halbpension?
5. Wieviel kosten 14 Tage Halbpension in diesen beiden Hotels?
6. Was ist in diesem Preis auch noch mit eingeschlossen?
7. Was für Leute machen hier Ferien?
8. Wie weit ist es vom Hotel zum Strand?
9. Warum bucht Günter nicht gleich?
10. Warum soll er mit dem Buchen nicht zu lange warten?
11. Wieviel müssen Günter und seine Freundin für diese Reise anzahlen?
12. Wann ist der Rest fällig?

IM REISEBÜRO

Sie haben nicht viel Geld, aber Sie möchten mit einer Freundin/einem Freund zusammen an irgendeinem° schönen Ort° Ferien machen. Gehen Sie deshalb ins Reisebüro Westermann, und fragen Sie dort nach preisgünstigen Sonderangeboten für Studenten.

some / place

Ihre Gesprächspartnerin/Ihr Gesprächspartner arbeitet beim Reisebüro Westermann und hilft Ihnen, den idealen Ferienort zu finden.

4. DESCRIBING PERSONS AND THINGS

ENDINGS OF UNPRECEDED ADJECTIVES

In *Kapitel 9* you learned that adjectives that appear before nouns have endings and that the **der**-words or **ein**-words that precede these adjectives determine what those endings will be.

Der neu**e** Golf braucht viel weniger Benzin als **der** alt**e**.	*The new Golf uses much less gas than the old one.*
Mein neu**er** Golf braucht viel weniger Benzin als **mein** alt**er**.	*My new Golf uses much less gas than my old one.*

Sometimes an adjective is not preceded by a **der**-word or an **ein**-word. In this case the adjective itself takes the **der**-word ending.

Ist Silkes neu**er** Wagen nicht toll?	*Isn't Silke's new car fantastic?*
Bei schlecht**em** Wetter bleiben wir zu Hause.	*In bad weather we stay at home.*
Haben Sie frisch**e** Brezeln?	*Do you have fresh pretzels?*

	masculine	feminine	neuter	plural
nominative	gut**er** Käse	gut**e** Wurst	gut**es** Brot	gut**e** Brezeln
accusative	gut**en** Käse	gut**e** Wurst	gut**es** Brot	gut**e** Brezeln
dative	gut**em** Käse	gut**er** Wurst	gut**em** Brot	gut**en** Brezeln

In modern German, unpreceded adjectives appear so rarely in the genitive case that it is unnecessary to learn these forms at this time.

H. LESEN SIE DIE FOLGENDEN SÄTZE OHNE DIE KURSIV GEDRUCKTEN WÖRTER!

Vergessen Sie nicht, daß Sie die Adjektivendungen ändern° müssen.

change

▶ *Dieser* deutsche Wein ist sehr gut.

Deutscher Wein ist sehr gut.

1. Bei *diesem* schönen Wetter kann ich einfach nicht richtig lernen.
2. Möchten Sie lieber *die* roten oder *die* gelben Rosen?
3. *Dieser* französische Käse ist sehr teuer.
4. Wasch den Pulli ja nicht in *diesem* heißen Wasser!
5. Mögen Sie *dieses* deutsche Bier?
6. *Die* amerikanischen Wagen sind meistens größer als *die* europäischen und *die* japanischen.
7. Mit *einem* trockenen° Wein schmecken *diese* frischen Brezeln ganz besonders gut.
8. So *eine* gute Leberwurst habe ich noch nie gegessen.
9. Mit *diesen* langen Haaren siehst du gar nicht gut aus.

dry (margin note)

I. WAS MAGST DU LIEBER? Ein Gespräch über ausländische Produkte. Verwenden Sie die Verben **trinken, essen, rauchen** oder **fahren.**

▶ der Tee: chinesisch / indisch

S1: Was für Tee trinkst du lieber, chinesischen oder indischen?

S2: Indischer Tee ist gut, aber chinesischen trinke ich lieber.
Chinesischer Tee ist gut, aber indischen trinke ich lieber.

1. die Schokolade: deutsch / schweizerisch
2. die Zigaretten: russisch / französisch
3. das Bier: holländisch / dänisch
4. der Käse: deutsch / französisch
5. die Oliven: spanisch / griechisch
6. die Wurst: polnisch / deutsch
7. der Wein: italienisch / französisch
8. der Kaviar: persisch / russisch
9. die Autos: deutsch / japanisch

THE PAST PARTICIPLE USED AS AN ADJECTIVE

In your reading you have frequently seen past participles used as adjectives. Before a noun the past participle takes the same endings as other adjectives.

Warum schläfst du immer bei **geschlossenem** Fenster?

Why do you always sleep with your window closed?

Gebrannte Kinder scheuen das Feuer.

Once bitten, twice shy. (literally: *Burned children shy away from the fire.*)

J. WAS IST DAS? Verwenden Sie in Ihren Antworten die unten gegebenen Partizipien mit den richtigen Adjektivendungen!

▶ eine elegant _____ Dame

gekleidet

Das ist eine elegant gekleidete Dame.

Sommerschlußverkauf!

1. frisch _____ Hemden

6. frisch _____ Äpfel

2. ein _____ Pferd *(n)*

7. ein schlecht _____ Mann

3. ein gut _____ junger Mann

8. ein _____ Fenster *(n)*

4. ein frisch _____ Brot *(n)*

9. eine _____ Jacke

5. ein _____ Brief *(m)*

gebaut	gesattelt	gebacken
gepflückt°	geschlossen°	gewaschen
rasiert	vergessen	angefangen

picked / closed

fashion show

are . . . wearing

Beschreiben Sie, was Ihre Mitstudenten/Mitstudentinnen tragen.°

▶ Tanja trägt eine hochelegante, blau und weiß[1] gestreifte Bluse.
David trägt einen schokoladenbraunen, handgestrickten Pullover.
Sandra trägt ein wunderbares, giftgrünes und ein bißchen zerrissenes Sweat-shirt.

fashionable / colorful / striped
plaid
flowered
das Gift: *poison / hand-knit*
ripped
worn (clothes)
worn (shoes)

modisch°	farbenfreudig°	gestreift°
hochelegant	grasgrün	kariert°
hochmodern	olivgrün	geblümt°
supermodern	giftgrün°	handgestrickt°
wunderschön	zitronengelb	zerrissen°
wunderbar	feuerrot	abgetragen°
ganz toll	dunkelblau	abgelaufen°
. . .	kornblumenblau	. . .
	schokoladenbraun	
	schneeweiß	
	taubengrau°	
	kohlrabenschwarz°	
	. . .	

die Taube: *dove*
die Kohle: *coal /* **der Rabe:** *raven*

THE PRESENT PARTICIPLE USED AS AN ADJECTIVE

In English the present participle has the ending **-ing:** *coming.* The German present participle is formed by adding **-d** to the infinitive: *kommend.* Before a noun, the present participle takes the same endings as other adjectives.

In der **kommenden** Woche fahren wir an den Bodensee.

*In the **coming** week we're going to Lake Constance.*

Bellende Hunde beißen nicht.

His bark is worse than his bite. (literally: **Barking** *dogs don't bite.*)

---

1. Here **blau** and **weiß** have no endings because they are adverbs.

K. WAS IST DAS? Verwenden Sie in Ihren Antworten die unten gegebenen Präsenspartizipien mit den richtigen Adjektivendungen!

▶ eine _____ Katze

schlafen

Das ist eine schlafende Katze.

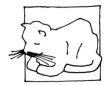

1. _____ Studenten

2. ein _____ Hund *(m)*

3. ein _____ Fisch *(m)*

4. ein _____ Mensch

5. _____ Kinder

6. ein _____ Auto *(n)*

7. ein _____ Kanarienvogel *(m)*

8. ein _____ Baum *(m)*

9. _____ Arbeiter

bellen	denken	sterben
fliegen	singen	fahren
spielen	lernen	streiken

2. SOMMERWOCHE FÜR ÄLTERE

23. 7. - 27. 7. 1990

*Was können die Senioren
in dieser Woche alles tun?*

ADJECTIVAL NOUNS

a. Adjectives used as nouns

In expressions like *the young and the restless* or *the rich and the famous,* adjectives are used as nouns. German uses adjectives as nouns much more frequently than English. These adjectival nouns are always capitalized and they take adjective endings.

Warum weint **die Kleine** denn?	*Why is **the little girl** crying?*
Wann kommt **Ihr Jüngster** in die Schule, Frau Schmidt?	*When does **your youngest boy** start school, Mrs. Schmidt?*
Ich möchte **ein kleines Dunkles.**	*I'd like **a small glass of dark beer.***
Die Kleinen fängt man, **die Großen** läßt man laufen.	*It's always **the little guy** that gets caught.*

In the singular, the articles and/or the adjective endings clearly indicate whether an adjectival noun refers to a male, a female, or a thing.

L. WER IST DAS? Verwenden Sie in Ihren Fragen die unten gebenen Adjektivpaare!

> | klein / dick | | der Hausmeister vom Studentenheim |

S1: Du Peter, wer ist denn der kleine Dicke dort? **S2:** Der kleine Dicke dort? Das ist der Hausmeister vom Studentenheim.

1.   meine neue Geographieprofessorin

2.   der Nachbarsjunge von nebenan°

next door

3.   die Kellnerin vom Café Stöpsel

4.   der Organist von der Marienkirche

5.   unsere neue Bibliothekarin°   *librarian*

bärtig / alt	hübsch / blond	süß / klein
klein / schwarzhaarig	groß / brünett	

b. Adjectival nouns that have become standard nouns

Some adjectival nouns are used so frequently that they are listed in dictionaries as standard nouns. However, they still take the regular adjective endings. All plural forms end in **-n.**

arbeitslos	*unemployed*	der Arbeitslose, die Arbeitslose	*unemployed person*
bekannt	*well-known*	der Bekannte, die Bekannte	*acquaintance*
deutsch	*German*	der Deutsche, die Deutsche	*German* (person)
grün	*green*	der Grüne, die Grüne	*member of the Green Party*
krank	*sick*	der Kranke, die Kranke	*sick person, patient*
tot	*dead*	der Tote, die Tote	*dead person*
verwandt	*related*	der Verwandte, die Verwandte	*relative*

M. WAS PASST WO?   Verwenden Sie die richtigen Adjektivendungen!

der (die) Bekannte   der (die) Grüne
der (die) Verwandte   der (die) Arbeitslose

1. Meine Kusine Andrea mag ich von allen meinen _____ am liebsten.
2. Ist Ralf dein Freund?
   Nein, er ist nur ein sehr guter _____.
3. Wissen Sie, wie viele Deutsche letztes Jahr für die _____ gestimmt haben?
4. 1933 gab es in Deutschland über sechs Millionen _____.

5. TALKING ABOUT QUANTITY

THE ADJECTIVES *VIEL* AND *WENIG*

When **viel** and **wenig** precede nouns in the singular, they usually take no endings.
When they precede nouns in the plural, they take the regular adjective endings.

Günter braucht **viel** Geld für seine **vielen** Freundinnen.	*Günter needs **a lot of** money for his **many** girl friends.*
Nur sehr **wenige** Menschen haben so **wenig** Geld wie wir Studenten.	*Only very **few** people have as **little** money as we students do.*

The comparative forms **mehr** and **weniger** never take endings. However, the superlative forms **meist-** and **wenigst-** take the regular adjective endings.

Ich habe **mehr** Hausaufgaben als du.	*I have **more** homework assignments than you do.*
Bei uns arbeiten **die meisten** Studenten im Sommer.	*Where I come from **most** students work in the summer.*

N. AUF EINER DEMONSTRATION. Ergänzen Sie die Endungen! Vergessen Sie nicht, daß oft gar keine Endungen nötig° sind.

necessary

1. Stephanie ist erst seit wenig___ Wochen in München und hat schon viel___ gut___ Freunde.
2. In ihrem Studentenheim wohnen viel___ ausländisch___ Studenten, und nur die wenigst___ von ihnen sind Amerikaner.
3. Ich glaube, dort wohnen mehr___ Ausländer als Deutsche.
4. Gestern war Stephanie mit viel___ ander___ Studenten aus ihrem Studentenheim auf einer Demonstration.
5. Als sie zum Marktplatz kamen, war dort viel___ Polizei° *(sing.)*, aber die meist___ Polizisten° waren sehr freundlich.

police
policemen

6. Ich glaube, da waren mehr___ Polizisten als Demonstranten.
7. Demonstrationen brauchen viel___ Zeit, und Stephanie weiß jetzt nicht, wie sie ihre viel___ Hausaufgaben fertigkriegen soll.
8. Sie hat viel___ Tage demonstriert und viel___ Nächte gearbeitet und nur wenig___ Schlaf bekommen.
9. Trink doch nicht immer so viel___ Kaffee, Stephanie!
10. Wenn ich weniger___ Kaffee trinke, schlafe ich ein.

ADJECTIVAL NOUNS AFTER *ETWAS, NICHTS, VIEL, WENIG*

When adjectival nouns follow **etwas, nichts, viel,** and **wenig,** they take the endings of neuter unpreceded adjectives.

Weißt du denn gar **nichts** Neu**es**?	*Don't you know anything new at all?*
Ich habe sehr **viel** Gut**es** über ihn gehört.	*I've heard a lot of good things about him.*
In diesem Artikel steht **wenig** Wichtig**es**.	*There is little of importance in this article.*

O. BEI DER ERÖFFNUNG° DES NEUEN STADTMUSEUMS. Herr Ziegler nimmt kein Blatt vor den Mund!° Verwenden Sie in den Antworten die Verben **sehen, hören, essen** oder **trinken.**

opening

nimmt . . . Mund: *doesn't mince words*

▶ dieser Picasso	häßlich
FRAU ZIEGLER: Was hältst° du von diesem Picasso?	**HERR ZIEGLER:** So etwas Häßliches habe ich noch nie gesehen.

hältst du von: *do you think of*

1. dieser Sekt°   fad°   *champagne / bland*
2. dieser Kaviar   abscheulich°   *awful*
3. Professor Kluges Rede°   blöd°   *speech / stupid*
4. Frau Krügers neues Kleid   geschmacklos°   *tasteless*
5. dieses Orchester   stümperhaft°   *amateurish*
6. dieser Film   doof
7. dieser Kaffee   bitter
8. dieser Kuchen   altbacken°   *stale*
9. Frau Hofmanns Frisur°   verrückt   *hairdo*

P. KLEINE GESPRÄCHE. Sagen Sie das auf deutsch!

1. MARTIN: How do you make soft-boiled° eggs, Claudia?

   CLAUDIA: I put the eggs in boiling water, and after five minutes I take them out and put them in ice-cold water (for) a moment.

   weichgekocht

2. CLAUDIA: Should I wash your sweaters too, Stephanie?

   STEPHANIE: Only the blue one, and please don't wash it in hot water. (Place **bitte** before **nicht.**)

3. HERR KUHN: What would you like for dessert, Christa?

   FRAU KUHN: Something very sweet, please.

   HERR KUHN: Perhaps a slice of° my freshly baked bread with butter and honey?°

   von / der Honig

   FRAU KUHN: Don't you have anything better? (*not anything = nothing;* flavor with **denn**)

4. FRAU HAAG: What should we give our oldest (daughter) for her twenty-first birthday, Hermann?

   HERR HAAG: Why don't you buy her a tennis racquet?

   FRAU HAAG: But she already has one. (Flavor with **doch** before **schon.**)

   HERR HAAG: It's always good to have a second one.

Wasserburg am Bodensee

CIV Bodensee und Rhein – Reise- und Autofähre
1 Personenkraftwagen bis 4 m oder 1 Motorrad mit Beiwagen oder 1 Kabinenroller
mit Fahrer oder 1 Anhänger zu Pkw
Friedrichshafen — Romanshorn oder umgekehrt
FrS 16,00
Gültig 1 Tag
Friedrichshafen 146 498-22
Nr: 0005361

Situated between Germany, Switzerland, and Austria, the **Bodensee** (Lake Constance) is Germany's largest lake. Its German name is derived from the village of **Bodman** on the north-west shore. Its English name comes from the city of **Konstanz** on the border between Germany and Switzerland. It is a busy lake, with frequent passenger and ferry service between the towns and cities on its shores.

The **Bodensee** is a mecca for tourists and vacationers. The area around the lake is one of the oldest and richest cultural regions in the German-speaking countries with many churches, monasteries, and other monuments to medieval culture. For vacationers the lake offers sailing and windsurfing, and the surrounding countryside has an abundance of hiking and bicycle paths.

The largest area of the lake belongs to Germany, and water from the **Bodensee** supplies large population centers like Stuttgart, some 100 kilometers to the north. The southern part of the lake falls under the jurisdiction of Switzerland, and a small section in the east belongs to Austria. All three countries work together to keep the lake clean.

ZUSAMMENSCHAU

URLAUBSPLÄNE°

vacation[1] plans

Gerd und Karin Vogel haben beide sehr stressige Berufe und brauchen dringend° Erholung.° Weil sie gerade ein Haus gekauft haben, haben sie nicht viel Geld und suchen eine möglichst billige Ferienwohnung.

urgently
rest and relaxation

Als Vertreter° für Büromöbel ist Gerd Vogel fast immer unterwegs.° Seine Frau Karin ist Krankenschwester,° und auch sie ist oft sehr gestreßt. Im August haben sie beide drei Wochen Urlaub, und sie träumen° von einem Urlaub ohne Auto und ohne Streß. Am liebsten möchten sie diese drei Wochen an irgendeinem See° verbringen und mal nichts tun als schlafen, lesen, am Strand liegen und schwimmen.

sales representative / on the road / nurse
are . . . dreaming
lake

Albert Merck, ein Arbeitskollege von Gerd, hat eine Ferienwohnung in dem kleinen Dorf Horn am Bodensee.° Die Wohnung ist im August noch frei, und Vogels können sie sehr billig bekommen. Das Haus liegt direkt am See, sagt Albert, und der Strand ist dort schön sandig. Die Wohnung ist schön möbliert und besteht aus° Wohnzimmer, Schlafzimmer, Küche und Bad. Das Badezimmer ist ein bißchen klein, aber es hat Dusche und Badewanne. Die Badewanne ist Gerd sehr wichtig, denn er hat oft Rückenschmerzen.° Seiner Meinung nach gibt es dagegen° nichts Besseres als ein heißes Bad am Morgen.

Lake Constance
consists of
back trouble / for that

Im Dorf ist ein guter Laden—fast ein Supermarkt, sagt Albert Merck—, wo man alles kaufen kann, was man braucht. Das ist Gerd besonders wichtig, denn er will den Wagen die ganzen drei Wochen in der Garage stehen lassen.

In Horn ist es sehr ruhig, es gibt nur wenige Feriengäste und kaum Touristen, und auch im Haus ist es immer ruhig. Die Leute in den anderen fünf Wohnungen sind alle schon älter, schon pensioniert. Da haben Sie wirklich mal Ihre Ruhe° sagt Albert Merck. Das ist den Vogels natürlich ganz besonders wichtig.

peace and quiet

Im vergangenen Sommer war Jutta Müller mit ihrem Mann drei Wochen in Albert Mercks Ferienwohnung in Horn. Jutta ist eine Arbeitskollegin von Karin, und Karin will heute nach der Arbeit mit ihr sprechen. Erst dann wollen Gerd und Karin entscheiden,° ob sie die Wohnung nehmen oder nicht.

decide

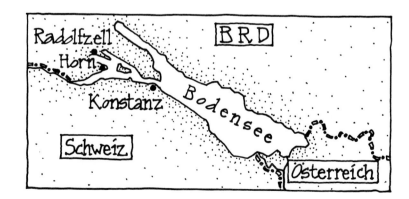

---

1. There are two German words for *vacation:* students have **Ferien** and people in the workforce have **Urlaub.**

ZUR ORIENTIERUNG UND ZUM ZUSAMMENFASSEN

is . . . dreaming

1. Was sind Gerd und Karin von Beruf? Warum träumt° Gerd von einem Urlaub ohne Auto? Wo möchten die beiden dieses Jahr ihren Urlaub verbringen? Was möchten sie dort tun?
2. Wo ist Horn? Wie weit ist es von Alberts Ferienwohnung bis zum Strand? Wie ist der Strand? Warum ist die Badewanne Gerd so wichtig?
3. Warum ist es Gerd so wichtig, daß der Laden in Horn fast ein Supermarkt ist? Warum ist es in Alberts Ferienwohnung so ruhig? Warum will Karin heute nach der Arbeit mit Jutta Müller sprechen?

 Sie hören vierzehn Aussagen zu *Urlaubspläne*. Entscheiden sie, ob diese Aussagen richtig oder falsch sind!

 Hören Sie, was Karin ihrem Mann nach dem Gespräch mit Jutta Müller erzählt, und beantworten Sie dann jede der folgenden Fragen zweimal! Beginnen Sie die erste Antwort mit „Albert sagt, daß . . . “ und die zweite mit „Jutta sagt, daß . . . “!

1. Wie weit ist es von Alberts Ferienwohnung bis zum Strand?
2. Wie ist das Badezimmer?
3. Wie gut ist der Laden in Horn?
4. Ist die Wohnung ruhig? Wenn ja, warum? Wenn nein, warum nicht?

Hören Sie die Unterhaltung zwischen Karin und Gerd noch einmal, und beantworten Sie die folgenden Fragen!

1. Wie reagiert Karin, als Gerd meint, daß sie mit dem Wagen zum Strand fahren müssen?

nicht . . . kommt:
is out of the question

2. Wie reagiert Karin, als Gerd sagt, daß ein Urlaub ohne heißes Bad für ihn nicht in Frage kommt°.
3. Warum findet Karin es gar nicht so schlimm, daß sie zum Einkaufen nach Radolfzell fahren müssen?
4. Warum ist Karin trotz aller Probleme so sehr für Alberts Wohnung?

in case

5. Was für eine Lösung hat sie, falls° jemand in einer der anderen fünf Wohnungen zu laut sein sollte?
6. Warum will Karin morgen selbst mit Albert sprechen?

composition

Schreiben Sie einen kleinen Aufsatz° zu einem der folgenden Themen:

a. **Ferienpläne.** Wohin möchten Sie in Ihren Sommerferien reisen? Was möchten Sie dort alles tun?

Nützliche Vokabeln

durch Europa trampen	*to hitchhike through Europe*
mit Rucksack und Schlafsack	*with a backpack and a sleeping bag*
eine Radtour durch Europa machen	*to go on a bicycle trip through Europe*
mit einem Eurail Youthpass durch Europa reisen	*to travel through Europe with a Eurail-pass*
viel von Europa sehen	*to see a lot of Europe*
in Jugendherbergen übernachten	*to sleep in youth hostels*
junge Leute aus anderen Ländern kennenlernen	*to get to know young people from other countries*
mein Deutsch ausprobieren	*to try out my German*

meine Ferien (an einem See, am Meer) verbringen	*to spend my vacation*[1] (at a lake, at the ocean)		
Ich möchte in meinen Ferien . . .	*During my vacation I would like . . .*		
schwimmen, segeln, Windsurfing gehen	*to go swimming, sailing, windsurfing*		
in der Sonne liegen	*to lie in the sun*		
faulenzen	*to do nothing*		
viel lesen	*to read a lot*		
gut essen	*to eat well*		
jeden Abend tanzen gehen	*to go dancing every night*		

b. **Meine schönsten (schlimmsten) Ferien.** Schreiben Sie eine kurze Erzählung. Vergessen Sie nicht, daß man in einer Erzählung das Präteritum verwendet.

Was muß man in Köln gesehen haben?

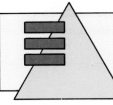

Wort, Sinn und Klang

Wörter under der Lupe

PREDICTING GENDER

All nouns with the suffixes **-heit** and **-keit** are *feminine.* Like most English nouns with the suffix *-ness,* most of these nouns are derived from adjectives. The suffix **-keit** is used whenever an adjective ends in **-lich** or **-ig.**

krank	*ill, sick*	**die** Krank**heit**	*illness, sickness*
freundlich	*friendly*	**die** Freundlich**keit**	*friendliness*
richtig	*right, correct*	**die** Richtig**keit**	*rightness, correctness*

Not all the English equivalents are formed with the suffix *-ness.*

wichtig	*important*	**die** Wichtig**keit**	*importance*
schön	*beautiful*	**die** Schön**heit**	*beauty*

Some adjectives have to be extended with **-ig** before the suffix **-keit** can be added. These adjectives will be marked with an asterisk in the exercise below.

arbeitslos*	*unemployed*	**die** Arbeitslos**igkeit**	*unemployment*

---

1. The German equivalent of *I would like to spend my vacation travel**ing**, do**ing** nothing, etc.* is **Ich möchte in meinen Ferien reisen, faulenzen,** etc.

An economical way for young people to see Europe is to purchase a Eurail Youthpass. This inexpensive pass offers unlimited rail travel for a predetermined amount of time, usually about a month.

Young people traveling through the German-speaking countries often choose to spend the night in the company of other young people in a youth hostel **(Jugendherberge).** In Germany there are about 820 of them, Austria has about 100 and Switzerland 85. The accommodations are simple but clean and inexpensive. The **Jugendherbergen** also rent or sell backpacks, sleeping bags, maps, and guide books, and they organize trips and courses for hikers and cyclists. Staying at a **Jugendherberge** is a wonderful way to meet young people from all over the world.

Welches Wort auf dem großen Schild hat nichts mit Freizeit zu tun?

- Form nouns from the following adjectives and give their English meanings.

1. dunkel   *dark*
2. hell*   *light, bright*
3. gesund   *healthy*
4. krank   *ill, sick*
5. klar   *clear*
6. selten   *rare*
7. süß*   *sweet*
8. klug   *intelligent*
9. dumm   *stupid*
10. schnell*   *fast*
11. verrückt   *crazy*
12. faul   *lazy*
13. schlecht*   *bad*
14. wirklich   *real*
15. blind   *blind*
16. mehr   *more*

WEITERE NÜTZLICHE WÖRTER UND AUSDRÜCKE

Die Ferien

die Ferien *(pl)*	vacation (*generally used for students*)
der Urlaub	vacation (*generally used for people in the work force*)
der Feriengast, die Feriengäste	vacationer
das Sonderangebot, die Sonderangebote	special package
die Übernachtung	overnight accommodation
die Halbpension	half-board (*bed, breakfast and a light supper*)
die Reise, die Reisen	trip
die Fahrt, die Fahrten	drive, trip

Die Ferien

der See, die Seen	lake
das Meer, die Meere	ocean
der Strand, die Strände	beach
der Sand	sand
das Gebirge	mountains
die Ruhe	peace and quiet
die Erholung	rest and relaxation
der Rucksack, die Rucksäcke	backpack
der Schlafsack, die Schlafsäcke	sleeping bag
die Jugendherberge, die Jugendherbergen	youth hostel
träumen	to dream
buchen	to book
an·zahlen	to pay down
übernachten, hat übernachtet	to spend the night
eine Radtour machen	to go on a bicycle trip
schwimmen, schwamm, ist geschwommen	to swim
faulenzen	to do nothing, to be lazy
günstig, preisgünstig	inexpensive, reasonable
eingeschlossen	included
bequem	comfortable
unterwegs	on the road

Kaufen und Verkaufen

der Kunde, die Kunden	customer (*male*)
die Kundin, die Kundinnen	customer (*female*)
der Vertreter, die Vertreter	sales representative (*male*)
die Vertreterin, die Vertreterinnen	sales representative (*female*)
der Verkäufer, die Verkäufer	salesman
die Verkäuferin, die Verkäuferinnen	saleswoman

Das Gegenteil

die Kälte—die Hitze	cold—heat
weich—hart	soft—hard
klug—doof	smart—stupid

Das Datum

Der wievielte ist heute?	What's the date today?
Den wievielten haben wir heute?	
Heute ist der fünfzehnte.	Today is the fifteenth.
Heute haben wir den fünfzehnten.	

WÖRTER IM KONTEXT

1. MIT ANDEREN WORTEN. Was paßt zusammen?

a.
preisgünstig	einen Platz reservieren
faulenzen	intelligent
klug	einen Teil bezahlen
buchen	dumm
anzahlen	billig
doof	nichts tun

b. das Meer   hohe Temperatur
    die Reise   billiges Hotel für junge Leute
    die Halbpension   der Ozean
    die Jugendherberge   Übernachtung, Frühstück und Abend-
                          essen
    die Hitze   die Fahrt

2. WAS PASST NICHT?

a.	b.	c.	d.
schlafen	der Vertreter	die Ferien	der Kunde
schwimmen	der Verkäufer	der Sonntag	der Strand
übernachten	der Verwandte	der Urlaub	der Sand
träumen	der Kunde	der Donnerstag	der See

Sprachnotizen

The preposition *bis*

The preposition **bis** indicates the end of a stretch of time *(until)* or space *(as far as)*. The object of **bis** appears in the accusative case.

Die Bibliothek ist **bis** nächsten Montag geschlossen.	*The library is closed **until** next Monday.*
Dieser Zug fährt nur **bis** Mannheim.	*This train only goes **as far as** Mannheim.*

Bis is often used in combination with other prepositions. In such cases, the second preposition determines the case.

Bis zum Anfang der Sommerferien sind es nur noch vierzehn Tage.	*It's only two weeks **until** the beginning of summer vacation.*
Vom Haus **bis zum** Strand sind es nur 500 Meter.	*It's only 500 meters from the house **to** the beach.*
Gestern war Karin wieder **bis nach** Mitternacht im Krankenhaus.	*Yesterday Karin was at the hospital **until after** midnight again.*

ZUR AUSSPRACHE

GERMAN *F, V,* AND *W*

In German the sound represented by the letter **f** is pronounced like English *f* and the sound represented by the letter **v** is generally also pronounced like English *f*.

- Hören Sie gut zu und wiederholen Sie!

für	vier
Form	vor
folgen	Volk

Familie **F**eldmann **f**ährt in den **F**erien nach **F**innland.
Volkmars **V**orlesung ist um **V**iertel **v**or **v**ier **v**orbei.
Volker ist **V**erkäufer **f**ür **F**arb**f**ernseher.

However, when the letter **v** appears in a word of foreign origin, it is pronounced like English *v*:

Im No**v**ember ist **V**eronika in einer **V**illa in **V**enedig.

In German the sound represented by the letter **w** is always pronounced like English *v*:

Walter **w**ill zu **W**eihnachten **zw**ei Flaschen **W**ein.
Wohnt **W**olfgang **w**ieder in einer **W**G?

In the following word pairs, distinguish clearly between German **f** and **w** sounds.

Vetter	**W**etter	**f**ort	**W**ort		
vier	**w**ir	**f**ein	**W**ein		
Vieh°	**w**ie	**F**arm	**w**arm	*cattle*	
voll	**W**olle	**F**elder	**W**älder		
Volk	**W**olke°	**F**est	**W**est	*cloud*	
		finden	**w**inden		

Wien: Blick über die Innenstadt

KAPITEL 12

■ **Kommunikationsziele**

*In **Kapitel 12** you will learn how to:*
express actions that you do to or for yourself
emphasize future actions
express probability
express feelings and emotions
talk about people and things without naming them

■ **Hör- und Sprechsituationen**

Berufstätige Eltern
Was kaufe ich mir mit diesem Geld?
Morgentoilette
Kleine Situationen
Wie sich Stephanie und Peter kennenlernten
Meine beste Freundin/mein bester Freund
Ich weiß es noch nicht genau
Ein paar persönliche Fragen
Karrieren
Ein ernster Konflikt

■ **Strukturen**

Reflexive pronouns
Reflexive verbs
Verb-preposition combinations
Wo-compounds
Da-compounds

■ **Wissenswertes**

Österreich

VORSCHAU

SIE HABEN IHN SEHR LIEB°
Ein Hörspiel° von Georg Kövary

Die Hauptperson in diesem Hörspiel ist ein etwa zehn Jahre altes Schlüsselkind° mit Namen Thomas. Thomas ist gerade von der Schule nach Hause gekommen, ist die Treppe zur Wohnung seiner Eltern hinaufgestiegen und steht jetzt vor der Wohnungstür.

Beachten Sie,° daß das Badezimmer und das Klo in dieser Wohnung separate Räume° sind und daß im Klo kein Waschbecken ist.

Personen: Thomas, Mutters Stimme,° Vaters Stimme

	Türklingel.° Pause. Türklingel, länger.
THOMAS:	*(ein kleiner Junge, unter Hall,° im Treppenhaus)°* Sie sind wieder nicht da — na, das hätt' ich mir denken können.° *(Schlüsselklirren.)°*
THOMAS:	Hoffentlich kenn' ich mich heute besser aus° mit den Schlüsseln, sonst dauert's° wieder eine halbe Stunde, bis ich in die Wohnung komme . . . Dabei muß ich schon so notwendig° . . . *Türaufschließen° mit Hindernissen.° Tür geht auf.*
THOMAS:	Na endlich!
10	*Einige Türen werden aufgemacht° und zugeschlagen.° Nach einer kurzen Pause Wasserspülung.°*
MUTTERS STIMME:	*(entfernt)°* Thomas!
THOMAS:	Na sowas° — du bist zu Hause, Mutti?
MUTTERS STIMME:	*(entfernt)* Thomas! Komm her, Thomas! Ich spreche zu dir aus
15	dem Badezimmer!
THOMAS:	Ja, ja, ich komm' ja schon . . .
MUTTERS STIMME:	*(erst jetzt merken° wir, daß die Stimme vom Tonband° kommt)* So ist's brav,° mein Kind.
THOMAS:	Ach so, der alte Trick mit dem Tonband. Und ich hab' geglaubt, du
20	bist wirklich da.
MUTTERS STIMME:	Du bist also gleich aufs Klo gegangen, wie du nach Hause gekommen bist. Das hast du richtig gemacht, denn es schadet° der Gesundheit, wenn man muß und es zurückhält. Ich wußte, daß ich einen klugen Sohn habe, und deshalb bat° ich Vati, das Ton-
25	bandgerät° mit der Wasserspülung° zu koppeln,° so daß es sich automatisch einschaltet,° nachdem du Lulu° gemacht hast. Weshalb° haben wir denn einen genialen° Techniker im Haus — wie Vati? So kannst du dich nicht darauf ausreden,° daß du vergessen hat-
30	test, das Gerät einzuschalten und ohne Nachtmahl° schlafen gehen mußtest wie neulich° . . . Du mußt niemals hungrig schlafen gehen, mein Schatz.° Mutti ist immer da und sorgt für°

Right margin notes:

they love him very much

radio play

latchkey child

note
rooms
voice

Das Glossar zu diesem Hörspiel finden Sie im Anhang.

dich! . . . Nun hör mir zu, Thomas . . . Ach nein, zuerst mußt du dir die Hände waschen! Na wird's bald?° Ich warte!°

THOMAS: Aber ja, ich mach' ja schon . . .
Wasser fließt,° wird abgestellt.°

MUTTERS STIMME: Schön abtrocknen,° sonst werden deine Hände rot. Wir sind heute abend zum Abendessen eingeladen, du mußt allein zu Bett. Aber du bist ja ein großer Junge, nicht wahr, mein Schatz? Und du

40 weißt, daß Mutti und Vati dich sehr lieb haben und immer nur an° dich denken, wie es dir dieser Text auch beweist.° Jetzt geh schön in die Küche. Wenn du die Tür aufmachst, geht der Kassettenrecorder los°, darauf° spricht Vati zu dir . . .

THOMAS: In die Küche, jawohl . . .

MUTTERS STIMME: Warte, nicht so hastig! Zuerst mußt du dieses Gerät abstellen. Siehst du, wie vergeßlich° du bist? Zum Glück° hast du eine Mutter, die sich um alles kümmert° und die dich sehr lie . . .
Gerät wird mitten im Wort abgestellt. Tür zu, Tür auf. Küche.

MUTTERS STIMME: Willkommen in der Küche, mein Kind! Mutti spricht weiter zu dir,

50 Vati hat keine Zeit mehr, er muß sich noch rasieren° und umziehen,° und wir sind sowieso° schon spät dran.° Wie du siehst, steht dein Essen auf dem Herd, du mußt es nur aufwärmen. Paß auf Liebling, daß du nicht auf den falschen Knopf° drückst,° sonst strömt Gas aus,° und du stirbst. Und das wollen wir doch nicht,

55 nicht wahr? Also, drück schon auf den Knopf, du wirst es nicht verfehlen,° du bist ja ein großer Junge! . . . Bis dein Essen warm wird, kannst du mir kurz erzählen, wenn du in der Schule irgendein Problem hast, du weißt, Thomas, deine Mutter ist immer für dich da. Ich höre, mein Schatz, stell auf Aufnahme um,° du

60 hast dreißig Sekunden Zeit!
Das Essen brutzelt.°

THOMAS: Huh, ist das heiß — das kann ich doch nicht anfassen!°
Geschirr mit Essen fällt mit Getöse° vom Herd.

THOMAS: Das Essen ist im Kübel.° Jetzt bleib' ich wieder hungrig wie

65 neulich.°

MUTTERS STIMME: Laß es dir schmecken,° mein Junge, Vati wünscht dir auch guten Appetit. Er ist gleich fertig zum Ausgehen, aber er hat stets ein Auge auf dich gerichtet° und leiht dir immer ein Ohr!° Apropos Vati: er hat eine Überraschung° für dich — wenn du in dein Zim-

70 mer gehst, findest du eine neue Platte° auf dem Plattenspieler. Hör dir das an . . .

THOMAS: Eine neue Platte?
Türen, Zimmer, Plattenspieler wird angestellt.°

VATERS STIMME: (*von der Platte, mit Zischgeräusch*)° Hallo, junger Mann, hier

75 spricht dein Vati! Höchstens° komm' ich ein bißchen spät zur Party, aber du kommst für mich zuerst, mein Sohn! Ich hab' für dich eine neue Platte gekauft, damit° du sie dir vorspielst vor dem Einschlafen, aber ich kann sie momentan nicht finden, und wir haben es schon so eilig.° Na, macht nichts, hier ein paar

80 Abschiedsworte° von mir, Thomas! Ich hab' dich sehr lieb, und es tut mir so leid, daß ich das nächste Wochenende wieder verreisen muß und nichts aus unserem Ausflug wird.° Wir werden es nachholen,° das Leben ist lang! Und wenn ich dir bei deinen Schular-

beiten helfen kann, dann sag's mir, und ich spreche es dir heute
85   nacht, wenn wir nach Hause kommen, auf Tonband. Denn du
mußt wissen, deine Mutter und ich sind nicht nur pflichtbewußte°
Eltern, sondern arbeiten nur für ihr Kind, für dich, Thomas! Du
bist für uns das Wichtigste, der Mittelpunkt° in unserem Leben!
Wir haben kein Verständnis° für Eltern, die° keine Zeit für ihre
90   Kinder haben — . . . keine Zeit für ihre Kinder haben — . . .
keine Zeit für ihre Kinder haben . . .

Sprachnotizen

Austrian words and expressions

In *Sie haben ihn sehr lieb* you met two typically Austrian words, **Nachtmahl** and
Kübel. A German author would have written **Abendessen** and **Eimer**. Here are
some other common Austrian words and expressions:

German	Austrian
Grüß dich!	Servus!
Tschüs!	Servus!
eine Tasse Kaffee	eine Schale Kaffee
die Kneipe	das Beisel

VOM LESEN ZUM SPRECHEN

ZUR ORIENTIERUNG UND ZUM ZUSAMMENFASSEN

Hören und lesen Sie das Hörspiel und beantworten Sie die folgenden
Fragen!

1. Die Eltern haben genau geplant, was Thomas tun soll, wenn er von der Schule
   nach Hause kommt. Welche drei Geräte spielen bei diesem Plan eine Rolle?

assume
Wie . . . gesorgt: *How did*
they make sure

2. Die Eltern nehmen an°, daß Thomas zuerst aufs Klo geht, wenn er nach Hause
   kommt. Wie haben sie dafür gesorgt°, daß Thomas nicht vergißt, vom Klo ins
   Badezimmer zu gehen und sich dort die Hände zu waschen?
3. Thomas mußte neulich ohne Abendessen schlafen gehen, weil er vergessen
   hatte, den Kassettenrecorder mit den Kochinstruktionen seiner Mutter ein-
   zuschalten. Was hat sein Vater getan, damit er heute weiß, wie er das Abendessen
   aufwärmen soll?
4. Woher wissen wir, daß die Eltern nicht eingeplant hatten, daß Thomas sein
   Essen auf den Boden fallen läßt?
5. Warum hört Thomas statt der neuen Platte die Stimme seines Vaters?

does . . . negate
shortly afterwards

6. Auf Zeile 58 sagt die Mutter, daß sie *immer* für Thomas da ist. Wie negiert° sie
   diese Aussage kurz darauf°?
7. Auf Zeile 88 sagt der Vater, daß Thomas für seine Eltern das Wichtigste und der
   Mittelpunkt in ihrem Leben ist. Wie negiert der Autor des Hörspiels diese Aussage kurz darauf sehr effektvoll?

in what way / **fassen**
. . . zusammen:
summarize

8. Inwiefern° fassen° der Titel und die dreimal wiederholte Phrase am Ende sehr
   gut zusammen, was der Autor mit diesem Hörspiel sagen will?

BERUFSTÄTIGE ELTERN

working

Besprechen Sie die folgenden Meinungen zum Thema *Berufstätige Eltern* zu zweit.

Mit welchen von diesen Meinungen sind Sie einverstanden°, und mit welchen sind Sie nicht einverstanden? Warum nicht?

in agreement

Wenn beide Eltern arbeiten, sollten sie dafür sorgen°, daß immer jemand zu Hause ist, wenn die Kinder von der Schule kommen.

dafür sorgen: *see to it*

Schlüsselkinder werden viel selbständigere° Menschen, weil sie schon so früh für sich selbst sorgen müssen.

more independent

Es kann zu schweren psychologischen Problemen führen°, wenn ein Kind nach der Schule regelmäßig in eine leere Wohnung kommt.

lead

Heutzutage gibt es im Fernsehen so gute Programme, daß es Kindern nie langweilig wird, wenn sie allein zu Hause sind.

Schlüsselkinder bekommen selten Hilfe bei den Schularbeiten und haben deshalb oft Probleme in der Schule.

Bis zum Alter von etwa zwölf Jahren sollten Kinder nicht den ganzen Abend allein sein.

Nachdem Sie die obigen Meinungen zu zweit besprochen und Ihre eigenen Meinungen formuliert haben, können Sie das Thema *Berufstätige Eltern* mit allen Ihren Klassenkameradinnen und Klassenkameraden diskutieren.

NÜTZLICHE WÖRTER UND AUSDRÜCKE

Nomen

das Hörspiel, die Hörspiele	radio play
die Stimme, die Stimmen	voice
das Tonband, die Tonbänder	(audio) tape
das Tonbandgerät, die Tonbandgeräte	tape recorder
die Kassette, die Kassetten	cassette
der Kassettenrecorder, die Kassettenrecorder	cassette recorder
der Knopf, die Knöpfe	button
die Aufnahme, die Aufnahmen	recording
die Klingel	doorbell
der Schlüssel, die Schlüssel	key
die Überraschung, die Überraschungen	surprise

Verben

klingeln	to ring	**dauern**	to take *(time)*
drücken	to press	**warten**	to wait
ein•schalten	to turn on *(radio, TV, etc.)*	**an•fassen**	to touch
		ab•trocknen	to dry off
ab•stellen	to turn off	**schaden (+ dative)**	to be bad for, to harm
merken	to notice	**schmecken**	to taste

Andere Wörter

vergeßlich	forgetful	**sowieso**	anyway
brav	good, well-behaved	**damit**	so that *(conjunction)*

Ausdrücke

Ich habe dich lieb.	I love you.	**Ich habe es eilig.**	I'm in a hurry.
zum Glück	luckily	**Ich bin spät dran.**	I'm late.

Synonyme

der Schatz — der Liebling	darling
die Schularbeiten — die Hausaufgaben	homework
momentan — im Moment	at the moment
einige — ein paar	a few, several
Laß es dir schmecken! — Guten Appetit!	Enjoy your meal!

WÖRTER IM KONTEXT

WAS PASST ZUSAMMEN?

a. Warum hast du denn geklingelt?

Ja, es ist wirklich eine sehr gute Aufnahme.

b. Hat das Hörspiel schon angefangen?

Daß er sehr vergeßlich geworden ist.

c. Wie lange dauert dieses Hörspiel?

Weil ich nicht weiß, auf welchen Knopf ich drücken muß.

d. Man kann die Stimmen der Sprecher sehr gut verstehen.

Weil ich meine Schlüssel nicht finden kann.

e. Warum hast du denn das Tonbandgerät nicht abgestellt?

Nur zehn Minuten.

f. Warte doch, bis ich meinen Kaffee ausgetrunken habe.

Da hast du recht. Die vielen Zigaretten haben seiner Gesundheit sehr geschadet.

g. Was hast du gemerkt, als du das letzte Mal mit Opa telefoniert hast?

Ja, schalte schnell das Radio ein!

h. Zum Glück hat er jetzt endlich das Rauchen aufgegeben.

Ich kann nicht. Ich bin sowieso schon viel zu spät dran.

1. TALKING ABOUT ACTIONS ONE DOES TO OR FOR ONESELF

REFLEXIVE PRONOUNS

To express the idea that one does an action to oneself or for oneself, English and German use reflexive pronouns. In German the reflexive pronoun can appear in the accusative case or the dative case. If a sentence starts with the subject, the reflexive pronoun follows directly after the conjugated verb.

ACCUSATIVE:	Ich habe **mich** geschnitten.	*I cut **myself**.*
DATIVE:	Ich hole **mir** jetzt eine Tasse Kaffee.	*I'm getting **myself** a cup of coffee now.*

a. Reflexive pronouns in the accusative case

Ich habe **mich** geschnitten.	*I cut **myself**.*
Tina hat **sich** geschnitten.	*Tina cut **herself**.*

The accusative reflexive pronoun is identical in form to the accusative personal pronoun, except in the 3rd person singular and plural and in the **Sie-**form, where it is **sich.**

Personal Pronouns		Reflexive Pronouns
Nominative	Accusative	Accusative
ich	mich	**mich**
du	dich	**dich**
er	ihn	
sie	sie	*sich*
es	es	
wir	uns	**uns**
ihr	euch	**euch**
sie	sie	*sich*
Sie	Sie	*sich*

Note that the reflexive pronoun that refers to **Sie** is not capitalized: **Haben Sie sich geschnitten?** Verbs that take a reflexive pronoun are listed as follows: **sich waschen** *to wash;* **sich baden** *to take a bath.*

Reflexive pronouns are used much more frequently in German than in English. Compare the following examples, where the English equivalents do not use reflexive pronouns at all.

Blick auf Salzburg

Wien
BURGENLAND
Kärnten
Niederösterreich
Ober
Österreich
SalzburgerLand
Steiermark
Tirol
VORARLBERG

Österreich (literally, the *Eastern Realm*) is located in the south-eastern corner of the German-speaking area of Europe. This peaceful country of only seven and a half million people has had a turbulent history and has often played a major role in the political evolution of Europe.

For many centuries Austria was a part of the **Heilige Römische Reich Deutscher Nation** *(The Holy Roman Empire of the German Nation),* a vast empire that at times encompassed most of continental Europe, and that was ruled by the Austrian House of Habsburg from 1438 to 1806. When this First German Empire collapsed, the Habsburgs proclaimed themselves "Emperors of Austria" and in 1867 became the rulers of the multi-national Austro-Hungarian Empire, a major European power of 60 million people, which included not only the Austrians and the Hungarians but also many Slavic peoples like the Czechs and the Slo-

vaks. At the end of World War I, the Austro-Hungarian Empire dissolved, and the Republic of Austria was born. Twenty years later this young republic was annexed by Hitler, the Austrian-born dictator of Nazi Germany. Together with the Germans, the Austrians experienced the short-lived nationalistic euphoria, as well as the terror and misery, of the Third Reich. After World War II, Austria again became an independent, democratic state and declared its permanent neutrality. By constitutional law, it cannot join a military alliance or permit the establishment of foreign military bases on its soil.

As a permanently neutral country, Austria plays a particularly active role in the peace-keeping efforts of the United Nations. Austrian medical teams and troops have served and are serving in trouble spots around the world such as the Congo, Cyprus, and the Middle East. Austria's capital, **Wien,** once the capital of a multi-ethnic empire, today continues

this tradition in a different way: it rivals Geneva as a center for international conferences and as the headquarters for many international organizations.

Austria, an alpine country with beautiful landscapes, attracts skiers, mountain-climbers, and vacationers from all over the world. Alpine skiing is the most popular winter sport in Austria because of the challenging slopes and the Austrian **Gemütlichkeit** offered in popular resorts such as Kitzbühel and Innsbruck. Kitzbühel has often hosted World Cup skiing events and Innsbruck was selected as the site for the Winter Olympics in 1964 and 1976. A network of hiking trails, comprising many thousands of kilometers, extends from Vienna at the eastern end of the country to the Swiss border in the west.

Vienna is an important academic and cultural center. In the field of psychology, it has become world-renowned as the home of Sigmund Freud, the founder of psychoanalysis. Austria is also a country with a great cultural tradition. Haydn, Mozart, Schubert, and Johann Strauß were born there. Beethoven, although born in Bonn, was attracted by the flourishing musical life of Vienna and lived and worked there until his death. Today Vienna's glittering **Staatsoper,** the **Wiener Philharmoniker,** the **Wiener Sängerknaben,** the **Burgtheater,** and in Salzburg, the **Festspiele** and the **Mozarteum** are synonymous with excellence to music and theater lovers throughout the world.

Ich habe **mich** noch nicht rasiert.   *I haven't shaved yet.*

Holger wäscht **sich** nur sehr selten.   *Holger washes very rarely.*

Zieh **dich** schnell an!   *Get dressed quickly.*

In sentences and clauses that do not begin with the subject, the reflexive pronoun usually precedes noun subjects, but always follows pronoun subjects:

Warum hat **sich Holger** denn nicht rasiert?   *Why didn't Holger shave?*

Warum hast **du dich** denn nicht rasiert, Holger?   *Why didn't you shave, Holger?*

Weißt du, ob **sich Stefanie** schon umgezogen hat?   *Do you know whether Stefanie has changed yet?*

Ich glaube nicht, daß **sie sich** schon umgezogen hat.   *I don't think that she has changed yet.*

Below is a list of common verbs that use reflexive pronouns in the accusative case.

sich waschen (wäscht sich), wusch sich, hat sich gewaschen	to wash
sich baden	to take a bath
sich duschen	to take a shower
sich kämmen	to comb one's hair
sich rasieren	to shave
sich anziehen, zog sich an, hat sich angezogen	to get dressed
sich ausziehen	to get undressed
sich umziehen	to change (one's clothes)

A. IN CLAUDIAS WG. Ergänzen Sie die Reflexivpronomen!

1. BERND: Dusch _____ schnell, Stefan! Ich muß _____ auch noch duschen.

   STEFAN: Wenn _____ Claudia stundenlang badet, kann ich _____ doch nicht duschen.

2. CLAUDIA: Du hast wieder mal vergessen, _____ zu rasieren, Bernd.

   BERND: Dafür° habe ich _____ heute mal richtig schön gekämmt.

3. MONIKA: Wenn ihr _____ nicht gleich umzieht, gehen wir ohne euch ins Kino.

   STEFAN: Wie können wir _____ denn umziehen, wenn unsere Hemden noch im Trockner sind?

4. BERND: Warum sind denn deine Kleider so zerknittert,° Stefan? Bist du gestern abend ins Bett gegangen, ohne _____ auszuziehen?

   STEFAN: Und du, Bernd? Ziehst du _____ immer an, bevor du _____ wäschst?

to make up for it

rumpled

B. BEI MEYERS

1. FRAU MEYER: Warum zieht ihr _____ denn nicht an, Kinder?

   NICOLE: Weil wir _____ noch nicht gewaschen haben.

   FRAU MEYER: Ja, dann wascht _____ doch mal endlich!

   OLIVER: Wie können wir _____ denn waschen, wenn _____ Vati stundenlang rasiert?

2. HERR MEYER: Wenn _____ die Kinder nicht sofort anziehen, kommen sie zu spät in die Schule.

FRAU MEYER: Wie können sie _____ denn anziehen, wenn du _____ stundenlang
rasierst und sie _____ nicht waschen können?

3. NICOLE: Warum zieht _____ Mutti denn um, Vati?

HERR MEYER: Weil Mutti und ich heute abend ausgehen.

OLIVER: Und wir? Was machen wir?

HERR MEYER: Ihr zieht _____ schnell aus und geht ins Bett.

C. BIST DU ENDLICH FERTIG? Ein ständiges° Problem in Claudias WG ist, daß sich   *constant*
Stefan im Badezimmer immer so viel Zeit läßt. Claudia schickt deshalb Holger, um
herauszufinden, ob Stefan endlich fertig ist. Arbeiten Sie zu dritt!

CLAUDIA: Du Holger, frag mal den Stefan, ob er sich jetzt endlich
geduscht hat.

HOLGER: Stefan, Claudia möchte wissen, ob du dich schon
geduscht hast.

STEFAN: Nein, noch nicht. Ich muß mich
erst rasieren.

1.

Du Holger, frag mal den Stefan, ob er
_____ jetzt endlich _____ hat.
Stefan, Claudia möchte wissen, ob du
_____ hast.

Nein, noch nicht. Ich muß _____ doch
erst _____.

2.

Du Holger, frag mal den Stefan, ob er
_____ jetzt endlich _____ hat.
Stefan, Claudia möchte wissen, ob du
_____ hast.

Nein, noch nicht. Ich muß _____ doch
erst _____.

3.

Du Holger, frag mal den Stefan, ob er
_____ jetzt endlich _____ hat.
Stefan, Claudia möchte wissen, ob du
_____ hast.

Nein, noch nicht. Ich muß _____ doch
erst _____.

4.

Du Holger, frag mal den Stefan, ob er
_____ jetzt endlich _____ hat.
Stefan, Claudia möchte wissen, ob du
_____ hast.

Nein, noch nicht. Ich muß _____ doch
erst _____.

5.

Du Holger, frag mal den Stefan, ob er
_____ jetzt endlich _____ hat.
Stefan, Claudia möchte wissen, ob du
_____ hast.

Nein, noch nicht. Ich muß _____ doch
erst _____.

D. ZWEI BRAVE KINDER! Jedesmal wenn Vater den Kindern sagt, was sie tun sollen, findet er heraus, daß sie es schon längst getan haben. Arbeiten Sie zu dritt.

MUTTER: Sag mal den Kindern, sie sollen sich schnell waschen.	
VATER: Mutter sagt, ihr sollt euch schnell waschen.	**STEFAN:** Aber wir haben uns doch schon längst gewaschen.

1.

Sag mal den Kindern, sie sollen _____ schnell _____.

Mutter sagt, ihr sollt _____ schnell _____.

Aber wir haben _____ doch schon längst _____.

2.

Sag mal den Kindern, sie sollen _____ schnell _____.

Mutter sagt, ihr sollt _____ schnell _____.

Aber wir haben _____ doch schon längst _____.

3.

Sag mal den Kindern, sie sollen _____ schnell _____.

Mutter sagt, ihr sollt _____ schnell _____.

Aber wir haben _____ doch schon längst _____.

4.

Sag mal den Kindern, sie sollen _____ schnell _____.

Mutter sagt, ihr sollt _____ schnell _____.

Aber wir haben _____ doch schon längst _____.

5.

Sag mal den Kindern, sie sollen _____ schnell _____.

Mutter sagt, ihr sollt _____ schnell _____.

Aber wir haben _____ doch schon längst _____.

6.

Sag mal den Kindern, sie sollen _____ schnell _____.

Mutter sagt, ihr sollt _____ schnell _____.

Aber wir haben _____ doch schon längst _____.

b. Reflexive pronouns in the dative case

In the examples below, the reflexive pronouns are indirect objects and are therefore in the dative case. A reflexive pronoun in the dative case often indicates that a person is doing something in her/his own interest. English uses the equivalent construction only occasionally.

Ich mache **mir** jetzt eine Tasse Kaffee.	*I'm going to make **myself** a cup of coffee now.*
Kaufst **du dir** jetzt auch einen Computer?	*Are you going to buy a computer now too?*

Note the difference in the way German and English refer to actions that involve one's own body.

Oliver wäscht **sich** nur selten **die** Hände.	***Oliver** washes **his** hands only rarely.*

Where English uses the possessive adjective (***his** hands*), German uses the dative reflexive pronoun and the definite article to express the same thing (***sich die Hände**).

The dative reflexive pronoun is identical in form to the dative personal pronoun except in the 3rd person singular and plural and in the **Sie**-form, where it is again **sich**.

Personal Pronouns		Reflexive Pronouns
Nominative	Dative	Dative
ich	mir	**mir**
du	dir	**dir**
er	ihm ⎫	
sie	ihr ⎬	*sich*
es	ihm ⎭	
wir	uns	**uns**
ihr	euch	**euch**
sie	ihnen	*sich*
Sie	Ihnen	*sich*

Stell Dir vor
es ist Krieg
und keiner geht hin

E. ERGÄNZEN SIE!

1. SABINE: Warum suchst du _____ denn keine größere Wohnung, Barbara?

   BARBARA: Wenn ich noch mehr Miete zahlen muß, kann ich _____ nichts mehr zu essen kaufen.

2. HERR KOCH: Warum kaufen _____ Müllers denn keinen zweiten Wagen?

   FRAU KOCH: Ich glaube, sie wollen _____ zuerst ein Haus kaufen.

3. CLAUDIA: Warum nimmst du _____ nicht ein Stück von meinem Kuchen, bevor du ins Bett gehst?

   MONIKA: Weil ich _____ die Zähne schon geputzt habe.

4. PETER: Warum bestellt ihr _____ denn kein Steak?

   CLAUDIA: Nicht in diesem Restaurant. Wir wollen _____ doch nicht die Zähne ausbeißen!°

   lose a tooth

5. ANTJE: Seit wann läßt _____ Sylvia die Haare beim Friseur waschen?

   HELGA: Seit sie _____ beim Schilaufen den Arm gebrochen hat.

6. FRAU BERGER: Warum soll ich _____ denn einen Videorecorder kaufen?

   HERR MÜNCH: Weil Sie _____ dann zu Hause die schönsten Filme anschauen können.

WAS KAUFE ICH MIR MIT DIESEM GELD?

Ihre Gesprächspartnerin/Ihr Gesprächspartner hat 500 Dollar und soll sich mit diesem Geld drei Dinge kaufen. Sie/er erzählt Ihnen, was die drei Dinge sind, und wieviel Geld sie/er für jedes ausgeben will. Berichten Sie der Klasse, was sie/er Ihnen erzählt hat!

S1: Zuerst kaufe ich mir . . .   Das kostet etwa . . .
Dann . . .   . . .
Und zuletzt . . .   . . .

S2: Zuerst kauft sie/er sich . . .

F. WAS MACHEN DIESE JUNGEN LEUTE?

▶ Anita

sich die Haare bürsten

Anita bürstet sich die Haare.

1. wir

3. Martin und Claudia

2. Peter

4. ich

sich einen Film anschauen	sich die Haare waschen
sich die Hände waschen	sich die Zähne putzen

5. Stephanie

7. Günter

6. wir

8. ich

sich einen Korb Äpfel kaufen	sich ein Stück Kuchen nehmen
sich eine Tasse Kaffee machen	sich ein frisches Hemd anziehen

Stellen Sie Ihrer Gesprächspartnerin/Ihrem Gesprächspartner ein paar Fragen über ihre/seine Morgentoilette. Berichten Sie dann Ihren Mitstudenten, was Sie herausgefunden haben.

Wann stehst du morgens auf?
Badest du dich, oder duschst du dich lieber?
Wie oft wäschst du dir die Haare?
Mit was für einem Shampoo wäschst du dir die Haare?
Ziehst du dich vor oder nach dem Frühstück an?
Putzt du dir vor oder nach dem Frühstück die Zähne?
Mit was für einer Zahnpasta putzt du dir die Zähne?
Was machst du dir alles zum Frühstück?

c. Reflexive pronouns used to express *each other*

German commonly uses the plural reflexive pronoun as a reciprocal pronoun corresponding to English *each other*. Note that the pronoun is not always expressed in English:

Wie habt ihr **euch** kennengelernt?   *How did you get to know **each other**?*
Wo sollen wir **uns** treffen?   *Where should we meet?*

G. WAS PASST ZUSAMMEN? Ergänzen Sie die Reflexivpronomen in den Fragen, und beantworten Sie die Fragen! Einige Antworten passen mehrmals.

1. Wie oft schreibt ihr _____?   Um acht.
2. Wie lange kennen _____ Claudia und Martin schon?   Durch Freunde.
       Seit einem halben Jahr.
3. Wie oft rufen _____ die beiden an?   Fast jeden Tag.
4. Wann sehen wir _____ wieder?   Hoffentlich sehr bald.
5. Wo sollen wir _____ heute abend treffen?   Am besten wieder bei mir.
6. Wann trefft ihr _____ heute abend?
7. Seit wann grüßen _____ Müllers und Maiers nicht mehr?
8. Wie haben Sie _____ kennengelernt?

H. KLEINE GESPRÄCHE. Sagen Sie das auf deutsch!

1. OLIVER: May I make myself a sandwich,° Mom?   **das Brot**
   MUTTI: Yes, but first you have to wash your hands.
2. PETER: Why are you changing? Are you going out?
   MARTIN: Yes, we're going to see the new Spielberg film. (Use **sich anschauen.**)
3. BERND: Why don't you get dressed, Stefan?
   STEFAN: Because I have to wash and shave first.
4. BERND: How did your brother and his wife get to know each other?
   STEFAN: David was a salesman in a computer store, and Eva bought her first computer there. (Use a reflexive pronoun.)

5. SABINE: When can we meet tomorrow? At ten?
   JULIE: Sorry.° Tomorrow at ten I'm having my hair cut.

REFLEXIVE VERBS

As was stated above, reflexive pronouns are used much more frequently in German than in English. Many German verbs are always or almost always accompanied by a reflexive pronoun; however their English equivalents are rarely reflexive. Note that in vocabulary lists the infinitives of these reflexive verbs are preceded by **sich.** Here are some important ones.

sich auf•regen	to get excited;	**sich setzen**	to sit down
	to get upset	**sich unterhalten**	to talk;
sich beeilen	to hurry (up)		to converse
sich benehmen	to behave	**sich verspäten**	to be late
sich entschuldigen	to apologize	**sich wohl fühlen**	to feel well
sich erkälten	to catch a cold		

I. WAS PASST IN DIE SPRECHBLASEN?

1. 2. 3. 4.

> Ich habe mich erkältet.   Reg dich doch nicht so auf!
> Sie haben sich verspätet.   Beeil dich doch ein bißchen!

5. 6. 7. 8.

> Komm, setz dich zu mir!
> Ich fühle mich nicht wohl.
>
> Du benimmst dich schlecht.
> Können Sie sich nicht wenigstens entschuldigen?

J. WAS PASST WO?   Ergänzen Sie die passenden reflexiven Verben!

▶

Weil er _____ immer so schlecht _____.

> sich benehmen

S1: Warum ladet ihr Günter nicht ein?

S2: Weil er sich immer so schlecht benimmt.

1. Ich will mit Stefan nichts mehr zu tun haben.
2. Warum war Stephanie heute nicht in der Vorlesung?
3. Warum denkst du denn, daß Holger in mich verknallt ist°?
4. Warum darf ich denn meinen Kaffee nicht austrinken?

Auch nicht, wenn er _____ _____?

Weil sie _____ _____ hat und mit hohem Fieber im Bett liegt.

Weil er _____ in der Cafeteria immer zu dir an den Tisch _____.

Weil wir _____ nicht _____ dürfen.

in . . . ist: *has a crush on me*

> sich verspäten/sich entschuldigen/sich setzen/sich erkälten

5. Warum hast du Vater nichts von dieser schlechten Zensur gesagt?
6. Warum habt ihr euch denn in diese Ecke gesetzt?
7. Warum darf ich denn meinen Tee nicht austrinken?
8. Warum willst du denn nicht mit uns tanzen gehen?

Weil er _____ immer so _____.

Weil wir _____ hier besser _____ können.

Weil wir _____ _____ müssen.

Weil ich _____ nicht _____.

Warum ist dieses Motorrad so eine „super Gelegenheit"?

> sich unterhalten/sich beeilen/sich aufregen/sich wohl fühlen

🎞 **KLEINE SITUATIONEN (1).**   Was paßt wo? Sie hören neun kleine Situationen. Ergänzen Sie die Reaktionen auf diese Situationen! Verwenden Sie die passenden reflexiven Verben!

sich verspäten   sich erkälten   sich setzen

1. Guten Tag! Bitte . . . !
2. Bitte, sei Punkt halb acht fertig! Wir dürfen . . . nicht . . .
3. Ich glaube, . . .

sich aufregen   sich entschuldigen   sich beeilen

4. Als erstes gehst du mal zu Schneiders, und . . .
5. . . . doch bitte ein bißchen, Gerhard!
6. Bitte, . . . nicht . . . !

sich unterhalten   sich wohl fühlen   sich benehmen

7. . . . doch nicht so schlecht, Günter!
8. Komm, wir gehen wieder! Hier können wir . . . nicht . . . !
9. Weil . . . nicht . . .

◣ ZUSAMMENSCHAU

WIE SICH STEPHANIE UND PETER KENNENLERNTEN

In den vergangenen acht Monaten sind Stephanie und Peter sehr gute Freunde geworden. Hören Sie, wie die beiden sich zu Anfang des Wintersemesters kennenlernten.

Neue Vokabeln

schade	*too bad*	Hau ab!	*Get lost!*
wozu?	*what for?*	an•haben	*to have on, to wear*
Raus mit dir!	*Get out!*	echt	*really*

locations

1. Die drei Szenen spielen an drei verschiedenen Orten°. Geben Sie jeder Szene den passenden Ort als Titel: *In der Wohnung von Peter und Martin / In der Cafeteria / Im Hörsaal.*

    Szene I: _____
    Szene II: _____
    Szene III: _____

2. Wer sind die Sprecher?

    Szene I: _____
    Szene II: _____
    Szene III: _____

3. Wer sagt das? In welcher Szene?

	Sprecher(in)	Szene
Willst du meinen neuen Pullover?	_____	____
Hast du Lust auf eine Tasse Kaffee?	_____	____
Sieht echt gut aus, der Pulli.	_____	____
Bist eine Süße, was?	_____	____
Viel Glück in der Liebe!	_____	____
Läßt der Professor euch immer so spät gehen?	_____	____
Dann treffen wir uns doch um halb zwei.	_____	____

▨▷ Hören Sie die drei Szenen noch einmal, und beantworten Sie die folgenden Fragen!

Szene I

1. Zu welcher Tageszeit findet° diese Unterhaltung statt?
2. Warum kann Stephanie jetzt nicht Kaffee trinken gehen?
3. Wann ist Stephanies Vorlesung zu Ende?
4. Warum können Peter und Stephanie auch dann nicht zusammen Kaffee trinken gehen?
5. Wie lange dauert Peters Seminar?
6. Wann und wo wollen sich die beiden treffen?

findet . . . statt: takes place

Szene II

1. Was macht Martin gerade, als Peter zur Tür hereinkommt?
2. Warum wundert sich° Martin, daß Peter jetzt nach Hause kommt?
3. Warum wundert sich Martin, daß sich Peter jetzt duschen will?
4. Warum will sich Peter umziehen?
5. Was soll Peter tun, während sich Martin fertigduscht?
6. Warum soll Peter Martins neuen Pullover anziehen?

is . . . surprised

Szene III

1. Wie lange muß Stephanie auf° Peter warten?
2. Warum hat sich Peter verspätet? Was sagt er? Was ist der wirkliche Grund?
3. Warum will Peter, daß sie sich auf den Platz in der Ecke setzen?
4. Warum sieht Peters Pullover so aus wie der von Martin? Was sagt Peter? Was ist der wirkliche Grund?
5. Warum nennt° Peter Stephanie „eine Süße"?

for

call

MEINE BESTE FREUNDIN/MEIN BESTER FREUND

Interviewen Sie Ihre Gesprächspartnerin/Ihren Gesprächspartner! Beginnen Sie mit den folgenden Fragen!

Wie heißt deine beste Freundin/dein bester Freund?
Was macht sie/er?
Wie lange kennt ihr euch schon?
Wo und wie habt ihr euch kennengelernt?
Warum seid ihr so gute Freunde? Was gefällt dir an ihr/ihm?
Wie oft seht ihr euch?
Streitet ihr euch° auch manchmal? Warum?
Wer entschuldigt sich zuerst, wenn ihr euch gestritten habt?
. . .

do you quarrel

 ## 2. EMPHASIZING FUTURE ACTIONS

THE FUTURE TENSE

In *Kapitel 3* you learned that future ideas are usually expressed with the present tense if the context clearly refers to future time.

Ich **besuche** dich nächste Woche.   I ***will visit*** you next week.

German does, however, have a future tense. Like the English future tense it consists of an auxiliary verb and an infinitive. The auxiliary verb is **werden.**

	Singular			Plural	
ich	**werde**	kommen	wir	**werden**	kommen
du	**wirst**	kommen	ihr	**werdet**	kommen
er/sie/es	**wird**	kommen	sie	**werden**	kommen
			Sie	**werden**	kommen

As was the case with other German tenses, the future tense has more than one English equivalent:

er wird kommen	*he will come* *he will be coming* *he is going to come*

The future tense is used to express a future event if the context does not clearly refer to future time.

Present Time: Du **siehst,** daß ich recht habe.   *You **see** that I'm right.*

Future Time: Du **wirst sehen,** daß ich recht habe.   *You **will see** that I'm right.*

The future tense is also used to *emphasize* that something is going to happen in the future.

Du **wirst** dieses Buch **lesen,** ob du willst oder nicht!   *You **will read** this book, whether you want to or not!*

The position of the auxiliary and the infinitive follow the pattern with which you are already familiar:

Statements: Ich **werde** euch jeden Tag eine Postkarte **schreiben.**   *I'll write you a postcard every day.*

Diesmal **werde** ich euch nicht so oft schreiben **können.**   *This time I won't be able to write you so often.*

Questions: Wann **wirst** du uns **schreiben?**   *When will you write us?*

Wirst du uns diesmal eine Postkarte **schreiben?**   *Will you write us a postcard this time?*

Dependent clauses: Glaubst du, daß Michael uns **schreiben wird?**   *Do you think that Michael will write us?*

K. WARUM FRAGST DU DENN? DAS IST DOCH GANZ KLAR! Ergänzen Sie das Futur des gegebenen Verbs in der Frage und in der Antwort.

▶ Glaubst du, daß Brigitte mit Professor Seidlmeyer ____? (sprechen)	Aber natürlich ____ sie mit ihm ____.
S1: Glaubst du, daß Brigitte mit Professor Seidlmeyer sprechen wird?	**S2:** Aber natürlich wird sie mit ihm sprechen.

1. Glaubst du, daß Holger uns ____? (schreiben)

   Aber natürlich ____ er uns ____.

2. Glaubst du, daß ____ Lilo und Thomas wieder ____? (sich verspäten)

   Aber natürlich ____ sie ____ wieder ____.

3. Glaubst du, daß Bernd mich rechtzeitig ____? (abholen)

   Aber natürlich ____ er dich rechtzeitig ____.

4. Glaubst du, daß ich mein Visum rechtzeitig ____? (bekommen)

   Aber natürlich ____ du es rechtzeitig ____.

5. Glaubst du, daß ____ Markus ____? (sich entschuldigen)

   Aber natürlich ____ er ____.

6. Glaubst du, daß Dieter ____? (zurückrufen)

   Aber natürlich ____ er ____.

7. Glaubst du, daß ____ Meyers den neuen Spielbergfilm ____? (sich anschauen)

   Aber natürlich ____ sie ihn ____.

3. EXPRESSING PROBABILITY

THE FUTURE TENSE TO EXPRESS PROBABILITY

The future tense is also used to express probability, often in conjunction with words like **wohl** *(probably)*.

Wo ist Professor Seidlmeyer? Er **wird** (wohl) in seinem Büro **sein.**	*Where is Professor Seidlmeyer? He's probably in his office.*

The example above refers to present time and the future tense expresses the idea that Professor Seidlmeyer is *probably* in his office at this moment. Here the use of the word **wohl** is optional.

If one wishes to express the idea that an event will probably take place in the *future*, **wohl** must be added.

Was macht ihr nächsten Sommer? Wir **werden wohl** wieder nach Österreich **trampen.**	*What will you be doing next summer? We're probably going to hitchhike to Austria again.*

Note that without **wohl** the response would mean *We're going to hitchhike to Austria again.*

L. ICH WEISS ES NICHT GENAU! Beginnen Sie Ihre Fragen mit **wo, wohin, warum** oder **was.** Ihre Gesprächspartnerin/Ihr Gesprächspartner kann die Information in ihrer/seiner Antwort nicht garantieren und verwendet deshalb das Futur und **wohl.**

In welche Länder fährt die Straße 191?

▶ _____ ist Martin?   Er ist in der Mensa.

S1: Wo ist Martin?   **S2:** Er wird wohl in der Mensa sein.

1. _____ machst du am Sonntag?   Ich besuche meinen Freund.
2. _____ kommt Holger nicht mit?   Er hat zu viel zu tun.
3. _____ ist Brigitte?   Sie spielt mit Ralf Tennis.
4. _____ sind Stephanie und Claudia?   Sie sind in der Bibliothek.
5. _____ geht ihr in den Sommer-   Wir trampen nach Schweden.
   ferien?
6. _____ hast du heute abend vor?   Ich muß lernen.
7. _____ ist denn Sabine?   Sie ist noch in der Vorlesung.
8. _____ fahrt ihr mit eurem Schiklub?   Wir fahren wieder nach Innsbruck.
9. _____ macht ihr heute abend?   Wir bleiben zu Hause.
10. _____ kommt Stefan heute abend   Er muß an seinem Referat arbeiten.
    nicht?

ICH WEISS ES NOCH NICHT GENAU

Stellen Sie Ihrer Gesprächspartnerin/Ihrem Gesprächspartner die folgenden Fragen, und berichten Sie dann, was Sie herausgefunden haben!

S1: Was machst du heute abend?   **S2:** Ich weiß es noch nicht genau, aber ich werde wohl ein bißchen Deutsch lernen und dann mit ein paar Freunden in die Kneipe gehen.

Weitere Fragen:
   Was machst du am Wochenende?
   Was machst du im Sommer?
   Was machst du, wenn du mit deinem Studium fertig bist?

Two notes on *werden*

Don't forget that as a verb in its own right, **werden** means *to get* or *to be* in the sense of *to become*.

Im Winter **wird** es schon sehr früh dunkel.   *In winter it **gets** dark very early.*

Nächste Woche **werde** ich fünfund-zwanzig.   *Next week I'll **be** twenty-five.*

Do not confuse **werden** with the modal verb **wollen,** which expresses a desire or a wish.

Ralf **wird** mich nach Hause fahren.   *Ralf **will** drive me home.*
Ralf **will** mich nach Hause fahren.   *Ralf **wants to** drive me home.*

M. TOBIAS HAT MORGEN GEBURTSTAG. Ergänzen Sie **werden** oder **wollen**.

1. Mein Bruder Tobias _____ morgen vierzehn.
2. Von den Eltern _____ er einen Computer zum Geburtstag.
3. Weil Vater sehr dafür° ist, _____ er ihn wohl auch kriegen.   *for it*
4. Mutter _____, daß Tobias die Hälfte selber bezahlt, aber so viel Geld _____ er wohl kaum haben.
5. Glaubst du, daß er den Computer viel benutzen _____?
6. Er _____ bestimmt den ganzen Tag damit° spielen _____.   *with it*
7. Vater _____, daß Tobias später mal Programmierer _____.
8. Vater denkt, daß Tobias als Programmierer sehr gut verdienen _____.
9. Mutter denkt, daß Tobias _____ soll, was er _____, und nicht, was sein Vater _____.
10. Wo ist Tobias jetzt?
    Er _____ in seinem Zimmer sein.
11. Was macht er denn dort?
    Er _____ wohl seine Hausaufgaben machen.
12. Wenn er dann seinen Computer hat, _____ er wohl nicht mehr so viel Zeit für seine Hausaufgaben haben.
13. Da hast du recht, und ich, ob ich es _____ oder nicht, _____ ihm bei seinen Hausaufgaben helfen müssen.

4. EXPANDING THE MEANING OF SOME VERBS

SPECIAL VERB-PREPOSITION COMBINATIONS

Ich habe **für** Schmidt gestimmt.	*I voted **for** Schmidt.*
Jede Oper beginnt **mit** einer Ouvertüre.	*Every opera begins **with** an overture.*
Ich habe bis morgens um drei **an** meinem Referat gearbeitet.	*I worked **on** my essay until 3 a.m.*

Many English and German verbs can be used in combination with specific prepositions. In the examples above, the prepositions used in both languages are direct equivalents. In most instances, however, the prepositions used in German do not correspond to those used in English.

Ich warte **auf** meinen Bruder.	*I'm waiting **for** my brother.*
Interessierst du dich **für** Musik?	*Are you interested **in** music?*

Below are some commonly used verb-preposition combinations. Note that the prepositions often lose their literal meanings. For the two-case prepositions, the test of **wo/wohin** that you learned in *Kapitel 9* does not apply, and the correct case is therefore given in parentheses. You will find that it is usually the accusative.

Angst haben vor *(+ dative)*	*to be afraid of*
arbeiten an *(+ dative)*	*to work on*
sich ärgern über *(+ accusative)*	*to be annoyed with*
sich auf•regen über *(+ accusative)*	*to get excited about; to get upset about*
denken an *(+ accusative)*	*to think of, about (i.e., to have in mind)*
erzählen von	*to tell about*

sich freuen auf *(+ accusative)*	*to look forward to*
sich freuen über *(+ accusative)*	*to be happy about; to be pleased with*
halten von	*to think of, about (i.e., to have an opinion of)*
sich interessieren für	*to be interested in*
lachen über *(+ accusative)*	*to laugh at, about*
sich verlieben in *(+ accusative)*	*to fall in love with*
warten auf *(+ accusative)*	*to wait for*
wissen von	*to know about*

N. WAS PASST ZUSAMMEN? Ergänzen Sie die Präpositionen in den Fragen und geben Sie passende Antworten! Einige Antworten passen mehrmals.

1. Wo soll ich _____ dich warten, Peter?
2. Was hältst du _____ unserer neuen Professorin?
3. Denkst du auch manchmal _____ mich?
4. Was weißt du _____ Einsteins Relativitätstheorie?
5. Wann erzählst du uns _____ deiner Deutschlandreise?
6. Seit wann interessierst du dich denn _____ Briefmarken?
7. Wie lange has du gestern _____ deinem Referat gearbeitet?

Vor der Bibliothek.
Gar nichts.
Seit vielen Jahren.
Von morgens bis abends.
Bald.

strange

8. Warum has du denn so Angst _____ Müllers Hund?
9. Warum ärgerst du dich denn so _____ Müllers Hund?
10. Warum freust du dich denn nicht _____ Onkel Pauls Besuch?
11. Warum regen sich deine Eltern _____ deinen Freund so auf?
12. Warum hat sich Bernd wohl _____ diese komische Frau verliebt?
13. Warum freut sich David denn nicht _____ seine gute Zensur?
14. Warum lacht Kurt _____ Lilos neue Frisur?

Weil er so viel raucht.
Weil er sie komisch° findet.
Weil er die ganze Nacht bellt.
Weil er eine bessere wollte.
Weil er beißt.
Weil er sie nett findet.

O. ERGÄNZEN SIE DIE DEUTSCHEN SÄTZE!

1. Who are you waiting for?
2. Tell us something about your trip.
3. He's afraid of my dog.
4. Are you laughing about me?
5. What do you know about her?
6. I don't think much of him.
7. Who are you thinking about?
8. Have you fallen in love with him?
9. I'm looking forward to the holidays.

. . . wartest du?
Erzähl uns etwas . . .
Er hat Angst . . .
Lacht ihr . . . ?
Was wissen Sie . . . ?
Ich halte nicht viel . . .
. . . denkst du?
Hast du dich . . . verliebt?
Ich freue mich . . .

10. I'm happy about my good grades.   Ich freue mich . . .
11. Günter's parents got very upset   Günters Eltern . . . sehr aufgeregt.
     about his bad grades.
12. Are you interested in modern   Interessierst du dich . . . ?
     music?
13. Did you work on your essay?   Hast du . . . gearbeitet?
14. Who was Claudia so annoyed with?   . . . hat sich Claudia so geärgert?

KLEINE SITUATIONEN (2). Was paßt wo? Sie hören zwölf kleine Situationen. Ergänzen Sie die Reaktionen auf diese Situationen! Verwenden Sie die passenden Verb-Präposition Kombinationen!

> sich freuen auf *(+ acc.)*   denken an *(+ acc.)*
> warten auf *(+ acc.)*   Angst haben vor *(+ dat.)*

1. Weil ich . . .
2. Jetzt habe ich wieder mal über . . .
3. Weil ich . . .
4. Warum bist du denn so unglücklich, Moritz? . . . nicht . . . ?

> sich ärgern über *(+ acc.)*   halten von
> erzählen von   arbeiten an *(+ dat.)*

5. Ich kann nicht. Ich muß . . .
6. Ich glaube, sie hat . . .
7. Aber Mutti, ich muß meinen Freunden doch . . .
8. Was . . . ?

> sich aufregen über *(+ acc.)*   sich verlieben in *(+ acc.)*
> sich interessieren für *(+ acc.)*   sich freuen über *(+ acc.)*

9. Glaubst du, daß . . . Florian . . . ?
10. Sag mal, Bettina, . . . ?
11. Bettina hat . . . sehr . . .
12. Vater hat . . .

5. ASKING QUESTIONS ABOUT PEOPLE OR THINGS

WO-COMPOUNDS

The interrogative pronouns **wem** and **wen** refer to persons.

Vor wem hast du Angst?   *Who are you afraid of?*
An wen denkst du?   *Who are you thinking of?*

If the object of a preposition is an interrogative pronoun which does *not* refer to a person, German uses a **wo**-compound:

Wovor hast du Angst?   *What are you afraid of?*
Woran denkst du?   *What are you thinking of?*

Note that an **r** is added to **wo** if the preposition begins with a vowel: **woran, worauf, worüber,** etc.

Note (handwritten sign):
WIR SIND UMGEZOGEN!
UNSERE NEUE ADRESSE:
HAUPTSTRASSE 48
WIR FREUEN UNS AUF IHREN BESUCH.
IHRE KREISSPARKASSE

P. AUF WEN WARTEST DU? / WORAUF WARTEST DU?

▶ warten auf *(+ acc.)*

_____ wartest du denn?   _____ mein_ Bruder.

S1: Auf wen wartest du denn?   **S2:** Auf meinen Bruder.

der Anruf

▶ warten auf *(+ acc.)*

_____ wartest du denn?   _____ ein_ Anruf° von Thomas.

S1: Worauf wartest du denn?   **S2:** Auf einen Anruf von Thomas.

der Haarschnitt

1. lachen über *(+ acc.)*
   _____ lacht ihr denn?   _____ dein_ Haarschnitt.°
2. Angst haben vor *(+ dat.)*
   _____ hat Monika so Angst?   _____ d_ Schlußprüfung natürlich.

das Benehmen: *behavior*

3. sich ärgern über *(+ acc.)*
   _____ hat sich Andrea so geärgert?   _____ dein schlecht_ Benehmen.°
4. denken an *(+ acc.)*
   _____ denkst du denn?   _____ mein_ Freund.

die Sammlung: *collection*

5. sich interessieren für *(+ acc.)*
   _____ interessiert sich dein Bruder   _____ sein_ Briefmarkensammlung.°
   am meisten?
6. sich verlieben in *(+ acc.)*
   _____ hat Hans-Georg sich diesmal   _____ mein_ Schwester.
   verliebt?
7. denken an *(+ acc.)*
   _____ denkst du denn?   _____ d_ Party morgen abend.
8. sich aufregen über *(+ acc.)*
   _____ hat sich dein Vater denn so auf-   _____ mein_ Zensuren.
   geregt?

Linz, die Hauptstadt von
Oberösterreich

Q. WIR KLATSCHEN ÜBER° GÜNTER. Erzählen Sie Ihrer Gesprächspartnerin / Ih- *gossip about*
rem Gesprächspartner den neuesten Klatsch über Günter Schlumberger.

▶ Günter wartet auf einen Brief von seiner Freundin in Montreal.

Weißt du, _____ Günter wartet?   _____ denn?

Auf _____.

S1: Weißt du, worauf Günter wartet?   *S2:* Worauf denn?

S1: Auf einen Brief von seiner Freundin
in Montreal.

1. Günter war gestern abend mit deiner Freundin im Kino.
   Weißt du, _____ Günter gestern   _____ denn?
   abend im Kino war?
   Mit _____.

2. Gestern hat Günter wieder mal den ganzen Tag an seinem Motorrad gearbeitet.
   Weißt du, _____ Günter gestern wie-   _____ denn?
   der mal den ganzen Tag gearbeitet
   hat?
   An _____.

3. Für sein Studium interessiert sich Günter am wenigsten.
   Weißt du, _____ sich Günter am   _____ denn?
   wenigsten interessiert?
   Für _____.

4. Auf seine Zensuren freut sich Günter gar nicht.
   Weißt du, _____ sich Günter gar nicht   _____ denn?
   freut?
   Auf _____.

5. Vor der mündlichen Prüfung hat Günter am meisten Angst.
   Weißt du, _____ Günter am meisten   _____ denn?
   Angst hat?
   Vor _____.

6. Seine schlechteste Zensur hat Günter von Professor Weber bekommen.
   Weißt du, _____ Günter seine
   schlechteste Zensur bekommen hat?
   Von _____.

7. Günter hat diesen Ferienjob durch seinen Onkel bekommen.
   Weißt du, _____ Günter diesen   _____ denn?
   Ferienjob bekommen hat?
   Durch _____.

8. Ich weiß das alles von Anita.
   Weißt du, _____ ich das alles weiß?   _____ denn?
   Von _____.

EIN PAAR PERSÖNLICHE FRAGEN

Stellen Sie Ihrer Gesprächspartnerin/Ihrem Gesprächspartner die folgenden Fragen und berichten Sie dann, was Sie herausgefunden haben!

Wofür interessierst du dich?
Hast du manchmal Angst? Wovor oder vor wem? Warum?
Ärgerst du dich manchmal? Worüber oder über wen? Warum?
Von wem hältst du viel oder nicht sehr viel? Warum?

6. TALKING ABOUT THINGS WITHOUT NAMING THEM

DA-COMPOUNDS

Was hast du **gegen Klaus?**	*What do you have **against Klaus?***
Ich habe überhaupt nichts **gegen ihn.**	*I have absolutely nothing **against him.***
Was hast du **gegen meinen Vorschlag?**	*What do you have **against my suggestion?***
Ich habe überhaupt nichts **dagegen.**	*I have absolutely nothing **against it.***

In German, personal pronouns that are objects of prepositions can refer *only* to people. For things or ideas, **da**-compounds must be used. As was the case with the **wo**-compounds, an **r** is added if the preposition begins with a vowel: **daran, darauf, darüber.**

sich beziehen auf: *to refer to*

R. ERGÄNZEN SIE! Entscheiden Sie, ob sich die Fragen Ihrer Gesprächspartnerin/Ihres Gesprächspartners auf Sachen oder Personen beziehen.°

S1:

S2:

1. Wo ist denn mein Kugelschreiber? Ich glaube, Günter schreibt _____.
2. Kommt ihr zu unserer Party? Ja, wir freuen uns schon sehr _____.
3. Schreibst du deinen Eltern oft? Nein, aber ich denke oft _____.
4. Hast du unsere Postkarte bekommen? Ja, ich habe mich sehr _____ gefreut.
5. Was halten Sie von moderner Musik? Ich interessiere mich sehr _____.
6. Ihr werdet doch nicht ohne Ralf wegfahren! Ich glaube, wir haben lange genug _____ gewartet.
7. Warum machst du nicht endlich mal deine Fahrprüfung? Ich habe Angst _____.
8. Sind deine Zensuren so schlecht, weil du so viel vor dem Fernseher sitzt? Aber das hat doch gar nichts _____ zu tun!
9. Wie hat euch die amerikanische Studentin gefallen? Peter hat sich sofort _____ verliebt.
10. Ist Bernds neuer Wagen nicht toll? Na hoffentlich. Er hat auch genug _____ bezahlt.

11. Was haltet ihr von Günters neuem Haarschnitt?

Wir haben uns fast totgelacht _____.

12. Hoffentlich kommt Karsten nicht zu eurer Party!

Nein, er weiß gar nichts _____.

DA-COMPOUND + *DASS*-CLAUSE OR INFINITIVE PHRASE

Ich bin **dagegen, daß** du Günter einlädst.

*I'm against your **inviting** Günter.*

Ich hatte mich so **darauf** gefreut, ihn wieder**zu**sehen.

*I had been looking forward so much to **seeing** him again.*

Sometimes the object of a preposition is a **daß**-clause or an infinitive phrase. Such clauses and phrases are frequently introduced by a **da**-compound. In the English equivalents of these clauses or phrases, the verb often appears in its *-ing* form.

S. EVA MÖCHTE MIT UNS NACH SCHLADMING. Ergänzen Sie die **da**-Formen!

1. MONIKA: Eva möchte mit uns nach Schladming. Seid ihr _____ oder _____, daß sie mitkommt?
2. STEFAN: Du denkst doch nicht im Ernst° _____, sie einzuladen?
3. MONIKA: Aber natürlich. Ich freue mich _____, sie mal wiederzusehen.
4. STEFAN: Eva hat keinen Humor, und sie fängt immer Streit° an. Ich bin ganz und gar° _____, daß wir sie mitnehmen.
5. MONIKA: Und du, Bernd? Was hältst du _____?
6. BERND: Ich glaube, wir sollten _____ denken, daß Eva es momentan nicht leicht hat.
7. MONIKA: Da hast du recht. Sie hat sicher große Angst _____, das ganze Wochenende allein zu sein.
8. BERND: Ich weiß, daß sie sehr _____ wartet, daß wir sie bald zurückrufen.
9. MONIKA: Was sagst du jetzt _____, Stefan?
10. STEFAN: Nun, wenn ihr beide so sehr _____ seid, habe ich auch nichts mehr _____.

seriously

arguments
ganz und gar: *completely*

T. AUF ENGLISCH, BITTE!

1. Ich freue mich gar nicht darauf, wieder zu Hause zu wohnen.
2. Denkt Peter wirklich daran, sich einen Bart wachsen° zu lassen?
3. Meine Eltern sind sehr dafür, daß ich ein Jahr in Deutschland studiere.
4. Als Kind habe ich oft davon geträumt, mal auf einem großen Schiff um die Welt zu reisen.

to grow

Was kostet eine Dauerwelle (*perm*) für Damen? Und für Herren?

Wie kommt man von München nach Schladming?

◨ ZUSAMMENSCHAU

📖 KARRIEREN

careers

Tanja und Dieter sind seit drei Jahren verheiratet. Sie haben beide studiert, haben interessante Berufe, und verdienen auch beide recht gut. Sie sind beide sehr ehrgeizig,° und sie haben hervorragende° Aussichten° auf erfolgreiche° Karrieren.

ambitious / excellent / prospects / successful

Lesen Sie, was Tanja und Dieter über sich selbst zu sagen haben und was für ein Ereignis° zu einem Konflikt zwischen ihnen führt.

event

Tanja

Ich heiße Tanja Schmidt-Müller. Ich bin 28 Jahre alt, bin verheiratet und habe keine Kinder. Ich habe in Hamburg Chemie studiert, und ich bin seit fünf Jahren Vertreterin einer großen pharmazeutischen Firma in Köln. Meine Arbeit gefällt mir sehr, ich bin sehr erfolgreich und verdiene auch gut. Ich habe einen Dienstwagen,° und ich besuche damit Ärzte und Apotheken in und um Köln. Der Leiter° der Verkaufsabteilung° meiner Firma ist sehr zufrieden mit meiner Arbeit. Er ist ein älterer Mann, und ich habe eine sehr gute Chance, in zwei Jahren seine Stellung° zu bekommen.

company car
head
sales division
position

Seit zwei Monaten wohnen mein Mann Dieter und ich in einer schönen und sehr gemütlichen Eigentumswohnung.° Es war sehr schwierig,° diese Wohnung zu finden, und wir waren beide sehr glücklich, als wir endlich einziehen konnten.

condominium apartment /
difficult

Mein Mann und ich sind beide in Köln geboren, und alle unsere Verwandten und Freunde leben in Köln oder in der Nähe von° Köln. Als ich noch in Hamburg studierte, hat es mir dort sehr gut gefallen. Und doch war ich froh,° als ich dann in meiner Heimatstadt Köln eine Stellung fand.

near
happy

Dieter

Ich heiße Dieter Müller. Ich bin 29 Jahre alt, bin verheiratet, aber wir haben noch keine Kinder. Ich bin Ingenieur und arbeite in der Motorenabteilung bei Ford in Köln. Meine Arbeit ist sehr interessant, und ich verdiene auch recht gut. Ich habe aber schon als Student davon geträumt, eines Tages als Motorenkonstrukteur° bei Porsche in Stuttgart zu arbeiten. Ich fahre auch einen Porsche, obwohl ich von meiner Firma einen luxuriösen Ford für viel weniger Geld bekommen kann.

engine designer

Weil ich in meinem Beruf sehr gut bin, hat der Chefkonstrukteur der Motorenabteilung bei Porsche von mir gehört, und ich habe heute mit der Mittagspost einen Brief von ihm bekommen. In diesem Brief bietet° er mir eine Stellung als Motorenkonstrukteur bei Porsche an. Rennwagenmotoren° konstruieren, das habe ich mir schon immer gewünscht! Und außerdem wird mein Gehalt° dort viel höher sein als hier bei Ford.

bietet . . . an: *offers*
racing car engines
salary

Ich habe ein bißchen Angst davor, heute abend mit Tanja über dieses Angebot° zu sprechen, denn ich weiß schon jetzt, daß sie in Köln bleiben will und daß sie viele sehr gute Gründe dafür hat. Natürlich möchte ich trotzdem° nach Stuttgart, denn so eine Chance kommt nur einmal im Leben. Außerdem werde ich dort so gut verdienen, daß Tanja eigentlich gar nicht mehr arbeiten muß. Wir kaufen uns dann bald ein schönes Haus, und irgendwann° wollen wir ja auch mal Kinder haben.

offer

anyway

some time or other

Situation

Es ist Freitag abend, acht Uhr. Tanja war heute seit acht Uhr morgens unterwegs und kommt gerade von der Arbeit. Dieter hat das Abendessen schon fast fertiggekocht — Lammkeule° mit grünen Bohnen,° Tanjas Lieblingsessen — und hat eine gute Flasche Wein entkorkt. Bei Kerzenlicht° beginnen sie dann zu essen, und nach einer Weile erzählt Dieter seiner Frau von dem phantastischen Angebot aus Stuttgart . . .

leg of lamb / beans
candle light

ZUR ORIENTIERUNG UND ZUM ZUSAMMENFASSEN

Zum Abschnitt *Tanja:* Versuchen Sie, sich mit Tanja zu identifizieren, und entscheiden Sie dann, welche drei der folgenden sechs Aussagen für Tanja die wichtigsten sind.

_____ Tanja hat in Hamburg studiert.

_____ Sie arbeitet bei einer großen pharmazeutischen Firma.

_____ Tanja ist in ihrem Beruf sehr erfolgreich.

_____ Sie hat eine gute Chance, in zwei Jahren Abteilungsleiterin zu werden.

_____ In Hamburg hat es Tanja sehr gut gefallen.

_____ Sie war sehr froh, als sie in ihrer Heimatstadt Köln eine Stellung fand.

Zum Abschnitt _Dieter:_ Welche drei der folgenden sechs Tatsachen° können Ihrer   _facts_
Meinung nach zu einem Konflikt zwischen Dieter und Tanja führen?

_____ Dieter ist Ingenieur und arbeitet bei Ford in Köln.

_____ Dieter hat schon als Student davon geträumt, eines Tages als Motorenkonstrukteur bei Porsche zu arbeiten.

_____ Dieter kann von Ford zu einem sehr günstigen Preis einen luxuriösen Wagen bekommen.

_____ Der Chefkonstrukteur von Porsche hat Dieter eine Stellung angeboten.

_____ In Stuttgart will Dieter bald ein schönes Haus kaufen.

_____ Tanja will in Köln bleiben, und sie hat sehr gute Gründe dafür.

Sie hören vierzehn Aussagen zu den Abschnitten _Tanja, Dieter_ und _Situation._ Entscheiden Sie, ob diese Aussagen richtig oder falsch sind!

Hören Sie die Unterhaltung zwischen Tanja und Dieter beim Abendessen!

Beantworten Sie die folgenden Fragen zu der Unterhaltung zwischen Tanja und Dieter!

1. Warum fühlt sich Tanja am Freitag abend wie im siebten Himmel? _Weil Dieter . . ._

2. Warum meint Dieter, daß Tanja es verdient hat, freitags zu einem fertigen Abendessen nach Hause zu kommen? _Weil sie . . ._

3. Warum sagt Tanja: „Ich habe doch erst nächste Woche Geburtstag!" _Weil Dieter . . ._

4. Was findet Dieter so toll? _Daß Tanja . . ._

5. Was findet Tanja so romantisch? _Daß . . ._

6. Warum bietet die Motorenabteilung der Firma Porsche Dieter eine Stellung an? _Weil sie . . ._

7. Warum meint Dieter, daß Tanja in Stuttgart gleich wieder eine Stellung finden wird? _Weil sie . . ._

8. Warum meint Tanja, daß ihre Stellung hier in Köln viel besser ist, als eine neue Stellung in Stuttgart? _Weil sie . . ._

9. Warum meint Dieter, daß Tanja in Stuttgart gar nicht mehr zu arbeiten und Geld zu verdienen braucht? _Weil die Firma Porsche . . ._

10. Was soll Tanja tun, wenn sie nicht mehr arbeitet? _Sie soll . . ._

11. Warum will Tanja nicht aufhören zu arbeiten? _Weil sie . . ._

12. Warum glaubt Dieter, daß sie in Stuttgart nicht wieder zwei Jahre lang eine Wohnung suchen müssen? _Weil er dort so gut verdient, daß . . ._

13. Warum findet Dieter es nicht so schlimm°, wenn sie in Stuttgart wohnen und   _bad_
ihre Eltern und Verwandten in Köln sind? _Weil . . ._

14. Warum will Tanja jetzt nicht mehr über Stuttgart und über Porsche sprechen? _Weil sie . . ._

Bei Porsche in Stuttgart

ROLLENSPIEL: EIN ERNSTER KONFLIKT

Übernehmen Sie mit Ihrer Gesprächspartnerin/Ihrem Gesprächspartner die Rollen von Tanja und Dieter. Tanja ist gerade von der Arbeit nach Hause gekommen und weiß noch nichts von dem Brief aus Stuttgart. Dieter ist in der Küche und macht das Abendessen fertig.

Finden Sie in der Unterhaltung beim Abendessen eine Lösung für Tanjas und Dieters Problem!

Präsentieren Sie Ihren Mitstudenten Ihre Auseinandersetzung und Ihre Lösung!

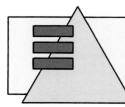

WORT, SINN UND KLANG

WÖRTER UNTER DER LUPE

GIVING LANGUAGE COLOR

Parts of the body are the basis for a wealth of interesting expressions that give color and flavor to a language. In this and the following chapter you will become acquainted with some of these expressions. The ones marked with an asterisk are more colloquial but are by no means slang.

Mir raucht der Kopf!	*I can't think straight anymore.*
Ich habe mir stundenlang den Kopf zerbrochen.°	*I racked my brain for hours.*
Peter hat Köpfchen.*	*Peter is very smart.*
Schläfst du wieder mit offenen Augen?	*Are you daydreaming again?*
Fahr mir doch nicht immer über den Mund!	*Don't always cut me short!*
Holger nimmt immer den Mund so voll!*	*Holger always talks so big!*
Er tanzt seinen Eltern auf der Nase herum.*	*He walks all over his parents.*
Hast du wieder mal die Nase zu tief ins Glas gesteckt?*	*Have you been drinking too much again?*
Ich glaube, der Kerl hat mich übers Ohr gehauen.°*	*I think that guy cheated me.*
Er findet immer ein Haar in der Suppe.	*He always finds something to complain about.*

zerbrechen: *to break*

hauen: *to hit*

WAS PASST ZUSAMMEN?

1. Warum benimmt sich Günter denn so schlecht?
2. Warum sagst du nichts, Eva? Hast du keine Meinung?
3. Was?! Dieser tolle Film hat deiner Schwester nicht gefallen?
4. Ich glaube, ich bin der beste Windsurfer in ganz Bayern.
5. Wie kommst du denn zu einer Eins° in Psychologie?

6. Warum hat Helga nicht gewußt, daß wir heute ein Quiz haben?
7. Warum kriegt Claudia denn immer Einsen für ihre Referate?
8. Warum meinst du denn, daß unsere Tochter keine gute Lehrerin wird?
9. Was schenkst du deinem Vater zum Geburtstag?
10. Wenn mein Vater mir das Geld borgt,° werde ich wohl Bernds alten Wagen kaufen.

Ach, die findet doch immer ein Haar in der Suppe.
Ich habe gelernt, bis mir der Kopf geraucht hat.
Nimm doch den Mund nicht so voll, Peter!
Ich glaube, er hat wieder mal die Nase zu tief ins Glas gesteckt.
Du fährst mir ja doch nur über den Mund, wenn ich etwas sage.   *an A*

Paß nur auf, daß er dich nicht übers Ohr haut.
Ich glaube, sie hat gestern wieder mal mit offenen Augen geschlafen.
Darüber zerbreche ich mir schon seit Tagen den Kopf.
Weil die Schüler ihr alle auf der Nase herumtanzen werden.
Sie hat Köpfchen.

lends

WEITERE NÜTZLICHE WÖRTER UND AUSDRÜCKE

Aus dem Berufsleben

die Firma, die Firmen	firm, company
die Stellung, die Stellungen	job, position
das Gehalt, die Gehälter	salary
die Abteilung, die Abteilungen	department
der Abteilungsleiter, die Abteilungsleiter	department head *(male)*
die Abteilungsleiterin, die Abteilungsleiterinnen	department head *(female)*
der Chef, die Chefs	boss *(male)*
die Chefin, die Chefinnen	boss *(female)*

Bei der Morgentoilette

sich duschen	to shower	**sich an•ziehen, zog sich an, hat sich angezogen**	to dress
sich baden	to bathe		
sich waschen	to wash	**sich aus•ziehen**	to undress
sich kämmen	to comb one's hair	**sich um•ziehen**	to change
sich rasieren	to shave		*(one's clothes)*

Gefühle° ausdrücken

feelings

sich ärgern über (+ acc.)	to be annoyed with
sich auf•regen über (+ acc.)	to get excited about, to get upset about
sich entschuldigen bei	to apologize to
sich freuen auf (+ acc.)	to look forward to
sich freuen über (+ acc.)	to be happy about; to be pleased with
sich interessieren für (+ acc.)	to be interested in
lachen über (+ acc.)	to laugh at, about

Gefühle ausdrücken

sich verlieben in *(+ acc.)*	to fall in love with
sich wundern über *(+ acc.)*	to be surprised about
sich wohl fühlen	to feel well

Denken

denken an *(+ acc.)*	to think of, about (i.e., *to have in mind*)
halten von	to think of, about (i.e., *to have an opinion of*)
wissen von	to know about

Sprechen

sagen	to say
reden	to speak, to talk
diskutieren	to discuss
besprechen (bespricht), besprach, hat besprochen	to discuss
erzählen von	to tell about
sich unterhalten (unterhält sich), unterhielt sich, hat sich unterhalten	to converse
sich unterhalten mit; über *(+ acc.)*	to talk to; about
quatschen	to gab; to talk

Wichtige Verben

arbeiten an *(+ dat.)*	to work on
sich beeilen	to hurry
sich benehmen (benimmt sich), benahm sich, hat sich benommen	to behave
sich erkälten	to catch a cold
sich setzen	to sit down
sich verspäten	to be late, to come late
warten auf *(+ acc.)*	to wait for

Andere wichtige Wörter und Ausdrücke

froh	happy, glad	**in der Nähe von**	near
trotzdem	anyway	**nach einer Weile**	after a while
		eines Tages	some day
		rechtzeitig	on time

Das Gegenteil

die Gesundheit — die Krankheit	health—illness
das Leben — der Tod	life—death
hoch — tief	high—low
schwierig — leicht	difficult — easy
ernst — lustig	serious—funny

WÖRTER IM KONTEXT

1. WAS PASST ZUSAMMEN?

a. Warum hast du dich denn so verspätet?   Weil wir uns nicht verspäten dürfen.

b. Warum soll ich mich denn bei Eva entschuldigen?   Er hat mir von seiner Europareise erzählt.

c. Warum soll ich mich denn so beeilen?
d. Wie hast du dich denn so erkältet?

e. Worüber hast du dich mit David so lange unterhalten?
f. Worüber wunderst du dich denn so?
g. Warum fühle ich mich denn so schlecht?

Weil ich über eine halbe Stunde auf den Bus warten mußte.
Daß du so rechtzeitig angefangen hast, an deinem Referat zu arbeiten.
Weil du dich auf ihrer Party so schlecht benommen hast.
Du wirst dich wohl erkältet haben.
Ich habe mich nicht warm genug angezogen.

2. WAS PASST WO?

besprechen   Gehalt   Stellung   über   Firma   Abteilungsleiterin   freut

a. Tanja hat eine sehr gute _____ bei einer großen pharmazeutischen _____ in Köln.
b. Wenn Tanja _____ wird, bekommt sie fast so viel _____ wie ihr Mann.
c. Dieter _____ sich sehr _____ das Stellenangebot von Porsche.
d. Dieter hat ein bißchen Angst davor, seine Pläne mit Tanja zu _____.

Leben   aufregen   in der Nähe von   über   trotzdem   schwieriges

e. Dieter weiß, daß Tanja sich _____ den Brief aus Stuttgart sehr _____ wird.
f. Das Stellenangebot von Porsche ist ein _____ Problem für die beiden.
g. Dieter möchte _____ nach Stuttgart, denn er denkt, daß so eine Chance nur einmal im _____ kommt.
h. Tanjas und Dieters Verwandte leben alle in Köln oder _____ Köln.

Klöße heißen in Österreich Knödel.

▦ ZUR AUSSPRACHE

GERMAN PF AND KN

In the German consonant cluster *pf* and *kn,* both consonants are pronounced.

- Hören Sie gut zu und wiederholen Sie!

Pfanne	**A**p**f**el	Dam**pf**°	*steam*
Pfennig	im**pf**en°	Ko**pf**	*to vaccinate*
Pfeffer	klo**pf**en°	To**pf**°	*pot*
Pflaume	tro**pf**en°	Kno**pf**	*to drip*
Pfund	Schnu**pf**en°	Strum**pf**°	*a cold / stocking*

1. Nimm diese Tro**pf**en für deinen Schnu**pf**en.
2. A**pf**el**pf**annkuchen mit **Pf**efferminztee? **Pf**ui!

Knast°	**kn**abbern°	**Kn**äckebrot°
Kneipe	**kn**ipsen°	**Kn**oblauch°
Knödel	**kn**utschen°	**Kn**ackwurst

jail / to nibble / crisp bread / to click / garlic to smooch

Herr **Kn**opf sitzt im **Kn**ast und **kn**abbert **Kn**äckebrot.

Fahnenschwingen, eine alte Schweizer Tradition

KAPITEL 13

■ **Kommunikationsziele**

*In **Kapitel 13*** you will learn how to:

use clauses to describe people, places, and things
give definitions
talk about hypothetical events
express regret
negotiate with a salesperson
negotiate a compromise

■ **Lesestück**

San Salvador

■ **Hör- und Sprechsituationen**

Beim Eheberater
Was ist das?
   Berufe und Tiere
   Gebäude und Geräte
Günter Schlumberger kauft einen Wagen
Der Autokauf
Was würdest du tun, wenn du eine Million hättest?
Wenn ich das nur (nicht) getan hätte!
Niemand ist perfekt!
Entlassen!
Ein Kompromiß

■ **Strukturen**

Relative clauses and relative pronouns
Subjunctive II: present time and past time
Würde + *infinitive*
The subjunctive with **als ob**
Modals in past-time subjunctive

■ **Wissenswertes**

Peter Bichsel
Die Schweiz

SAN SALVADOR°
Peter Bichsel

one of the Galapagos Islands off the coast of Ecuador

Die Notiz,° die° ein Mann mit seiner neuen Füllfeder° auf ein Blatt° Papier schreibt, faßt mit wenigen Worten seine ganzen Probleme zusammen.

note / that / fountain pen / sheet

Sie finden unter Zur Orientierung und zum Zusammenfassen *ein paar Fragen zu den zwei Hauptabschnitten dieser Geschichte.*

Er hatte eine Füllfeder gekauft.

Nachdem er mehrmals seine Unterschrift,° dann seine Initialen, seine Adresse, einige Wellenlinien,° dann die Adresse seiner Eltern auf ein Blatt gezeichnet hatte, nahm er einen neuen Bogen,° faltete ihn sorgfältig° und schrieb: „Mir ist es hier zu

5 kalt", dann „ich gehe nach Südamerika", dann hielt° er inne, schraubte° die Kappe auf die Feder, betrachtete° den Bogen und sah, wie die Tinte° eintrocknete und dunkel wurde (in der Papeterie° garantierte man, daß sie schwarz werde°), dann nahm er seine Feder erneut° zur Hand und setzte noch großzügig° seinen Namen darunter.

10 Dann saß er da.

Später räumte° er die Zeitungen vom Tisch, überflog° dabei die Kinoinserate,° dachte an irgend etwas, schob° den Aschenbecher° beiseite, zerriß den Zettel° mit den Wellenlinien, entleerte seine Feder und füllte sie wieder. Für die Kinovorstel-lung° war es jetzt zu spät.

Das Glossar zu dieser Erzählung finden Sie im Anhang.

15 Die Probe° des Kirchenchors dauerte bis neun Uhr, um halb zehn würde Hildegard zurück sein. Er wartete auf Hildegard. Zu all dem° Musik aus dem Radio. Jetzt drehte° er das Radio ab.

Auf dem Tisch, mitten auf dem Tisch, lag nun der gefaltete Bogen, darauf stand in blauschwarzer Schrift° sein Name Paul.

20 „Mir ist es hier zu kalt", stand auch darauf.

Nun würde also Hildegard heimkommen, um halb zehn. Es war jetzt neun Uhr. Sie läse° seine Mitteilung,° erschräke° dabei, glaubte wohl das mit Südamerika nicht, würde dennoch° die Hemden im Kasten° zählen, etwas müßte ja geschehen sein.°

Sie würde in den „Löwen"° telefonieren.

25 Der „Löwen" ist mittwochs geschlossen. Sie würde lächeln° und verzweifeln° und sich damit abfinden,° vielleicht.

Sie würde sich mehrmals die Haare aus dem Gesicht streichen,° mit dem Ringfinger der linken Hand beidseitig der Schläfe° entlangfahren,° dann langsam den Mantel aufknöpfen.

30 Dann saß er da, überlegte,° wem er einen Brief schreiben könnte, las die
Gebrauchsanweisung° für den Füller noch einmal — leicht° nach rechts drehen° —
las auch den französischen Text, verglich° den englischen mit dem deutschen, sah
wieder seinen Zettel, dachte an Palmen, dachte an Hildegard.

Saß da.

35 Und um halb zehn kam Hildegard und fragte: „Schlafen die Kinder?"

Sie strich sich die Haare aus dem Gesicht.

VOM LESEN ZUM SPRECHEN

ZUR ORIENTIERUNG UND ZUM ZUSAMMENFASSEN

1. Hauptabschnitt (Z. 1–14)

VOR DEM LESEN. Stellen° Sie sich vor, Sie hätten sich eine neue Füllfeder gekauft
und wollten sie ausprobieren. Was würden Sie *außer Ihrem Namen* noch damit
schreiben?

Ich würde . . . schreiben.
Dann würde ich . . .

. . .

stellen . . . vor:
imagine

NACH DEM LESEN. Haken° Sie die vier Aussagen ab, die° zu dem Mann mit der
Füllfeder zu passen scheinen!

Ich glaube, der Autor erzählt in diesem Abschnitt von einem Mann, . . .

haken . . . ab: *check /
that*

_____ der° den Winter nicht mag und deshalb nach Südamerika auswandern will.

_____ der sich eine neue Füllfeder gekauft hat, um seiner Freundin einen
Abschiedsbrief° zu schreiben.

_____ der sich eine neue Füllfeder gekauft hat, um seinen Eltern einen
Abschiedsbrief zu schreiben.

_____ der viele Freunde und Bekannte hat.

_____ der glücklich verheiratet ist.

_____ der nicht sehr glücklich ist.

_____ der sehr gelangweilt° ist und deshalb daran denkt, ins Kino zu gehen.

who

farewell letter

bored

2. Hauptabschnitt (Z. 15–Ende)

VOR DEM LESEN. Jeder Mensch hat gewisse° typische Gewohnheiten° und Ge-
sten°. Wenn man sich sehr gut und sehr lange kennt, gehen einem° solche°
Gewohnheiten und Gesten manchmal auf die Nerven. Denken Sie an Ihre Familie,
Freunde und Mitstudenten, und geben Sie ein paar Beispiele von Gewohnheiten
und Gesten, die° Ihnen manchmal auf die Nerven gehen.

certain / habits
*gestures / **einem . . .**
auf die Nerven: *on
one's nerves / such*
which

Lesen Sie jetzt den zweiten Hauptabschnitt von Peter Bichsels Kurzgeschichte. Ach-
ten° Sie auf typische Gewohnheiten und Gesten der beiden Personen.

achten . . . auf: *pay
attention to*

Peter Bichsel was born in 1935 in Lucerne, Switzerland. While he was still an elementary school teacher, he received critical acclaim as a writer with his short story collection *Eigentlich möchte Frau Blum den Milchmann kennenlernen*. "San Salvador" is taken from this collection. Since 1968 he has been able to devote himself fully to his writing, and has established himself as one of Switzerland's leading authors.

Bichsel's stories tell about common people and commonplace situations, and his child-like, repetitive prose is deceptively simple. Many of the stories are marked by an underlying note of sadness and deal with a recurring theme: the increasing isolation, boredom, and loneliness that result from the inability of people to communicate with one another.

NACH DEM LESEN. Beantworten Sie die folgenden Fragen!

predictable / refer to

Im Leben von Paul und Hildegard gibt es keine Überraschungen, und alles ist genau vorhersagbar°. Die folgenden Fragen beziehen sich auf° diese Vorhersagbarkeit und Monotonie.

does expect
actually
mention

1. Um wieviel Uhr erwartet° Paul seine Frau, und um wieviel Uhr kommt sie tatsächlich° nach Hause?
2. Wie oft erwähnt° der Autor diese Uhrzeit?
3. Was für eine Geste ist typisch für Hildegard?
4. Warum weiß Hildegard so genau, wo sie Paul zu suchen hat, wenn er abends nicht zu Hause ist?

common

marriage

Paul und Hildegard scheinen keine gemeinsamen° Interessen zu haben und sich auch nicht für einander zu interessieren. Die folgenden Fragen beziehen sich auf diesen Aspekt ihrer Ehe°.

1. Wie zeigt der Autor, daß Hildegard sich nicht dafür interessiert, was Paul an diesem Abend gemacht hat?
2. Hildegard scheint sich sehr für ihre Kinder zu interessieren. Wie zeigt der Autor, daß die Kinder in Pauls Leben keine sehr wichtige Rolle spielen?
3. Was will Paul mit dem „mir ist es hier zu kalt" eigentlich sagen?

escape

4. Paul will sich aus der Kälte seiner Ehe nach Südamerika retten°. Warum hat der Autor seiner Geschichte den Titel *San Salvador* gegeben? Was bedeutet *San Salvador?*

marriage counselor

ROLLENSPIEL: BEIM EHEBERATER°

married couple

Personen: ein Ehepaar°
eine Eheberaterin/ein Eheberater

Sie sind seit etwa zehn Jahren verheiratet, und finden Ihre Ehe sehr langweilig. Sie und Ihre Frau/Ihr Mann wissen oft nicht, worüber Sie miteinander sprechen sollen, und einige schlechte Gewohnheiten Ihrer Partnerin/Ihres Partners gehen

Ihnen ziemlich auf die Nerven. Sie gehen deshalb zusammen zu einer Eheberaterin/einem Eheberater, erzählen ihr/ihm Ihre Probleme und bitten um Rat.°   *ask for advice*

Ein paar schlechte Gewohnheiten

Meine Frau/Mein Mann:

liest beim Essen immer die Zeitung.
hilft nie bei der Hausarbeit.
tut nichts für die Kinder.
sitzt immer vor dem Fernseher.
telefoniert stundenlang mit ihren Freundinnen/seinen Freunden.
interessiert sich nur für ihre/seine Arbeit, für Sport, schöne Kleider usw.
liegt samstags und sonntags immer den halben Tag im Bett.
. . .

NÜTZLICHE WÖRTER UND AUSDRÜCKE

Nomen

die Füllfeder, die Füllfedern	fountain pen
der Füller, die Füller	fountain pen
die Tinte	ink
die Gebrauchsanweisung, die Gebrauchsanweisungen	instructions, directions
die Schrift, die Handschrift	handwriting
die Unterschrift, die Unterschriften	signature
der Name, des Namens, die Namen	name
das Blatt, die Blätter	sheet of paper; leaf
der Zettel, die Zettel	piece of paper; note
die Notiz, die Notizen	note
das Inserat, die Inserate	ad
der Chor, die Chöre	choir
die Probe, die Proben	rehearsal
die Geste, die Gesten	gesture
die Gewohnheit, die Gewohnheiten	habit
der Aschenbecher, die Aschenbecher	ashtray

Verben

erschrecken (erschrickt), erschrak, ist erschrocken	to be frightened, to be alarmed
erwarten	to expect
falten	to fold
füllen	to fill
lächeln	to smile
überlegen	to think about
vergleichen, verglich, hat verglichen	to compare
zeichnen	to draw

Verben

zerreißen, zerriß, hat zerrissen	to tear up, to rip up
zusammen•fassen	to summarize

Andere Wörter und Ausdrücke

sorgfältig	carefully
mehrmals	several times
irgend etwas	something or other
Das geht mir auf die Nerven.	That gets on my nerves.

Sprachnotizen

Irgend

To express *some . . . or other,* German affixes **irgend** to the beginning of many words:

irgendwo	somewhere or other	**irgendein** Mann	some man or other
irgendwann	sometime or other	**irgendeine** Frau	some woman or other
irgendwie	somehow or other		

With **etwas** and **jemand, irgend** is written as a separate word:

irgend etwas	something or other
irgend jemand	someone or other

WÖRTER IM KONTEXT

WAS PASST WO?

Unterschrift	Blatt	Füller	Gebrauchsanweisung	überlegte
Namen	zeichnete	Tinte		

Peter hatte sich einen neuen ＿＿＿ gekauft. Als er nach Hause kam, las er zuerst sehr sorgfältig die ＿＿＿. Dann füllte er den Füller mit ＿＿＿, nahm ein ＿＿＿ Papier, ＿＿＿ ein paar Wellenlinien und schrieb mehrmals seine ＿＿＿ und den ＿＿＿ seiner Freundin. Dann saß er da und ＿＿＿, was er noch schreiben könnte.

gerettet	Kinoinserate	gelangweilt	Chorprobe	Aschenbecher
Zettel	auf die Nerven	erwartet	erschrak	

Als Sabine aus der ＿＿＿ nach Hause kam, war Jens weg. Auf der Couch lagen die ＿＿＿, und zuerst dachte sie, daß er wohl ins Kino gegangen war. Aber dann sah sie auf dem Tisch unter dem ＿＿＿ einen ＿＿＿ mit der kurzen Mitteilung „Mir ist es hier zu kalt, ich gehe nach Südamerika." Sabine ＿＿＿. Sie wußte, daß sie einander in letzter Zeit oft sehr ＿＿＿ gegangen waren, daß Jens oft sehr ＿＿＿ war und daß auch sonst in ihrer Ehe vieles nicht in Ordnung war. Aber daß Jens plötzlich nach Südamerika gehen würde, das hatte sie nicht ＿＿＿. Sie kannte eine gute Eheberaterin, die schon viele Ehen ＿＿＿ hatte. Aber dazu war es jetzt zu spät.

For the Swiss people, the symbol of freedom and individual rights is their national hero, Wilhelm Tell. The beginnings of the **Confoederatio Helvetica** date back to his act of rebellion and defiance against the Habsburg governor who forced him to shoot an apple from his son's head. A legendary marksman, Tell hit the apple without harming his son, but subsequently shot the governor, thereby initiating the successful alliance in 1291 of the Swiss peasants from the **Kantone** *(provinces)* of **Schwyz, Uri,** and **Unterwalden** against the Habsburgs. It is from the first of these cantons that Switzerland **(die Schweiz)** gets its name. Over the centuries this nucleus of three cantons has grown into a confederation of twenty-six cantons with four official languages: German, French, Italian, and Rhaeto-Romanic.

Since 1515 Switzerland has not participated in foreign wars, and since 1815 it has been internationally recognized as a permanently neutral country. Despite the country's neutrality, the Swiss feel that they should be able to defend their own borders. The Swiss army is a modern, well-equipped force of 620,000 that can be mobilized within 48 hours to protect the country. Switzerland's military strength, combined with a mountainous terrain that serves as a natural fortress, deterred even Hitler from invading the country. Switzerland's permanent neutrality allows it to play a unique role in international politics. Geneva, for example, has long been the headquarters for many international organizations and has also been the neutral site for dialogue between opposing ideologies. The Inter-

Alpenmilch ist besonders gut.

national Red Cross was founded in Geneva, and the League of Red Cross Societies is still based in this city.

The Swiss constitution requires the government to be a "direct democracy", i.e., all important decisions must be reached by popular vote, even matters of foreign policy. Thus the proposal that Switzerland should join the United Nations was put to a vote in 1986 and was rejected by the people. In the area of domestic policy, it is interesting to note that the (male) electorate did not give women the right to vote until 1971. In the canton of Appenzell, the men continue to defy the country's equal rights law by denying women this basic right.

Switzerland is extremely rich in mountains, lakes, and breathtaking scenery, but apart from hydro-electric power, it has no natural resources. It has so little arable land that it has to import a full 40% of its food supply. In order to survive, the Swiss have had to be very inventive. They have built a prosperous food industry on milk, the only product that mountain pastures have enabled them to produce in large quantities. Swiss cheeses, milk chocolate, and baby foods are famous the world over. Switzerland also has a highly developed machine and metal industry that produces everything from enormous diesel engines to watches and other precision instruments, and a research-intensive chemical industry. Add to this a flourishing tourist trade and the world-wide services of the Swiss banking and insurance industries, and it will come as no surprise that Switzerland has one of the highest standards of living in the world.

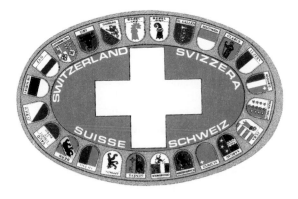

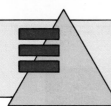

FUNKTIONEN UND FORMEN

1. DESCRIBING PEOPLE, PLACES, AND THINGS

RELATIVE CLAUSES AND RELATIVE PRONOUNS

Like adjectives, relative clauses are used to describe people, places, and things.

	ADJECTIVE	NOUN	
Our	*expensive*	*computer*	has already broken down.

	NOUN	RELATIVE CLAUSE	
The	*computer*	*that cost us so much money*	has already broken down.

Relative clauses are introduced by relative pronouns. The noun to which a relative pronoun refers is called its *antecedent*.

		RELATIVE CLAUSE		
	ANTECEDENT	RELATIVE PRONOUN		
Do you know	*the boy*	*who*	is sitting over there?	
	The sweater	*that*	I bought at Karstadt's	has a hole.
Is	*the girl*	*whom*	I'm supposed to help in math	here yet?
Are those	*the people*	*whose*	dog barks so much at night?	
Show me	*the records*	*that*	you bought yesterday.	

Most forms of the German relative pronoun are identical to those of the definite article.

		RELATIVE CLAUSE		
	ANTECEDENT	RELATIVE PRONOUN		
Kennst du	**den Jungen,**	**der**	dort drüben sitzt?	
	Der Pulli,	**den**	ich bei Karstadt gekauft habe,	hat ein Loch.
Ist	**das Mädchen,**	**dem**	ich in Mathe helfen soll,	schon hier?
Sind das	**die Leute,**	**deren**	Hund nachts so viel bellt?	
Zeig mir	**die Platten,**	**die**	du gestern gekauft hast.	

The gender and number of the antecedent determine whether a relative pronoun is masculine, feminine, or neuter and whether it is singular or plural. The case of the relative pronoun reflects its function within the relative clause.

Der Pulli, **den** ich bei Karstadt gekauft habe, hat ein Loch.

*The sweater **that** I bought at Karstadt's has a hole.*

The relative pronoun **den,** like its antecedent **Pulli,** is masculine and singular. It is in the accusative case because it is the direct object of the verb within the relative clause.

Sind das die Leute, **deren** Hund so viel bellt?	*Are those the people, **whose** dog barks so much?*

The relative pronoun **deren,** like its antecedent **Leute,** is plural. It is in the genitive case because it expresses a possessive relationship between **Leute** and **Hund.**

Because relative clauses are subordinate clauses, they are marked off by commas, and the conjugated verb appears at the end of the clause. In contrast to English, the German relative pronoun can never be omitted:

Der Pulli, **den** ich gekauft habe, hat ein Loch.	*The sweater I bought has a hole.*
Zeig mir die Platten, **die** du gekauft hast.	*Show me the records you bought.*

Forms of the Relative Pronoun			
	Masculine	Feminine	Neuter	Plural
Nominative	der	die	das	die
Accusative	den	die	das	die
Dative	dem	der	dem	**denen**
Genitive	**dessen**	**deren**	**dessen**	**deren**

A. KENNST DU DEN TYP? Ergänzen Sie die Relativpronomen!

1. Kennst du den Typ,° _____ immer bei Tina zu Besuch ist?
2. Kennst du den Typ, _____ wir gestern mit Tina im Kino gesehen haben?
3. Kennst du den Typ, _____ Bild auf Tinas Schreibtisch steht?
4. Kennst du den Typ, _____ sie den schönen Pullover strickt?°

5. Wie heißt die Professorin, _____ Vorlesungen du so interessant findest?
6. Wie heißt die Professorin, _____ so gute Zensuren gibt?
7. Wie heißt die Professorin, _____ du heute nachmittag im Labor° helfen sollst?
8. Wie heißt die Professorin, _____ ihr zu unserer Fete einladen wollt?

9. Wer ist das kleine Mädchen, _____ immer mit unseren Kindern im Garten spielt?
10. Wer ist das kleine Mädchen, _____ Dreirad vor unserer Garage herumsteht?
11. Wer ist das kleine Mädchen, _____ unser Sohn zu seiner Geburtstagsparty einladen will?
12. Wer ist das kleine Mädchen, _____ unser Sohn seinen Hamster zeigt?

13. Die Touristen, _____ aus dem tollen Reisebus dort aussteigen, sind Amerikaner.
14. Die Touristen, _____ Bus dort steht, sind Amerikaner.
15. Die Touristen, _____ ich heute nachmittag das Schloß° zeigen soll, sind Amerikaner.
16. Die Touristen, _____ ich letzten Sommer durch ganz Europa gefahren habe, waren Amerikaner.

der Typ: *guy*

is knitting

lab

Wir laden alle ein, die in den Ferien im Ländle bleiben – radeln Sie mit !

Radfahren im eigenen Land macht Spaß!

castle

B. DEFINITIONEN. Ergänzen Sie die Relativpronomen!

▶ Ein Flaschner ist ein Handwerker *(m),*° . . .

_____ man braucht, wenn das Klo kaputt ist.

Ein Flaschner ist ein Handwerker, den man braucht, wenn das Klo kaputt ist.

---

1. Ein Kabriolett ist ein Auto *(n),* . . .

3. Ein Schreiner ist ein Handwerker, . . .

2. Ein Tausendfüßler ist ein Tier *(n),* . . .

4. Schnecken sind Tiere, . . .

_____ Möbel baut.   _____ Dach° man bei schönem Wetter aufmachen kann.
_____ viele Beine hat.   _____ ihr Haus auf dem Rücken tragen.

5. Ein Staubsauger ist ein elektrischer Apparat *(m),* . . .

8. Hühner sind Tiere, . . .

6. Eine Verkehrsampel ist eine Lampe, . . .

9. Ein Psychiater ist ein Arzt, . . .

7. Ein Hocker ist ein Stuhl *(m),* . . .

_____ keine Lehne° hat.   _____ man alles erzählen kann.   *back*
_____ Eier wir essen.   _____ man zum Putzen braucht.
_____ den Autofahrern zeigt, ob sie fahren dürfen oder warten müssen.

C. KLEINE GESPRÄCHE. Ergänzen Sie die Relativpronomen!

S1:

1. Ist das die Platte, _____ du von Martin gekriegt hast?
2. Ist das der Weißwein, _____ Peter uns empfohlen° hat?
3. Sind das die ausländischen Studenten, _____ wir die Bibliothek zeigen sollen?
4. Ist das das Bücherregal, _____ du selber gebaut hast?
5. Ist das die amerikanische Studentin, _____ du Deutsch beibringen° sollst?
6. Ist das der Mann, _____ das Blumengeschäft in der Gartenstraße gehört?
7. Ist das die Professorin, _____ ihr alle so mögt?
8. Ist das das Nachbarskind, _____ Dreirad du reparieren sollst?
9. Ist das der Pulli, _____ Anita dir gestrickt hat?
10. Sind das die beiden alten Damen, _____ Wohnung wir putzen sollen?

S2:

Nein, das ist die, _____ ich in Berlin gekauft habe.

Nein, das ist der, _____ noch im Kühlschrank war.   *recommended*

Nein, das sind die, _____ sich fürs Studentenheim interessieren.

Nein, das ist das, _____ wir bei Möbel-Maier gekauft haben.

Nein, das ist die, _____ ich in Mathe helfen soll.   *teach*

Nein, das ist der, _____ dort als Verkäufer arbeitet.

Nein, das ist die, _____ uns immer zu viel Hausaufgaben gibt.

Nein, das ist das, _____ ich den Drachen° gebaut habe.   *kite*

Nein, das ist der, _____ ich aus Schweden mitgebracht habe.

Nein, das sind die, _____ wir im Garten helfen müssen.

WAS IST DAS?

Beschreiben Sie mit einem Relativsatz irgendeinen Beruf oder irgendein Tier! Ihre Mitstudenten müssen erraten,° was Sie meinen.   *guess*

S1: Was ist das? Ein Tier, das „muh" sagt, und Milch gibt.   *S2:* Das ist eine Kuh.

S2: Was ist das? Eine Frau, die Zähne repariert.
S3: Was ist das? . . .

S3: Das ist eine Zahnärztin.

S4: . . .

Berufe

ein Student/eine Studentin
ein Professor/eine Professorin
ein Arzt/eine Ärztin
ein Architekt/eine Architektin
ein Automechaniker/eine Automechanikerin
ein Fabrikarbeiter/eine Fabrikarbeiterin
ein Bäcker/eine Bäckerin
. . .

Tiere

ein Fisch
eine Katze
ein Hund
eine Giraffe
ein Nashorn°
ein Huhn°
ein Hase
. . .

rhinoceros
chicken

THE RELATIVE PRONOUN AS OBJECT OF A PREPOSITION

If a relative pronoun is the object of a preposition, its case is determined by that preposition.

Kennst du den Typ, **mit dem** Sabine am Sonntag zum Starnberger See fährt?

*Do you know the guy **with whom** Sabine is going to Lake Starnberg on Sunday?*

Ist das der CD-Spieler, **für den** du nur 250 Mark bezahlt hast?

*Is that the CD player **for which** you paid only 250 marks?*

Relative pronouns never contract with prepositions.

Preposition + definite article:

Meine Großmutter wohnt **im** Seniorenheim in der Panoramastraße.

*My grandmother lives **in the** senior citizens' home on Panorama Street.*

Preposition + relative pronoun:

Das Seniorenheim, **in dem** meine Großmutter wohnt, ist in der Panoramastraße.

*The senior citizens' home **in which** my grandmother lives is on Panorama Street.*

D. DEFINITIONEN. Ergänzen Sie die Relativpronomen!

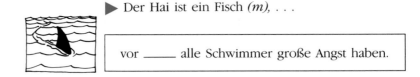

▶ Der Hai ist ein Fisch *(m),* . . .

vor _____ alle Schwimmer große Angst haben.

Der Hai ist ein Fisch, vor dem alle Schwimmer große Angst haben.

1. Ein Lastwagen ist ein Fahrzeug
   (n),° . . .

3. Ein Spiegel ist eine Glasscheibe,° . . .   *sheet of glass*
                                                 vehicle

2. Bienen sind Insekten, . . .

4. Eine Schneiderin ist eine Frau, . . .

---

bei _____ man Kleider machen läßt.   mit _____ man große, schwere Dinge transportieren kann.
von _____ wir Honig bekommen.   in _____ man schaut, wenn man sich selbst sehen will.

---

5. Eine Waage ist ein Gerät (n),° . . .   8. Eine Untertasse ist ein kleiner   *device*
                                              Teller, . . .

6. Schafe sind Tiere, . . .

9. Eine Säge ist ein Werkzeug
   (n),° . . .   *tool*

7. Ein Kinderwagen ist ein Fahrzeug, . . .

---

mit _____ man Bäume fällen kann.   von _____ wir Wolle bekommen.
in _____ man Babys spazierenfährt.   auf _____ man seine Tasse stellt.
   mit _____ man herausfinden kann, wie schwer etwas ist.

E. EIN FERIENJOB IN DER SCHWEIZ. Ergänzen Sie die Relativpronomen!

1. An dem Tag, an _____ ich in Zürich ankam, war es schon sehr schön warm.
2. Der Freund meines Vaters, durch _____ ich den Ferienjob bekommen hatte, holte mich vom Bahnhof ab und brachte mich zu den Leuten, bei _____ ich wohnen sollte.
3. Das Zimmer, in _____ ich bei diesen Leuten einzog, war klein, und das Bett, in _____ ich schlief, war ein bißchen zu kurz für mich.
4. Die Leute hatten zwei nette kleine Söhne, mit _____ ich später an Tagen, an _____ ich nicht arbeiten mußte, oft im Zürichsee schwimmen ging.
5. Die Firma, bei _____ ich arbeitete, machte Roboter, für _____ sie von Autofabriken in Deutschland und in Frankreich viel Geld bekam.
6. Der Meister,° unter _____ ich arbeitete, war ein sehr netter Mann, von _____ ich viel lernte.
7. Er besorgte° mir auch ein tolles Fahrrad, für _____ ich nur hundert Franken bezahlen mußte und auf _____ ich dann im August mit ein paar jungen Arbeitskollegen eine Radtour durch die ganze Schweiz machte.
8. In den Hochalpen lag auf den Pässen, über _____ wir fuhren, oft noch tiefer Schnee.
9. Der höchste Paß, über _____ wir kamen, war der St.° Bernhard.
10. Natürlich besuchten wir hier auch das Kloster° St. Bernhard, aus _____ die bekannten Bernhardinerhunde stammen.°
11. In den Jugendherbergen, in _____ wir übernachteten, trafen wir junge Leute aus aller Welt.
12. Dieser Sommer in der Schweiz war eine Zeit, in _____ ich mehr gesehen und gelernt habe als je zuvor° in meinem Leben.

foreman

got

= Sankt
monastery
originate

ever before

In den Hochalpen lag oft noch tiefer Schnee.

 **WAS IST DAS?**

building

Beschreiben Sie irgendein Gebäude° oder Gerät mit einem Relativsatz! Ihre Mitstudenten müssen erraten, was Sie meinen.

S1: Was ist das? Ein Gebäude, in dem man fast alles kaufen kann.

S2: Das ist ein Kaufhaus.

S2: Was ist das? Ein Gerät, mit dem man Fotos macht.

S3: Das ist eine Kamera.

S3: Was ist das? . . .

S4: . . .

Gebäude	Geräte	
eine Bibliothek	ein Mikroskop	
eine Disco	ein Filmprojektor	
eine Bank	eine Kochplatte	
ein Postamt°	ein Dosenöffner	*post office*
ein Gasthaus	eine Schreibmaschine	
ein Krankenhaus	ein Rasierapparat	
ein Supermarket	ein Telefon	
. . .	. . .	

F. ES IST NICHT ALLES GOLD, WAS GLÄNZT!° Sagen Sie das auf deutsch!   *glitters*

FRAU ZIEGLER:	Just° think, Mrs. Krüger, the used car° we bought last week is already broken.°
HERR ZIEGLER:	Yes, and the dealer° from whom we bought it is sitting in jail.°
FRAU KRÜGER:	Is that the good-looking° young man whose picture was in the paper yesterday?
FRAU ZIEGLER:	Yes. Almost all (the) cars he sold were defective.°
HERR ZIEGLER:	And all the° money he got from his customers is gone.°
FRAU KRÜGER:	I don't understand how a man who looks so good can cheat so much.°
HERR ZIEGLER:	There° you see it again, Mrs. Krüger. All that glitters is not gold! (Flavor with **mal** after *again*.)

**nur / der Gebraucht-
wagen / kaputt**

**der Händler / im
Gefängnis / gut
aussehend**

defekt

all the: **das ganze / weg**

so much: **so**

da

 # ZUSAMMENSCHAU

🔊 GÜNTER SCHLUMBERGER KAUFT EINEN WAGEN

Günter ist beim Autohändler° und möchte sich einen Wagen kaufen. Die drei Gebrauchtwagen, die der Verkäufer ihm zeigt, sind ein Opel und zwei VWs. Lesen Sie bitte zuerst die *Neuen Vokabeln*. Hören Sie dann, was Günter und der Verkäufer miteinander sprechen, und finden Sie für jeden der drei Wagen das Baujahr°, den Kilometerstand° und den Preis heraus.   *car dealer*

year of manufacture / mileage

Neue Vokabeln

der Mittelklassewagen	*medium-sized car*
der Kleinwagen	*compact car*
die Benzinpreise *(pl)*	*price of gas*
in dieser Preislage	*in this price range*
frisch lackiert	*freshly painted*
Hat nur 80 000 drauf.	*The mileage is only 80,000 km.*
aus erster Hand	*one owner*
dreisieben = dreitausendsiebenhundert	
zwoacht = zweitausendachthundert	
geräumig	*roomy*

TÜV?[1]
durch den TÜV sein
probe•fahren
die Probefahrt
sich Zeit lassen

Inspected?
to have passed inspection
to take for a test drive
test drive
to take one's time

Warum verkauft Berkenkamp so viele Gebrauchtwagen?

possibilities

	Baujahr	Kilometerstand	Preis
Opel Kadett			
VW Polo			
VW Golf			

WAS PASST ZUSAMMEN? Bei Nummer 5 gibt es zwei Möglichkeiten°.

1. Der Wagen, den sich Günter zuerst anschaut, — sind alle durch den TÜV.
2. Die Gebrauchtwagen, die dieser Autohändler verkauft, — ist ein VW Polo.
3. Der Wagen, für den sich Günter am meisten interessiert, — kosten alle unter viertausend.
4. Der Wagen, den Günter ein bißchen zu klein findet, — ist ein VW Golf.
5. Die Gebrauchtwagen, die sich Günter anschaut, — ist ein Opel Kadett.

Hören Sie die Unterhaltung zwischen Günter und dem Verkäufer noch einmal, und beantworten Sie dann die folgenden Fragen!

1. Warum kauft Günter keinen Mittelklassewagen?
2. Wieviel Geld möchte Günter für den Wagen ausgeben?
3. Warum sieht der Opel Kadett so gut aus?
4. Finden Sie zwei weitere Dinge, die den Opel Kadett besonders attraktiv machen!

Was für Pluspunkte hat dieser Käfer (beetle)?

---

1. **Technischer Überwachungsverein:** Name of the agency that does periodic safety checks that are mandatory for all motor vehicles in Germany.

5. Warum kauft Günter den Kadett nicht?
6. Warum kauft Günter den Polo nicht?
7. Warum meint der Verkäufer, daß ein Kilometerstand von 120 000 für einen Golf nicht viel ist?

 ## ROLLENSPIEL: DER AUTOKAUF

Sie sind Autoverkäufer, und Ihre Gesprächspartnerin/Ihr Gesprächspartner interessiert sich für einen guten Gebrauchtwagen. Fragen Sie, was sie/er ausgeben möchte, und zeigen Sie ihr/ihm ein paar Wagen in dieser Preislage. Nachdem Ihre Gesprächspartnerin/Ihr Gesprächspartner den richtigen Wagen gefunden hat, schaut sie/er ihn sich ganz genau an und findet ein paar Kleinigkeiten°, die nicht   *little things*
ganz in Ordnung sind (siehe die Liste unten). Natürlich möchte sie/er den Wagen jetzt zu einem günstigeren Preis, und Sie müssen versuchen, trotzdem noch ein paar Mark zu verdienen.

Ein paar Kleinigkeiten, die an einem Gebrauchtwagen oft nicht ganz in Ordnung sind:

Die rechte Tür schließt nicht richtig.	*The right door doesn't close properly.*
Das Handschuhfach schließt nicht richtig.	*The glove compartment doesn't close properly.*
Die Antenne läßt sich nicht ausziehen.	*The antenna can't be pulled out.*
Der linke Scheibenwischer funktioniert nicht.	*The left windshield wiper doesn't work.*
Der Zigarettenanzünder funktioniert nicht.	*The cigarette lighter doesn't function.*
Die Sitze sind voller Flecken.	*The seats are full of stains.*
Im Kofferraum sind ein paar Roststellen.	*There are some rust spots in the trunk.*
Der Reservereifen hat nicht genug Profil.	*The spare time doesn't have enough tread.*
. . .	. . .

2. EXPRESSING THE HYPOTHETICAL

SUBJUNCTIVE II

To express wishful thinking you use verb forms that you would not use if you were talking about facts:

Wishful thinking: If only I *had* a million dollars!
Fact: I *have* only fifty dollars.

The form *had* in the first example is not the simple past but a *subjunctive* form of the verb *to have*. By using subjunctive forms the speaker indicates that what she/he says is *contrary-to-fact* or *hypothetical*.

Expressing the Factual	**Expressing the Hypothetical**
I *have* no time tonight.	If only I *had* time tonight!
Peter *is*n't here.	If only Peter *were* here!
Martin *has* to work tomorrow and he *can't* help us.	If Martin *did*n't have to work tomorrow, he *could* help us.

The subjunctive forms that German uses to express the hypothetical are also very similar to the simple past.

Expressing the Factual	**Expressing the Hypothetical**
Ich **habe** heute abend keine Zeit.	Wenn ich nur heute abend Zeit **hätte!**
Peter **ist** nicht hier.	Wenn Peter nur hier **wäre!**
Martin **muß** morgen arbeiten und **kann** uns nicht helfen.	Wenn Martin morgen nicht arbeiten **müßte, könnte** er uns helfen.

These forms are called *subjunctive II* because they are derived from the *second* principal part of the verb, i.e., the simple past.

The subjunctive II forms of **haben, sein,** and **werden** are umlauted:

Infinitive	Simple Past	Subjunctive II
haben	hatte	hätte
sein	war	wäre
werden	wurde	würde

The subjunctive II forms of those modals that have an umlaut in the infinitive are umlauted:

dürfen	durfte	dürfte
können	konnte	könnte
mögen	mochte	möchte
müssen	mußte	müßte
sollen	sollte	sollte
wollen	wollte	wollte

Of the irregular and mixed verbs, colloquial German commonly uses only the following in subjunctive II. Note that the subjunctive II forms of **kommen** and **wissen** are umlauted.

Infinitive	Simple Past	Subjunctive II
kommen	kam	käme
gehen	ging	ginge
bleiben	blieb	bliebe
wissen	wußte	wüßte

Wenn Claudia nur nicht immer eine halbe Stunde zu spät **käme!**	*If only Claudia **didn't** always **come** half an hour late!*
Wenn Günter nur bald **ginge!**	*If only Günter **would go** soon!*

Wenn ich nur die richtige Antwort **wüßte!**

*If only I **knew** the right answer!*

Wenn meine Uhr nur nicht immer **stehenbliebe!**

*If only my watch **didn't stop** all the time!*

To express the hypothetical with most irregular and mixed verbs and with *all* regular verbs, colloquial German tends to use an alternate form that you will learn on page 439.

In subjunctive II *all* verbs have the following set of personal endings:

Singular	Plural
ich hätt**e**	wir hätt**en**
du hätt**est**	ihr hätt**et**
er/sie/es hätt**e**	sie hätt**en**
Sie hätt**en**	

G. WENN DAS LEBEN NUR NICHT SO KOMPLIZIERT WÄRE! Ergänzen Sie die Konjunktivformen° der passenden Verben!

subjunctive forms

1. Holger hat kein Fahrrad und will deshalb immer mein Fahrrad leihen. Ich mag das gar nicht, aber ich kann nicht nein sagen.

   Wenn Holger nur ein Fahrrad _____!
   Wenn Holger nur nicht immer mein Fahrrad leihen _____!
   Wenn ich nur nein sagen _____!

2. Es ist Winter, und es wird schon um fünf dunkel. Ich habe bis halb sechs Vorlesungen, und muß zu Fuß nach Hause.

   Wenn es nur nicht so früh dunkel _____!
   Wenn ich nur nicht bis halb sechs Vorlesungen _____!
   Wenn ich nur nicht zu Fuß nach Hause _____!

3. Günter ist sehr faul. Er geht nur selten in die Vorlesung und will deshalb immer mein Skript.°

   lecture notes

   Wenn Günter nur nicht so faul _____!
   Wenn er nur öfter in die Vorlesung _____!
   Wenn er nur nicht immer mein Skript _____!

4. Es ist sehr heiß, aber weil ich eine Ohreninfektion habe, darf ich nicht schwimmen gehen.

   Wenn es nur nicht so heiß _____!
   Wenn ich nur keine Ohreninfektion _____!
   Wenn ich nur schwimmen gehen _____!

5. Ich ärgere mich darüber, daß ich morgen eine Prüfung habe, daß ich den ganzen Abend lernen muß und daß ich deshalb nicht auf Davids Party gehen kann.

   Wenn ich nur morgen keine Prüfung _____!
   Wenn ich nur nicht den ganzen Abend lernen _____!
   Wenn ich nur auf Davids Party gehen _____!

6. Es ist sehr kalt, ich habe keinen warmen Wintermantel, muß aber trotzdem in die Vorlesung.

Wenn es nur nicht so kalt ＿＿！
Wenn ich nur einen warmen Wintermantel ＿＿！
Wenn ich nur nicht in die Vorlesung ＿＿！

7. Meine Zimmerkollegin Sabine bleibt immer bis nachts um zwei auf. Ich kann dann oft nicht einschlafen, bekomme nie genug Schlaf und bin deshalb immer sehr müde.

Wenn Sabine nur nicht immer bis nachts um zwei ＿＿！
Wenn sie nur früher ins Bett ＿＿！
Wenn ich nur nicht immer so müde ＿＿！

8. Ich werde in letzter Zeit immer sehr schnell müde. Ich möchte gern wissen, was mit mir los ist, aber ich habe momentan keine Zeit, zum Arzt zu gehen.

Wenn ich nur nicht immer so schnell müde ＿＿！
Wenn ich nur ＿＿, was mit mir los ist!
Wenn ich nur Zeit ＿＿, zum Arzt zu gehen!

9. Ich bin mit meinem Freund Paul im Kino und wir schauen uns einen deutschen Film an. Weil der Film keine englischen Untertitel hat und weil Paul kein Deutsch kann, muß ich ihm immer alles übersetzen.

Wenn der Film nur englische Untertitel ＿＿！
Wenn Paul nur Deutsch ＿＿！
Wenn ich ihm nur nicht immer alles übersetzen ＿＿！

10. Ich darf nicht rauchen, weil der Arzt es mir verboten hat. Meine Zimmerkollegin weiß das, und ich warte deshalb sehr darauf, daß sie endlich in die Vorlesung geht.

Wenn ich nur rauchen ＿＿！
Wenn Julia nur nicht ＿＿, daß der Arzt mir das Rauchen verboten hat.
Wenn sie nur endlich in die Vorlesung ＿＿！

H. UNGLÜCKLICHE LIEBE! Ergänzen Sie die Konjunktivformen der gegebenen Verben!

too bad

Tilmann denkt: Schade,° daß ich Nicoles Telefonnummer nicht weiß!
Wenn ich ihre Nummer ＿＿, ＿＿ ich sie anrufen. (wissen / können)
Wenn sie zu Hause ＿＿, ＿＿ ich sie besuchen. (sein / gehen)
Wenn sie zuviel Hausaufgaben ＿＿, ＿＿ ich ihr helfen. (haben / können)
Wenn wir die Hausaufgaben fertig ＿＿, ＿＿ wir dann zusammen fernsehen und dabei eine Pizza essen. (haben / können)

Nicole denkt: Gott sei Dank, daß Tilmann meine Telefonnummer nicht weiß!
Wenn er meine Nummer ＿＿, ＿＿ er mich anrufen. (wissen / können)
Wenn er mich dann besuchen ＿＿, ＿＿ ich lügen und sagen, ich ＿＿ zuviel Hausaufgaben. (wollen / müssen / haben)
Was ＿＿ ich denn sagen, wenn er mir bei den Hausaufgaben helfen ＿＿? (können / wollen)
Es ＿＿ schrecklich, wenn er mich besuchen ＿＿ und wieder stundenlang ＿＿! (sein / kommen / bleiben)

Würde + infinitive

To express the hypothetical, colloquial German commonly uses the subjunctive II forms for **haben, sein, werden,** the modals, and **wissen.** It frequently also uses subjunctive II forms for the irregular verbs **kommen, gehen,** and **bleiben.** All other verbs tend to appear in a construction that is parallel to English *would + infinitive:* **würde + infinitive.**

Was **würdest** du **tun,** wenn du so schreckliche Kopfschmerzen hättest?

*What **would** you **do** if you had such a terrible headache?*

Ich **würde** sofort den Arzt **anrufen.**

*I **would call** the doctor immediately.*

Was **würdest** du **tun,** wenn du sehr reich wärest?

*What **would** you **do** if you were very rich?*

Ich **würde** eine Weltreise **machen.**

*I **would take** a trip around the world.*

Ich würde sofort Dr. Dobler anrufen.

Singular		Plural	
ich würde	machen	wir	würden machen
du würdest	machen	ihr	würdet machen
er/sie/es würde	machen	sie	würden machen
	Sie würden machen		

I. WENN ES NUR WAHR° WÄRE!

true

▶ du · mir einen Porsche kaufen

S1: Was würdest du tun, wenn du reich wärest?

S2: Ich würde mir einen Porsche kaufen.

1. Claudia · versuchen, den Menschen in der Dritten Welt zu helfen
2. ihr · nach Europa fliegen
3. deine Eltern · eine Weltreise machen
4. Martin · sein Geld gut investieren
5. Anita · ihr ganzes Geld den Armen geben
6. Peter und Stephanie · heiraten und sich ein schönes Haus kaufen
7. Günter · sofort aufhören zu studieren
8. Sie · meinen Eltern eine Villa an der Riviera kaufen

J. UM RAT FRAGEN *(ASKING FOR ADVICE).* Fragen Sie Ihre Gesprächspartnerin/Ihren Gesprächspartner um Rat!

▶ Ich bin immer so nervös.

> . . . weniger Kaffee trinken

S1: Was würdest du tun, wenn du immer so nervös wärest?

S2: Ich würde weniger Kaffee trinken.

1. Ich habe kein Geld mehr.
2. Ich bin immer so müde.
3. Mein neuer Pulli hat ein Loch.
4. Ich will nicht zu Günters Fete gehen.

cough
5. Ich muß immer husten.°

... ihn sofort zurückbringen.   ... mir einen Job suchen.
... das Rauchen aufgeben.   ... mal richtig ausschlafen.
          ... ihm sagen, daß ich ein Referat fertigschreiben muß.

---

6. Ich kann nachts nicht schlafen.
7. Ich weiß Anitas Telefonnummer nicht.
8. Meine Freundin geht mit Günter in die Disco.
9. Ich darf in meinem Zimmer keine laute Musik spielen.
10. Ich kann kein Zimmer finden.
11. Ich muß ein Referat fertigschreiben, und meine Eltern kommen zu Besuch.

---

headphones
tell her off
information

... sie ins Kino schicken.   ... mir ein Paar Kopfhörer° kaufen.
... ihr die Meinung sagen.°   ... eine Schlaftablette nehmen.
... die Auskunft° anrufen.   ... eine Anzeige in die Zeitung setzen.

WAS WÜRDEST DU TUN, WENN DU EINE MILLION DOLLAR HÄTTEST?

Stellen Sie Ihrer Gesprächspartnerin/Ihrem Gesprächspartner diese Frage, und berichten Sie dann Ihren Mitstudenten, was Sie herausgefunden haben!

S1: Was würdest du tun, wenn du eine Million Dollar hättest?

S2: Ich würde meinen Eltern ein Haus kaufen, würde den Rest des Geldes auf die Bank legen und von den Zinsen° leben.

interest

S2: Und du? Was würdest du tun?

S1: Ich würde . . .

SUBJUNCTIVE II: PAST TIME

In past-time factual statements or questions German uses the perfect tense or the simple past tense. In past-time hypothetical statements or questions the verb always appears as a past participle with the auxiliary in subjunctive II. German does not use the **würde**-construction in past-time hypothetical statements and questions.

Expressing the Factual	Expressing the Hypothetical
Es **hat** den ganzen Tag **geregnet.** *It **rained** all day.*	Wenn es nur nicht den ganzen Tag **geregnet hätte!** *If only it **hadn't rained** all day!*
Es **war** kalt, und wir **sind** nicht schwimmen **gegangen.** *It **was** cold and we **didn't go** swimming.*	Wenn es nicht so kalt **gewesen wäre, wären** wir schwimmen **gegangen.** *If it **hadn't been** so cold, we **would have gone** swimming.*
Weil ich heute morgen um acht eine Vorlesung **hatte, bin** ich um sieben **aufgestanden.** *Because I **had** a lecture at eight this morning, I **got up** at seven.*	Wenn ich heute morgen um acht keine Vorlesung **gehabt hätte, wäre** ich nicht schon um sieben **aufgestanden.** *If I **hadn't had** a lecture at eight this morning, I **wouldn't have gotten up** at seven.*

K. WENN ICH NUR NICHT SO BLÖD° GEWESEN WÄRE! Ergänzen Sie die Konjunktivformen der passenden Verben!   *stupid*

1. Statt meine Hausaufgaben zu machen, habe ich bis ein Uhr nachts vor dem Fernseher gesessen und mir einen blöden Film angeschaut.

   Wenn ich nur meine Hausaufgaben _____ _____!
   Wenn ich nur nicht bis ein Uhr nachts vor dem Fernseher _____ _____!
   Wenn ich mir nur diesen blöden Film nicht _____ _____!

2. Statt meiner Schwester einen Geburtstagsbrief zu schreiben, bin ich zu Stefan gegangen und habe die halbe Nacht Karten gespielt.

   Wenn ich nur meiner Schwester _____ _____!
   Wenn ich nur nicht zu Stefan _____ _____!
   Wenn ich nur nicht die halbe Nacht Karten _____ _____!

3. Statt in meine Vorlesungen zu gehen, habe ich Günter angerufen und dann den ganzen Nachmittag mit ihm Billard gespielt.

   Wenn ich nur in meine Vorlesungen _____ _____!
   Wenn ich nur Günter nicht _____ _____!
   Wenn ich nur nicht den ganzen Nachmittag mit ihm Billard _____ _____!

4. Statt mein Referat fertigzuschreiben, habe ich mich auf die Couch gelegt und bin eingeschlafen.

   Wenn ich nur mein Referat _____ _____!
   Wenn ich mich nur nicht auf die Couch _____ _____!
   Wenn ich nur nicht _____ _____!

FERNSEHEN - SONNTAG /

Schweiz

13.50 Ich, Christian Hahn · 5. (von 13)
14.15 Formel-1-Rennen · Großer Preis von Deutschland **16.15** Vogelperspektive Amerika **17.05** Der Fall Eichhörnchen **17.45** Gutenacht-Geschichte **18.00** Die Seidenstraße · 4. (von 6) **18.45** Sport am Wochenende
19.30 Tagesschau/Kultur
20.10 ★ ⑦ **Drei Männer und ein Baby** · Franz. Komödie, 1985 (105 Min.)
Mit Roland Giraud, Michel Boujenah, André Dussollier u.a.
Pierre, Jacques und Michel leben in einer komfortablen Wohngemeinschaft. Eines Tages finden sie ein Kinderkörbchen samt Säugling vor der Tür.
21.55 Tagesschau/Sport
22.15 21. Internat. **Schachfestival in Biel**
23.05 ★ ■□ **Sackgasse**
US-Drama, 1937 (85 Min.)
Mit Humphrey Bogart, Sylvia Sidney, Joel McCrea u.a.
ca. 0.30 Nachtbulletin

5. Statt um sieben aufzustehen und joggen zu gehen, bin ich bis zehn im Bett geblieben.

Wenn ich nur um sieben ____ ____!
Wenn ich nur joggen ____ ____!
Wenn ich nur nicht bis zehn im Bett ____ ____!

thriller

6. Statt rechtzeitig ins Bett zu gehen, bin ich bis zwei Uhr nachts aufgeblieben und habe einen Krimi° gelesen.

Wenn ich nur rechtzeitig ins Bett ____ ____!
Wenn ich nur nicht bis zwei Uhr nachts ____ ____!
Wenn ich nur nicht diesen blöden Krimi ____ ____!

L. WAS HÄTTEST DU GEMACHT?

▶ Jemand hat meinen Wagen gestohlen.

> . . . sofort zur Polizei gegangen.

S1: Was hättest du gemacht, wenn jemand deinen Wagen gestohlen hätte?

S2: Ich wäre sofort zur Polizei gegangen.

1. Meine Freundin ist mit Günter ausgegangen.
2. Professor Huber hat mir so eine schlechte Zensur gegeben.
3. Ich habe in Europa meinen Paß verloren.

gave change

4. Die Verkäuferin hat mir drei Mark zu viel herausgegeben.°

mir ist . . .
ausgegangen: *I ran out of*

5. Mir ist in Europa das Geld ausgegangen.°
6. Meine Verwandten haben mich in Frankfurt nicht abgeholt.

> . . . mit dem Zug nach Stuttgart gefahren.
> . . . sofort zum nächsten Konsulat gegangen.

borrowed money from
told her off
complained

> . . . meine deutschen Verwandten angepumpt.°
> . . . ihr die Meinung gesagt.°
> . . . mich beschwert.°
> . . . sie ihr gleich zurückgegeben.

WENN ICH DAS NUR (NICHT) GETAN HÄTTE!

regrets

Jeder Mensch tut manchmal Dinge, die er später bereut.° Erzählen Sie Ihren Mitstudenten etwas, was Sie bereuen!

S1: Wenn ich nur gestern nacht nicht so lange aufgeblieben wäre!
S2: Wenn ich nur keinen Gebrauchtwagen gekauft hätte!
S3: Wenn ich nur die Konjunktivformen gelernt hätte!
S4: Wenn ich nur . . .

THE SUBJUNCTIVE WITH *ALS OB* OR *ALS*

The conjunction **als ob** (*as if, like*) and its variant **als** introduce clauses that express something hypothetical and they are therefore followed by the subjunctive.

Robert tut immer so, **als ob** er kein Geld **hätte**.

*Robert always acts **as if** he didn't have any money.*

Sabine tut so, **als ob** sie das ganze Wochenende lernen **müßte**.

*Sabine acts **as if** she had to study all weekend.*

When **ob** is omitted, the verb form in the subjunctive follows directly after **als**.

Dieter sieht aus, **als wäre** er gerade **aufgestanden**.

*Dieter looks **like** he just got up.*

M. WAS IST DENN BEI ZIEGLERS LOS? Übernehmen Sie mit Ihrer Gesprächspartnerin/Ihrem Gesprächspartner die Rollen von Uwe, Helga und Herrn und Frau Ziegler! Ergänzen Sie in den Fragen die Verbformen **hätte, wäre, könnte, müßte** oder **wüßte**.

▶ *HELGA:* Warum tut Uwe so, als _____ er keinen Hunger?

MUTTER: Weil . . .

> Er mag keine Brokkoli.

HELGA: Warum tut Uwe so, als hätte er keinen Hunger?

MUTTER: Weil er keine Brokkoli mag.

1. Helga: Warum tut Uwe so, als ob er die halbe Nacht lernen _____?

   Mutter: Weil . . .

2. Uwe: Warum tut Helga so, als ob sie schwer krank _____?

   Mutter: Weil . . .

3. Uwe: Warum tut Helga so, als _____ sie plötzlich wieder ganz gesund?

   Vater: Weil . . .

4. Mutter: Warum tut Uwe denn so, als ob er von dem zerbrochenen° Fenster bei Krügers nichts _____?

   Vater: Weil . . .

   broken

5. Helga: Warum tut Vati so, als ob er schreckliche Kopfschmerzen _____?

   Mutter: Weil . . .

6. Helga: Warum tut Mutti so, als ob sie plötzlich keine Zahnschmerzen mehr _____?

   Vater: Weil . . .

7. Helga: Warum tut Uwe so, als _____ er kaum gehen?°

   Mutter: Weil . . .

   walk

> Sie will mit ihrem Freund in ein Rockkonzert.
> Wir sind heute abend bei Krügers eingeladen.
> Er will nicht beim Abwaschen° helfen.
> Sie will nicht in die Schule.
> Er will nicht dafür bezahlen.
> Sie will nicht zum Zahnarzt.
> Er will Vati nicht im Garten helfen.

with the dishes

MODAL VERBS IN THE PAST-TIME SUBJUNCTIVE

The German equivalent of the mouthful of English verbs in the following sentence is quite simple:

Wenn sie nicht auf der Intensivstation gewesen wäre, **hätten** wir sie **besuchen dürfen.**

If she hadn't been in intensive care, we ***would have been permitted to visit*** *her.*

The pattern is **hätte** + *double infinitive.* Note that the infinitive of the modal follows the infinitive of the main verb. This pattern is standard for all past-time hypothetical sentences that contain modal verbs:

Ich **hätte** das nicht **bezahlen können.**

*I **wouldn't have been able to pay** for that. (I **couldn't have paid** for that.)*

Ich **hätte** das nicht **bezahlen mögen.**

*I **wouldn't have liked to pay** for that.*

Wir **hätten** zu viel **bezahlen müssen.**

*We **would have had to pay** too much.*

Ich **hätte** das nicht **bezahlen wollen.**

*I **wouldn't have wanted to pay** for that.*

Sie **hätten** ihn nicht so gut **bezahlen sollen.**

*You **shouldn't have paid** him so well.*

N. AUF ENGLISCH, BITTE!

1. Ich hätte den Kerl nicht heiraten wollen.
2. Sie hätte den Kerl nicht heiraten sollen.
3. Ich hätte das nicht essen mögen.
4. Wir hätten dir helfen können.
5. Wenn du kein Fieber gehabt hättest, hättest du aufstehen dürfen.
6. Wenn du kein Fieber gehabt hättest, hättest du nicht im Bett bleiben müssen.

O. WAS PASST ZUSAMMEN?

1. Wenn ich bessere Zensuren gehabt hätte,
2. Wenn ich Evas Telefonnummer gehabt hätte,
3. Wenn ich mich heute so schlecht gefühlt hätte wie gestern,
4. Wenn ich Onkel Bernhards Adresse gehabt hätte,

hätte ich bei ihm übernachten können.

hätte ich ein Jahr in der Schweiz studieren dürfen.

hätte ich sie anrufen können.

hätte ich die Prüfung nicht schreiben wollen.

5. Wenn deine Mutter immer mit dir Deutsch gesprochen hätte,
6. Wenn du kein Fieber gehabt hättest,
7. Wenn du den Wagen vor einem Jahr gekauft hättest,
8. Wenn du nicht so spät aufgestanden wärest,

hättest du nicht ohne Frühstück aus dem Haus rennen müssen.

hättest du keinen Deutschkurs zu nehmen brauchen.

hättest du nicht im Bett bleiben müssen.

hättest du tausend Mark weniger dafür bezahlen müssen.

9. Wenn Claudia gestern nicht so spät ins Bett gegangen wäre,

hätte sie die Prüfung nicht zu schreiben brauchen.

10. Wenn Claudia das Loch in ihrem Pulli erst viel später gesehen hätte,

hätte sie heute viel besser denken können.

11. Wenn Claudia ein Referat geschrieben hätte,

hätte sie nicht in Deutschland studieren wollen.

12. Wenn Stephanie nicht schon in Amerika so gut Deutsch gelernt hätte,

hätte sie ihn nicht zurückbringen dürfen.

P. REAKTIONEN. Lesen Sie die folgenden Situationen, und ergänzen Sie dann **hätt-** und doppelte Infinitive!

1. Nicole ist fünfzehn, und wenn sie manchmal erst nach Mitternacht nach Hause kommt, sagen ihre Eltern kein Wort.

   Nicoles neunzehnjährige Schwester Silke denkt: „Ich ＿＿＿ mit fünfzehn nicht so spät nach Haus ＿＿＿ ＿＿＿.“

2. Eva hat kurz vor ihrer Amerikareise eine Kamera gekauft und, ohne sie vorher auszuprobieren, in Amerika Hunderte von Fotos damit gemacht. Zu Hause in Zürich bringt sie die Filme dann ins Fotogeschäft. Als sie sie wieder abholen will, sagt der Verkäufer: „Ihre Filme sind leider alle total überbelichtet.“° *overexposed*

   Als Eva mit ihren überbelichteten Filmen nach Hause kommt, sagt ihr Vater: „Du ＿＿＿ die Kamera natürlich vor deiner Amerikareise ＿＿＿ ＿＿＿, Eva.“

3. Sylvia hat das winzige° Häuschen gesehen, in dem ihre Eltern in den ersten Jahren ihrer Ehe lebten. *tiny*

   Sylvia denkt: „In so einem winzigen Häuschen ＿＿＿ ich nicht ＿＿＿ ＿＿＿.“

4. Weil Bernd zu spät aufgestanden ist, fährt ihm der Bus vor der Nase weg. Das Taxi, das er nimmt, um rechtzeitig in die Vorlesung zu kommen, kostet so viel, daß er später von Stefan fünf Mark leihen muß, um in der Cafeteria frühstücken zu können.

   Bernd denkt: „Wenn ich ein paar Minuten früher aufgestanden wäre, ＿＿＿ ich ＿＿＿ ＿＿＿, ohne mir von Stefan fünf Mark zu leihen.“

5. Christa zeigt ihren Eltern Fotos von einer Reise durch Südamerika. Eines der Fotos zeigt ein ziemlich elendes Hotel, in dem Christa übernachtet hat.

   Ihre Mutter denkt: „Hier ＿＿＿ ich nicht ＿＿＿ ＿＿＿.“

6. Nina war sehr krank, ist aber gestern aufgestanden, um eine wichtige Prüfung zu schreiben. Das Resultat ist, daß es ihr heute wieder viel schlechter geht.

   Ihre Zimmerkollegin sagt: „Du ＿＿＿ noch ein paar Tage länger im Bett ＿＿＿ ＿＿＿, Nina.“

7. Bergers machen eine Kanadareise. Sie haben Quebec gesehen und wollen zum Schluß noch Freunde in Vancouver besuchen. Weil sie nicht wissen, wie groß Kanada eigentlich ist, fliegen sie nicht, sondern fahren mit dem Zug.

   In Winnipeg sagt Frau Berger zu ihrem Mann: „Du, Oskar, vielleicht ＿＿＿ wir doch lieber ＿＿＿ ＿＿＿.“

8. Nadine möchte gern auf Barbaras Party, aber weil ihre ältere Schwester beim Abendessen erzählt hat, daß Günter Schlumberger auch dort sein wird, haben ihre Eltern sie nicht gehen lassen.

Nadine sagt zu ihrer Schwester: „Wenn du nicht gesagt hättest, daß Günter dort sein wird, ـــــ ich bestimmt ـــــ ـــــ .“

9. Gerhard wohnt schon lange nicht mehr zu Hause. Heute abend ist Tante Emma bei seinen Eltern zu Besuch, und obwohl seine Mutter weiß, daß Gerhard die Tante nicht mag, hat sie ihn auch zum Abendessen eingeladen. Als seine Mutter ihm die Tür aufmacht und keinen Wagen sieht, fragt sie: „Warum kommst du denn heute zu Fuß, Gerhard?“

Gerhard antwortet: "Wenn ich mit dem Wagen gekommen wäre, ـــــ ich sicher Tante Emma nach Hause ـــــ ـــــ .“

NIEMAND IST PERFEKT!

Was hätten Sie heute oder in den vergangenen Tagen alles tun oder nicht tun sollen? Erzählen Sie es Ihren Mitstudenten! Seien Sie ehrlich!°

honest

S1: Ich hätte die Konjunktivformen besser lernen sollen!
S2: Ich hätte gestern abend nicht so lange vor dem Fernseher hocken° sollen!
S3: Ich hätte . . . sollen!

hocken: *to sit*

 ZUSAMMENSCHAU

 ENTLASSEN!°

fired

Frau Schmidt ist die Besitzerin eines Möbelgeschäfts in der Ritterstraße in Köln. In den vergangenen Jahren ging das Geschäft sehr gut, und als im Herbst 1983 ihr alter Buchhalter in den Ruhestand trat,° stellte° Frau Schmidt noch im gleichen° Jahr zwei neue Buchhalter ein: den jung° verheirateten Stefan Wendel und Brigitte Schneider, eine alleinstehende° Enddreißigerin.° Die beiden verstehen° sich sehr gut und arbeiten gut zusammen, und Frau Schmidt ist mit beiden gleich° zufrieden.

*retired / **stellte . . . ein:** hired / same / recently*

*single / woman in her late thirties / **verstehen sich . . . gut:** get along / equally*

Brigitte versteht sich auch mit Stefans Frau sehr gut, und sie ist oft bei Wendels eingeladen. Nina Wendel, die früher einmal Krankenschwester in der Kölner Universitätsklinik war, hat dort nach dem ersten Kind noch halbtags gearbeitet und ist nach dem zweiten dann ganz zu Hause geblieben. Inzwischen° hat Nina drei kleine Kinder, und sie wäre manchmal recht froh, wenn sie nicht immer den ganzen Tag mit ihnen zusammen sein müßte. Sie freut sich deshalb immer sehr, wenn Brigitte zu Besuch kommt und mit den Kindern spielt.

in the meantime

Im vergangenen Frühjahr hat in der Ritterstraße ein zweites Möbelgeschäft aufgemacht, und die Firma Schmidt hat viele Kunden verloren. Frau Schmidt, die ein sehr freundschaftliches Verhältnis° zu ihren Angestellten° hat, möchte am liebsten

relationship / employees

niemand entlassen. Aber die Firma verliert inzwischen so viel Geld, daß Frau Schmidt gestern doch mehrere° Entlassungsbriefe schreiben mußte, einen davon an Brigitte. Das war keine leichte° Entscheidung,° und Frau Schmidt erwartet, daß Brigitte heute gleich° zu ihr ins Büro kommt, denn Frauen betrachten° solche° Entscheidungen heutzutage oft als diskriminierend.

several

easy / decision

right away / regard / such

Sie hören zwölf Aussagen zu *Entlassen!* Entscheiden Sie, ob diese Aussagen richtig oder falsch sind.

Hören Sie jetzt die Auseinandersetzung zwischen Brigitte und Frau Schmidt. In welcher Reihenfolge° hören Sie die folgenden Aussagen und Fragen, und wer ist die Sprecherin?

sequence

	Reihenfolge	Sprecherin
Ich möchte ja gar nicht, daß Sie ihn entlassen.	_____	_____
Das ist kein Argument mehr? Eine Frau und drei kleine Kinder sind kein Argument mehr?	_____	_____
Ja, und ich habe mich sehr darüber aufgeregt.	_____	_____
Sie sind beide gleich gut, und Sie haben auch beide im gleichen Jahr bei mir angefangen.	_____	_____
Eine andere Lösung? An was für eine andere Lösung denken Sie denn?	_____	_____
Wie können Sie als Frau so etwas tun?	_____	_____

Hören Sie die Auseinandersetzung zwischen Brigitte und Frau Schmidt noch einmal, und beantworten Sie die folgenden Fragen!

1. Warum muß Frau Schmidt einen von ihren beiden Buchhaltern entlassen?
2. Warum will Frau Schmidt nicht Stefan entlassen, sondern Brigitte?
3. Was denkt Brigitte, warum Frau Schmidt sie entlassen will?
4. Wer ist der bessere Buchhalter, Brigitte oder Stefan?
5. Warum kann Nina Wendel viel leichter Arbeit finden als Brigitte?
6. Warum will Brigitte mit Stefan und Nina sprechen?

ROLLENSPIEL: EIN KOMPROMISS

Personen: Brigitte, Nina, Stefan

Brigitte hat Nina und Stefan zum Abendessen eingeladen (natürlich ohne die Kinder). Die beiden wissen noch nichts von dem Entlassungsbrief, den Brigitte heute morgen bekommen hat, und von Brigittes Gespräch mit Frau Schmidt. Nachdem Brigitte ihnen alles erzählt hat, versuchen sie zu dritt, eine gerechtere° Lösung zu finden.

fairer

Präsentieren Sie Ihren Mitstudenten Ihr Gespräch und Ihre Lösung!

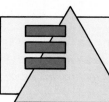

WORT, SINN UND KLANG

1. WORDS AS CHAMELEONS: *GLEICH*

Gleich has a variety of meanings:

a. As an adjective, **gleich** means *same*.

Monika und ich sind im **gleichen** Jahr geboren.	*Monika and I were born in the **same** year.*

b. As an adverb, **gleich** has three meanings:
  1. Expressing the idea of sameness, **gleich** means *equally*.

Monika und ich sind beide **gleich** intelligent.	*Monika and I are both **equally** intelligent.*

  2. Expressing time, **gleich** means *right (away), immediately*.

Ich komme **gleich** nach dem Essen.	*I'm coming **right** after lunch.*
Ich komme **gleich.**	*I'm coming **right away (immediately).***

  3. Expressing location, **gleich** means *right, directly*.

Die Aktentasche steht **gleich** neben dem Schreibtisch.	*The briefcase is **right** beside the desk.*

- What is the correct English equivalent of **gleich** in each of the sentences below: *same, equally, right (right away), right (directly)*?

  1. Wo ist der Tennisplatz?
     Gleich hinter dem Studentenheim.
  2. Die Schuhe waren so schön und so billig, daß ich gleich zwei Paar gekauft habe.
  3. Du hast ja genau das gleiche Kleid wie ich.
  4. Ich wohne gleich neben der Bäckerei Biehlmaier.
  5. Steh gleich auf, Holger! Es ist schon zehn nach zehn.
  6. Wer spielt besser Klavier, du oder deine Schwester?
     Wir spielen etwa gleich gut.
  7. Meine Freundin hat für den gleichen Pulli zwanzig Mark mehr bezahlt als ich.
  8. Wann wollen Sie das Geld?
     Gleich jetzt!

9. Sind die beiden Hotels gleich teuer?

10. Mach doch nicht immer die gleichen Fehler!° *mistake*

2. GIVING LANGUAGE COLOR

There are so many expressions based on the names of the parts of the body, that another sampling is added here. To help you develop your skill in using a dictionary, the expressions are given as they would be listed there: the verbs are given in their infinitive form and the pronouns **jemanden** or **jemandem** (often abbreviated to **jdn** or **jdm** in dictionaries) indicate whether the expression contains an accusative or dative object.[1]

The expressions marked with an asterisk are a bit more colloquial.

unter vier Augen	*in private*
Hals über Kopf abreisen	*to leave in a terrible rush*
Hals- und Beinbruch!*	*Good luck!*
jemanden auf den Arm nehmen*	*to pull someone's leg*
für jemanden die Hand ins Feuer legen	*to vouch for someone*
die Hände in den Schoß° legen	*to sit back and do nothing* *lap*
weder Hand noch Fuß haben	*to make no sense*
lange Finger machen*	*to steal, to pilfer*
jemandem ein Loch in den Bauch fragen*	*to pester the living daylights out of someone (with questions)*
jemandem Beine machen*	*to make someone get a move on*
mit dem linken Bein zuerst aufstehen*	*to get out of bed on the wrong side*
auf großem Fuß leben	*to live in luxury*

WAS PASST ZUSAMMEN?

1. Warum haben Sie mir denn so eine schlechte Zensur gegeben, Professor Seidlmeyer?

   Dann paß nur auf, daß die Kinder dir kein Loch in den Bauch fragen.

2. Was will denn der Polizist bei unseren Nachbarn?

   Aber natürlich. Für den lege ich die Hand ins Feuer.

3. Weißt du schon, daß Martin eine Million gewonnen hat?

   Ihr Ältester wird wohl wieder lange Finger gemacht haben.

4. Heute abend gehe ich zum erstenmal bei Müllers babysitten.

   Er wird wohl mit dem linken Bein zuerst aufgestanden sein.

5. Ist dieser Mann ein guter Arbeiter?

   Ich glaube, du nimmst mich auf den Arm.

6. Warum ist Holger denn so schlecht gelaunt?°

   Weil Ihre Argumente weder Hand noch Fuß haben.   *in a bad mood*

7. Wo ist denn Herr Ziegler?

   Ja, aber nur unter vier Augen.

8. Ich muß jetzt zu meinem Examen.

   Der ist heute morgen Hals über Kopf nach Bonn zurückgefahren.

9. Was machst du in den Semesterferien?

   Ja, dann geh doch mal, und mach ihr Beine!

---

1. In spoken German, the pronoun **jemand** is increasingly used without case endings.

10. Warum haben Bergers denn bankrott gemacht?

11. Erzählst du mir, worüber ihr gestern Abend gesprochen habt?

12. Sabine sitzt immer noch beim Frühstück.

Zuerst werde ich mal eine Woche lang die Hände in den Schoß legen, und dann suche ich mir einen guten Job. Na, dann tschüs, und Hals- und Beinbruch!

Weil sie seit Jahren auf zu großem Fuß gelebt haben.

WEITERE NÜTZLICHE WÖRTER UND AUSDRÜCKE

Fahrzeuge

das Fahrzeug, die Fahrzeuge	vehicle
der Lastwagen, die Lastwagen	truck
der Personenwagen, die Personenwagen	passenger car
der Kleinwagen, die Kleinwagen	compact car
das Kabriolett, die Kabrioletts	convertible (*car*)
der Gebrauchtwagen, die Gebrauchtwagen	used car
aus erster Hand	one owner
das Baujahr, die Baujahre	year (*of manufacture*)
die Bremse, die Bremsen	brake
der Reifen, die Reifen	tire
der Scheibenwischer, die Scheibenwischer	windshield wiper
das Handschuhfach	glove compartment
das Benzin	gas
ein•steigen — aus•steigen	to get in—to get out

Im Geschäft

das Geschäft, die Geschäfte	business; store
der Besitzer, die Besitzer	owner (*male*)
die Besitzerin, die Besitzerinnen	owner (*female*)
der (die) Angestellte, die Angestellten	employee
sich gut verstehen	to get along well
ein•stellen — entlassen	to hire—to fire
halbtags — ganztags	part-time—full-time

Ehe

die Hochzeit, die Hochzeiten	wedding
die Ehe, die Ehen	marriage
das Ehepaar, die Ehepaare	married couple
der Eheberater, die Eheberater	marriage counselor (*male*)
die Eheberaterin, die Eheberaterinnen	marriage counselor (*female*)

Das Gegenteil

verheiratet — alleinstehend	married—single
früher — heutzutage	in the past—nowadays
verlieren — finden	to lose—to find

WÖRTER IM KONTEXT

WAS PASST WO?

Lastwagen	Bremsen	Gebrauchtwagen	Eheberaterin
Angestellte	Kabriolett		

1. Eine Frau, deren Beruf es ist, Ehepaaren zu helfen, ihre Probleme zu lösen, ist eine _____.
2. Leute, die für den Besitzer eines Geschäfts arbeiten, heißt man _____.
3. Die Teile eines Fahrzeugs, mit denen man es zum Halten bringt, heißen _____.
4. Ein Fahrzeug, mit dem man schwere Dinge transportiert, heißt man einen _____.
5. Ein Auto, dessen Dach man bei schönem Wetter aufmachen kann, heißt man ein _____.
6. Einen Wagen, der nicht mehr seinem ersten Besitzer gehört, heißt man einen _____.

> alleinstehend   aus erster Hand   einstellen   Baujahr
> entlassen   Ehepaar

7. Das Jahr, in dem eine Autofabrik einen Wagen gebaut hat, ist das _____ dieses Wagens.
8. Ein Mensch, der nicht verheiratet ist, ist _____.
9. Ein Mann und eine Frau, die verheiratet sind, sind ein _____.
10. Ein Gebrauchtwagen, der nur einen Besitzer gehabt hat, ist ein Gebrauchtwagen _____.
11. Der Besitzer eines Geschäfts, das Kunden verliert, muß oft Angestellte _____.
12. Der Besitzer eines Geschäfts, das viele neue Kunden hat, muß oft mehr Angestellte _____.

▮ 📼 ZUR AUSSPRACHE

THE GLOTTAL STOP

In order to distinguish *an ice boat* from *a nice boat* in pronunciation, you must use a glottal stop, i.e., you must momentarily close and then reopen the vocal chords before saying the word *ice*. The glottal stop is used much more frequently in German than in English. It occurs before words and syllables that begin with a vowel.

- Hören Sie gut zu und wiederholen Sie!

  1. Onkel •Alfred •ist •ein •alter •Esel!
  2. Tante •Emma will •uns •alle •ent•erben!°   *disinherit*
  3. Be•eilt •euch! •Eßt •eure •Erbsen° •auf!   *peas*
  4. Lebt •ihr •in •Ober•ammergau •oder •in •Unter•ammergau?

Das Ende des kalten Krieges

KAPITEL 14

■ **Kommunikationsziele**

*In **Kapitel 14** you will learn how to:*
focus on the receiver of an action
focus on an activity as such
report what someone else has said
deal with some challenges of literary and scientific
  prose

■ **Lesestücke**

Forgive me!
Geschichte ohne Moral

■ **Hör- und Sprechsituationen**

Zum Thema Krieg
Gute Vorsätze fürs Neue Jahr
Was alles noch getan werden muß
Wie gut ist Ihr Gedächtnis?
Spekulationen
Reaktionen

■ **Strukturen**

The passive voice
Other ways of focusing on the receiver of an action
Indirect quotation
Extended participial modifiers

■ **Wissenswertes**

Hans Bender
The division and reunification of Germany
The GDR: Forty years of Marxist socialism
Alfred Polgar

VORSCHAU

FORGIVE ME!
von Hans Bender

Diese Geschichte spielt am Ende des Zweiten Weltkriegs, und der Autor erzählt sie aus der Perspektive einer fiktiven° Erzählerin, die damals vierzehn Jahre alt war.   *fictitious*

Auf Seite 456 finden Sie unter Zur Orientierung *und zum* Zusammenfassen *ein paar Fragen zu den drei Hauptabschnitten dieser Geschichte.*

Herr Studienrat° Runge sagte mit einschläfernder Stimme: „Forgive me" ist ein starker Ausdruck. Der Engländer gebraucht ihn eigentlich nur Gott gegenüber,° im Gebet,° in der höchsten Gefühlsaufwallung.° Ihr werdet ihn selten hören, selten gebrauchen. Häufiger° kommen vor „excuse me" und „sorry", ja vor allem „sorry".
5 „Sorry" könnt ihr bei jeder Entschuldigung anwenden.° Wenn ihr an jemandem vorbeigehen° wollt, wenn ihr jemandem auf den Fuß getreten° seid, sagt „I'm sorry" . . .

Ich war vierzehn Jahre alt. Ich saß in der letzten Bank° und war nicht besonders aufmerksam.° Vor mir auf der polierten° Platte° lag ein blaues Oktavheftchen,° in
10 das ich die neuen Wörter eintragen° sollte. Doch ich malte rechts und links von meinem Namen eine Blume. Unter dem Oktavheftchen lag ein Spiegel,° in den ich ab und zu sah. Ich sah gern in den Spiegel, zupfte° an meinen Haaren vor der Stirne und schnitt° Gesichter. Ich wollte nämlich Schauspielerin° werden. Auf dem Heimweg überholten° mich, drei Jungen von der Parallelklasse, Walter, Horst und
15 Siegbert. Siegbert sagte: „Da geht die Brigitte Horney!"° Die anderen lachten.—Was hatte nur dieser Siegbert gegen mich? Er reizte,° neckte° mich, blies die Backen auf,° ich aber freute mich, wenn ich ihn sah . . .

Es war Anfang April. Der Krieg ging dem Ende zu. Von Vater kamen keine Briefe mehr. Mutter saß am Abend ohne Worte an meinem Bett.

20 Einige Tage später wurden° wir aus der Schule nach Hause geschickt. Um die Mittagszeit surrten° amerikanische Tiefflieger° über die Dächer. In der Nacht fuhren Lastwagen mit SS-Leuten[1] der Rheinbrücke zu,° und die Fenster schütterten° vom Gedröhn° der Front. Dann drängten° sich Autos, Pferdewagen und Panzer° durch die Straßen, über die Trottoirs,° Infanteristen zogen zurück, in Gruppen, vereinzelt,° abgerissen,° verwundet.

Unsere kleine Stadt wurde aufgewühlt° von Angst, Unruhe,° Ungewißheit° und der Erwartung,° daß alles zu Ende sei. Beck, ein fanatischer Anhänger Hitlers, bewaffnete° junge Leute und alte Leute. Er verteilte° Gewehre° und Panzerfäuste,° er ließ Sperren° errichten,° Gräben° ausheben.° Die Alten machten nur widerwillig°
30 mit, aber die Jungen hatten keine Ahnung,° und deshalb waren sie vielleicht sogar begeistert.° Auch Siegbert. Siegbert lag unter dem Befehl° eines ehemaligen°

Das Glossar zu dieser Erzählung finden Sie im Anhang.

---

1. The **Schutzstaffel** was the elite military unit of the Nazi party. It was greatly feared by all opponents of Hitler's regime.

Weltkriegsoffiziers° auf einem Hügel° vor der Stadt. Ich trug Wasser zum Hügel, Kaffee, Kuchen, Zigaretten, und die letzte Tafel Schokolade, die Vater zu Weihnachten geschickt hatte, brachte ich zu Siegbert. Ich saß im Graben neben ihm. Er sagte: „Du, ich habe mich getäuscht,° du bist kein Flittchen°—eher° ein Junge." Das machte mich stolz.° Ich rauchte kurz danach, ohne zu husten, meine erste Zigarette. Aber ich war kein Junge! Nein, ich war kein Junge.

An einem frühen Vormittag ging ich wieder zum Hügel. Die Wege und die Felder lagen wie ausgestorben, nur die Lerchen° stiegen° aus den Furchen.° Seit diesem Morgen weiß ich, wie schön Gesang der Lerchen ist. Auf dem Hügel wurde ich nicht gerade freundlich empfangen.° Einer sagte: „So'n Wahnsinn."° Und der Weltkriegsoffizier sagte: „Tolles° Mädchen, du kannst nicht mehr zurück."

„Warum?" fragte ich.

„Es geht los," sagte er.

„Was? Was geht los?"

Niemand antwortete. Eine unheimliche° Stille. Ich stolperte° über den Hügel zu Siegbert. Er riß° mich in den Graben, neben sich, preßte meinen Kopf in seine Arme und sagte: „Warum bist du nur gekommen! Warum bist du nur heute gekommen!"

Dann explodierte die Ruhe. Einschläge° schüttelten den Hügel. Zornige° Granaten durchwühlten° die Erde, die wenigen Leben herauszuwerfen,° herauszupflügen° wie Kartoffeln aus dem Felde. Hatte ich Angst? Hatte ich keine Angst? Ich weiß es nicht.

Erdfontänen sprangen hoch. Splitter° regneten und der Rauch nahm den Atem.°

Eine Stimme gellte: „Sie sind auf der Straße!"

Dann wurde es ruhig, doch in der Ruhe war ein dunkles Rollen.°

Siegbert sagte: „Mal nachsehen." Er richtete sich auf° und schaute, den Kopf über den Grabenrand,° zur Straße hinüber. Ich sah zu ihm auf und sagte: „Siehst du etwas? Siehst du—?" Da schoß° Blut aus seinem Hals, ein roter Strahl,° wie aus einer Röhre° . . .

In der Kirche war ein Bild: das Lamm Gottes über einem Kelch.° Blut, ein roter Bogen, wölbte sich aus einer klaffenden Halswunde zum Kelchrand.° Ich hatte das Bild in der Kirche lange nicht gesehen. Jetzt sah ich es genau. Das Bild war mein einziger Gedanke,° ein dummer deplazierter° Gedanke. Lähmend.° Ich konnte nicht schreien, nichts tun. Ich sah das Blut aus seinem Hals stoßen°—und dachte an das Bild in der Kirche . . . Dann brach sein Körper zusammen,° nach vorn,° zu mir, sackte in die Hocke,° die Stirn schlug° auf die Knie, und die Hände legten sich nach unten geöffnet° neben die Füße auf die Erde.

In die Unheimlichkeit° meiner Angst fiel ein Schatten.° Oben, am Grabenrand, stand ein Soldat, ein fremder° Soldat, in fremder Uniform, mit einem fremden Stahlhelm und einer fremden Waffe,° die noch nach Siegbert zielte.°

Sein Mörder!

Aber der senkte° die Waffe, warf° sie zur Erde und sagte: „Forgive me." Er beugte sich herab,° riß meine Hände an seine Brust und sagte: „Forgive me."

Hans Bender was born in Mühlhausen near Heidelberg in 1919. The outbreak of World War II interrupted his university studies, and he served in the German infantry for five years until he was taken prisoner by the Russians in 1944. He was a prisoner of war in the Soviet Union until 1949. Bender presently resides in **Köln.** He works extensively as an editor and anthologist, and many young writers owe much to him.

The motto at the beginning of one of his collections of short stories reads: „Geh nach Hause und schreibe über Sachen, die sich vor deinen Augen abspielen." Bender is a keen observer and he has drawn on his war-time experiences to portray realistically and very eloquently the reactions of ordinary people to the larger events that intrude upon their lives.

VOM LESEN ZUM SPRECHEN

ZUR ORIENTIERUNG UND ZUM ZUSAMMENFASSEN

1. Hauptabschnitt (Z. 1–17)

VOR DEM LESEN: Stellen Sie sich vor, Sie wären Englischlehrer an einem deutschen Gymnasium und müßten Ihrer Englischklasse den Unterschied zwischen den Ausdrücken *Forgive me* und *Sorry* erklären. Besprechen Sie mit Ihrer Gesprächspartnerin/Ihrem Gesprächspartner, wie Sie das so interessant wie möglich erklären könnten. Präsentieren Sie dann Ihren Mitstudenten, was Sie sich ausgedacht haben.

NACH DEM LESEN: Beantworten Sie die folgenden Fragen!

1. Woher wissen wir, daß Siegbert etwa vierzehn Jahre alt war?
2. Warum schnitt die Erzählerin Gesichter, wenn sie während der Englischklasse *secretly* ab und zu heimlich° in den Spiegel sah?
3. Warum sagte Siegbert „Da geht die Brigitte Horney!", als er, Walter und Horst die Erzählerin überholten?

2. Hauptabschnitt (Z. 18–37)

VOR DEM LESEN: Stellen Sie sich die folgende Situation vor: Sie sind ein Junge im Alter von dreizehn oder vierzehn Jahren. Es ist Krieg, die Armee Ihres Landes ist *defeated / has fled* geschlagen° und geflohen°, und der Feind ist schon ganz in der Nähe von Ihrer *order* Stadt. Sie bekommen den Befehl°, zusammen mit alten Männern und mit anderen *equipped* Jungen in Ihrem Alter die Stadt gegen die modern ausgerüstete° Armee des *defend* Feindes zu verteidigen°. Wie würden Sie auf diesen Befehl reagieren?

Ich würde . . .

NACH DEM LESEN: Was paßt zusammen?

1. Die Mutter saß abends wortlos am   weil sie keine Ahnung hatten, wie
   Bett der Erzählerin,   *dangerous* gefährlich° das alles war.
2. Die alten Männer machten nur   weil Siegbert sie jetzt respektierte.
   widerwillig mit,

3. Die Jungen waren begeistert,

4. Die Kinder wurden aus der Schule nach Hause geschickt,

5. Die Erzählerin war stolz,

weil sie Angst hatte, daß der Vater nicht mehr lebte.

weil sie wußten, daß der Krieg verloren war.

weil sie zu Hause sicherer° waren als in der Schule.   *safer*

3. Hauptabschnitt (Z. 38–Ende)

VOR DEM LESEN: Stellen Sie sich die folgende Situation vor: Sie sind Soldat°, und Sie stehen plötzlich einem feindlichen Soldaten gegenüber°. Sie haben beide Gewehre° in der Hand, und der andere könnte Sie jeden Moment erschießen°. Was würden Sie tun, um Ihr Leben zu retten?   *soldier* *opposite* *guns / shoot*

Ich würde . . .

NACH DEM LESEN: Was paßt zusammen?

1. Woran könnte man denken, wenn man liest, wie die Erzählerin den frühen Vormittag beschreibt?

2. Warum wurde die Erzählerin an diesem Morgen nicht so freundlich empfangen wie sonst?

3. Womit vergleicht die Erzählerin die Menschen im Graben?

4. Was ist der Pflug, der die Menschen aus dem Graben herauspflügt?

5. Warum mußte die Erzählerin an das Bild in der Kirche denken?

6. Woher kam der Schatten, der plötzlich in den Graben fiel?

7. Warum zielte der fremde Soldat mit seiner Waffe immer noch nach dem toten Siegbert?

8. Warum warf der fremde Soldat plötzlich seine Waffe zur Erde und sagte „Forgive me"?

Mit Kartoffeln, die noch in der Erde sind.

Die feindlichen Granaten.

An den Ausdruck „die Ruhe° vor dem Sturm."   *calm*

Die Leute im Graben wußten, daß der Feind bald angreifen° würde.   *attack*

Von dem fremden Soldaten.

Er hatte Angst.

Weil die Anwesenheit° des Mädchens ihm klarmachte, was es bedeutet, einen Menschen zu töten°.   *presence* *kill*

Weil das Blut aus Siegberts Halswunde so herausschoß wie das Blut aus der Halswunde des Lammes.

ZUM THEMA KRIEG

Der Soldat, der Siegbert getötet hat, kämpft° gegen Hitler und deshalb für eine gute Sache. Trotzdem denkt das Mädchen im Graben instinktiv „Sein Mörder!", als sie ihn sieht. Denken Sie, daß dieser Soldat ein Mörder ist?   *is fighting*

Siegbert war zu jung, um zu wissen, daß er für eine schlechte Sache kämpfte. Würden Sie Siegbert einen Mörder nennen°, wenn er den fremden Soldaten getötet hätte?   *call*

Wie Sie wissen, ist die Schweiz ein permanent neutrales Land und hat trotzdem eine große und modern ausgerüstete Armee. Wenn die Schweiz angegriffen würde,

---

würden Schweizer Soldaten schießen und fremde Soldaten töten. Würden Sie diese Schweizer Soldaten Mörder nennen?

circumstances

Darf ein Soldat töten? Wenn ja, unter welchen Umständen°? Besprechen Sie dieses Problem mit Ihren Mitstudenten!

Nützliche Wörter und Ausdrücke

Nomen

der Schauspieler, die Schauspieler	actor
die Schauspielerin, die Schauspielerinnen	actress
der Ausdruck, die Ausdrücke	expression
der Spiegel, die Spiegel	mirror
der Soldat, des Soldaten, die Soldaten	soldier
der Befehl, die Befehle	command
die Waffe, die Waffen	weapon
das Gewehr, die Gewehre	gun, rifle
die Wunde, die Wunden	wound
das Blut	blood
der Weg, die Wege	way, path, road
die Brücke, die Brücken	bridge
der Graben, die Gräben	ditch
die Erde	earth, ground
der Hügel, die Hügel	hill
das Dach, die Dächer	roof
der Rauch	smoke
der Schatten, die Schatten	shade, shadow
die Bank, die Bänke	bench

Verben

schießen, schoß, hat geschossen	to shoot
erschießen, erschoß, hat erschossen	to shoot dead
werfen (wirft), warf, hat geworfen	th throw
schlagen (schlägt), schlug, hat geschlagen	to hit, to beat
nennen, nannte, hat genannt	to call, to name
malen	to draw, to paint *(a picture)*
überholen	to pass
verteilen	to distribute
stolpern, ist gestolpert	to stumble
schütteln	to shake

Andere Wörter

widerwillig	reluctant	genau	distinct, exact
stolz (auf + *accusative*)	proud (of)	verwundet	wounded
fremd	foreign	gefährlich	dangerous
häufig	frequent		

Ausdrücke

ab und zu	now and then
kurz danach	shortly afterwards
eine Tafel Schokolade	a chocolate bar
Du bist mir auf den Fuß getreten.	You stepped on my toe.
Ich sehe mal nach.	I'll check.
Ich habe keine Ahnung.	I have no idea.

WÖRTER IM KONTEXT

1. ASSOZIATIONEN

a. der Rauch   der Krieg   c. die Wunde   gehen
   der Spiegel   das Theater   das Gewehr   sitzen
   der Soldat   das Feuer   der Weg   bluten
   der Schauspieler   das Glas   die Bank   schießen

b. die Waffe   rot   d. malen   der Fuß
   der Hügel   tief   stolpern   der Mörder
   der Graben   gefährlich   werfen   das Bild
   das Blut   hoch   erschießen   der Ball

2. WAS PASST WO?

überholen   ab und zu   genaue   Schatten   schütteln   häufig   Ahnung

a. _____ ist ein Synonym von „oft".
b. _____ ist ein Synonym von „manchmal".
c. Statt „Ich weiß es nicht" kann man auch sagen: „Ich habe keine _____".
d. Statt nein zu sagen, kann man auch den Kopf _____.
e. Wenn ich schneller fahren will, als der Wagen vor mir, muß ich ihn _____.
f. Im _____ ist es kühler als in der Sonne.
g. Können Sie mir bitte die _____ Zeit sagen?

FUNKTIONEN UND FORMEN

1. FOCUSING ON THE RECEIVER OF AN ACTION

THE PASSIVE VOICE

In grammatical terms, the doer of an action is usually the subject of the sentence:

Peter holt mich um sieben ab.   **Peter** *is picking me up at seven.*

After the defeat of the Nazi regime in World War II, the Allies (Great Britain, France, the USA, and the USSR) divided Germany into four occupation zones and Berlin into four sectors. As differing ideologies led to increasingly strained relations between East and West, Germany, and especially Berlin, became the stage for a confrontation that came to be known as the Cold War. In 1948 the Soviets blockaded all road and rail routes to the three western sectors of Berlin. The Western Allies responded with the Berlin Airlift **(die Luftbrücke):** for ten months food and basic supplies were flown into the beleaguered city. As it became clear to the Western powers that they would not be able to work together with the USSR on the German question, they decided to combine their three zones into a German state. In May 1949, the **Bundesrepublik Deutschland** was born, with Bonn as its capital. A few months later, in October 1949, the USSR responded by declaring the Soviet zone a second German state, the **Deutsche Demokratische Republik.**

The Federal Republic maintained that it was a country for *all* Germans, and it granted full citizenship to every citizen of the German Democratic Republic who chose to move to the west. This policy, combined with a booming West German economy and the antipathy of many East Germans for communism, led to a mass exodus to the FRG in the 1950s. In an effort to halt this exodus of mostly young and highly qualified people, the government of the GDR constructed a virtually impenetrable barrier of barbed wire fences and land mines along its western border. But Berlin, situated like an island deep in the territory of the GDR remained a problem. The boundaries between the four sectors of the city were open, and thousands of citizens of the GDR escaped to the West via Berlin. This exodus came to an abrupt end in 1961, when the government of the GDR sealed the last gateway to the West with a wall **(die Mauer),** dividing the Soviet sector from the other three. With the building of the Wall, East/West dialogue came to a standstill for

Berliner Kinder winken einem amerikanischen „Rosinenbomber".

1961: Bau der Berliner Mauer

1989: Abbruch der Berliner Mauer

a decade. It was not until the Four Power Agreement of 1971 that a degree of normalcy returned to Berlin. The GDR acknowledged the right of the West to maintain military forces in West Berlin and agreed that the FRG should be the representative of West Berlin to the world. Telephone service between the two parts of the city was restored. West Berliners were no longer prohibited from traveling to East Berlin and the GDR.

For the next eighteen years, the two Germanies lived more or less peacefully side by side. In September 1989, Hungary opened its border to Austria and fifteen thousand citizens of the GDR fled through Hungary to the West. Tens of thousands more came via Czechoslovakia and Poland. The government of the GDR was in crisis. In an attempt to stem the flow, it ordered the opening of the Berlin Wall on November 9, 1989, less than a year after Erich Honecker, then Party Secretary, declared that it would still be standing in fifty or a hundred years. The process of German reunification had begun.

A sentence in which the *doer of an action* functions as the subject of the sentence is said to be in the *active voice.*

If, however, you find it unnecessary or unimportant to mention the doer of the action or if the receiver of the action is more important, you can make the receiver of the action the subject of the sentence:

Ich werde um sieben abgeholt.   *I*'m being picked up at seven.

A sentence in which the *receiver of the action* functions as subject is said to be in the *passive voice.* Note that in such a sentence the receiver of the action does not appear in the accusative case but in the *nominative case.* Note also that in the passive voice the verb appears as a *past participle* with a form of **werden** as auxiliary.

TENSES IN THE PASSIVE VOICE

In the passive voice the different tenses are indicated by the auxiliary **werden.** English uses the auxiliary verb *to be.*

Present	ich **werde** abgeholt	*I'm being picked up*
Simple Past	ich **wurde** abgeholt	*I was picked up*
Perfect	ich **bin** abgeholt **worden**	
Past Perfect	ich **war** abgeholt **worden**	*I had been picked up*
Future	ich **werde** abgeholt **werden**	*I will be picked up*

Note that as an auxiliary for the passive voice, **werden** uses **worden** as a participle instead of **geworden.**

USE OF THE PASSIVE VOICE

In the passive voice, the attention is focused on the receiver of the action and on the action itself. In the examples below, what happens to the receiver of the action is more important than who does it. The passive voice is therefore the more natural mode of expression.

Passive	**Active**
Ich **werde** nächste Woche **operiert.**	Der Chirurg **operiert** mich nächste Woche.
I'm being operated on next week.	*The surgeon is operating on me next week.*
Ist Ihr Buch jetzt endlich **veröffentlicht worden?**	**Hat** der Verlag Ihr Buch jetzt endlich **veröffentlicht?**
Has your book finally been published?	*Has the publisher finally published your book?*

18. März 1990: Die ersten freien Wahlen in der DDR

The peaceful revolution that began in the **German Democratic Republic** in the fall of 1989 culminated in its first free elections on March 18, 1990. The conservative three-party **Allianz für Deutschland** won 48.2 per cent of the vote. Lothar de Maizière, leader of the **Ost-CDU** and an advocate of early reunification, became Prime Minister. Of the eligible voters, 93.39 per cent went to the polls.

During the forty-odd years of its existence, the **G**DR considered itself a socialist democracy of workers and farmers allied to, but independent of, the Soviet Union. Its government, based on Marxist ideology, was controlled by the **SED, the Sozialistische Einheitspartei Deutschlands.** The **G**DR was one of the ten strongest industrial countries in the world, and it had the highest standard of living of all the East Bloc countries. This was a remarkable feat for a country of only 17 million that had received no aid to help it rebuild after World War II.

Under the Marxist regime, every citizen of the **G**DR was guaranteed the right to work and everyone, from doctor to blue collar worker, worked for the state. Unemployment was virtually non-existent. All education, including vocational training and post-secondary education, was free of charge. Living expenses, including rents and health insurance, were very low because everything was subsidized by the state. Day care for children was provided free of charge and most children between the ages of three and six were enrolled in a local nursery school **(Kinderkrippe).**

On paper the **G**DR looked like a Utopian state. However, a fundamental element was lacking: the freedom of personal choice. As well, central planning had provided consumers with poor quality goods in a "feast or famine" fashion. By their votes in the March 1990 election, the majority of East Germans said no to any further socialist experiments. They clearly showed that they preferred personal freedom and the competition of a market economy to the cradle-to-grave security of a Marxist welfare state. They also wanted a speedy reunification with West Germany. The first step toward reunification was taken on July 2, 1990, when monetary union between East and West Germany took place, with the **Deutsche Mark** the sole currency. This was followed on October 3, 1990, by the political union of the two countries.

2. Juli 1990: Dieselbe Mark für Ost und West

A. WAS WIRD HIER GEMACHT?

ein Haus/bauen

Hier wird ein Haus gebaut.

1.

2.

3.

4.

5.

6.

7.

> Blumen / gießen   der Rasen / mähen
> Eis / verkaufen   Tennis / spielen
> Kleider / anprobieren   ein Auto / reparieren
>   Schi / laufen

B. WAS WURDE HIER GEMACHT? WAS IST HIER GEMACHT WORDEN?

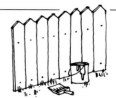

ein Zaun / streichen

Hier wurde ein Zaun gestrichen.
Hier ist ein Zaun gestrichen worden.

1.

2.

3.

4.

5.

6.

7.

Äpfel / pflücken	Holz / spalten
ein Baum / fällen	Bier / trinken
Schnee / schaufeln	ein Feld / pflügen
Fenster *(pl)* / putzen	

C. ERGÄNZEN SIE DIE PASSENDEN VERBEN!

▶ bezahlen / arbeiten

Warum _____ du jeden Sommer für dieselbe° Firma?

Weil ich dort gut _____.

the same

S1: Warum arbeitest du jeden Sommer für dieselbe Firma?

S2: Weil ich dort gut bezahlt werde.

---

1. haben / kaufen
   Warum _____ Frau Wagner plötzlich so viel Geld?

   Weil ihr Buch viel _____.

2. umbauen° / suchen
   Warum _____ Schneiders eine möblierte Wohnung?

   to remodel

   Weil ihr Haus _____.

3. reparieren / fahren
   Warum _____ du denn mit dem Bus?

   Weil mein Wagen gerade _____.

4. streiken / bezahlen
   Warum _____ diese Leute?

   Weil sie so schlecht _____.

to bloom

5. gießen / blühen°
   Warum _____ die Orchideen denn   Weil sie nicht regelmäßig _____.
   nicht?
6. essen / abholen
   Warum _____ du keinen Nachtisch?   Weil ich gleich _____.

THE IMPERSONAL PASSIVE

In German the passive voice is sometimes used to focus attention on an activity as such. This construction is called the *impersonal passive*. It does not exist in English. Note the absence of a subject. Note also that in such sentences the verb is always in the 3rd person singular.

Bei meinen Eltern **wird** jeden Morgen   *At my parents' house, breakfast is at*
Punkt sieben **gefrühstückt.**   *seven on the dot every morning.*

D. WAS WIRD HIER GEMACHT?

laut lachen

Hier wird laut gelacht.

1.

2.

3.

4.

5.

6.

7.

8.

baden	kochen
singen	zu viel rauchen
fernsehen	essen und trinken
putzen	tanzen

GUTE VORSÄTZE° FÜRS NEUE JAHR

resolutions

Wenn es in der Silvesternacht zwölf Uhr schlägt°, fassen° viele Menschen allerhand° gute Vorsätze. Sie sagen oder denken aber meistens nicht „Von heute ab **rauche ich** nicht mehr" oder „Von heute ab **stehe ich** jeden Morgen um sieben **auf**", sondern „Von heute ab **wird** nicht mehr **geraucht**" oder „Von heute ab **wird** jeden Morgen um sieben **aufgestanden.**"

strikes / make / all kinds of

Stellen Sie sich vor, die heutige Deutschstunde wäre eine Silvesterparty, und Sie hätten beschlossen°, einander um Mitternacht allerhand gute Vorsätze fürs neue Jahr zu erzählen. Jetzt ist es fünf vor zwölf, und Sie haben noch fünf Minuten Zeit, sich auszudenken, wie Sie Ihr Leben ändern wollen. Schreiben Sie sich ein paar gute Vorsätze auf, und erzählen Sie sie dann Ihren Mitstudenten!

decided

Von heute ab wird Von heute ab werden	regelmäßig Sport alle Hausaufgaben pünktlich viel mehr Obst und Gemüse jeden Morgen rechtzeitig jeden Tag eine Stunde Deutsch alle Referate pünktlich keine Süßigkeiten° mehr täglich nur noch eine Stunde jeden Abend rechtzeitig ins Bett viel weniger Kaffee jeden Morgen eine halbe Stunde kein Bier mehr . . .	gegessen getrunken gegangen abgegeben° gejoggt ferngesehen gelernt gemacht aufgestanden getrieben . . .

handed in

sweets

THE PASSIVE WITH A MODAL VERB

In *Kapitel 4* you learned that a verb that is modified by a modal verb appears in the infinitive form. In the passive voice this infinitive will be a *passive infinitive*.

Du **mußt** heute den Rasen **mähen.**

*You **have to cut** the lawn today.*

Sie **dürfen** den Patienten jetzt nicht **stören.**

*You **may** not **disturb** the patient now.*

Der Rasen **muß** heute **gemäht werden.**

*The lawn **has to be cut** today.*

Der Patient **darf** jetzt nicht **gestört werden.**

*The patient **may** not **be disturbed** now.*

The passive infinitive consists of a *past participle* plus the infinitive **werden.**

Active Infinitive	fragen	*to ask*
Passive Infinitive	gefragt werden	*to be asked*

Was darf nicht überholt werden?

E. NICHT NUR MENSCHEN HABEN WÜNSCHE! Ergänzen Sie die passenden passiven Infinitive!

▶ Ich möchte schnellstens . . .

gegossen werden

Ich möchte schnellstens gegossen werden!

1. Wir möchten
   endlich . . .

3. Wir möchten
   heute noch . . .

2. Ich möchte
   so gern . . .

4. Ich möchte
   so bald wie
   möglich . . .

5. Ich möchte
bald mal . . .

7. Ich möchte
endlich mal
wieder . . .

6. Ich möchte
sofort . . .

gefüttert werden	geflickt werden
gegessen werden	gespielt werden
gewaschen werden	repariert werden
zurückgegeben werden	

F. MÜSSEN WIR NICHT TANJA ABHOLEN? Ergänzen Sie die passenden aktiven oder passiven Infinitive!

▶ Müssen wir nicht Tanja _____?   Nein, sie will heute nicht _____ _____.

> abholen

S1: Müssen wir nicht Tanja abholen?   *S2:* Nein, sie will heute nicht abgeholt werden.

1. Soll ich den Brief _____?   Ja, er muß sofort _____ _____.
2. Kann ich den Rasen denn nicht morgen _____?   Nein, er muß heute noch _____ _____.
3. Wann soll ich Thomas morgen früh _____?   Er will Punkt sechs _____ _____.
4. Kann man diese Bluse in heißem Wasser _____?   Nein, sie darf nur in lauwarmem Wasser _____ _____.
5. Dürfen wir die Möbel _____, Frau Wild?   Nein, die Möbel dürfen auf keinen Fall° _____ _____.   *under no circumstances*
6. Wie oft sollen wir diese Orchideen _____?   Die müssen jeden zweiten Tag _____ _____.
7. Sollen wir die Katze morgens oder abends _____?   Sie muß morgens *und* abends _____ _____.

umstellen	wecken	füttern	gießen	mähen	wegschicken	waschen

WAS ALLES NOCH GETAN WERDEN MUSS

put

Versetzen° Sie sich in eine der folgenden Situationen, und machen Sie eine Liste von allem, was noch schnell getan werden muß. Sie können auch selbst eine

similar / invent

ähnliche° Situation erfinden°.

lesen . . . vor: *read to*

Lesen Sie die Liste Ihren Mitstudenten vor°!

Situationen:

1. Ihre Mutter hat gerade angerufen und Ihnen gesagt, daß sie Sie heute nachmittag besuchen kommt.

prepared

2. Sie haben ein paar Freunde auf heute abend zu sich eingeladen und haben noch nichts vorbereitet°.

3. . . .

Mein Bett	muß	aufgehängt werden
Eine Pizza	müssen	abgestaubt° werden
Mein Zimmer		gebacken werden
Ein Kuchen		geputzt werden
Die Möbel		gekocht werden
Meine Kleider		gemacht werden
Bier		abgewaschen werden
Mein Schreibtisch		aufgeräumt° werden
Der Teppich		gesaugt° werden
Die Fenster		gekauft werden
Das Abendessen		. . .
Das Badezimmer		
Die Küche		
Das Geschirr		
. . .		

dusted

tidied up
vacuumed

MENTIONING THE AGENT IN A PASSIVE SENTENCE

In most passive sentences the agent (the doer of the action) is omitted. However if the agent is mentioned, it appears in the dative case after the proposition **von.**

Dieses Buch ist mir **von einem Freund** empfohlen worden.

This book was recommended to me by a friend.

culprit

G. WER IST DER TÄTER?°

▶ Weißt du, wie dieser Diplomat ums Leben gekommen° ist?

Er ist von . . . worden.

died

Ein Terrorist hat ihn ermordet.

S1: Weißt du, wie dieser Diplomat ums Leben gekommen ist?

S2: Er ist von einem Terroristen ermordet worden.

1. Weißt du, was mit Rotkäppchen° passiert ist? — Es ist von . . . worden. — *Little Red Ridinghood*
2. Weißt du, wie Müllers Hund gestorben ist? — Er ist von . . . worden.
3. Weißt du, wo unser Kanarienvogel ist? — Er ist von . . . worden.
4. Weißt du, warum Kathrin ein verbundenes° Bein hat? — Sie ist von . . . worden. — *bandaged*
5. Weißt du, warum Herr Metzger so deprimiert ist? — Er ist von . . . worden.

Ein Hund hat sie gebissen.　　　Ein Wolf hat es gefressen.
Ein Lastwagen hat ihn überfahren.　　Frau Wilds Katze hat ihn gefressen.
Seine Firma hat ihn entlassen.

---

6. Weißt du, warum der kleine Moritz so schrecklich weint? — Er ist von . . . worden.
7. Weißt du, warum Günter nicht mehr zu Hause wohnt? — Er ist von . . . worden.
8. Weißt du, warum sich Tina diesen miserablen Film anschauen will? — Er ist ihr von . . . worden.
9. Weißt du, wie die Polizei den Bankräuber so schnell kriegen konnte? — Er ist von . . . worden.
10. Weißt du, wie Abel ums Leben gekommen ist? — Er ist von . . . worden.

Sein großer Bruder hat ihn verhauen.°　　Seine Eltern haben ihn rausgeworfen.°　　*beat up / threw out*
Eine Freundin hat ihn ihr empfohlen.°　　Sein Bruder Kain hat ihn erschlagen.°　　*recommended / slew*
Eine versteckte Kamera hat ihn fotografiert.

OTHER WAYS OF FOCUSING ON THE RECEIVER OF AN ACTION

Apart from the passive voice, German has some other ways of focusing on the receiver of an action or on the action itself.

Man + the active voice

Wie schreibt **man** dieses Wort?　　　*How do **you** write this word?*

Using the impersonal subject **man** signals that the doer of the action is not important and shifts the focus to the receiver of the action or to the action itself.

H. MAN KANN ES SO ODER SO SAGEN. Verwenden Sie in den Fragen das Passiv!
Ihre Gesprächspartnerin/Ihr Gesprächspartner antwortet mit **man** und aktiven Verbformen.

▶ sprechen

_____ in Quebec viel Französisch _____ ?   In Quebec _____ man fast nur Französisch.

S1: Wird in Quebec viel Französisch gesprochen?   **S2:** In Quebec spricht man fast nur Französisch.

1. gebrauchen
   Was _____ häufiger _____, „sorry" oder „forgive me"?   „Sorry" _____ man viel häufiger.
2. schreiben
   _____ „heißen" mit Eszett _____ ?   Ja, „heißen" _____ man mit Eszett.
3. aussprechen
   _____ das Eszett anders _____ als ein Doppel-s?   Nein, das Eszett und das Doppel-s _____ man genau gleich aus.
4. bauen
   _____ in dieser Fabrik auch Personenwagen _____ ?   Nein, hier _____ man nur Lastwagen.
5. trinken
   _____ in Frankreich auch so viel Bier _____ wie in Deutschland?   Nein, dort _____ man mehr Wein.
6. schreiben
   _____ an deutschen Unis auch so viele Prüfungen _____ wie hier bei uns?   Nein, dort _____ man bei weitem nicht so viele Prüfungen.

Sein + *zu*-infinitive

Hunde **sind** an der Leine **zu führen.**   *Dogs **are to be (must be) kept** on a leash.*

Unser Rasenmäher **war** nicht mehr **zu reparieren.**   *Our lawnmower **couldn't be repaired** any more.*

This highly idiomatic construction also focuses on the receiver of the action. Note that the English equivalents of this construction usually consist of a form of the verb *to be* with a passive infinitive, or of the modals *can* or *must* with a passive infinitive.

I. AUF ENGLISCH, BITTE!

nowhere
clean

1. Mein Geldbeutel ist nirgends° zu finden.
2. Die Jacke war nicht mehr sauber° zu kriegen.
3. Sind denn wirklich keine Theaterkarten mehr zu haben?
4. Dein Benehmen ist nicht zu entschuldigen.
5. Sein Wunsch war nicht zu erfüllen.
6. Da sind noch ein paar Briefe zu tippen, Frau Meyer.

bills
to reach

7. Diese Rechnungen° sind sofort zu bezahlen.
8. Sind Sie in Deutschland telefonisch zu erreichen?°

Sich lassen + infinitive

Glauben Sie, daß **sich** das **machen läßt?**   *Do you think that this **can be done?***

The English equivalent of this construction is a form of the modal *can* with a passive infinitive.

J. AUF ENGLISCH, BITTE!

1. Diese Sätze lassen sich nicht wörtlich° ins Englische übersetzen.°   *literally / to translate*
2. Diese Frage läßt sich nicht beantworten.
3. Läßt sich das denn nicht vermeiden?°   *to avoid*
4. Lassen sich diese Probleme denn wirklich nicht lösen?
5. Wie läßt sich das erklären?
6. Das läßt sich alles automatisieren.

ZUSAMMENSCHAU

WIE GUT IST IHR GEDÄCHTNIS?

In diesem Buch sind Sie in den vergangenen Monaten immer wieder denselben° fünf Studenten begegnet°: Stephanie, Claudia, Peter, Martin und Günter. Was wissen Sie noch von ihnen? Ergänzen Sie die passenden Namen!   *the same* / *met*

Günter

_____ wohnt im zweiten Semester in einer WG.
_____ verbringt seine Ferien gern in warmen Ländern,
     besonders in Florida und in Spanien.
_____ geht gern Windsurfing.
_____ ist nicht Deutsche, hat aber väterlicherseits deutsche Vorfahren.
_____ interessiert sich für Technik und alte Maschinen.
_____ verbringt ihre Semesterferien bei ihrem Onkel in Köln.
_____ hat viele Freundinnen.
_____ kann gut flicken.
_____ läßt sich bei Referaten gern helfen.
_____ hat im College sehr gut Deutsch gelernt.
_____ wohnen zu Beginn ihres Studiums in einem Zimmer in der Zennerstraße.
_____ denkt daran, im zweiten Semester ein Zimmer in einem Privathaus zu
     mieten.
_____ hat letzten Sommer bei einem Maler gearbeitet.
_____ schenkt gern Blumen.
_____ mieten die Wohnung einer Frau, die auf ein Jahr zu ihrem Sohn nach Texas
     reist.
_____ läßt sich im Kaufhaus nicht übers° Ohr hauen.   **übers Ohr hauen:** *be cheated*
_____ ißt und schläft zu viel und arbeitet zu wenig.
_____ wohnt immer noch bei seinen Eltern.
_____ zieht den Pullover eines Zimmerkollegen an, um eine Mitstudentin zu
     beeindrucken°.   *impress*
_____ wohnen im ersten Semester im Studentenheim.
_____ will sich einen Wagen kaufen.

say good-bye
choose

Sie müssen sich jetzt von Stephanie, Claudia, Peter, Martin und Günter verabschieden°. Spekulieren Sie, wie das Leben dieser Studenten weitergeht. Wählen° Sie eine/einen von den fünf und arbeiten Sie mit zwei oder drei Mitstudenten ihre/seine weitere Lebensgeschichte aus. Erzählen Sie diese Lebensgeschichte Ihren Klassenkameraden.

Sprachnotizen

Derselbe, dieselbe, dasselbe

The English equivalent of **derselbe, (dieselbe, dasselbe)** is *the same*. Both **der-** and **selb-** take case endings:

Helga und Eva wohnen in **derselben** Straße.	*Helga and Eva live on **the same** street.*
Sag doch nicht immer **dasselbe**!	*Don't always say **the same** thing!*
Ich habe jetzt schon drei Jahre lang **dieselbe** Mathelehrerin.	*I've had **the same** math teacher for three years.*

The forms of **derselbe** are written as one word, unless the defiite article is contracted with a preposition:

Helga und Eva sind als Kinder **zur selben** Schule gegangen.	*As children Helga and Eva went **to the same** school.*

2. REPORTING IN YOUR OWN WORDS WHAT SOMEONE ELSE HAS SAID

Ich bin ein Berliner.

INDIRECT QUOTATION: COLLOQUIAL GERMAN

In *direct quotation* you report the original and unchanged words of a speaker. Quotation marks indicate the beginning and the end of the quotation.

Im Jahr 1963 sagte Präsident Kennedy vor dem Rathaus in Berlin-Schöneberg: „Ich bin ein Berliner."

In *indirect quotation* you report in your own words what someone else has said.

What Eva said:	**Your report of what she said:**
„**Mein** Freund arbeitet diesen Sommer bei der Post."	Eva hat mir erzählt, daß **ihr** Freund diesen Sommer bei der Post arbeitet.
„Arbeitet **dein** Freund wieder bei McDonald's?"	Sie fragte mich, ob **mein** Freund wieder bei McDonald's arbeitet.
„Warum sucht er sich denn keinen besseren Job?"	Sie fragte, warum er sich denn keinen besseren Job sucht.
„**Vergiß** nicht, zu meiner Fete zu kommen!"	Sie sagte, daß **ich** nicht **vergessen soll,** zu **ihrer** Fete zu kommen.

Note the change of pronouns and possessive adjectives. Note also that **sollen** is used to report imperatives.

K. BETTINA IST IM STRESS. Sie waren bei Bettina und wollten sie zum Tanzen einladen. Berichten Sie, wie Bettina reagierte!

Bettinas Reaktionen:	Ihr Bericht:
1. Ich kann heute nicht mit dir tanzen gehen.	Sie sagte, daß . . .
2. Ich habe viel zu viel zu tun.	Sie sagte, daß . . .
3. Ich bin zur Zeit sehr gestreßt.	Sie sagte, daß . . .
4. Ich habe fast kein Geld mehr.	Sie sagte, daß . . .
5. Ich muß meinen Eltern schreiben.	Sie sagte, daß . . .
6. Ich bekomme viel zu wenig Geld von ihnen.	Sie sagte, daß . . .
7. Kannst du mir hundert Mark leihen?	Sie fragte, . . .
8. Warum willst du mir denn nichts leihen?	Sie fragte, . . .
9. Laß mich jetzt in Ruhe!	Sie sagte, daß . . .
10. Ruf mich heute abend an!	Sie sagte, daß . . .

In colloquial language, speakers of German also use *subjunctive II* to report what someone else has said. The conjunction **daß** is then frequently omitted.

What Bettina said:	Your report of what she said:
„Es **geht mir** schon wieder viel besser."	Als ich Bettina heute abend anrief, sagte sie, es **ginge ihr** schon wieder viel besser.

L. BETTINA HAT SICH WIEDER ERHOLT°. Am Abend haben Sie Bettina angerufen, und mit einer ganz anderen Bettina gesprochen. Berichten Sie, was sie diesmal alles fragte und sagte! Verwenden Sie den Konjunktiv II!

recovered

Was Bettina diesmal sagte:	Ihr Bericht:
1. Willst du immer noch tanzen gehen?	Sie fragte, . . .
2. Wann kommst du mich abholen?	Sie fragte, . . .
3. Der Brief an meine Eltern ist weg.	Sie sagte, . . .
4. Meine Hausaufgaben kann ich auch morgen früh noch machen.	Sie sagte, . . .
5. Ich habe noch fünfzig Mark.	Sie sagte, . . .
6. Das ist genug für heute abend.	Sie sagte, . . .
7. Zieh deinen neuen Pulli an!	Sie sagte, . . .
8. Komm so schnell wie möglich!	Sie sagte, . . .

INDIRECT QUOTATION: LITERARY AND JOURNALISTIC GERMAN

In literary and journalistic German, reporting what someone else has said is usually restricted to the 3rd person singular and the 3rd person plural. The 3rd person plural appears in subjunctive II and the 3rd person singular appears in *subjunctive I.*

The term *subjunctive I* indicates that this verb form is derived from the first principal part, i.e., the infinitive. In the 3rd person singular, subjunctive I is formed by adding the personal ending **-e** to the infinitive stem.

Infinitive	Subjunctive I (3rd person singular)	Subjunctive II (3rd person plural)
haben	er/sie/es habe	sie hätten
werden	werde	würden
können	könne	könnten
müssen	müsse	müßten
sollen	solle	sollten
wissen	wisse	wüßten
gehen	gehe	gingen

The verb **sein** is an exception. It appears in subjunctive I in the plural as well as in the singular. Note that the singular form has no personal ending.

3rd person singular: er/sie/es **sei**
3rd person plural: sie **seien**

There is no difference in meaning between subjunctive I and subjunctive II.

Ein Zeitungsbericht:

Anläßlich seines hundertsten Geburtstags sagte Herr Maier, er **habe** sein langes Leben in erster Linie seiner lieben Frau Elisabeth zu verdanken. Obwohl sie selbst schon über neunzig **sei, versorge** sie ihn getreulich, und sie **sehe** immer darauf, daß er jeden Tag ein gesundes Essen **bekomme.** Er **sei** auch sehr glücklich, daß alle seine Kinder, Enkel und Urenkel heute hier **seien** und dieses Fest mit ihm und seiner Frau **feierten.** Er **hoffe,** sie **kämen** nächstes Jahr alle wieder, um seinen hundertersten Geburtstag zu feiern.

A newspaper report:

*On the occasion of his hundredth birthday, Mr. Maier said that it was above all his dear wife Elizabeth whom he **had** to thank for his longevity. Although she **was** over ninety herself, she **took** care of him faithfully, and she **saw** to it that he always **got** a healthy meal. He **was** also very happy that all his children, grandchildren, and great-grandchildren **were** here today and **celebrating** this party with him and his wife. He **hoped** they **were** all **coming** again next year to celebrate his hundred and first birthday.*

Herr Maier und seine Frau Elisabeth an seinem 100. Geburtstag

M. SAGEN SIE DASSELBE IN WENIGER LITERARISCHEM DEUTSCH! Verwenden Sie Konjunktiv II statt Konjunktiv I!

1. Der Student sagte, er sei sehr arm und er habe großen Hunger.
2. Als der Student sagte, er komme vom Paradies, fragte die Bauersfrau, wie es den Leuten dort gehe.
3. Der Student erzählte ihr, daß die meisten Leute dort sehr arm seien. Sie müßten fast den ganzen Tag Halleluja singen, und sie bekämen oft nicht einmal genug zu essen. Nur ein paar, die noch Verwandte hätten und manchmal Pakete bekämen, hätten es ein bißchen besser.
4. Die Bauersfrau fragte, ob der Student ihrem ersten Mann Geld und Kleider mitnehmen könne, wenn seine Ferien zu Ende seien und er wieder ins Paradies zurückgehe.
5. Sie sagte, er solle ihrem Hans dieses Bündel geben und ihm sagen, daß sie ihn nie vergessen werde.
6. Der Bauer hielt sein Pferd an und fragte den Wanderer, ob er wisse, wo der Student mit dem Bündel auf dem Rücken jetzt sei.
7. Als der Bauer hörte, daß der Student jetzt in dem Wald dort drüben sei, sagte er, er müsse diesen Kerl fangen, und der Wanderer solle doch bitte solange sein Pferd halten.

INDIRECT QUOTATION: PAST TIME

When *direct quotation* appears in a past tense (simple past, perfect, past perfect), *indirect quotation* uses past-time subjunctive, i.e., the past participle of the verb with the auxiliaries **haben** or **sein** in the subjunctive.

	Colloquial
Brigitte sagte: „Gerhard **hat** mir einen langen Brief **geschrieben**.“	Brigitte sagte, Gerhard **hätte** ihr einen langen Brief **geschrieben.**
	Literary
	Brigitte sagte, Gerhard **habe** ihr einen langen Brief **geschrieben.**
	Colloquial
Gerhard schrieb: „Gestern abend **waren** wir zum erstenmal im Theater.“	Gerhard schrieb, gestern abend **wären** sie zum erstenmal im Theater **gewesen.**
	Literary
	Gerhard schrieb, gestern abend **seien** sie zum erstenmal im Theater **gewesen.**

When *direct quotation* refers to past time and contains a modal and infinitive, *indirect quotation* uses the auxiliary **haben** in the subjunctive together with a double infinitive:

	Colloquial
Helga schrieb: „Ich **mußte** wegen einer schweren Erkältung fast eine ganze Woche im Bett **bleiben**.“	Helga schrieb, sie **hätte** wegen einer schweren Erkältung fast eine ganze Woche im Bett **bleiben müssen.**

Helga schrieb, sie **habe** wegen einer schweren Erkältung fast eine ganze Woche im Bett **bleiben müssen.**

N. WAS HABEN DIESE LEUTE WÖRTLICH GESAGT ODER GESCHRIEBEN?

▶ Stephanie sagte, sie hätte für ihr Referat eine Eins bekommen. „Ich habe für mein Referat eine Eins bekommen."

1. Tina sagte, sie hätte die ganze Nacht nicht geschlafen.
2. Tina sagte, sie hätte die ganze Nacht nicht schlafen können.
3. Meine Freunde schrieben, sie seien gestern zum erstenmal in Dresden gewesen, und sie hätten es dort sehr interessant gefunden.
4. Sabine sagte, ihr kleiner Bruder hätte wegen seiner schlechten Zensuren gestern nicht zum Fußballmatch gehen dürfen.
5. Meine Eltern schrieben, sie seien von Frankfurt sofort nach Wien weitergeflogen.
6. Stephanie sagte, sie hätte eine halbe Stunde auf den Bus warten müssen.

3. DESCRIBING PEOPLE, PLACES, AND THINGS

EXTENDED PARTICIPIAL MODIFIERS

In *Kapitel 13* you learned how to describe people, places, and things with relative clauses:

Die Instrumente, **die von dieser Firma hergestellt werden,** sind von hervorragender Qualität.

*The instruments **that are manufactured by this company** are of superior quality.*

Die Passagiere, **die schon seit vielen Stunden auf ihre Maschine warteten,** wurden immer ungeduldiger.

*The passengers, **who had been waiting for their plane for many hours,** became increasingly impatient.*

German journalists and writers of scientific prose often condense such information in an *extended participial modifier.* Whereas a relative clause follows the noun, an extended participial modifier *precedes* it.

Relative Clause

Die Instrumente, **die von dieser Firma hergestellt werden,** sind von hervorragender Qualität.

Die Passagiere, **die schon seit vielen Stunden auf ihre Maschine warteten,** wurden immer ungeduldiger.

Extended Participial Modifier

Die *von dieser Firma hergestellten Instrumente sind von hervorragender Qualität.*

Die *schon seit vielen Stunden auf ihre Maschine wartenden* Passagiere wurden immer ungeduldiger.

Note that in an extended participial modifier the verb appears as a present or past participle used as an adjective.

O. AUF ENGLISCH, BITTE! In translating the following sentences take the information contained in the participial modifier and place it after the noun. Express this information in the form of a relative clause.

Dresden mit Hofkirche und
Semper Oper

> Die **in den letzten Kriegstagen von britischen und amerikanischen
> Bombern total zerstörte** Stadt Dresden ist heute wieder fast so schön wie
> vor dem Krieg.

*The city of Dresden, **which had been totally destroyed by British and American bombers in the last days of the war,** is almost as beautiful today as it was before the war.*

1. Die Werke dieser **seit vielen Jahren in Italien lebenden** Autorin werden immer noch viel gelesen.
2. Dieses **vor fünfzig Jahren viel gelesene** Buch ist heute nur noch in wenigen Bibliotheken zu finden.
3. Je° tiefer der Dollarkurs° fällt, desto teurer werden alle **aus Übersee nach Nordamerika kommenden** Waren.°
4. Die **in diesem Artikel beschriebenen** Experimente zeigen wieder einmal, wie schädlich° Zigarettenrauch ist.
5. In seinem **nächsten Monat in „Geo"[1] erscheinenden°** Artikel versucht der Autor zu zeigen, daß Elefanten jetzt zu den am meisten gefährdeten° Spezies gehören.
6. Die **im Jahr 1961 von der DDR gebaute** Mauer war viele Jahre lang eine der größten Sehenswürdigkeiten° Berlins.
7. Der Rhein ist der größte der **von Süden nach Norden fließenden°** deutschen Flüsse.°
8. Das Fleisch der **mit Fischmehl gefütterten** Schweine war total ungenießbar.°

je . . . desto: *the . . . the /*
der Kurs: *rate of exchange*
merchandise
harmful
erscheinen: *to appear*
endangered

tourist attractions
fließen: *to flow*
rivers
inedible

---

1. The German equivalent of "National Geographic."

GESCHICHTE OHNE MORAL

von Alfred Polgar

according to
manner / bourgeois

Obwohl diese Geschichte dem Titel nach° „ohne Moral" ist, erzählt der Autor in einer humorvollen, leicht ironischen Weise° von der Moral einer bürgerlichen° Familie der dreißiger Jahre.

Sie finden unter Zur Orientierung und zum Zusammenfassen *ein paar Fragen zu den zwei Hauptabschnitten dieser Geschichte.*

Sonntag, drei Uhr nachmittags, sagte der Gymnasiast° Leopold, jetzt müsse er fort,° denn der Autobus zum Fußballmatch fahre Punkt drei Uhr fünfzehn von seinem Standplatz ab.

Das Glossar zu dieser Erzählung finden Sie im Anhang.

„Und deine Schularbeiten für morgen?" fragte die Mutter.

5 „Die mache ich am Abend."

Tante Alwine meinte, es sei schade ums° Geld für die Autofahrt, so ein junger Mensch könne auch zu Fuß gehen.

Es wurde Abend, und Leopold war noch nicht zu Hause. Und dann kam die Nachricht,° daß der fahrplanmäßig° um drei Uhr fünfzehn von seinem Standplatz 10 abgegangene° Autobus in einen Graben gestürzt° und sämtliche° Insassen° schwer verletzt° seien.

Die Mutter, aus der Ohnmacht° erwacht, klagte sich immerzu an,° sie hätte Leopold nie und nimmer erlauben dürfen, seine Schularbeiten erst am Abend zu machen. Jetzt büße° sie für ihre elterliche Schwäche.°

15 Der Vater verfluchte° das Fußballspiel und den Götzen° Sport überhaupt.

Tante Alwine schrie: „Hätte er nicht zu Fuß gehen können wie tausend andere Jungen?"

Ihr Mann schüttelte bedeutsam° den Kopf: „Heute ist der dritte August, der Sterbetag unseres seligen° Großvaters. Daran hätte man denken müssen."

20 Die Großmutter mütterlicherseits sprach zu sich selbst: „Kürzlich bin ich ihm auf eine Lüge gekommen.° Ich ermahnte° ihn: „Wer lügt, sündigt,° und wer sündigt, wird bestraft."° Da hat er mir ins Gesicht gelacht!"

Das Mädchen für alles° sagte dem Kohlenmann: „Na, sehen Sie? Wie ich Ihnen erzählt habe, daß mir heute früh zwei Nonnen begegnet sind[1], da haben Sie sich 25 über mich lustig gemacht!"°

Hernach ging das Mädchen für alles hinunter zu den Portiersleuten,° um mit ihnen den traurigen° Fall° zu bereden.° „Ja", sagte sie, „am Ersten wollten wir aufs Land° fahren. Aber weil die Schneiderin° mit den Kleidern der Gnädigen° nicht fertig war, sind sie noch dageblieben. Wegen der dummen Fetzen."°

---

1. The nuns' black habit is facetiously compared to a black cat. A black cat crossing one's path is considered by some to be a sign of bad luck.

30 Die Portiersfrau meinte: „Am Sonntag sollten Kinder und Eltern zusammenbleiben . . . Aber bei den besseren Leuten gibt's ja kein Familienleben mehr."

Emma, das eine der beiden Fräulein vom Konditor° im Nebenhaus, machte sich bittere Vorwürfe° wegen ihrer Prüderie.° Hätte sie dem armen jungen Mann nicht nein gesagt, dann wäre er heute nachmittag mit ihr gewesen und nicht beim
35 Fußballspiel.

Bobby, der Dobermann, dachte: „Gestern hat er mir einen Tritt gegeben.° In der ersten Wut° wollte ich ihn ins Bein beißen. Leider, leider hab' ich es nicht getan. Sonst wäre es ihm heute kaum möglich gewesen, zum Fußballmatch zu gehen."

Spätabends kam, vergnügt,° Leopold nach Hause. Das mit dem Fußballmatch hatte
40 er nur vorgeschwindelt.° In Wirklichkeit war er mit Rosa, dem anderen Fräulein vom Konditor nebenan, auf einer Landpartie° gewesen, die, schien es, einen zufriedenstellenden° Verlauf° genommen hatte.

Die Mutter umarmte ihren Sohn in hemmungsloser° Rührung.°

Der Vater gab ihm ein paar Ohrfeigen.°

45 Die Großmutter mütterlicherseits faltete die Hände und betete° stumm:° „Lieber Gott, ich danke Dir, daß er wieder gelogen hat."

ZUR ORIENTIERUNG UND ZUM ZUSAMMENFASSEN

1. Hauptabschnitt (Z. 1–11)

VOR DEM LESEN: Erzählen Sie Ihren Mitstudenten, was Sie an einem typischen Sonntagnachmittag machen!

NACH DEM LESEN: Was paßt wo? Einige Namen passen mehrmals.

die Fahrgäste° Tante Alwine der Bus Leopold die Mutter   *passengers*

1. _____ meinte, junge Leute sollten zu Fuß gehen, statt mit dem Bus zu fahren.
2. _____ waren alle schwer verletzt.
3. _____ meinte, er könne seine Schularbeiten auch noch am Abend machen.
4. _____ stürzte in einen Graben.
5. _____ sagte, er fahre jetzt zum Fußballmatch.
6. _____ meinte, es sei schade ums Geld für die Busfahrt.
7. _____ sagte, der Bus fahre um Viertel nach drei ab.

8. _____ fragte, wann Leopold denn seine Schularbeiten machen wolle.
9. _____ war Gymnasiast.

2. Hauptabschnitt (Z. 12–Ende)

superstitious

VOR DEM LESEN: Sind Sie abergläubisch°? Stellen Sie sich die folgende Situation vor: Sie wollen so billig wie möglich nach Europa fliegen. Kurz bevor Sie zum Reisebüro kommen, läuft Ihnen eine große schwarze Katze über den Weg. Im Reisebüro finden Sie heraus, daß die billigste Chartergesellschaft fast ganz ausgebucht ist, und daß der einzige Tag, an dem Sie noch einen Platz bekommen können, ein Freitag und der dreizehnte ist. Mit anderen Gesellschaften können Sie fliegen, wann Sie wollen, aber der Flug kostet Sie dann mindestens° 200 Dollar mehr. Wer von Ihnen würde den billigeren Flug am Freitag nehmen?

at least

NACH DEM LESEN: Als die Nachricht kommt, der Bus sei in einen Graben gestürzt und alle Fahrgäste seien schwer verletzt, suchen Leopolds Verwandte und Bekannte nach Erklärungen für sein Unglück. Sagen Sie, wer welche der folgenden Erklärungen hat!

1. Weil ich ihm nein gesagt habe.
2. Weil mir heute früh zwei Nonnen begegnet sind.
3. Weil Leopold nicht zu Fuß zum Fußballmatch gegangen ist.　　　die Mutter
4. Weil niemand daran gedacht hat, daß heute Großvaters Sterbetag ist.　　　der Vater
5. Weil Leopold gelogen hat.　　　die Großmutter
6. Weil ich ihn nicht ins Bein gebissen habe.　　　die Tante
7. Weil es bei den besseren Leuten kein Familienleben mehr gibt.　　　der Onkel
8. Weil die Familie wegen der Kleider von Leopolds Mutter nicht schon am ersten aufs Land gefahren ist.　　　Bobby, der Dobermann
9. Weil Fußball und Sport den jungen Leuten heutzutage viel zu wichtig sind.　　　die Hausgehilfin°

maid

10. Weil ich ihm erlaubt habe, seine Schularbeiten erst am Abend zu machen.　　　Emma
Die Portiersfrau

REAKTIONEN

Am Ende seiner Geschichte erzählt der Autor, wie Leopolds Mutter, Vater und Großmutter reagierten, als er spät abends ganz vergnügt nach Hause kam. Am lustigsten ist wohl die Reaktion der Großmutter, die kurz vorher moralisierte: „Wer lügt, sündigt, und wer sündigt, wird bestraft", und die jetzt stumm betet: „Lieber Gott, ich danke Dir, daß er wieder gelogen hat." Wie die anderen Personen und Bobby, der Dobermann, reagierten, erfahren° wir nicht.

find out

Denken Sie sich mit zwei Gesprächspartnern zusammen aus, wie die Tante, der Onkel, die Hausgehilfin, die Portiersfrau, Emma und Bobby auf Leopolds uner-wartetes° Erscheinen° reagiert haben könnten. Erzählen Sie Ihren Mitstudenten, was sie sich ausgedacht haben.

unexpected / appearance

WORT, SINN UND KLANG

WÖRTER UNTER DER LUPE

EXPANDING VOCABULARY:
THE VERB *GEHEN* IN COMBINATION WITH PREFIXES

In *Kapitel 5* you learned that the meaning of verbs can be modified or changed by the addition of a prefix. In the small sampling below, you will see how the meaning of the verb **gehen** is changed by a number of separable prefixes. You will also see that within each set the meaning of the separable verb changes according to the context in which it is used.

WAS PASST ZUSAMMEN?   Suchen Sie die passenden englischen Verben!

ausgehen

1. Warum ist es so kalt? Ist das Feuer ausgegangen?	to end
2. Wenn mir das Geld ausgeht, verkaufe ich einfach meinen Wagen.	to go out
3. Ich muß jetzt gehen. Ihr könnt mir dann erzählen, wie der Film aus-gegangen ist.	to go out
4. Gehst du heute abend schon wieder aus, oder bleibst du endlich mal zu Hause und schreibst dein Referat fer-tig?	to run out of

eingehen

1. Professor Seidlmeyer sagte, er würde in seiner nächsten Vorlesung auf die-ses Problem eingehen.	to die
2. Warum hat meine Hose denn plötzlich so kurze Beine? Sie ist beim Waschen eingegangen.	to sink in; to understand
3. Wo ist denn dein Hamster? Der arme Kerl war krank und ist ge-stern eingegangen.	to shrink

4. Wann geht es dir endlich ein, daß ich mit dir nichts mehr zu tun haben will?	to go into

nachgehen

1. Warum bist du mir nachgegangen? Ich habe dir doch gesagt, daß ich allein sein möchte.	to be slow
2. Warum kommst du denn so spät? Ich glaube, meine Uhr geht mal wieder nach.	to haunt
3. Gehen Sie dieser Sache bitte nach, und lassen Sie mich dann wissen, was Sie herausgefunden haben.	to follow
experience 4. Dieses schreckliche Erlebnis° wird mir noch viele Jahre lang nachgehen.	to investigate

vorgehen

tougher 1. Die Polizei sollte gegen betrunkene Fahrer viel schärfer° vorgehen.	to go on
2. Wenn ich wüßte, was in Sandras Kopf vorgeht, könnte ich ihr vielleicht helfen.	to be fast
3. Warum kommst du denn so früh? Ich glaube, meine Uhr geht mal wieder vor.	to be

aufgehen

locked 1. Warum geht denn die Tür nicht auf? Weil sie abgeschlossen° ist.	to be involved in
sowed 2. Von den Karotten, die ich gesät° habe, sind nur sehr wenige aufgegangen.	to go up
3. Claudia geht in ihrem Studium so auf, daß sie fast keine Zeit für Martin hat.	to open
4. 18 geteilt durch 6 geht auf, aber 20 geteilt durch 6 geht nicht auf.	to rise
5. Wann geht morgen die Sonne auf?	to divide evenly
6. Das Haus ist in Flammen aufgegangen.	to germinate

WEITERE NÜTZLICHE WÖRTER UND AUSDRÜCKE

die Landschaft *(the landscape)*

der Hügel, die Hügel	hill
der Berg, die Berge	mountain
das Gebirge	mountain range
das Tal, die Täler	valley

die Landschaft *(the landscape)*

der Bach, die Bäche	stream
der Fluß, die Flüsse	river
der Wasserfall, die Wasserfälle	waterfall
die Brücke, die Brücken	bridge
der See, die Seen	lake
das Süßwasser	fresh water
das Meer	sea, ocean
das Salzwasser	salt water
die Welle, die Wellen	wave
die Küste, die Küsten	coast
der Strand, die Strände	beach
der Sand	sand
die Bucht, die Buchten	bay
der Hafen, die Häfen	harbor
die Insel, die Inseln	island
die Halbinsel, die Halbinseln	peninsula
der Wald, die Wälder	forest
der Nadelbaum, die Nadelbäume	coniferous tree
der Laubbaum, die Laubbäume	deciduous tree
die Wiese, die Wiesen	meadow
das Feld, die Felder	field
die Erde	earth; soil
der Weg, die Wege	way; road
der Pfad, die Pfade	path

WÖRTER IM KONTEXT

WAS IST DAS?

a. Die Grenze zwischen Land und Meer nennt man die _____.

b. Einen sehr kleinen Weg nennt man einen _____.

c. Viele Bäume sind ein _____.

d. Einen Baum, der im Winter seine Blätter° verliert, nennt man einen _____.   *leaves*

e. Ein Stück Land, das mitten im Meer oder mitten in einem See liegt, nennt man eine _____.

f. Das Wasser im Meer ist _____.

g. Das Wasser in einem See ist _____.

h. Einen nicht sehr hohen Berg nennt man einen _____.

i. Ein Stück Land, das weit ins Meer oder in einen See hineinreicht° aber noch mit   *juts into* dem Festland° verbunden ist, nennt man eine _____.   *mainland*

j. Eine zum Landen von Schiffen ausgebaute Bucht nennt man einen _____.

k. Bäume die ihre Blätter auch im Winter nicht verlieren, nennt man _____.

l. Ein Stück Land, auf dem nur Gras und wilde Blumen wachsen, nennt man eine _____.

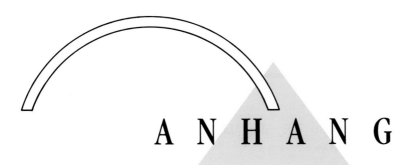

A N H A N G

GRAMMATICAL TABLES

1. *DER*-WORDS

The **der**-words are **der, die, das** (the), **dieser** (this), **jeder** (each, every), **welcher** (which).

	Masculine	Feminine	Neuter	Plural
Nominative	der	die	das	die
	dieser	diese	dieses	diese
Accusative	den	die	das	die
	diesen	diese	dieses	diese
Dative	dem	der	dem	den
	diesem	dieser	diesem	diesen
Genitive	des	der	des	der
	dieses	dieser	dieses	dieser

2. *EIN*-WORDS

The **ein**-words are **ein** (a, an), **kein** (not a, not any, no), and the possessive adjectives **mein** (my), **dein** (your), **sein** (his), **ihr** (her), **sein** (its), **unser** (our), **euer** (your), **ihr** (their), **Ihr** (your).

	Masculine	Feminine	Neuter	Plural
Nom.	ein	eine	ein	—
	mein	meine	mein	meine
Acc.	einen	eine	ein	—
	meinen	meine	mein	meine
Dat.	einem	einer	einem	—
	meinem	meiner	meinem	meinen
Gen.	eines	einer	eines	—
	meines	meiner	meines	meiner

3. PRONOUNS

a. Personal pronouns

Nom.	Acc.	Dat.	Subj.	Dir. Obj.	Ind. Obj.
ich	mich	mir	*I*	*me*	*me*
du	dich	dir	*you*	*you*	*you*
er	ihn	ihm	*he*	*him*	*him*
sie	sie	ihr	*she*	*her*	*her*
es	es	ihm	*it*	*it*	*it*
wir	uns	uns	*we*	*us*	*us*
ihr	euch	euch	*you*	*you*	*you*
sie	sie	ihnen	*they*	*them*	*them*
Sie	Sie	Ihnen	*you*	*you*	*you*

b. Reflexive pronouns

	Acc.	Dat.	Dir. Obj./Ind. Obj.
ich	mich	mir	*myself*
du	dich	dir	*yourself*
er	sich	sich	*himself*
sie	sich	sich	*herself*
es	sich	sich	*itself*
wir	uns	uns	*ourselves*
ihr	euch	euch	*yourselves*
sie	sich	sich	*themselves*
Sie	sich	sich	*yourself*
			yourselves

c. Definite articles used as pronouns

der (he, it, this one, that one), **die** (she, it, this one, that one), **das** (it, this one, that one), **die** (they, these, those)

	Masculine	Feminine	Neuter	Plural
Nom.	der	die	das	die
Acc.	den	die	das	die
Dat.	dem	der	dem	den**en**

d. *Ein*-words used as pronouns

einer (one), **keiner** (no one, none), **meiner** (mine), **deiner** (yours), **seiner** (his, its), **ihrer** (hers), **unserer** (ours), **eurer** (yours), **ihrer** (theirs), **Ihrer** (yours)

	Masculine	Feminine	Neuter	Plural
Nom.	keiner	keine	kein(e)s	keine
Acc.	keinen	keine	kein(e)s	keine
Dat.	keinem	keiner	keinem	keinen

e. Interrogative pronouns

	For Persons	For Things
Nom.	wer	was
Acc.	wen	was
Dat.	wem	—
Gen.	wessen	—

f. Relative pronouns

	Masculine	Feminine	Neuter	Plural
Nom.	der	die	das	die
Acc.	den	die	das	die
Dat.	dem	der	dem	den**en**
Gen.	des**sen**	der**en**	des**sen**	der**en**

4. ADJECTIVE ENDINGS

a. After *der*-words

	Masculine	Feminine	Neuter	Plural
Nom.	der jung**e** Mann	die jung**e** Frau	das lieb**e** Kind	die jung**en** Männer
Acc.	den jung**en** Mann	die jung**e** Frau	das lieb**e** Kind	die jung**en** Männer
Dat.	dem jung**en** Mann	der jung**en** Frau	dem lieb**en** Kind	den jung**en** Männern
Gen.	des jung**en** Mannes	der jung**en** Frau	des lieb**en** Kindes	der jung**en** Männer

b. After *ein*-words

	Masculine	Feminine	Neuter	Plural
Nom.	ein jung**er** Mann	eine jung**e** Frau	ein lieb**es** Kind	keine jung**en** Männer
Acc.	einen jung**en** Mann	eine jung**e** Frau	ein lieb**es** Kind	keine jung**en** Männer
Dat.	einem jung**en** Mann	einer jung**en** Frau	einem lieb**en** Kind	keinen jung**en** Männern
Gen.	eines jung**en** Mannes	einer jung**en** Frau	eines lieb**en** Kindes	keiner jung**en** Männer

c. For unpreceded adjectives

	Masculine	Feminine	Neuter	Plural
Nom.	gut**er** Käse	gut**e** Wurst	gut**es** Brot	gut**e** Würste
Acc.	gut**en** Käse	gut**e** Wurst	gut**es** Brot	gut**e** Würste
Dat.	gut**em** Käse	gut**er** Wurst	gut**em** Brot	gut**en** Würsten

5. *N*-NOUNS

All *n*-nouns are masculine. They are listed in dictionaries as follows: der Student, -en, -en.

	Singular	Plural
Nom.	der Student	die Student**en**
Acc.	den Student**en**	die Student**en**
Dat.	dem Student**en**	den Student**en**
Gen.	des Student**en**	der Student**en**

6. PREPOSITIONS

With Acc.	With Dat.	With Acc. or Dat.	With Gen. or Dat.
durch	aus	an	statt
für	außer	auf	trotz
gegen	bei	hinter	während
ohne	mit	in	wegen
um	nach	neben	
	seit	über	
	von	unter	
	zu	vor	
		zwischen	

7. ADJECTIVES AND ADVERBS WITH IRREGULAR COMPARATIVES AND SUPERLATIVES

Base Form	Comparative	Superlative
gern	lieber	liebst-
gut	besser	best-
hoch	höher	höchst-
nah	näher	nächst-
viel	mehr	meist-

B. VERBS

a. Present tense

	lernen[1]	arbeiten[2]	reisen[3]	geben[4]	backen[5]	laufen[6]
ich	lerne	arbeite	reise	gebe	backe	laufe
du	lernst	arbeit**est**	reis**t**	**gi**bst	**bä**ckst	**läu**fst
er/sie/es	lernt	arbeit**et**	reist	**gi**bt	**bä**ckt	**läu**ft
wir	lernen	arbeiten	reisen	geben	backen	laufen
ihr	lernt	arbeit**et**	reist	gebt	backt	lauft
sie	lernen	arbeiten	reisen	geben	backen	laufen
Sie	lernen	arbeiten	reisen	geben	backen	laufen

1. Regular verbs
2. Verbs with expanded endings
3. Verbs with contracted endings
4. Irregular verbs with stem vowel change **e** to **i (ie)**
5. Irregular verbs with stem vowel change **a** to **ä**
6. Irregular verbs with stem vowel change **au** to **äu**

b. Present tense of the auxiliaries *haben, sein, werden*

	haben	sein	werden
ich	habe	bin	werde
du	hast	bist	wirst
er/sie/es	hat	ist	wird
wir	haben	sind	werden
ihr	habt	seid	werdet
sie	haben	sind	werden
Sie	haben	sind	werden

c. Present tense of the modal verbs

	dürfen	können	mögen (möcht-)		müssen	sollen	wollen
ich	darf	kann	mag	(möchte)	muß	soll	will
du	darfst	kannst	magst	(möchtest)	mußt	sollst	willst
er/sie/es	darf	kann	mag	(möchte)	muß	soll	will
wir	dürfen	können	mögen	(möchten)	müssen	sollen	wollen
ihr	dürft	könnt	mögt	(möchtet)	müßt	sollt	wollt
sie	dürfen	können	mögen	(möchten)	müssen	sollen	wollen
Sie	dürfen	können	mögen	(möchten)	müssen	sollen	wollen

d. Imperatives

Familiar Singular	Lern(e)!	Gib!	Sei!
Familiar Plural	Lernt!	Gebt!	Seid!
Formal	Lernen Sie!	Geben Sie!	Seien Sie!

e. Simple past tense

	Regular Verbs		**Irregular Verbs**
ich	lernte	arbeitete	ging
du	lerntest	arbeitetest	gingst
er/sie/es	lernte	arbeitete	ging
wir	lernten	arbeiteten	gingen
ihr	lerntet	arbeitetet	gingt
sie	lernten	arbeiteten	gingen
Sie	lernten	arbeiteten	gingen

f. Present perfect tense

	Regular Verbs				**Irregular Verbs**			
ich	habe	gelernt	bin	gereist	habe	gesungen	bin	gegangen
du	hast	gelernt	bist	gereist	hast	gesungen	bist	gegangen
er/sie/es	hat	gelernt	ist	gereist	hat	gesungen	ist	gegangen
wir	haben	gelernt	sind	gereist	haben	gesungen	sind	gegangen
ihr	habt	gelernt	seid	gereist	habt	gesungen	seid	gegangen
sie	haben	gelernt	sind	gereist	haben	gesungen	sind	gegangen
Sie	haben	gelernt	sind	gereist	haben	gesungen	sind	gegangen

g. Past perfect tense

	Regular Verbs				**Irregular Verbs**			
ich	hatte	gelernt	war	gereist	hatte	gesungen	war	gegangen
du	hattest	gelernt	warst	gereist	hattest	gesungen	warst	gegangen
er/sie/es	hatte	gelernt	war	gereist	hatte	gesungen	war	gegangen
wir	hatten	gelernt	waren	gereist	hatten	gesungen	waren	gegangen
ihr	hattet	gelernt	wart	gereist	hattet	gesungen	wart	gegangen
sie	hatten	gelernt	waren	gereist	hatten	gesungen	waren	gegangen
Sie	hatten	gelernt	waren	gereist	hatten	gesungen	waren	gegangen

h. Future tense

ich	werde	lernen
du	wirst	lernen
er/sie/es	wird	lernen
wir	werden	lernen
ihr	werdet	lernen
sie	werden	lernen
Sie	werden	lernen

i. Subjunctive mood: Present and future time

	Subjunctive II			Subjunctive I: Indirect Discourse		
ich	ginge	käme	könnte	(ginge)	(käme)	könne
du	gingest	kämest	könntest	gehest	kommest	könnest
er/sie/es	ginge	käme	könnte	gehe	komme	könne
wir	gingen	kämen	könnten	(gingen)	(kämen)	(könnten)
ihr	ginget	kämet	könntet	gehet	kommet	könnet
sie	gingen	kämen	könnten	(gingen)	(kämen)	(könnten)
Sie	gingen	kämen	könnten	(gingen)	(kämen)	(könnten)

For verbs other than **haben, sein, werden, gehen, kommen, bleiben, wissen,** and the modals use **würde** + infinitive:

	Subjunctive II		Subjunctive I: Indirect Discourse	
ich	würde	lernen	(würde)	lernen
du	würdest	lernen	werdest	lernen
er/sie/es	würde	lernen	werde	lernen
wir	würden	lernen	(würden)	lernen
ihr	würdet	lernen	(würdet)	lernen
sie	würden	lernen	(würden)	lernen
Sie	würden	lernen	(würden)	lernen

Past time

	Subjunctive II				Subjunctive I: Indirect Discourse			
ich	hätte	gelernt	wäre	gegangen	(hätte)	gelernt	sei	gegangen
du	hättest	gelernt	wärest	gegangen	habest	gelernt	seiest	gegangen
er/sie/es	hätte	gelernt	wäre	gegangen	habe	gelernt	sei	gegangen
wir	hätten	gelernt	wären	gegangen	(hätten)	gelernt	seien	gegangen
ihr	hättet	gelernt	wäret	gegangen	habet	gelernt	seiet	gegangen
sie	hätten	gelernt	wären	gegangen	(hätten)	gelernt	seien	gegangen
Sie	hätten	gelernt	wären	gegangen	(hätten)	gelernt	seien	gegangen

Modal Verbs

	Subjunctive II			Subjunctive I: Indirect Discourse		
ich	hätte	lernen	sollen	(hätte)	lernen	sollen
du	hättest	lernen	sollen	habest	lernen	sollen
er/sie/es	hätte	lernen	sollen	habe	lernen	sollen
wir	hätten	lernen	sollen	(hätten)	lernen	sollen
ihr	hättet	lernen	sollen	habet	lernen	sollen
sie	hätten	lernen	sollen	(hättet)	lernen	sollen
Sie	hätten	lernen	sollen	(hätten)	lernen	sollen

j. Passive Voice

	Present Tense		Simple Past Tense	
ich	werde	abgeholt	wurde	abgeholt
du	wirst	abgeholt	wurdest	abgeholt
er/sie/es	wird	abgeholt	wurde	abgeholt
wir	werden	abgeholt	wurden	abgeholt
ihr	werdet	abgeholt	wurdet	abgeholt
sie	werden	abgeholt	wurden	abgeholt
Sie	werden	abgeholt	wurden	abgeholt

	Present Perfect Tense			Past Perfect Tense		
ich	bin	abgeholt	worden	war	abgeholt	worden
du	bist	abgeholt	worden	warst	abgeholt	worden
er/sie/es	ist	abgeholt	worden	war	abgeholt	worden
wir	sind	abgeholt	worden	waren	abgeholt	worden
ihr	seid	abgeholt	worden	wart	abgeholt	worden
sie	sind	abgeholt	worden	waren	abgeholt	worden
Sie	sind	abgeholt	worden	waren	abgeholt	worden

	Future Tense		
ich	werde	abgeholt	werden
du	wirst	abgeholt	werden
er/sie/es	wird	abgeholt	werden
wir	werden	abgeholt	werden
ihr	werdet	abgeholt	werden
sie	werden	abgeholt	werden
Sie	werden	abgeholt	werden

PRINCIPAL PARTS OF IRREGULAR AND MIXED VERBS

The following list contains the principal parts of the irregular and mixed verbs in *Treffpunkt Deutsch*. With only a few exceptions, compound verbs are not listed.

Infinitive	Irr. Present	Simple Past	Perfect Tense	
Irregular verbs				
bleiben		bleib	ist geblieben	to stay; to remain
leihen		lieh	hat geliehen	to lend
reiten		ritt	ist geritten	to ride
scheinen		schien	hat geschienen	to shine; to seem
schneiden		schnitt	hat geschnitten	to cut
schreiben		schrieb	hat geschrieben	to write
schreien		schrie	hat geschrieen	to shout
steigen		stieg	ist gestiegen	to climb

Infinitive	Irr. Present	Simple Past	Perfect Tense	
Irregular verbs				
betrügen		betrog	hat betrogen	to betray; to cheat
fliegen		flog	ist geflogen	to fly
frieren		fror	hat gefroren	to be cold
gießen		goß	hat gegossen	to water
lügen		log	hat gelogen	to tell a lie
riechen		roch	hat gerochen	to smell
schießen		schoß	hat geschossen	to shoot
verbieten		verbot	hat verboten	to forbid
verlieren		verlor	hat verloren	to lose
ziehen		zog	hat gezogen	to pull
finden		fand	hat gefunden	to find
singen		sang	hat gesungen	to sing
springen		sprang	ist gesprungen	to jump
trinken		trank	hat getrunken	to drink
helfen	(hilft)	half	hat geholfen	to help
nehmen	(nimmt)	nahm	hat genommen	to take
sprechen	(spricht)	sprach	hat gesprochen	to speak
sterben	(stirbt)	starb	ist gestorben	to die
treffen	(trifft)	traf	hat getroffen	to meet
werfen	(wirft)	warf	hat geworfen	to throw
essen	(ißt)	aß	hat gegessen	to eat
fressen	(frißt)	fraß	hat gefressen	to eat (of animals)
geben	(gibt)	gab	hat gegeben	to give
lesen	(liest)	las	hat gelesen	to read
sehen	(sieht)	sah	hat gesehen	to see
vergessen	(vergißt)	vergaß	hat vergessen	to forget
backen	(bäckt)	backte	hat gebacken	to bake
einladen	(lädt ein)	lud ein	hat eingeladen	to invite
fahren	(fährt)	fuhr	ist gefahren	to drive
schlagen	(schlägt)	schlug	hat geschlagen	to hit
tragen	(trägt)	trug	hat getragen	to carry; to wear
waschen	(wäscht)	wusch	hat gewaschen	to wash
fallen	(fällt)	fiel	ist gefallen	to fall
fangen	(fängt)	fing	hat gefangen	to catch
halten	(hält)	hielt	hat gehalten	to hold; to stop
lassen	(läßt)	ließ	hat gelassen	to let; to leave
schlafen	(schläft)	schlief	hat geschlafen	to sleep
laufen	(läuft)	lief	ist gelaufen	to run
gehen		ging	ist gegangen	to go
hängen		hing	hat gehangen	to be hanging
heißen		hieß	hat geheißen	to be called
kommen		kam	ist gekommen	to come
liegen		lag	hat gelegen	to lie, to be situated
rufen		rief	hat gerufen	to call
saufen	(säuft)	soff	hat gesoffen	to drink heavily
schwimmen		schwamm	ist geschwommen	to swim

Infinitive	Irr. Present	Simple Past	Perfect Tense	
Irregular verbs				
sitzen		saß	hat gesessen	to sit
stehen		stand	hat gestanden	to stand
Mixed Verbs				
bringen		brachte	hat gebracht	to bring
denken		dachte	hat gedacht	to think
kennen		kannte	hat gekannt	to be acquainted with
rennen		rannte	ist gerannt	to run
wissen	(weiß)	wußte	hat gewußt	to know (a fact)
Modal Verbs				
dürfen	(darf)	durfte	hat gedurft	to be allowed to
können	(kann)	konnte	hat gekonnt	to be able to
mögen	(mag)	mochte	hat gemocht	to like
müssen	(muß)	mußte	hat gemußt	to have to
sollen	(soll)	sollte	hat gesollt	to be supposed to
wollen	(will)	wollte	hat gewollt	to want to
Auxiliary Verbs				
haben	(hat)	hatte	hat gehabt	to have
sein	(ist)	war	ist gewesen	to be
werden	(wird)	wurde	ist geworden	to become, to get

SUPPLEMENTARY WORD SETS

Kapitel 3

Fächer (*Fields of Study*)

art history	**Kunstgeschichte**
biology	**Biologie**
business	**Betriebswirtschaft**
chemistry	**Chemie**
chemical engineering	**Chemotechnik**
computer science	**Informatik**
economics	**Volkswirtschaft**
electrical engineering	**Elektrotechnik**
English language and literature	**Anglistik**
finance	**Finanzwirtschaft**
geography	**Geographie**
geology	**Geologie**
history	**Geschichte**
humanities	**Geisteswissenschaften**
mathematics	**Mathematik**

Kapitel 3

Fächer (*Fields of Study*)

mechanical engineering	**Maschinenbau**
medicine	**Medizin**
nursing	**Krankenpflege**
philosophy	**Philosophie**
physical education	**Leibeserziehung**
physics	**Physik**
political science	**Politikwissenschaft**
psychology	**Psychologie**
religious studies	**Religionswissenschaft**
Romance languages and literatures	**Romanistik**
sociology	**Soziologie**

Berufe (*Occupations*)

accountant	**Wirtschaftsprüfer**
bus driver	**Busfahrer**
chemist	**Chemiker**
computer programmer	**Programmierer**
doctor	**Arzt (Ärztin)**
factory worker	**Fabrikarbeiter**
teacher	**Lehrer (Lehrerin)**
housewife	**Hausfrau (Hausmann)**
lawyer	**Rechtsanwalt**
mailman	**Briefträger**
musician	**Musiker**
nurse	**Krankenschwester**
pharmacist	**Apotheker**
police officer	**Polizist**
professor	**Professor**
sales clerk	**Verkäufer**
social worker	**Sozialarbeiter**

Hobbys

to cook	**kochen**
(I like to cook.)	**(Ich koche gern.)**
to ski	**Schi laufen**
(I like to ski.)	**(Ich laufe gern Schi.)**
to go dancing	**tanzen gehen**
(I like to go dancing.)	**(Ich gehe gern tanzen.)**
to play cards	**Karten spielen**
(I like to play cards.)	**(Ich spiele gern Karten.)**
to bake	**backen**
to read	**lesen**
to sing	**singen**
to travel	**reisen**
to take photos	**fotografieren**
to go swimming	**schwimmen gehen**
to go hiking	**wandern gehen**
to go windsurfing	**Windsurfing gehen**
to go to concerts	**ins Konzert gehen**
to go to movies	**ins Kino gehen**
to go to the theater	**ins Theater gehen**
to play chess	**Schach spielen**

Hobbys

to play soccer	**Fußball spielen**
to play hockey	**Hockey spielen**
to play tennis	**Tennis spielen**
to play table tennis	**Tischtennis spielen**
to play the flute	**Flöte spielen**
to play the guitar	**Gitarre spielen**
to play the piano	**Klavier spielen**

Kapitel 4

Essen und Trinken

a glass of apple juice	**ein Glas Apfelsaft**
a glass of tomato juice	**ein Glas Tomatensaft**
a cup of tea	**eine Tasse Tee**
a can of cola	**eine Dose Cola**
a bottle of beer	**eine Flasche Bier**
muesli	**Müsli**
Cornflakes[1]	**Cornflakes**
toast	**Toast**
with butter	**mit Butter**
with jam	**mit Marmelade**
with honey	**mit Honig**
with peanut butter	**mit Erdnußbutter**
a hamburger	**ein Hamburger**
a hotdog	**ein Hotdog**
a cheese sandwich	**ein Käsebrot**
a liverwurst sandwich	**ein Leberwurstbrot**
a ham sandwich	**ein Schinkenbrot**
cutlet	**ein Schnitzel**
a steak	**ein Steak**
rice	**Reis**
noodles	**Nudeln**
fried potatoes	**Bratkartoffeln**
potato salad	**Kartoffelsalat**
coleslaw	**Krautsalat**
vegetables	**Gemüse**
carrots	**Karotten**
peas	**Erbsen**
beans	**Bohnen**
corn	**Mais**
a piece of apple pie or cake	**ein Stück Apfelkuchen**
a piece of cheese cake	**ein Stück Käsekuchen**
a piece of (layer) cake	**ein Stück Torte**
a cup of yogurt with fruit	**ein Becher Fruchtjoghurt**
(a dish of) ice cream	**ein Eis**
fruit	**Obst**
an apple	**ein Apfel**
a pear	**eine Birne**
a banana	**eine Banane**
an orange	**eine Apfelsine**

---

1. Since World War II many of the North American breakfast cereals have become available in Germany, Austria, and Switzerland.

GLOSSAR ZU DEN LESESTÜCKEN

Kapitel 12: Sie haben ihn sehr lieb

line 1: (ringing of) a door bell
line 2: amid echoing / on the stairs
line 3: **na ... können:** I might have known
line 4: rattling of keys
line 5: **kenn' ... aus:** I'll be able to manage
line 6: it will take
line 7: **Dabei ... notwendig:** I have to go (to the toilet) so badly
line 8: unlocking of the door / difficulty
line 10: are opened / slammed shut
line 11: (sound of) flushing
line 12: from a distance
line 13: I don't believe it!
line 17: notice / (audio) tape
line 18: good
line 22: it is bad for
line 24: asked
line 25: tape recorder / flushing mechanism / hook up
line 26: turns itself on / pee
line 27: why / brilliant
line 29: have the excuse
line 30: Austrian for **Abendessen**
line 31: the other day
line 32: darling / looks after
line 34: **wird's bald:** are you going to? / am waiting
line 36: flows / is turned off
line 37: dry off
line 40: about
line 41: proves
line 43: **geht ... los:** will turn on / on it
line 46: forgetful / luckily
line 47: **die ... kümmert:** who takes care of everything
line 50: shave
line 51: change / anyway / running late
line 53: button / press
line 54: **strömt ... aus:** will escape
line 56: **wirst ... verfehlen:** won't do the wrong thing
line 59: **stell ... um:** switch to record
line 61: sizzles
line 62: touch
line 63: a crash
line 64: done for (*lit.* in the trash can)
line 65: the other day
line 66: **Laß schmecken:** enjoy your meal
line 68: **er ... gerichtet:** he's always watching over you / **leiht ... Ohr:** is always ready to listen

line 69: surprise
line 70: record
line 73: is turned on
line 74: hissing sound
line 75: at worst
line 77: so that
line 79: **wir ... eilig:** we're in such a hurry
line 80: words of farewell
line 82: **nichts ... wird:** nothing will come of our outing
line 83: **wir ... nachholen:** we'll make up for it
line 87: conscientious
line 88: center
line 89: sympathy / who

Kapitel 13: San Salvador

line   2: signature
line   3: wavy lines
line   4: sheet / carefully
line   5: **hielt ... inne:** paused / screwed
line   6: looked at / ink
line   7: stationery store / would turn
line   8: again / with a flourish
line 11: cleared / glanced over / movie ads
line 12: **schob ... beiseite:** pushed aside / ashtray / piece of paper
line 14: show
line 15: rehearsal
line 16: on top of all that
line 17: **drehte ... ab:** turned off
line 19: handwriting
line 22: would read / message / would be alarmed
line 23: nevertheless / chest of drawers / have happened
line 24: The Lion (*name of a pub*)
line 25: smile / despair
line 26: **sich ... abfinden:** resign herself to it
line 27: brush
line 28: temple / run along
line 29: thought about
line 30: instructions / slightly / turn
line 31: compared

Kapitel 14: Forgive me!

line   1: high school teacher
line   2: when addressing God
line   3: prayer / **in ... Gefühlsaufwallung:** in moments of intense emotion
line   4: more frequently
line   5: use
line   6: go past / stepped
line   8: on a bench in the last row
line   9: attentive / polished / desk-top / small notebook
line 10: write down

line 11: mirror
line 12: pulled
line 13: made / actress
line 14: passed
line 15: German movie star
line 16: nettled / teased
line 17: **blies ... auf:** puffed up his cheeks
line 20: **wurden ... geschickt:** were sent
line 21: buzzed / low-flying fighter planes
line 22: **der ... zu:** toward the bridge over the Rhine / rattled
line 23: rumbling / crowded / tanks
line 24: sidewalks
line 25: singly / tattered
line 26: **wurde ... aufgewühlt:** was in a turmoil / agitation / uncertainty
line 27: anticipation
line 28: armed / distributed / guns / bazookas
line 29: roadblocks / set up / ditches / dug / reluctantly
line 30: idea
line 31: enthusiastic / command / former
line 32: World War I officer / hill
line 35: I was mistaken / flirt / but more like
line 36: proud
line 39: larks / rose / furrows
line 41: welcomed / What insanity.
line 42: crazy
line 46: eerie / stumbled
line 47: pulled
line 50: explosions / angry
line 51: churned up / to throw out / to plow out
line 54: fragments / breath
line 56: rumbling
line 57: stood up
line 58: edge of the ditch
line 59: shot / stream
line 60: pipe
line 61: chalice
line 62: **ein ... Kelchrand:** a red arch formed a curve from a gaping wound in its neck to the edge of the chalice
line 64: thought / out-of-place / paralyzing
line 65: gushing
line 66: **brach ... zusammen:** his body collapsed / forward
line 67: **sackte ... Hocke:** sank into a crouching position / hit
line 68: **nach ... geöffnet:** palms down
line 69: horror / shadow
line 70: foreign
line 71: weapon / **nach ... zielte:** aimed at Siegbert
line 72: murderer
line 73: lowered / threw
line 74: bent down / pulled

Kapitel 14: Geschichte ohne Moral

line 1: high school student / **= fortgehen:** to go away
line 6: it was a waste of
line 9: news / as scheduled
line 10: departed / plunged / all / passengers
line 11: wounded
line 12: faint / **klagte ... an:** reproached herself incessantly
line 14: was atoning / weakness
line 15: cursed / idol
line 18: meaningfully
line 19: dearly departed
line 21: **bin ... gekommen:** I caught him telling a lie / admonished / sins
line 22: punished
line 23: maid
line 25: **haben ... lustig gemacht:** you made fun of me
line 26: caretakers
line 27: sad / case / discuss / to the country
line 28: seamstress / my lady's
line 29: rags
line 32: pastry shop
line 33: **machte ... Vorwürfe:** reproached herself / prudishness
line 36: **hat ... gegeben:** he kicked me
line 37: rage
line 39: in a good mood
line 40: made up
line 41: outing
line 42: satisfactory / course
line 43: unrestrained / emotion
line 44: slaps
line 45: prayed / silently

GERMAN-ENGLISH VOCABULARY

This German-English vocabulary includes all the words used in *Treffpunkt Deutsch* except numbers. Chapter numbers (and E for *Einleitung*) are given for all words and expressions occurring in the chapter vocabularies. The letters A and B following the chapter numbers refer to *Nützliche Wörter und Ausdrücke* and *Weitere Nützliche Wörter und Ausdrücke* respectively. Passive vocabulary does not have a chapter reference.

Nouns are listed with their plural forms: **die Studentin, -nen.** No plural entry is given if the plural is rarely used or nonexistent. When two entries follow a noun, the first one indicates the genitive and the second indicates the plural: **der Student, -en, -en.**

Irregular and mixed verbs are listed with their principal parts. Vowel changes in the present tense are noted in parentheses and auxiliaries for the perfect tense are given: **lesen (liest), las, hat gelesen.** Separable prefixes are indicated by a raised dot between the prefix and the verb stem: **an•fangen.**

The following abbreviations are used:

acc	accusative	*dat*	dative
adj	adjective	*gen*	genitive
adv	adverb	*pl*	plural
coll	colloquial	*prep*	preposition
conj	conjunction	*sing*	singular

A

ab und zu now and then (14A)
der **Abend**
  Guten Abend! Good evening!
  (E)
  Wann eßt ihr zu Abend? When
  do you eat supper? (4A)
abend
  heute abend tonight (2B)
  morgen abend tomorrow night
  (2B)
das **Abendessen** evening meal,
  supper
  zum Abendessen for supper
abends in the evening (4B)
aber but (1B)
**ab•fahren (fährt ab), fuhr ab, ist
  abgefahren** to leave, to depart
  (5B)
**ab•geben (gibt ab), gab ab, hat
  abgegeben** to hand in
abgelaufen worn (of shoes)
abgenutzt worn
abgetragen worn (of clothes)
ab•hauen to clear out
  Hau ab! Get lost! (12B)
ab•holen to pick up (5A)
das **Abitur** high school diploma
  (10B)
ab•sägen to saw off
abscheulich awful
der **Abschied** departure
**ab•schließen, schloß ab, hat
  abgeschlossen** to lock
**ab•schreiben, schrieb ab, hat
  abgeschrieben** to copy (7A)
**ab•steigen, stieg ab, ist abge-
  stiegen** to get off, (dismount)
ab•stellen to turn off (12A)
ab•trocknen to dry off (12A)
die **Abteilung, -en** department
  (12B)
der **Abteilungsleiter, - / die Abteilungsleiterin, -nen**
  department manager (12B)

**ab•waschen (wäscht ab), wusch
  ab, hat abgewaschen** to do
  the dishes
die **Abwechslung** change
achten auf (+ *acc*) to pay attention to
die **Adresse, -n** address (9B)
der **Affe, -n** ape, monkey
ähnlich similar
die **Ahnung**
  Ich habe keine Ahnung. I
  have no idea. (14A)
die **Aktentasche, -n** briefcase
  (9B)
der **Akzent, -e** accent
alarmieren to alert
das **Album, Alben** album
der **Alkohol** alcohol
alle everybody
  Es ist alle. It's all gone.
  alle vierzehn Tage every two
  weeks (9A)
allein alone
alleinstehend single (not married)
  (13B)
alles all, everything
  vor allem above all (9B)
die **Alpen** the Alps
als than (2A); when (*conj*) (10A)
  nichts als nothing but (2A)
  als Kind as a child (6A)
also then
alt old (2B)
altbacken stale
das **Alter** age
das **Altersheim, -e** old people's
  home
ältlich elderly
altmodisch old-fashioned
(das) **Amerika** America
der **Amerikaner, - / die
  Amerikanerin, -nen**
  American (person) (1B)
amerikanisch American

die **Ampel, -n** traffic light
an on; to (9B)
an•bieten, bot an, hat angeboten
  to offer
ander- other; different (7A)
ändern to change
anders different
an•deuten to indicate
der **Anfang** beginning (10B)
  Anfang Mai at the beginning of
  May
**an•fangen (fängt an), fing an,
  hat angefangen** to begin (5B)
der **Anfänger, -** beginner
an•fassen to touch (12A)
das **Angebot, -e** offer
die **Angel, -n** hinge
Angenommen! Agreed!
der (die) **Angestellte, -n** employee
  (13B)
die **Angst, ̈e** fear
  Angst haben (vor + *dat*) to be
  afraid (of) (10A)
**an•haben (hat an), hatte an, hat
  angehabt** to wear, to have on
**an•halten (hält an), hielt an, hat
  angehalten** to stop
der **Anhalter, -** hitchhiker
  per Anhalter (fahren) to hitchhike
der **Anhänger, -** follower
an•hören to listen to (5B)
**an•kommen, kam an, ist an-
  gekommen** to arrive (5B)
die **Anlage, -n** park
**an•nehmen (nimmt an), nahm
  an, hat angenommen** to assume
an•probieren to try on (5A)
an•pumpen to borrow money
  from
der **Anruf, -e** (telephone) call
an•rufen, rief an, hat angerufen
  to call (on the telephone) (5A)

an•schauen to look at (5A)

die **Antenne, -n** antenna

antik antique

die **Antwort, -en** answer (10B)

antworten (+ *dat*) to answer (3B)

die **Anweisung, -en** instruction

an•zahlen to pay down (11B)

die **Anzahlung, -en** down payment

die **Anzeige, -n** ad (10B)

an•ziehen, zog an, hat an-gezogen to put on (7B)

  sich an•ziehen to dress (12B)

der **Apfel, ̈** apple

der **Apfelkuchen, -** apple cake, apple pie

der **Apfelsaft** apple juice (3B)

der **Apfelstrudel** apple strudel

die **Apotheke, -n** pharmacy (8B)

der **Apotheker, -** / die **Apothekerin, -nen** pharmacist

der **Apparat, -e** apparatus, appliance

der **Appetit** appetite

  Guten Appetit! Enjoy your meal! (8A)

der **April** April (2B)

das **Aquarium** aquarium

die **Arbeit** work (6A)

arbeiten to work (3A)

  arbeiten an (+ *dat*) to work on (12B)

der **Arbeiter, -** / die **Arbeiterin, -nen** worker

die **Arbeitserfahrung** work experience (10B)

arbeitslos unemployed (6A)

der/die **Arbeitslose, -n** unemployed person

die **Arbeitslosigkeit** unemployment

der **Architekt, -en** / die **Architektin, -nen** architect

der **Ärger** annoyance, trouble

ärgern to annoy, to make angry

sich ärgern über (+ *acc*) to get annoyed with (12B)

das **Argument, -e** argument

arm poor (5A)

der **Arm, -e** arm (10B)

das **Armband, ̈er** bracelet (7B)

die **Armbanduhr, -en** wristwatch (7B)

arrangieren to arrange

der **Artikel, -** article (5B)

der **Arzt, ̈e** / die **Ärztin, -nen** doctor (8B)

der **Aschenbecher, -** ashtray (13A)

der **Assistent, -en** / die **Assistentin, -nen** assistant

der **Ast, ̈e** branch

der **Atem** breath

  außer Atem out of breath

der **Athlet, -en, en** / die **Athletin, -nen** athlete

attraktiv attractive

auch too, also (2A)

auf on, onto; to (9B)

  Auf Wiederhören! Good-bye! (on the telephone) (1B)

  Auf Wiedersehen! Good-bye! (E)

auf•bleiben to stay up

auf•essen (ißt auf), aß auf, hat aufgegessen to eat up

die **Aufgabe, -n** task

auf•geben (gibt auf), gab auf, hat aufgegeben to give up

auf•gehen, ging auf, ist aufgegangen to open; to rise

auf•hängen to hang up

auf•hören to stop (5B)

auf•machen to open (9B)

aufmerksam attentive

die **Aufnahme, -n** recording (12A)

auf•passen to pay attention (6B)

auf•räumen to tidy up

sich auf•regen über (+ *acc*) to get excited about, to get upset with (12B)

sich auf•richten to stand up

auf•schließen, schloß auf, hat aufgeschlossen to unlock

auf•sehen (sieht auf), sah auf, hat aufgesehen to look up

auf•springen, sprang auf, ist aufgesprungen to jump up

auf•stehen, stand auf, ist aufgestanden to get up (5A)

auf•wachen to wake up (6B)

auf•wärmen to warm up

auf•wecken to wake (someone) up

auf•ziehen, zog auf, hat aufgezogen to wind (a clock)

das **Auge, -n** eye (10B)

der **August** August (2B)

aus from (E); out of (7B)

aus•arbeiten to work out, to prepare

aus•breiten to spread out

der **Ausdruck, ̈e** expression (14A)

die **Auseinandersetzung, -en** argument

aus•essen (ißt aus), aß aus, hat ausgegessen to finish (eating)

aus•fallen (fällt aus), fiel aus, ist ausgefallen to be canceled

  ausfallen lassen to skip

der **Ausflug, ̈e** outing

aus•füllen to fill out (11A)

aus•geben (gibt aus), gab aus, hat ausgegeben to spend (8B)

ausgebucht booked up

aus•gehen, ging aus, ist ausgegangen to go out (5B)

  Mir ist das Geld ausgegangen. I ran out of money.

ausgezeichnet excellent

sich aus•kennen, kannte sich aus, hat sich ausgekannt to know one's way around

die **Auskunft** information

die **Auslage, -n** window display

der **Ausländer, -** foreigner

ausländisch foreign

das **Auslandsamt** foreign students' office

aus•packen to unpack (6A)

aus•probieren to try out (5A)

die **Ausrede, -n** excuse

die **Aussage, -n** statement

aus•schlafen (schläft aus), schlief aus, hat ausgeschlafen to sleep in (5A)

  mal richtig ausschlafen to sleep in for a change

aus•schreiben, schrieb aus, hat ausgeschrieben to write out

außer except for (7B)

  außer sich sein to be beside oneself

außerdem besides (2A)

aus•sehen (sieht aus), sah aus, hat ausgesehen

  aus•sehen wie to look like

  Das sieht gut aus. That looks good. (8A)

aus•setzen mit to interrupt

die **Aussicht** view

die **Aussprache** pronunciation

aus•stehen, stand aus, hat ausgestanden to endure

aus•stehen *(cont.)*

Ich kann den Kerl nicht ausstehen. I can't stand that guy. (7A)

aus•steigen, stieg aus, ist ausgestiegen to get out (13B)

(das) **Australien** Australia

aus•strömen to escape, leak

aus•suchen to select

der **Austauschschüler, -** / die **Austauschschülerin, -nen** exchange student

aus•trinken, trank aus, hat ausgetrunken to finish (drinking)

der **Auswanderer, -** emigrant

aus•wandern to emigrate (6A)

aus•ziehen, zog aus, hat (ist) ausgezogen to take off (7B); to move out (9B)

sich **aus•ziehen** to undress (12B)

das **Auto, -s** car (3B)

die **Autobahn, -en** highway (11A)

automatisch automatic

automatisieren to automate

die **Automatisierung** automation

der **Automechaniker, -** / die **Automechanikerin, -nen** auto mechanic

der **Autor, -en** / die **Autorin, -nen** author

der **Autostopp**

per Autostopp reisen to hitch-hike

der **Autounfall, ⁻e** car accident

B

das **Baby, -s** baby

der **Bach, ⁻e** stream (14B)

backen (bäckt), backte (buk), hat gebacken to bake (3B)

der **Bäcker, -** baker (8B)

die **Bäckerei** bakery (8B)

das **Bad, ⁻er** bath; bathroom (9A)

(sich) **baden** to bathe, to have a bath; to swim (6B)

die **Badewanne, -n** bathtub (9A)

das **Badewetter** swimming weather (1A)

das **Badezimmer, -** bathroom (9A)

die **Bahn** railway (13A)

der **Bahnhof, ⁻e** railway station (8B)

bald soon (4B)

der **Balkon, -s** balcony (9A)

der **Ball, ⁻e** ball

die **Banane, -n** banana

die **Bank, ⁻e** bench (14A)

die **Bank, -en** bank (8A)

der **Bankier, -s** banker

der **Bankräuber, -** bank robber

bankrott bankrupt

der **Bär, -en, -en** bear

Ich habe einen Bärenhunger. I'm famished.

das **Barometer, -** barometer

der **Bart, ⁻e** beard

bärtig bearded

der **Bauarbeiter, -** / die **Bauarbeiterin, -nen** construction worker

der **Bauch, ⁻e** stomach, belly (10B)

bauen to build (8A)

der **Bauer, -n, -n** farmer (10A)

das **Baujahr, -e** year of manufacture (13B)

der **Baum, ⁻e** tree (6B)

die **Baumwolle** cotton

beantworten (+ *acc*) to answer

der **Becher**

ein **Becher Joghurt** a carton of yogurt (4A)

bedeuten to mean

die **Bedeutung** meaning

sich **beeilen** to hurry (12B)

der **Befehl, -e** command (14A)

befreundet sein to be friends

begegnen (+ *dat*) to meet

der **Beginn** beginning

beginnen, begann, hat begonnen to begin

behalten (behält), behielt, hat behalten to keep

bei at, at the home of (7B); with

bei euch where you come from, where you live (2A); at your house (6A)

bei IBM at IBM (3A)

bei Monika at Monika's (6A)

bei uns where I (we) come from, where I (we) live, back home (2A); at our house (6A)

bei•bringen, brachte bei, hat beigebracht to teach

beide both, two (8A)

das **Bein, -e** leg (10B)

das **Beispiel** example (6B)

zum Beispiel (z.B.) for example

(e.g.) (6B)

beißen, biß, hat gebissen to bite

der **Beistelltisch, -e** end table

beizen to stain wood

bekannt well-known

der (die) **Bekannte, -n** acquaintance

bekommen, bekam, hat bekommen to get, to receive (5B)

bellen to bark

sich **benehmen (benimmt sich), benahm sich, hat sich benommen** to behave (12B)

das **Benehmen** behavior

das **Benzin** gasoline (13B)

benutzen to use

bequem comfortable (11B)

berechnen to calculate

die **Berechnung, -en** calculation

bereits already (11A)

der **Berg, -e** mountain

bergsteigen to go mountain climbing

berichten to report (14B)

der **Beruf** occupation, profession (3B)

Was sind Sie von Beruf? What do you do for a living? (3B)

berufstätig working

berühmt famous

bescheiden modest

beschließen, beschloß, hat beschlossen to decide

beschreiben, beschrieb, hat beschrieben to describe (5B)

die **Beschreibung, -en** description

sich **beschweren** to complain

besichtigen to tour, to view

der **Besitzer, -** / die **Besitzerin, -nen** owner (13B)

besonders especially

besorgen to get

besprechen (bespricht), besprach, hat besprochen to discuss (11A)

besser better

das **Besteck** cutlery (8B)

bestehen aus to consist of

bestellen to order (5B)

bestimmt certain(ly); for sure (2A)

bestrafen to punish

der **Besuch, -e** visit; company

zu Besuch kommen to come for a visit, to visit (8B)

besuchen to visit (3B)

der **Besucher, -** visitor
beten to pray
betrachten to regard
das **Bett, -en** bed (9A)
  ins Bett to bed (2B)
betrügen, betrog, hat betrogen to betray, to deceive, to cheat (11A)
betrunken drunk
bevor before (*conj*) (10B)
bewaffnen to arm
der **Bewerber, - /** die **Bewerberin, -nen** applicant
beweisen to prove
die **Bewerbung, -en** application (10B)
bewundern to admire
bewußt consciously, knowingly
bezahlen to pay (6B)
die **Bibliothek, -en** library (4A)
  in die Bibliothek to the library (2B)
die **Biene, -n** bee
das **Bier** beer (3B)
der **Bierbauch, ⁻e** beer belly
das **Bild, -er** picture (5A)
die **Bildunterschrift, -en** caption
das **Billard** billiards
billig cheap (2B)
die **Biochemie** biochemistry
die **Biologie** biology
die **Birne, -n** pear; light bulb (13A)
bis until (3A)
  bis dahin by then
  Bis heute abend! See you tonight! (5A)
  Bis nachher! See you later! (3A)
  von ... bis from . . . to (4B)
bisher up to now
bißchen
  ein bißchen a bit (4A)
der **Bissen, -** bite (to eat)
bitte please (1B)
  Wie bitte? Pardon? (E)
bitten, bat, hat gebeten to ask
bitter bitter
Bitte schön? May I help you? (6B)
Bitte schön! You're welcome! (6B)
der **Bizeps** biceps
das **Blatt, ⁻er** leaf; sheet of paper
blau blue (1B); drunk
bleiben, blieb, ist geblieben to stay, to remain (6B)
blind blind
die **Blindheit** blindness

blöd stupid
blond blonde
blühen to bloom
die **Blume, -n** flower (8B)
das **Blumengeschäft** flower shop (8B)
die **Bluse, -en** blouse (7B)
das **Blut** blood (14A)
blutig bloody
der **Boden, ⁻** ground
der **Bodensee** Lake Constance
der **Bogen, ⁻** arch
  der **Bogen Papier** sheet of paper
die **Bohne, -n** bean
bohren to drill
der **Bohrer, -** drill
der **Bomber, -** bomber
das **Boot, -e** boat
borgen to borrow; to lend
böse bad, evil (11A)
der **Boß, Bosse** boss
der **Braten, -** roast
die **Bratkartoffeln** (*pl*) fried potatoes
die **Bratwurst, ⁻e** (frying) sausage
brauchen to need (3B); to take (of time)
  Du brauchst nicht zu kommen. You don't have to come.
braun brown (7B)
brav good, well-behaved (12A)
die **BRD (die Bundesrepublik Deutschland)** the FRG (the Federal Republic of Germany) (1B)
brechen (bricht), brach, hat gebrochen to break
die **Bremse, -n** brake (13B)
brennen, brannte, hat gebrannt to burn
das **Brett, -er** board
  das schwarze Brett bulletin board (9B)
die **Brezel, -n** pretzel
der **Brief, -e** letter (5B)
die **Briefmarke, -n** stamp (6A)
der **Brieföffner, -** letter opener
der **Briefträger, -** mailman
die **Brille** (eye)glasses (9B)
bringen, brachte, hat gebracht to bring (10B)
die **Brokkoli** (*pl*) broccoli
das **Brot** bread; sandwich (4A)
  eine Scheibe Brot a slice of

bread (4A)
das **Brötchen, -** roll (4A)
die **Brücke, -n** bridge (14A)
der **Bruder, ⁻** brother (3B)
brüderlich brotherly
brünett brunette
die **Brust** chest (10B)
brutzeln to sizzle
das **Buch, ⁻er** book (5B)
buchen to book (11B)
das **Bücherregal, -e** book case (9A)
die **Bücherstütze, -n** bookend
der **Bücherwurm** bookworm
der **Buchhalter, -** accountant
die **Buchhandlung** bookstore (8B)
buchstabieren to spell
die **Bucht, -en** bay (14B)
das **Büfett, -s** buffet (9A)
das **Bügeleisen, -** iron
bügeln to iron
der **Bulle, -n** bull
das **Bündel, -** bundel
die **Bundesbahn** Federal Railway
die **Bundesrepublik Deutschland (die BRD)** the Federal Republic of Germany (the FRG) (1B)
der **Bürgermeister, -** mayor
das **Büro, -s** office (10B)
bürsten to brush
der **Bus, -se** bus (3B)
die **Busfahrt, -en** bus trip
der **Busch, ⁻e** bush (10A)
buschig bushy
der **Busfahrer, - /** die **Busfahrerin, -nen** bus driver
die **Bushaltestelle, -n** bus stop
die **Butter** butter

C

die **Cafeteria** university cafeteria (*for light meals and snacks*) (4A)
  in die Cafeteria to the cafeteria (2B)
campen gehen to go camping
die **CD-Platte, -n;** die **Cd, -s** compact disc; CD
der **CD-Spieler** CD player
das **Cello, -s** cello
der **Champagner** champagne
der **Champignon, -s** mushroom
die **Chance, -n** chance

der **Chef, -s**/die **Chefin, -innen** boss (12B)
die **Chemie** chemistry
chinesisch Chinese
der **Chirurg, -en** surgeon
der **Chor, ⁻e** choir (13A)
das **Cockpit** cockpit
die **Cola** cola (3B)
der **Computer, -** computer
die **Couch, -es** sofa, couch (9A)
der **Couchtisch, -e** coffee table (9A)

D

da there; then
das **Dach, ⁻er** roof (14A); top (of a car)
dafür in exchange
dahin
  bis dahin by then
damals at that time (10A)
die **Dame, -n** lady (8A)
  Dame spielen to play checkers
damit so that (*conj*) (12A)
der **Dampf, ⁻e** steam
danach afterwards
  kurz danach shortly afterwards (14A)
der **Dank** thanks
  Gott sei Dank! Thank God!
  Vielen Dank! Thank you very much! Thanks a lot!
danke, danke schön thanks (E)
danken (+ *dat*) to thank (7B)
dann then (2B)
darauf
  kurz darauf shortly afterwards
das this, that (E)
daß that (*conj*) (8B)
das **Datum**, die **Daten** date (11B)
dauern to take (time) (12A)
dauernd constantly
die **Dauerwelle, -n** perm
der **Daumen, -** thumb (10B)
  Halt mir die Daumen. Keep your fingers crossed for me.
dazu with it; in addition
die **DDR (die Deutsche Demokratische Republik)** the GDR (the German Democratic Republic)
die **Debatte, -n** debate

die **Decke, -n** ceiling (9A)
defekt defective
definieren to define
die **Definition, -en** definition
dein your
die **Demokratie, -n** democracy
der **Demonstrant, -en** / die **Demonstrantin, -nen** demonstrator
die **Demonstration, -en** demonstration
demonstrieren to demonstrate
denken, dachte, hat gedacht to think (5A)
  denken an (+ *acc*) to think of, about (*to have in mind*) (12B)
das **Denkmal, ⁻er** monument
Denkste! Ja denkste! That's what you think!
denn because, for (5A)
deprimierend depressing (2A)
derselbe, dieselbe, dasselbe the same
deshalb therefore, for that reason, that's why (4B)
deswegen therefore, for that reason
deutsch German
das **Deutsch** German (language)
der (die) **Deutsche, -n** German (person)
die **Deutsche Demokratische Republik (die DDR)** the German Democratic Republic (the GDR)
(das) **Deutschland** Germany
deutschsprachig German-speaking
die **Deutschstunde, -n** German class
der **Dezember** December (2B)
der **Dialog, -e** dialogue
dick fat (2A)
  dicke Freunde close friends
  Kuchen macht dick. Cake is fattening. (4A)
der **Dienstag** Tuesday (2B)
das **Dienstmädchen, -** maid
der **Dienstwagen, -** company car
dies this
dieser, diese, dieses this (5B)
diesmal this time (6A)
das **Ding, -e** thing (5A)
der **Diplomat, -en, -en** diplomat
direkt directly
der **Direktor, -en** / die **Direk-**

torin, -nen director
der **Dirndlrock, ⁻e** colorful skirt typical of Bavaria or Austria
der **Discjockey, -s** disk jockey
die **Disco, -s** disco (7A)
  in die Disco to the disco
die **Diskette, -n** disk
diskriminierend discriminatory
diskutieren to discuss (9B)
die **Distel, -n** thistle
doch yes (*in response to a negative statement or question*); anyway; but
die **Donau** Danube (*river*)
der **Donnerstag** Thursday (2B)
doof stupid (11B)
doppelt double
  doppelt so weit twice as far
das **Dorf, ⁻er** village (10A)
der **Dorn, -en** thorn
dort there (2A)
die **Dose, -n** can (9B)
der **Dosenöffner, -** can opener
der **Drachen, -** kite
draußen outside
das **Drehbuch, ⁻er** screenplay
dreimal three times (6A)
das **Dreirad, ⁻er** tricycle
die **Drogerie** drugstore (8B)
drüben over there, on the other side (8A)
drücken to press (12A)
  drücken auf (+ *acc*) to press (something)
dumm stupid (2B)
die **Dummheit, -en** stupidity
der **Dummkopf, ⁻e** dimwit
dunkel dark (9A)
  im Dunkeln in the dark
dunkelblau dark blue
die **Dunkelheit** darkness
dünn thin (2B)
durch through (5B)
  Die Kartoffeln sind nicht durch. The potatoes aren't done.
durch•lesen (liest durch), las durch, hat durchgelesen to read through
durchstudieren to look through
dürfen (darf), durfte, hat gedurft to be allowed to, may (4B)
  Was darf's sein? What would you like? (8A)

der **Durst** thirst (5B)
  Ich habe Durst. I am thirsty.
    (5B)
die **Dusche, -n** shower (9A)
(sich) **duschen** to shower (6B)

E

eben just
echt typically; really
die **Ecke, -n** corner (8A)
  gleich um die Ecke right
    around the corner (8A)
egal
  Das ist mir egal. I don't care.
    (7B)
die **Ehe, -n** marriage (13B)
der **Eheberater, -** / die
  Eheberaterin, -nen marriage
    counselor (13B)
das **Ehepaar, -e** married couple
    (13B)
ehrlich honest
das **Ei, -er** egg (4A)
eigen own
eigenartig unique
eigentlich actually (6A)
die **Eigentumswohnung, -en**
    condominium apartment
die **Eile** hurry
eilig
  Ich habe es eilig. I'm in a
    hurry. (12A)
ein a, an
einander one another, each other
    (10B)
einfach simply, just (7A)
**ein•fallen (fällt ein), fiel ein, ist
  eingefallen**
  Mir fällt nichts ein. I can't
    think of anything. (7A)
einfältig simple-minded
das **Einfamilienhaus, ̈-er** single
    family dwelling (9B)
der **Eingang, ̈-e** entrance (7A)
**ein•gehen, ging ein, ist ein-
  gegangen** to go into
eingeschlossen included (11B)
einige a few, several (12A)
  nach einiger Zeit after a while
ein•kaufen to shop, to go shop-
    ping (6B)
die **Einkaufsliste, -n** shopping list

das **Einkommen** income (3B)
**ein•laden (lädt ein), lud ein, hat
  eingeladen** to invite (5B)
die **Einleitung, -en** introduction
einmal once (6A)
  noch einmal (over) again, once
    more (7A)
ein•mauern to put a wall around
ein•packen to pack
die **Eins, -en** A (*grade*)
ein•schalten to turn on (*radio, TV,
    etc.*) (12A)
ein•schenken to pour
**ein•schlafen (schläft ein),
  schlief ein, ist eingeschlafen**
    to fall asleep (6B)
einschläfernd monotonous
**ein•schlagen (schlägt ein),
  schlug ein, hat ein-
  geschlagen** to drive in; to
    wrap; to shake (on an agree-
    ment)
**ein•sehen (sieht ein) sah ein,
  hat eingesehen** to realize, see
**ein•steigen, stieg ein, ist ein-
  gestiegen** to get in (13B)
ein•stellen to turn on; to adjust; to
    hire (13B)
**ein•tragen (trägt ein), trug ein,
  hat eingetragen** to write
    down, to enter
einverstanden sein to be in
    agreement
der **Einwanderer, -** immigrant
ein•wandern to immigrate
    (6A)
die **Einwanderung** immigration
ein•zeichnen to sketch in
**ein•ziehen, zog ein, ist ein-
  gezogen** to move in (9B)
einzig only
das **Eis** ice (2A); ice cream
eisern iron
eisig icy
eiskalt ice cold
der **Elefant, -en, -en** elephant
das **Elektrizitätswerk** power sta-
    tion
elend miserable
der **Ellbogen, -** elbow
elterlich parental
die **Eltern** (*pl*) parents (3B)
**empfangen (empfängt), emp-
  fing, hat empfangen** to wel-
    come

**empfehlen (empfiehlt),
  empfahl, hat empfohlen** to
    recommend
das **Ende, -n** end (10B)
  Ende August at the end of Au-
    gust
  zu Ende sein to be over (4B)
endlich finally (6B); at last
die **Endung, -en** ending
energisch tough (*of a person*)
eng close, crowded
der **Engel, -** angel
(das) **England** England
der **Engländer, -** / die **Engländerin, -nen** English (person)
das **Enkelkind, -er** grandchild
enterben to disinherit
entfernt from a distance
entgeistert flabbergasted
entkorken to uncork
**entlassen (entläßt), entließ, hat
  entlassen** to fire (13B)
entscheiden to decide (11A)
die **Entscheidung, -en** decision
sich **entschuldigen bei** to apolo-
    gize to (12B)
die **Entschuldigung, -en** excuse
    (14A)
  Entschuldigung! Excuse me!
    (E)
die **Erde** earth, ground (14A)
die **Erfahrung, -en** experience
der **Erfinder, -** inventor
die **Erfindung, -en** invention
erfolgreich successful
erfrieren, erfror, ist erfroren to
    freeze to death
die **Erfrischung, -en** refreshment
erfüllen to fulfill
ergänzen to complete; to supply
sich **erkälten** to catch a cold (12B)
die **Erkältung, -en** cold
erklären to explain (6B)
die **Erklärung, -en** explanation
erlauben to allow
das **Erlebnis, -se** experience
ermahnen to admonish
ernst serious (12B)
die **Ernte, -n** harvest
ernten to harvest
eröffnen to open
die **Eröffnung** opening
erreichen to reach
**erscheinen, erschien, ist
  erschienen** to appear

erschießen, erschoß, hat erschossen to shoot dead (14A)

erschlagen (erschlägt), erschlug, hat erschlagen to beat to death

erschrecken (erschrickt), erschrak, ist erschrocken to be frightened, to be alarmed (13A)

erst only; not until (4B)

erst first (4B)
  zum erstenmal for the first time (13A)

ertrinken, ertrank, ist ertrunken to drown

erwachen to awaken

erwähnen to mention

erwarten to expect (13A)

die Erwartung, -en expectation

erwünscht desirable

erzählen to tell (a story) (6B)
  erzählen von to tell about (12B)

der Erzähler, - / die Erzählerin, -nen narrator

die Erzählung, -en story, narrative

der Esel, - donkey; jackass; idiot

essen (ißt), aß, hat gegessen to eat (4B)

das Essen meal (7A)

etwa approximately (6A)

etwas something (4A)

euer your

(das) Europa Europe

europäisch European

ewig forever

das Examen, - exam

exotisch exotic

das Experiment, -e experiment

explodieren to explode

extrem extreme (2A)

das Extrem, -e extreme
  Was für Extreme! What extremes! (2A)

F

die Fabel, -n fable

die Fabrik, -en factory (10B)

der Fabrikarbeiter, - / die Fabrikarbeiterin, -nen factory worker

das Fach, ¨er course

fad bland

fahren (fährt), fuhr, ist gefahren to drive (4B)

der Fahrer, - driver

der Fahrplan, ¨e schedule (*bus, train*)

fahrplanmäßig as scheduled

die Fahrprüfung, -en driving test

das Fahrrad, ¨er bicycle (3B)

die Fahrt, -en drive, trip (11B)

das Fahrzeug, -e vehicle (13B)

die Fakultät, -en faculty

Fall: auf keinen Fall under no circumstances

fallen (fällt), fiel, ist gefallen to fall (4B)

fällen to fell

fällig due

falsch wrong (5B)

falten to fold (13A)

die Familie family (3B)

fanatisch fanatical

fangen (fängt), fing, hat gefangen to catch (10A)

die Farbe, -n color (1B)

farbenblind color blind

farbenfreudig colorful

der Farbfernseher, - color TV

der Farbton, ¨e grade of color

die Farm, -en farm

das Faß barrel
  Bier vom Faß draft beer

fast almost (1A)

faszinierend fascinating

faul lazy (6B)

faulenzen to do nothing, to be lazy (11B)

die Faulheit laziness

die Faust, ¨e fist

der Februar February (2B)

die Feder, -n feather

fehlen to be missing

der Fehler, - mistake

feiern to celebrate

die Feige, -n fig

der Feind, -e enemy (11A)

das Feld, -er field (10A)

das Fenster, - window (9A)

die Ferien (*pl*) vacation (11B)

der Feriengast, ¨e vacationer (11B)

der Ferienjob, -s summer job

fern•sehen (sieht fern), sah fern, hat ferngesehen to watch TV (6B)

das Fernsehen television (13A)

der Fernseher, - TV set (9A)

fertig finished, done, ready (1A)

fertig•kriegen to get done

fertig•machen to finish, complete

fertig•schreiben, schrieb fertig, hat fertiggeschrieben to finish writing (5B)

das Fest, -e party, festival

die Fete, -n party

fett fat

fettig fatty

der Fetzen, - rag

das Feuer, - fire

das Fieber fever

der Film, -e film

das Finanzamt tax office

finanziell financial

finden, fand, hat gefunden to find (3B)
  Wie findest du...? What do you think of . . . ?

der Finger, - finger (10B)

der Fingernagel, ¨ fingernail

die Firma, -en company (12B)

der Fisch, -e fish

fischen to fish

das Fischmehl fish meal

die Flamme, -en flame

die Flasche, -n bottle
  eine Flasche Wein a bottle of wine (7B)

der Flaschenöffner, - bottle opener

der Flaschner, - plumber

der Fleck, -en stain

das Fleisch meat (4A)

der Fleischer, - butcher (8B)

die Fleischerei butcher shop (8B)

fleißig hard-working (6B)

flicken to mend

die Flickwolle mending yarn

fliegen, flog, ist geflogen to fly (3A)

fliehen, floh, ist geflohen to flee

fließen, floß, ist geflossen to flow

das Flittchen, - flirt

flott stylish

der Flughafen, ¨ airport (8B)

das Flugzeug, -e airplane (3B)

der Flur hallway (9A)

der Fluß, Flüsse river (14B)

folgen (+ *dat*) to follow

die Form, -en shape

fort away

---

fort•fahren (fährt fort), fuhr fort, ist fortgefahren to leave, drive away

das Foto, -s photo

fotografieren to photograph

die Frage, -n question (10B)

der Fragebogen, - questionnaire (11A)

fragen to ask (a question) (4A)

das Fragewort, ¨er question word

der Franken, - (Swiss) franc

frankieren to put postage on

(das) Frankreich France

französisch French

das Französisch French (language)

Frau Mrs., Ms. (E)

die Frau, -en woman; wife (1B)

das Fräulein, - Miss

frech fresh, impudent

frei free (11A)

    Heute habe ich frei. Today I have a day off. (5A)

frei•halten (hält frei), hielt frei, hat freigehalten to keep clear

der Freitag Friday (2B)

die Freizeit leisure time

fremd foreign (14A)

der/die Fremde, -n stranger (8A)

fressen (frißt), fraß, hat gefressen to eat (*of animals*) (4B)

sich **freuen auf** (+ *acc*) to look forward to (12B)

sich **freuen über** (+ *acc*) to be happy about, to be pleased with (12B)

der Freund, -e (male) friend, boyfriend (6A)

die Freundin -nen (female) friend, girl friend (6A)

freundlich friendly (10B)

die Freundlichkeit friendliness

die Freundschaft, -en friendship

freundschaftlich friendly

frieren, fror, hat gefroren to be cold (10A)

das Frisbee, -s frisbee

frisch fresh

der Friseur, -e hairdresser

die Frisur, -en hairdo

froh happy (12B)

fröhlich cheerful

fromm pious

die Frucht, ¨e fruit

früh early (4A)

morgen früh tomorrow morning (4B)

früher in the past (13B)

der Frühling spring (2B)

das Frühstück breakfast (4A)

    zum Frühstück for breakfast (4A)

frühstücken to eat breakfast, to have breakfast (4A)

der Fuchs, ¨e fox

fühlen to feel

    sich wohl fühlen to fell well (12B)

führen to lead

der Führerschein driver's license (10B)

füllen to fill (13A)

der Füller fountain pen (13A)

die Füllfeder, -n fountain pen (13A)

funktionieren to function

für for (3A)

    Was für ein Instrument spielst du? What instrument do you play? (3A)

die Furche, -n furrow

fürchten to fear

der Fuß, ¨e foot (10B)

    Du bist mir auf den Fuß getreten. You stepped on my toe. (14A)

    zu Fuß gehen to go on foot, to walk (8B)

der Fußball, ¨e soccer ball

    Fußball spielen to play soccer

das Fußballmatch, -es football match

der Fußboden, ¨ floor

das Futter food (*for an animal*)

füttern to feed (9A)

G

die Gabel, -n fork (8B)

galoppieren to gallop

ganz all, whole, very, quite, completely, absolutely

    den ganzen Tag all day (5A)

ganztags full-time (employment) (13B)

gar nicht not at all (1A)

die Garage, -n garage (9B)

garantieren to guarantee

die Garderobe, -n front hall closet (9A)

der Garten, ¨ garden, yard (6B)

der Gärtner, - gardener

das Gas, - gas (*for cooking and heating*)

der Gast, ¨e guest, customer (*in a restaurant*) (8A)

das Gasthaus, ¨er restaurant (8A)

das Gebäude, - building

geben (gibt), gab, hat gegeben to give (4B)

    Das gibt's doch nicht! That's impossible! That can't be! (9A)

    es gibt there is, there are (4B)

das Gebirge mountain (11B)

geblümt flowered

geboren

    Ich bin am 1. (ersten) September 1967 geboren. I was born on September 1, 1967. (6A)

gebrauchen to use

die Gebrauchsanweisung, -en instructions, directions

der Gebrauchtwagen, - used car (13B)

der Geburtstag, -e birthday (7B)

    zum Geburtstag for one's birthday (7B)

der Geburtstagskuchen, - birthday cake

das Gedächtnis memory

der Gedanke, -n thought (14A)

gefährdet endangered

gefährlich dangerous (14A)

gefallen (gefällt), gefiel, hat gefallen (+ *dat*) to like (7B)

    Deine Jeans gefallen mir. I like your jeans. (7B)

    Was gefällt dir an ihm? What do you like about him?

das Gefühl, -e feeling (12B)

gegen against; around (5B)

    gegen sieben (Uhr) around seven (o'clock) (5A)

die Gegend, -en area

das Gegenteil, -e opposite

gegenüber across from (7B)

das Gehalt, ¨er salary (12B)

gehen, ging, ist gegangen to go (3A)

    Geht das? Is that possible?

    Wie geht es Ihnen? / Wie geht's? How are you? (E)

der **Gehilfe, -n** helper, assistant
gehören (+ *dat*) to belong to (7B)
gekleidet dressed
gelb yellow (1B)
das **Geld** money (3B)
der **Geldbeutel, -** wallet (7B)
gelingen, gelang, ist gelungen
    to succeed
das **Gelüst, -e** craving
das **Gemüse** vegetables (8B)
gemütlich cozy, comfortable (8B)
genau exact; distinct; careful (14A)
    genauso gut just as good
    genauso ... wie exactly like
der **General, -e** general
die **Genetik** genetics
genial brilliant
das **Genie, -s** genius
genug enough (6B)
gerade just, just now (6B)
die **Geranie, -n** geranium
das **Gerät, -e** device
geräumig roomy
die **Germanistik** study of German
    language and literature
gern (lieber, am liebsten) gladly
    Hörst du gern Musik? Do you
    like to listen to music? (3A)
die **Gerste** barley
das **Gerücht, -e** rumor (11A)
die **Gesamtnote, -n** average grade
der **Gesang, -e** song
das **Geschäft, -e** business (13B)
geschehen (geschieht), geschah,
    ist geschehen to happen
das **Geschenk, -e** gift
die **Geschichte, -n** story (10A); his-
    tory
das **Geschirr** dishes, china (8B)
geschlossen closed
der **Geschmack, -er** taste
geschmackvoll tasteful
geschmacklos tasteless
die **Geschwister** (*pl*) sisters and
    brothers (3B)
das **Gesicht, -er** face (10B)
    Gesichter schneiden to make
    faces
das **Gespräch, -e** conversation
der **Gesprächspartner, -** / die
    Gesprächspartnerin, -nen
    partner in conversation
die **Geste, -n** gesture (13A)
gestern yesterday (2B)
gestreift striped

gesund healthy (4A)
die **Gesundheit** health (12B)
das **Getränk, -e** beverage
getrennt separate
gewaltig mighty
    ganz gewaltig tremendously
das **Gewehr, -e** rifle (14A)
geweiht holy
gewinnen, gewann, hat gewon-
    nen to win
die **Gewohnheit, -en** habit (13A)
gießen, goß, hat gegossen to
    water (6B)
die **Gießkanne, -n** watering can
das **Gift, -e** poison
die **Giraffe, -n** giraffe
die **Gitarre, -n** guitar
glänzen to glitter
das **Glas, -er** glass (4A)
    ein Glas Orangensaft a glass of
    orange juice (4A)
die **Glasscheibe** sheet of glass
glauben (+ *dat*) to believe, to
    think (6A)
gleich just about, right away (1A);
    same (10B); equally; immedi-
    ately; right, directly
    gleich jetzt right now (6A)
    gleich um die Ecke right
    around the corner
gleichzeitig at the same time
glitzern to glitter
das **Glück** luck (12A)
    Du hast Glück. You're lucky.
    (7B)
    zum Glück luckily (12A)
glücklich happy (10A)
das **Gold** gold
golden gold
die **Goldmedaille, -n** gold medal
das **Goldstück, -e** gold coin
(der) **Gott** God
    Gott sei Dank! Thank God!
graben (gräbt), grub, hat
    gegraben to dig
der **Graben, -** ditch (14A)
der **Grad** degree
    dreißig Grad thirty degrees (1A)
das **Gramm** gram
das **Grammophon** gramophone
die **Grammatik, -en** grammar
die **Granate, -n** grenade, shell
die **Grapefruit, -s** grapefruit
das **Gras** grass (6B)
grasig grassy

grau gray (1B)
grausam cruel
die **Grenze, -n** border (10A)
groß large, tall (2B)
    groß schreiben to capitalize
die **Größe, -n** size
die **Großeltern** (*pl*) grandparents
    (3B)
die **Großmutter, -** grandmother
    (3B)
der **Großvater, -** grandfather (3B)
Grüezi! Hello! (*Swiss dialect*)
grün green (1B)
    der (die) **Grüne, -n** member of
    the Green Party
der **Grund, -e** reason (8A)
der **Grundriß, Grundrisse** floor
    plan
die **Grundschule, -en** elementary
    school (10B)
grunzen to grunt
die **Gruppe, -n** group
der **Gruß, -e** greeting
grüßen to greet, to say hello (10A)
    Grüß dich! Hi! (E)
    Grüß Gott! Hello! (in Southern
    Germany and Austria)
das **Gulasch** goulash
günstig inexpensive, reasonable
    (11B)
die **Gurke, -n** cucumber
gut good, well (2B)
gutherzig good-hearted
der **Gymnasiast, -en, -en** student
    in an academic high school
das **Gymnasium, -ien** college pre-
    paratory high school (10B)

H

das **Haar, -e** hair (10B)
haarig hairy
der **Haarschnitt, -e** haircut
haben (hat), hatte, hat gehabt to
    have (3A)
das **Hackmesser, -** meat cleaver
der **Hafen, -** harbor (14B)
der **Hahn, -e** rooster
der **Hai, -e** shark
halb half
    halb zwölf eleven thirty (4B)
die **Halbinsel, -n** peninsula (14B)
die **Halbpension** bed, breakfast,
    and a light supper (11B)

halbtags part-time (employment) (13B)

die **Hälfte, -n** half

Hallo! Hi! (E)

der **Hals, -̈e** neck (10B)

die **Halskette, -n** necklace

halten (hält), hielt, hat gehalten to hold; to stop (4B); to keep

  halten von to think of, about (*to have an opinion about*) (12B)

der **Hamburger, -** hamburger

der **Hammer, -̈** hammer

der **Hamster, -** hamster

die **Hand, -̈e** hand (10B)

  aus erster Hand one owner (13B)

der **Händler, -** dealer

die **Handschrift, -en** handwriting; manuscript

der **Handschuh, -e** glove (7B)

das **Handschuhfach** glove compartment (13B)

der **Handwerker, -** craftsman

hängen to put (in a hanging position), to hang (up)

hängen, hing, hat gehangen to be hanging

die **Harfe, -n** harp

hart hard, firm (11B)

der **Hase, -n, -n** rabbit

hassen to hate

häßlich ugly (9A)

hastig hasty, fast

hauen to hit

häufig frequent (14A)

der **Hauptbahnhof** main railway station (7A)

das **Hauptfach, -̈er** major (*field of study*)

das **Hauptgericht, -e** main course

die **Hauptstadt, -̈e** capital city (11A)

das **Haus, -̈er** house (6B)

  nach Hause gehen to go home (4B)

  Bist du heute abend zu Hause? Will you be (at) home tonight? (6A)

der **Hausarzt, -̈e** / die **Hausärztin, -nen** family doctor (8B)

die **Hausaufgabe, -n** homework assignment (10B)

der **Hausmann, -̈er** house husband

der **Hausmeister, -** superintendent (of a building)

der **Hausschuh, -e** slipper (7B)

das **Haustier, -e** pet

die **Haustür** front door

der **Hauswirt, -e** / die **Hauswirtin, -nen** landlord / landlady (9B)

die **Hecke, -n** hedge (6B)

das **Heft, -e** notebook

heilen to heal

die **Heilung** healing

die **Heimatstadt** home town

heim•kommen, kam heim, ist heimgekommen to come home (5B)

der **Heimweg** way home

heiraten to marry, to get married (6A)

heiß hot (1A)

heißen, hieß, hat geheißen to be called (E); to mean

  das heißt, d.h. that is, i.e.

  Ich heiße ... My name is . . . (E)

  Was heißt das? What does that mean?

  Wie heißen Sie? / Wie heißt du? What is your name? (E)

heizen to heat

die **Heizung** heating

helfen (hilft), half, hat geholfen (+ *dat*) to help (7A)

hell light, bright (9A)

hellblau light blue

die **Helligkeit** brightness

das **Hemd, -en** shirt (7B)

hemmungslos unrestrained

der **Henkel, -** handle

heraus•geben (gibt heraus), gab heraus, hat herausgegeben to give change

heraus•finden, fand heraus, hat herausgefunden to find out

der **Herbst** fall (2B)

der **Herd, -e** stove (9A)

Herein! Come in!

hereinkommen, kam herein, ist hereingekommen to come in

Herr Mr. (E)

der **Herr, -n, -en** gentleman

  mein Herr sir

her•stellen to manufacture

herum•stehen, stand herum, hat herumgestanden to stand around

hervorragend superior

das **Herz, -ens, -en** heart

der **Herzanfall, -̈e** heart attack

Herzlichst With best regards (in a letter)

heute today (1A)

  heute abend tonight (2B)

  heute morgen this morning (4B)

  heute nachmittag this afternoon

heutzutage nowadays (13B)

hier here (2B)

hierher here (*to this place*)

die **Hilfe** help

hilfsbereit helpful

der **Himmel** sky (1A); heaven

hinaus•gehen, ging hinaus, ist hinausgegangen to go out

hinaus•werfen (wirft hinaus), warf hinaus, hat hinausgeworfen to throw out

das **Hindernis, -se** hindrance

hindurch•stecken to put through

hinein•gehen, ging hinein, ist hineingegangen to go in (8A)

sich **hin•setzen** to sit down

hinter behind (9B)

die **Hitze** heat (11A)

das **Hobby, -s** hobby (3B)

hoch (hoh-) high (12B)

das **Hochhaus, -̈er** high-rise (9B)

hochqualifiziert highly qualified

die **Hochzeit, -en** wedding

hocken to sit

der **Hocker, -** stool

der **Höcker, -̈** hump (of a camel)

der **Hockeyschläger, -** hockey stick

hoffen to hope

hoffentlich hopefully, I hope (8B)

holen to get, to fetch (10A)

höllisch hellish

das **Holz, -̈er** wood

der **Holzfäller, -** lumberjack

der **Honig** honey

hören to hear, to listen to (3A)

der **Hörsaal, -säle** lecture hall (10B)

das **Hörspiel, -e** radio play (12A)

die **Hose, -n** pants, trousers (7B)

  ein Paar Hosen a pair of pants (7B)

der **Hotdog, -s** hot dog

das **Hotel, -s** hotel (7A)

hübsch pretty

der **Hügel, -** hill (14A)

das **Huhn, -̈er** hen

der **Humor** humor
der **Hund, -e** dog (3B)
das **Hundewetter** rotten weather (1A)
  Was für ein Hundewetter! What rotten weather! (1A)
der **Hunger** hunger (5B)
  Ich habe Hunger. I am hungry. (5B)
hungern to go hungry (10A)
hungrig hungry
hupen to honk (5A)
huschen to scurry
husten to cough
das **Hustenmittel** cough medicine
der **Hut, ̈-e** hat (7B)
der **Hüttenkäse** cottage cheese (4A)

I

das **Ideal, -e** ideal
der **Idiot, -en, -en** idiot
der **Igel, -** hedgehog
ihr her, their
Ihr your
immer always (2B)
  immer mehr more and more (6A)
  immer noch still (4B)
impfen to vaccinate
in in, into (9B)
indisch (*East*) Indian
die **Infektion, -en** infection
der **Ingenieur, -e** engineer
das **Insekt, -en** insect
die **Insel, -n** island (14B)
das **Inserat, -e** ad (13A)
das **Instrument, -e** instrument (3A)
intellektuell intellectual
intelligent intelligent (2B)
die **Intensivstation, -en** Intensive Care Unit
interessant interesting (5B)
sich **interessieren für** to be interested in (12B)
interviewen to interview
investieren to invest
inzwischen in the meantime
irgendein some . . . (or other)
irgend etwas something (or other) (13A)

irgendwann sometime (or other)
irgendwo somewhere (or other)
(das) **Irland** Ireland
(das) **Italien** Italy
italienisch Italian
das **Italienisch** Italian (language)

J

ja yes (E)
die **Jacke, -n** jacket (7B)
das **Jahr, -e** year (2B)
die **Jahreszeit, -en** season (2B)
das **Jahrhundert, -e** century (10A)
-jährig -year-old
jährlich yearly
der **Januar** January (2B)
japanisch Japanese
jawohl yes indeed
der **Jazz** jazz
je each, every
je ... desto the . . . the
die **Jeans** (*pl*) jeans (7B)
jeder, jede, jedes each, every (5B)
jedesmal every time
jemand somebody (5A)
jetzt now (1A)
der **Job, -s** part-time job
joggen gehen to go jogging
der **Joghurt** yogurt (4A)
  ein Becher Joghurt a carton of yogurt (4A)
der **Jude, -n, -n** Jew
die **Jugendherberge, -n** youth hostel (11B)
der **Juli** July (2B)
jung young (2B)
der **Junge, -n, -n** boy (9B)
der **Juni** June (2B)

K

das **Kabriolett, -e** convertible (*car*) (13B)
der **Kaffee** coffee (3B)
die **Kaffeekanne** coffee pot
der **Käfig, -e** cage
die **Kaktee, -n** cactus
das **Kalb, ̈-er** calf
der **Kalender, -** calendar (9B)
(das) **Kalifornien** California

kalifornisch Californian
kalt cold (1A)
die **Kälte** cold (11B)
das **Kamel, -e** camel
die **Kamera, -s** camera
sich **kämmen** to comb one's hair (12B)
(das) **Kanada** Canada (1B)
der **Kanadier, -** / die **Kanadierin, -nen** Canadian (*person*)
kanadisch Canadian
der **Kanarienvogel, ̈** canary
das **Kännchen, -** little pot
der **Kapitalismus** capitalism
der **Kapitän, -e** captain
das **Kapitel, -** chapter
kaputt broken
kariert plaid, checkered
der **Karfreitag** Good Friday
die **Karotte, -n** carrot
die **Karriere, -n** career
die **Karte, -n** ticket; card (3A)
die **Kartoffel, -n** potato (4A)
der **Karton, -s** box, carton
der **Käse** cheese (4A)
das **Kasseler Rippchen, -** (das **Kaßler**) smoked pork chop
die **Kassette, -n** cassette (12A)
der **Kassettenrecorder, -** cassette recorder (12A)
der **Kassierer, -** / die **Kassiererin, -nen** cashier, teller
der **Kasten, -** box
der **Kater** tomcat
die **Katze, -n** cat (3B)
kaufen to buy (3B)
das **Kaufhaus** department store (8B)
kaum scarcely, hardly (6A)
der **Kaviar** caviar
kein not a, not any, no
der **Keller, -** basement, cellar
der **Kellner, -** / die **Kellnerin, -nen** waiter / waitress (8A)
kennen, kannte, hat gekannt to know, to be acquainted with, to be familiar with (3B)
kennen•lernen to get to know (5B)
der **Kenner, -** connoisseur
die **Kenntnisse** (*pl*) experience; knowledge
das **Kennzeichen, -** license plate number

der **Kerl, -e** guy (5A)
die **Kerze, -n** candle
der **Kessel, -** kettle
die **Kette, -n** chain
das **Kilogramm** kilogram
der **Kilometer, -** kilometer
der **Kilometerstand** mileage
das **Kind, -er** child (3B)
die **Kindergärtnerin, -nen**
    kindergarten teacher
der **Kinderwagen, -** baby carriage
kindisch childish
das **Kinn** chin (10B)
das **Kino, -s** cinema
  ins Kino to the movies (2B)
die **Kirche, -n** church (10A)
der **Kirchenchor, ̈e** church choir
die **Kirsche, -n** cherry
klar clear
  Klar! Of course! (5A)
die **Klarheit** clarity
die **Klarinette, -n** clarinette
die **Klasse, -en** class
der **Klassenkamerad, -en** / die
  Klassenkameradin, -nen
  classmate
das **Klavier, -e** piano (3A)
die **Klavierstunde, -n** piano lesson
kleben to stick
der **Klee** clover
das **Kleid, -er** dress (5A)
  die **Kleider** clothes (5A)
kleiden to dress
das **Kleidungsstück, -e** article of
  clothing
klein small, little (2B)
der **Kleinwagen, -** compact car
  (13B)
das **Klima** climate (2A)
die **Klingel** doorbell (12A)
klingeln to ring (12A); to sound
klinisch clinically
klirren to rattle
das **Klo, -s** toilet (9A)
  aufs Klo to the toilet
klopfen to knock
das **Kloster, ̈** monastery, convent
der **Klub, -s** club
klug smart (11B)
die **Klugheit** intelligence, clever-
  ness
der **Klumpen, -** lump
knabbern to nibble
das **Knäckebrot** crispbread

knackig crisp
die **Knackwurst, ̈e** knackwurst
knallig loud (*of colors*)
der **Knast** jail
die **Kneipe, -n** pub
  in die Kneipe to the pub
  (2B)
das **Knie, -e** knee (10B)
knipsen to click
der **Knoblauch** garlic
der **Knopf, ̈e** button (12A)
knutschen to smooch
der **Koch, ̈e**/die **Köchin, -nen**
  cook
das **Kochbuch, ̈er** cookbook
kochen to cook (3B); to boil
die **Kochplatte, -n** hot plate (9B)
koffeinfrei decaffeinated
der **Koffer, -** suitcase (6A)
der **Kofferraum** trunk (*of a car*)
der **Kognak** cognac
der **Kohl** cabbage
die **Kohle, -n** coal
der **Kollege, -en, -en** / die **Kol-**
  legin, -nen colleague
(das) **Köln** Cologne
komisch strange
kommen, kam, ist gekommen to
  come (E)
die **Kommode, -n** dresser (9A)
der **Kommunismus** communism
der **Kommunist, -en, -en**
  Communist
kommunistisch Communist
kompliziert complicated
der **Kompromiß,** die
  Kompromisse compromise
der **Konditor** pastry chef
der **Konjunktiv** subjunctive
können (kann), konnte, hat
  gekonnt to be able to, can
  (4B)
der **Könner, -** expert
konservativ conservative
konstruieren to design
der **Konstrukteur, -e** designer
das **Konsulat** consulate
der **Kontrast, -e** contrast
kontrollieren to control
das **Konzert, -e** concert (3A)
  ins Konzert to a concert, to concerts (2B)
der **Kopf, ̈e** head (10B)
der **Kopfhörer, -** headphone

der **Kopfsalat** head lettuce
die **Kopfschmerzen** (*pl*) headache
koppeln to couple, join
der **Korb, ̈e** basket
der **Kork, -en** cork
der **Korkenzieher, -** corkscrew
die **Kornblume, -n** cornflower
der **Körper** body (10B)
der **Körperteil, -e** part of the body
  (10B)
korrigieren to correct
kosten to cost (3B)
krabbeln to crawl
der **Krampf, ̈e** cramp
krank sick, ill (4A)
der (die) **Kranke, -n** sick person
das **Krankenhaus** hospital (8B)
die **Krankenschwester, -n** nurse
die **Krankheit, -en** illness
kränklich sickly
die **Krawatte, -n** tie
die **Kreatur -en** creature
der **Kredit** credit
  auf Kredit on credit
der **Krieg, -e** war (11A)
kriegen to get (5A)
der **Krimi, -s** thriller, detective
  story
kritisch critical
kritisieren to criticize
das **Krokodil, -e** crocodile
krumm crooked
die **Küche, -n** kitchen (9A)
der **Kuchen, -** cake (4A)
die **Küchenbenutzung** kitchen
  privileges (9B)
der **Kugelschreiber, -** ballpoint
  pen (7B)
die **Kuh, ̈e** cow
kühl cool (1A)
der **Kühlschrank, ̈e** refrigerator
  (9A)
sich **kümmern um** to take care of
der **Kunde, -n, -n** / die **Kundin,**
  -nen customer
der **Kurs, -e** course; rate of exchange
kursiv gedruckt italicized
kurz short (2B)
  kurz darauf shortly afterwards
die **Kurzfassung, -en** shortened
  version
die **Kurzgeschichte, -n** short story
kürzlich recently

die **Kusine** (female) cousin (3B)
die **Küste, -n** coast (14b)

___L___

das **Labor, -s** lab
lächeln to smile (13A)
lachen to laugh (10B)
    lachen über (+ *acc*) to laugh about, at (12B)
    lächerlich ridiculous
lackieren to paint (a car)
der **Laden, ⁻** store (8B)
laden (**lädt**), **lud, hat geladen** to load
lahm lame
das **Lamm, ⁻er** lamb
die **Lammkeule** leg of lamb
die **Lampe, -n** lamp (9A)
das **Land, ⁻er** land, country
    aufs Land to the country
landen to land
die **Landung, -en** landing
das **Landschaftsbild, -er** landscape painting
lang long (2B)
    ein Jahr lang for a year
    schon längst a long time ago
    sein Leben lang all his life
langsam slow (5B)
langweilig boring (5B)
lassen (**läßt**), **ließ, hat gelassen** to let, to leave (4B); to have something done
    sich Zeit lassen to take one's time
    Wo lassen Sie Ihren Wagen reparieren? Where do you have your car repaired?
der **Lastwagen, -** truck (13B)
das **Latein** Latin (*language*)
der **Laubbaum, ⁻e** deciduous tree (14B)
der **Lauf** motion, sprint
    in vollem Lauf at top speed
laufen (**läuft**), **lief, ist gelaufen** to run (4B)
    Schi laufen to go skiing (3B)
die **Laus, ⁻e** louse
lausig lousy
laut loud, aloud (6A)
lauwarm lukewarm
leben to live (in a country or city) (3B)

das **Leben** life (12B)
    ums Leben kommen to die
die **Lebensgewohnheit, -en** lifestyle
der **Lebenslauf, ⁻e** resumé, curriculum vitae (10B)
die **Lebensmittel** (*pl*) groceries
der **Lebensunterhalt** living expenses
die **Leber** liver
die **Leberwurst, ⁻e** liver sausage
lebhaft lively, vigorously
das **Leder** leather
die **Lederhose, -n** leather pants
ledern (made of) leather
leer empty (8A)
legen to put (in a lying position), to lay (down) (9A)
die **Lehne** back (of a chair)
die **Lehre, -n** apprenticeship
    eine Lehre machen to serve an apprenticeship
der **Lehrer, -** / die **Lehrerin, -nen** teacher (10B)
leicht easy, light (12B); slight
leid
    Es tut mir leid. I'm sorry. (7B)
leider unfortunately (6B)
leihen, lieh, hat geliehen to lend, to borrow (8B)
die **Leine, -n** leash
leise softly
leisten to do
der **Leiter, -** head, leader
der **Lektor, -en**/die **Lektorin, -nen** editor
die **Lerche, -n** lark
lernen to learn (3A)
das **Lesebuch, ⁻er** reader
lesen (**liest**), **las, hat gelesen** to read (4B)
der **Leser, -** reader
die **Leseratte, -n** bookworm
leserlich legible
der **Lesestoff** reading material
letzt last (6B)
die **Leute** (*pl*) people (6B)
das **Licht, -er** light
der **Lichtschalter, -** light switch (9B)
lieb dear (9A)
    Ich habe dich lieb. I love you. (12A)
die **Liebe** love (12A)
lieben to love

lieber
    Lieber Regen als Eis und Schnee. I'd rather have rain than ice and snow. (2A)
der **Liebling** darling (12A)
das **Lieblingsessen, -** favorite meal
das **Lied, -er** song
der **Lieferwagen, -** delivery truck
liegen, lag, hat gelegen to lie, to be lying, to be situated (6B)
liegen•lassen (**läßt liegen**), **ließ liegen, hat liegengelassen** to leave behind
lila purple (1B)
die **Lilie, -n** lily
die **Limonade** soft drink
links left, to the left (10B)
die **Lippe, -n** lip (10B)
der **Lippenstift, -e** lipstick
lispeln to lisp
die **Liste, -n** list
literarisch literary
das **Loch, ⁻er** hole
der **Löffel, -** spoon (8B)
los
    Was ist denn los? What's the matter? (7A)
lösen to solve
los•gehen, ging los, ist losgegangen to start; to set out
die **Lösung, -en** solution (10B)
die **Luft** air
die **Lüge, -n** lie
lügen, log, hat gelogen to tell a lie (10A)
    Er lügt wie gedruckt. He lies through his teeth. (7A)
das **Lulu** pee
der **Lumpen, -** rag
die **Lupe, -n** magnifying glass
die **Lust** enjoyment
    Hast du Lust? Do you feel like it? (3A)
    Ich habe Lust auf Fisch. I feel like having fish. (8A)
lustig funny; happy (12B)
    sich lustig machen über (+ *acc*) to make fun of
luxuriös luxurious

___M___

machen to do, to make (3A)
    Das macht nichts. That doesn't

matter. (8A)

Mach's gut! Good luck!

die **Macht, ⁻e** power (11A)

an die Macht kommen to gain power

das **Mädchen** girl (9B)

mähen to mow (6B)

die **Mahlzeit, -en** meal

der **Mai** May (2B)

der **Makler, -** real estate agent

das **Mal** time (10G)

zum erstenmal for the first time

malen to draw, to paint (a picture) (14A)

der **Maler, -** painter

man one (6B)

manchmal sometimes (2A)

der **Mann, ⁻er** man; husband (5B)

der **Mantel, ⁻** coat (7B)

das **Märchen, -** fairy tale

die **Mark, -** mark (*German currency*)

der **Markt, ⁻e** market

der **Marktplatz, ⁻e** market square

der **März** March (2B)

die **Maschine, -n** machine; airplane

der **Maßstab, ⁻e** yardstick

die **Mathe** math

die **Mauer, -n** wall

der **Maurer, -** bricklayer

die **Maus, ⁻e** mouse

der **Mechaniker, -** mechanic

die **Medaille** medal

medizinisch medical

das **Meer, -e** ocean, sea (11B)

mehr more

mehrere several

die **Mehrheit** majority

mehrmals several times (13A)

mein my (E)

meinen to mean; to think (8A); to say (11A)

meinetwegen if you like

die **Meinung, -en** opinion

die Meinung sagen to tell off

Ich bin der Meinung, daß ... I'm of the opinion that . . .

Meiner Meinung nach ... In my opinion . . .

meist most

meistens mostly, most of the time (2B)

der **Meister, -** foreman; master

die **Mensa** university cafeteria (*for full meals*) (4A)

der **Mensch, -en, -en** person, man, human being, (6B)

die **Menschen** (*pl*) people (6B)

Mensch! Wow! Boy! (1A)

Menschenskind! Good grief! (4A)

merken to notice (12A)

die **Messe, -n** trade fair

das **Messer, -** knife (8B)

das **Metall** metal

der **Meter, -** meter

(das) **Mexiko** Mexico

die **Miete, -n** rent (9B)

mieten to rent (9B)

die **Mikrobiologie** microbiology

das **Mikrophon** microphone

das **Mikroskop, -e** microscope

der **Mikrowellenherd, -e** microwave oven

die **Milch** milk (3B)

mild mild (2A)

die **Million, -en** million

der **Millionär, -e** millionaire

der **Millimeter, -** millimeter

der **Minister, -** minister (*in govt.*)

der **Ministerpräsident, -en, -en** Prime Minister

die **Minute, -n** minute (2B)

mischen to mix

die **Mischung, -en** mixture

miserabel miserable

die **Mistgabel, -n** manure fork

mit with; at the age of (4A)

mit•arbeiten to work along

mit•bringen, brachte mit, hat mitgebracht to bring along

miteinander with each other (8A)

mit•fahren (fährt mit), fuhr mit, ist mitgefahren to go along

mit•gehen, ging mit, ist mitgegangen to go along

mit•kommen, kam mit, ist mitgekommen to come along

mit•machen to join in

Das mache ich nicht nochmal mit! I'm not putting up with that again! (5A)

mit•nehmen (nimmt mit), nahm mit, hat mitgenommen to take along (5B)

mitschuldig partly responsible

mit•singen, sang mit, hat mitgesungen to sing along

der **Mitstudent, -en** / die **Mitstudentin, -nen** classmate, fellow student

der **Mittag** noon

Wann eßt ihr zu Mittag? When do you eat lunch? (4A)

das **Mittagessen** lunch, noon meal (4A)

mittags (at) noon (4B)

die **Mitte** middle

Mitte Oktober the middle of October

der **Mittelklassewagen, -** medium-sized car

der **Mittelpunkt** center

mitten middle of (2A)

mitten im Winter in the middle of winter (2A)

die **Mitternacht** midnight

der **Mittwoch** Wednesday (2B)

die **Möbel** (*pl*) furniture (9A)

das **Möbelstück, -e** piece of furniture

möbliert furnished (9A)

die **Modenschau** fashion show

mögen (mag), mochte, hat gemocht to like (4B)

ich möchte I would like (4B)

modern modern

modisch fashionable

möglich possible (10A)

so schnell wie möglich as quickly as possible (10A)

der **Moment, -e** moment

im Moment at the moment (12A)

momentan at the moment (12A)

der **Monat, -e** month (2B)

der **Mond, -e** moon

monatlich monthly

der **Montag** Monday (2B)

am Montag on Monday

die **Moral** moral

der **Mörder, -** murderer

der **Morgen** morning

bis Morgen until tomorrow, by tomorrow

Guten Morgen! / Morgen! Good morning! (E)

morgen morning (2B)

heute morgen this morning (4B)

morgen abend tomorrow evening, tomorrow night (2B)

morgen früh tomorrow morning (4B)

morgens in the morning (4B)

der **Most** cider

der **Motor, -en** motor
die **Motorenabteilung** engine division
der **Motorenkonstrukteur, -e** engine designer
das **Motorrad, ⸚er** motorcycle (3B)
müde tired (4B)
(das) **München** Munich
der **Mund, ⸚er** mouth (10B)
mürrisch moody, sulky
das **Museum, Museen** museum
die **Musik** music (3A)
musikalisch musical
müssen (muß), mußte, hat gemußt to have to, must (4B)
die **Mutter, ⸚** mother (3B)
mütterlich motherly
mütterlicherseits maternal
die **Mutti** mom
die **Mütze, -n** hat, cap

N

Na! Well!
nach to (2A); after (7B); adapted from
  nach Hause gehen to go home (4B)
der **Nachbar, -n, -n** / die **Nachbarin, -nen** neighbor (9B)
nachdem after (*conj*) (10B)
nach•denken, dachte nach, hat nachgedacht to think, ponder
nach•gehen, ging nach, ist nachgegangen to follow; to be slow (*of clocks*)
nachher later, afterwards
  Bis nachher! See you later! (3A)
nach•holen to make up for
der **Nachmittag, -e** afternoon
  heute nachmittag this afternoon
nachmittags in the afternoon (4B)
nach•prüfen to check, to verify
die **Nachricht, -en** news
nach•sehen (sieht nach), sah nach, hat nachgesehen to check (14A)
  Ich sehe mal nach. I'll check. (14A)
nächst next (3A)
  nächstes Jahr next year (3A)
die **Nacht, ⸚e** night
  Gute Nacht! Good night! (E)

der **Nachteil, -e** disadvantage
der **Nachtisch, -e** dessert (4A)
  zum Nachtisch for dessert (4A)
nachts at night (4B)
der **Nachttisch, -e** night table
der **Nadelbaum, ⸚e** coniferous tree (14B)
der **Nagel, ⸚** nail
nah close
die **Nähe** proximity
  in der Nähe von near (12B)
nähen to sew
die **Nähmaschine, -n** sewing machine
der **Name, -ns, -n** name (E)
  Mein Name ist ... My name is . . . (E)
nämlich you see
der **Narr, -en, -en** court jester
die **Nase, -n** nose (10B)
naß wet (10B)
der **Nationalismus** nationalism
die **Nationalität** nationality
die **Natur** nature
  von Natur by nature
natürlich of course (3A)
neben beside (9B)
nebenan next door
das **Nebenhaus, ⸚er** house next door
der **Neffe, -n** nephew
nehmen (nimmt), nahm, hat genommen to take (4B)
nein no (E)
nennen, nannte, hat genannt to call, to name (14A)
der **Nerv, -en** nerve
  Das geht mir auf die Nerven. That gets on my nerves. (13A)
nervös nervous
nett nice (4B)
das **Netz, -e** net
neu new (2B)
neugierig nosy
das **Neujahr** New Year
neulich recently, the other day
(das) **Neuseeland** New Zealand
nicht not
  gar nicht not at all (4A)
  nicht? nicht wahr? isn't it? (*transforms positive statements into questions*)
  nicht mehr no longer
  noch nicht not yet (4B)
  überhaupt nicht not at all

die **Nichte, -n** niece
nichts nothing (2A)
  Das macht nichts. That doesn't matter. (8A)
  gar nichts nothing at all
  nichts als Regen nothing but rain (2A)
nie, niemals never (2B)
niemand nobody (5B)
nirgends nowhere
noch still (1A); even
  noch ein another
  noch nicht not yet (4B)
  was noch? what else?
nochmal, noch einmal (over) again, once more (7A)
das **Nomen, -** noun
die **Nonne, -n** nun
der **Norden** north
nördlich (von) north (of)
(das) **Norwegen** Norway
die **Notiz, -en** note
notwendig necessary; urgent
der **November** November (2B)
die **Nummer, -n** number (1B)
die **Nudel, -n** noodle
die **Null, -en** zero (2A)
nur only, just (1A)
die **Nuß, Nüsse** nut
nützlich useful

O

ob whether (*conj*) (8B)
oben at the top (10B)
ober upper
der **Ober, -** waiter
  Herr Ober! Waiter!
die **Oboe, -n** oboe
das **Obst** fruit (8B)
obwohl although (*conj*) (10B)
der **Ochse, -n** ox
oder or (1B)
der **Ofen, ⸚** stove
offen open (8A)
der **Offizier, -e** officer (*army*)
öffnen to open (6B)
die **Öffnung, -en** opening
oft often (2A)
ohne without (4A)
die **Ohnmacht** fainting
das **Ohr, -en** ear (10B)
die **Ohrfeige, -n** slap

der **Ohrring, -e** earring (7B)
der **Oktober** October (2B)
das **Oktoberfest** Octoberfest
  aufs Oktoberfest to the Octo-
    berfest
ölig oily
die **Oma, -s** grandma (3B)
der **Onkel, -** uncle (3B)
der **Opa, -s** grandpa (3B)
die **Oper, -n** opera
operieren to operate
die **Orange, -n** orange
der **Orangensaft** orange juice (3B)
das **Orchester, -** orchestra
die **Orchidee, -n** orchid
ordentlich decent
ordnen to put in order
die **Ordnung** order (7B)
  in Ordnung O.K. (7B)
der **Organist, -en, -en** organist
der **Osten** east
östlich (von) east (of)
(das) **Ostern** Easter
(das) **Österreich** Austria (2B)
der **Österreicher, -** / die **Öster-
    reicherin, -nen** Austrian (*per-
    son*) (1B)
österreichisch Austrian
die **Ouvertüre, -n** overture
der **Ozean, -e** ocean

P

das **Paar** pair, couple
  ein Paar Hosen a pair of pants
    (7B)
paar
  ein paar a couple of, a few (4A)
  auf ein paar Tage for a few days
    (8A)
packen to pack
die **Packung, -en** package
das **Paket, -e** parcel
der **Panzer, -** tank
das **Papier, -e** paper
der **Papierkorb, ⁻e** wastepaper
  basket (9A)
das **Paradies** paradise
das **Parfüm** perfume (7B)
der **Park, -s** park
parken to park
der **Parkplatz, ⁻e** parking lot
der **Partner, -** / die **Partnerin,
  -nen** partner

das **Partizip, -ien** participle
das **Partizip Perfekt** past participle
die **Party, -s** party
  auf eine Party to a party
der **Paß, Pässe** passport; mountain
  pass
passen to fit
  Das paßt mir nicht. That
    doesn't suit me.
passend appropriate
passieren, passierte, ist passiert
  to happen
der **Patient, -en** / die **Patientin,
  -nen** patient
die **Pause, -n** break, intermission
  (3A)
der **Pazifik** Pacific Ocean
der **Pazifist, -en, en** pacifist
das **Pedal, -e** pedal
der **Pelzmantel, ⁻** fur coat
pensioniert retired
perfekt perfect
der **Personenwagen, -** passenger
  car (13B)
persönlich personal
die **Persönlichkeit, -en**
  personality
pessimistisch pessimistic
der **Pfad, -e** path (14B)
die **Pfanne, -n** pan
der **Pfannkuchen, -** pancake
  der Berliner Pfannkuchen
    jelly doughnut
der **Pfeffer** pepper
die **Pfeife, -n** pipe
der **Pfennig, -e** penny
das **Pferd, -e** horse (10A)
die **Pflanze, -n** plant
pflanzen to plant
die **Pflaume, -n** plum
pflichtbewußt conscientious
pflücken to pick
pflügen to plow
der **Pfosten, -** post
die **Pfote, -n** paw
das **Pfund, -e** pound
phantastisch fantastic
pharmazeutisch pharmaceutical
die **Philosophie** philosophy
die **Physik** physics
der **Pilot, -en, -en** pilot
die **Pistole, -n** pistol
die **Pizza, -s** pizza
der **Plan, ⁻e** plan (11A)
planen to plan

die **Planung** planning
das **Plastik** plastic
die **Platte, -n** record (3A); desktop
der **Plattenspieler, -** record player
der **Platz, ⁻e** place, seat, room;
  (town) square (8A)
plötzlich suddenly, all of a sudden
  (7A)
das **Plusquamperfekt** past perfect
poliert polished
die **Politikwissenschaft** political
  science
politisch political
die **Polizei** police
der **Polizist, -en, -en** / die **Polizistin, -nen** police officer
polnisch Polish
die **Pommes frites** French fries
  (4A)
der **Portier** caretaker
die **Portion, -en** helping, serving,
  order (4A)
  eine Portion Pommes frites an
    order of French fries (4A)
das **Porzellan** porcelain
die **Post** post office (8B); mail
das **Poster, -** poster (9B)
das **Postfach** P.O. Box
die **Postkarte, -n** postcard (6A)
praktisch practical
die **Präposition, -en** preposition
der **Präsident, -en, -en** president
das **Präteritum** simple past tense
der **Preis, -e** price
preisgünstig inexpensive (11B)
die **Preislage, -n** price range
die **Presse** press (11A)
pressen to press
die **Privatsphäre** privacy
pro per
die **Probe, -n** rehearsal
**probe•fahren (fährt probe), fuhr
  probe, ist probegefahren** to
  take for a test drive
die **Probefahrt, -en** test drive
probieren to try (7A)
das **Problem, -e** problem (6A)
der **Professor, -en** / die **Professorin, -nen** professor
das **Profil** tread (of a tire)
der **Programmierer, -** / die
  Programmiererin, -nen
  programmer
das **Projekt, -e** project
die **Propaganda** propaganda

Prost! Cheers!

protestieren to protest

protzig ostentatious, swanky

die **Provinz, -en** province

die **Prüderie** prudishness

prüfen to examine

die **Prüfung, -en** examination (10B)

der **Psychiater** psychiatrist

der **Pudding, -s** pudding

der **Pudel, -n** poodle

der **Pulli, -s** sweater (7B)

der **Pullover, -** sweater (7B)

Punkt elf at eleven on the dot (4B)

pünktlich punctual

putzen to clean (6B)

die **Putzfrau, -en** cleaning lady

Q

die **Qualifikation, -en** qualification

die **Qualität, -en** quality

Quatsch! nonsense (6A)

quatschen to gab; to talk (9B)

das **Quiz, -** quiz

R

der **Rabe, -n** raven

das **Rad, ¨er** wheel; bike

eine **Radtour machen** to go on a bicycle trip (11B)

das **Radio, -s** radio

die **Radtour, -en** bicycle trip

der **Rand, ¨er** edge

der **Rasen** lawn (6B)

der **Rasenmäher, -** lawn mower (6B)

der **Rasierapparat, -e** shaver (7B)

(sich) **rasieren** to shave (12B)

rasseln to rattle

der **Rat** advice

um Rat fragen to ask for advice

raten (rät) riet, hat geraten to advise

das **Rathaus** city hall

das **Rätsel, -** riddle

die **Ratte, -n** rat

der **Rauch** smoke (14A)

rauchen to smoke (6B)

Mir raucht der Kopf. I can't think straight.

das **Rauchen** smoking

raus•gehen, ging raus, ist rausgegangen to go out

reagieren (auf + acc) to react (to)

die **Reaktion, -en** reaction

rechnen to calculate

die **Rechnung, -en** bill

recht quite (8A)

Du hast recht. You are right.

rechts right, to the right (10B)

rechtzeitig on time (12B)

die **Rede, -n** speech

reden to talk

das **Referat, -e** report, paper (4A)

das **Reformhaus, ¨er** health food store

regelmäßig regular (9B)

der **Regen** rain (2A)

der **Regenschirm, -e** umbrella

das **Regenwetter** rainy weather

regieren to govern (11A)

die **Regierung, -en** government (11A)

regnen to rain (1A)

Es regnet. It's raining. (1A)

Es regnet in Strömen. It's pouring rain. (1A)

reich rich (5B)

der **Reichskanzler** German Chancellor

der **Reichstag** German Parliament

reif ripe

der **Reifen, -** tire (13B)

die **Reihe, -n** row

der Reihe nach in order

die **Reihenfolge** sequence

rein pure

rein•gehen, ging rein, ist reingegangen to go in

der **Reis** rice

die **Reise, -n** trip (11B)

das **Reisebüro, -s** travel agency

der **Reisebus, -se** touring bus

reisen to travel (3B)

reißen, riß, hat gerissen to pull, yank

reiten, ritt, ist geritten to ride (10A)

der **Reiter** horseback rider

reklamieren to complain

die **Relativitätstheorie** theory of relativity

rennen, rannte, ist gerannt to run (10B)

der **Rennwagen, -** racing car

die **Rente, -n** pension

reparieren to repair (6B)

der **Reservereifen, -** spare tire

der **Rest, -e** rest, remainder

das **Restaurant, -s** restaurant

das **Resultat, -e** result

retten to save (11A)

die **Revolution** revolution

der **Rhein** Rhine (*river*)

richtig right; really; properly (5A)

die **Richtigkeit** rightness, correctness

riechen, roch, hat gerochen to smell (8B)

riesig huge

der **Ring, -e** ring

rings um ... herum all around

riskieren to risk

der **Roboter, -** robot

der **Rock** rock music

der **Rock, ¨e** skirt (7B)

roh raw

rollen to roll

das **Rollenspiel, -e** role play

der **Roman, -e** novel (5B)

romantisch romantic

rosa pink

die **Rose, -n** rose

der **Rost** rust

rostig rusty

rot red (1B)

rothaarig red-haired

(das) **Rotkäppchen** Little Red Ridinghood

das **Rotkraut** red cabbage

die **Rübe, -n** turnip

der **Rücken, -** back

der **Rucksack, ¨e** backpack (11B)

rücksichtsvoll considerate

rufen, rief, hat gerufen to call, to exclaim (7A)

die **Ruhe** peace and quiet (11B)

der **Ruhestand** retirement

in den Ruhestand treten to retire

ruhig quiet (9B)

die **Rührung** emotion

ruinieren to ruin

der **Rüssel, -** trunk (*of an elephant*)

der **Saal, Säle** hall
die **Sache, -n** thing, matter
der **Sack, ⸚e** sack
säen to sow
der **Saft, ⸚e** juice
saftig juicy
sägen to saw
sagen to say, to tell (4A)
  sag mal say, tell me (1A)
der **Salat, -e** salad (4A)
das **Salz** salt
salzig salty
das **Salzwasser** salt water
die **Sammlung, -en** collection
der **Samstag** Saturday (2B)
sämtliche all
der **Sand** sand (11B)
sandig sandy
der **Sänger, - / die Sängerin, -nen** singer
sarkastisch sarcastic
satteln to saddle
der **Satz, ⸚e** sentence
sauber clean
sauer sour (2B)
das **Sauerkraut** sauerkraut
saufen (säuft), soff, hat gesoffen to drink heavily (4B)
saugen to suck
das **Sauwetter** rotten weather
das **Saxophon, -e** saxophone
die **S-Bahn** rapid transit commuter train
schäbig shabby
das **Schach** chess (3B)
  Schach spielen to play chess (3B)
die **Schachtel, -n** (cardboard) box
schade too bad
  Es ist schade ums Geld. It's a waste of money.
schaden (+ *dat*) to be bad for (12A)
der **Schaden, ⸚** damage
das **Schaf, -e** sheep
der **Schäferhund, -e** German shepherd dog
der **Schafskopf, ⸚e** dimwit, blockhead
der **Schal, -e** scarf (7B)
die **Schallplatte, -n** record
schalten (auf) to switch (to)
scharf sharp; spicy; tough

der **Schatten, -** shade, shadow (14A)
schattig shady
der **Schatz** darling (12A)
schauen to look, see
schaufeln to shovel
das **Schaufenster, -** display window (8A)
einen Schaufensterbummel machen to go window shopping
der **Schaukelstuhl, ⸚e** rocking chair
das **Schaumbad, ⸚er** bubble bath
der **Schauspieler, - / die Schauspielerin, -nen** actor / actress (14A)
der **Scheck, -s** check
das **Scheckheft, -e** checkbook
die **Scheibe, -en** slice (4A)
  eine Scheibe Brot a slice of bread (4A)
der **Scheibenwischer, -** windshield wiper (13B)
scheinen, schien, hat geschienen to shine (1A)
der **Schellfisch** haddock
schenken to give (as a gift) (7B)
scheuen to shy away from
der **Schi, -er** ski (3B)
  Schi laufen to go skiing (3B)
schick chic
schicken to send (7B)
schieben, schob, hat geschoben to push
schief crooked
schießen, schoß, hat geschossen to shoot (14A)
das **Schiff, -e** ship
das **Schild, -er** road sign
schimpfen to scold
die **Schinkenwurst** ham sausage
der **Schirm, -e** umbrella
der **Schlaf** sleep
schlafen (schläft), schlief, hat geschlafen to sleep (4B)
die **Schlafratte, -en** sleepyhead
schläfrig sleepy
der **Schlafsack, ⸚e** sleeping bag (11B)
die **Schlaftablette, -n** sleeping pill
das **Schlafzimmer, -** bedroom (9A)
schlagen (schlägt), schlug, hat geschlagen to hit, to beat (14A)

das **Schlagzeug** drums
schlampig sloppy
die **Schlange, -n** snake
schlank slim
die **Schlankheitskur, -en** diet
schlau smart, cunning, sly
schlecht bad (2B)
die **Schlechtigkeit** badness
schleimig slimy
schleppen to drag (5A)
schließen, schloß, hat geschlossen to close
schließlich after all; finally (10B)
schlimm bad
der **Schlips, -e** tie (7B)
der **Schlittschuh, -e** skate
das **Schloß, Schlösser** castle
der **Schlosser, -** toolmaker
schlüpfrig slippery
der **Schluß, Schlüsse** end (5A)
  Schluß! That's all!
  zum **Schluß** to top it off; finally (5A)
der **Schlüssel, -** key (12A)
die **Schlußprüfung, -en** final exam
schmecken to taste (12A)
  Laß es dir schmecken! Enjoy your meal! (12A)
der **Schmerz, -en** pain
schmutzig dirty
der **Schnaps** hard liquor
die **Schnecke, -n** snail
der **Schnee** snow (2A)
der **Schneesturm, ⸚e** snowstorm
schneiden, schnitt, hat geschnitten to cut (6B)
der **Schneider, - / die Schneiderin, -nen** tailor / seamstress
schneien to snow (2A)
schnell quick, fast (5B)
  schnell machen to hurry up
die **Schnelligkeit** speed
der **Schnellimbiß** hot snack stand
das **Schnitzel, -** cutlet
  das Wiener Schnitzel breaded veal cutlet
der **Schnupfen** cold
der **Schnurrbart, ⸚e** moustache
schockiert shocked
die **Schokolade** chocolate
  eine Tafel Schokolade a chocolate bar (14A)
schön nice, beautiful (1A)

die **Schönheit** beauty
schon already (3A)
schonen to protect
der **Schrank, ¨-e** wardrobe, cabinet, closet (9A)
schrecklich terrible, awful (11A)
schreiben, schrieb, hat geschrieben to write (4A)
  schreiben an (+ *acc*) to write to
die **Schreibmaschine, -n** typewriter
der **Schreibtisch, -e** desk (9A)
die **Schreibtischlampe, -n** desk lamp
schreien, schrie, hat geschrieen to shout
der **Schreiner, -** cabinet maker
die **Schrift** handwriting
schriftlich in writing
der **Schuh, -e** shoe (7B)
die **Schularbeit, -en** homework (12A)
schuldig guilty
die **Schule, -n** school (6A)
das **Schulenglisch** high school English
der **Schüler, -** / die **Schülerin, -nen** pupil, student in a high school (10B)
die **Schulter, -n** shoulder (10B)
schütteln to shake (14A)
schwach weak
die **Schwäche** weakness
schwarz black (1B)
  das schwarze Brett bulletin board (9B)
das **Schwarzbrot** dark rye bread
der **Schwarzwald** Black Forest
(das) **Schweden** Sweden
das **Schwein, -e** pig
  Schwein haben to be lucky
der **Schweinebraten** pork roast
der **Schweinestall, ¨-e** pigpen
der **Schweiß** sweat
die **Schweiz** Switzerland (1B)
der **Schweizer, -** / die **Schweizerin, -nen** Swiss (*person*) (1B)
schweizerisch Swiss
schwellen to swell
die **Schwellung, -en** swelling
schwer hard, difficult; heavy (6A); seriously
  Es fällt mir schwer, so früh aufzustehen. I find it hard to get up so early.

die **Schwester, -n** sister (3B)
schwierig difficult (12B)
die **Schwierigkeit, -en** difficulty
schwimmen, schwamm, ist geschwommen to swim (3B)
  schwimmen gehen to go swimming (3B)
das **Schwyzerdütsch** dialect word for Swiss German
der **See, -n** lake (11B)
das **Segelboot, -e** sailboat (3B)
segeln gehen to go sailing (3B)
sehen (sieht), sah, hat gesehen to see (4B)
  Ich sehe schlecht. My eyesight is bad.
die **Sehenswürdigkeit, -en** tourist attraction
sehr very (1A)
die **Seifenoper, -n** soap opera
sein his, its
sein (ist), war, ist gewesen to be (E)
seit since; for (a period of time) (7B)
die **Seite, -n** side, page
der **Sekretär, -e** / die **Sekretärin, -nen** secretary
der **Sekt** champagne
die **Sekunde, -n** second (2B)
selber myself, yourself, himself, etc. (5A)
selbst myself, yourself, himself, etc. (5A)
selten rarely, seldom (2B)
die **Seltenheit, -en** rarity
das **Semester, -** semester
das **Seminar, -e** seminar
sensibel sensitive
der **September** September (2B)
der **Sessel, -** armchair (9A)
setzen to set
sich setzen to sit down (12B)
das **Shampoo** shampoo
(das) **Sibirien** Siberia
sicher sure, certainly; probably (5A)
silbern (made of) silver
singen, sang, hat gesungen to sing (3B)
die **Sitte, -n** custom
der **Sitz, -e** seat (11A)
sitzen, saß, hat gesessen to sit (6B)
das **Skript** lecture notes
der **Slum, -s** slum
so such

so ... wie as . . . as (2A)
die **Socke, -n** sock (7B)
sofort immediately (9A)
sogar even
der **Sohn, ¨-e** son (3B)
solang(e) as long as; in the meantime
solcher, solche, solches such
der **Soldat, -en, -en** soldier (14A)
sollen (soll), sollte, hat gesollt to be supposed to; should; to be said to be (4B)
der **Sommer** summer (2A)
das **Sonderangebot, -e** special offer (11B)
sondern but (*rather*) (8B)
der **Sonnabend** Saturday (2B)
die **Sonne** sun (1A)
sonnig sunny
der **Sonntag** Sunday (2B)
sonst or else, otherwise (5A); apart from that
die **Sorge, -n** worry
sorgen für to look after
sorgfältig carefully (13A)
die **Soße, -n** sauce
das **Souvenir, -s** souvenir
sowieso anyway (12A)
der **Sozialarbeiter, -** / die **Sozialarbeiterin, -nen** social worker
der **Sozialismus** socialism
die **Spaghetti** (*pl*) spaghetti
spalten to split
(das) **Spanien** Spain
das **Spanisch** Spanish (*language*)
das **Sparbuch, ¨-er** bankbook
sparen to save (8B)
die **Spargel** (*pl*) asparagus
sparsam thrifty
der **Spaß** enjoyment
  Es macht mir Spaß, Deutsch zu lernen. I enjoy learning German.
spät late (5B)
  Wie spät ist es? What time is it? (4B)
  Ich bin spät dran. I'm running late. (12A)
spazieren•fahren (fährt spazieren), fuhr spazieren, ist spazierengefahren to go for a ride (7A)
spazieren•gehen, ging spazieren, ist spazieren-

gegangen to go for a walk (5A)

der **Spaziergang, ⸚e** walk

der **Spazierstock, ⸚e** walking stick

die **Speisekarte, -n** menu (8A)

die **Spezies, -** species

der **Spiegel, -** mirror (14A)

spielen to play (3A)

der **Spinat** spinach

spinnen to be crazy

der **Sport** sport, athletics

  Sport treiben to be active in sports (4A)

sportlich athletic

der **Sportwagen, -** sports car

spöttisch mockingly

die **Sprache, -n** language

die **Sprachkenntnisse** (*pl*) knowledge of foreign languages

die **Sprechblase, -n** speech bubble

sprechen (spricht), sprach, hat gesprochen to speak (4B)

der **Sprecher, -** speaker

die **Sprechstunde, -n** office hour

springen, sprang, ist gesprungen to jump

das **Spülbecken, -** kitchen sink (9A)

der **Staat, -en** state (8A)

die **Staatskasse** state treasury

die **Stadt, ⸚e** city, town (8B)

  in die Stadt to town (8B)

der **Stadtbummel** stroll through town

  einen Stadtbummel machen to stroll through town

der **Stadtpark** city park

der **Stahlhelm, -e** steel helmet

der **Stall, ⸚e** stable (10A)

der **Stamm, ⸚e** tree trunk

stammen aus to come from, to originate from

ständig constant

stark strong (11A)

statt instead of (9B)

statt•finden, fand statt, hat stattgefunden to take place

der **Staub** dust

der **Staubsauger, -** vacuum cleaner

staunen to be astonished

das **Steak, -s** steak

stecken to put, to stick (10A)

stehen, stand, hat gestanden to stand (6B)

  Steht mir diese Jacke? Does this jacket suit (look good on) me? (7B)

stehen•bleiben, blieb stehen, ist stehengeblieben to stop (10A)

die **Stehlampe, -n** floor lamp (9A)

stehlen (stiehlt), stahl, hat gestohlen to steal

steigen, stieg, ist gestiegen (auf + *acc*) to climb (on) (10A); to rise

der **Stein, -e** stone

stellen to put (in an upright position), to stand (9A)

das **Stellenangebot, -e** job offer (10B)

die **Stellung, -en** job, position (12B)

sterben (stirbt), starb, ist gestorben to die (6A)

die **Stereoanlage, -n** stereo (9A)

die **Steuer, -n** tax

still quiet

die **Stille** stillness

die **Stimme, -n** voice (12A)

stimmen to vote (11A); to be right

  da stimmt etwas nicht ganz that doesn't quite make sense

stinken, stank, hat gestunken to stink

stinkig stinky

die **Stirn, -en** forehead

der **Stock, ⸚e** cane, stock; floor, story

stolpern to stumble (14A)

stolz (auf + *acc*) proud (of) (14A)

stoppen to stop

stören to disturb

der **Strand, ⸚e** beach (11B)

  am Strand on the beach

die **Straße, -n** street (8B)

die **Straßenbahn** streetcar

streichen, strich, hat gestrichen to paint (6B)

streiken to strike, to go on strike

der **Streit** fight

sich **streiten, stritt sich, hat sich gestritten** to fight

der **Streß** stress

stressig stressful

stricken to knit

der **Strumpf, ⸚e** stocking

das **Stück, ⸚e** piece (4A)

  ein Stück Kuchen a piece of cake (4A)

fünf Mark das Stück five marks a piece

der **Student, -en** / die **Studentin, -nen** student

der **Studentenchor, ⸚e** student choir

das **Studentenheim, -e** / das **Studentenwohnheim, -e** dormitory, student residence (9B)

das **Studentenwerk** student center

der **Studienrat, ⸚e** / die **Studienrätin, -nen** high school teacher

studieren to study (3A)

das **Studium** studies

der **Stuhl, ⸚e** chair (9A)

stümperhaft amateurish

die **Stunde, -n** hour (2B)

  auf eine Stunde for an hour

  vor zwei Stunden two hours ago (9A)

stundenlang for hours

der **Stundenplan, ⸚e** timetable

stündlich hourly

der **Sturm, ⸚e** storm

stürzen to fall; to plunge

suchen to look for (5B)

der **Süden** south

südlich (von) south (of)

die **Summe, -n** sum

summen to buzz, to hum

sündigen to sin

der **Supermarkt** supermarket (8B)

die **Suppe, -n** soup (4A)

das **Surfbrett, -er** surfboard, windsurfer (5A)

süß sweet (2B)

die **Süßigkeiten** (*pl*) sweets

das **Süßwasser** fresh water (14B)

das **Sweatshirt, -s** sweatshirt (7B)

sympathisch likeable

die **Symphonie, -n** symphony

das **Symphonieorchester** symphony orchestra

die **Szene, -n** scene

T

der **Tabak** tobacco

die **Tablette, -n** pill

die **Tafel, -n** blackboard (10B)

  eine Tafel Schokolade chocolate bar (14A)

der **Tag, -e** day (2B)
    auf ein paar Tage for a few days (8A)
    den ganzen Tag all day (5A)
    eines Tages some day, one day (12B)
    alle vierzehn Tage every two weeks (9A)
    Guten Tag! Hello! (E)
das **Tagebuch, ̈-er** diary
tagelang for days (13B)
das **Tagesgericht, -e** special of the day
der **Tagesjob, -s** job for a day
der **Tageslauf** daily routine
das **Tagesmenü, -s** special of the day
täglich daily
tagsüber during the day
taktlos tactless (10B)
taktvoll tactful (10B)
das **Tal, ̈-er** valley (14B)
die **Tante, -n** aunt (3B)
tanzen to dance
der **Tänzer, -** / die **Tänzerin, -nen** dancer
tapezieren to wallpaper
tapfer brave
die **Tasche, -n** pocket (10A)
das **Taschenbuch, ̈-er** paperback
der **Taschenrechner, -** calculator
die **Tasse, -n** cup (4A)
    eine Tasse Kaffee a cup of coffee (4A)
der **Täter, -** culprit
tatsächlich really, actually
die **Taube, -n** dove
sich **täuschen** to be mistaken
der **Tausendfüßler, -** millipede
das **Taxi, -s** taxi
    per Taxi by taxi
der **Techniker, -** technician
der **Tee** tea (3B)
die **Teekanne, -n** teapot
der **Teekessel, -** teakettle
der **Teil, -e** part (11A)
teilen to divide
das **Telefon, -e** telephone (1B)
telefonieren (mit) to talk on the phone (with) (6B)
telefonisch by telephone
die **Telefonnummer, -n** telephone number (9B)
das **Teleskop, -e** telescope
der **Teller, -** plate (4A)

ein Teller Suppe a bowl of soup (4A)
die **Temperatur, -en** temperature
das **Tennis** tennis (3B)
    Tennis spielen to play tennis (3B)
der **Tennisschläger, -** tennis racquet
der **Teppich, -e** carpet, rug (9A)
der **Terrorist, -en, -en** / die **Terroristin, -nen** terrorist
der **Test, -s** test
teuer expensive (2B)
der **Teufel** devil
der **Text, -e** text
das **Textverarbeitungssystem, -en** word processor
das **Theater** theater
    ins Theater to the theater (2B)
das **Thema, -en** topic
die **Theorie, -n** theory (8A)
das **Thermometer, -** thermometer (1A)
der **Thunfisch, -e** tuna fish
tief deep (12B)
das **Tier, -e** animal
die **Tinte** ink
tippen to type; to tap
der **Tisch, -e** table (8A)
der **Toast** toast
der **Toaster, -** toaster
die **Tochter, ̈** daughter (3B)
der **Tod** death (12B)
todmüde dead tired
todschick very stylish, snazzy
die **Toilette, -n** toilet (9A)
tolerant tolerant
toll fantastic (1A); crazy
die **Tomate, -n** tomato
der **Ton, ̈-e** tone, sound, note
das **Tonband, ̈-er** (audio) tape (12A)
das **Tonbandgerät, -e** tape recorder (12A)
der **Topf, ̈-e** pot
die **Torte** cake
    Schwarzwälder Kirschtorte Black Forest cherry cake
tot dead
der (die) **Tote, -n** dead person
töten to kill
sich **tot•lachen** to die laughing
der **Tourist, -en, -en** / die **Touristin, -nen** tourist

tragen (trägt), trug, hat getragen to carry (10A)
trainieren to train
trampen to hitchhike (6B)
transportieren to transport
der **Traum, ̈-e** dream
träumen to dream (11B)
traurig sad (14B)
(sich) **treffen (trifft), traf, hat getroffen** to meet (7A)
treiben
    Sport treiben to be active in sports (4A)
trennen to separate
    getrennt bezahlen to pay separately
die **Treppe, -n** stair (9A)
das **Treppenhaus** staircase
treten (tritt), trat, ist getreten to step
    Du bist mir auf den Fuß getreten. You stepped on my toe. (14A)
trinken, trank, hat getrunken to drink (3B)
das **Trinkgeld** tip
der **Tritt, -e** kick
    einen Tritt geben to kick
trocken dry (10B)
der **Trockner, -** dryer
die **Trompete, -n** trumpet
tropfen to drip
das **Trottoir, -s** sidewalk
trotz in spite of (9B)
trotzdem anyway, nevertheless (12B)
Tschüs! So long! (E)
tüchtig capable; thoroughly
die **Tulpe, -n** tulip
tun, tat, hat getan to do, to make (3B)
    Das tut gut. That feels good. (8A)
    Du tust mir leid. I feel sorry for you. (12A)
    Es tut mir leid. I'm sorry. (7B)
    so tun, als ob to act as if
die **Tür, -en** door (8A)
die **Türkei** Turkey
türkisch Turkish
TÜV *Technischer Überwachungsverein*
    durch den TÜV gehen to pass inspection (of a car)

der **Typ, -en** guy
typisch typical (6A)

U

üben to practice (6B)
über over, above (2A)
überall everywhere (8A)
überbelichtet overexposed
überfahren to run over
überhaupt at all
überholen to pass (14A)
überlegen to think about (13A)
übermorgen the day after tomorrow (4B)
übernächst
  übernächste Woche the week after next
übernachten to stay overnight (11B)
die **Übernachtung** overnight accommodation (11B)
übernehmen (übernimmt), übernahm, hat übernommen to take on
überrascht surprised
die **Überraschung, -en** surprise (12A)
überreden to persuade
Übersee overseas
  aus Übersee from overseas
übersetzen to translate
die **Übersetzung, -en** translation
überzeugend convincing
übrigens by the way (4A)
die **Übung, -en** exercise; seminar (10B)
die **Uhr, -en** clock (2B)
  Es ist sieben Uhr. It's seven o'clock. (3A)
  Wieviel Uhr ist es? What time is it? (4B)
  um wieviel Uhr (at) what time (4B)
  um zwei Uhr at two o'clock (4B)
um at, around (5B)
  um wieviel Uhr? (at) what time? (4B)
um ... zu in order to
umarmen to embrace
die **Umgebung** surrounding area (11A)

um•graben (gräbt um), grub um, hat umgegraben to dig up
umsonst for nothing (8B)
um•stellen to rearrange (9A); to switch
der **Umweltschutz** protection of the environment
um•ziehen, zog um, ist umgezogen to move
  sich um•ziehen to change (one's clothes) (12B)
und and (1A)
uneben uneven
unfreundlich unfriendly (10B)
ungarisch Hungarian
(das) **Ungarn** Hungary
ungeduldig impatient
ungefähr approximately
ungeheuer tremendously
ungenießbar inedible
ungesund unhealthy (4A)
unglücklich unhappy; unrequited
die **Uni, -s** university (10B)
  zur Uni to the university (6B)
die **Uniform, -en** uniform
die **Universität, -en** university
unmöglich impossible
unpolitisch unpolitical
unregelmäßig irregular (9B)
die **Unruhe** agitation
unser our
unten at the bottom (10B); below
unter under, below (2A); lower; among
die **Untergrundbahn, die U-Bahn** subway
sich **unterhalten (unterhält sich) unterhielt sich, hat sich unterhalten** to converse
sich **unterhalten mit; über** (+ *acc*) to talk to; about
die **Unterhaltung, -en** conversation (8A)
die **Unterkunft** living accommodation
untergeschlagen crossed
der **Unterricht** teaching
der **Unterschied, -e** difference (8A)
die **Unterschrift, -en** signature (13A)
die **Untertasse, -n** saucer (8A)
der **Untertitel, -** subtitle

unterwegs on the way; on the road (11B)
unwahr untrue
die **Unwahrheit, -en** untruth
unwichtig unimportant (5B)
unzufrieden dissatisfied (9A)
die **Urgroßmutter** great-grandmother
der **Urgroßvater** great-grandfather
der **Urlaub** (*sing*) holidays, vacation (11B)
usw. (und so weiter) etc. (and so on) (1B)

V

die **Vase, -n** vase
der **Vater, ¨** father (3B)
väterlich fatherly
väterlicherseits paternal
der **Vati** dad
Venedig Venice
sich **verändern** to change
das **Verb, -en** verb
verbessern to correct
die **Verbesserung, -en** correction
verbieten, verbot, hat verboten to forbid
verblüfft baffled
verbringen, verbrachte, hat verbracht to spend (time) (11A)
verbunden bandaged
verdienen to earn (3B)
die **Vereinigten Staaten (die USA)** the United States (the USA) (1B)
Verflixt! Darn it!
verfluchen to curse
vergangen past
vergessen (vergißt), vergaß, hat vergessen to forget (4B)
vergeßlich forgetful (12A)
der **Vergleich, -e** comparison
vergleichen, verglich, hat verglichen to compare (13A)
vergnügt happy, in a good mood
das **Verhältnis** relationship
verhauen to beat up
verheiratet (mit) married (to) (8A)
verkaufen to sell (3B)

der **Verkäufer, -** / die
Verkäuferin, -nen sales clerk,
salesman / saleslady (11B)
die **Verkaufsabteilung** sales division
der **Verkehr** traffic
die **Verkehrsampel, -n** traffic light
verkratzt scratched
der **Verlag, -e** publisher
**verlassen (verläßt), verließ, hat
verlassen** to leave
verletzt wounded
sich **verlieben in** (+ *acc*) to fall in
love with (12B)
verlieren, verlor, hat verloren to
lose (13B)
verlobt engaged (to be married)
vermeiden, vermied, hat vermieden to avoid
vermieten to rent out (9B)
veröffentlichen to publish
verreisen to go out of town
verrückt crazy, mad (4A)
die **Verrücktheit** craziness, madness
versalzen oversalted
**verschieben, verschob, hat
verschoben** to postpone
verschieden different, various
(10B)
sich **verspäten** to be late (12B)
verspotten to ridicule
**versprechen (verspricht),
versprach, hat versprochen**
to promise (9A)
das **Verständnis** sympathy, understanding
verstecken to hide (10A)
verstehen, verstand, hat verstanden to understand (5B)
sich gut verstehen to get along
well (13B)
versuchen to try (5B)
verteilen to distribute (14A)
der **Vertreter, -** / die **Vertreterin,
-nen** sales representative (11B)
vertrocknet dried up
verwandt related
der (die) **Verwandte, -n** relative
(11A)
verwenden to use
verwundet wounded (14A)
der **Vetter** (male) cousin (3B)
der **Videorecorder, -** video cassette recorder, VCR

das **Vieh** cattle
viel much, a lot (2B)
vielleicht perhaps (5A)
vielseitig varied
das **Viertel** quarter (4B)
Viertel nach a quarter after (4B)
Viertel vor a quarter to (4B)
das **Vierteljahr** three months
die **Viertelstunde, -n** fifteen minutes
das **Visum, Visen** visa
der **Vizepräsident, -en, -en** vice
president
der **Vogel, ⁻** bird
die **Vokabeln** vocabulary
das **Volk, ⁻er** nation, people (11A)
voll full (8A)
voller full of
völlig completely
vollständig completely
von from; of (7B)
von ... bis from . . . to (4B)
von jetzt ab from now on
vor in front of; before (9B)
fünf vor neun five to nine
vor allem above all (9B)
vor sich hin to oneself
vor zwei Stunden two hours
ago (9A)
vorbei sein to be over
**vorbei•kommen, kam vorbei, ist
vorbeigekommen** to come by
vor•bereiten to prepare
die **Vorfahren** (*pl*) ancestors
vor•gehen, ging vor, ist vorgegangen to be fast (*of a
clock*)
vorgestern the day before yesterday (4B)
der **Vorgang, ⁻e** event
**vor•haben (hat vor), hatte vor,
hat vorgehabt** to plan, to have
planned (5A)
vorher before (4A)
vor•kommen, kam, vor, ist vorgekommen to occur, happen
vor•legen to submit
**vor•lesen (liest vor), las vor, hat
vorgelesen** to read to
die **Vorlesung, -en** lecture (4A)
in die Vorlesung to a lecture
(2B)
vormittags in the morning (4B)
der **Vorname, -ens, -en** first name
der **Vorschlag, ⁻e** suggestion

**vor•schlagen (schlägt vor),
schlug vor, hat vorgeschlagen** to suggest
der **Vorteil, -e** advantage
die **Vorwahl** area code (1B)
der **Vorwurf, ⁻e** reproach
sich **Vorwürfe machen** to reproach oneself

W

die **Waage, -n** scale (for weighing)
das **Wachs** wax
wachsen to grow
die **Waffe, -n** weapon (14A)
der **Wagen, -** car (3B)
der **Wahnsinn** insanity
wahr true
nicht wahr? isn't it? aren't you?
(*transforms positive statements
into questions*)
während during (9B)
wahrhaftig surely
die **Wahrheit, -en** truth (10A)
der **Wald, ⁻er** woods, forest (10A)
der **Walzer, -** waltz
die **Wand, ⁻e** wall (9A)
wandern gehen to go hiking (3B)
wann? when? (2B)
die **Ware, -n** merchandise
warm warm (1A)
warnen to warn
die **Warnung, -en** warning
warten to wait (12A)
warten (auf + *acc*) to wait (for)
(12B)
warum? why? (2B)
die **Warze, -n** wart
was? what? (1A)
**Was für ein Instrument spielst
du?** What instrument do you
play? (3A)
Was für Extreme! What extremes! (2A)
das **Waschbecken, -** sink (9A)
die **Wäsche** laundry
**waschen (wäscht), wusch, hat
gewaschen** to wash (4B)
der **Wäschetrockner** clothes dryer
die **Waschmaschine, -n** washer
der **Waschsalon** laundromat
das **Wasser** water (3B)
der **Wasserfall, ⁻e** waterfall (14B)

wässerig watery
die **Wasserratte, -n** water rat
wecken to waken
der **Wecker, -** alarm clock
weder ... noch neither . . . nor (10B)
weg away; gone
der **Weg, -e** way, path (14A)
wegen because of (9B)
weg•fahren (fährt weg), fuhr weg, ist weggefahren to drive away, go away
weg•fliegen, flog weg, ist weg-geflogen, er fliegt weg to fly away, to go away (*in a plane*)
weg•gehen, ging weg, ist weg-gegangen to go away, to leave (5B)
weg•schicken to send away
weich soft (11B)
weichgekocht soft-boiled
das **Weihnachten** Christmas (7B)
  an Weihnachten at Christmas
  zu Weihnachten at, for Christmas (7B)
das **Weihnachtsgeschenk, -e** Christmas present (7B)
weil because (8B)
die **Weile** while
  nach einer Weile after a while (12B)
der **Wein** wine (3B)
  eine Flasche Wein a bottle of wine (7B)
das **Weinglas, ¨er** wine glass
weinen to cry (10B)
weiß white (1B)
die **Weißwurst, ¨e** veal sausage
weit far (7A)
weiter further, additional
weiter•geben (gibt weiter), gab weiter, hat weitergegeben to pass on
weiter•lesen (liest weiter), las weiter, hat weitergelesen to continue reading (7A)
weiter•spielen to continue playing
weiter•schlafen (schläft weiter), schlief weiter, hat weiter-geschlafen to continue sleeping
weiter•studieren to continue studying
welcher, welche, welches which (5B)

die **Welle, -n** wave (14B)
die **Welt** world (11A)
  zur Welt kommen to be born
der **Weltkrieg, -e** world war (11A)
weltlich worldly
die **Weltreise, -n** trip around the world
wenig little (2B)
wenigstens at least
wenn when (*conj*); if (*conj*) (8B)
wer? who? (E)
werden (wird), wurde, ist geworden to become; to get (4B)
werfen (wirft), warf, hat gewor-fen to throw (14A)
das **Werkzeug, -e** tool
wertvoll valuable
weshalb why
der **Westen** west
westlich (von) west (of)
die **Wette, -n** bet
  um die Wette laufen to run a race
  Was gilt die Wette? What are you betting?
wetten um to bet on
der **Wettlauf, ¨e** race
das **Wetter** weather (1A)
die **WG, -s** / die **Wohngemeinschaft, -en** shared housing (9B)
wichtig important (5B)
die **Wichtigkeit** importance
widerwillig reluctant (14A)
wie like, as (4A)
  so ... wie as . . . as (4B)
wie? how? (E)
  Wie bitte? Pardon? (E)
  Wie geht es Ihnen? / Wie geht's? How are you? (E)
  Wie spät ist es? What time is it?
wieder again (5A)
der **Wiederaufbau** reconstruction
wiederholen to repeat (3B)
das **Wiederhören**
  Auf Wiederhören! Good-bye (*on the telephone*) (1B)
wieder•sehen (sieht wieder), sah wieder, hat wieder-gesehen to see again
  Auf Wiedersehen! Good-bye! (E)
(das) **Wien** Vienna
die **Wiese, -n** meadow (14B)

wieviel? how much? (2B)
  Den wievielten haben wir heute? What's the date today? (11B)
  Der wievielte ist heute? What's the date today? (11B)
  Wieviel Uhr ist es? What time is it? (4B)
wie viele? how many? (2B)
Willkommen! Welcome!
der **Wind, -e** wind
windig windy (1A)
windstill calm, windless (1A)
das **Windsurfing** windsurfing (3B)
  Windsurfing gehen to go wind-surfing (3B)
der **Winter** winter (2A)
winzig tiny
wirklich really (7A)
die **Wirklichkeit** reality
der **Wirtschaftsprüfer, -** / die **Wirtschaftsprüferin, -nen** accountant
wissen (weiß), wußte, hat gewußt to know (6A)
  wissen von to know about (12B)
wissenschaftlich scientific
der **Witz, -e** joke
wo? where? (in what place?) (2B)
die **Woche, -n** week (2B)
das **Wochenende, -n** weekend
das **Wochenendhaus, ¨er** cottage (9B)
der **Wochenmarkt, ¨e** weekly market
wöchentlich weekly
woher? / wo ... her? where? (from what place?) (2B)
wohin? / wo ... hin? where? (to what place?) (2B)
wohl well; probably (4B)
  sich wohl fühlen to feel well (12B)
wohnen to live (to live in a build-ing or street) (3B)
die **Wohngemeinschaft, -en** / die **WG, -s** shared housing (9B)
die **Wohnmöglichkeit, -en** types of living accommodation
die **Wohnung, -en** apartment (9A)
das **Wohnzimmer, -** livingroom (9A)
der **Wolf, ¨e** wolf
  ein Wolf im Schafspelz a wolf in sheep's clothing

die **Wolke, -n** cloud
die **Wolle** wool
wollen (made of) wool
wollen (will), wollte, hat gewollt to want to (4B)
das **Wort, ¨er** word (5B)
das **Wörterbuch, ¨er** dictionary
wörtlich literally
der **Wortschatz, ¨e** vocabulary
wozu? what for?
die **Wunde, -n** wound (14A)
das **Wunder, -** miracle
wunderbar wonderful
sich **wundern über (+ acc)** to be surprised about
wunderschön very beautiful
der **Wunsch, ¨e** wish
das **Wunschdenken** wishful thinking
wünschen to wish (8A)
   Sie wünschen? May I help you?
der **Wurm, ¨er** worm
wurmig wormy
die **Wurst** sausage; cold cuts (4A)
die **Wut** rage

Z

---

zäh tough
die **Zahl, -en** number
zahlen to pay
zählen to count
der **Zahn, ¨e** tooth (10B)
der **Zahnarzt, ¨e** / die **Zahnärztin, -nen** dentist (8B)
die **Zahnpasta** toothpaste
die **Zahnschmerzen** (*pl*) toothache
zart tender
der **Zaun, ¨e** fence (6B)
die **Zehe, -en** toe (10B)
zeichnen to draw, to draft (13A)
die **Zeichnung, -en** drawing
zeigen to show (7B)
   Das Thermometer zeigt 30 Grad. The thermometer reads thirty degrees. (1A)

die **Zeile -n** line
die **Zeit, -en** time (2B)
   sich Zeit lassen to take one's time
die **Zeitung, -en** newspaper (5B)
zelten to camp
die **Zensur, -en** grade, mark (7A)
der **Zentimeter, -** centimeter
zerbrechen (zerbricht), zerbrach, hat zerbrochen to break
zerreißen, zerriß, hat zerrissen to rip up (13A)
zerrissen ripped
zerstören to destroy (14B)
der **Zettel, -** piece of paper; note
die **Ziege, -n** goat
ziehen, zog, hat gezogen to pull; to move
das **Ziel, -e** goal, finish line
ziemlich fairly, quite, rather (9A)
die **Zigarre, -n** cigar
die **Zigarette, -n** cigarette
   der **Zigarettenanzünder** cigarette lighter (*in a car*)
das **Zimmer, -** room
der **Zimmerkollege, -n, -n** / die **Zimmerkollegin, -nen** roommate (E)
die **Zimmerpflanze, -n** houseplant (9A)
die **Zimmersuche** looking for a room
der **Zins, -en** interest
das **Zitat, -e** quotation
die **Zitrone, -n** lemon
der **Zivildienst** community service (*in lieu of military service*)
der **Zoll** customs
der **Zollbeamte, -n** customs officer
der **Zoo, -s** zoo
zornig angry
zu too; to; to the home of (7B); closed (8A)
   Bist du heute abend zu Hause? Will you be (at) home tonight? (6A)
der **Zucker** sugar (4A)

zuerst (at) first (4B)
zufrieden satisfied (9A)
der **Zug, ¨e** train (3B)
zu•geben (gibt zu), gab zu, hat zugegeben to admit
zu•gehen (auf + acc), ging zu, ist zugegangen to approach
zu•hören to listen
die **Zukunft** future
zuletzt last (*adv*) (9B)
zu•machen to close (8A)
die **Zunge, -n** tongue
(das) **Zürich** Zurich
zurück back
zurück•bringen, brachte zurück, hat zurückgebracht to bring back
zurück•geben (gibt zurück), gab zurück, hat zurückgegeben to give back
zurück•halten (hält zurück), hielt zurück, hat zurückgehalten to hold back
zurück•kommen, kam zurück, ist zurückgekommen to come back (5A)
zurück•rufen, rief zurück, hat zurückgerufen to call back
zusammen together (8A)
zusammen•binden, band zusammen, hat zusammengebunden to tie together
zusammen•fassen to summarize (13A)
zusammen•passen to go together, to match
zu•schlagen (schlägt zu), schlug zu, hat zugeschlagen to slam shut
die **Zuschlagskarte, -n** additional ticket
zwar to be sure
zweimal twice (6A)
zwischen between (9B)

ENGLISH-GERMAN VOCABULARY

A

A (*grade*) die Eins, -en
a lot viel
able: to be able können (kann), konnte, hat gekonnt
above über (+ *acc* or *dat*)
　above all vor allem
absolutely ganz
accident der Unfall, ̈e
according to nach (+ *dat*)
acquaintance der / die Bekannte, -n
to **act**
　to **act as if** so tun, als ob
actor / actress der Schauspieler, -/die Schauspielerin, -nen
actually eigentlich; tatsächlich
ad die Anzeige, -n; das Inserat, -e
address die Adresse, -n
afraid: to be afraid (of) Angst haben (**vor** + *dat*)
after (*prep*) nach; (*conj*) nachdem
　after a while nach einer Weile
　after all schließlich
afternoon
　in the afternoon nachmittags
　this afternoon heute nachmittag
afterwards nachher; danach
again wieder
　over again noch einmal, nochmal
against gegen (+ *acc*)
ago vor
　two hours ago vor zwei Stunden
air die Luft
airplane das Flugzeug, -e; die Maschine, -n
airport der Flughafen, ̈
alarm clock der Wecker, -
to **be alarmed** erschrecken (erschrickt) erschrak, ist erschrocken
album das Album, -en
alcohol der Alkohol
all alles; ganz
　all day den ganzen Tag
allowed: to be allowed to dürfen (darf), durfte, hat gedurft
almost fast
alone allein

Alps die Alpen
already schon; bereits
also auch
although obwohl (*conj*)
always immer
America (das) Amerika
American amerikanisch; (person) der Amerikaner, - / die Amerikanerin, -nen
among unter
and und
angry zornig
　to be angry (with/about) sich ärgern (**über** + *acc*)
animal das Tier, -e
another noch ein
to **annoy** ärgern
annoyed: to get annoyed (with) sich ärgern (**über** + *acc*)
answer die Antwort, -en
to **answer** antworten (+ *dat*); beantworten (+ *acc*)
antenna die Antenne, -n
antique antik
anyway sowieso; trotzdem
apartment die Wohnung, -en
to **apologize** sich entschuldigen
apparatus der Apparat, -e
appetite der Appetit
apple der Apfel, ̈
　apple cake, apple pie der Apfelkuchen, -
　apple juice der Apfelsaft
appropriate passend
approximately etwa; ungefähr
April der April
area code die Vorwahl
arm der Arm, -e
armchair der Sessel, -
around (*place*) um (+ *acc*); (*time*) gegen (+ *acc*)
　around five o'clock gegen fünf
to **arrive** ankommen, kam an, ist angekommen
article der Artikel, -
as wie
　as . . . as so . . . wie
　as a child als Kind
　as if als ob
ashtray der Aschenbecher, -
to **ask (a question)** fragen

assistant der Assistent, -en, -en / die Assistentin, -nen
to **assume** an•nehmen (nimmt an), nahm an, hat angenommen
at (*time*) um (+ *acc*); (*at the home of*) bei (+ *dat*)
　at IBM bei IBM
　at Monika's bei Monika
　at that time damals
athletic sportlich
athletics der Sport
attractive attraktiv
August der August
aunt die Tante, -n
Austria (das) Österreich
Austrian österreichisch; (*person*) der Österreicher, - / die Österreicherin, -nen
auto mechanic der Automechaniker, -
away fort; weg
awful schrecklich; abscheulich

B

baby das Baby, -s
back (*adv.*) zurück
back der Rücken, -
backpack der Rucksack, ̈e
bad schlecht; schlimm; (evil) böse
　to **be bad for** schaden (+ *dat*)
　Too bad! Schade!
to **bake** backen (bäckt), backte, hat gebacken
baker der Bäcker, -
bakery die Bäckerei, -en
balcony der Balkon, -s
ball der Ball, ̈e
ballpoint pen der Kugelschreiber, -
bank die Bank, -en
bankbook das Sparbuch, ̈er
bankrupt bankrott
to **bark** bellen
basement der Keller, -
bath das Bad, ̈er
to **bathe, have a bath** baden
bathroom das Bad, ̈er; das Badezimmer, -
bathtub die Badewanne, -n

bay die Bucht, -en
to **be** sein (ist), war, ist gewesen
to **be canceled** aus•fallen (fällt aus), fiel aus, ist ausgefallen
to **be right** stimmen
beach der Strand, ⁻e
  on the beach am Strand
beard der Bart, ⁻e
to **beat** schlagen (schlägt), schlug, hat geschlagen
beautiful schön
because (*coord. conj*) denn; (*subord. conj*) weil
  because of wegen (+ *gen*)
to **become** werden (wird), wurde, ist geworden
bed das Bett, -en
  to bed ins Bett
bed, breakfast, and a light supper die Halbpension
bedroom das Schlafzimmer, -
beer das Bier
before (*prep + acc or dat*) vor; (*conj*) bevor; (*adv*) vorher
to **begin** an•fangen (fängt an), fing an, hat angefangen; beginnen, begann, hat begonnen
beginner der Anfänger, -
beginning der Anfang, ⁻e
to **behave** sich benehmen (benimmt sich), benahm sich, hat sich benommen
behavior das Benehmen
behind hinter (+ *acc or dat*)
to **believe** glauben (+ *dat*)
belly der Bauch, ⁻e
to **belong to** gehören (+ *dat*)
below unter (+ *acc or dat*)
  below zero unter Null
bench die Bank, ⁻e
beside neben (+ *acc or dat*)
besides außerdem
to **betray** betrügen, betrog, hat betrogen
better besser
between zwischen (+ *acc or dat*)
beverage das Getränk, -e
bicycle das Fahrrad, ⁻er
  to go on a bicycle trip eine Radtour machen
bike das Rad, ⁻er
bill die Rechnung, -en
biochemistry die Biochemie
biology die Biologie
bird der Vogel, ⁻

birthday der Geburtstag, -e
  for one's birthday zum Geburtstag
bit: a bit ein bißchen
bite (to eat) der Bissen, -
to **bite** beißen, biß, hat gebissen
black schwarz
Black Forest der Schwarzwald
blackboard die Tafel, -n
blonde blond
blood das Blut
blouse die Bluse, -n
blue blau
body der Körper, -
to **boil** kochen
book das Buch, ⁻er
to **book** buchen
bookcase das Bücherregal, -e
bookstore die Buchhandlung, -en
border die Grenze, -n
boring langweilig
born geboren
  I was born on March 1st. Ich bin am 1. März geboren.
to **borrow** borgen; leihen, lieh, hat geliehen
boss der Boß, Bosse; der Chef, -s/ die Chefin, -nen
both beide
bottle die Flasche, -n
  a bottle of wine eine Flasche Wein
bottle opener der Flaschenöffner, -
bottom: at the bottom unten
bowl: a bowl of soup ein Teller Suppe
box die Schachtel, -n; der Karton, -s
boy der Junge, -n, -n
boyfriend der Freund, -e
bracelet das Armband, ⁻er
brake die Bremse, -n
bread das Brot
  dark rye bread das Schwarzbrot
break die Pause, -n
to **break** brechen (bricht), brach, hat gebrochen; zerbrechen; kaputt•machen
to **break down** kaputt•gehen, ging kaputt, ist kaputtgegangen
breakfast das Frühstück
  for breakfast zum Frühstück
  to have breakfast frühstücken
briefcase die Aktentasche, -n
bright hell

to **bring** bringen, brachte, hat gebracht
to **bring along** mit•bringen
broken kaputt
brother der Bruder, ⁻
brothers and sisters die Geschwister (*pl*)
brown braun
brunette brünett
to **brush** bürsten
  to brush one's teeth sich die Zähne putzen
buffet das Büffet, -s
to **build** bauen
building das Gebäude, -
bulletin board das schwarze Brett
bus der Bus, -se
bus stop die Bushaltestelle, -en
bush der Busch, ⁻e
business das Geschäft, -e
but aber; (*in the sense of* rather) sondern
butcher der Fleischer, -
butcher shop die Fleischerei, -en
butter die Butter
button der Knopf, ⁻e
to **buy** kaufen
by (*near*) an (+ *acc or dat*)
  by Beethoven von Beethoven
  by the way übrigens
  by then bis dahin

C

cafeteria (*at a university*) (*for light meals and snacks*) die Cafeteria; (*for full meals*) die Mensa
  to the cafeteria in die Cafeteria
cake der Kuchen, -; (*layer cake*) die Torte, -n
to **calculate** rechnen
calculator der Taschenrechner, -
calender der Kalender, -
California (das) Kalifornien
call (*on the telephone*) der Anruf, -e
to **call** rufen, rief, hat gerufen; (*on the telephone*) an•rufen, rief an, hat angerufen; (*name*) nennen, nannte, hat genannt
called: to be called heißen, hieß, hat geheißen
calm (*windless*) windstill

camera die Kamera, -s
camping: to go camping campen
    gehen
can die Dose, -
can opener der Dosenöffner, -
can (*to be able to*) können (kann),
    konnte, hat gekonnt
Canada (das) Kanada
Canadian kanadisch
Canadian (*person*) der Kanadier,
    - / die Kanadierin, -nen
canceled: to be canceled
    ausfallen (fällt aus) fiel aus, ist
    ausgefallen
capital city die Hauptstadt, ¨e
car das Auto, -s; der Wagen, -
    medium-sized car der Mit-
    telklassewagen
card die Karte, -n
care: I don't care. Das ist mir
    egal.
career die Karriere, -n
carefully sorgfältig
carpet der Teppich, -e
to **carry** tragen (trägt), trug, hat
    getragen
case der Fall, ¨e
cassette die Kassette, -n
cassette recorder der Kassetten-
    recorder, -
cat die Katze, -n
to **catch** fangen (fängt), fing, hat
    gefangen
    to **catch a cold** sich erkälten
CD die CD-Platte, -n; die CD, -s
CD player der CD-Spieler, -
ceiling die Decke, -n
cellar der Keller, -
center of town das Stadtzentrum
century das Jahrhundert, -e
certainly bestimmt; sicher
chain die Kette, -n
chair der Stuhl, ¨e
to **change** (*one's clothes*) sich
    um•ziehen, zog sich um, hat
    sich umgezogen
chapter das Kapitel, -
cheap billig
to **cheat** betrügen, betrog, hat
    betrogen
to **check** nach•sehen (sieht nach),
    sah nach, hat nachgesehen
   I'll check. Ich sehe mal nach.
checkered kariert
cheerful fröhlich

Cheers! Prost!
cheese der Käse, -
chemistry die Chemie
check der Scheck, -s
chess das Schach
    to **play chess** Schach spielen
chest die Brust
chic schick
    very chic todschick
child das Kind, -er
childish kindisch
chin das Kinn
china das Geschirr
chocolate die Schokolade
    a chocolate bar eine Tafel
    Schokolade
choir der Chor, ¨e
Christmas (das) Weihnachten
    at Christmas an (zu) Weih-
    nachten
    Christmas present das Weih-
    nachtsgeschenk, -e
    for Christmas zu Weihnachten
church die Kirche, -n
cigarette die Zigarette, -n
cinema das Kino, -s
circumstance: under no circum-
    stances auf keinen Fall
city die Stadt, ¨e
city hall das Rathaus, ¨er
clarinet die Klarinette, -n
class die Klasse, -n
classmate der Mitstudent, -en / die
    Mitstudentin, -nen
clean sauber
to **clean** putzen
climate das Klima
to **climb (on)** steigen **(auf +**
    acc)**,** stieg, ist gestiegen
clock die Uhr, -en
    at two o'clock um zwei
    It's seven o'clock. Es ist sieben
    Uhr.
to **close** zu•machen; schließen,
    schloß, hat geschlossen
closed zu; geschlossen
closet der Schrank, ¨e
clothes die Kleider
club der Klub, -s
coast die Küste, -n
coat der Mantel, ¨
coffee der Kaffee
coffee table der Couchtisch, -e
cola die Cola, -s
cold kalt; die Kälte; (illness) die

Erkältung; der Schnupfen
   to be cold frieren, fror, hat
    gefroren
   to catch a cold sich erkälten
cold cuts die Wurst
Cologne (das) Köln
color die Farbe, -n
colorful farbenfreudig
color TV der Farbfernseher, -
to **comb one's hair** sich kämmen
to **come** kommen, kam, ist gekom-
    men
   where I/we come from bei uns
   where you come from bei
    euch
to **come along** mit•kommen, kam
    mit, ist mitgekommen
to **come back** zurück•kommen,
    kam zurück, ist zurückgekom-
    men
to **come home** heim•kommen,
    kam heim, ist heimgekommen
comfortable bequem; gemütlich
command der Befehl, -e
to **command** befehlen (befiehlt),
    befahl, hat befohlen
compact car der Kleinwagen, -
company die Firma, -en; der Be-
    such
to **compare** vergleichen, verglich,
    hat verglichen
completely ganz
complicated kompliziert
computer der Computer, -
concert das Konzert, -e
   to a concert ins Konzert
conservative konservativ
to **continue reading** weiter•lesen
    (liest weiter), las weiter, hat
    weitergelesen
to **converse** sich unterhalten, (un-
    terhält sich) unterhielt sich, hat
    sich unterhalten
conversation das Gespräch, -; die
    Unterhaltung, -en; die Konversa-
    tion, -en
convertible (*car*) das Kabriolett, -e
to **cook** kochen
cookbook das Kochbuch, ¨er
cool kühl
to **copy** ab•schreiben, schrieb ab,
    hat abgeschrieben
corner die Ecke, -n
   right around the corner gleich
    um die Ecke

---

to **correct** korrigieren; verbessern

to **cost** kosten

cottage das Wochenendhaus, ⸚er

cottage cheese der Hüttenkäse

to **count** zählen

country das Land, ⸚er

   to the country aufs Land

couple (*pair*) das Paar, -e

   a couple of (*a few*) ein paar

course der Kurs, -e; das Fach, ⸚er

cousin (female) die Kusine, -n; (male) der Vetter, -n

cozy gemütlich

crazy verrückt

to **criticize** kritisieren

to **cry** weinen

cunning schlau

cup die Tasse, -n

   a cup of coffee eine Tasse Kaffee

curriculum vitae der Lebenslauf, ⸚e

curtain der Vorhang, ⸚e

customer der Kunde, -n, -n / die Kundin, -nen; (*in a restaurant*) der Gast, ⸚e

to **cut** schneiden, schnitt, hat geschnitten

cutlery das Besteck

cutlet das Schnitzel, -

   veal cutlet das Wiener Schnitzel

D

Dad der Vati, -s

daily täglich

   daily routine der Tageslauf

to **dance** tanzen

dangerous gefährlich

dark dunkel

darling der Liebling; der Schatz

date: What's the date today? Der wievielte ist heute? Den wievielten haben wir heute?

daughter die Tochter, ⸚

day der Tag, -e

   during the day tagsüber

   for a few days auf ein paar Tage

   for days tagelang

   job for a day der Tagesjob, -s

one day, some day eines Tages

   the day after tomorrow übermorgen

dead tot

dead (*person*) der/die Tote, -n

dear lieb

to **deceive** betrügen, betrog, hat betrogen

December der Dezember

to **decide** beschließen, beschloß, hat beschlossen; (sich) entscheiden, entschied, hat entschieden

decision die Entscheidung, -en

deep tief

degree der Grad

   thirty degrees dreißig Grad

dentist der Zahnarzt, ⸚e/die Zahnärztin, -nen

to **depart** ab•fahren (fährt ab), fuhr ab, ist abgefahren

department die Abteilung, -en

department store das Kaufhaus, ⸚er

depressing deprimierend

to **describe** beschreiben, beschrieb, hat beschrieben

description die Beschreibung, -en

desk der Schreibtisch, -e

desk lamp die Schreibtischlampe, -n

dessert der Nachtisch, -e

   for dessert zum Nachtisch

diary das Tagebuch, ⸚er

dictionary das Wörterbuch, ⸚er

to **die** sterben (stirbt), starb, ist gestorben

difference der Unterschied, -e

different (*adj*) ander -; verschieden; (*adv*) anders

difficult schwierig; schwer

dimwit der Dummkopf, ⸚e

directions die Gebrauchsanweisung, -en

directly direkt

dirty schmutzig

disco die Disco, -s

   to the Disco in die Disco

to **discuss** diskutieren; besprechen (bespricht), besprach, hat besprochen

dishes das Geschirr

   to do the dishes ab•waschen (wäscht ab), wusch ab, hat abgewaschen

dissatisfied unzufrieden

to **disturb** stören

disturbance die Störung, -en

ditch der Graben, ⸚

divorce die Scheidung, -en

   to get a divorce sich scheiden lassen

   divorced geschieden

to **do** machen; tun, tat, hat getan

doctor der Arzt, ⸚e/die Ärztin, -nen

   family doctor der Hausarzt

dog der Hund, -e

done fertig

   to have something done etwas machen lassen

donkey der Esel, -

door die Tür, -en

doorbell die Klingel, -n

dormitory das Studentenheim, -e; das Studentenwohnheim, -e

dot: at twelve on the dot Punkt zwölf

to **drag** schleppen

to **draw** zeichnen; malen

dream der Traum, ⸚e

to **dream** träumen

dress das Kleid, -er

to **dress** sich an•ziehen, zog sich an, hat sich angezogen

dressed gekleidet

dresser die Kommode, -n

to **drink** trinken, trank, hat getrunken

   to drink heavily saufen (säuft), soff, hat gesoffen

drive, trip die Fahrt, -en

to **drive** fahren (fährt), fuhr, ist gefahren

   to go for a drive spazieren•fahren (fährt spazieren), fuhr spazieren, ist spazierengefahren

driver der Fahrer, -/die Fahrerin, -nen

driver's license der Führerschein, -e

driving test die Fahrprüfung, -en

drugstore die Drogerie, -n

drunk betrunken; (*coll*) besoffen; blau

dry trocken

to **dry off** ab•trocknen

(*clothes*) **dryer** der Trockner, -; der Wäschetrockner, -

during während (+ *gen*)

E

each jeder, jede, jedes
   each other einander
ear das Ohr, -en
early früh
to **earn** verdienen
earring der Ohrring, -e
earth die Erde
Easter (das) Ostern
easy leicht
to **eat** essen (ißt), aß, hat gegessen;
   (*of animals*) fressen (frißt),
   fraß, hat gefressen
   **When do you eat lunch/
   supper?** Wann eßt ihr zu
   Mittag/zu Abend?
to **eat breakfast** frühstücken
to **eat up** auf•essen (ißt auf), aß
   auf, hat aufgegessen
egg das Ei, -er
   fried egg, sunny side up das
   Spiegelei, -er
elbow der Ellbogen
elementary school die
   Grundschule, -n
to **emigrate** aus•wandern
employee der/die Angestellte, -n
empty leer
end das Ende, -n; der Schluß,
   Schlüsse
end table der Beistelltisch, -e
ending die Endung, -en
enemy der Feind, -e
engaged (*to be married*) verlobt
England (das) England
English englisch
English (*person*) der Engländer,
   - / die Engländerin, -nen
enjoy
   Enjoy your meal! Guten Appetit!
   I enjoy learning German. Es
   macht mir Spaß, Deutsch zu
   lernen.
enough genug
entrance der Eingang, ⁼e
equally gleich
especially besonders
etc. usw.
Europe (das) Europa
European europäisch
even sogar
   even better noch besser

evening der Abend
   Good evening! Guten Abend!
   in the evening abends
every jeder, jede, jedes
   every time jedesmal
   every two weeks alle vierzehn
   Tage
everybody alle
everything alles
everywhere überall
exact genau
   exactly like genauso wie
examination das Examen, -; die
   Prüfung, -en
   final exam die Schlußprüfung,
   -en
example das Beispiel, -e
   for example, e.g. zum Beispiel,
   z.B.
except for außer (+ *dat*)
excellent ausgezeichnet
exchange student der Austauschschüler, - / die Austauschschülerin, -nen
excited aufgeregt
   to get excited (about) sich
   auf•regen (über + *acc*)
excuse die Ausrede; die Entschuldigung, -en
   Excuse me! Entschuldigung!
exercise die Übung, -en
expensive teuer
experience die Erfahrung, -en; das
   Erlebnis, -se; die Kenntnisse (*pl*)
to **explain** erklären
explanation die Erklärung, -en
expression der Ausdruck, ⁼e
extreme extrem; das Extrem, -e
eye das Auge, -n
eyesight: My eyesight is bad. Ich
   sehe schlecht.

F

face das Gesicht, -er
factory die Fabrik, -en
fairy tale das Märchen, -
fall (*autumn*) der Herbst
to **fall** fallen (fällt), fiel, ist gefallen
to **fall asleep** ein•schlafen (schläft
   ein), schlief ein, ist eingeschlafen
to **fall in love (with)** sich ver-

   lieben (**in** + *acc*)
family die Familie, -n
family doctor der Hausarzt, ⁼e /
   die Hausärztin, -nen
famous berühmt
Fantastic! Toll! Phantastisch!
far weit
farm die Farm, -en
farmer der Bauer, -n, -n
fascinating faszinierend
fashionable modisch
fast schnell
   to be fast (*of clocks*) vor•gehen,
   ging vor, ist vorgegangen
fat dick; fett
father der Vater, ⁼
fattening: to be fattening dick
   machen
fear die Angst, ⁼e
February der Februar
**Federal Republic of Germany
   (the FRG)** die Bundesrepublik
   Deutschland (die BRD)
to **feed** füttern
to **feel** fühlen
   to feel well sich wohl fühlen
   Do you feel like it? Hast du
   Lust?
   I feel like having fish. Ich
   habe Lust auf Fisch.
   I feel sorry for you. Du tust
   mir leid.
   That feels good. Das tut gut.
feeling das Gefühl, -e
fellow student der Mitstudent, -en,
   -en / die Mitstudentin, -nen
fence der Zaun, ⁼e
to **fetch** holen
fever das Fieber
few wenige
   a few ein paar; einige
field das Feld, -er
fight der Streit
to **fight** (sich) streiten, stritt, hat
   gestritten
to **fill** füllen
to **fill out** aus•füllen
film der Film, -e
final exam die Schlußprüfung, -en
finally endlich; schließlich; zum
   Schluß
to **find** finden, fand, hat gefunden
   I find it hard, . . . Es fällt mir
   schwer, . . .

to **find out** heraus•finden
finger der Finger, -
fingernail der Fingernagel, ¨
to **finish drinking** aus•trinken,
   trank aus, hat ausgetrunken
to **finish eating** aus•essen (ißt
   aus), aß aus, hat ausgegessen
to **finish writing** fertig•schreiben,
   schrieb fertig, hat fertiggeschrieben
finished fertig
fire das Feuer, -
to **fire** entlassen (entläßt), entließ,
   hat entlassen
first (*adj*) erst; (*adv*) erst, zuerst
  at first zuerst
  for the first time zum erstenmal
fish der Fisch, -e
fist die Faust, ¨e
flashlight die Taschenlampe, -n
floor der Fußboden, ¨; (*story in a*
  building) der Stock
floor lamp die Stehlampe, -n
to **flow** fließen, floß, ist geflossen
flower die Blume, -n
flower shop das Blumengeschäft, -e
flowered geblümt
flute die Flöte, -n
to **fly** fliegen, flog, ist geflogen
foot der Fuß, ¨e
  on foot zu Fuß
for für (+ *acc*); (*a period of time*)
  seit (+ *dat*); (*because*) denn
  for a year ein Jahr lang
  for days/hours
    tagelang/stundenlang
  for supper zum Abendessen
  for sure bestimmt
to **forbid** verbieten, verbot, hat verboten
forehead die Stirn, -en
foreign ausländisch; fremd
foreign students' office das Auslandsamt
foreigner der Ausländer, - / die
  Ausländerin, -nen
forest der Wald, ¨er
to **forget** vergessen (vergißt),
  vergaß, hat vergessen
forgetful vergeßlich
fork die Gabel, -n
fountain pen der Füller, -; die
  Füllfeder, -n
France (das) Frankreich
French französisch

French (*language*) (das) Französisch
Frenchman/woman der Franzose,
  -n / die Französin, -nen
free frei
freeway die Autobahn, -en
French fries die Pommes frites
  (*pl*)
frequent häufig
fresh (*impudent*) frech
fresh frisch
Friday der Freitag
friend der Freund, -e / die Freundin, -nen
  to **be friends** befreundet sein
friendly freundlich
to **be frightened** erschrecken
  (erschrickt) erschrak, ist
  erschrocken
from aus (+ *dat*); von (+ *dat*)
  from . . . to von . . . bis
  from now on von jetzt ab
front: in front of vor (+ *acc* or
  dat)
front hall closet die Garderobe, -n
fruit die Frucht, ¨e; das Obst
full voll
  full of voller
full-time ganztags
fun: to make fun of sich lustig
  machen über (+ *acc*)
funny lustig
fur coat der Pelzmantel, ¨
furnished möbliert
furniture die Möbel (*pl*)
  piece of furniture das
   Möbelstück, -e
future die Zukunft

G

to **gab** quatschen
garage die Garage, -n
garden der Garten, ¨
gasoline das Benzin
genius das Genie, -s
German deutsch; (*language*) (das)
  Deutsch; (*person*) der/die Deutsche
**German Democratic Republic
  (the GDR)** die Deutsche
  Demokratische Republik (die
  DDR)

German class die Deutschstunde, -n
German language and literature
  (*study of*) die Germanistik
German-speaking deutschsprachig
German teacher der Deutschleh-
  rer, - / die Deutschlehrerin,
  -nen
Germany (das) Deutschland
gesture die Geste, -n
to **get** (*receive*) bekommen, bekam,
  hat bekommen; kriegen; (*fetch*)
  holen; (*become*) werden (wird),
  wurde, ist geworden
Get lost! Hau ab!
to **get along well** sich gut
  verstehen, verstand sich gut, hat
  sich gut verstanden
to **get excited (about)** sich
  auf•regen (**über** + *acc*)
to **get in** ein•steigen, stieg ein, ist
  eingestiegen
to **get off, out of** aus•steigen, stieg
  aus, ist ausgestiegen
to **get to know** kennen•lernen
to **get up** auf•stehen, stand auf, ist
  aufgestanden
to **get upset (with)** sich auf•regen
  (**über** + *acc*)
gift das Geschenk, -e
girl das Mädchen, -
girlfriend die Freundin, -nen
to **give** geben (gibt), gab, hat
  gegeben; (*as a gift*) schenken
to **give back** zurück•geben (gibt
  zurück), gab zurück, hat
  zurückgegeben
to **give up** auf•geben (gibt auf),
  gab auf, hat aufgegeben
glass das Glas, ¨er
  a glass of orange juice ein Glas
   Orangensaft
glasses die Brille (*sing*)
glove der Handschuh, -e
glove compartment das Handschuhfach, ¨er
to **go** gehen, ging, ist gegangen
to **go away** weg•gehen, ging weg,
  ist weggegangen
to **go camping** campen gehen
to **go in** hinein•gehen, ging hinein,
  ist hineingegangen
to **go out** aus•gehen, ging aus, ist
  ausgegangen; hinaus•gehen
gold(en) golden
gone fort; weg

good gut; (*well-behaved*) brav
Good grief! Menschenskind!
Good-bye! Auf Wiedersehen!
Tschüs! (*on the telephone*) Auf
Wiederhören!
to **govern** regieren
government die Regierung, -en
grade die Zensur, -en
gram das Gramm
grandchild das Enkelkind, -er
grandfather der Großvater, ⸚
grandma die Oma, -s
grandmother die Großmutter, ⸚
grandpa der Opa, -s
grandparents die Großeltern
grass das Gras
gray grau
green grün
member of the Green Party
der/die Grüne, -n
to **greet** grüßen
grief: Good grief! Menschenskind!
groceries die Lebensmittel (*pl*)
ground die Erde; der Boden
group die Gruppe, -n
to **grow** wachsen (wächst), wuchs,
ist gewachsen
guest der Gast, ⸚e
guilty schuldig
guitar die Gitarre, -n
guy der Kerl, -e; der Typ, -en

H

habit die Gewohnheit, -en
hair das Haar, -e
haircut der Haarschnitt, -e
hairdo die Frisur
hairdresser der Friseur, -e
half halb; die Hälfte, -n
half past ten halb elf
hall (*corridor*) der Flur, -e
hamburger der Hamburger, -
hand die Hand, ⸚e
handwriting die Handschrift, die
Schrift
to **hang** (*put in a hanging position*) hängen; (*be in a hanging
position*) hängen, hing, hat
gehangen
to **hang up** auf•hängen
to **happen** geschehen (geschieht),
geschah, ist geschehen;

passieren (ist passiert)
happy froh; glücklich
to be happy (about) sich
freuen (**über** + *acc*)
harbor der Hafen, ⸚
hard hart; (*difficult*) schwierig;
schwer
hard-working fleißig
hardly kaum
hat der Hut, ⸚e
to **have** haben (hat), hatte, hat
gehabt
to **have on** an•haben (hat an),
hatte an, hat angehabt
to **have planned** vor•haben (hat
vor), hatte vor, hat vorgehabt
to **have to, must** müssen (muß),
mußte, hat gemußt
You don't have to come. Du
brauchst nicht zu kommen.
head der Kopf, ⸚e
headache die Kopfschmerzen (*pl*)
headphone der Kopfhörer, -
health die Gesundheit
healthy gesund
to **hear** hören
heart das Herz, -ens, -en
heat die Hitze
heaven der Himmel
heavy schwer
hedge die Hecke, -n
Hello! Guten Tag! Grüß Gott!
to **say hello** grüßen
help die Hilfe
to **help** helfen (hilft), half, hat
geholfen (+ *dat*)
May I help you? Bitte schön?
Sie wünschen?
helpful hilfsbereit
her ihr
here hier; hierher
Hi! Grüß dich! Hallo! Tag!
to **hide** verstecken
high hoch, hoh-
high rise (*building*) das Hochhaus, ⸚er
high school das Gymnasium, Gym-
nasien
high school diploma das Abitur
high school student der Schüler,
- / die Schülerin, -nen; der
Gymnasiast, -en / die Gym-
nasiastin, -nen
to **hike** wandern
to **go hiking** wandern gehen

to **hire** ein•stellen
his sein
to **hit** schlagen (schlägt), schlug, hat
geschlagen; hauen
to **hitchhike** per Anhalter fahren;
trampen
hitchhiker der Anhalter, -
hobby das Hobby, -s
hockey stick der Hockeyschläger
to **hold** halten (hält), hielt, hat
gehalten
hole das Loch, ⸚er
holidays der Urlaub (*sing*); die
Ferien (*pl*)
home
to be at home zu Hause sein
to come home heim•kommen,
kam heim, ist heimgekommen
to go home nach Hause gehen
hometown die Heimatstadt
homework assignment die
Schularbeit, -en; die Hausaufgabe, -n
honey der Honig
to **honk** hupen
to **hope** hoffen
hopefully, I hope hoffentlich
horse das Pferd, -e
hospital das Krankenhaus, ⸚er
hot heiß
hotdog der Hotdog, -s
hot plate die Kochplatte, -n
hotel das Hotel, -s
hour die Stunde, -n
house das Haus, ⸚er
at our house bei uns
house husband der Hausmann, ⸚er
houseplant die Zimmerpflanze, -n
how? wie?
How are you? Wie geht es
Ihnen? / Wie geht's?
how many? wie viele?
how much? wieviel?
huge riesig
human being der Mensch, -en, -en
hunger der Hunger
hungry hungrig
I'm hungry. Ich habe Hunger. /
Ich bin hungrig.
I'm very hungry. Ich habe
einen Bärenhunger.
to **go hungry** hungern
hurry: I'm in a hurry. Ich habe
es eilig.

to **hurry (up)** sich beeilen; schnell machen
husband der Mann, ¨er

I

ice das Eis
ice cream das Eis
ice cold eiskalt
idea die Idee, -n
  I have no idea. Ich habe keine Ahnung.
idiot der Idiot, -en, -en; der Esel, -
if wenn (*conj*)
ill krank
illness die Krankheit, -en
immediately sofort; gleich
to **immigrate** ein•wandern
impatient ungeduldig
important wichtig
impossible unmöglich
in, into in (+ *acc* or *dat*)
income das Einkommen, -
inexpensive günstig; preisgünstig
ink die Tinte
instead statt (+ *gen*)
instruction die Gebrauchsanweisung, -en
instrument das Instrument, -
intelligent intelligent
interested: to be interested in sich interessieren für (+ *acc*)
interesting interessant
intermission die Pause, -n
to **interview** interviewen
to **invest** investieren
to **invite** ein•laden (lädt ein), lud ein, hat eingeladen
iron das Bügeleisen, -
to **iron** bügeln
irregular unregelmäßig
Italian italienisch; (*language*) (das) Italienisch; (*person*) der Italiener, - / die Italienerin, -nen
Italy (das) Italien

J

jacket die Jacke, -n
January der Januar
Japanese japanisch

jazz das Jazz
jeans die Jeans (*pl*)
jog die Stellung, -en; (*casual*) der Job, -s; der Ferienjob, -s
to **jog** joggen
joke der Witz, -e
juice der Saft, ¨e
July der Juli
June der Juni
to **jump** springen, sprang, ist gesprungen
just einfach; nur
  just about gleich
  just now gerade

K

to **keep** behalten (behält), behielt, hat behalten
key der Schlüssel, -
to **kill** töten
kilometer der Kilometer, -
kitchen die Küche, -n
kitchen privileges die Küchenbenutzung
kitchen sink das Spülbecken, -
knee das Knie, -
knife das Messer, -
to **knit** stricken
to **knock** klopfen
to **know** (*a fact*) wissen (weiß), wußte, hat gewußt; (*be acquainted / familiar with*) kennen, kannte, hat gekannt; (*a language*) können (kann), konnte, hat gekonnt
  to know about wissen von (+ *dat*)
  to get to know kennen•lernen
knowledge of foreign languages die Sprachkenntnisse (*pl*)

L

lab das Labor, -s
lake der See, -n
lamp die Lampe, -n
to **land** landen
landlady die Hauswirtin, -nen
landlord der Hauswirt, -e
language die Sprache, -n

large groß
last letzt; (*adv*) zuletzt
  at last endlich; schließlich
late spät
  I'm running late. Ich bin spät dran.
  to be late sich verspäten
later nachher
  See you later! Bis nachher!
to **laugh (about, at)** lachen (**über** + *acc*)
laundry die Wäsche
lawn der Rasen, -
lawn mower der Rasenmäher, -
lazy faul
  to be lazy faul sein; faulenzen
to **learn** lernen
least: at least wenigstens
to **leave** (*depart*) ab•fahren (fährt ab), fuhr ab, ist abgefahren; weg•gehen, ging weg, ist weggegangen; (*someone/something*) lassen (läßt), ließ, hat gelassen
lecture die Vorlesung, -en
  to a lecture in die Vorlesung
lecture hall der Hörsaal, Hörsäle
lecture notes das Skript
left, to the left links
leg das Bein, -e
leisure time die Freizeit
to **lend** leihen, lieh, hat geliehen; borgen
to **let** lassen (läßt), ließ, hat gelassen
letter der Brief, -e; (*of alphabet*) der Buchstabe, -n
library die Bibliothek, -en
  to the library in die Bibliothek
license plate number das Kennzeichen, -
lie die Lüge, -n
to **lie** (*be situated*) liegen, lag, hat gelegen; (*tell a lie*) lügen, log, hat gelogen
  He lies through his teeth. Er lügt wie gedruckt.
life das Leben, -
light hell; leicht; das Licht, -er
light bulb die Birne, -n; die Glühbirne, -n
light switch der Lichtschalter, -
like wie
to **like** mögen (mag), mochte, hat gemocht; gefallen (gefällt), gefiel, hat gefallen (+ *dat*)

I like your jeans. Deine Jeans gefallen mir.

Do you like to go to concerts? Gehst du gern ins Konzert?

I would like . . . ich möchte ...

What do you like about him? Was gefällt dir an ihm?

What would you like? Was darf's sein?

lip die Lippe, -n

lipstick der Lippenstift, -e

to **listen** zu•hören

  to listen to hören; sich etwas an•hören

little (*size*) klein; (*amount*) wenig

to **live** (*in a country or city*) leben; (*in a building or street*), wohnen

lively lebhaft

living: What do you do for a living? Was sind Sie von Beruf?

living room das Wohnzimmer, -

long lang

  as long as solang(e)

to **look good** (gut) aus•sehen (sieht aus), sah aus, hat ausgesehen

to **look at** an•schauen

to **look for** suchen

to **look forward to** sich freuen auf (+ *acc*)

to **look like** aus•sehen wie

to **lose** verlieren, verlor, hat verloren

loud laut; (*of colors*) knallig

love die Liebe

  I love you. Ich habe dich lieb. Ich liebe dich.

luck das Glück

luckily zum Glück

lucky: You're lucky. Du hast Glück. (*coll*) Du hast Schwein.

lunch (*noon meal*) das Mittagessen, -

M

machine die Maschine, -n

mad (*crazy*) verrückt

mail die Post

major (*field of study*) das Hauptfach, ¨er

to **make** machen; tun, tat, hat getan

to **make angry** ärgern

man der Mann, ¨er; (*human being*) der Mensch, -en, -en

March der März

mark (*currency*) die Mark, -; (*grade*) die Zensur, -en

  ten marks a piece zehn Mark das Stück

marriage die Ehe, -n

marriage counselor der Eheberater, -/die Eheberaterin, -nen

market der Markt, ¨e

married (to) verheiratet (mit + *dat*)

  married couple das Ehepaar, -e

to **marry, get married** heiraten

math die Mathe

matter die Sache, -n

  That doesn't matter. Das macht nichts.

  What's the matter? Was ist denn los?

May der Mai

may: to be allowed to dürfen (darf), durfte, hat gedurft

meadow die Wiese, -n

meal das Essen

to **mean** meinen

  What does that mean? Was heißt das?

meaning die Bedeutung, -en

meat das Fleisch

mechanic der Mechaniker, -

to **meet** (sich) treffen (trifft), traf, hat getroffen; begegnen (+ *dat*)

to **mend** flicken

menu die Speisekarte, -n

meter der Meter, -

microwave oven der Mikrowellenherd, -e

middle die Mitte

  the middle of October Mitte Oktober

in the middle mitten

  in the middle of winter mitten im Winter

midnight die Mitternacht

mild mild

milk die Milch

million die Million, -en

minute die Minute, -n

  in a minute gleich

miracle das Wunder, -

mirror der Spiegel, -

miserable miserabel, elend

Miss (das) Fräulein, -

mistake der Fehler, -

modest bescheiden

Mom die Mutti, -s

moment der Moment, -e

  at the moment im Moment; momentan

Monday der Montag

  on Monday am Montag

money das Geld

month der Monat, -e

more mehr

  more and more immer mehr

morning der Morgen; der Vormittag

  Good morning! Guten Morgen!

  in the morning morgens; vormittags

  this morning heute früh, heute morgen

most meist

mostly, most of the time meistens

mother die Mutter, ¨

motorcycle das Motorrad, ¨er

mountain der Berg, -e

mountain range das Gebirge

mouse die Maus, ¨e

moustache der Schnurrbart, ¨e

mouth der Mund, ¨er

to **move** (*change place of residence*) um•ziehen, zog um, ist umgezogen

to **move in** ein•ziehen, zog ein, ist eingezogen

to **move out** aus•ziehen, zog aus, ist ausgezogen

movie theater das Kino, -s

  to go to the movies ins Kino gehen

to **mow** mähen

Mr. Herr

Mrs., Ms. Frau

much viel

Munich (das) München

murderer der Mörder, -

museum das Museum, Museen

music die Musik

musical musikalisch

must (*to have to*) müssen (muß), mußte, hat gemußt

my mein

N

name der Name, -ns, -n
   first name der Vorname, -ns, -n
   My name is . . . Ich heiße . . . ;
     Mein Name ist . . .
   What is your name? Wie
     heißen Sie? Wie heißt du?
nation (*people*) das Volk, ¨er
near in der Nähe von
neck der Hals, ¨e
to **need** brauchen
neighbor der Nachbar, -n, -n / die
   Nachbarin, -nen
neither . . . nor weder . . . noch
nephew der Neffe, -n, -n
nerve der Nerv, -en
That gets on my nerves. Das geht
   mir auf die Nerven.
nervous nervös
never nie, niemals
nevertheless trotzdem
new neu
newspaper die Zeitung, -en
next nächst
nice nett; (*weather*) schön
niece die Nichte, -n
night die Nacht, ¨e
   at night nachts
   Good night! Gute Nacht!
no nein
   no longer nicht mehr
nobody niemand
Nonsense! Quatsch!
noon der Mittag
   at noon mittags
nose die Nase, -n
not nicht
   not a, not any, no kein
   not at all gar nicht; überhaupt
     nicht
   not until erst
   not yet noch nicht
notebook das Heft, -e
note die Notiz, -en; der Zettel, -
notes (*from lecture*) das Skript
nothing nichts
   nothing at all gar nichts
   nothing but nichts als
   for nothing umsonst
to **notice** merken
novel der Roman, -e
November der November
now jetzt
   now and then ab und zu

nowadays heutzutage
nowhere nirgends
nurse die Krankenschwester, -n
number die Nummer, -n; die
   Zahl, -en

O

O.K. in Ordnung
occupation der Beruf, -e
   What is your occupation? Was
     sind Sie von Beruf?
to **occur** vor•kommen, kam vor, ist
   vorgekommen
ocean das Meer; der Ozean
o'clock: seven o'clock sieben Uhr
October der Oktober
Octoberfest das Oktoberfest
   to the Octoberfest aufs Okto-
     berfest
of von
of course natürlich
off: Today I have a day off. Heute
   habe ich frei.
office das Büro, -s
office hour die Sprechstunde, -n
often oft
old alt
old-fashioned altmodisch
on, onto auf (+ *acc* or *dat*); an
   (+ *acc* or *dat*)
on the other side drüben
once einmal
   once more noch einmal, noch-
     mal
one (*you, people*) man
one another einander
one day, some day eines Tages
oneself (*myself, yourself, etc.*)
   selber; selbst
only nur; erst; einzig
open offen
to **open** auf•machen; öffnen
opinion die Meinung, -en
or oder
or else sonst
orange juice der Orangensaft
order die Ordnung; (*of food*) die
   Portion, -en
   an order of French fries eine
     Portion Pommes frites
   in order to um... zu

to **order** bestellen; befehlen
   (befiehlt), befahl, hat befohlen
ostentatious protzig
other ander
otherwise sonst
our unser
out of aus (+ *dat*)
outside draußen
over über (+ *acc* or *dat*)
   over again noch einmal, noch-
     mal
   over there drüben
   to be over zu Ende sein
overnight accommodation die
   Übernachtung, -en
   to stay overnight übernachten
owner der Besitzer, - / die Besitzerin, -nen

P

to **pack** packen
page die Seite, -n
to **paint** (*a picture*) malen; (*a
   fence*) streichen, strich, hat
   gestrichen
pair das Paar
   a pair of pants ein Paar Hosen
pants die Hose, -n
paper das Papier; (*essay*) das
   Referat, -e
piece of paper der Zettel, -
paperback das Taschenbuch, ¨er
parcel das Paket, -e
Pardon? Wie bitte?
parents die Eltern
park der Park, -s
to **park** parken
parking lot der Parkplatz, ¨e
part der Teil, -e
to **participate** mit•machen
partner der Partner, -
part-time: I have a part-time job.
   Ich habe einen Teilzeitjob.
party die Party, -s; die Fete, -n
   to a party auf ein Party
to **pass** überholen
passenger car der Personenwagen, -
passport der Paß, Pässe
past: in the past früher
patient geduldig; der Patient,
   -en, -en /

die Patientin, -nen; der/die Kranke, -n
path der Weg, -e; der Pfad, -e
to **pay** bezahlen; zahlen
to **pay attention** auf•passen
to **pay down** an•zahlen
peace and quiet die Ruhe
peninsula der Halbinsel, -n
penny der Pfennig, -e
people die Leute (*pl*); die Menschen (*pl*)
pepper der Pfeffer
perfect perfekt
perfume das Parfüm
perhaps vielleicht
person der Mensch, -en, -en
personal persönlich
pet das Haustier, -e
pharmacist der Apotheker, - / die Apothekerin, -nen
pharmacy die Apotheke, -n
philosophy die Philosophie
photo das Foto, -s
to **photograph** fotografieren
physics die Physik
piano das Klavier, -e
piano lesson die Klavierstunde, -n
to **pick up** ab•holen
picture das Bild, -er
piece das Stück, -e
  a piece of cake ein Stück Kuchen
  five marks a piece fünf Mark das Stück
pigpen der Schweinestall, ¨e
pill die Tablette, -n
pink rosa
pizza die Pizza, -s
place der Platz, ¨e
plaid kariert
plan der Plan, ¨e
to **plan, to have planned** vor•haben (hat vor), hatte vor, hat vorgehabt; planen
plate der Teller, -
to **play** spielen
please bitte
pleased: to be pleased (with) sich freuen (**über** + *acc*)
pleasure die Lust
pocket die Tasche, -n
police die Polizei (*sing*)
policeman / policewoman der Polizist, -en, -en / die Polizistin, -nen

political politisch
political science die Politikwissenschaft
poor arm
position (*job*) die Stellung, -en
possible möglich
  as quickly as possible so schnell wie möglich
post office die Post
postcard die Postkarte, -n
poster das Poster, -
pot der Topf, ¨e
potato die Kartoffel, -n
power die Macht, ¨e
practical praktisch
to **practice** üben
to **pray** beten
present das Geschenk, -e
to **press** drücken
pretty hübsch
price der Preis, -e
probably sicher; wohl
problem das Problem, -e
profession der Beruf, -e
professor der Professor, -en / die Professorin, -nen
programmer der Programmierer, - / die Programmiererin, -en
to **promise** versprechen (verspricht), versprach, hat versprochen
to **pronounce** aus•sprechen (spricht aus), sprach aus, hat ausgesprochen
pronunciation die Aussprache
properly richtig
to **protest** protestieren
proud (of) stolz (**auf** + *acc*)
proximity die Nähe
pub die Kneipe, -n
  to the pub in die Kneipe
to **pull** ziehen, zog, hat gezogen
punctual pünktlich
pupil der Schüler, - / die Schülerin, -nen
purple lila
to **put** (*in a hanging position*) hängen; (*in a lying position*) legen; (*in an upright position*) stellen; (*to stick*) stecken
to **put on** an•ziehen, zog an, hat angezogen
to **put up with: I'm not putting up with that again.** Das mache ich nicht noch mal mit.

Q

quarter das Viertel
  quarter after Viertel nach
  quarter to Viertel vor
question die Frage, -n
questionnaire der Fragebogen, -
quick schnell
quiet ruhig; still
quite recht; ganz; ziemlich
quiz das Quiz, -

R

radio das Radio, -s
radio play das Hörspiel, -e
railway die Bahn, -en
  railway station der Bahnhof, ¨e
  main railway station der Hauptbahnhof
rain der Regen
to **rain** regnen
  It's pouring rain. Es regnet in Strömen.
rarely selten
rather (*preference*) lieber; (*quite*) ziemlich
  I'd rather have rain than ice and snow. Lieber Regen als Eis and Schnee.
to **read** lesen (liest), las, hat gelesen
  What does the thermometer read? Was zeigt das Thermometer?
ready fertig
really wirklich; tatsächlich; echt; richtig
to **rearrange** um•stellen
reason der Grund, ¨e
to **receive** bekommen, bekam, hat bekommen
to **recommend** empfehlen (empfiehlt), empfahl, hat empfohlen
record die Platte, -n; die Schallplatte, -n
record player der Plattenspieler, -
recording die Aufnahme, -n
red rot
red-haired rothaarig
refrigerator der Kühlschrank, ¨e

regular regelmäßig
rehearsal die Probe, -n
related verwandt
relative der/die Verwandte, -n
reluctant widerwillig
to **remain** bleiben, blieb, ist geblieben
rent die Miete, -n
to **rent** mieten
to **rent out** vermieten
to **repair** reparieren
to **repeat** wiederholen
report das Referat, -e
to **report** berichten
restaurant das Restaurant, -s; das Gasthaus, ˚er
resumé der Lebenslauf, ˚e
to **return** zurück•geben (gibt zurück), gab zurück, hat zurückgegeben; zurück•bringen, brachte zurück, hat zurückgebracht
Rhine (*river*) der Rhein
rice der Reis
rich reich
to **ride** reiten, ritt, ist geritten
 to go for a ride spazieren•fahren (fährt spazieren), fuhr spazieren, ist spazierengefahren
rifle das Gewehr, -e
right richtig
 You are right. Du hast recht.
 That's not right. Das stimmt nicht.
 right around the corner gleich um die Ecke
 right away gleich; sofort
right, to the right rechts
ring der Ring, -e
to **ring** klingeln
to **rip up** zerreißen, zerriß, hat zerrissen
ripe reif
ripped zerrissen
to **risk** riskieren
river der Fluß, Flüsse
road die Straße, -n
 on the road unterwegs
rock group die Rockgruppe, -n
rock music der Rock
rocking chair der Schaukelstuhl, ˚e
roll das Brötchen, -
roof das Dach, ˚er
room das Zimmer, -

 We have no room. Wir haben keinen Platz.
roommate der Zimmerkollege, -n, -n/die Zimmerkollegin, -nen
rose die Rose, -n
rug der Teppich, -e
to **ruin** ruinieren
to **run** laufen (läuft), lief, ist gelaufen; rennen, rannte, ist gerannt
 I ran out of money. Mir ist das Geld ausgegangen.

S

sailboat das Segelboot, -e
sailing: to go sailing segeln gehen
salad der Salat, -e
salary das Gehalt, ˚er
sales clerk der Verkäufer, - / die Verkäuferin, -nen
sales representative der Vertreter, - / die Vertreterin, -nen
salt das Salz
same gleich
sand der Sand
sandwich das Sandwich, -es
satisfied zufrieden
Saturday der Samstag; der Sonnabend
saucer die Untertasse, -n
sausage die Wurst, ˚e
to **save** (*a life*) retten; (*money*) sparen
saxophone das Saxophon, -e
to **say** sagen
 to say hello grüßen
scarcely kaum
scarf der Schal, -e
schedule (*bus, train*) der Fahrplan, ˚e
school die Schule, -n
sea das Meer
season die Jahreszeit, -en
seat der Sitz, -e; der Platz, ˚e
second die Sekunde, -n
secretary der Sekretär, -e / die Sekretärin, -nen
to **see** sehen (sieht), sah, hat gesehen; schauen
 See you later! Bis später! Bis nachher!

 See you on Monday! Bis Montag!
to **see again** wieder•sehen (sieht wieder), sah wieder, hat wiedergesehen
to **seem** scheinen, schien, hat geschienen
seldom selten
to **sell** verkaufen
semester das Semester, -
seminar die Übung, -en
to **send** schicken
to **send away** weg•schicken
sense der Sinn
sentence der Satz, ˚e
to **separate** trennen
September der September
serious ernst
serving die Portion, -en
several einige; mehrere
several times mehrmals
to **sew** nähen
shade, shadow der Schatten, -
shady schattig
to **shake** schütteln
shampoo das Shampoo
shared housing die WG, -s; die Wohngemeinschaft, -en
sharp scharf
to **shave** sich rasieren
shaver der Rasierapparat, -e
to **shine** scheinen, schien, hat geschienen
ship das Schiff, -e
shirt das Hemd, -en
shoe der Schuh, -e
to **shoot** schießen, schoß, hat geschossen; (*dead*) erschießen
to **shop, to go shopping** ein•kaufen
short kurz; (*stature*) klein
 shortly afterwards kurz darauf, kurz danach
short story die Kurzgeschichte, -n
should (*to be supposed to*) sollen, sollte, hat gesollt
shoulder die Schulter, -n
to **shout** schreien, schrie, hat geschrieen
to **show** zeigen
shower die Dusche, -n
to **shower** (sich) duschen
sick krank
side die Seite, -n
signature die Unterschrift, -en

simple einfach

since seit

to **sing** singen, sang, hat gesungen

single (*not married*) ledig; alleinstehend

single family dwelling das Einfamilienhaus, ¨er

sister die Schwester, -n

sisters and brothers die Geschwister (*pl*)

to **sit** sitzen, saß, hat gesessen

to **sit down** sich setzen

size die Größe, -n

skate der Schlittschuh, -e

to **go skating** Schlittschuh laufen

ski der Schi, -er

skiing: to go skiing Schi laufen

skirt der Rock, ¨e

sky der Himmel

to **sleep** schlafen (schläft), schlief, hat geschlafen

to **sleep in** aus•schlafen (schläft aus), schlief aus, hat ausgeschlafen

sleeping bag der Schlafsack, ¨e

sleeping pill die Schlaftablette, -n

slice die Scheibe, -n

a slice of bread eine Scheibe Brot

slim schlank

slipper der Hausschuh, -e

slow langsam

to be slow (*of clocks*) nach•gehen, ging nach, ist nachgegangen

small klein

smart intelligent; klug; schlau

to **smell** riechen, roch, hat gerochen

to **smile** lächeln

smoke der Rauch

to **smoke** rauchen

snow der Schnee

to **snow** schneien

snowstorm der Schneesturm, ¨e

So long! Tschüs!

so that damit (*conj*)

soap opera die Seifenoper

soccer: *to play soccer* Fußball spielen

sock die Socke, -n

sofa die Couch, -es

soft weich

soft-boiled weichgekocht

soldier der Soldat, -en, -en

solution die Lösung, -en

somebody jemand

something etwas

something or other irgend etwas

sometimes manchmal

somewhere (*or other*) irgendwo

son der Sohn, ¨e

song das Lied, -er

soon bald

sorry

I'm sorry. Es tut mir leid.

I feel sorry for you. Du tust mir leid.

soup die Suppe, -n

sour sauer

Southern California Südkalifornien

spaghetti die Spaghetti (*pl*)

Spain (das) Spanien

Spaniard der Spanier, - / die Spanierin, -nen

Spanish spanisch; (*language*) (das) Spanisch

to **speak** sprechen (spricht), sprach, hat gesprochen

special (offer) das Sonderangebot, -e

to **spell** buchstabieren

to **spend** (*money*) aus•geben (gibt aus), gab aus, hat ausgegeben; (*time*) verbringen, verbrachte, hat verbracht

spicy scharf

spite: in spite of trotz

spoon der Löffel, -

sports der Sport

to be active in sports Sport treiben, trieb, hat getrieben

sports car der Sportwagen, -

spring der Frühling

stable der Stall, ¨e

stair die Treppe, -n

staircase das Treppenhaus

stamp die Briefmarke, -n

to **stand** stehen, stand, hat gestanden; (put in an upright position) stellen; (bear) aus•stehen, stand aus, hat ausgestanden

I can't stand that guy. Ich kann den Kerl nicht ausstehen.

state der Staat, -en

to **stay** bleiben, blieb, ist geblieben

to **steal** stehlen (stiehlt), stahl, hat gestohlen

steak das Steak, -s

to **step** treten (tritt), trat, ist getreten

You stepped on my toe. Du bist mir auf den Fuß getreten.

stereo die Stereoanlage, -n

still noch; immer noch

stomach der Bauch, ¨e

to **stop** (*doing something*) auf•hören; (*moving*) halten (hält), hielt, hat gehalten; (*walking*) stehen•bleiben, blieb stehen, ist stehengeblieben; (*someone, something*) an•halten (hält an), hielt an, hat angehalten; stoppen

store der Laden, ¨

storm der Sturm, ¨e

story die Geschichte, -n; die Erzählung, -en; (*floor*) der Stock

stove der Herd, -e

strange komisch

strange der (die) Fremde, -n

stream der Bach, ¨e

street die Straße, -n

streetcar die Straßenbahn, -en

stress der Streß

stressful stressig

to **strike** streiken

striped gestreift

stroll: to stroll through town einen Stadtbummel machen

strong stark

student (*university*) der Student, -en, -en / die Studentin, -nen; (*elem. or high school*) der Schüler, - / die Schülerin, -nen

student center das Studentenwerk

student choir der Studentenchor

studies das Studium

to **study** (*at a university*) studieren; (*do homework*) lernen

to **stumble** stolpern

stupid blöd; dumm; doof

stupidity die Dummheit, -en

stylish flott

subtitle der Untertitel, -

subway die Untergrundbahn, -en; die U-Bahn, -en

such (a) so (ein)

suddenly plötzlich

sugar der Zucker

to **suit** passen; stehen, stand, hat gestanden

That doesn't suit me. Das paßt mir nicht.

Does this dress look good on me? Steht mir diese Jacke?

suitcase der Koffer, -

to **summarize** zusammen•fassen

summer der Sommer

sun die Sonne, -n

Sunday der Sonntag

sunny sonnig

supermarket der Supermarkt, ⁻e

supper das Abendessen

for supper zum Abendessen

When do you eat supper? Wann eßt ihr zu Abend?

supposed: to be supposed to sollen, sollte, hat gesollt

(for) sure sicher; bestimmt

surfboard das Surfbrett, -er

surprise die Überraschung, -en

surprised überrascht

to be surprised about sich wundern über (+ acc)

swanky protzig

sweater der Pulli, -s; der Pullover, -

sweatshirt das Sweatshirt, -s

sweet süß

sweets die Süßigkeiten

to **swim** baden; schwimmen, schwamm, ist geschwommen

swimming: to go swimming schwimmen/baden gehen

swimming weather das Bade-wetter

Swiss cheese Schweizer Käse

Swiss (person) der Schweizer, - / die Schweizerin, -nen

to **switch** um•stellen

Switzerland die Schweiz

symphony orchestra das Symphonieorchester

scene die Szene, -n

T

table der Tisch, -e

tactful taktvoll

tactless taktlos

to **take** nehmen (nimmt), nahm, hat genommen; (time) brauchen; dauern

to **take along** mit•nehmen (nimmt mit), nahm mit, hat mitgenommen

to **take off (clothing)** aus•ziehen, zog aus, hat ausgezogen

to **take out** heraus•nehmen (nimmt heraus), nahm heraus, hat herausgenommen

to **talk** reden; sprechen (spricht), sprach, hat gesprochen; (gab) quatschen

tall groß

tape (audio) das Tonband, ⁻er

tape recorder das Tonbandgerät, -e

taste der Geschmack, ⁻er

to **taste** schmecken

tasteful geschmackvoll

tasteless geschmacklos

taxi das Taxi, -s

tea der Tee

teakettle der Teekessel, -

teacher der Lehrer, - / die Lehrerin, -nen

telephone das Telefon, -e

telephone number die Telefon-nummer, -n

television das Fernsehen

television set der Fernsehapparat, -e; der Fernseher, -

to **tell** sagen; (a lie) lügen, log, hat gelogen; (a story) erzählen

tell me sag mal

to **tell about** erzählen von (+ dat)

temperature die Temperatur, -en

tennis das Tennis

to play tennis Tennis spielen

tennis racquet der Tennis-schläger, -

terrible schrecklich

test der Test, -s

than als

to **thank** danken (+ dat)

Thank God! Gott sei Dank!

thank you, thanks danke, danke schön

thanks der Dank

that das; (conj) daß

that is, i.e. das heißt, d.h.

the . . . the je . . . desto

theater das Theater, -

to the theater ins Theater

their ihr

then dann; (at that time) damals

by then bis dahin

there dort; da

there is, there are es gibt

therefore, for that reason deshalb; deswegen

thermometer das Thermometer, -

thick dick

thin dünn

thing das Ding, -e; die Sache, -n

to **think** denken, dachte, hat gedacht; glauben (+ dat); meinen

That's what you think! Denkste! Ja denkste!

to **think of, about** (have in mind) denken an (+ acc); (have an opinion about) halten von

I can't think of anything. Mir fällt nichts ein.

thirst der Durst

thirsty: I'm thirsty. Ich habe Durst.

this dieser, diese, dieses; das

this time diesmal

thriller der Krimi, -s

through durch (+ acc)

to **throw** werfen (wirft), warf, hat geworfen

thumb der Daumen, -

Thursday der Donnerstag

ticket die Karte, -n

tie die Krawatte, -n; der Schlips, -e

time die Zeit, -en

(at) what time? um wieviel Uhr?

on time rechtzeitig

this time diesmal

three times dreimal

What time is it? Wieviel Uhr ist es? Wie spät ist es?

timetable der Stundenplan, ⁻e

tiny winzig

tire der Reifen, -

tired müde

to (a country or city) nach (+ dat); (an institution) auf (+ acc or dat); zu (+ dat); (the edge of something) an (+ acc or dat)

five to nine fünf vor neun

toast der Toast

toaster der Toaster, -

today heute

toe die Zehe, -n

You stepped on my toe. Du bist mir auf den Fuß getreten.

together zusammen

toilet die Toilette, -n; das Klo, -s

tomato die Tomate, -n

tomorrow morgen

tomorrow evening morgen abend

tomorrow morning morgen früh; morgen vormittag

tomorrow night morgen abend

the day after tomorrow übermorgen

---

tongue die Zunge, -n
tonight heute abend; heute nacht
too zu; (*also*) auch
tooth der Zahn, ¨e
toothache die Zahnschmerzen (*pl*)
toothpaste die Zahnpasta
top
  at the top oben
topic das Thema, Themen
to **touch** an•fassen
tough (*of meat*) zäh; (*of a person*) energisch
tourist der Tourist, -en, -en
town die Stadt, ¨e
  to town in die Stadt
traffic der Verkehr
traffic light die Ampel, -n
train der Zug, ¨e
to **translate** übersetzen
translation die Übersetzung, -en
to **travel** reisen
travel agency das Reisebüro, -s
tree der Baum, ¨e; (*deciduous*) der Laubbaum, ¨e; (*coniferous*) der Nadelbaum, ¨e
trip die Reise, -n; die Fahrt, -en
  trip around the world die Weltreise
trousers die Hose, -n
truck der Lastwagen, -
true wahr
trunk (*of a car*) der Kofferraum
truth die Wahrheit
to **try** probieren
to **try on** an•probieren
to **try out** aus•probieren
Tuesday der Dienstag
to **turn off** ab•stellen
to **turn on** (*radio, TV, etc.*) ein•schalten; an•machen
twice zweimal
  twice as far doppelt so weit
to **type** tippen
typewriter die Schreibmaschine, -n
typical typisch

U

ugly häßlich
umbrella der Schirm, -e
uncle der Onkel, -
under unter (+ *acc* or *dat*)

to **understand** verstehen, verstand, hat verstanden
to **undress** sich aus•ziehen, zog sich aus, hat sich ausgezogen
unemployed arbeitslos
unemployed person der/die Arbeitslose, -en
unemployment die Arbeitslosigkeit
unfortunately leider
unfriendly unfreundlich
unhappy unglücklich
unhealthy ungesund
unimportant unwichtig
United States (USA) die Vereinigten Staaten (die USA)
university die Universität, -en; die Uni, -s
  to the university zur Uni
to **unpack** aus•packen
until bis
  not until erst
upset: to get upset (about) sich auf•regen (**über** + *acc*)
use: It's no use. Es hat keinen Sinn.
to **use** benutzen; verwenden
used car der Gebrauchtwagen, -

V

vacation der Urlaub (*sing*), die Ferien (*pl*)
vacationer der Feriengast, ¨e
vacuum cleaner der Staubsauger, -
valley das Tal, ¨er
valuable wertvoll
vegetables das Gemüse (*sing*)
vehicle das Fahrzeug, -e
verb das Verb, -en
very sehr; ganz
vicinity die Nähe
  in the vicinity of in der Nähe von
video cassette recorder (VCR) der Videorecorder, -
Vienna (das) Wien
village das Dorf, ¨er
visa das Visum, Visen
to **visit** zu Besuch kommen; (*someone*) besuchen
vocabulary der Wortschatz; das Vokabular
voice die Stimme, -n
to **vote** stimmen

W

to **wait (for)** warten (**auf** + *acc*)
waiter der Ober, -; der Kellner, -
Waiter! Herr Ober!
waitress die Kellnerin, -nen
to **wake up** auf•wachen; (*someone*) auf•wecken
to **walk, go on foot** zu Fuß gehen
  to go for a walk spazieren•gehen, ging spazieren, ist spazierengegangen
wall die Mauer, -n; die Wand, ¨e
wallet der Geldbeutel, -
wallpaper die Tapete, -n
to **wallpaper** tapezieren
to **want to** wollen (will), wollte, hat gewollt
war der Krieg, -e
wardrobe (*closet*) der Schrank, ¨e
warm warm
to **warm up** auf•wärmen
to **warn** warnen
to **wash** waschen (wäscht), wusch, hat gewaschen
washbasin das Waschbecken, -
washer die Waschmaschine, -n
waste: It's a waste of money. Es ist schade ums Geld.
wastepaper basket der Papierkorb, ¨e
to **watch TV** fern•sehen (sieht fern), sah fern, hat ferngesehen
water das Wasser
to **water** gießen; goß, hat gegossen
waterfall der Wasserfall, ¨e
wave die Welle, -n
way der Weg, -e
  by the way übrigens
  on the way unterwegs
weak schwach
weapon die Waffe, -n
to **wear** an•haben (hat an), hatte an, hat angehabt; tragen (trägt), trug, hat getragen
weather das Wetter
  rotten weather (das) Hundewetter
  What's the weather like? Wie ist das Wetter?
Wednesday der Mittwoch
wedding die Hochzeit, -en
week die Woche, -n
  every two weeks alle vierzehn Tage
weekend das Wochenende, -n

welcome: You're welcome! Bitte schön!

well gut; wohl

well-behaved brav

well-known bekannt

wet naß

what? was?

  What extremes! Was für Extreme!

  what for? wozu?

  What (kind of) instrument do you play? Was für ein Instrument spielst du?

  What rotten weather! Was für ein Hundewetter!

wheel das Rad, ¨er

when (*conj*) als; (*conj*) wenn; (*question word*) wann

where? (*from what place?*) woher?; wo . . . her?

Where are you from? Woher bist du / kommst du?

where? (*in what place?*) wo?

where? (*to what place?*) wohin?; wo . . . hin?

whether ob (*conj*)

which welcher, welche, welches

while die Weile

  after a while nach einer Weile

white weiß

who? wer?

whole ganz

why? warum? weshalb?

wife die Frau, -en

to **win** gewinnen, gewann, hat gewonnen

wind der Wind, -e

windshield wiper der Scheibenwischer, -

window das Fenster, -

  display window das Schaufenster, -

  to go window shopping einen Schaufensterbummel machen

windsurfing: to go windsurfing Windsurfing gehen

windsurfer das Surfbrett, -er

windy windig

wine der Wein, -e

winter der Winter

wish der Wunsch, ¨e

to **wish** wünschen

with mit (+ *dat*); (*at the home of*) bei (+ *dat*)

without ohne (+ *acc*)

woman die Frau, -en

wonderful wunderbar, wundervoll

woods der Wald, ¨er

word das Wort, ¨er

work die Arbeit

to **work (on)** arbeiten **(an** + *dat*)

worker der Arbeiter, - / die Arbeiterin, -nen

world die Welt, -en

world war der Weltkrieg, -e

worn (*of clothes*) abgetragen; (*of shoes*) abgelaufen

wound die Wunde, -n

Wow! Mensch!

wristwatch die Armbanduhr, -en

to **write** schreiben, schrieb, hat geschrieben

  to write to schreiben an (+ *acc*)

  in writing schriftlich

wrong falsch

Y

yard der Garten, ¨

year das Jahr, -e

  year of manufacture das Baujahr, -e

yellow gelb

yes ja; (*in response to negative statement or question*) doch

yesterday gestern

  the day before yesterday vorgestern

yogurt der Joghurt

young jung

your dein; euer; Ihr

youth hostel die Jugendherberge, -n

Z

zero die Null, -en

Zurich Zürich

CREDITS

The authors and editors would like to thank the following authors and publishers for permission to use copyrighted material.

Text Material

pages 382–384: Georg Kövary, Kurzhörspiel "Sie haben ihn sehr lieb," © Georg Kövary. Reprinted by kind permission of the author. Recording of "Sie haben ihn sehr lieb" aus der Hörspiel-Edition des ORF Landesstudio Niederösterreich, Band 6: Kurzhörspiele.   pages 420–421: Peter Bichsel, "San Salvador," from *Eigentlich möchte Frau Blum den Milchmann kennenlernen,* © Walter-Verlag AG, Olten.   pages 454–455: Hans Bender, "Forgive Me," from *Worte, Bilder, Menschen,* © 1969 Carl Hanser Verlag, Munchen, Wien.   pages 480–481: Alfred Polgar, "Geschichte ohne Moral," in *Kleine Schriften,* Band III, © Rowohlt Verlag, Reinbek.

Photos

facing page 1: Eckebrecht/Bavaria.   page 4: Owen Franken/German Information Center.   page 7: F. and R. Widmaier.

page 8: Institut für Auslandsbeziehungen, Stuttgart.   page 12: F. and R. Widmaier.   F. and R. Widmaier.   page 13: F. and R. Widmaier.   page 20 (left): Inter Nationes.   page 20 (right): Inter Nationes.   page 21 (top) Inter Nationes.   page 21 (bottom): Inter Nationes.   page 24: F. and R. Widmaier.   page 25: Volkswagen Canada; Deutsche Zentrale für Tourismus; BMW Canada Inc.; Deutsche Postreklame GMBH.   page 29: F. and R. Widmaier.

page 32: Owen Franken/German Information Center.   page 36: Zeitverlag, Gerd Bucerius GMBH; Gruner und Jahr A.G. (Stern Magazin); SPIEGEL-Verlag; Axel Springer Verlag, Hamburg; photo from Inter Nationes.   page 39: F. and R. Widmaier.   page 41: Owen Franken/German Information Center.   page 43: Swiss National Tourist Office.   page 47: F. and R. Widmaier.   page 48: F. and R. Widmaier.   page 52: F. and R. Widmaier.   page 55. F. and R. Widmaier.

page 58: Owen Franken/German Information Center.   page 69: F. and R. Widmaier.   page 70: Swiss National Tourist Office   page 71 (left): Inter Nationes.   page 71 (right): c. ÖFVW.   page 73: Owen Franken/German Information Center.   page 74: F. and R. Widmaier.   page 76: F. and R. Widmaier.   page 80: F. and R. Widmaier.   page 81: F. and R. Widmaier.   page 93: Inter Nationes.

page 94: Pasdzior/Penner/Inter Nationes.   page 98: Owen Franken/German Information Center.   page 99: F. and R. Widmaier.   page 100: Inter Nationes. page 101: F. and R. Widmaier.   page 102: F. and R. Widmaier.   page 103: F. and R. Widmaier.   page 112: F. and R. Widmaier.   page 113: F. and R. Widmaier.   page 114: Inter Nationes.   page 116: Owen Franken/German Information Center.

page 124: Inter Nationes.   page 127: Inter Nationes.   page 128: Inter Nationes.   page 129: Deutsche Bundespost TELEKOM.   page 131: Inter Nationes.   page 137: Owen Franken/German Information Center.   page 140: F. and R. Widmaier.   page 146: F. and R. Widmaier.   page 147 (top): Inter Nationes.   page 147 (bottom): F. and R. Widmaier.   page 148: die Bundesregierung,

Bonn.　page 153: F. and R. Widmaier.　page 154: F. and R. Widmaier.　page 155; Inter Nationes. page 156: F. and R. Widmaier.

page 158: Museum of the City of New York.　page 161: Amerika Woche; California Staats-Zeitung und Herold; Deutsche Presse.　page 162: F. and R. Widmaier.　page 165 (left): The Cleveland Orchestra.　page 165 (right): AIP Niels Bohr Library.　page 177 (top): Owen Franken/German Information Center.　page 177 (bottom): F. and R. Widmaier.　page 181: Ricker Fruchtsäfte GmbH. page 187: F. and R. Widmaier.　page 189: F. and R. Widmaier.　page 190: F. and R. Widmaier. page 191: F. and R. Widmaier.

page 194: Institut für Auslandsbeziehungen, Stuttgart.　page 198: Verlag Dominique GmbH.　page 202: F. and R. Widmaier.　page 203 (top): F. and R. Widmaier.　pager 203 (bottom): Inter Nationes. page 211: F. and R. Widmaier.　page 212: Inter Nationes.　page 215: F. and R. Widmaier.　page 216: Inter Nationes.　page 217: F. and R. Widmaier.　page 218: Inter Nationes.　page 219: F. and R. Widmaier.　page 231: Inter Nationes.　page 232: F. and R. Widmaier.

page 236: F. and R. Widmaier.　page 240 (left): F. and R. Widmaier.　page 240 (right): Familie Bofinger/Sonne-Post.　page 242: Inter Nationes.　page 247: Inter Nationes.　page 248 (left): M. Knuttel/Apotheke am Kirchplatz, Welzheim.　page 248 (right): F. and R. Widmaier.　page 255: Inter Nationes.　page 258: Inter Nationes.　page 260: F. and R. Widmaier/Federal Express.　page 262: F. and R. Widmaier.　page 266: F. and R. Widmaier.　page 267: F. and R. Widmaier.　page 268 (left): Inter Nationes.　page 271: F. and R. Widmaier.

page 276: F. and R. Widmaier.　page 279: F. and R. Widmaier.　page 280: F. and R. Widmaier. page 281: F. and R. Widmaier.　page 283 (top): Institut für Auslandsbeziehungen, Stuttgart.　page 283 (bottom): F. and R. Widmaier.　page 285: F. and R. Widmaier.　page 292: F. and R. Widmaier. page 294: Inter Nationes.　page 297: F. and R. Widmaier.　page 299: F. and R. Widmaier.　page 303: F. and R. Widmaier.　page 306: F. and R. Widmaier.

page 312: Inter Nationes.　page 318: F. and R. Widmaier.　page 319: German Information Center. page 320: Inter Nationes.　page 321: Inter Nationes.　page 329: F. and R. Widmaier.　page 333: F. and R. Widmaier.　page 341: F. and R. Widmaier.

page 346: German Information Center.　page 350: UPI/ Bettmann Archives.　page 356: F. and R. Widmaier.　page 357: Inter Nationes.　page 360: F. and R. Widmaier.　page 361: F. and R. Widmaier.　page 362: F. and R. Widmaier.　page 363: Ricker Fruchtsäfte GmbH.　page 364: F. and R. Widmaier.　page 366: Die Grünen.　page 368: F. and R. Widmaier.　page 370: F. and R. Widmaier.　page 372: Inter Nationes.　page 375: Owen Franken/German Information Center. page 376; F. and R. Widmaier.

page 380: J. Grossauer/c. ÖFVW.　page 388: Bernard Debow.　page 395: F. and R. Widmaier.　page 399: F. and R. Widmaier.　page 402: Greenpeace.　page 404: F. and R. Widmaier.　page 407: F. and R. Widmaier.　page 408: Bonnacke/c. ÖFVW.　page 411: F. and R. Widmaier.　page 413: Inter Nationes.　page 417: Inter Nationes.

page 418: Swiss National Tourist Office.　page 425: Swiss National Tourist Office.　page 427: F. and R. Widmaier.　page 429: F. and R. Widmaier.　page 432: Bernard Debow.　page 434: F. and R. Widmaier.　page 436: F. and R. Widmaier.　page 439: F. and R. Widmaier.　page 440: F. and R. Widmaier.

page 452: Presse- und Informationsamt der Bundesregierung, Bonn.　page 460: UPI/Bettmann Newsphotos.　page 461 (top): German Information Center.　page 461 (bottom): Gamma.　page 462: Inter Nationes.　page 463 (top): Gamma.　page 463 (bottom): Inter Nationes.　page 468: F. and R. Widmaier.　page 472: F. and R. Widmaier.　page 474: UPI/Bettmann Newsphotos.　page 476: Susanne Widmaier.　page 479: Jürgens Ost und Europa Photo.　page 485: Die Grünen.

INDEX

Cultural information *(Wissenswertes)* is listed under *Kultur.*

Future tense *(cont.)*
 to express probability, 403
 uses of, 402

G

ganz, meanings of, 190
gehen with prefixes, 483
Gender of nouns, 14, 119–120, 231, 307, 341, 375
Genitive case, 294
 prepositions with, 298
gern, 69
 comparative of, 69
gleich, meanings of, 448

H

haben
 as auxiliary of the perfect tense, 168, 175
 present tense of, 82–83
 simple past tense of, 183
hängen, 288, 289
hin / her, 333

I

ihr / Sie / du, 6
Imperatives
 du-imperative, 200–201
 ihr-imperative, 202
 Sie-imperative, 203
Indefinite article, 45
 accusative forms, 78
 negative forms of, 47
 nominative forms of, 78
 omission of, 74
Indirect object, 204–205
Indirect quotation, 474–477
 in colloquial German, 474
 in literary and journalistic German, 475–476
 past time, 477
Infinitive
 as alternative to passive, 472
 da-compound with, 411
 definition of, 65
 ohne + zu-infinitive, 250
 passive, 467
 um + zu-infinitive, 249
 used as a noun, 231
 with modals, 101
 würde with, 439
 zu-infinitive, 246
Inseparable-prefix verbs, 134, 181
Interrogative pronouns, 141
 dative case of 206

J

ja vs. **doch,** 84

K

kein, 47, 78
kennen vs. **wissen,** 167
Kultur
 air transportation, 114
 Anglo-Saxons, 30
 Apotheke / Drogerie / Reformhaus, 248
 apprenticeship system, 189
 Austria, 388–389
 Bach, J.S., 62
 Beethoven, L.v., 62
 Bender, Hans, 456
 Bichsel, Peter, 422
 Bodensee, 372
 Christmas, 212
 city transit, 114
 climate, 43
 division and reunification of Germany, 460–461
 du, ihr, Sie and their social implications, 6
 eating out in restaurants, 240
 Fußball, 147
 Gastarbeiter, 218
 German Democratic Republic, 463
 Grimm brothers, 338
 Hamburg, 36
 health food stores, 248
 Hitler and the Third Reich, 350–351
 holidays, 229
 housing, 280
 immigration to North America, 165
 invitations and gifts, 215
 landscapes, 20–21
 license plates, 76
 Liechtenstein, 357
 Ludwig II of Bavaria, 131
 Luther, Martin, 319
 Mitbringsel, 215
 Munich, 128
 Polgar, Alfred, 481
 political parties, 148
 postal and telephone service, 24
 railway system, 114
 Sachs, Hans, 316
 Schoenberg, A., 62
 Schrebergärten, 283
 shaking hands, 6
 student housing, 306
 supermarkets and specialty stores, 268
 Switzerland, 425
 table etiquette, 255
 transportation, 114

 universities, 98
 university life, 116
 use of first names, 6
 why German and English are similar, 30
 Würstchenbuden / Schnellimbiß, 258
 youth hostels, 376

L

lassen, 243–244, 472
legen, 288
lieber vs. **besser,** 120
liegen, 289

M

man, 471
Mixed verbs, 330
Modal auxiliaries, 101–105
 meaning of, 101–102
 omission of infinitive after, 102
 passive voice with, 467
 past-time subjunctive, 444
 position of, 101–102
 position of **nicht** with, 102
 present tense of, 103–105
 simple past tense of, 322

N

n-nouns, 296–297
nach vs. **zu,** 219
nicht, position of, 17, 83–84, 102, 169
nicht brauchen zu, 252
Nominative case, 78, 139
 definite article, 139
 subject, 78
Nouns
 adjectives used as, 368, 369, 371
 compound, 270
 functioning like separable prefixes, 135
 gender of, 14, 119–120, 231, 307, 341, 375
 omission after an adjective, 354
 plural forms of, 44
Numbers
 cardinal, 14
 ordinal, 360
nur vs. **erst,** 153

O

Objects
direct, 77

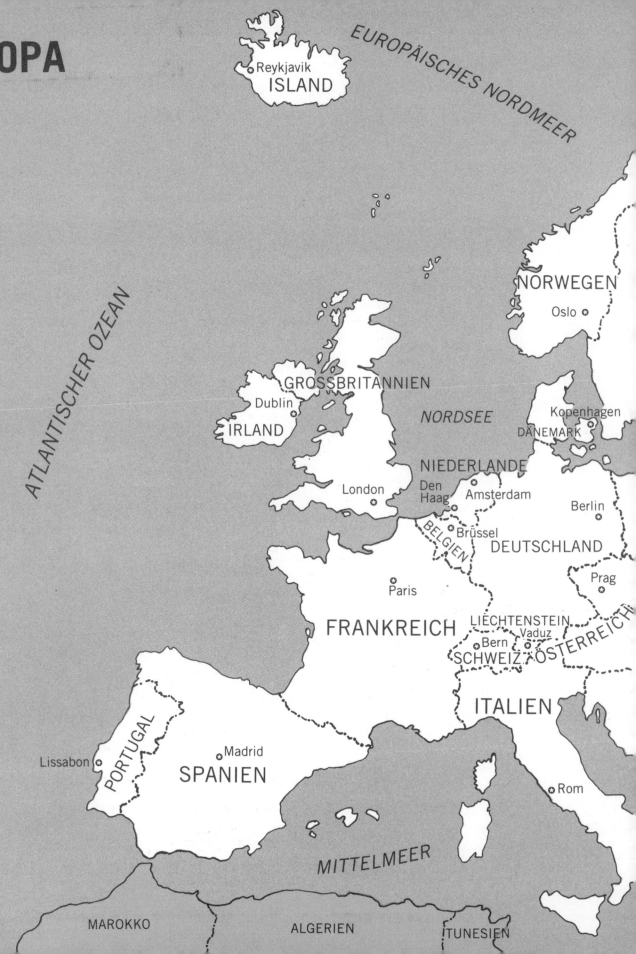

EUROPA

ISLAND
Reykjavik

EUROPÄISCHES NORDMEER

NORWEGEN
Oslo

ATLANTISCHER OZEAN

GROSSBRITANNIEN

NORDSEE

Kopenhagen
DÄNEMARK

Dublin

IRLAND

London

NIEDERLANDE
Den Haag
Amsterdam

Berlin

BELGIEN
Brüssel

DEUTSCHLAND

Prag

Paris

LIECHTENSTEIN
Vaduz

FRANKREICH

Bern
SCHWEIZ

ÖSTERREICH

ITALIEN

PORTUGAL

Madrid

Lissabon

SPANIEN

Rom

MITTELMEER

MAROKKO

ALGERIEN

TUNESIEN